A Dictionary of Famous Quotations

Robin Hyman, the son of a well-known antiquarian bookseller, was born in London in 1931. After taking an Honours degree in English, he went into publishing in 1955 and is now Joint Managing Director of Evans Brothers Limited. He spent several years compiling *A Dictionary of Famous Quotations*, and is joint author of the very successful *Boys' and Girls' First Dictionary*. He has also compiled an anthology of nursery rhymes, *Three Bags Full*, and, with his wife Inge, written the stories for a number of children's picture books, notably *Barnabas Ball at the Circus*, *Runaway James and the Night Owl* and *Run, Run, Chase the Sun*. He lives in Hampstead Garden Suburb with his wife, two sons and a daughter.

Pan Reference Books

A Dictionary of Famous Quotations

compiled by Robin Hyman

revised edition

Pan Books London and Sydney

First published 1962 as *The Modern Dictionary of Quotations* by Evans Brothers Ltd
Published 1967 by Pan Books Ltd, Cavaye Place, London SW10 9PG
Revised 1973
Reprinted 1974, 1976
© Robin Hyman 1962, 1973
ISBN 0 330 43120 X
Printed in Great Britain by
Richard Clay (The Chaucer Press) Ltd, Bungay, Suffolk

Introduction

A Dictionary of Famous Quotations has been planned as a useful and comprehensive work of reference and also as a book which I hope will give pleasure to readers who use it as an anthology. The selection of entries, as well as the arrangement in single rather than double column, is intended to encourage the browser in addition to anyone looking up specific quotations. The number of quotations selected from an author is not, of course, any indication of the author's popularity or literary merit. Some authors, like Pope and Wilde, wrote in an epigrammatic form which lends itself well to quotation; by comparison few novelists, apart from Dickens, have this particular quality. The criterion in selection is what is likely to be familiar to the general reader whose mother tongue is English. A few quotations are included from French, German, Greek, Italian, Latin and Spanish sources which seem likely to be known to many readers and in all such cases a translation is given. As well as quotations over one thousand proverbs are included. Often one does not know whether a familiar phrase is proverbial or whether it has a specific literary origin. Because of this it seemed helpful to include the best-known proverbs.

It is often extremely difficult to assess the degree of familiarity of quotations and this is particularly true when considering what to include from contemporary writing and speech. Which of the following, for example, are likely to be remembered in, say, 1980?

'*One small step for man, one giant leap for mankind.*' Neil Armstrong, the first man on the moon, 21 July 1969

'*The trouble with senior management, I notice as an outsider, is that there are too many one-ulcer men holding down two-ulcer men's jobs.*' Prince Philip, Duke of Edinburgh, Speech, 7 May 1963

'*As I look ahead, I am filled with foreboding. Like the Roman I seem to see "the river Tiber foaming with much blood".*' Enoch Powell, Speech on immigration, Birmingham, 20 April 1968

'*I have lived seventy-eight years without hearing of bloody places like Cambodia.*' Sir Winston Churchill, 28 April 1953, as quoted in Lord Moran's book on Churchill in 1966

'*From now, the pound is worth 14 per cent or so less in terms of other currencies. It does not mean, of course, that the pound here in Britain, in your pocket or purse or in your bank, has been devalued.*' Harold Wilson, Speech after devaluation of the pound, 20 Nov. 1967

'*In a hierarchy every employee tends to rise to his level of incompetence.*' Laurence J. Peter and Raymond Hull, *The Peter Principle*, 1969

'*Three passions, simple but overwhelmingly strong, have governed my life: the longing for love, the search for knowledge, and unbearable pity for the suffering of mankind.*' Bertrand Russell, *Autobiography*, Vol. 1, Prologue, 1967

Many quotations from the twentieth century are included in this book but, as the test for selection is that a quotation is likely to remain well known for several years, I have, of course, excluded most current television and radio sayings, advertising slogans and political phrases. I hope in a future edition to have the opportunity of considering whether the seven quotations above and many others from literature and speech of the 1960s and 1970s show signs of standing the test of time.

The quotations in the book have been arranged alphabetically by author and, wherever possible, line references have been given in poems, and act and scene references in plays. The name of the speaker has been given in all quotations from plays, and this enables one to find out without reference to the original test that, for example, it was Marcellus, and not Hamlet or Horatio as one might have supposed, who said, 'Something is rotten in the state of Denmark'.

A comprehensive index with over 25,000 entries has been provided at the end of the dictionary and this contains the key words in each quotation. It gives not only the page reference, but the number of the quotation on the page. From this index it is easy to trace quickly a half-remembered quotation by looking up one of the key words and, also, should one refer to individual words in the index like *man* or *beauty*, to find quotations on these subjects. References in most cases are to the Oxford Editions of Standard Authors, but line references obviously vary from edition to edition with authors, like Shakespeare, who wrote partly in prose and partly in poetry.

ROBIN HYMAN, London, 1972

Acknowledgements

Many friends gave encouragement and helpful advice during the five years of preparation of this book. Thanks are due in particular to the Rev. S. R. Cutt for his assistance in the selection of quotations from the Bible; Mrs. E. M. Hatt who undertook the immense task of compiling the index; and Miss Barbara Hall and Miss Pamela Jones for their careful checking of the proofs. Librarians in England and the United States have answered numerous enquiries with great courtesy, and the staff of the British Museum have been especially helpful. The verification of contemporary references has in many cases been made easier by the ready co-operation of the writers and speakers themselves.

A Dictionary of Famous Quotations

ACTON, John Emerich Edward Dalberg, 1st Baron 1834–1902

1 Power tends to corrupt, and absolute power corrupts absolutely. Great men are almost always bad men . . . There is no worse heresy than that the office sanctifies the holder of it.
Historical Essays and Studies, Appendix,
Letter to Bishop Mandell Creighton

ADAMS, John Quincy, 1767–1848

2 Think of your forefathers! Think of your posterity!   *Speech,*
Plymouth, Massachusetts, 22 Dec. 1802

ADAMS, Sarah Flower, 1805–1848

3 Nearer, my God to thee,
    Nearer to thee!
  E'en though it be a cross
    That raiseth me.   *Nearer, my God, to Thee*

ADDISON, Joseph, 1672–1719

4 'Tis not in mortals to command success,
  But we'll do more, Sempronius; we'll deserve it. PORTIUS
Cato, Act 1, Scene 2

5 The woman that deliberates is lost. MARCIA *Ib, Act 4, Scene 1*

6 Thus I live in the world rather as a Spectator of mankind, than as one of the species, by which means I have made myself a speculative statesman, soldier, merchant, and artisan, without ever meddling with any practical part of life.   *The Spectator,*
No. 1, 1 March 1711

7 Sunday clears away the rust of the whole week.   *Ib, No. 112*
9 July 1711

8 [*Sir Roger*] told them, with the air of a man who would not give his judgment rashly, that 'much might be said on both sides'.
Ib, No. 122, 20 July 1711

9 The spacious firmament on high,
  With all the blue ethereal sky,
  And spangled heavens, a shining frame,
  Their great Original proclaim. *Ib, No. 465, 23 Aug. 1712, Ode*

10 A woman seldom asks advice until she has bought her wedding clothes.   *Ib, No. 475, 4 Sept. 1712*

11 We are always doing something for posterity, but I would fain see posterity do something for us. *The Spectator, No. 583, 20 Aug. 1714*

12 See in what peace a Christian can die. *Last words*

ADY, Thomas, c. 1655

13 Matthew, Mark, Luke and John,
The bed be blest that I lie on.
Four angels to my bed,
Four angels round my head,
One to watch, and one to pray,
And two to bear my soul away. *A Candle in the Dark*

AKINS, Zoë, 1886–1958

14 The Greeks Had a Word for It. *Title of play, 1930*

ALCUIN, 735–804

15 *Vox populi, vox dei.* The voice of the people is the voice of God. *Letter to Charlemagne*

ALDRICH, Henry, 1647–1710

16 If all be true that I do think,
There are five reasons we should drink:
Good wine – a friend – or being dry –
Or lest we should be by and by –
Or any other reason why. *Reasons for Drinking*

ALEXANDER, Cecil Frances, 1818–1895

17 All things bright and beautiful,
All creatures great and small,
All things wise and wonderful,
The Lord God made them all
All Things Bright and Beautiful

18 The rich man in his castle,
The poor man at his gate,
God made them, high or lowly,
And order'd their estate. *Ib*

19 Once in royal David's city
Stood a lowly cattle shed,
Where a Mother laid her Baby
In a manger for His bed:
Mary was that Mother mild,
Jesus Christ her little child. *Once in Royal David's City*

20 There is a green hill far away,
    Without a city wall,
  Where the dear Lord was crucified,
    Who died to save us all.   *There is a Green Hill*

ALLAINVAL, Abbé Léonor d', 1700–1753
21 *L'embarras des richesses*. A superfluity of good things.
                                        Title of play, 1726

ALLINGHAM, William, 1824–1889
22 Up the airy mountain
  Down the rushy glen,
  We daren't go a-hunting,
  For fear of little men.   *The Fairies*

AMBROSE, St, 340?–397?
23 *Si fueris Romae, Romano vivito more;*
  Si fueris alibi, vivito sicut ibi.
  When in Rome, live as the Romans do: when elsewhere, live as
  they live elsewhere. *Advice to St Augustine, quoted by Jeremy
                                             Taylor*

ANDERSEN, Hans Christian, 1805–1875
24 The Ugly Duckling.   *Title of Story*

ANONYMOUS
Advertisements
25 Daddy, what did you do in the Great War?
                                Recruiting Poster, 1914–1918 War
26 Drinka pinta milka day.   *Milk Marketing Board*
27 Friday night is Amami night.
28 Guinness is good for you.
29 Is your journey really necessary? *Railway Poster, 1939–1945 War*
30 That schoolgirl complexion.   *Palmolive Soap*
31 Stop me and buy one.   *Wall's Ice Cream*
32 They come as a boon and a blessing to men,
  The Pickwick, The Owl, and the Waverley pen.
33 Top People take *The Times*.
34 Worth a guinea a box.   *Beecham's Pills*
35 You want the best seats; we have them   *Keith Prowse & Co.
                                                  Ltd*

Ballads

36 In Scarlet town, where I was born,
    There was a fair maid dwellin',
    Made every youth cry *Well-a-way!*
    Her name was Barbara Allen.   *Barbara Allen's Cruelty*
                                              Stanza 1

37 The King sits in Dunfermline town
    Drinking the blude red wine.   *Sir Patrick Spens, 1*

38 To Noroway, to Noroway,
    To Noroway o'er the faem;
    The King's daughter o' Noroway,
    'Tis thou must bring her hame.   *Ib, 13*

39 There were three ravens sat on a tree,
    They were as black as they might be.
    The one of them said to his make,
    'Where shall we our breakfast take?'   *The Three Ravens, 1*

40 As I was walking all alane
    I heard twa corbies making a mane:
    The tane unto the tither did say,
    'Whar shall we gang and dine the day?'   *The Twa Corbies*

Epitaphs

41 Here lie I and my four daughters,
    Killed by drinking Cheltenham waters.
    Had we but stick to Epsom salts,
    We wouldn't have been in these here vaults.
                                     Cheltenham Waters

42 Here lies a man who was killed by lightning;
    He died when his prospects seemed to be brightening.
    He might have cut a flash in this world of trouble,
    But the flash cut him, and he lies in the stubble.   *At Great*
                                     Torrington, Devon

43 Here lies a poor woman who was always tired,
    She lived in a house where help wasn't hired:
    Her last words on earth were: 'Dear friends, I am going
    To where there's no cooking, or washing, or sewing,
    For everything there is exact to my wishes,
    For where they don't eat there's no washing of dishes.
    I'll be where loud anthems will always be ringing,
    But having no voice I'll be quit of the singing.
    Don't mourn for me now, don't mourn for me never,
    I am going to do nothing for ever and ever.'
                                     On a Tired Housewife

44 Here lies my wife,
   Here lies she;
   Hallelujah!
   Hallelujee!   *At Leeds*

45 Here lies the body of Richard Hind,
   Who was neither ingenious, sober, nor kind.   *On Richard Hind*

46 Here lies the body of Mary Ann Lowder,
   She burst while drinking a seidlitz powder.
   Called from the world to her heavenly rest,
   She should have waited till it effervesced.   *On Mary Ann*
                                                              Lowder

47 Here lies Will Smith – and, what's something rarish,
   He was born, bred, and hanged, all in the same parish.
                                                        On Will Smith

48 Mary Ann has gone to rest,
   Safe at last on Abraham's breast,
   Which may be nuts for Mary Ann,
   But is certainly rough on Abraham.   *Mary Ann*

49 Stranger! Approach this spot with gravity!
   John Brown is filling his last cavity.   *A Dentist*

50 This is the grave of Mike O'Day
   Who died maintaining his right of way.
   His right was clear, his will was strong.
   But he's just as dead as if he'd been wrong.   *20th century*

Limericks

51 There was a faith-healer of Deal,
   Who said, 'Although pain isn't real,
      If I sit on a pin
      And it punctures my skin,
   I dislike what I fancy I feel.'

52 There was a young lady of Riga,
   Who went for a ride on a tiger;
      They returned from the ride
      With the lady inside,
   And a smile on the face of the tiger.

53 There was a young man of Boulogne
   Who sang a most topical song.
      It wasn't the words
      That frightened the birds,
   But the horrible *double entendre*.

54 There was a young man of Japan
   Whose limericks never would scan;

When they said it was so,
He replied, 'Yes, I know,
But I always try to get as many words into the last line as ever I
   possibly can.'

55 There was a young woman called Starkie,
Who had an affair with a darky.
   The result of her sins
   Was quadruplets, not twins –
One black, and one white, and two khaki.

56 There was an old man from Darjeeling,
Who boarded a bus bound for Ealing,
   He saw on the door:
   'Please don't spit on the floor',
So he stood up and spat on the ceiling.

57 There's a wonderful family called Stein,
There's Gert and there's Epp and there's Ein;
   Gert's poems are bunk,
   Epp's statues are junk,
And no one can understand Ein.

For other limericks, see Arnold Bennett (33:12), A. H. R. Buller
(76:52), A. H. Euwer (134:53), M. E. Hare (158:68), R. A. Knox
(191:20), Edward Lear (195:65 and 66), D. L. Merritt (209:38)
and W. C. Monkhouse (224:52).

Play

58 Everyman, I will go with thee and be thy guide,
In thy most need to go by thy side. KNOWLEDGE *Everyman*
                                        (*15th century morality play*)

Poems and Sayings

59 A beast, but a just beast. *Of Dr Temple, Headmaster of Rugby*

60 From ghoulies and ghosties and long-leggety beasties
And things that go bump in the night,
Good Lord, deliver us!   *Scottish prayer*

61 He that fights and runs away
May live to fight another day.   *Musarum Deliciae (17th
                                        century)*

62 'How different, how very different, from the home life of our own
   dear Queen!'   *Irvin S. Cobb, A Laugh a Day. Remark of
         Victorian lady after a performance of Anthony and
                                        Cleopatra*

63 I always eat peas with honey
   I've done it all my life,
   They do taste kind of funny,
   But it keeps them on the knife.   *Peas*

64 I know two things about the horse,
   And one of them is rather coarse.   *The Horse (20th century)*

65 If all the world were paper,
   And all the sea were ink,
   And all the trees were bread and cheese,
   What should we do for drink?   *If All the World were Paper*
                                              (17th century)

66 King Charles the First walked and talked
   Half an hour after his head was cut off.   *Peter Puzzlewell,*
              A Choice Collection of Riddles, Charades, and
                                  Rebuses (18th century)

67 Lizzie Borden took an axe
   And gave her mother forty whacks;
   When she saw what she had done,
   She gave her father forty-one.   *On an American Trial of the*
                                                   1890's

68 Miss Buss and Miss Beale
   Cupid's darts do not feel.
   How different from us,
   Miss Beale and Miss Buss   *On Two Victorian Headmistresses*

69 Please to remember
   The Fifth of November,
   Gunpowder treason and plot.   *Guy Fawkes Day*

70 The rabbit has a charming face;
   Its private life is a disgrace.   *The Rabbit (20th century)*

71 Sumer is icumen in
   Lhude sing cucu!
   Groweth sed and bloweth med
   And springth the wude nu.   *Sumer is Icumen In (13th century)*

Songs

72 Absence makes the heart grow fonder.   *Davison, Poetical*
                                              Rhapsody, 1602

73 The animals went in one by one,
   There's one more river to cross.   *One More River*

74 As I sat on a sunny bank,
   On Christmas Day in the morning,
   I spied three ships come sailing by.   *Carol, As I sat on a*
                                              Sunny Bank

75 Begone, dull care! I prithee begone from me!
   Begone, dull care, you and I shall never agree.   *Begone Dull*
                                                      Care

76 The bells of hell go ting-a-ling-a-ling
   For you but not for me.   *Song of 1914–1918 War*

77 The Campbells are comin', oho, oho.   *The Campbells are*
                                                      Comin'

78 Come landlord, fill the flowing bowl,
   Until it doth run over . . .
       For tonight we'll merry, merry be,
       Tomorrow we'll be sober.   *Come, Landlord, Fill the*
                                              Flowing Bowl

79 Come lasses and lads, get leave of your dads,
   And away to the Maypole hie,
   For every he has got him a she,
   And the fiddler's standing by.   *Come Lasses and Lads*

80 Early one morning, just as the sun was rising,
   I heard a maid singing in the valley below:
   'Oh, don't deceive me; Oh, never leave me!
   How could you use a poor maiden so?'   *Early One Morning*

81 Frankie and Johnny were lovers, lordee, and how they could love,
   Swore to be true to each other, true as the stars above;
   He was her man, but he done her wrong.   *Frankie and Johnny*

82 God rest you merry, gentlemen,
   Let nothing you dismay.   *God Rest you Merry*

83 Greensleeves was all my joy,
     Greensleeves was my delight,
   Greensleeves was my heart of gold,
     And who but Lady Greensleeves.   *Greensleeves*

84 Ha, ha, ha, you and me,
   Little brown jug, don't I love thee!   *The Little Brown Jug*

85 Here's a health unto his Majesty. . . .
   Confusion to his enemies, . . .
   And he that will not drink his health,
   I wish him neither wit nor wealth,
   Nor yet a rope to hang himself.   *Here's a Health unto his*
                                                   Majesty

86 Here we come gathering nuts in May
      Nuts in May,
   On a cold and frosty morning.   *Children's Song*

87 The holly and the ivy,
   When they are both full grown,

Of all the trees that are in the wood,
The holly bears the crown.
The rising of the sun
And the running of the deer,
The playing of the merry organ,
Sweet singing in the choir.   *Carol, The Holly and the Ivy*

88 I feel no pain, dear mother, now
But oh, I am so dry!
O take me to a brewery
And leave me there to die.   *Shanty*

89 In Dublin's fair city, where the girls are so pretty,
I first set my eyes on sweet Molly Malone,
As she wheeled her wheelbarrow, through streets broad and
      narrow,
Crying, Cockles and mussels! alive, alive, O!   *Cockles and*
                                                   Mussels

90 She was a fishmonger, but sure 'twas no wonder,
For so were her father and mother before.   *Ib*

91 In good King Charles's golden days,
When loyalty no harm meant,
A zealous High Churchman was I,
And so I got preferment.   *The Vicar of Bray*

92 And this is law, that I'll maintain,
Unto my dying day, Sir,
That whatsoever King shall reign,
I'll be the Vicar of Bray, Sir.   *Ib*

93 It is good to be merry and wise,
It is good to be honest and true,
It is best to be off with the old love,
Before you are on with the new.   *Songs of England and*
                                      Scotland, 1835

94 My Bonnie is over the ocean,
My Bonnie is over the sea,
My Bonnie is over the ocean,
Oh, bring back my Bonnie to me.   *My Bonnie*

95 Now I am a bachelor, I live by myself and I work at the weaving
      trade,
And the only only thing that I ever did wrong
Was to woo a fair young maid.   *Weaver's Song*

96 She sighed, she cried, she damned near died: she said 'What
      shall I do?'
So I took her into bed and covered up her head
Just to save her from the foggy, foggy dew.   *Ib*

97 Oh, I went down South for to see my Sal,
Sing 'Polly-wolly-doodle' all the day!   *Polly-Wolly-Doodle*

98 Oh, 'tis my delight on a shining night, in the season of the year.
     The Lincolnshire Poacher

99 Old soldiers never die;
They only fade away.   *War Song, 1914–1918*

1 O, Shenandoah, I long to hear you
Away, you rolling river.   *Shenandoah*

2 O ye'll tak' the high road, and I'll tak' the low road,
And I'll be in Scotland afore ye,
But me and my true love will never meet again,
On the bonnie, bonnie banks o' Loch Lomon'.
     The Bonnie Banks o' Loch Lomon'

3 She was poor but she was honest
Victim of a rich man's game.
First he loved her, then he left her,
And she lost her maiden name.   *She was Poor but she was Honest*

4 See her on the bridge at midnight,
Saying 'Farewell, blighted love.'
Then a scream, a splash and goodness,
What is she a-doin' of?   *Ib*

5 It's the same the whole world over,
It's the poor wot gets the blame,
It's the rich wot gets the gravy.
Ain't it all a bleedin' shame?   *Ib*

6 Some talk of Alexander, and some of Hercules,
Of Hector and Lysander, and such great names as these;
But of all the world's brave heroes there's none that can compare
With a tow, row, row, row, row, row for the British Grenadier.
     The British Grenadiers

7 The sons of the prophet were brave men and bold,
And quite unaccustomed to fear,
But the bravest by far in the ranks of the Shah
Was Abdul the Bulbul Amir.   *Abdul the Bulbul Amir*

8 Swing low sweet chariot,
Comin' for to carry me home,
I looked over Jordan an' what did I see?
A band of Angels coming after me,
Comin' for to carry me home.   *Swing Low, Sweet Chariot*

9 There is a lady sweet and kind,
Was never face so pleased my mind;
I did but see her passing by,
And yet I love her till I die.   *Passing By*

10 There is a tavern in the town,
And there my dear love sits him down,
And drinks his wine 'mid laughter free,
And never, never thinks of me. *There is a Tavern in the Town*

11 Fare thee well, for I must leave thee,
Do not let this parting grieve thee,
And remember that the best of friends must part. *Ib*

12 Tom Pearse, Tom Pearse, lend me your grey mare,
All along, down along out along Lee.
For I want for to go to Widdicombe Fair,
Wi' Bill Brewer, Jan Stewer, Peter Gurney, Peter Davey, Dan'l
Whiddon, Harry Hawk, Old Uncle Tom Cobbleigh and all.
Widdicombe Fair

13 We're here because we're here because we're here because we're
here. *Army Song, 1914–1918*

14 What shall we do with the drunken sailor
Early in the morning?
Hoo-ray and up she rises
Early in the morning. *What shall we do with the Drunken
Sailor?*

French

15 *Liberté! Égalité! Fraternite!* Liberty! Equality! Fraternity!
French Revolution

16 *Revenons à nos moutons.* Let us return to our sheep (i.e. to the
subject). *Maistre Pierre Pathelin*

Greek

17 Nothing in excess *In the temple at Delphi*

Latin

18 *Ad majorem Dei gloriam.* To the greater glory of God.
Motto of the Society of Jesus

19 *Et in Arcadia ego.* I too am in Arcadia. *Inscription on tomb*

20 *Gaudeamus igitur,*
Iuvenes dum sumus
Let us be happy while we are young. *Students' song (13th
century)*

21 *Tempora mutantur, et nos mutamur in illis.* Times change, and we
change with them. *Quoted in Harrison, Description of Britain,
1577*

ARABIAN NIGHTS

22 Who will change old lamps for new ones?... new lamps for
old ones?   *The History of Aladdin*

23 Open Sesame!   *The History of Ali Baba*

ARCHIMEDES, 287–212 B.C.

24 Give me a firm place to stand, and I will move the earth.
On the Lever

25 I have found it! [Eureka!]   *On making a discovery*

ARISTOTLE, 384–322 B.C.

26 Man is by nature a political animal.   *Politics, Book 1*

27 Inferiors revolt in order that they may be equal, and equals that
they may be superior. Such is the state of mind which creates
revolutions.   *Ib, Book 5*

28 Plato is dear to me, but dearer still is truth.   *Attributed*

ARNOLD, George, 1834–1865

29 The living need charity more than the dead.   *The Jolly Old
Pedagogue*

ARNOLD, Matthew, 1822–1888

30 The sea is calm to-night,
The tide is full, the moon lies fair
Upon the Straits.   *Dover Beach*

31 Is it so small a thing
To have enjoy'd the sun,
To have lived light in the spring,
To have loved, to have thought, to have done?
Empedocles on Etna

32 Come, dear children, let us away;
Down and away below.   *The Forsaken Merman*

33 Children dear, was it yesterday
(Call yet once) that she went away?   *Ib*

34 She left lonely for ever
The kings of the sea.   *Ib*

35 Who saw life steadily, and saw it whole:
The mellow glory of the Attic stage.   *Sonnets, To a Friend*

36 Wandering between two worlds, one dead,
The other powerless to be born.   *The Grande Chartreuse*

37 Strew on her roses, roses,
   And never a spray of yew.
   In quiet she reposes:
   Ah! would that I did too. *Requiescat*

38 Tonight it doth inherit
   The vasty Hall of Death. *Ib*

39 Go, for they call you, Shepherd, from the hill. *The Scholar Gipsy, 1*

40 All the live murmur of a summer's day. *Ib, 20*

41 Tired of knocking at Preferment's door. *Ib, 35*

42 Before this strange disease of modern life,
   With its sick hurry, its divided aims. *Ib, 203*

43 Still nursing the unconquerable hope,
   Still clutching the inviolable shade. *Ib, 211*

44 Others abide our question. Thou art free.
   We ask and ask: Thou smilest and art still,
   Out-topping knowledge. *Shakespeare*

45 Truth sits upon the lips of dying men. *Sohrab and Rustum*

46 And that sweet City with her dreaming spires
   She needs not June for beauty's heightening. *[Of Oxford] Thyrsis, 19*

47 The pursuit of perfection, then, is the pursuit of sweetness and light. *Culture and Anarchy*

48 Thus we have got three distinct terms, Barbarians, Philistines, Populace, to denote roughly the three great classes into which our society is divided. *Ib*

49 Home of lost causes, and forsaken beliefs, and unpopular names, and impossible loyalties! *[Of Oxford] Essays in Criticism, First Series, Preface*

50 I am bound by my own definition of criticism: a disinterested endeavour to learn and propagate the best that is known and thought in the world. *Ib, Functions of Criticism at the Present Time*

51 In poetry, no less than in life, he is 'a beautiful and ineffectual angel, beating in the void his luminous wings in vain.' *[Of Shelley] Ib, Second Series*

52 Culture is the passion for sweetness and light, and (what is more) the passion for making them prevail. *Literature and Dogma, Preface*

53 Culture, the acquainting ourselves with the best that has been known and said in the world, and thus with the history of the human spirit. *Ib*

ARNOLD, Thomas, 1795–1842

54 What we must look for here is, first, religious and moral principles; secondly, gentlemanly conduct; thirdly, intellectual ability.   *Address to his Scholars at Rugby*

55 My object will be, if possible to form Christian men, for Christian boys I can scarcely hope to make.   *Letter on appointment as Headmaster of Rugby, 1828*

ASAF, George (George H. Powell), 1880–1951

56 What's the use of worrying?
   It never was worth while,
So, pack up your troubles in your old kit-bag,
   And smile, smile, smile.
                    Pack up your Troubles in your old Kit-Bag (1915)

ASQUITH, Herbert Henry, 1st Earl of Oxford and Asquith, 1852–1928

57 Wait and see.   *Various Speeches, 1910*

AUDEN, Wystan Hugh, 1907–1973

58 To save your world you asked this man to die:
   Would this man, could he see you now, ask why?
                    Epitaph for an Unknown Soldier

59 When statesmen gravely say – 'We must be realistic –'
   The chances are they're weak and therefore pacifistic:
   But when they speak of Principles – look out – perhaps
   Their generals are already poring over maps.   *Footnotes*

60 Lay your sleeping head, my love,
   Human on my faithless arm.   *Lullaby*

61 To the man-in-the-street, who, I'm sorry to say
   Is a keen observer of life,
   The word Intellectual suggests straight away
   A man who's untrue to his wife.   *Note on Intellectuals*

62 Our researchers into Public Opinion are content
   That he held the proper opinions for the time of year;
   When there was peace, he was for peace; when there was war,
      he went.   *The Unknown Citizen*

AUGUSTINE, St, 354–430

63 Give me chastity and continence, but not yet.   *Confessions, 8*

AUSTEN, Jane, 1775–1817

64 The yeomanry are precisely the order of people with whom I feel I can have nothing to do. A degree or two lower, and ... I might hope to be useful to their families in some way or other. EMMA
Emma, Ch. 4

65 One half of the world cannot understand the pleasures of the other. EMMA *Ib, Ch. 9*

66 Nobody is healthy in London, nobody can be. MR WOODHOUSE
Ib, Ch. 12

67 Human nature is so well disposed towards those who are in interesting situations, that a young person, who either marries or dies, is sure of being kindly spoken of. *Ib, Ch. 22*

68 Business, you know, may bring money, but friendship hardly ever does. JOHN KNIGHTLEY *Ib, Ch. 34*

69 It will, I believe, be everywhere found, that as the clergy are, or are not what they ought to be, so are the rest of the nation. EDMUND *Mansfield Park, Ch. 9*

70 To sit in the shade on a fine day, and look upon verdure is the most perfect refreshment. FANNY *Ib, Ch. 9*

71 Let other pens dwell on guilt and misery. *Ib, Ch. 48*

72 But are they all horrid, are you sure they are all horrid? CATHERINE MORLAND *Northanger Abbey, Ch. 6*

73 A woman, especially if she have the misfortune of knowing anything, should conceal it as well as she can. *Ib, Ch. 14*

74 One does not love a place the less for having suffered in it, unless it has all been suffering, nothing but suffering.
Persuasion, Ch. 20

75 It is a truth universally acknowledged, that a single man in possession of a good fortune must be in want of a wife.
Pride and Prejudice, Ch. 1

76 Happiness in marriage is entirely a matter of chance. *Ib, Ch. 6*

77 How can you contrive to write so even? MISS BINGLEY *Ib, Ch. 10*

78 It is happy for you that you possess the talent of flattering with delicacy. May I ask whether these pleasing attentions proceed from the impulse of the moment, or are the result of previous study? MR BENNET *Ib, Ch. 14*

79 Nobody is on my side, nobody takes part with me: I am cruelly used, nobody feels for my poor nerves. MRS BENNET *Ib, Ch. 48*

80 'I am afraid' replied Elinor, 'that the pleasantness of an employment does not always evince its propriety.' *Sense and Sensibility, Ch. 13*

81 What dreadful hot weather we have! It keeps me in a continual state of inelegance. *Letter, 18 Sept. 1796*

AUSTIN, Alfred, 1835–1913

82 An earl by right, by courtesy a man. *The Season*

83 Across the wires the electric message came:
'He is no better, he is much the same.' *On the Illness of the Prince of Wales, Attributed*

BACON, Francis, 1st Baron Verulam, 1561–1626

84 My Essayes ... come home, to Mens Businesse, and Bosomes. *Essays. Dedication*

85 What is truth? said jesting Pilate, and would not stay for an answer. *Essay 1. Of Truth*

86 Men fear death, as children fear to go in the dark; and as that natural fear in children is increased with tales, so is the other. *2. Of Death*

87 It is natural to die as to be born; and to a little infant, perhaps, the one is as painful as the other. *Ib*

88 All colours will agree in the dark. *3. Of Unity in Religion*

89 Revenge is a kind of wild justice; which the more man's nature runs to, the more ought law to weed it out. *4. Of Revenge*

90 Prosperity is the blessing of the Old Testament; adversity is the blessing of the New. *5. Of Adversity*

91 Prosperity is not without many fears and distastes; and adversity is not without comforts and hopes. *Ib*

92 Prosperity doth best discover vice; but adversity doth best discover virtue. *Ib*

93 He that talketh what he knoweth, will also talk what he knoweth not. *6. Of Simulation and Dissimulation*

94 The joys of parents are secret, and so are their griefs and fears. *7. Of Parents and Children.*

95 Children sweeten labours, but they make misfortunes more bitter. *Ib*

96 He that hath wife and children hath given hostages to fortune; for they are impediments to great enterprises, either of virtue or mischief. *8. Of Marriage and Single Life*

97 Wives are young men's mistresses; companions for middle age; and old men's nurses. *Ib*

98 He was reputed one of the wise men, that made answer to the question, when a man should marry? A young man not yet, an elder man not at all.   *8. Of Marriage and Single Life*

99 Nuptial love maketh mankind; friendly love perfecteth it; but wanton love corrupteth and embaseth it.   *10. Of Love*

1 Men in great places are thrice servants: servants of the sovereign or state; servants of fame; and servants of business.
                                        11. Of Great Place

2 There is in human nature generally more of the fool than of the wise.   *12. Of Boldness*

3 If the hill will not come to Mahomet, Mahomet will go to the hill.   *Ib*

4 In charity there is no excess.   *13. Of Goodness, and Goodness of Nature*

5 If a man be gracious and courteous to strangers, it shews he is a citizen of the world.   *Ib*

6 New nobility is but the act of power; but ancient nobility is the act of time.   *14. Of Nobility*

7 So when any of the four pillars of government are mainly shaken or weakened (which are religion, justice, counsel, and treasure), men had need to pray for fair weather.
                                        15. Of Seditions and Troubles

8 Money is like muck, not good except it be spread.   *Ib*

9 The remedy is worse than the disease.   *Ib*

10 A little philosophy inclineth man's mind to atheism; but depth in philosophy bringeth men's minds about to religion.
                                        16. Of Atheism

11 It were better to have no opinion of God at all, than such an opinion as is unworthy of him.   *17. Of Superstition*

12 Travel, in the younger sort, is a part of education; in the elder, a part of experience.   *18. Of Travel*

13 It is a miserable state of mind to have few things to desire and many things to fear.   *19. Of Empire*

14 Nothing destroyeth authority so much as the unequal and untimely interchange of power pressed too far, and relaxed too much.   *Ib*

15 There be that can pack the cards, and yet cannot play well.
                                        22. Of Cunning

16 Be so true to thyself, as thou be not false to others.
                                        23. Of Wisdom for a Man's Self

17 He that will not apply new remedies must expect new evils: for time is the greatest innovator. *24. Of Innovations*

18 To choose time is to save time. *25. Of Dispatch*

19 The French are wiser than they seem, and the Spaniards seem wiser than they are. *26. Of Seeming Wise*

20 Whosoever is delighted in solitude is either a wild beast or a god. *27. Of Friendship*

21 Riches are for spending. *28. Of Expense*

22 Age will not be defied. *30. Of Regiment of Health*

23 Suspicions amongst thoughts are like bats amongst birds, they ever fly by twilight. *31. Of Suspicion*

24 Of great riches there is no real use, except it be in the distribution. *34. Of Riches*

25 Nature is often hidden, sometimes overcome, seldom extinguished. *38. Of Nature in Men*

26 A man that is young in years may be old in hours, if he have lost no time. *42. Of Youth and Age*

27 Virtue is like a rich stone, best plain set. *43. Of Beauty*

28 Houses are built to live in, and not to look on. *45. Of Building*

29 God Almighty first planted a garden. And indeed it is the purest of human pleasures. *46. Of Gardens*

30 Studies serve for delight, for ornament, and for ability. *50. Of Studies*

31 To spend too much time in studies is sloth. *Ib*

32 Some books are to be tasted, others to be swallowed, and some few to be chewed and digested. *Ib*

33 Reading maketh a full man; conference a ready man; and writing an exact man. *Ib*

34 Histories make men wise; poets witty; the mathematics subtile; natural philosophy deep; moral grave; logic and rhetoric able to contend. *Ib*

35 Fame is like a river, that beareth up things light and swoln, and drowns things weighty and solid. *53. Of Praise*

36 The place of justice is an hallowed place. *56. Of Judicature*

37 If a man will begin with certainties, he shall end in doubts, but if he will be content to begin with doubts, he shall end in certainties. *The Advancement of Learning, 1, 5, 8*

38 Hope is a good breakfast, but it is a bad supper. *Apophthegms, 36*

39 I have taken all knowledge to be my province.   *Letter to Lord Burleigh, 1592*

40 God's first creature, which was light.   *The New Atlantis*

41 There are four classes of Idols which beset men's minds. To these for distinction sake I have assigned names – calling the first class, Idols of the Tribe; the second, Idols of the Cave; the third, Idols of the Market-place; the fourth, Idols of the Theatre.
Novum Organum

42 Nature, to be commanded, must be obeyed.   *Ib*

BAGEHOT, Walter, 1826–1877

43 *The Times* has made many ministries.   *The English Consitution, Ch. 1*

44 Women – one half the human race at least – care fifty times more for a marriage than a ministry.   *Ib, Ch. 2*

45 Of all nations in the World, the English are perhaps the least a nation of pure philosophers.   *Ib*

46 Poverty is an anomaly to rich people. It is very difficult to make out why people who want dinner do not ring the bell.
Literary Studies, 2

BAIRNSFATHER, Charles Bruce, 1888–1959

47 Well, if you knows of a better 'ole, go to it.   *Fragments from France, 1*

BALFOUR, Arthur James, 1848–1930

48 The energies of our system will decay, the glory of the sun will be dimmed, and the earth, tideless and inert, will no longer tolerate the race which has for a moment disturbed its solitude. Man will go down into the pit, and all his thoughts will perish.
The Foundations of Belief, Part 1, Ch. 1

49 It is unfortunate, considering that enthusiasm moves the world, that so few enthusiasts can be trusted to speak the truth.
Letter to Mrs Drew, 1918

BALL, John, ?–1381

50 When Adam delved and Eve span,
Who was then the gentleman?   *Text for sermon on Peasants' Revolt*

BARHAM, Richard Harris, 1788–1845

51 A servant's too often an impudent elf;
– If it's business of consequence, *do it yourself!* *The Ingoldsby Legends, The Ingoldsby Penance, Moral*

52 The Jackdaw sat on the Cardinal's chair!
  Bishop and abbot, and prior were there.   *The Ingoldsby*
                          Legends, The Jackdaw of Rheims

53   Never, I ween,
              Was a prouder seen,
  Read of in books, or dreamt of in dreams,
  Than the Cardinal Lord Archbishop of Rheims!   *Ib*

54 He long lived the pride of that country side,
  And at last in the odour of sancity died.   *Ib*

55 He smiled and said, 'Sir, does your mother know that you are
  out?'   *Ib, Misadventures at Margate*

BARING-GOULD, Sabine, 1834–1924

56 Now the day is over,
    Night is drawing nigh,
    Shadows of the evening
    Steal across the sky.   *Now the Day is over*

57 Onward Christian soldiers
    Marching as to war,
    With the Cross of Jesus
    Going on before.   *Onward Christian Soldiers*

BARNUM, Phineas Taylor, 1810–1891

58 There's a sucker born every minute.   *Attributed*

BARRIE, Sir James Matthew, 1860–1937

59 When the first baby laughed for the first time, the laugh broke
  into a thousand pieces and they all went skipping about, and
  that was the beginning of fairies. PETER PAN *Peter Pan, Act 1*

60 Every time a child says 'I don't believe in fairies' there is a little
  fairy somewhere that falls down dead. PETER PAN   *Ib*

61 To die will be an awfully big adventure. PETER PAN *Ib, Act 3*

62 Do you believe in fairies? Say quick that you believe. If you
  believe, clap your hands! PETER PAN   *Ib, Act 4*

63 One's religion is whatever he is most interested in, and yours is
  Success. KATE   *The Twelve-Pound Look*

64 You've forgotten the grandest moral attribute of a Scotsman,
  Maggie, that he'll do nothing which might damage his career.
  JOHN SHAND   *What Every Woman Knows, Act 2*

BARRINGTON, George, 1755–1810?

65 True patriots we; for be it understood,
We left our country for our country's good.   *Prologue for
opening of Playhouse, Sydney, 16 Jan. 1796 by company
of convicts*

BATEMAN, Edgar, 19th century

66 Wiv a ladder and some glasses,
You could see to 'Ackney Marshes,
If it wasn't for the 'ouses in between.   *If it wasn't for the
'Ouses in between*

BATES, Katherine Lee, 1859–1929

67 America! America!
God shed His grace on thee
And crown thy good with brotherhood
From sea to shining sea!   *America the Beautiful*

BAYLY, Thomas Haynes, 1797–1839

68 Absence makes the heart grow fonder,
Isle of Beauty, Fare thee well!   *Isle of Beauty*

BEATTY, David, 1st Earl Beatty, 1871–1936

69 There's something wrong with our bloody ships today.
Remark during Battle of Jutland, 1916

BEAUMONT, Francis, 1584–1616

70   What things we have seen,
Done at the Mermaid! heard words that have been
So nimble, and so full of subtle flame,
As if that everyone from whence they came
Had meant to put his whole wit in a jest,
And had resolved to live a fool the rest
Of his dull life.   *Letter to Ben Jonson*

71 Mortality, behold and fear!
What a change of flesh is here.   *On the Tombs in Westminster
Abbey*

**BEAUMONT, Francis, 1584–1616, and FLETCHER, John,
1579–1625**

72 But what is past my help is past my care.   *The Double
Marriage, Act 1, Scene 1*

73 There is no other purgatory but a woman.   ELDER LOVELESS
The Scornful Lady, Act 3, Scene 1

BECKETT, Samuel, 1906–

74 Nothing happens, nobody comes, nobody goes, it's awful!
ESTRAGON *Waiting for Godot, Act 1*

75 VLADIMIR: That passed the time.
ESTRAGON: It would have passed in any case.
VLADIMIR: Yes, but not so rapidly. *Ib, Act 1*

76 Habit is a great deadener. VLADIMIR *Ib, Act 3*

BECKFORD, William, 1759–1844

77 I am not over-fond of resisting temptation. *Vathek*

BECON, Thomas, 1512–1567

78 For when the wine is in, the wit is out. *Catechism, 375*

BEE, Bernard Elliott, 1823–1861

79 There is Jackson standing like a stone wall. *First Battle of Bull Run, 1861*

BEECHING, Henry Charles, 1859–1919

80 First come I; my name is Jowett.
There's no knowledge but I know it.
I am Master of this College:
What I don't know isn't knowledge. *The Masque of Balliol*

BEERBOHM, Sir Max, 1872–1956

81 Most women are not so young as they are painted.
A Defence of Cosmetics

82 Zuleika, on a desert island, would have spent most of her time in looking for a man's footprint. *Zuleika Dobson, Ch. 2*

83 She was one of the people who say, 'I don't know anything about music really, but I know what I like.' *Ib, Ch. 9*

BEERS, Ethel Lynn, 1827–1879

84 All quiet along the Potomac tonight,
    No sound save the rush of the river,
While soft falls the dew on the face of the dead –
    The picket's off duty forever. *All Quiet Along the Potomac*

BEHN, Aphra, 1640–1689

85 Love ceases to be a pleasure, when it ceases to be a secret.
La Montre, or The Lover's Watch, Four o'clock

86 Variety is the soul of pleasure. WILLMORE *The Rover, Part 2, Act 1*

87 Fine clothes, rich furniture, jewels and plate are more inviting
than beauty unadorn'd.   PETRONELLA *The Rover, Part 4, Act 2*

BELLOC, Hilaire, 1870–1953

88 Child! do not throw this book about;
  Refrain from the unholy pleasure
Of cutting all the pictures out!
  Preserve it as your chiefest treasure.   *The Bad Child's Book*
  of Beasts, Dedication

89 When people call this beast to mind,
They marvel more and more
At such a little tail behind,
So large a trunk before.   *Ib, The Elephant*

90 The Chief Defect of Henry King
Was chewing little bits of String.   *Cautionary Tales, Henry*
  King

91 Physicians of the Utmost Fame
Were called at once; but when they came
They answered, as they took their Fees,
'There is no Cure for this Disease.'   *Ib*

92 'Oh, my Friends, be warned by me,
That Breakfast, Dinner, Lunch and Tea
Are all the Human Frame requires. . . .'
With that the Wretched Child expires.   *Ib*

93 When I am dead, I hope it may be said:
'His sins were scarlet, but his books were read.'   *Epigrams,*
  On His Books

94 Lord Finchley tried to mend the Electric Light
Himself. It struck him dead: And serve him right!
It is the business of the wealthy man
 To give employment to the artisan.   *Ib, Lord Finchley*

95 The accursèd power which stands on Privilege
(And goes with Women, and Champagne and Bridge)
Broke – and Democracy resumed her reign:
(Which goes with Bridge, and Women and Champagne).
  Ib, On a General Election

96 The Devil, having nothing else to do,
Went off to tempt My Lady Poltagrue.
My Lady, tempted by a private whim,
To his extreme annoyance, tempted him.   *Ib, On Lady*
  Poltagrue, A Public Peril

97 I said to Heart, 'How goes it?' Heart replied:
'Right as a Ribstone Pippin!' But it lied.   *The False Heart*

98 I'm tired of Love: I'm still more tired of Rhyme.
 But Money gives me pleasure all the Time.   *Fatigue*

99 Birds in their little nests agree
 With Chinamen, but not with me.   *On Food*

 1 Remote and ineffectual Don
 That dared attack my Chesterton.   *Lines to a Don*

 2 The Microbe is so very small
 You cannot make him out at all.   *More Beasts for Worse*
                                         Children, The Microbe

 3 Lord Hippo suffered fearful loss
 By putting money on a horse
 Which he believed, if it were pressed,
 Would run far faster than the rest.   *More Peers, Lord Hippo*

 4 Lord Lucky, by a curious fluke,
 Became a most important duke,
 From living in a vile Hotel
 A long way east of Camberwell
 He rose in less than half an hour
 To riches, dignity and power.   *More Peers, Lord Lucky*

 5 When I am living in the Midlands
  That are sodden and unkind,
 I light my lamp in the evening:
  My work is left behind;
 And the great hills of the South Country
  Come back into my mind.   *The South Country*

 6 If I ever become a rich man,
  Or if ever I grow to be old,
 I will build a house with deep thatch
  To shelter me from the cold,
 And there shall the Sussex songs be sung
  And the story of Sussex told.   *Ib*

 7 I will hold my house in the high wood
  Within a walk of the sea,
 And the men that were boys when I was a boy
  Shall sit and drink with me.   *Ib*

 8 Do you remember an Inn,
 Miranda?   *Tarantella*

BENNETT, Enoch Arnold, 1867–1931

 9 'Ye can call it influenza if ye like,' said Mrs Machin. 'There was
 no influenza in my young days. We called a cold a cold.'
                                          The Card, Ch. 8

10 'And yet,' demanded Councillor Barlow . . . 'what great cause is
he identified with?'
'He is identified,' said the speaker, 'with the great cause of
cheering us all up.'   *The Card, Ch. 12*

11 Being a husband is a whole-time job. That is why so many
husbands fail. They cannot give their entire attention to it.
CULVER   *The Title, Act 1*

12 There was a young man of Montrose,
Who had pockets in none of his clothes,
  When asked by his lass
  Where he carried his brass,
He said, 'Darling, I pay through the nose.'   *Limerick*

BENSON, Arthur Christopher, 1862–1925

13 Land of Hope and Glory, Mother of the Free,
How shall we extol thee, who are born of thee?
Wider still and wider shall thy bounds be set;
God who made thee mighty, make thee mightier yet.
    Land of Hope and Glory (Music by Sir Edward Elgar)

BENTHAM, Jeremy, 1748–1832

14 The greatest happiness of the greatest number is the foundation
of morals and legislation.   *The Commonplace Book*

BENTLEY, Edmund Clerihew, 1875–1956

15 The Art of Biography
Is different from Geography.
Geography is about Maps,
But Biography is about Chaps.   *Biography for Beginners,*
                                          Introductory Remarks

16 Sir Christopher Wren
Said, 'I am going to dine with some men.
If anybody calls
Say I am designing St Paul's.'   *Ib, Sir Christopher Wren*

17 What I like about Clive
Is that he is no longer alive.
There is a great deal to be said
For being dead.   *Ib, Clive*

18 Sir Humphry Davy
Detested gravy.
He lived in the odium
Of having discovered Sodium.   *Ib, Sir Humphry Davy*

19 George the Third
Ought never to have occurred.

One can only wonder
At so grotesque a blunder. *More Biography, George the Third*

20 When their lordships asked Bacon
How many bribes he had taken
He had at least the grace
To get very red in the face. *Baseless Biography, Bacon*

BENTLEY, Nicolas Clerihew, 1907–

21 Cecil B. de Mille,
Rather against his will,
Was persuaded to leave Moses
Out of 'The Wars of the Roses'. *Clerihew*

BERLIN, Irving, 1888–

22 Come on and hear, come on and hear, Alexander's Ragtime
Band. *Alexander's Ragtime Band*

BERNARD, William Bayle, 1807–1875

23 A Storm in a Teacup. *Title of Farce*

BETJEMAN, Sir John, 1906–

24 The Church's Restoration
In eighteen-eighty-three
Has left for contemplation
Not what there used to be. *Hymn*

25 Miss J. Hunter Dunn, Miss J. Hunter Dunn,
Furnish'd and burnish'd by Aldershot sun. *A Subaltern's Love-song*

THE BIBLE

(Quotations are from the Authorised Version, 1611, unless otherwise stated)

OLD TESTAMENT
Genesis

26 In the beginning God created the heaven and the earth.
And the earth was without form, and void. *1, 1–2*

27 And God said, Let there be light: and there was light. *1, 3*

28 So God created man in his own image, in the image of God
created he him; male and female created he them. *1, 27*

29 Be fruitful, and multiply, and replenish the earth. *1, 28*

30 And God saw everything that he had made, and, behold, it was
very good.   *Genesis, 1, 31*

31 And the Lord God took the man, and put him into the garden of
Eden to dress it and to keep it.   *2, 15*

32 And the Lord God said, It is not good that the man should be
alone; I will make him an help meet for him.   *2, 18*

33 And the rib, which the Lord God had taken from man, made he
a woman.   *2, 22*

34 This is now bone of my bones, and flesh of my flesh.   *2, 23*

35 And they were both naked, the man and his wife, and were not
ashamed.   *2, 25*

36 Ye shall be as gods, knowing good and evil.   *3, 5*

37 And they sewed fig leaves together, and made themselves
aprons.   *3, 7*

38 In the sweat of thy face shalt thou eat bread.   *3, 19*

39 For dust thou art, and unto dust shalt thou return.   *3, 19*

40 The mother of all living.   *3, 20*

41 Am I my brother's keeper?   *4, 9*

42 And the Lord set a mark upon Cain.   *4, 15*

43 And all the days of Methuselah were nine hundred sixty and
nine years.   *5, 27*

44 There were giants in the earth in those days.   *6, 4*

45 There went in two and two unto Noah into the ark, the male
and the female.   *7, 9*

46 And the ark rested in the seventh month, on the seventeenth day
of the month, upon the mountains of Ararat.   *8, 4*

47 And the dove came in to him in the evening; and, lo, in her
mouth was an olive leaf pluckt off.   *8, 11*

48 While the earth remaineth, seedtime and harvest, and cold and
heat, and summer and winter, and day and night shall not cease.
8, 22

49 Whoso sheddeth man's blood, by man shall his blood be shed.
9, 6

50 I do set my bow in the cloud.   *9, 13*

51 Even as Nimrod the mighty hunter before the Lord.   *10, 9*

52 Therefore is the name of it called Babel; because the Lord did
there confound the language of all the earth.   *11, 9*

53 His hand will be against every man, and every man's hand
against him.   *16, 12*

54 Shall not the Judge of all the earth do right?   *18, 25*

55 If I find in Sodom fifty righteous within the city, then I will spare all the place for their sakes. *Genesis, 18, 26*

56 But his wife looked back from behind him, and she became a pillar of salt. *19, 26*

57 In thy seed shall the nations of the earth be blessed. *22, 18*

58 He sold his birthright unto Jacob. *25, 33*

59 Esau my brother is a hairy man, and I am a smooth man. *27, 11*

60 The voice is Jacob's voice, but the hands are the hands of Esau. *27, 22*

61 A ladder set up on the earth, and the top of it reached to heaven. *28, 12*

62 He made him a coat of many colours. *37, 3*

63 Behold, this dreamer cometh. *37, 19*

64 Jacob saw that there was corn in Egypt. *42, 1*

65 Ye shall eat the fat of the land. *45, 18*

66 Unstable as water, thou shalt not excel. *49, 4*

Exodus

67 Now there arose up a new king over Egypt, which knew not Joseph. *1, 8*

68 I have been a stranger in a strange land. *2, 22*

69 Behold, the bush burned with fire, and the bush was not consumed. *3, 2*

70 A land flowing with milk and honey. *3, 8*

71 I AM THAT I AM. *3, 14*

72 Ye shall no more give the people straw to make brick. *5, 7*

73 Let my people go, that they may serve me. *8, 1*

74 This is the finger of God. *8, 19*

75 Darkness which may be felt. *10, 21*

76 But the Lord hardened Pharaoh's heart, and he would not let them go. *10, 27*

77 The Lord smote all the firstborn in the land of Egypt. *12, 29*

78 And the children of Israel went into the midst of the sea upon the dry ground. *14, 22*

79 Would to God we had died by the hand of the Lord in the land of Egypt, when we sat by the flesh pots, and when we did eat bread to the full. *16, 3*

80 And when the children of Israel saw it, they said one to another, It is manna: for they wist not what it was. And Moses said unto them, This is the bread which the Lord hath given you to eat.
Exodus, 16, 15

81 I am the Lord thy God, which have brought thee out of the land of Egypt, out of the house of bondage. *20, 2*

82 Thou shalt have no other gods before me. *20, 3*

83 Thou shalt not make unto thee any graven image. *20, 4*

84 For I the Lord thy God am a jealous God, visiting the iniquity of the fathers upon the children unto the third and fourth generation of them that hate me. *20, 5*

85 Thou shalt not take the name of the Lord thy God in vain. *20, 7*

86 Remember the sabbath day, to keep it holy.
Six days shalt thou labour, and do all thy work:
But the seventh day is the sabbath of the Lord thy God. *20, 8–10*

87 Honour thy father and thy mother: that thy days may be long unto the land which the Lord thy God giveth thee. *20, 12*

88 Thou shalt not kill. *20, 13*

89 Thou shalt not commit adultery. *20, 14*

90 Thou shalt not steal. *20, 15*

91 Thou shalt not bear false witness against thy neighbour. *20, 16*

92 Thou shalt not covet thy neighbour's house, thou shalt not covet thy neighbour's wife, nor his manservant, nor his maidservant, nor his ox, nor his ass, nor any thing that is thy neighbour's. *20, 17*

93 Thou shalt give life for life,
Eye for eye, tooth for tooth, hand for hand, foot for foot. *21, 23–24*

94 Thou shalt not suffer a witch to live. *22, 18*

95 Thou art a stiffnecked people. *33, 3*

Leviticus

96 Let him go for a scapegoat into the wilderness. *16, 10*

97 Ye shall be holy; for I the Lord your God am holy. *19, 2*

98 And thou shalt not glean thy vineyard, neither shalt thou gather every grape of thy vineyard; thou shalt leave them for the poor and stranger. *19, 10*

99 Thou shalt love thy neighbour as thyself. *19, 18*

1 Thou shalt rise up before the hoary head, and honour the face
of the old man. *Leviticus, 19, 32*

Numbers

2 The Lord bless thee, and keep thee: The Lord make his face
shine upon thee, and be gracious unto thee: the Lord lift up
his countenance upon thee, and give thee peace. *6, 24–26*

3 We will go by the king's high way. *20, 17*

4 Let me die the death of the righteous, and let my last end be
like his! *23, 10*

Deuteronomy

5 Hear, O Israel: The Lord our God is one Lord. *6, 4*

6 And thou shalt love the Lord thy God with all thine heart, and
with all thy soul, and with all thy might. *6, 5*

7 Man doth not live by bread only, but by every word that proceedeth out of the mouth of the Lord doth man live. *8, 3*

8 As a man chasteneth his son, so the Lord God chasteneth thee.
8, 5

9 And now, Israel, what doth the Lord thy God require of thee,
but to fear the Lord thy God, to walk in all his ways, and to love
him and to serve the Lord thy God with all thy heart and with all
thy soul. *10, 12*

10 Love ye therefore the stranger: for ye were strangers in the land
of Egypt. *10, 19*

11 For the poor shall never cease out of the land. *15, 11*

12 Thou shalt not muzzle the ox when he treadeth out the corn.
25, 4

13 I have set before you life and death, blessing and cursing: therefore choose life, that both thou and thy seed may live. *30, 19*

14 He kept him as the apple of his eye. *32, 10*

15 Jeshurun waxed fat, and kicked. *32, 15*

16 As thy days, so shall thy strength be. *33, 25*

17 The eternal God is thy refuge, and underneath are the everlasting
arms. *33, 27*

Joshua

18 Be strong and of a good courage. *1, 6*

19 Hewers of wood and drawers of water. *9, 21*

20 Sun, stand thou still upon Gibeon; and thou, Moon, in the
valley of Ajalon. *10, 12*

Judges

21 I arose a mother in Israel.   5, 7
22 The stars in their courses fought against Sisera.   5, 20
23 She brought forth butter in a lordly dish.   5, 25
24 Have they not divided the prey; to every man a damsel or two?
                                                              5, 30
25 Faint, yet pursuing.   8, 4
26 Say now Shibboleth.   12, 6
27 Out of the eater came forth meat, and out of the strong came forth sweetness.   14, 14
28 He smote them hip and thigh.   15, 8
29 If I be shaven, then my strength will go from me.   16, 17
30 He bowed himself with all his might; and the house fell upon the lords, and upon all the people that were therein.   16, 30
31 From Dan even to Beer-sheba.   20, 1
32 Every man did that which was right in his own eyes.   21, 25

Ruth

33 Whither thou goest, I will go; and where thou lodgest, I will lodge: thy people shall be my people, and thy God my God.
                                                              1, 16
34 The Lord do so to me, and more also, if ought but death part thee and me.   1, 17
35 And she went, and came, and gleaned in the field after the reapers.   2, 3

1 Samuel

36 Speak, Lord; for thy servant heareth.   3, 9
37 It is the Lord: let him do what seemeth him good.   3, 18
38 Quit yourselves like men.   4, 9
39 Is Saul also among the prophets?   10, 11
40 The Lord hath sought him a man after his own heart.   13, 14
41 Agag came unto him delicately.   15, 32
42 Man looketh on the outward appearance, but the Lord looketh on the heart.   16, 7
43 David took an harp, and played with his hand.   16, 23
44 Saul hath slain his thousands, and David his ten thousands.
                                                              18, 7
45 David therefore departed thence, and escaped to the cave Adullam.   22, 1

2 Samuel

46 How are the mighty fallen!   *1, 19*

47 Tell it not in Gath, publish it not in the streets of Askelon;
lest the daughters of the Philistines rejoice, lest the daughters of
the uncircumcised triumph.   *1, 20*

48 Saul and Jonathan were lovely and pleasant in their lives, and in
their death they were not divided: they were swifter than eagles,
they were stronger than lions.   *1, 23*

49 Thy love to me was wonderful, passing the love of women.
                                                                    1, 26

50 Abner with the hinder end of the spear smote him under the
fifth rib.   *2, 23*

51 Would God I had died for thee, O Absalom, my son, my son!
                                                                   18, 33

52 The sweet psalmist of Israel.   *23, 1*

1 Kings

53 Divide the living child in two.   *3, 25*

54 There came of all people to hear the wisdom of Solomon.
                                                                    4, 34

55 The barrel of meal shall not waste, neither shall the cruse of oil
fail.   *17, 14*

56 How long halt ye between two opinions?   *18, 21*

57 There ariseth a little cloud out of the sea, like a man's hand.
                                                                   18, 44

58 A still small voice.   *19, 12*

59 Elijah passed by him, and cast his mantle upon him.   *19, 19*

2 Kings

60 Go up, thou bald head.   *2, 23*

61 There is death in the pot.   *4, 40*

62 The driving is like the driving of Jehu the son of Nimshi; for he
driveth furiously.   *9, 20*

Esther

63 Let it be written among the laws of the Persians and the Medes,
that it be not altered.   *1, 19*

64 The king loved Esther above all the women.   *2, 17*

Job

65 Naked came I out of my mother's womb, and naked shall I return thither: the Lord gave, and the Lord hath taken away; blessed be the name of the Lord.   *1, 21*

66 Shall mortal man be more just than God? shall a man be more pure than his maker?   *4, 17*

67 Man is born unto trouble, as the sparks fly upward.   *5, 7*

68 Though he slay me, yet will I trust in him.   *13, 15*

69 Man that is born of a woman is of few days, and full of trouble.
                                                              14, 1

70 Miserable comforters are ye all.   *16, 2*

71 I am escaped with the skin of my teeth.   *19, 20*

72 I know that my redeemer liveth.   *19, 25*

73 The price of wisdom is above rubies.   *28, 18*

74 I was eyes to the blind, and feet was I to the lame.   *29, 15*

75 Great men are not always wise.   *32, 9*

76 Who is this that darkeneth counsel by words without knowledge?
                                                              38, 2

77 Hath the rain a father?   *38, 28*

78 Canst thou draw out leviathan with an hook?   *41, 1*

79 I have heard of thee by the hearing of the ear: but now mine eye seeth thee.   *42, 5*

Psalms

80 Why do the heathen rage, and the people imagine a vain thing?
                                                              2, 1

81 Out of the mouth of babes and sucklings hast thou ordained strength.   *8, 2*

82 What is man, that thou art mindful of him?   *8, 4*

83 Thou hast made him a little lower than the angels.   *8, 5*

84 The fool hath said in his heart, There is no God.   *14, 1*

85 Keep me as the apple of the eye, hide me under the shadow of thy wings.   *17, 8*

86 The heavens declare the glory of God; and the firmament sheweth his handywork.   *19, 1*

87 Day unto day uttereth speech, and night unto night sheweth knowledge.   *19, 2*

88 More to be desired are they than gold, yea, than much fine gold: sweeter also than honey and the honeycomb.   *19, 10*

89 Let the words of my mouth, and the meditation of my heart, be acceptable in thy sight, O Lord, my strength, and my redeemer.
Psalms, 19, 14

90 Some trust in chariots, and some in horses: but we will remember the name of the Lord our God. *20, 7*

91 The Lord is my shepherd; I shall not want. *23, 1*

92 He maketh me to lie down in green pastures: he leadeth me beside the still waters. *23, 2*

93 Yea, though I walk through the valley of the shadow of death, I will fear no evil: for thou art with me; thy rod and thy staff they comfort me. *23, 4*

94 The earth is the Lord's, and the fulness thereof; the world, and they that dwell therein. *24, 1*

95 Weeping may endure for a night, but joy cometh in the morning.
30, 5

96 Into thy hands I commend my spirit. *31, 6, Book of Common Prayer version*

97 Praise the Lord with harp: sing unto him with the psaltery and an instrument of ten strings. *33, 2*

98 Sing unto him a new song, play skilfully with a loud noise. *33, 3*

99 O taste and see that the Lord is good. *34, 8*

1 The Lord is nigh unto them that are of a broken heart. *34, 18*

2 But the meek shall inherit the earth. *37, 11*

3 I have been young, and now am old; yet have I not seen the righteous forsaken, nor his seed begging bread. *37, 25*

4 I myself have seen the ungodly in great power: and flourishing like a green bay-tree. *37, 36, Book of Common Prayer version*

5 Lord, make me to know mine end, and the measure of my days.
39, 4

6 Blessed is he that considereth the poor. *41, 1*

7 God is our refuge and strength, a very present help in trouble.
46, 1

8 Purge me with hyssop, and I shall be clean, wash me, and I shall be whiter than snow. *51, 7*

9 The sacrifices of God are a broken spirit: a broken and a contrite heart, O God, thou wilt not despise. *51, 17*

10 Oh that I had wings like a dove! *55, 6*

11 They are like the deaf adder that stoppeth her ear. *58, 4*

12 They grin like a dog, and run about through the city.
59, 6, Book of Common Prayer version

13 Make a joyful noise unto God.   *Psalms, 66, 1*

14 They go from strength to strength.   *84, 7*

15 I had rather be a doorkeeper in the house of my God, than to
dwell in the tents of wickedness.   *84, 10*

16 For a thousand years in thy sight are but as yesterday when it is
past, and as a watch in the night.   *90, 4*

17 The days of our years are threescore years and ten; and if by
reason of strength they be fourscore years, yet is their strength
labour and sorrow; for it is soon cut off, and we fly away. *90, 10*

18 So teach us to number our days, that we may apply our hearts
unto wisdom.   *90, 12*

19 He shall cover thee with his feathers, and under his wings shalt
thou trust.   *91, 4*

20 Thou shalt not be afraid for the terror by night; nor for the
arrow that flieth by day.   *91, 5*

21 Nor for the pestilence that walketh in darkness: nor for the
destruction that wasteth at noonday.   *91, 6*

22 Like as a father pitieth his children, so the Lord pitieth them
that fear him.   *103, 13*

23 As for man, his days are as grass: as a flower of the field, so he
flourisheth.   *103, 15*

24 Wine that maketh glad the heart of man.   *104, 15*

25 The iron entered into his soul.   *105, 18, Book of Common
                                                   Prayer version*

26 They that go down to the sea in ships, that do business in great
waters.   *107, 23*

27 They reel to and fro, and stagger like a drunken man, and are at
their wits' end.   *107, 27*

28 The fear of the Lord is the beginning of wisdom.   *111, 10*

29 The mountains skipped like rams, and the little hills like lambs.
                                                         114, 4

30 They have mouths, but they speak not: eyes have they, but they
see not.   *115, 5*

31 They have ears, but they hear not: noses have they, but they
smell not.   *115, 6*

32 I said in my haste, All men are liars.   *116, 11*

33 Precious in the sight of the Lord is the death of his saints.
                                                         116, 15

34 It is better to trust in the Lord than to put confidence in man.
                                                         118, 8

35 The stone which the builders refused is become the head stone of the corner. *Psalms, 118, 22*

36 I am for peace: but when I speak, they are for war. *120, 7*

37 I will lift up mine eyes unto the hills, from whence cometh my help. *121, 1*

38 The sun shall not smite thee by day, nor the moon by night. *121, 6*

39 The Lord shall preserve thy going out and thy coming in from this time forth, and even for evermore. *121, 8*

40 They that sow in tears shall reap in joy. *126, 5*

41 Except the Lord build the house, they labour in vain that build it. *127, 1*

42 It is vain for you to rise up early, to sit up late, to eat the bread of sorrows: for so he giveth his beloved sleep. *127, 2*

43 Behold, how good and how pleasant it is for brethren to dwell together in unity! *133, 1*

44 By the rivers of Babylon, there we sat down, yea, we wept, when we remembered Zion. *137, 1*

45 We hanged our harps upon the willows in the midst thereof. *137, 2*

46 Sing us one of the songs of Zion. *137, 3*

47 How shall we sing the Lord's song in a strange land? *137, 4*

48 If I forget thee, O Jerusalem, let my right hand forget her cunning. *137, 5*

49 If I do not remember thee, let my tongue cleave to the roof of my mouth. *137, 6*

50 I am fearfully and wonderfully made. *139, 14*

51 Set a watch, O Lord, before my mouth; keep the door of my lips. *141, 3*

52 The eyes of all wait upon thee; and thou givest them their meat in due season. *145, 15*

53 Put not your trust in princes. *146, 3*

Proverbs

54 The fear of the Lord is the beginning of knowledge. *1, 7*

55 Whom the Lord loveth he correcteth. *3, 12*

56 Her ways are ways of pleasantness, and all her paths are peace. *3, 17*

57 Go to the ant, thou sluggard; consider her ways, and be wise. *6, 6*

58 For wisdom is better than rubies.   *Proverbs, 8, 11*

59 Wisdom hath builded her house, she hath hewn out her seven
pillars.   *9, 1*

60 Stolen waters are sweet, and bread eaten in secret is pleasant.
                                                   9, 17

61 A wise son maketh a glad father: but a foolish son is the heaviness of his mother.   *10, 1*

62 The memory of the just is blessed.   *10, 7*

63 In the multitude of counsellers there is safety. *11, 14*

64 As a jewel of gold in a swine's snout, so is a fair woman which is
without discretion.   *11, 22*

65 A virtuous woman is a crown to her husband: but she that
maketh ashamed is as rottenness in his bones.   *12, 4*

66 Hope deferred maketh the heart sick.   *13, 12*

67 He that spareth his rod hateth his son: but he that loveth him
chasteneth him betimes.   *13, 24*

68 Righteousness exalteth a nation.   *14, 34*

69 A soft answer turneth away wrath.   *15, 1*

70 A merry heart maketh a cheerful countenance.   *15, 13*

71 Better is a dinner of herbs where love is, than a stalled ox and
hatred therewith.   *15, 17*

72 Pride goeth before destruction, and an haughty spirit before a
fall.   *16, 18*

73 Even a fool, when he holdeth his peace, is counted wise. *17, 28*

74 Wealth maketh many friends.   *19, 4*

75 Wine is a mocker, strong drink is raging: and whosoever is
deceived thereby is not wise.   *20, 1*

76 Even a child is known by his doings.   *20, 11*

77 It is naught, it is naught, saith the buyer; but when he is gone
his way, then he boasteth.   *20, 14*

78 The glory of young men is their strength.   *20, 29*

79 A good name is rather to be chosen than great riches.   *22, 1*

80 Train up a child in the way he should go: and when he is old,
he will not depart from it.   *22, 6*

81 If thine enemy be hungry, give him bread to eat; and if he be
thirsty, give him water to drink:
For thou shalt heap coals of fire upon his head, and the Lord
shall reward thee.   *25, 21–22*

82 As cold waters to a thirsty soul, so is good news from a far
country.   *25, 25*

83 A whip for the horse, a bridle for the ass, and a rod for the fool's
back. *Proverbs, 26, 3*

84 As a dog returneth to his vomit, so a fool returneth to his folly.
26, 11

85 Whoso diggeth a pit shall fall therein. *26, 27*

86 Open rebuke is better than secret love. *27, 5*

87 Faithful are the wounds of a friend. *27, 6*

88 He that maketh haste to be rich shall not be innocent. *28, 20*

89 Where there is no vision, the people perish. *29, 18*

90 Give me neither poverty nor riches; feed me with food convenient for me. *30, 8*

91 There be three things which are too wonderful for me, yea, four
which I know not: The way of an eagle in the air; the way of a
serpent upon a rock; the way of a ship in the midst of the sea;
and the way of a man with a maid. *30, 18–19*

92 Who can find a virtuous woman? for her price is far above
rubies. *31, 10*

Ecclesiastes

93 Vanity of vanities, saith the Preacher, vanity of vanities; all is
vanity. *1, 2*

94 What profit hath a man of all his labour which he taketh
under the sun? *1, 3*

95 One generation passeth away, and another generation cometh:
but the earth abideth for ever. *1, 4*

96 There is no new thing under the sun. *1, 9*

97 For in much wisdom is much grief: and he that increaseth
knowledge increaseth sorrow. *1, 18*

98 To every thing there is a season, and a time to every purpose
under the heaven. *3, 1*

99 A threefold cord is not quickly broken. *4, 12*

1 God is in heaven, and thou upon earth: therefore let thy words
be few. *5, 2*

2 The sleep of a labouring man is sweet. *5, 12*

3 A good name is better than precious ointment; and the day
of death than the day of one's birth. *7, 1*

4 For as the crackling of thorns under a pot, so is the laughter of
the fool. *7, 6*

5 Say not thou, What is the cause that the former days were better
than these? for thou dost not inquire wisely concerning this.
7, 10

6 Be not righteous over much.   *Ecclesiastes, 7, 16*

7 Whatsoever thy hand findeth to do, do it with thy might.
9, 10

8 The race is not to the swift, nor the battle to the strong, neither yet bread to the wise, nor yet riches to men of understanding, nor yet favour to men of skill; but time and chance happeneth to them all.   *9, 11*

9 Cast thy bread upon the waters: for thou shalt find it after many days.   *11, 1*

10 Rejoice, O young man, in thy youth.   *11, 9*

11 Remember now thy Creator in the days of thy youth, while the evil days come not, nor the years draw nigh, when thou shalt say, I have no pleasure in them.   *12, 1*

12 Man goeth to his long home.   *12, 5*

13 Of making many books there is no end; and much study is a weariness of the flesh.   *12, 12*

14 Let us hear the conclusion of the whole matter: Fear God, and keep his commandments: for this is the whole duty of man.
12, 13

The Song of Solomon

15 Let him kiss me with the kisses of his mouth: for thy love is better than wine.   *1, 2*

16 I am black, but comely, O ye daughters of Jerusalem.   *1, 5*

17 I am the rose of Sharon, and the lily of the valleys.   *2, 1*

18 His banner over me was love.   *2, 4*

19 Stay me with flagons, comfort me with apples: for I am sick of love.   *2, 5*

20 Rise up, my love, my fair one, and come away.   *2, 10*

21 For, lo, the winter is past, the rain is over and gone.   *2, 11*

22 The flowers appear on the earth; the time of the singing of birds is come, and the voice of the turtle is heard in our land.   *2, 12*

23 Our vines have tender grapes.   *2, 15*

24 Until the day break, and the shadows flee away.   *2, 17*

25 I sleep, but my heart waketh.   *5, 2*

26 Terrible as an army with banners.   *6, 4*

27 Love is strong as death; jealousy is cruel as the grave.   *8, 6*

28 Many waters cannot quench love.   *8, 7*

Isaiah

29 The ox knoweth his owner, and the ass his master's crib.   *1, 3*

30 Though your sins be as scarlet, they shall be as white as snow.
1, 18

31 They shall beat their swords into plowshares, and their spears into pruning-hooks: nation shall not lift up sword against nation, neither shall they learn war any more.   *2, 4*

32 What mean ye that ye beat my people to pieces, and grind the faces of the poor?   *3, 15*

33 Woe unto them that call evil good, and good evil.   *5, 20*

34 A virgin shall conceive, and bear a son, and shall call his name Immanuel.   *7, 14*

35 The people that walked in darkness have seen a great light.   *9, 2*

36 For unto us a child is born, unto us a son is given: and the government shall be upon his shoulder: and his name shall be called Wonderful, Counseller, The mighty God, The everlasting Father, The Prince of Peace.   *9, 6*

37 The wolf also shall dwell with the lamb, and the leopard shall lie down with the kid; and the calf and the young lion and the fatling together; and a little child shall lead them.   *11, 6*

38 How art thou fallen from heaven, O Lucifer, son of the morning!
14, 12

39 Watchman, what of the night?   *21, 11*

40 Let us eat and drink; for to-morrow we shall die.   *22, 13*

41 Set thine house in order: for thou shalt die.   *38, 1*

42 All flesh is grass.   *40, 6*

43 Behold, the nations are as a drop of a bucket.   *40, 15*

44 A bruised reed shall he not break, and the smoking flax shall he not quench.   *42, 3*

45 There is no peace, saith the Lord, unto the wicked.   *48, 22*

46 How beautiful upon the mountains are the feet of him that bringeth good tidings.   *52, 7*

47 He is despised and rejected of men; a man of sorrows, and acquainted with grief.   *53, 3*

48 All we like sheep have gone astray.   *53, 6*

49 He is brought as a lamb to the slaughter.   *53, 7*

50 Seek ye the Lord while he may be found, call ye upon him while he is near.   *55, 6*

51 For my thoughts are not your thoughts, neither are your ways my ways, saith the Lord.   *55, 8*

52 Is it such a fast that I have chosen? a day for a man to afflict his soul?   *Isaiah, 58, 5*

53 To give unto them beauty for ashes, the oil of joy for mourning, the garment of praise for the spirit of heaviness.   *61, 3*

Jeremiah

54 They have healed also the hurt of the daughter of my people slightly, saying, Peace, peace; when there is no peace.   *6, 14*

55 Is there no balm in Gilead; is there no physician there? *8, 22*

56 Can the Ethiopian change his skin, or the leopard his spots?   *13, 23*

57 As the clay is in the potter's hand, so are ye in mine hand, O house of Israel.   *18, 6*

58 The fathers have eaten a sour grape, and the children's teeth are set on edge.   *31, 29*

Lamentations

59 Is it nothing to you, all ye that pass by? behold, and see if there be any sorrow like unto my sorrow.   *1, 12*

60 Remembering mine affliction and my misery, the wormwood and the gall.   *3, 19*

61 His compassions fail not. They are new every morning.   *3, 22–23*

62 It is good for a man that he bear the yoke in his youth. *3, 27*

Ezekiel

63 They four had one likeness, as if a wheel had been in the midst of a wheel.   *10, 10*

64 The king of Babylon stood at the parting of the way.   *21, 21*

65 O ye dry bones, hear the word of the Lord.   *37, 4*

66 Son of man, set thy face against Gog, the land of Magog.   *38, 2*

Daniel

67 And he commanded the most mighty men that were in his army to bind Shadrach, Meshach, and Abed-nego, and to cast them into the burning fiery furnace.   *3, 20*

68 MENE, MENE, TEKEL, UPHARSIN.   *5, 25*

69 Thou art weighed in the balances, and art found wanting.   *5, 27*

70 Thy kingdom is divided, and given to the Medes and Persians.   *5, 28*

71 The law of the Medes and Persians, which altereth not.
Daniel, 6, 12

72 They brought Daniel, and cast him into the den of lions. *6, 16*

73 The Ancient of days. *7, 13*

74 O Daniel, a man greatly beloved. *10, 11*

Hosea

75 I desired mercy, and not sacrifice; and the knowledge of God more than burnt offerings. *6, 6*

76 They have sown the wind, and they shall reap the whirlwind. *8, 7*

77 I drew them with cords of a man, with bands of love. *11, 4*

Joel

78 Rend your heart, and not your garments. *2, 13*

79 The years that the locust hath eaten. *2, 25*

80 Your old men shall dream dreams, your young men shall see visions. *2, 28*

81 Multitudes in the valley of decision. *3, 14*

Amos

82 Can two walk together, except they be agreed? *3, 3*

83 Prepare to meet thy God. *4, 12*

84 Woe to them that are at ease in Zion. *6, 1*

Jonah

85 So they cast lots, and the lot fell upon Jonah. *1, 7*

86 Jonah was in the belly of the fish three days and three nights. *1, 17*

87 And God said to Jonah, Doest thou well to be angry for the gourd? *4, 9*

88 And should not I spare Nineveh, that great city, wherein are more than sixscore thousand persons that cannot discern between their right hand and their left hand; and also much cattle? *4, 11*

Micah

89 They shall sit every man under his vine and under his fig tree. *4, 4*

90 O my people, what have I done unto thee? and wherein have I wearied thee? *6, 3*

91 What doth the Lord require of thee, but to do justly, and to love mercy, and to walk humbly with thy God? *Micah, 6, 8*

Habakkuk

92 Thou art of purer eyes than to behold evil. *1, 13*
93 Write the vision, and make it plain upon tables, that he may run that readeth it. *2, 2*

Haggai

94 The glory of this latter house shall be greater than of the former. *2, 9*

Zechariah

95 Is not this a brand plucked out of the fire? *3, 2*
96 Who hath despised the day of small things? *4, 10*
97 What are these wounds in thine hands? Then he shall answer, Those with which I was wounded in the house of my friends. *13, 6*

Malachi

98 Have we not all one father? hath not one God created us? *2, 10*
99 The Lord, whom ye seek, shall suddenly come to his temple. *3, 1*

1 Unto you that fear my name shall the Sun of righteousness arise with healing in his wings. *4, 2*

THE NEW TESTAMENT
St Matthew

2 Where is he that is born King of the Jews? for we have seen his star in the east, and are come to worship him. *2, 2*
3 Rachel weeping for her children, and would not be comforted, because they are not. *2, 18*
4 Repent ye: for the kingdom of heaven is at hand. *3, 2*
5 The voice of one crying in the wilderness. *3, 3*
6 O generation of vipers, who hath warned you to flee from the wrath to come? *3, 7*
7 Man shall not live by bread alone, but by every word that proceedeth out of the mouth of God. *4, 4*
8 Follow me, and I will make you fishers of men. *4, 19*
9 Blessed are the meek: for they shall inherit the earth. *5, 5*

10 Blessed are the pure in heart: for they shall see God.
St Matthew, 5, 8

11 Ye are the salt of the earth: but if the salt have lost his savour, wherewith shall it be salted? *5, 13*

12 An eye for an eye, and a tooth for a tooth. *5, 38*

13 Resist not evil: but whosoever shall smite thee on thy right cheek, turn to him the other also. *5, 39*

14 Love your enemies. *5, 44*

15 He maketh his sun to rise on the evil and on the good, and sendeth rain on the just and on the unjust. *5, 45*

16 Let not thy left hand know what thy right hand doeth. *6, 3*

17 Use not vain repetitions. *6, 7*

18 After this manner therefore pray ye: Our Father which art in heaven, Hallowed be thy name. Thy kingdom come. Thy will be done in earth, as it is in heaven. Give us this day our daily bread. And forgive us our debts, as we forgive our debtors. And lead us not into temptation, but deliver us from evil: For thine is the kingdom, and the power, and the glory, for ever. Amen. *6, 9–13*

19 No man can serve two masters. *6, 24*

20 Ye cannot serve God and mammon. *Ib*

21 Consider the lilies of the field, how they grow; they toil not, neither do they spin. *6, 28*

22 Sufficient unto the day is the evil thereof. *6, 34*

23 Judge not, that ye be not judged. *7, 1*

24 Neither cast ye your pearls before swine. *7, 6*

25 Therefore all things whatsoever ye would that men should do to you, do ye even so to them: for this is the law and the prophets.
7, 12

26 Enter ye in at the strait gate. *7, 13*

27 Beware of false prophets, which come to you in sheep's clothing, but inwardly they are ravening wolves. *7, 15*

28 A man under authority. *8, 9*

29 What went ye out into the wilderness to see? A reed shaken with the wind? *11, 7*

30 He that is not with me is against me. *12, 30*

31 One pearl of great price. *13, 46*

32 A prophet is not without honour, save in his own country.
13, 57

33 If the blind lead the blind, both shall fall into the ditch. *15, 14*

34 Thou art Peter, and upon this rock I will build my church; and the gates of hell shall not prevail against it. *St Matthew, 16, 18*

35 The keys of the kingdom of heaven.   *16, 19*

36 Get thee behind me, Satan.   *16, 23*

37 Except ye be converted, and become as little children, ye shall not enter into the kingdom of heaven.   *18, 3*

38 But whoso shall offend one of these little ones which believe in me, it were better for him that a millstone were hanged about his neck, and that he were drowned in the depth of the sea.
                                                                     18, 6

39 If thine eye offend thee, pluck it out.   *18, 9*

40 Until seventy times seven.   *18, 22*

41 It is easier for a camel to go through the eye of a needle, than for a rich man to enter into the kingdom of God.   *19, 24*

42 For many are called, but few are chosen.   *22, 14*

43 Render therefore unto Caesar the things which are Caesar's; and unto God the things that are God's.   *22, 21*

44 Ye blind guides, which strain at a gnat, and swallow a camel.
                                                                    23, 24

45 Wars and rumours of wars.   *24, 6*

46 For unto every one that hath shall be given, and he shall have abundance: but from him that hath not shall be taken away even that which he hath.   *25, 29*

47 As a shepherd divideth his sheep from the goats.   *25, 32*

48 Inasmuch as ye have done it unto one of the least of these my brethren, ye have done it unto me.   *25, 40*

49 Ye have the poor always with you.   *26, 11*

50 Watch and pray, that ye enter not into temptation: the spirit indeed is willing, but the flesh is weak.   *26, 41*

51 He took water, and washed his hands before the multitude, saying, I am innocent of the blood of this just person.   *27, 24*

52 I am with you alway, even unto the end of the world.   *28, 20*

St Mark

53 They that are whole have no need of the physician, but they that are sick.   *2, 17*

54 The sabbath was made for man, and not man for the sabbath.
                                                                     2, 27

55 If a house be divided against itself, that house cannot stand.
                                                                     3, 25

56 He that hath ears to hear, let him hear. *St Mark, 4, 9*

57 My name is Legion: for we are many. *5, 9*

58 For what shall it profit a man, if he shall gain the whole world and lose his own soul? *8, 36*

59 I believe: help thou mine unbelief. *9, 24*

60 What therefore God hath joined together, let not man put asunder. *10, 9*

61 Suffer the little children to come unto me, and forbid them not: for of such is the kingdom of God. *10, 14*

62 Is it not written, My house shall be called of all nations the house of prayer? but ye have made it a den of thieves. *11, 17*

63 And there came a certain poor widow, and she threw in two mites, which make a farthing. *12, 42*

64 Take ye heed, watch and pray. *13, 33*

65 Before the cock crow twice, thou shalt deny me thrice. *14, 30*

66 Crucify him. *15, 13*

St Luke

67 There was no room for them in the inn. *2, 7*

68 And there were in the same country shepherds abiding in the field, keeping watch over their flock by night. *2, 8*

69 Ye shall find the babe wrapped in swaddling clothes, lying in a manger. *2, 12*

70 Glory to God in the highest, and on earth peace, good will toward men. *2, 14*

71 Be content with your wages. *3, 14*

72 Physician, heal thyself. *4, 23*

73 No man putteth new wine into old bottles. *5, 37*

74 No man, having put his hand to the plough, and looking back, is fit for the kingdom of God. *9, 62*

75 The labourer is worthy of his hire. *10, 7*

76 Fell among thieves. *10, 30*

77 He passed by on the other side. *10, 31*

78 Friend, go up higher. *14, 10*

79 The poor, and the maimed, and the halt, and the blind. *14, 21*

80 Joy shall be in heaven over one sinner that repenteth, more than over ninety and nine just persons, which need no repentance. *15, 7*

81 And he would fain have filled his belly with the husks that the
swine did eat.   *St Luke, 15, 16*

82 Bring hither the fatted calf, and kill it.   *15, 23*

83 I cannot dig; to beg I am ashamed.   *16, 3*

84 The children of this world are in their generation wiser than the
children of light.   *16, 8*

85 Make to yourselves friends of the mammon of unrighteousness.
                                               16, 9

86 The crumbs which fell from the rich man's table.   *16, 21*

87 Between us and you there is a great gulf fixed.   *16, 26*

88 Remember Lot's wife.   *17, 32*

89 I thank thee, that I am not as other men are.   *18, 11*

90 Out of thine own mouth will I judge thee.   *19, 22*

91 Father, forgive them; for they know not what they do.   *23, 34*

St John

92 In the beginning was the Word, and the Word was with God,
and the Word was God.   *1, 1*

93 The true Light, which lighteth every man that cometh into the
world.   *1, 9*

94 He came unto his own, and his own received him not.   *1, 11*

95 The Word was made flesh, and dwelt among us.   *1, 14*

96 Can there any good thing come out of Nazareth?   *1, 46*

97 Ye must be born again.   *3, 7*

98 The wind bloweth where it listeth.   *3, 8*

99 For God so loved the world, that he gave his only begotten Son,
that whosoever believeth in him should not perish, but have
everlasting life.   *3, 16*

1 Men loved darkness rather than light, because their deeds were
evil.   *3, 19*

2 Judge not according to the appearance, but judge righteous
judgment.   *7, 24*

3 He that is without sin among you, let him first cast a stone at her.
                                               8, 7

4 I am the light of the world.   *8, 12*

5 The night cometh, when no man can work.   *9, 4*

6 The good shepherd giveth his life for the sheep.   *10, 11*

7 Jesus wept.   *11, 35*

8 A new commandment I give unto you, That ye love one another.
St John, 13, 34

9 In my Father's house are many mansions.   *14, 2*

10 Greater love hath no man than this, that a man lay down his life for his friends.   *15, 13*

11 Whither goest thou?   *16, 5*

12 Pilate saith unto him, What is truth?   *18, 38*

13 What I have written I have written.   *19, 22*

14 Blessed are they that have not seen, and yet have believed.
20, 29

Acts of the Apostles

15 Silver and gold have I none; but such as I have give I thee.
3, 6

16 Thy money perish with thee, because thou hast thought that the gift of God may be purchased with money.   *8, 20*

17 He went on his way rejoicing.   *8, 39*

18 It is hard for thee to kick against the pricks.   *9, 5*

19 God is no respecter of persons.   *10, 34*

20 In him we live, and move, and have our being.   *17, 28*

21 Great is Diana of the Ephesians.   *19, 34*

22 It is more blessed to give than to receive.   *20, 35*

23 A citizen of no mean city.   *21, 39*

24 Brought up in this city at the feet of Gamaliel.   *22, 3*

25 I appeal unto Caesar.   *25, 11*

26 Hast thou appealed unto Caesar? unto Caesar shalt thou go.
25, 12

27 I was not disobedient unto the heavenly vision.   *26, 19*

28 Almost thou persuadest me to be a Christian.   *26, 28*

Romans

29 The just shall live by faith.   *1, 17*

30 These, having not the law, are a law unto themselves.   *2, 14*

31 Death hath no more dominion over him.   *6, 9*

32 The wages of sin is death.   *6, 23*

33 For the good that I would I do not: but the evil which I would not, that I do.   *7, 19*

34 And we know that all things work together for good to them that love God.   *8, 28*

35 If God be for us, who can be against us?   *Romans, 8, 31*

36 So we, being many, are one body in Christ, and every one members one of another.   *12, 5*

37 Let love be without dissimulation. Abhor that which is evil; cleave to that which is good.   *12, 9*

38 Rejoice with them that do rejoice, and weep with them that weep.
12, 15

39 Be not wise in your own conceits.   *12, 16*

40 Vengeance is mine; I will repay, saith the Lord.   *12, 19*

41 Be not overcome of evil, but overcome evil with good. *12, 21*

42 The powers that be are ordained of God.   *13, 1*

43 Love worketh no ill to his neighbour: therefore love is the fulfilling of the law.   *13, 10*

44 None of us liveth to himself, and no man dieth to himself.
14, 7

45 We then that are strong ought to bear the infirmities of the weak.
15, 1

1 Corinthians

46 I have planted, Apollos watered; but God gave the increase.
3, 6

47 Absent in body, but present in spirit.   *5, 3*

48 Know ye not that a little leaven leaveneth the whole lump?
5, 6

49 All things are lawful unto me, but all things are not expedient.
6, 12

50 It is better to marry than to burn.   *7, 9*

51 All things to all men.   *9, 22*

52 If a woman have long hair, it is a glory to her.   *11, 15*

53 When I become a man, I put away childish things.   *13, 11*

54 Now we see through a glass, darkly; but then face to face.
13, 12

55 And now abideth faith, hope, charity, these three; but the greatest of these is charity.   *13, 13*

56 Let your women keep silence in the churches.   *14, 34*

57 Let all things be done decently and in order.   *14, 40*

58 One born out of due time.   *15, 8*

59 By the grace of God I am what I am.   *15, 10*

60 O death, where is thy sting? O grave, where is thy victory?
15, 55

2 Corinthians

61 The letter killeth, but the spirit giveth life. *3, 6*

62 We walk by faith, not by sight. *5, 7*

63 God loveth a cheerful giver. *9, 7*

64 For ye suffer fools gladly, seeing ye yourselves are wise.
11, 19

65 A thorn in the flesh. *12, 7*

66 My grace is sufficient for thee: for my strength is made perfect in weakness. *12, 9*

Galatians

67 The right hands of fellowship. *2, 9*

68 Ye are fallen from grace. *5, 4*

69 Bear ye one another's burdens. *6, 2*

70 Be not deceived; God is not mocked: for whatsoever a man soweth, that shall he also reap. *6, 7*

Ephesians

71 Be ye angry, and sin not; let not the sun go down upon your wrath. *4, 26*

72 For this cause shall a man leave his father and mother, and shall be joined unto his wife, and they two shall be one flesh. *5, 31*

73 Put on the whole armour of God. *6, 11*

74 For we wrestle not against flesh and blood, but against principalities, against powers, against the rulers of the darkness of this world, against spiritual wickedness in high places. *6, 12*

Philippians

75 Work out your own salvation with fear and trembling. *2, 12*

76 Whose God is their belly, and whose glory is in their shame.
2, 19

77 Our conversation is in heaven. *3, 20*

78 The peace of God, which passeth all understanding. *4, 7*

79 Whatsoever things are true, whatsoever things are honest, whatsoever things are just, whatsoever things are pure, whatsoever things are lovely, whatsoever things are of good report; if there be any virtue, and if there be any praise, think on these things.
4, 8

80 I have learned, in whatsoever state I am, therewith to be content.
4, 11

Colossians

81 Touch not; taste not; handle not.   *2, 21*

82 Set your affection on things above, not on things on the earth.
                                                               3, 2

1 Thessalonians

83 Remembering without ceasing your work of faith, and labour
   of love.   *1, 3*

84 Pray without ceasing.   *5, 17*

85 Prove all things: hold fast that which is good.   *5, 21*

2 Thessalonians

86 If any would not work, neither should he eat.   *3, 10*

1 Timothy

87 Not greedy of filthy lucre.   *3, 3*

88 Refuse profane and old wives' fables.   *4, 7*

89 Let no man despise thy youth.   *4, 12*

90 Drink no longer water, but use a little wine for thy stomach's
   sake and thine often infirmities.   *5, 23*

91 For we brought nothing into this world, and it is certain we can
   carry nothing out.   *6, 7*

92 The love of money is the root of all evil.   *6, 10*

93 Fight the good fight of faith.   *6, 12*

2 Timothy

94 All scripture is given by inspiration of God.   *3, 16*

95 I have fought a good fight, I have finished my course, I have kept
   the faith.   *4, 7*

Titus

96 Unto the pure all things are pure.   *1, 15*

Hebrews

97 It is appointed unto men once to die, but after this the judgment.
                                                               9, 27

98 It is a fearful thing to fall into the hands of the living God.
                                                               10, 31

99 Faith is the substance of things hoped for, the evidence of things
   not seen.   *11, 1*

1 Whom the Lord loveth he chasteneth.   *Hebrews, 12, 6*

2 Let brotherly love continue.   *13, 1*

3 Jesus Christ the same yesterday, and today, and for ever.

    13, 8

James

4 Faith without works is dead.   *2, 20*

5 The tongue can no man tame; it is an unruly evil.   *3, 8*

6 Resist the devil, and he will flee from you.   *4, 7*

7 Ye have heard of the patience of Job.   *5, 11*

1 Peter

8 All flesh is as grass.   *1, 24*

9 Honour all men. Love the brotherhood. Fear God. Honour the king.   *2, 17*

10 Giving honour unto the wife, as unto the weaker vessel.   *3, 7*

11 Charity shall cover the multitude of sins.   *4, 8*

12 Be sober, be vigilant; because your adversary the devil, as a roaring lion, walketh about, seeking whom he may devour.

    5, 8

2 Peter

13 The dog is turned to his own vomit again; and the sow that was washed to her wallowing in the mire.   *2, 22*

14 One day is with the Lord as a thousand years, and a thousand years as one day.   *3, 8*

1 John

15 Shutteth up his bowels of compassion.   *3, 17*

16 God is love.   *4, 8*

17 There is no fear in love; but perfect love casteth out fear.

    4, 18

2 John

18 The elder unto the elect lady.   *1, 1*

Revelation

19 I am Alpha and Omega, the beginning and the ending.   *1, 8*

20 Be thou faithful unto death, and I will give thee a crown of life.

    2, 10

21 He shall rule them with a rod of iron.   *2, 27*

22 I will not blot out his name out of the book of life. *Revelation, 3, 5*

23 Because thou art lukewarm, and neither cold nor hot, I will spue
    thee out of my mouth.   *3, 16*

24 Behold, I stand at the door, and knock.   *3, 20*

25 He went forth conquering, and to conquer.   *6, 2*

26 Behold a pale horse: and his name that sat on him was Death,
    and Hell followed with him.   *6, 8*

27 And when he had opened the seventh seal, there was silence in
    heaven about the space of half an hour.   *8, 1*

28 The bottomless pit.   *9, 1*

29 They had tails like unto scorpions, and there were stings in their
    tails.   *9, 10*

30 Let him that hath understanding count the number of the beast:
    for it is the number of a man; and his number is Six hundred
    threescore and six.   *13, 18*

31 A place called in the Hebrew tongue Armageddon.   *16, 16*

32 And I saw a new heaven and a new earth: for the first heaven
    and the first earth were passed away; and there was no more sea.
                                                                   21, 1

33 The holy city, new Jerusalem, coming down from God out of
    heaven, prepared as a bride adorned for her husband.   *21, 2*

34 And God shall wipe away all tears from their eyes; and there
    shall be no more death, neither sorrow, nor crying, neither shall
    there be any more pain: for the former things are passed away.
                                                                   21, 4

35 If any man shall add unto these things, God shall add unto him
    the plagues that are written in this book.   *22, 18*

APOCRYPHA

1 Esdras

36 The first wrote, Wine is the strongest.
    The second wrote, The King is strongest.
    The third wrote, Women are strongest: but above all things Truth
    beareth away the victory.   *3, 10*

37 Great is Truth, and mighty above all things.   *4, 41*

2 Esdras

38 I shall light a candle of understanding in thine heart, which shall
    not be put out.   *14, 25*

Tobit

39 If thou hast abundance, give alms accordingly: if thou have but a little, be not afraid to give according to that little.   *4, 8*

40 So they went forth both, and the young man's dog with them.
    5, 16

Wisdom of Solomon

41 Let us crown ourselves with rosebuds, before they be withered.
    2, 8

42 Through envy of the devil came death into the world.   *2, 24*

43 The souls of the righteous are in the hand of God, and there shall no torment touch them.   *3, 1*

44 The corruptible body presseth down the soul.   *9, 15*

45 O Lord, thou lover of souls.   *11, 26*

Ecclesiasticus

46 My son, if thou come to serve the Lord, prepare thy soul for temptation.   *2, 1*

47 A faithful friend is the medicine of life.   *6, 16*

48 Miss not the discourse of the elders.   *8, 9*

49 Open not thine heart to every man.   *8, 19*

50 Give not thy soul unto a woman.   *9, 2*

51 Forsake not an old friend.   *9, 10*

52 Judge none blessed before his death.   *11, 28*

53 He that toucheth pitch shall be defiled therewith.   *13, 1*

54 Be not made a beggar by banqueting upon borrowing.   *18, 33*

55 All wickedness is but little to the wickedness of a woman.
    25, 19

56 Let thy speech be short, comprehending much in few words.
    32, 8

57 Honour a physician with the honour due unto him.   *38, 1*

58 How can he get wisdom . . . whose talk is of bullocks?   *38, 25*

59 Let us now praise famous men, and our fathers that begat us.
    44, 1

60 Rich men furnished with ability, living peaceably in their habitations.   *44, 6*

61 And some there be, which have no memorial.   *44, 9*

62 Their bodies are buried in peace, but their name liveth for evermore.   *44, 14*

1 Maccabees

63 Consider ye throughout all ages, that none that put their trust
   in him shall be overcome.   *2, 61*

2 Maccabees

64 When he was at the last gasp.   *7, 9*
65 It was an holy and good thought.   *12, 45*

THE BOOK OF COMMON PRAYER

66 We have erred, and strayed from thy ways like lost sheep.
                          Morning Prayer, General Confession

67 We have left indone those things which we ought to have done;
   And we have done those things which we ought not to have
   done.   *Ib, Ib*

68 As it was in the beginning, is now, and ever shall be: world
   without end.   *Ib, Gloria*

69 The noble army of Martyrs.   *Ib, Te Deum*

70 Give peace in our time, O Lord.   *Ib, Versicles*

71 Whose service is perfect freedom. *Ib, Second Collect, for Peace*

72 In Quires and Places where they sing.   *Ib, Rubric after Third
                                                             Collect*

73 When two or three are gathered together in thy Name thou wilt
   grant their requests.   *Ib, Prayer of St Chrysostom*

74 Lighten our darkness.   *Evening Prayer, Third Collect, for Aid
                                              Against all Perils*

75 Defend us from all perils and dangers of this night.   *Ib, Ib*

76 Have mercy upon us miserable sinners.   *Litany*

77 Envy, hatred, and malice, and all uncharitableness.   *Ib*

78 All the deceits of the world, the flesh, and the devil.   *Ib*

79 In the hour of death, and in the day of judgement.   *Ib*

80 Preserve to our use the kindly fruits of the earth.   *Ib*

81 All sorts and conditions of men.   *Prayer for all Conditions of
                                                             men*

82 All who profess and call themselves Christians.   *Ib*

83 Those who are any ways afflicted, or distressed, in mind, body,
   or estate.   *Ib*

84 Patience under their sufferings, and a happy issue out of all
   their afflictions.   *Ib*

85 Our creation, preservation, and all the blessings of this life.
A General Thanksgiving

86 Read, mark, learn and inwardly digest.
Collect, 2nd Sunday in Advent

87 All our doings without charity are nothing worth.
Ib Quinquagesima Sunday

88 Jews, Turks, Infidels, and Hereticks. *Ib, Third Collect for Good Friday*

89 A right judgement in all things. *Ib, Whit-Sunday*

90 The author and giver of all good things.
Ib, 7th Sunday after Trinity

91 Whom truly to know is everlasting life. *Ib, St Philip and St James's Day*

92 Constantly speak the truth, boldly rebuke vice, and patiently suffer for the truth's sake. *Ib, St John Baptist's Day*

93 An open and notorious evil liver. *Holy Communion, Introductory Rubric*

94 Grant that the old Adam in this Child may be so buried, that the new man may be raised up in him. *Publick Baptism of Infants, Blessing*

95 Renounce the devil and all his works. *Ib*

96 The pomps and vanity of this wicked world. *Catechism*

97 To order myself lowly and reverently to all my betters. *Ib*

98 To keep my hands from picking and stealing. *Ib*

99 To do my duty in that state of life, unto which it shall please God to call me. *Ib*

1 An outward and visible sign of an inward and spiritual grace. *Ib*

2 Being now come to the years of discretion.
Order of Confirmation

3 If any of you know cause, or just impediment. *Solemnization of Matrimony*

4 Brute beasts that have no understanding. *Ib*

5 Let him now speak, or else hereafter for ever hold his peace. *Ib*

6 Wilt thou have this Woman to thy wedded wife? *Ib*

7 To have and to hold from this day forward, for better for worse, for richer for poorer, in sickness and in health, to love and to cherish, till death us do part. *Ib*

8 To love, cherish, and to obey. *Ib*

9 With this ring I thee wed, with my body I thee worship, and with all my worldly goods I thee endow. *Solemnization of Matrimony*

10 Those whom God hath joined together let no man put asunder.
Ib

11 I pronounce that they be Man and Wife together.   *Ib*

12 The Office ensuing is not to be used for any that die unbaptized, or excommunicate, or have laid violent hands upon themselves.
Burial of the Dead, Introductory Rubric

13 Man that is born of a woman hath but a short time to live, and is full of misery.   *Ib*

14 In the midst of life we are in death.   *Ib*

15 We therefore commit his body to the ground; earth to earth, ashes to ashes, dust to dust.   *Ib*

BICKERSTAFFE, Isaac, 1735?–1812?

16 There was a jolly miller once
   Lived on the river Dee;
He worked and sang from morn till night;
   No lark more blithe than he.   *Love in a Village, Act, 1,*
Scene 5

17 I care for nobody, not I,
   If no one cares for me.   *Ib*

18 But if I'm content with a little
   Enough is as good as a feast.   *Ib, Act 3, Scene 1*

BICKERSTETH, Edward Henry, 1825–1906

19 Peace, perfect peace, in this dark world of sin?
The blood of Jesus whispers peace within.   *Songs in the House*
of Pilgrimage

BINYON, Laurence Robert, 1869–1943

20 They shall grow not old, as we that are left grow old:
   Age shall not weary them, nor the years condemn.
At the going down of the sun and in the morning
   We will remember them.   *For the Fallen (1914–1918)*

BIRRELL, Augustine, 1850–1933

21 That great dust-heap called 'history'.   *Obiter Dicta, 1st series,*
Carlyle

BISMARCK, Otto von, 1815–1898

22 *Nach Canossa gehen wir nicht.* We will not go to Canossa.
Speech, Reichstag, 14 May 1872

23 *Blut und Eisen.* Blood and Iron.   *Speech, Prussian Chamber, 28 Jan. 1886*

BLACKSTONE, Sir William, 1723–1780

24 The king never dies.   *Commentaries on the Laws of England, Book 1, 7*

25 That the king can do no wrong, is a necessary and fundamental principle of the English constitution.   *Ib, Book 3, 17*

26 It is better that ten guilty persons escape than one innocent suffer.   *Ib, Book, 4, 27*

BLAIR, Eric, see ORWELL, George

BLAKE, William, 1757–1827

27 To see a World in a grain of sand,
And a Heaven in a wild flower,
Hold Infinity in the palm of your hand,
And Eternity in an hour.   *Auguries of Innocence, 1*

28 A robin redbreast in a cage
Puts all Heaven in a rage.   *Ib, 5*

29 A truth that's told with bad intent
Beats all the lies you can invent.   *Ib, 53*

30 Man was made for joy and woe;
And when this we rightly know,
Thro' the world we safely go.   *Ib, 56*

31 God appears, and God is Light,
To those poor souls who dwell in Night;
But does a Human Form display
To those who dwell in realms of Day.   *Ib, 129*

32 Does the Eagle know what is in the pit
Or wilt thou go ask the Mole?
Can Wisdom be put in a silver rod,
Or love in a golden bowl?   *The Book of Thel, Thel's Motto*

33 Mutual Forgiveness of each vice,
Such are the Gates of Paradise.   *The Gates of Paradise, Prologue*

34 He who bends himself a Joy,
Doth the wingèd life destroy;
But he who kisses the Joy as it flies
Lives in Eternity's sunrise.
  Gnomic Verses, XVII, Several Questions Answered

35 For a Tear is an Intellectual thing;
And a Sigh is the sword of an angel king;

And the bitter groan of a Martyr's woe
Is an arrow from the Almighty's bow.   *Jerusalem, f. 52*

36 He who would do good to another must do it in Minute
Particulars.
General Good is the plea of the scoundrel, hypocrite, and
flatterer.   *Ib, f. 55*

37 I care not whether a man is Good or Evil; all that I care
Is whether he is a Wise Man or a Fool. Go! put off Holiness,
And put on Intellect.   *Ib, f. 91*

38 And did those feet in ancient time
Walk upon England's mountains green?
And was the holy lamb of God
On England's pleasant pastures seen?

Bring me my bow of burning gold!
Bring me my arrows of desire!
Bring me my spear! O clouds, unfold!
Bring me my chariot of fire!

I will not cease from mental fight,
Nor shall my sword sleep in my hand,
Till we have built Jerusalem
In England's green and pleasant land.   *Milton, Preface*

39 Mock on, mock on, Voltaire, Rousseau;
Mock on, mock on; 'tis all in vain!
You throw the sand against the wind,
And the wind blows it back again.   *Mock on, mock on,*
                                              Voltaire, Rousseau

40 Never seek to tell thy love,
Love that never told can be;
For the gentle wind does move
Silently, invisibly.   *Never seek to tell thy Love*

41 Soon as she was gone from me,
A traveller came by,
Silently, invisibly:
He took her with a sigh.   *Ib*

42 A petty sneaking knave I knew –
O! Mr Cromek, how do ye do?   *On Cromek*

43 Love seeketh not itself to please,
Nor for itself hath any care,
But for another gives its ease,
And builds a Heaven in Hell's despair.
         Songs of Experience, The Clod and the Pebble

44 My mother groan'd, my father wept,
Into the dangerous world I leapt;

Helpless, naked, piping loud,
Like a fiend hid in a cloud. *Songs of Experience, Infant Sorrow*

45 But if at the Church they would give us some ale,
And a pleasant fire our souls to regale,
We'd sing and we'd pray all the livelong day,
Nor ever once wish from the Church to stray.
Ib, The Little Vagabond

46 Tiger! Tiger! burning bright
In the forests of the night,
What immortal hand or eye
Could frame thy fearful symmetry? *Ib, The Tiger*

47 When the stars threw down their spears,
And water'd heaven with their tears,
Did he smile his work to see?
Did he who made the Lamb make thee? *Ib*

48 Piping down the valleys wild,
Piping songs of pleasant glee,
On a cloud I saw a child. *Songs of Innocence, Introduction*

49 'Pipe a song about a Lamb!'
So I piped with merry cheer. *Ib*

50 Little Lamb, who made thee?
Dost thou know who made thee? *Ib, The Lamb*

51 My mother bore me in the southern wild,
And I am black, but O! my soul is white. *Ib, The Little Black Boy*

52 When the voices of children are heard on the green,
And laughing is heard on the hill. *Ib, Nurse's Song*

53 Can I see another's woe,
And not be in sorrow too? *Ib, On Another's Sorrow*

54 Whether on Ida's shady brow,
Or in the chambers of the East,
The chambers of the sun, that now
From ancient melody have ceas'd. *To the Muses*

55 How have you left the ancient love
That bards of old enjoy'd in you!
The languid strings do scarcely move!
The sound is forc'd, the notes are few! *Ib*

56 Without Contraries is no progression. Attraction and Repulsion,
Reason and Energy, Love and Hate, are necessary to Human
existence. *The Marriage of Heaven and Hell, The Argument*

57 Energy is Eternal Delight. *Ib, The Voice of the Devil*

58 The road of excess leads to the palace of Wisdom.
                 The Marriage of Heaven and Hell, Proverbs of Hell

59 He who desires but acts not, breeds pestilence.   *Ib*

60 A fool sees not the same tree that a wise man sees.   *Ib*

61 Damn braces. Bless relaxes.   *Ib*

62 Exuberance is Beauty.   *Ib*

63 Where man is not, nature is barren.   *Ib*

64 If the doors of perception were cleansed everything would appear to man as it is, infinite.   *Ib, A Memorable Fancy*

BORROW, George Henry, 1803–1881

65 There's night and day, brother, both sweet things; sun, moon, and stars, brother, all sweet things; there's likewise a wind on the heath. Life is very sweet, brother; who would wish to die?
                             Lavengro, Ch. 25

BOSQUET, Marshal Pierre, 1810–1861

66 *C'est magnifique, mais ce n'est pas la guerre.* It is magnificent, but it is not war.   *Watching the Charge of the Light Brigade,*
                                Balaclava, 1854

BOSSIDY, John Collins, 1860–1928

67 And this is good old Boston,
   The Home of the bean and the cod,
   Where the Lowells talk to the Cabots,
   And the Cabots talk only to God.   *On the Aristocracy of*
                                Harvard

BOULTON, Sir Harold Edwin, 1859–1935

68 When Adam and Eve were dispossessed
   Of the garden hard by Heaven,
   They planted another one down in the West,
   'Twas Devon, glorious Devon!   *Glorious Devon*

69 Speed, bonny boat, like a bird on the wing;
   'Onward!' the sailors cry;
   Carry the lad that's born to be king
   Over the sea to Skye.   *Skye Boat Song*

BOURDILLON, Francis William, 1852–1921

70 The night has a thousand eyes,
    And the day but one;
   Yet the light of the bright world dies
    With the dying sun.   *Light*

BOWEN, Charles, 1st Baron, 1835–1894

71 The rain it raineth on the just
   And also on the unjust fella:
   But chiefly on the just, because
   The unjust steals the just's umbrella. *Sichel, Sands of Time*

BOWEN, Edward Ernest, 1836–1901

72 Forty years on, growing older and older,
   Shorter in wind, as in memory long,
   Feeble of foot, and rheumatic of shoulder,
   What will it help you that once you were strong?
                                    Forty Years on,
                                    Harrow School Song

BRADFORD, John, 1510?–1555

73 There, but for the grace of God, goes John Bradford. *Remark*
                        on seeing some criminals led to execution

BRATHWAITE, Richard, 1588?–1673

74 To Banbury came I, O profane one!
   Where I saw a Puritane-one
   Hanging of his cat on Monday,
   For killing of a mouse on Sunday. *Barnabee's Journal, 1*

BRIDGES, Robert, 1844–1930

75 Awake, my heart, to be loved, awake, awake!
   The darkness silvers away, the morn doth break,
   It leaps in the sky: unrisen lustres slake
   The o'ertaken moon. Awake, O heart, awake!
                            Awake, My Heart, to be Loved

76 I heard a linnet courting
       His lady in the spring. *I heard a Linnet courting*

77 I never shall love the snow again
       Since Maurice died. *I never shall love the Snow again*

78 Perfect little body, without fault or stain on thee,
   With promise of strength and manhood full and fair!
                                    On a Dead Child

79 When Death to either shall come, –
       I pray it be first to me. *When Death to either shall come*

BRIGHT, John, 1811–1889

80 The Angel of Death has been abroad throughout the land; you
   may almost hear the beating of his wings. *Speech, House of*
                                    Commons, 23 Feb. 1855

81 England is the mother of parliaments.   *Speech, Birmingham,*
                                                   18 Jan. 1865

82 The right honourable gentleman... has retired into what may be
called his political Cave of Adullam.   *Speech, House of*
                                         Commons, 13 March 1866

83 Force is not a remedy.   *Speech, Birmingham, 16 Nov. 1880*

BRONTË, Emily, 1818–1848

84   No coward soul is mine,
No trembler in the world's storm-troubled sphere:
        I see Heaven's glories shine,
And faith shines equal, arming me from fear.   *Last Lines*

85   Vain are the thousand creeds
That move men's hearts: unutterably vain;
        Worthless as wither'd weeds.   *Ib*

86 Riches I hold in light esteem,
        And Love I laugh to scorn;
And lust of fame was but a dream
        That vanish'd with the morn.   *The Old Stoic*

87 O! dreadful is the check – intense the agony –
When the ear begins to hear, and the eye begins to see;
When the pulse begins to throb – the brain to think again –
The soul to feel the flesh, and the flesh to feel the chain.
                                              The Prisoner

BROOKE, Rupert, 1887–1915

88 Blow out, you bugles, over the rich Dead.   *The Dead*

89 Just now the lilac is in bloom
All before my little room.   *The Old Vicarage, Grantchester*

90 For England's the one land, I know,
Where men with Splendid Hearts may go.   *Ib*

91 Stands the Church clock at ten to three?
And is there honey still for tea?   *Ib*

92 If I should die, think only this of me:
That there's some corner of a foreign field
That is forever England.   *The Soldier*

93 A dust whom England bore, shaped, made aware,
Gave, once, her flowers to love, her ways to roam,
A body of England's, breathing English air,
Washed by the rivers, blest by suns of home.   *Ib*

94 And laughter, learnt of friends; and gentleness,
In hearts at peace, under an English heaven.   *Ib*

BROOKS, Phillips, 1835–1893

95 O little town of Bethlehem,
　　How still we see thee lie;
　　Above thy deep and dreamless sleep
　　　The silent stars go by.　　　*O Little Town of Bethlehem*

BROWN, Thomas, 1663–1704

96 I do not love thee, Doctor Fell,
　　The reason why I cannot tell;
　　But this alone I know full well,
　　I do not love thee, Doctor Fell.　　*Translation of Martial*
　　　　　　　　　　　　　　　　　　　　　　Epigrams, 1, 32

BROWN, Thomas Edward, 1830–1897

97 A garden is a lovesome thing, God wot!　　　*My Garden*

BROWNE, Charles Farrar, see WARD, Artemus

BROWNE, Sir Thomas, 1605–1682

98 He who discommendeth others obliquely commendeth himself.
　　　　　　　　　　　　　　　　　　　　　　Christian Morals

99 I dare, without usurpation, assume the honourable style of
　　Christian.　　　　　　　　　　　*Religio Medici, Part, 1, 1*

1 All things are artificial, for nature is the art of God.　　*Ib, 16*

2 I am of a constitution so general that it consorts and sympa-
　thizeth with all things. I have no antipathy, or rather idiosyncrasy,
　in diet, humour, air, any-thing.　　　　　　　*Ib, Part 2, 1*

3 It is the common wonder of all men, how among so many
　million of faces, there should be none alike.　　　　*Ib, 2*

4 No man can justly censure or condemn another, because indeed
　no man truly knows another.　　　　　　　　　*Ib, 4*

5 I could be content that we might procreate like trees, without
　conjunction, or that there were any way to perpetuate the world
　without this trivial and vulgar way of coition.　　*Ib, Part 2, 9*

6 Lord, deliver me from myself.　　　　　　　　*Ib, 10*

7 Man is a noble animal, splendid in ashes, and pompous in the
　grave.　　　　　　　　　　　　　　　　*Urn Burial, Ch. 5*

BROWNE, Sir William, 1692–1774

8 The King to Oxford sent a troop of horse,
　For Tories own no argument but force:

With equal skill to Cambridge books he sent,
For Whigs admit no force but argument.   *Reply to Trapp's*
Epigram (see 393 : 54)

BROWNING, Elizabeth Barrett, 1806–1861

9   Let no one till his death
Be called unhappy. Measure not the work
Until the day's out and the labour done.   *Aurora Leigh,*
Book 5

10 Since when was genius found respectable?   *Ib, Book 6*

11 Do you hear the children weeping, O my brothers,
Ere the sorrow comes with years?   *The Cry of the Children*

12 I tell you hopeless grief is passionless.   *Grief*

13 What was he doing, the great god Pan,
Down in the reeds by the river?   *A Musical Instrument*

BROWNING, Robert, 1812–1889

14   Love, we are in God's hand.
How strange now, looks the life he makes us lead!
So free we seem, so fettered fast we are!   *Andrea del Sarto*

15 Ah, but a man's reach should exceed his grasp,
Or what's a heaven for?   *Ib*

16 One who never turned his back but marched breast forward,
        Never doubted clouds would break,
Never dreamed, though right were worsted, wrong would
    triumph,
Held we fall to rise, are baffled to fight better,
        Sleep to wake.   *Asolando, Epilogue*

17 Just when we are safest, there's a sunset-touch,
A fancy from a flower-bell, some one's death,
A chorus-ending from Euripides, –
And that's enough for fifty hopes and fears
As old and new at once as Nature's self,
To rap and knock and enter in our soul.   *Bishop Blougram's*
Apology

18 No, when the fight begins within himself,
A man's worth something.   *Ib*

19 Oh, the little more, and how much it is!
        And the little less, and what worlds away!
By The Fire-side, 39

20   We loved, sir – used to meet:
How sad and bad and mad it was –
        But then, how it was sweet!   *Confessions*

21 Oh, to be in England
Now that April's there,
And whoever wakes in England
Sees, some morning, unaware,
That the lowest boughs and the brushwood sheaf
Round the elm-tree bole are in tiny leaf,
While the chaffinch sings on the orchard bough
In England – now! *Home-Thoughts, from Abroad*

22 And after April, when May follows,
And the whitethroat builds, and all the swallows! *Ib*

23 That's the wise thrush; he sings each song twice over,
Lest you should think he never could recapture
The first fine careless rapture! *Ib*

24 Nobly, nobly Cape Saint Vincent to the North-west died away;
Sunset ran, one glorious blood-red, reeking into Cadiz Bay.
Home-Thoughts, from the Sea

25 Whoso turns, as I, this evening, turn to God to praise and pray,
While Jove's planet rises yonder, silent over Africa. *Ib*

26 I sprang to the stirrup, and Joris, and he;
I galloped, Dirck galloped, we galloped all three.
How they brought the Good News from Ghent to Aix

27   Escape me?
       Never –
       Beloved!
While I am I, and you are you. *Life in a Love*

28 Just for a handful of silver he left us,
       Just for a riband to stick in his coat. *The Lost Leader*

29 Never glad confident morning again! *Ib*

30 Ah, did you once see Shelley plain,
       And did he stop and speak to you?
And did you speak to him again,
       How strange it seems, and new! *Memorabilia*

31 Never the time and the place
       And the loved one all together! *Never the Time and
                                       the Place*

32 Dante, who loved well because he hated,
Hated wickedness that hinders loving. *One Word More, 5*

33 Where my heart lies, let my brain lie also! *Ib, 14*

34 God be thanked, the meanest of his creatures
Boasts two soul-sides, one to face the world with,
One to show a woman when he loves her. *Ib, 17*

35 It was roses, roses all the way. *The Patriot*

36   Hamelin Town's in Brunswick,
       By famous Hanover city;
          The river Weser, deep and wide,
          Washes its wall on the southern side.
                              The Pied Piper of Hamelin, 1

37   Rats!
       They fought the dogs and killed the cats,
          And bit the babies in the cradles.   *Ib, 2*

38   With shrieking and squeaking
       In fifty different sharps and flats.   *Ib, 2*

39 'If I can rid your town of rats
    Will you give me a thousand guilders?'
    'One? fifty thousand!' – was the exclamation
    Of the astonished Mayor and Corporation.   *Ib, 6*

40 And the muttering grew to a grumbling;
    And the grumbling grew to a mighty rumbling;
    And out of the houses the rats came tumbling.   *Ib, 7*

41 So, munch on, crunch on, take your nuncheon,
    Breakfast, supper, dinner, luncheon!   *Ib*

42 'You threaten us, fellow? Do your worst,
    Blow your pipe there till you burst!'   *Ib, 9*

43 All the little boys and girls,
    With rosy cheeks and flaxen curls,
    And sparkling eyes, and teeth like pearls,
    Tripping and skipping, ran merrily after
    The wonderful music with shouting and laughter.   *Ib, 12*

44 The year's at the spring,
    And day's at the morn;
    Morning's at seven;
    The hill-side's dew-pearled;
    The lark's on the wing;
    The snail's on the thorn;
    God's in His heaven –
    All's right with the world.   *Pippa Passes, 1, Morning*

45 All service ranks the same with God –
    With God, whose puppets, best and worst,
    Are we: there is no last nor first.   *Ib, 4, Night*

46 Grow old along with me.
    The best is yet to be,
    The last of life, for which the first was made:
    Our times are in His hand

Who saith 'A whole I planned,
Youth shows but half; trust God: see all nor be afraid!'
Rabbi Ben Ezra

47 Let age approve of youth, and death complete the same! *Ib*

48 What of soul was left, I wonder, when the kissing had to stop?
A Toccata of Galuppi's, 14

BUCHANAN, Robert Williams, 1841–1901

49 The Fleshly School of Poetry. *Title of article in the Contemporary Review, Oct. 1871*

50 She just wore
Enough for modesty – no more. *White Rose and Red, Part 1, 5*

BUFFON, Georges Louis Leclerc, Comte de, 1707–1788

51 *Le style est l'homme même.* Style is the man himself.
Discours sur le style

BULLER, Arthur Henry Reginald, 1874–1944

52 There was a young lady named Bright,
Whose speed was far faster than light;
She set out one day
In a relative way,
And returned home the previous night. *Limerick*

BULWER-LYTTON, Edward, 1803–1873

53 Here Stanley meets, – how Stanley scorns, the glance!
The brilliant chief, irregularly great,
Frank, haughty, rash, – the Rupert of Debate.
The New Timon, 1, 6

54 Beneath the rule of men entirely great,
The pen is mightier than the sword. *Richelieu, 2, 2*

BUNN, Alfred, 1796?–1860

55 I dreamt that I dwelt in marble halls,
With vassals and serfs at my side. ARLINE *The Bohemian Girl,
Act 2*

BUNYAN, John, 1628–1688

56 Some said, John, print it; others said, Not so;
Some said, It might do good; others said, No..
Pilgrim's Progress, Author's Apology

57 As I walked through the wilderness of this world. *Ib, Part 1*

58 The name of the slough was Despond. *Pilgrim's Progress, Part 1*

59 The gentleman's name that met him was Mr Worldly Wiseman.
Ib

60 It beareth the name of Vanity Fair, because the town where 'tis
kept is lighter than vanity.   *Ib*

61 Mr Facing-both-ways.   *Ib*

62 A castle called Doubting Castle, the owner whereof was Giant
Despair.   *Ib*

63 So I awoke, and behold it was a dream.   *Ib*

64 He who would valiant be
'Gainst all disaster,
Let him in constancy
    Follow the Master.
There's no discouragement
Shall make him once relent
His first avowed intent
        To be a pilgrim.   *Ib, Part 2, English Hymnal Version*

65 I'll fear not what men say,
I'll labour night and day
        To be a pilgrim.   *Ib*

66 He that is down needs fear no fall;
    He that is low, no pride.   *Ib, Shepherd Boy's Song*

67 So he passed over, and all the trumpets sounded for him on the
other side.   *Ib*

BURGESS, Gelett, 1866–1951

68 I never saw a Purple Cow,
I never hope to see one;
But I can tell you, anyhow,
I'd rather see than be one.   *The Purple Cow*

69 Ah, yes, I wrote 'Purple Cow' –
I'm sorry, now, I wrote it!
But I can tell you anyhow,
I'll kill you if you quote it.   *Reply*

BURGON, John William, 1813–1888

70 Match me such marvel save in Eastern clime,
A rose-red city half as old as time.   *Petra, 132*

BURKE, Edmund, 1729–1797

71 The concessions of the weak are the concessions of fear.
Speech on Conciliation with America, 22 March 1775

72 The use of force alone is but *temporary*. It may subdue for a moment; but it does not remove the necessity of subduing again: and a nation is not governed, which is perpetually to be conquered.   *Speech on Conciliation with America, 22 March 1775*

73 I do not know the method of drawing up an indictment against an whole people.   *Ib*

74 All government, indeed every human benefit and enjoyment, every virtue, and every prudent act, is founded on compromise and barter.   *Ib*

75 The people are the masters.   *Speech on the Economical Reform, 11 Feb. 1780*

76 He was not merely a chip of the old block, but the old block itself.   *Of Pitt's first speech, 26 Feb. 1781*

77 There is, however, a limit at which forbearance ceases to be a virtue.   *Observations on 'The Present State of the Nation', 1769*

78 But the age of chivalry is gone. That of sophisters, economists, and calculators, has succeeded; and the glory of Europe is extinguished for ever.   *Reflections on the Revolution in France*

79 Man is by his constitution a religious animal.   *Ib*

80 Superstition is the religion of feeble minds.   *Ib*

81 Good order is the foundation of all good things.   *Ib*

82 Example is the school of mankind, and they will learn at no other.   *Letters on a Regicide Peace, 1, 1796*

83 And having looked to government for bread, on the very first scarcity they will turn and bite the hand that fed them.   *Thoughts and Details on Scarcity*

84 If any ask me what a free government is, I answer, that, for any practical purpose, it is what the people think so.   *Letter to the Sheriffs of Bristol, 1777*

85 Liberty, too, must be limited in order to be possessed.   *Ib*

86 Among a people generally corrupt, liberty cannot long exist. *Ib*

87 The greater the power, the more dangerous the abuse.   *Speech, House of Commons, 7 Feb. 1771*

88 I am convinced that we have a degree of delight, and that no small one, in the real misfortunes and pains of others.   *On the Sublime and Beautiful, 1, 14*

89 Power gradually extirpates from the mind every humane and gentle virtue.   *A Vindication of Natural Society*

BURNET, Bishop Gilbert, 1643–1715

90 There was a sure way to see it lost, and that was to die in the last
   ditch.   *History of his own Times, 1*

BURNEY, Fanny (Mme D'Arblay), 1752–1840

91 Dancing? Oh, dreadful! How it was ever adopted in a civilized
   country I cannot find out; 'tis certainly a Barbarian exercise,
   and of savage origin. MR MEADOWS   *Cecilia, Book 3*

92 'True, very true ma'am,' said he, yawning, 'one really lives nowhere; one does but vegetate and wish it all at an end.' MR
   MEADOWS   *Ib, Book 4*

93 Indeed, the freedom with which Dr Johnson condemns whatever
   he disapproves is astonishing.   *Diary, 23 Aug. 1778*

BURNS, John, 1858–1943

94 Every drop of the Thames is liquid history.
                               Attributed by Sir Frederick Whyte

BURNS, Robert, 1759–1796

95 Ae fond kiss, and then we sever!   *Ae Fond Kiss, 1*

96 But to see her was to love her,
   Love but her, and love for ever.   *Ib, 11*

97 Had we never lov'd sae kindly,
   Had we never lov'd sae blindly,
   Never met – or never parted,
   We had ne'er been broken-hearted.   *Ib, 13*

98 Flow gently, sweet Afton, among thy green braes,
   Flow gently, I'll sing thee a song in thy praise. *Afton Water, 1*

99 Should auld acquaintance be forgot,
   And never brought to min'?   *Auld Lang Syne, 1*

1 We'll tak a cup o' kindness yet,
   For auld lang syne.   *Ib, 7*

2 Freedom and Whisky gang thegither!   *The Author's Earnest*
                                            Cry and Prayer, 185

3 Gin a body meet a body
   Coming through the rye;
   Gin a body kiss a body,
   Need a body cry?   *Coming through the Rye, 5*

4 I wasna fou, but just had plenty.
                             Death and Doctor Hornbrook, 14

5 On ev'ry hand it will allow'd be,
He's just – nae better than he should be.
A Dedication to Gavin Hamilton, 25

6 A man's a man for a' that. *For a' that and a' that, 12*

7 Green grow the rashes O,
Green grow the rashes O;
The sweetest hours that e'er I spent,
Are spent amang the lasses O! *Green Grow the Rashes, 1*

8 The wisest man the warl' saw,
He dearly lov'd the lasses O. *Ib, 19*

9 The golden hours on angel wings
Flew o'er me and my dearie;
For dear to me as light and life
Was my sweet Highland Mary. *Highland Mary, 13*

10 There's some are fou o' love divine,
There's some are fou o' brandy. *The Holy Fair, 239*

11 John Anderson my jo, John,
When we were first acquent,
Your locks were like the raven,
Your bonnie brow was brent. *John Anderson My Jo, 1*

12 True it is, she had one failing,
Had a woman ever less?
Lines, written under picture of Miss Burns

13 Nature's law,
That man was made to mourn. *Man was Made to Mourn, 31*

14 Man's inhumanity to man
Makes countless thousands mourn! *Ib, 55*

15 O Mary, at thy window be,
It is the wish'd, the trysted hour! *Mary Morison, 1*

16 Wee, sleekit, cow'rin', tim'rous beastie,
O what a panic's in thy breastie! *To a Mouse, 1*

17 I'm truly sorry man's dominion
Has broken Nature's social union. *Ib, 7*

18 The best laid schemes o' mice an' men
Gang aft a-gley,
An' lea'e us nought but grief an' pain
For promis'd joy. *Ib, 39*

19 Still thou art blest compar'd wi' me!
The present only toucheth thee:
But oh! I backward cast my e'e
On prospects drear!

An' forward tho' I canna see,
    I guess an' fear! *To a Mouse, 43*

20 My heart's in the Highlands, my heart is not here;
My heart's in the Highlands a-chasing the deer;
Chasing the wild deer, and following the roe,
My heart's in the Highlands, wherever I go.
       My Heart's in the Highlands, 1

21 My love is like a red red rose
  That's newly sprung in June:
My love is like the melodie
  That's sweetly play'd in tune. *A Red, Red Rose*

22 Scots, wha hae wi' Wallace bled,
Scots, wham Bruce has aften led,
Welcome to your gory bed,
  Or to victorie.   *Scots, Wha Hae, 1*

23 Liberty's in every blow!
  Let us do or die!   *Ib, 23*

24 Some hae meat, and canna eat,
  And some wad eat that want it;
But we hae meat and we can eat,
  And sae the Lord be thankit. *The Selkirk Grace*

25 But pleasures are like poppies spread –
You seize the flow'r, its bloom is shed;
Or like the snow falls in the river –
A moment white, then melts for ever. *Tam o' Shanter, 59*

26 Ye banks and braes o' bonnie Doon,
  How can ye bloom sae fresh and fair?
How can ye chant, ye little birds,
  And I sae weary fu' o' care? *Ye Banks and Braes, 1*

27 Thou minds me o' departed joys,
  Departed never to return. *Ib, 7*

28 And my fause lover stole my rose,
  But ah! he left the thorn wi' me. *Ib, 15*

BURTON, Robert, 1577–1640

29 All my joys to this are folly,
Naught so sweet as Melancholy. *Anatomy of Melancholy,*
       Author's Abstract of Melancholy

30 *Hinc quam sit calamus saevior ense patet.* From this it is clear
how much more cruel the pen is than the sword. *Ib, Part 1*

31 England is a paradise for women, and hell for horses: Italy a
paradise for horses, hell for women. *Ib, Part 3*

32 One religion is as true as another. *Anatomy of Melancholy, Part 3*
33 Be not solitary, be not idle. *Ib, Last words*

BUSSY-RABUTIN, Comte de, 1618–1693

34 *L'absence est à l'amour ce qu'est au feu le vent; il éteint le petit, il allume le grand.* Absence is to love what wind is to fire; it extinguishes the small, it inflames the great.
Histoire Amoureuse des Gaules

BUTLER, Samuel, 1612–1680

35 When civil fury first grew high,
And men fell out they knew not why. *Hudibras, 1, 1, 1*

36 For every why he had a wherefore. *Ib, 1, 1, 132*

37 Oaths are but words, and words but wind. *Ib, 2, 2, 107*

38 What makes all doctrines plain and clear?
About two hundred pounds a year.
And that which was prov'd true before
Prove false again? Two hundred more. *Ib, 3, 1, 1277*

39 He that complies against his will,
Is of his own opinion still. *Ib, 3, 3, 547*

40 The souls of women are so small,
That some believe they've none at all. *Miscellaneous Thoughts*

BUTLER, Samuel, 1835–1902

41 It has been said that the love of money is the root of all evil.
The want of money is so quite as truly. *Erewhon, Ch. 20*

42 I keep my books at the British Museum and at Mudie's.
The Humour of Homer, Ramblings in Cheapside

43 Life is one long process of getting tired. *Note-books, Life, 7*

44 Life is the art of drawing sufficient conclusions from insufficient premises. *Ib, 9*

45 All progress is based upon a universal innate desire on the part of every organism to live beyond its income. *Ib, 16*

46 To live is like love, all reason is against it, and all healthy instinct for it. *Ib, Higgledy-Piggledy, Life and Love*

47 Stowed away in a Montreal lumber room
The Discobolus standeth and turneth his face to the wall;
Dusty, cobweb-covered, maimed and set at naught,
Beauty crieth in an attic and no man regardeth.
O God! O Montreal! *A Psalm of Montreal*

48 The advantage of doing one's praising for oneself is that one can lay it on so thick and exactly in the right places.
The Way of All Flesh, Ch. 34

49 A man's friendships are, like his will, invalidated by marriage – but they are also no less invalidated by the marriage of his friends. *Ib, Ch. 75*

50 'Tis better to have loved and lost than never to have lost at all.
Ib, Ch. 77 (see also 103 : 31 and 386 : 59)

51 Brigands demand your money or your life; women require both.
Attributed

BYROM, John, 1692–1763

52 Christians awake, salute the happy morn,
Whereon the Saviour of the world was born.
Hymn for Christmas Day

53 God bless the King, I mean the Faith's Defender;
God bless – no harm in blessing – the Pretender;
But who Pretender is, or who is King,
God bless us all – that's quite another thing.
To an Officer in the Army

BYRON, George Gordon, 6th Baron, 1788–1824

54 In short, he was a perfect cavaliero,
And to his very valet seem'd a hero. *Beppo, 33*

55 I like the weather, when it is not rainy,
That is, I like two months of every year. *Ib, 48*

56 Maidens, like moths, are ever caught by glare,
And Mammon wins his way where Seraphs might despair.
Childe Harold's Pilgrimage, Canto 1, 9

57 Adieu, adieu! my native shore
Fades o'er the waters blue. *Ib, 1, 13*

58 My native Land – Good Night! *Ib*

59 There was a sound of revelry by night,
And Belgium's capital had gather'd then
Her Beauty and her Chivalry, and bright
The lamps shone o'er fair women and brave men.
Ib, Canto 3, 21

60 On with the dance! let joy be unconfined;
No sleep till morn, when Youth and Pleasure meet
To chase the glowing Hours with flying feet. *Ib, 3, 22*

61 I have not loved the world, nor the world me;
I have not flatter'd its rank breath, nor bow'd
To its idolatrics a patient knee. *Ib, 3, 113*

62 I stood in Venice, on the Bridge of Sighs;
A palace and a prison on each hand. *Childe Harold's*
Pilgrimage, Canto 4, 1

63 Yet, Freedom! yet thy banner, torn, but flying,
Streams like the thunder-storm *against* the wind. *Ib, 4, 98*

64 While stands the Coliseum, Rome shall stand;
When falls the Coliseum, Rome shall fall;
And when Rome falls – the World. *Ib, 4, 145*

65 There is a pleasure in the pathless woods,
There is a rapture on the lonely shore,
There is society, where none intrudes,
By the deep Sea, and music in its roar:
I love not Man the less, but Nature more. *Ib, 4, 178*

66 What men call gallantry, and gods adultery,
Is much more common where the climate's sultry.
Don Juan, Canto 1, 63

67 A little still she strove, and much repented,
And whispering 'I will ne'er consent' – consented. *Ib, 1, 117*

68 Sweet is revenge – especially to women. *Ib, 1, 124*

69 Pleasure's a sin, and sometimes sin's a pleasure. *Ib, 1, 133*

70 Man's love is of man's life a thing apart,
'Tis woman's whole existence. *Ib, 1, 194*

71 Man, being reasonable, must get drunk;
The best of life is but intoxication. *Ib, Canto 2, 179*

72 Alas! the love of women! it is known
To be a lovely and a fearful thing. *Ib, 2, 199*

73 In her first passion woman loves her lover,
In all the others all she loves is love. *Ib, Canto 3, 3*

74 'Tis melancholy, and a fearful sign
Of human frailty, folly, also crime,
That love and marriage rarely can combine. *Ib, 3, 5*

75 All tragedies are finish'd by a death,
All comedies are ended by a marriage. *Ib, 3, 9*

76 Dreading that climax of all human ills
The inflammation of his weekly bills. *Ib, 3, 35*

77 The isles of Greece, the isles of Greece!
Where burning Sappho loved and sung,
Where grew the arts of war and peace,
Where Delos rose, and Phoebus sprung!
Eternal summer gilds them yet,
But all, except their sun, is set. *Ib, 3, 86, 1*

78 The mountains look on Marathon –
And Marathon looks on the sea;

And musing there an hour alone,
   I dream'd that Greece might still be free.   *Don Juan,*
                                                                  Canto, 3, 86, 3

79 And if I laugh at any mortal thing,
   'Tis that I may not weep.   *Ib, Canto, 4, 4*

80 There is a tide in the affairs of women,
   Which, taken at the flood, leads – God knows where.
                                               Ib, Canto 6, 2

81 A lady of a 'certain age', which means
   Certainly aged.   *Ib, 6, 69*

82 And, after all, what is a lie? 'Tis but
   The truth in masquerade.   *Ib, Canto 11, 37*

83 'Tis strange the mind, that very fiery particle,
   Should let itself be snuff'd out by an article.   [*John Keats*]
                                                Ib, 11, 60

84 Now hatred is by far the longest pleasure;
   Men love in haste, but they detest at leisure.   *Ib, Canto 13, 6*

85 The English winter – ending in July,
   To recommence in August.   *Ib, 13, 42*

86 Society is now one polish'd horde,
   Form'd of two mighty tribes, the *Bores* and *Bored*.
                                            Ib, 13, 95

87 'Tis strange – but true; for truth is always strange;
   Stranger than fiction: if it could be told,
   How much would novels gain by the exchange!
                               Ib, Canto 14, 101

88   I'll publish, right or wrong:
   Fools are my theme, let satire be my song.
              English Bards and Scotch Reviewers, 5

89 'Tis pleasant, sure, to see one's name in print;
   A book's a book, although there's nothing in't.   *Ib, 51*

90 A man must serve his time to every trade
   Save censure – critics all are ready made.   *Ib, 63*

91   As soon
   Seek roses in December – ice in June;
   Hope constancy in wind, or corn in chaff;
   Believe a woman or an epitaph,
   Or any other thing that's false, before
   You trust in critics, who themselves are sore.   *Ib, 75*

92 Better to err with Pope, than shine with Pye.   *Ib, 102*

93 Fare thee well! and if for ever,
   Still for ever, fare thee well.   *Fare Thee Well, 1*

94 Who kill'd John Keats?
  'I,' says the Quarterly,
  So savage and Tartarly;
   ' 'Twas one of my feats.'   *John Keats*

95 Maid of Athens, ere we part,
  Give, oh give me back my heart!
                  Maid of Athens, ere we Part

96 She walks in beauty, like the night
   Of cloudless climes and starry skies;
  And all that's best of dark and bright
   Meet in her aspect and her eyes.   *She Walks in Beauty*

97 So, we'll go no more a roving
   So late into the night,
  Though the heart be still as loving,
   And the moon be still as bright.
               So, we'll go no more a roving

98 Though the night was made for loving,
   And the day returns too soon,
  Yet we'll go no more a roving
   By the light of the moon.   *Ib*

99 When we two parted
   In silence and tears,
  Half broken-hearted
   To sever for years,
  Pale grew thy cheek and cold,
   Colder thy kiss;
  Truly that hour foretold
   Sorrow to this.   *When we two parted*

1 If I should meet thee
  After long years,
  How should I greet thee? –
  With silence and tears.   *Ib*

2 I awoke one morning and found myself famous.   *Entry in*
        Memoranda after publication of Childe Harold

BYRON, Henry James, 1834–1884

3 Life's too short for chess.   *Our Boys, Act 1*

CAESAR, Augustus, 63 B.C.–A.D. 14

4 *Quintili Vare, legiones redde.* Quintilius Varus, give me back my
  legions.   *Suetonius, Divus Augustus, 23*

5 *Ad Kalendas Graecas soluturos.* To be paid at the Greek Kalends.
                    Ib, 87

CAESAR, Julius, 102?–44 B.C.

6 *Gallia est omnis divisa in partes tres.* All Gaul is divided into
   three parts.   *De Bello Gallico, 1, 1*

7 *Iacta alea est.* The die is cast.   *On Crossing the Rubicon,*
                                                            49 B.C.

8 *Veni, vidi, vici.* I came, I saw, I conquered.   *After Victory at*
                                                       Zela, 47 B.C.

9 *Et tu, Brute.* You too, Brutus?   *Last Words, attributed*

10 Caesar's wife must be above suspicion.   *Plutarch,*
                                                  Life of Caesar

CALVERLEY, Charles Stuart, 1831–1884

11 The auld wife sat at her ivied door
    (Butter and eggs and a pound of cheese)
    A thing she had frequently done before;
    And her spectacles lay on her aproned knees.   *Ballad*

12 The heart which grief hath cankered
    Hath one unfailing remedy – the Tankard.   *Beer*

13 For I've read in many a novel that, unless they've souls that
    grovel,
    Folks *prefer* in fact a hovel to your dreary marble halls.
                                                  In the Gloaming

14 How Eugene Aram, though a thief, a liar, and a murderer
    Yet, being intellectual, was amongst the noblest of mankind.
                                                       Of Reading

15 I have a liking old
    For thee, though manifold
    Stories, I know, are told,
      Not to thy credit.   *Ode to Tobacco*

CAMDEN, William, 1551–1623

16 Betwixt the stirrup and the ground
    Mercy I asked, mercy I found.   *Epitaph for a Man killed*
                                           by falling from his Horse

CAMPBELL, Roy, 1902–1957

17 You praise the firm restraint with which they write,
    I'm with you there, of course:
    They use the snaffle and the curb all right,
    But where's the bloody horse?
                              On Some South African Novelists

CAMPBELL, Thomas, 1777–1844

18 O leave this barren spot to me!
Spare, woodman, spare the beechen tree.
The Beech-Tree's Petition

19 A chieftain to the Highlands bound
Cries 'Boatman, do not tarry!
And I'll give thee a silver pound
To row us o'er the ferry.' *Lord Ullin's Daughter*

20 'Tis distance lends enchantment to the view,
And robes the mountain in its azure hue.
Pleasures of Hope, 1, 7

21 Ye mariners of England
That guard our native seas,
Whose flag has braved, a thousand years,
The battle and the breeze. *Ye Mariners of England*

22 Now Barabbas was a publisher. *Attributed*

CAMPION, Thomas, 1567–1620

23 Follow thy fair sun, unhappy shadow. *Follow thy Fair Sun*

24 There is a garden in her face,
Where roses and white lilies grow.
There is a Garden in her Face

25 There cherries grow, which none may buy
Till 'Cherry Ripe' themselves do cry. *Ib*

CANNING, George, 1770–1827

26 I called the New World into existence to redress the balance of
the Old. *Speech, 12 Dec. 1826*

27 But of all plagues, good Heaven, thy wrath can send,
Save me, oh, save me, from the candid friend.
New Morality, 209

28 Pitt is to Addington
As London is to Paddington. *The Oracle*

CAREY, Henry, 1693?–1743

29 God save our Gracious King,
Long live our noble King,
God save the King.
Send him victorious,
Happy and glorious. *God Save the King. Origin is disputed.*
See Dr Percy A. Scholes, God Save the Queen, 1954

30 Confound their politics
Frustrate their knavish tricks *Ib*

31 Of all the girls that are so smart
   There's none like pretty Sally;
   She is the darling of my heart
   And she lives in our alley.   *Sally in our Alley*

CARLYLE, Thomas, 1795–1881

32 A witty statesman said, you might prove anything by figures.
                                          Essay on Chartism

33 Genius (which means transcendent capacity of taking trouble,
   first of all).   *Frederick the Great, Book 4, Ch. 3*

34 A whiff of grapeshot. *History of the French Revolution, 1, 5, 3*

35 The seagreen Incorruptible. (*Robespierre*)   *Ib, 2, 4, 4*

36 No great man lives in vain. The history of the world is but the
   biography of great men.   *Heroes and Hero-Worship, 1,*
                                          The Hero as Divinity

37 The true University of these days is a collection of books.
                              Ib, 5, The Hero as Man of Letters

38 History is the essence of innumerable biographies.
                                          Essay on History

39 No man who has once heartily and wholly laughed can be
   altogether irreclaimably bad. *Sartor Resartus, Book 1, Ch. 4*

CARNEGIE, Dale, 1888–

40 How to Win Friends and Influence People.   *Title of Book*

CARNEY, Julia A. Fletcher, 1823–1908

41 Little drops of water, little grains of sand,
   Make the mighty ocean and the pleasant land.
   So the little minutes, humble though they be,
   Make the mighty ages of eternity   *Little Things*

CARROLL, Lewis (Charles Lutwidge Dodgson), 1832–1898

42 'What is the use of a book,' thought Alice, 'without pictures or
   conversation?'   *Alice's Adventures in Wonderland, Ch. 1*

43 She found a little bottle on it, ('which certainly was not here
   before,' said Alice,) and round its neck a paper label, with the
   words 'DRINK ME' beautifully printed on it in large letters.
                                          Ib, Ch. 1

44 'Curiouser and curiouser!' cried Alice.   *Ib, Ch. 2*

45 How doth the little crocodile
   Improve his shining tail,

And pour the waters of the Nile
  On every golden scale!
How cheerfully he seems to grin,
  How neatly spread his claws,
And welcomes little fishes in
  With gently smiling jaws! ALICE   *Alice's Adventures in Wonderland, Ch. 2*

46 'I'll be judge, I'll be jury,' said cunning old Fury: 'I'll try the whole cause, and condemn you to death.'   *Ib, Ch. 3*

47 The Duchess! The Duchess! Oh my dear paws! Oh my fur and whiskers! THE WHITE RABBIT   *Ib, Ch. 4*

48 'You are old, Father William,' the young man said,
  'And your hair has become very white;
And yet you incessantly stand on your head –
  Do you think at your age, it is right?'
'In my youth,' Father William replied to his son,
  'I feared it might injure the brain;
But, now that I'm perfectly sure I have none,
  Why, I do it again and again.' ALICE   *Ib, Ch. 5*

49 'I have answered three questions, and that is enough.'
  Said his father; 'don't give yourself airs!
Do you think I can listen all day to such stuff?
  Be off or I'll kick you downstairs!' ALICE   *Ib, Ch. 5*

50 'If everybody minded their own business,' the Duchess said in a hoarse growl, 'the world would go round a deal faster than it does.'   *Ib, Ch. 6*

51 Speak roughly to your little boy,
  And beat him when he sneezes:
He only does it to annoy,
  Because he knows it teases. THE DUCHESS   *Ib, Ch. 6*

52 I speak severely to my boy,
  I beat him when he sneezes;
For he can thoroughly enjoy
  The pepper when he pleases! THE DUCHESS   *Ib. Ch. 6*

53 Twinkle, twinkle, little bat!
  How I wonder what you're at! THE HATTER   *Ib, Ch. 7*

54 Up above the world you fly,
  Like a tea-tray in the sky. THE HATTER   *Ib, Ch. 7*

55 'Take some more tea,' the March Hare said to Alice, very earnestly.
'I've had nothing yet,' Alice replied in an offended tone, 'so I can't take more.'
'You mean you can't take *less*,' said the Hatter: 'it's very easy to take *more* than nothing.'   *Ib, Ch. 7*

56 The Queen was in a furious passion, and went stamping about, and shouting 'Off with his head!' or 'Off with her head!' about once in a minute.   *Alice's Adventures in Wonderland, Ch. 8*

57 Everything's got a moral, if only you can find it.   THE DUCHESS
Ib. Ch. 9

58 Take care of the sense, and the sounds will take care of themselves.   THE DUCHESS   *Ib, Ch. 9*

59 'Why did you call him Tortoise, if he wasn't one?' Alice asked. 'We called him Tortoise because he taught us,' said the Mock Turtle angrily: 'really you are very dull!'   *Ib, Ch. 9*

60 'Reeling and Writhing, of course, to begin with,' the Mock Turtle replied; 'and then the different branches of Arithmetic – Ambition, Distraction, Uglification, and Derision.'   *Ib, Ch. 9*

61 'That's the reason they're called lessons,' the Gryphon remarked: 'because they lessen from day to day.'   *Ib, Ch. 9*

62 'Will you walk a little faster?' said a whiting to a snail.
'There's a porpoise close behind us, and he's treading on my tail.'
THE MOCK TURTLE   *Ib, Ch. 10*

63 Will you, won't you, will you, won't you, will you join the dance?   THE MOCK TURTLE   *Ib, Ch. 10*

64 'Tis the voice of the Lobster; I heard him declare,
'You have baked me too brown, I must sugar my hair.'   ALICE
Ib, Ch. 10

65 Soup of the evening, beautiful Soup!   THE MOCK TURTLE
Ib, Ch. 10

66 'The Queen of Hearts, she made some tarts,
     All on a summer day:
The Knave of Hearts, he stole those tarts,
     And took them quite away!'   THE WHITE RABBIT (reading)
Ib, Ch. 11

67 They told me you have been to her,
     And mentioned me to him:
She gave me a good character,
     But said I could not swim.   THE WHITE RABBIT (reading)
Ib, Ch. 12

68 'No, no!' said the Queen. 'Sentence first – verdict afterwards.'
'Stuff and nonsense!' said Alice loudly.   *Ib, Ch. 12*

69 'Twas brillig, and the slithy toves
     Did gyre and gimble in the wabe;
All mimsy were the borogoves,
     And the mome raths outgrabe.   ALICE (reading)
Through the Looking-Glass, Ch. 1

70 One, two! One, two! And through and through
   The vorpal blade went snicker-snack!
He left it dead, and with its head
   He went galumphing back. ALICE (reading)   *Through the*
                                                Looking Glass, Ch. 1

71 'And hast thou slain the Jabberwock?
   Come to my arms, my beamish boy!
   O frabjous day! Callooh! Callay!'
   He chortled in his joy. ALICE (reading)   *Ib, Ch. 1*

72 Now, *here*, you see, it takes all the running *you* can do, to keep
   in the same place. If you want to get somewhere else, you must
   run at least twice as fast as that! THE QUEEN   *Ib, Ch. 2*

73 'If you think we're wax-works,' he said, 'you ought to pay, you
   know.
   Wax-works weren't made to be looked at for nothing. Nohow!'
   TWEEDLEDUM   *Ib, Ch. 4*

74 Tweedledum and Tweedledee
      Agreed to have a battle;
   For Tweedledum said Tweedledee
      Had spoiled his nice new rattle. ALICE   *Ib, Ch. 4*

75 'Contrariwise,' continued Tweedledee, 'if it was so, it might be;
   and if it were so, it would be: but as it isn't, it ain't. That's logic.'
                                                       Ib, Ch. 4

76 The sun was shining on the sea,
      Shining with all his might:
   He did his very best to make
      The billows smooth and bright –
   And this was odd, because it was
      The middle of the night. TWEEDLEDEE (reciting *The Walrus*
                                        and The Carpenter) *Ib, Ch. 4*

77 'It's very rude of him,' she said,
      'To come and spoil the fun!' TWEEDLEDEE   *Ib, Ch. 4*

78 The Walrus and the Carpenter
      Were walking close at hand;
   They wept like anything to see
      Such quantities of sand:
   'If this were only cleared away,'
      They said, 'it *would* be grand!' TWEEDLEDEE   *Ib, Ch. 4*

79 'If seven maids with seven mops
      Swept it for half a year,
   Do you suppose,' the Walrus said,
      'That they could get it clear?'
   'I doubt it,' said the Carpenter,
      And shed a bitter tear. TWEEDLEDEE   *Ib, Ch. 4*

80 'The time has come,' the Walrus said,
   'To talk of many things:
Of shoes – and ships – and sealing-wax –
Of cabbages – and kings –
And why the sea is boiling hot –
   And whether pigs have wings.' TWEEDLEDEE (reciting *The Walrus and the Carpenter*) *Through the Looking Glass, Ch. 4*

81 'I weep for you,' the Walrus said:
   'I deeply sympathize.'
With sobs and tears he sorted out
   Those of the largest size,
Holding his pocket-handkerchief
   Before his streaming eyes. TWEEDLEDEE   *Ib, Ch. 4*

82 'O Oysters,' said the Carpenter,
   'You've had a pleasant run!
Shall we be trotting home again?'
   But answer came there none –
And this was scarcely odd, because
   They'd eaten every one. TWEEDLEDEE   *Ib, Ch. 4*

83 The rule is, jam tomorrow and jam yesterday – but never jam today. THE QUEEN   *Ib, Ch. 5*

84 Humpty Dumpty sat on a wall:
Humpty Dumpty had a great fall.
All the King's horses and all the King's men
Couldn't put Humpty Dumpty in his place again. ALICE
                          Ib, Ch. 6

85 'They gave it me,' Humpty Dumpty continued thoughtfully,
… 'for an un-birthday present.'   *Ib, Ch. 6*

86 'When *I* use a word,' Humpty Dumpty said in rather a scornful tone, 'it means just what I choose it to mean – neither more nor less.'   *Ib, Ch. 6*

87 In winter, when the fields are white,
I sing this song for your delight – HUMPTY DUMPTY *Ib, Ch. 6*

88 In spring, when woods are getting green,
I'll try and tell you what I mean. HUMPTY DUMPTY *Ib, Ch. 6*

89 I sent a message to the fish:
I told them 'This is what I wish.' HUMPTY DUMPTY *Ib, Ch. 6*

90 The little fishes of the sea,
They sent an answer back to me.
The little fishes' answer was
'We cannot do it, Sir, because – '. HUMPTY DUMPTY *Ib, Ch. 6*

91 I said it very loud and clear;
I went and shouted in his ear. HUMPTY DUMPTY   *Ib, Ch. 6*

92 He's an Anglo-Saxon Messenger – and those are Anglo-Saxon
   attitudes. THE KING   *Through the Looking Glass, Ch. 7*

93 It's as large as life, and twice as natural! HAIGHA   *Ib, Ch. 7*

94 The Lion looked at Alice wearily. 'Are you animal – or vegetable – or mineral?' he said, yawning at every other word.
                                                          Ib, Ch. 7

95 I'll tell thee everything I can;
       There's little to relate.
   I saw an aged aged man,
       A-sitting on a gate. THE KNIGHT   *Ib, Ch. 8*

96 'Speak when you're spoken to!' the Red Queen sharply inter-
   rupted her.   *Ib, Ch. 9*

97 No admittance till the week after next! CREATURE WITH A LONG
   BEAK   *Ib, Ch. 9*

98 'You look a little shy; let me introduce you to that leg of
   mutton,' said the Red Queen. 'Alice – Mutton; Mutton – Alice.'
                                                          Ib, Ch. 9

CARY, Phoebe, 1824–1871

99 And though hard be the task,
     'Keep a stiff upper lip.'   *Keep a Stiff Upper Lip*

CASTLING, Harry, 19th century

 1 Let's all go down the Strand.   *Title of Song*

CATO, Marcus Porcius, 234–149 B.C.

 2 *Delenda est Carthago*. Carthage must be destroyed.
                                           Plutarch, Life of Cato

CATULLUS, Gaius Valerius, 87–54? B.C.

 3 *Vivamus, mea Lesbia, atque amemus*
   Rumoresque senum severiorum
   Omnes unius aestimemus assis.
   Let us live, my Lesbie, and love, and pay no heed to all the talk
   of censorious old men.   *Carmina, 5*

 4 *Da mi basia mille.*
   Give me a thousand kisses.   *Ib*

 5 *Odi et amo. Quare id faciam, fortasse requiris.*
   Nescio, sed fieri sentio et excrucior.
   I hate and love. Why I do so, perhaps you ask.
   I do not know, but I feel it and am in torment.   *Ib, 85*

 6 *Atque in perpetuum, frater, ave atque vale.*
   And for ever, brother, hail and farewell!   *Ib, 101*

CAVELL, Edith, 1865–1915

7 I realize that patriotism is not enough. I must have no hatred or
bitterness towards anyone.   *Last Words*

CERVANTES, Miguel de, 1547–1616

8 The knight of the sorrowful countenance.
Don Quixote, Part 1, Ch. 19

9 Every man is as Heaven made him, and sometimes a great deal
worse.   *Ib, Part 2, Ch. 4*

10 There are only two families in the world, my old grandmother
used to say, The *Haves* and the *Have-Nots*.   *Ib, Ch. 20*

11 A private sin is not so prejudicial in the world as a public
indecency.   *Ib, Ch. 22*

12 Tell me what company thou keepest, and I'll tell thee what thou
art.   *Ib, Ch. 23*

CHAMBERLAIN, Joseph, 1836–1914

13 Provided that the City of London remains as at present, the
Clearing-house of the World
Speech, Guildhall, London, 19 Jan. 1904

14 The day of small nations has long passed away. The day of
Empires has come.   *Speech, Birmingham, 12 May 1904*

CHAMBERLAIN, Neville, 1869–1940

15 In war, whichever side may call itself the victor, there are no
winners, but all are losers.   *Speech, Kettering, 3 July 1938*

16 I believe it is peace for our time . . . peace with honour.
Broadcast after Munich Agreement, 1 Oct. 1938

17 Hitler has missed the bus.   *Speech, House of Commons,*
4 April 1940

CHANDLER, John, 1806–1876

18 Conquering kings their titles take
From the foes they captive make:
Jesu, by a nobler deed
From the thousands He hath freed.
Conquering Kings their Titles Take

CHARLES I of Great Britain, 1600–1649

19 Never make a defence or apology before you be accused.
Letter to Lord Wentworth, 3 Sept. 1636

CHARLES II of Great Britain, 1630–1685

20 He had been, he said, a most unconscionable time dying; but he hoped that they would excuse it.
Macaulay, History of England, Vol. 1, Ch. 4

21 Not a religion for gentlemen. [*Presbyterianism*]
Burnet, History of My Own Time, Vol. 1, Book 2, Ch. 2

22 Let not poor Nelly starve. [*Said on his death-bed*]
Ib, Vol. 2, Book 3, Ch. 17

23 Better than a play.
On House of Lords Debate on Divorce Bill, 1670

CHARLES V, Holy Roman Emperor, 1500–1558

24 I speak Spanish to God, Italian to women, French to men, and German to my horse.
Attributed

CHARLES, Hughie, see PARKER, Ross

CHAUCER, Geoffrey, 1340?–1400

25 Whan that Aprille with his shoures sote
The droghte of Marche hath perced to the rote.
The Canterbury Tales, Prologue, 1

26 He was a verray parfit gentil knight.
Ib, 72

27 He was as fresh as is the month of May.
Ib, 92 (Squire)

28 And Frensh she spak ful faire and fetisly,
After the scole of Stratford atte Bowe,
For Frensh of Paris was to hir unknowe.
Ib, 124 (Prioress)

29 He yaf nat of that text a pulled hen,
That seith, that hunters been nat holy men.
Ib, 177 (Monk)

30 What sholde he studie, and make himselven wood,
Upon a book in cloistre alwey to poure,
Or swinken with his handes, and laboure,
As Austin bit? How shal the world be served?
Lat Austin have his swink to him reserved.
Ib, 184 (Monk)

31 A Clerk ther was of Oxenford also,
That un-to logik hadde longe y-go.
Ib, 285

32 As lene was his hors as is a rake.
Ib, 287 (Clerk)

33 For him was lever have at his beddes heed
Twenty bokes, clad in blak or reed,
Of Aristotle and his philosophye,
Than robes riche, or fithele, or gay sautrye.
But all be that he was a philosophre,
Yet hadde he but litel gold in cofre.
Ib, 293 (Clerk)

34 Souninge in moral vertu was his speche,
   And gladly wolde he lerne, and gladly teche.   *The Canterbury
                                       Tales, Prologue, 307 (Clerk)*

35 No-wher so bisy a man as he ther nas,
   And yet he semed bisier than he was.   *Ib, 321 (Man of Law)*

36 It snewed in his hous of mete and drinke.   *Ib, 345 (Franklin)*

37 His studie was but litel on the bible.   *Ib, 438 (Doctor)*

38 For gold in phisik is a cordial,
   Therfore he lovede gold in special.   *Ib, 443 (Doctor)*

39 She was a worthy womman al hir lyve,
   Housbondes at chirche-dore she hadde fyve,
   Withouten other companye in youthe.   *Ib, 459 (Wife of Bath)*

40 This noble ensample to his sheep he yaf,
   That first he wroghte, and afterward he taughte.
                                       Ib, 496 (Parson)

41 If gold ruste, what shal iren do?   *Ib, 500 (Parson)*

42 But Cristes lore, and his apostles twelve,
   He taughte, and first he folwed it himselve.   *Ib, 527 (Parson)*

43 His walet lay biforn him in his lappe,
   Bret-ful of pardoun come from Rome al hoot.
                                       Ib, 686 (Pardoner)

44 The smyler with the knyf under the cloke.
                                       Ib, The Knight's Tale, 1141

45 This world nis but a thurghfare ful of wo,
   And we ben pilgrimes, passinge to and fro;
   Deeth is an ende of every worldly sore.   *Ib, Ib, 1989*

46 So was hir joly whistle wel y-wet.   *Ib, The Reve's Tale, 235*

47 Tragedie is to seyn a certeyn storie,
   As olde bokes maken us memorie,
   Of him that stood in greet prosperitee
   And is y-fallen out of heigh degree
   Into miserie, and endeth wrecchedly.
                                       Ib, The Monk's Prologue, 85

48 Mordre wol out, that see we day by day.
                                       Ib, The Nun's Priest's Tale, 232

49 My sone, keep wel thy tongue and keep thy freend.
                                       Ib, The Maunciple's Tale, 319

50 The lyf so short, the craft so long to lerne,
   Th'assay so hard, so sharp the conquering.
                                       The Parlement of Foules, 1

51 For of fortunes sharp adversitee
   The worst kinde of infortune is this,

A man to have ben in prosperitee,
And it remembren, what it passed is.
Troilus and Criseyde, 3, 1625

52 Go, litel book, go litel myn tragedie.   *Ib, 5, 1786*

53 O moral Gower, this book I directe
To thee.   *Ib, 5, 1856*

CHESTERFIELD, Philip Dormer Stanhope, 4th Earl of, 1694–1773

54 Be wiser than other people if you can, but do not tell them so.
Letter to his Son, 19 Nov. 1745

55 Whatever is worth doing at all is worth doing well.
Ib, 10 March 1746

56 An injury is much sooner forgotten than an insult.
Ib, 9 Oct. 1746

57 Take the tone of the company you are in.   *Ib, 9 Oct. 1747*

58 Advice is seldom welcome; and those who want it the most
always like it the least.   *Ib, 29 Jan. 1748*

59 In my mind, there is nothing so illiberal and so ill-bred, as
audible laughter.   *Ib, 9 March 1748*

60 A man of sense only trifles with them [*women*], plays with them,
humours and flatters them, as he does with a sprightly and
forward child; but he neither consults them about, nor trusts
them with, serious matters.   *Ib, 5 Sept. 1748*

61 Idleness is only the refuge of weak minds.   *Ib, 20 July 1749*

62 Women are much more like each other than men: they have, in
truth, but two passions, vanity and love; these are their universal
characteristics.   *Ib, 19 Dec. 1749*

63 Every woman is infallibly to be gained by every sort of flattery,
and every man by one sort or other.   *Ib, 16 March 1752*

64 Unlike my subject will I frame my song,
It shall be witty and it shan't be long.
Epigram on 'Long' Sir Thomas Robinson

65 Give Dayrolles a chair.   *Last words*

CHESTERTON, Gilbert Keith, 1874–1936

66 The strangest whim has seized me . . . After all
I think I will not hang myself today.   *A Ballade of Suicide*

67 When fishes flew and forests walked
And figs grew upon thorn,
Some moment when the moon was blood
Then surely I was born.   *The Donkey*

68 The devil's walking parody
   On all four-footed things   *The Donkey*

69 Fools! For I also had my hour;
   One far fierce hour and sweet;
   There was a shout about my ears,
   And palms before my feet.   *Ib*

70 White founts falling in the Courts of the sun,
   And the Soldan of Byzantium is smiling as they run.   *Lepanto*

71 Strong gongs groaning as the guns boom far,
   Don John of Austria is going to the war.   *Ib*

72 Before the Roman came to Rye or out to Severn strode,
   The rolling English drunkard made the rolling English road.
                                    The Rolling English Road

73 The night we went to Birmingham by way of Beachy Head.   *Ib*

74 For there is good news yet to hear and fine things to be seen,
   Before we go to Paradise by way of Kensal Green.   *Ib*

75 Smile at us, pay us, pass us, but do not quite forget,
   For we are the people of England, that never have spoken yet.
                                          The Secret People

76 God made the wicked Grocer
   For a mystery and a sign,
   That men might shun the awful shops
   And go to inns to dine.   *The Song Against Grocers*

77 And Noah he often said to his wife when he sat down to dine,
   'I don't care where the water goes if it doesn't get into the wine'.
                                            Wine and Water

78 The human race, to which so many of my readers belong.
   The Napoleon of Notting Hill, Book 1, Ch. 1, Opening Words

CHEVALIER, Albert, 1861–1923

79   'Wot cher!' all the neighbours cried,
     'Who're yer goin' to meet Bill?
     Have yer bought the street Bill?'
   Laugh! I thought I should have died,
   Knock'd 'em in the Old Kent Road.
                      Knock'd 'em in the Old Kent Road

80 We've been together now for forty years,
   An' it don't seem a day too much;
   There ain't a lady livin' in the land
   As I'd 'swop' for my dear old Dutch!   *My Old Dutch*

CHEVALIER, Maurice, 1888–1972

81 I prefer old age to the alternative.   *Remark, 1962*

CHURCHILL, Charles, 1731–1764

82   Be England what she will,
With all her faults, she is my country still.   *The Farewell, 27*

83 The danger chiefly lies in acting well;
No crime's so great as daring to excel.
                         Epistle to William Hogarth

84 He for subscribers baits his hook,
And takes your cash, but where's the book?
No matter where; wise fear, you know,
Forbids the robbing of a foe;
But what, to serve our private ends,
Forbids the cheating of our friends?
         [Dr Johnson and his Dictionary] The Ghost, 3, 801

CHURCHILL, Lord Randolph Spencer, 1849–1894

85 The old gang. *[Members of the Conservative Government]*
                Speech, House of Commons, 7 March 1878

86 An old man in a hurry. *[Gladstone]*   *Speech, June 1886*

87 I never could make out what those damned dots meant. *[The decimal point]*   *Quoted in Winston Churchill's Biography*

CHURCHILL, Sir Winston Leonard Spencer, 1874–1965

88 It cannot in the opinion of His Majesty's Government be classified as slavery in the extreme acceptance of the word without some risk of terminological inexactitude.
              Speech, House of Commons, 22 Feb. 1906

89 The maxim of the British people is 'Business as usual'.
              Speech, Guildhall, London, 9 Nov. 1914

90 The German dictator, instead of snatching the victuals from the table, has been content to have them served to him course by course.   *Speech, House of Commons, 5 Oct. 1938*

91 I cannot forecast to you the action of Russia. It is a riddle wrapped in a mystery inside an enigma.
              Broadcast, 1 Oct. 1939

92 I would say to the House, as I said to those who have joined the Government: 'I have nothing to offer but blood, toil, tears and sweat.'   *Speech, House of Commons, 13 May 1940*

93 Victory at all costs, victory in spite of all terror, victory however long and hard the road may be; for without victory there is no survival.   *Ib*

94 We shall not flag or fail. We shall fight in France, we shall fight on the seas and oceans, we shall fight with growing confidence

and growing strength in the air, we shall defend our island, whatever the cost may be, we shall fight on the beaches, we shall fight on the landing grounds, we shall fight in the fields and in the streets, we shall fight in the hills; we shall never surrender.
Speech, House of Commons, 4 June 1940

95 Let us therefore brace ourselves to our duties, and so bear ourselves that, if the British Empire and its Commonwealth last for a thousand years, men will still say, 'This was their finest hour'.
Speech, House of Commons, 18 June 1940

96 Never in the field of human conflict was so much owed by so many to so few.
Speech, House of Commons, 20 Aug. 1940
on R.A.F. in Battle of Britain

97 *Nous attendons l'invasion promise de longue date. Les poissons aussi.*
We are waiting for the long-promised invasion. So are the fishes.
Broadcast to the French People, 21 Oct. 1940

98 Here is the answer which I will give to President Roosevelt. . . . Give us the tools, and we will finish the job.
Broadcast, 9 Feb. 1941

99 What kind of a people do they [*the Japanese*] think we are?
Speech, U.S. Congress, 26 Dec. 1941

1 When I warned them [*the French Government*] that Britain would fight on alone whatever they did, their generals told their Prime Minister and his divided Cabinet: 'In three weeks England will have her neck wrung like a chicken.' Some chicken! Some neck!
Speech, Canadian Parliament, 30 Dec. 1941

2 This is not the end. It is not even the beginning of the end. But it is, perhaps, the end of the beginning.
Speech, Mansion House, London, 10 Nov. 1942

3 Let me, however, make this clear, in case there should be any mistake about it in any quarter. We mean to hold our own. I have not become the King's First Minister in order to preside over the liquidation of the British Empire.
Ib

4 The soft under-belly of the Axis.
Speech, House of Commons, 11 Nov. 1942

5 The problems of victory are more agreeable than those of defeat, but they are no less difficult.
Ib

6 There is no finer investment for any community than putting milk into babies. Healthy citizens are the greatest asset any country can have.
Broadcast: A Four Years' Plan, 21 March 1943

7 I view with profound misgivings the retreat of the American Army to our line of occupation in the central sector, thus bringing Soviet power into the heart of Western Europe and the descent of an iron curtain between us and everything to the eastward. *Cable to President Truman, 4 June 1945*
Quoted in The Second World War, Vol. 6, Triumph and Tragedy,
1954, p. 523

8 From Stettin in the Baltic to Trieste in the Adriatic, an iron curtain has descended across the Continent.
Speech, Westminster College, Fulton, U.S.A., 5 March 1946

9 This is the sort of English up with which I will not put.
Attributed. Marginal comment on document,
quoted by Sir Ernest Gowers in Plain Words, 1948, p. 74

10 In War: Resolution. In Defeat: Defiance. In Victory: Magnanimity. In Peace: Goodwill. *The Second World War, Vol. 1,*
The Gathering Storm, 1948, Moral of the Work

11 I have never accepted what many people have kindly said, namely that I inspired the nation. It was the nation and the race dwelling all round the globe that had the lion heart. I had the luck to be called upon to give the roar.
Speech on 80th birthday, Westminster Hall, 30 Nov. 1954

CIBBER, Colley, 1671–1757

12 One had as good be out of the world, as out of the fashion.
Love's Last Shift, Act 2

13 Stolen sweets are best. *The Rival Fools, Act 1*

CICERO, Marcus Tullius, 106–43 B.C.

14 *Nihil tam absurde dici potest, quod non dicatur, ab alique philosophorum.* There is nothing so absurd but some philosopher has said it. *De Divinatione, 2, 58*

15 *Salus populi suprema est lex.* The good of the people is the chief law. *De Legibus, 3, 3, 8*

16 *Summum bonum.* The greatest good. *De Officiis, 1, 2*

17 *Cedant arma togae, concedant laurea laudi.* Let wars give way to peace, laurels to paeans. *Ib, 1, 22*

18 *Mens cuiusque is est quisque.* The mind of each man is the man himself. *De Republica, 6, 26*

19 *O tempora! O mores!* What times! What customs!
In Catilinam, 1, 1

20 *Civis Romanus sum.* I am a Roman citizen.
In Verrem, 5, 57, 147

21 *O fortunatam natam me consule Romam!* O happy Rome, born
when I was consul.   *Quoted in Juvenal, 10, 22*

CLAY, Henry, 1777–1852
22 I had rather be right than be President.   *Speech,   1850*

CLEMENS, Samuel Langhorne, see TWAIN, Mark

CLEVELAND, Stephen Grover, 1837–1908
23 However plenty silver dollars may become, they will not be
distributed as gifts among the people.
                 First Annual Message as President of U.S.A., 8 Dec. 1885

CLIVE, Lord Robert, 1725–1774
24 By God, Mr Chairman, at this moment I stand astonished at
my own moderation! *Reply during Parliamentary Inquiry, 1773*

CLOUGH, Arthur Hugh, 1819–1861
25 A world where nothing is had for nothing.
                           The Bothie of Tober-na-Vuolich, 8, 5
26 How pleasant it is to have money. *Dipsychus, Part 1, Scene 4*
27 And almost every one when age,
    Disease, or sorrows strike him,
  Inclines to think there is a God,
    Or something very like Him.   *Ib, Part 1, Scene 5*
28 Thou shalt have one God only; who
  Would be at the expense of two?   *The Latest Decalogue, 1*
29 Thou shalt not kill; but needst not strive
  Officiously to keep alive.   *Ib, 11*
30 Thou shalt not covet; but tradition
  Approves all forms of competition.   -   *Ib, 19*
31 'Tis better to have fought and lost,
  Than never to have fought at all.   *Peschiera*
32 Say not the struggle naught availeth,
    The labour and the wounds are vain.
  The enemy faints not, nor faileth,
    And as things have been, things remain.
                       Say not the struggle naught availeth
33 For while the tired waves, vainly breaking,
    Seem here no painful inch to gain,
  Far back through creeks and inlets making
    Comes silent, flooding in, the main.   *Ib*

34 And not by eastern windows only,
　　When daylight comes, comes in the light,
　In front the sun climbs slow, how slowly,
　　But westward, look, the land is bright. *Say not the struggle*
naught availeth

COBBETT, William, 1762–1835

35 To be poor and independent is very nearly an impossibility.
Advice to Young Men

36 But what is to be the fate of the great wen [*London*] of all?
Rural Rides

COBORN, Charles, 1852–1945

37 Two lovely black eyes,
　Oh, what a surprise!
　Only for telling a man he was wrong,
　Two lovely black eyes! *Two Lovely Black Eyes*

COKE, Sir Edward, 1552–1634

38 How long soever it hath continued, if it be against reason, it is
　of no force in law. *First Institute*

39 A man's house is his castle. *Third Institute*

40 Six hours in sleep, in law's grave study six,
　Four spend in prayer, the rest on Nature fix. *Pandects*

COLERIDGE, Hartley, 1796–1849

41 She is not fair to outward view
　　As many maidens be;
　Her loveliness I never knew
　　Until she smiled on me. *Song, She is not Fair*

COLERIDGE, Samuel Taylor, 1772–1834

42 It is an ancient Mariner,
　And he stoppeth one of three.
　'By thy long grey beard and glittering eye,
　Now wherefore stopp'st thou me?'
The Rime of the Ancient Mariner, Part 1, 1

43 He holds him with his glittering eye. *Ib, 1, 13*

44 The Sun came up upon the left,
　Out of the sea came he!
　And he shone bright, and on the right
　Went down into the sea. *Ib, 1, 25*

45 The bride hath paced into the hall,
　Red as a rose is she. *Ib, 1, 33*

46 The ice was here, the ice was there,
   The ice was all around:
   It cracked and growled, and roared and howled,
   Like noises in a swound!   *The Rime of the Ancient Mariner,*
                                                      Part, 1, 59

47 With my cross-bow
   I shot the albatross.   *Ib, 1, 81*

48 The fair breeze blew, the white foam flew,
   The furrow followed free;
   We were the first that ever burst
   Into that silent sea.   *Ib, Part 2, 103*

49 As idle as a painted ship
   Upon a painted ocean.   *Ib, 2, 117*

50 Water, water, every where,
   And all the boards did shrink;
   Water, water, every where,
   Nor any drop to drink.   *Ib, 2, 119*

51 I bit my arm, I sucked the blood,
   And cried, A sail! a sail!   *Ib, Part 3, 160*

52 Her lips were red, her looks were free,
   Her locks were yellow as gold:
   Her skin was as white as leprosy,
   The Night-mare Life-in-Death was she,
   Who thicks man's blood with cold.   *Ib, 3, 190*

53 I fear thee, ancient Mariner!
   I fear thy skinny hand!   *Ib, Part 4, 224*

54 Alone, alone, all, all alone,
   Alone on a wide wide sea!
   And never a saint took pity on
   My soul in agony.   *Ib, 4, 232*

55 The many men, so beautiful!
   And they all dead did lie:
   And a thousand thousand slimy things
   Lived on; and so did I.   *Ib, 4, 236*

56 The moving Moon went up the sky,
   And no where did abide:
   Softly she was going up,
   And a star or two beside.   *Ib, 4, 263*

57 Oh sleep! it is gentle thing,
   Beloved from pole to pole!   *Ib, Part 5, 292*

58 We were a ghastly crew.   *Ib, 5, 340*

59 Quoth he, 'The man hath penance done,
   And penance more will do.'   *Ib, 5, 408*

60 Like one, that on a lonesome road
  Doth walk in fear and dread,
  And having once turned round walks on,
  And turns no more his head;
  Because he knows, a frightful fiend
  Doth close behind him tread.   *The Rime of the Ancient
    Mariner, Part 6, 446*

61 No voice; but oh! the silence sank
  Like music on my heart.   *Ib, 6, 498*

62 O Wedding-Guest! this soul hath been
  Alone on a wide wide sea:
  So lonely 'twas, that God himself
  Scarce seemed there to be.   *Ib, Part, 7, 597*

63 He prayeth well, who loveth well
  Both man and bird and beast.   *Ib, 7, 612*

64 He prayeth best, who loveth best
  All things both great and small;
  For the dear God who loveth us,
  He made and loveth all.   *Ib, 7, 614*

65 A sadder and a wiser man,
  He rose the morrow morn.   *Ib, 7, 624*

66 A sight to dream of, not to tell!   *Christabel, 1, 253*

67 And constancy lives in realms above;
  And life is thorny; and youth is vain;
  And to be wroth with one we love
  Doth work like madness in the brain.   *Ib, 2, 410*

68 I see, not feel, how beautiful they are!   *Dejection: An Ode, 38*

69 I may not hope from outward forms to win
  The passion and the life, whose fountains are within.   *Ib, 45*

70 Swans sing before they die – 'twere no bad thing
  Should certain persons die before they sing.
    Epigram on a Volunteer Singer

71 In Xanadu did Kubla Khan
  A stately pleasure-dome decree:
  Where Alph, the sacred river, ran
  Through caverns measureless to man
    Down to a sunless sea.   *Kubla Khan, 1*

72 A savage place! as holy and enchanted
  As e'er beneath a waning moon was haunted
  By woman wailing for her demon-lover!   *Ib, 14*

73 Through wood and dale the sacred river ran,
  Then reached the caverns measureless to man.   *Ib, 26*

74 And 'mid this tumult Kubla heard from far
   Ancestral voices prophesying war!   *Kubla Khan*, 29

75 It was a miracle of rare device,
   A sunny pleasure-dome with caves of ice!   *Ib, 35*

76 Weave a circle round him thrice,
   And close your eyes with holy dread,
   For he on honey-dew hath fed,
   And drunk the milk of Paradise.   *Ib, 51*

77 This Lime-tree Bower my Prison   *Title of Poem*

78 Tranquillity! thou better name
   Than all the family of Fame!   *Ode to Tranquillity*

79 That willing suspension of disbelief for the moment, which
   constitutes poetic faith.   *Biographia Literaria, Ch. 14*

80 Our myriad-minded Shakespeare.   *Ib, Ch. 15*

81 Summer has set in with its usual severity.
      Remark quoted in C. Lamb's letter to V. Novello, 9 May 1826

82 I wish our clever young poets would remember my homely
   definitions of prose and poetry; that is, prose = words in their
   best order;—poetry = the best words in the best order.
                               Table Talk, 12 July 1827

83 No mind is thoroughly well organized that is deficient in a sense
   of humour.   *Table Talk*

84 What comes from the heart, goes to the heart.   *Ib*

COLLINGS, Jesse, 1831–1921

85 Three acres and a cow.   *Slogan for Land Reform, 1885*

COLLINS, Mortimer, 1827–1876

86 A man is as old as he's feeling,
   A woman as old as she looks.   *The Unknown Quantity*

COLLINS, William, 1721–1759

87 To fair Fidele's grassy tomb
      Soft maids, and village hinds shall bring
   Each op'ning sweet, of earliest bloom,
      And rifle all the breathing Spring.   *Dirge in Cymbeline, 1*

88 Hamlets brown, and dim-discover'd spires.   *Ode to Evening, 37*

89 How sleep the brave, who sink to rest,
   By all their country's wishes blest!
                          Ode written in the Year 1746, 1

90 By fairy hands their knell is rung,
   By forms unseen their dirge is sung;

There Honour comes, a Pilgrim grey,
To bless the turf that wraps their clay,
And Freedom shall a-while repair,
To dwell a weeping hermit there! *Ode written in the*
Year 1746, 7

91 When Music, heavenly maid, was young.
The Passions, An Ode for Music, 1

92 With eyes up-rais'd, as one inspir'd,
Pale Melancholy sate retir'd. *Ib, 57*

93 O Music, sphere-descended Maid,
Friend of Pleasure, Wisdom's aid. *Ib, 95*

COLMAN, George, 1762–1836

94 Mum's the word. *The Battle of Hexham, Act 2, Scene 1*

95 When taken
To be well shaken. *Newcastle Apothecary*

COLTON, Charles Caleb, 1780?–1832

96 Men will wrangle for religion; write for it; fight for it; anything
but – live for it. *Lacon, 1, No. 25*

97 When you have nothing to say, say nothing. *Ib, No. 183*

98 Imitation is the sincerest form of flattery. *Ib, No. 217*

99 Examinations are formidable even to the best prepared, for the
greatest fool may ask more than the wisest man can answer.
Ib, No. 322

 1 The debt which cancels all others. *Ib, 2, No. 66*

CONFUCIUS, 551–479 B.C.

 2 Men's natures are alike; it is their habits that carry them far
apart. *Analects*

 3 Study the past, if you would divine the future. *Ib*

 4 Learning without thought is labour lost; thought without
learning is perilous. *Ib*

CONGREVE, William, 1670–1729

 5 Music has charms to soothe a savage breast,
To soften rocks, or bend a knotted oak. ALMERIA
The Mourning Bride, Act 1

 6 Heaven has no rage like love to hatred turned,
Nor hell a fury like a woman scorned. ZARA *Ib, Act 3*

 7 They come together like the coroner's inquest, to sit upon the
murdered reputations of the week. FAINALL
The Way of the World, Act 1, Scene 1

8 'Tis for the honour of England, that all Europe should know
that we have blockheads of all ages.   FAINALL
The Way of the World, Act 1, Scene 5

9 A wit should no more be sincere, than a woman constant; one
argues a decay of parts, as t'other of beauty.   WITWOUD
Ib, Act 1, Scene 6

10 Here she comes i' faith full sail, with her fan spread and
streamers out, and a shoal of fools for tenders.   MIRABELL
Ib, Act 2, Scene 5

11 I am persecuted with letters – I hate letters – nobody knows
how to write letters; and yet one has 'em, one does not know
why. – They serve one to pin up one's hair.   MRS MILLAMENT
Ib

12 MRS MILLAMENT: I believe I gave you some pain.
MIRABEL: Does that please you?
MRS MILLAMENT: Infinitely; I love to give pain.   *Ib*

13 Lord, what is a lover, that it can give? Why, one makes lovers
as fast as one pleases, and they live as long as one pleases, and
they die as soon as one pleases: and then if one pleases one
makes more.   MRS MILLAMENT *Ib*

14 Love's but the frailty of the mind,
When 'tis not with ambition join'd.   SONG *Ib, Act 3, Scene 12*

15 O, nothing is more alluring than a levee from a couch in some
confusion.   LADY WISHFORT   *Ib, Act 4, Scene 1*

16 I nauseate walking; 'tis a country diversion, I loathe the country
and everything that relates to it.   MRS MILLAMENT
Ib, Act 4, Scene 4

17 Let us never visit together, nor go to a play together, but let us
be very strange and wellbred: let us be as strange as if we had
been married a great while; and as wellbred as if we were not
married at all.   MRS MILLAMENT   *Ib, Act 4, Scene 5*

18 These articles subscribed, if I continue to endure you a little
longer, I may by degrees dwindle into a wife.
MRS MILLAMENT   *Ib*

19 I hope you do not think me prone to any iteration of
nuptials.   LADY WISHFORT   *Ib, Act 4, Scene 12*

20 O, she is the antidote to desire.   WAITWELL   *Ib, Act 4,
Scene 14*

CONNELL, James, 1852–1929
21 Then raise the scarlet standard high!
Beneath its shade we'll live and die!

Though cowards flinch, and traitors jeer,
We'll keep the Red Flag flying here!   *The Red Flag*

CONNOLLY, Cyril, 1903–1974

22 As repressed sadists are supposed to become policemen or
butchers so those with irrational fear of life become publishers.
Enemies of Promise

CONNOR, T. W., 19th century

23 She was one of the early birds,
And I was one of the worms.
She was a Dear Little Dickie-Bird

CONRAD, Joseph, 1857–1924

24 You shall judge of a man by his foes as well as by his friends.
Lord Jim, Ch. 34

25 A work that aspires, however humbly, to the condition of art
should carry its justification in every line.
The Nigger of the Narcissus, Preface

26 The sea never changes and its works, for all the talk of men, are
wrapped in mystery.   *Typhoon, Ch. 2*

27 The belief in a supernatural source of evil is not necessary;
men alone are quite capable of every wickedness.
Under Western Eyes, Part 2

COOLIDGE, Calvin, 1872–1933

28 There is no right to strike against the public safety by anybody,
anywhere, any time.   *On the Boston police strike, 14 Sept. 1919*

29 He said he was against it.   *When asked what a clergyman
had said in a sermon on sin*

COOPER, James Fenimore, 1789–1851

30 The Last of the Mohicans.   *Title of Novel*

CORBUSIER, Le, 1887–1965

31 *Une maison est une machine-à-habiter.* A house is a machine for
living in.   *Vers une architecture, 1923*

CORNEILLE, Pierre, 1606–1684

32 *À vaincre sans péril, on triomphe sans gloire.* We triumph without glory when we conquer without danger.   DON GOMÈS
Le Cid, Act 2, Scene 2

33 *Faites votre devoir, et laissez faire aux dieux.* Do your duty and
leave the rest to the Gods.   LE VIEIL HORACE

Horace, Act 2, Scene 8

CORNFORD, Frances Crofts, 1886–1960

34 O why do you walk through the fields in gloves.
    Missing so much and so much?
O fat white woman whom nobody loves
Why do you walk through the fields in gloves
When the grass is as soft as the breast of doves
And shivering-sweet to the touch?

To a Fat Lady Seen from a Train

CORNUEL, Anne Bigot de, 1605–1694

35 *Il n'y a pas de héros pour son valet de chambre.* No man is a hero
to his valet.   *Lettres de Mlle. Aissé, 13 Aug. 1728*

COUBERTIN, Baron Pierre de, 1863–1937

36 *L'important dans ces olympiades, c'est moins d'y gagner que d'y
prendre part. . . . L'important dans la vie ce n'est point le triomphe
mais le combat.*
The most important thing in the Olympic Games is not winning
but taking part. . . . The essential thing in life is not conquering
but fighting well.   *Speech at Banquet to Officials of Olympic
Games, London, 24 July 1908*

COUÉ, Émile, 1857–1926

37 *Tous les jours, à tous points de vue, je vais de mieux en mieux.*
Every day, in every way, I am getting better and better.

Formula for his cures by auto-suggestion

COUSIN, Victor, 1792–1867

38 *L'art pour l'art.* Art for art's sake.   *Lecture at Sorbonne, 1818*

COWARD, Noel, 1899–1973

39 The Stately Homes of England
How beautiful they stand,
To prove the upper classes
Have still the upper hand.   *Operette, Act 1, Scene 7,
The Stately Homes of England*

40 And tho' if the Van Dycks have to go
And we pawn the Bechstein Grand,
We'll stand by the Stately Homes of England.   *Ib*

41 A room with a view – and you
    And no one to worry us
  No one to hurry us.
                    This Year of Grace, Act 1, A Room with a View

42 At twelve noon the natives swoon
  And no further work is done.
  But mad dogs and Englishmen
  Go out in the midday sun.
                    Words and Music, Mad Dogs and Englishmen

43 Don't let's be Beastly to the Germans.   *Title of Song*

44 Don't put your Daughter on the Stage, Mrs Worthington.
                                        Title of song

45 Poor Little Rich Girl.   *Title of song*

COWLEY, Abraham, 1618–1667
46 God the first garden made, and the first city Cain.
                                        The Garden

47 This only grant me, that my means may lie
  Too low for envy, for contempt too high.   *Of Myself*

COWLEY, Hannah, 1743–1809
48 But what is woman?–only one of Nature's agreeable blunders.
              DOILEY   *Who's the Dupe? Act 2, Scene 2*

COWPER, William, 1731–1800
49 Hark! the Gaul is at her gates!   *Boadicea*

50 Regions Caesar never knew
      Thy posterity shall sway,
  Where his eagles never flew,
      None invincible as they.   *Ib*

51 He found it inconvenient to be poor.   *Charity, 189*

52 A moral, sensible, and well-bred man
  Will not affront me, and no other can.   *Conversation, 193*

53 Pernicious weed! whose scent the fair annoys,
  Unfriendly to society's chief joys,
  Thy worst effect is banishing for hours
  The sex whose presence civilizes ours.   *Ib, 251*

54 John Gilpin was a citizen
    Of credit and renown,
  A train-band captain eke was he,
    Of famous London town.   *John Gilpin, 1*

55 Tomorrow is our wedding day
   And we will then repair
   Unto the Bell at Edmonton
   All in a chaise and pair.   *John Gilpin, 2*

56 O'erjoyed was he to find
   That, though on pleasure she was bent,
   She had a frugal mind.   *Ib, 8*

57 Away went Gilpin – who but he?
   His fame soon spread around;
   He carries weight! he rides a race,
   'Tis for a thousand pound!   *Ib, 29*

58 The dinner waits, and we are tired:
   Said Gilpin, So am I!   *Ib, 37*

59 Said John, 'It is my wedding-day,
   And all the world would stare,
   If wife should dine at Edmonton,
   And I should dine at Ware.'   *Ib, 49*

60 'Twas for your pleasure you came here,
   You shall go back for mine.   *Ib, 50*

61 Now let us sing, Long live the King,
   And Gilpin long live he;
   And when he next doth ride abroad,
   May I be there to see!   *Ib, 63*

62 What peaceful hours I once enjoyed!
      How sweet their memory still!
   But they have left an aching void,
      The world can never fill.   *Olney Hymns, 1*

63 God moves in a mysterious way,
      His wonders to perform;
   He plants His footsteps in the sea,
      And rides upon the storm.   *Ib, 35*

64 Toll for the brave,
   The brave that are no more:
   All sunk beneath the wave,
   Fast by their native shore. *On the Loss of the Royal George*

65 How much a dunce that has been sent to roam
   Excels a dunce that has been kept at home.
                              Progress of Error, 415

66 Thou god of our idolatry, the press.   *Ib, 461*

67 Absence of occupation is not rest,
   A mind quite vacant is a mind distressed.   *Retirement, 623*

68 I sing the Sofa.   *The Task, 1, The Sofa, 1*

69 God made the country, and man made the town. *The Task 1,*
The Sofa, 749

70 England, with all thy faults, I love thee still,
My country. *Ib, 2, The Timepiece, 206*

71 Variety's the very spice of life
That gives it all its flavour. *Ib, 2, 606*

72 Detested sport,
That owes its pleasure to another's pain. *Ib, 3, The Garden, 326*

73 Now stir the fire, and close the shutters fast,
Let fall the curtains, wheel the sofa round,
And, while the bubbling and loud-hissing urn
Throws up a steamy column, and the cups,
That cheer but not inebriate, wait on each,
So let us welcome peaceful evening in.
Ib, 4, The Winter Evening, 36

74 Nature is but a name for an effect
Whose cause is God. *Ib, 6, The Winter Walk at Noon, 223*

75 I would not enter on my list of friends
(Though graced with polished manners and fine sense,
Yet wanting sensibility) the man
Who needlessly sets foot upon a worm. *Ib, 6, 560*

76 The twentieth year is well-nigh past,
Since first our sky was overcast:
Ah, would that this might be the last
My Mary! *To Mary*

77 I am monarch of all I survey
My right there is none to dispute.
Verses supposed to be written by Alexander Selkirk

78 O Solitude! Where are the charms
That sages have seen in thy face?
Better dwell in the midst of alarms
Than reign in this horrible place. *Ib*

CRABBE, George, 1754–1832

79 Habit with him was all the test of truth,
'It must be right: I've done it from my youth.'
The Borough, Letter 3, The Vicar, 138

80 Books cannot always please, however good;
Minds are not ever craving for their food.
Ib, Letter 24, Schools, 402

81 A master-passion is the love of news. *The Newspaper, 279*

82 Secrets with girls, like loaded guns with boys,
Are never valued till they make a noise.
Tales of the Hall, 11, The Maid's Story, 84

CRASHAW, Richard, 1612?–1649

83 I would be married but I'd have no wife,
I would be married to a single life.   *On Marriage*

84 Whoe'er she be,
That not impossible she
That shall command my heart and me.
                              Wishes to his Supposed Mistress

CREIGHTON, Mandell, 1843–1901

85 No people do so much harm as those who go about doing good.
                              Life, 1904

CROKER, John Wilson, 1780–1857

86 A game which a sharper once played with a dupe, entitled 'Heads
I win, tails you lose.'   *Croker Papers*

87 We now are, as we always have been, decidedly and conscienti-
ously attached to what is called the Tory, and which might with
more propriety be called the Conservative, party.
                              Quarterly Review, Jan, 1830

CROMWELL, Oliver, 1599–1658

88 I beseech you, in the bowels of Christ, think it possible you may
be mistaken.   *Letter to the General Assembly of the Church
                              of Scotland, 3 Aug. 1650*

89 What shall we do with this bauble? There, take it away.
                              Speech dismissing Parliament, 20 April 1653

90 It is not fit that you should sit here any longer! . . . you shall
now give place to better men.
                              Speech to the Rump Parliament, 22 Jan. 1654

91 Mr Lely, I desire you would use all your skill to paint my
picture truly like me, and not flatter me at all; but remark all
these roughnesses, pimples, warts, and everything as you see me,
otherwise I will never pay a farthing for it.
                              Horace Walpole's Anecdotes of Painting, Ch. 12

CUMBERLAND, Bishop Richard, 1631–1718

92 It is better to wear out than to rust out.
                              Quoted in G. Horne, The Duty of Contending for the Faith

CUMMINGS, Edward Estlin, 1894–1962

93 a politician is an arse upon
which everyone has sat except a man.   *a politician*

94 anyone lived in a pretty how town
   (with up so floating many bells down)
   spring summer autumn winter
   he sang his didn't he danced his did.

   anyone lived in a pretty how town

95 Humanity i love you because
   when you're hard up you pawn your
   intelligence to buy a drink.

   humanity i love you

CUNNINGHAM, Allan, 1784–1842

96 A wet sheet and a flowing sea,
   A wind that follows fast,
   And fills the white and rustling sail,
   And bends the gallant mast. *A Wet Sheet and a Flowing Sea*

97 It's hame and it's hame, hame fain wad I be,
   Oh, hame, hame, hame to my ain countree!

   It's Hame and It's Hame

CURRAN, John Philpot, 1750–1817

98 The condition upon which God hath given liberty to man is
   eternal vigilance. *Speech on the Right of Election of
   Lord Mayor of Dublin, 10 July 1790*

DACRE, Harry, 19th century

99 Daisy, Daisy, give me your answer, do!
   I'm half crazy, all for the love of you!
      It won't be a stylish marriage,
      I can't afford a carriage,
   But you'll look sweet upon the seat
   Of a bicycle made for two! *Daisy Bell*

DANA, Charles Anderson, 1819–1897

1 When a dog bites a man that is not news, but when a man bites
   a dog, that is news. *What is News? The New York Sun, 1882*

DANTE, Alighieri, 1265–1321

2 *Lasciate ogni speranza voi ch'entrate.* Abandon hope, all ye who
   enter here. *Divine Comedy, Inferno, 3, 9*

3   *Nessun maggior dolore,
   Che ricordarsi del tempo felice
   Nella miseria.*
   There is no greater sorrow than to recall a time of happiness
   when in misery. *Ib, 5, 121*

4 *L'amor che muove il sole e l'altre stelle.* The love that moves the
sun and the other stars. *Divine Comedy, Paradiso, 33, 145*

DANTON, Georges Jaques, 1759–1794

5 *De l'audace, encore de l'audace, et toujours de l'audace!* Boldness,
and again boldness, and always boldness!
Speech, French Legislative Committee, 2 Sept. 1792

DARWIN, Charles Robert, 1809–1882

6 Man with all his noble qualities . . . still bears in his bodily
frame the indelible stamp of his lowly origin.
The Descent of Man, Last Words

7 I have called this principle, by which each slight variation, if
useful, is preserved, by the term of Natural Selection.
The Origin of Species, Ch. 3

8 The expression often used by Mr Herbert Spencer of the Survival
of the Fittest is more accurate, and is sometimes equally convenient. *Ib, Ch. 3*

DAVENANT, Sir William, 1606–1668

9 I shall sleep like a top. CELANIA *The Rivals, Act 3*

10 Awake, awake! the morn will never rise,
Till she can dress her beauty at your eyes. *Song*

DAVIES, William Henry, 1871–1940

11 What is this life if, full of care,
We have no time to stand and stare? *Leisure*

12 Sweet Stay-at-Home, sweet Well-content. *Sweet Stay-at-Home*

DAVIS, Jefferson, 1808–1889

13 All we ask is to be let alone. *Attributed remark, Inaugural
Address as President of Confederated States of America, 1861*

DAY LEWIS, Cecil, 1904–1972

14 Nothing so sharply reminds a man he is mortal
As leaving a place
In a winter morning's dark, the air on his face
Unkind as the touch of sweating metal.
Departure in the Dark

15 Tempt me no more; for I
Have known the lightning's hour,
The poet's inward pride,
The certainty of power. *Tempt me no more*

DECATUR, Stephen, 1779–1820

16 Our country! In her intercourse with foreign nations, may she
always be in the right; but our country, right or wrong.
Speech, Norfolk, Virginia, April 1816

DEFOE, Daniel, 1660?–1731

17 I takes my man Friday with me.   *Robinson Crusoe, Part 1*

18 Wherever God erects a house of prayer,
The Devil always builds a chapel there;
And 'twill be found, upon examination,
The latter has the largest congregation.
The True-Born Englishman, Part 1, 1

19 And of all plagues with which mankind are curst,
Ecclesiastic tyranny's the worst.   *Ib, Part 2, 299*

DEKKER, Thomas, 1570?–1641?

20 Golden slumbers kiss your eyes,
Smiles awake you when you rise.
Patient Grissil, Act 4, Scene 2

21 Brave shoemakers, all gentlemen of the gentle craft.
The Shoemaker's Holiday, Act 3, Scene 1

DE LA MARE, Walter, 1873–1956

22 Look thy last on all things lovely,
Every hour.   *Farewell*

23 'Is there anybody there?' said the Traveller,
Knocking on the moonlit door.   *The Listeners*

24 'Tell them I came, and no one answered,
That I kept my word,' he said.   *Ib*

25 Softly along the road of evening,
In a twilight dim with rose,
Wrinkled with age, and drenched with dew,
Old Nod, the shepherd, goes.   *Nod*

26 Three jolly Farmers
Once bet a pound
Each dance the others would
Off the ground.   *Off the Ground*

27 Slowly, silently, now the moon
Walks the night in her silver shoon.   *Silver*

DENMAN, Thomas, 1st Baron, 1779-1854

28 Trial by jury itself, instead of being a security to persons who
are accused, will be a delusion, a mockery, and a snare.
Judgment in O'Connell v. The Queen, 4 Sept. 1844

DENNIS, John, 1657-1734

29 A man who could make so vile a pun would not scruple to pick
a pocket.   *The Gentleman's Magazine, 1781*

DE QUINCEY, Thomas, 1785-1859

30 Murder considered as one of the Fine Arts.   *Title of Essay*

DESCARTES, René, 1596-1650

31 *Cogito, ergo sum.* I think, therefore I am.   *Le Discours de la
Méthode*

DICKENS, Charles, 1812-1870

32 'There are strings', said Mr Tappertit, 'in the human heart that
had better not be wibrated.'   *Barnaby Rudge, Ch. 22*

33 This is a London particular . . . A fog, miss.   *Bleak House,
Ch. 3*

34 I expect a judgment. Shortly. MISS FLITE   *Ib*

35 It is a melancholy truth that even great men have their poor
relations.   *Ib, Ch. 28*

36 'God bless us every one!' said Tiny Tim, the last of all.
A Christmas Carol, Stave 3

37 'I am a lone lorn creetur',' were Mrs Gummidge's words . . .
'and everythink goes contrairy with me.'   *David Copperfield,
Ch. 3*

38 Barkis is willin'. BARKIS   *Ib, Ch. 5*

39 I have known him [*Mr Micawber*] come home to supper with a
flood of tears, and a declaration that nothing was now left but
a jail; and go to bed making a calculation of the expense of
putting bow-windows to the house, 'in case anything turned
up,' which was his favourite expression.   *Ib, Ch. 11*

40 Annual income twenty pounds, annual expenditure nineteen
nineteen six, result happiness. Annual income twenty pounds,
annual expenditure twenty pounds ought and six, result misery.
MR MICAWBER   *Ib, Ch. 12*

41 We are so very 'umble. URIAH HEEP   *Ib, Ch. 17*

42 I only ask for information. ROSA DARTLE   *Ib, Ch. 20*

43 'It was as true', said Mr Barkis, 'as taxes is. And nothing's
   truer than them.'   *David Copperfield, Ch. 21*

44 Accidents will occur in the best-regulated families.
                          MR MICAWBER *Ib, Ch. 28*

45 I'm Gormed – and I can't say no fairer than that.
                          MR PEGGOTTY *Ib, Ch. 63*

46 When found, make a note of. CAPTAIN CUTTLE
                          Dombey and Son, Ch. 15

47 Whatever was required to be done, the Circumlocution Office
   was beforehand with all the public departments in the art of
   perceiving – HOW NOT TO DO IT. *Little Dorrit, Book 1, Ch. 10*

48 Let us be moral. Let us contemplate existence. MR PECKSNIFF
                          Martin Chuzzlewit, Ch. 10

49 Here's the rule for bargains: 'Do other men, for they would do
   you.' That's the true business precept. JONAS CHUZZLEWIT
                                        Ib, Ch. 11

50 He'd make a lovely corpse. MRS GAMP   *Ib, Ch. 25*

51 Oh Sairey, Sairey, little do we know what lays afore us!
                          MRS GAMP *Ib, Ch. 40*

52 At Mr Wackford Squeers' Academy, Dotheboys Hall . . .
   Youth are boarded, clothed, booked, furnished with pocket-
   money, provided with all necessaries, instructed in all languages
   living and dead . . . No extras, no vacations, and diet unparalleled.   *Nicholas Nickleby, Ch. 3*

53 Every baby born into the world is a finer one than the last.
                                        Ib, Ch. 36

54 My life is one demd horrid grind! MR MANTALINI *Ib, Ch. 64*

55 Oliver Twist has asked for more. BUMBLE *Oliver Twist, Ch. 2*

56 Known by the *sobriquet* of 'The artful Dodger.'   *Ib, Ch. 8*

57 I only know two sorts of boys. Mealy boys, and beef-faced boys.
                          MR GRIMWIG *Ib, Ch. 14*

58 'If the law supposes that,' said Mr Bumble . . ., 'the law is a
   ass – a idiot.'   *Ib, Ch. 51*

59 The question about everything was, would it bring a blush to the
   cheek of a young person? *Our Mutual Friend, 1, II*

60 Not presume to dictate, but broiled fowl and mushrooms –
   capital thing! JINGLE   *Pickwick Papers, Ch. 2*

61 Kent, sir – everybody knows Kent – apples, cherries, hops and
   women. JINGLE   *Ib*

62 I wants to make your flesh creep. JOE, THE FAT BOY *Ib, Ch. 8*

63 'It's always best on these occasions to do what the mob do.'
'But suppose there are two mobs?' suggested Mr Snodgrass.
'Shout with the largest,' replied Mr Pickwick.
Pickwick Papers, Ch. 13

64 Can I unmoved see thee dying
On a log,
Expiring frog! MRS LEO HUNTER *Ib, Ch. 15*

65. 'Sir,' said Mr Tupman, 'you're a fellow.' 'Sir,' said Mr Pickwick,
'you're another!' *Ib*

66 Mr Weller's knowledge of London was extensive and peculiar.
Ib, Ch. 20

67 Take example by your father, my boy, and be very careful o'
vidders all your life, specially if they've kept a public house,
Sammy. MR WELLER *Ib*

68 Poverty and oysters always seem to go together. SAM WELLER
Ib, Ch. 22

69 Wery glad to see you indeed, and hope our acquaintance may
be a long 'un, as the gen'l'm'n said to the fi' pun' note.
SAM WELLER *Ib, Ch. 25*

70 Wen you're a married man, Samivel, you'll understand a good
many things as you don't understand now; but vether it's worth
goin' through so much, to learn so little, as the charity-boy said
ven he got to the end of the alphabet, is a matter o' taste.
MR WELLER *Ib, Ch. 27*

71 A double glass o' the inwariable. MR WELLER *Ib, Ch. 33*

72 Poetry's unnat'ral; no man ever talked poetry 'cept a beadle on
boxin' day. MR WELLER *Ib*

73 It's my opinion, sir, that this meeting is drunk. STIGGINS *Ib*

74 Chops and Tomata sauce. Yours, Pickwick. *Ib, Ch. 34*

75 Put it down a we, my lord, put it down a we! MR WELLER *Ib*

76 Oh Sammy, Sammy vy worn't there a alleybi! MR WELLER *Ib*

77 Anythin' for a quiet life, as the man said wen he took the sitivation at the lighthouse. SAM WELLER *Ib, Ch. 43*

78 A smattering of everything, and a knowledge of nothing.
Sketches by Boz, Tales, Ch. 3, Sentiment, Minerva House

79 It is a far, far, better thing that I do, than I have ever done; it
is a far, far, better rest that I go to, than I have ever known.
SIDNEY CARTON *A Tale of Two Cities, Ch. 15*

DICKINSON, Emily, 1830–1886

80 Success is counted sweetest
By those who ne'er succeed. *Poems, Part 1, Life*

81 How dreary to be somebody!
  How public, like a frog
  To tell your name the livelong day
  To an admiring bog!   *Poems, Part 1, Life*

82 Parting is all we know of heaven,
  And all we need of hell.   *Ib*

83 There's a certain slant of light,
  On winter afternoons,
  That oppresses, like the weight
  Of Cathedral tunes.   *Ib, Part 2, Nature*

84 Because I could not stop for Death,
  He kindly stopped for me;
  The carriage held but just ourselves
  And Immortality.   *Ib, Part 4, Time and Eternity*

85 If I shouldn't be alive
  When the robins come,
  Give the one in red cravat
  A memorial crumb.   *Ib*

DIOGENES, 412?–323? B.C.

86 Stand a little less between me and the sun.   *Plutarch, Life of*
                                            Alexander, 14

DIONYSIUS of Halicarnassus, 40?–8 B.C.

87 History is philosophy teaching by examples.   *Ars rhetorica, 11, 2*

DISRAELI, Benjamin, 1st Earl of Beaconsfield, 1804–1881

88 I will sit down now, but the time will come when you will hear
  me.   *Maiden Speech, House of Commons, 7 Dec. 1837*

89 The right honourable gentleman [*Sir Robert Peel*] caught the
  Whigs bathing, and walked away with their clothes.   *Speech,*
                          House of Commons, 28 Feb. 1845

90 A Conservative government is an organized hypocrisy.
                                    Ib, 17 March 1845

91 The question is this: Is man an ape or an angel? I, my lord, am
  on the side of the angels.   *Speech, 25 Nov. 1864*

92 An author who speaks about his own books is almost as bad as
  a mother who talks about her own children.   *Speech, Glasgow,*
                                         19 Nov. 1873

93 Lord Salisbury and myself have brought you back peace – but
  a peace I hope with honour.   *Speech, House of Commons,*
                                        16 July 1878

94 A sophistical rhetorician [*Gladstone*] inebriated with the exuberance of his own verbosity.   *Speech, 27 July, 1878*

95 Youth is a blunder; manhood a struggle; old age a regret.
SIDONIA   *Coningsby, Book 3, Ch. 1*

96 Every woman should marry – and no man.   HUGO BOHUN
Lothair, Ch. 30

97 To be conscious that you are ignorant is a great step to knowledge.   *Sybil, Book 1, Ch. 5*

98 I was told that the Privileged and the People formed Two Nations.   *Ib, Book 4, Ch. 8*

99 Variety is the mother of enjoyment.   *Vivian Grey, Book 5,
Ch. 4*

1 She is an excellent creature, but she never can remember which came first, the Greeks or the Romans.   [*Of his wife*]
Attributed

2 When I want to read a novel I write one.   *Attributed*

DODGSON, Charles Lutwidge, see CARROLL, Lewis

DONNE, John, 1573–1631

3 And new Philosophy calls all in doubt,
The Element of fire is quite put out;
The Sun is lost, and th' earth, and no man's wit
Can well direct him where to look for it.   *An Anatomy of the
World, 205*

4 Come live with me, and be my love,
And we will some new pleasures prove
Of golden sands, and crystal brooks,
With silken lines, and silver hooks.   *The Bait*

5 Reason is our Soul's left hand, Faith her right,
By these we reach divinity.   *To the Countess of Bedford, 1*

6 Love built on beauty, soon as beauty, dies.
Elegies, No. 2, The Anagram, 27

7 No Spring, nor Summer beauty hath such grace,
As I have seen in one Autumnal face.   *Ib, No. 9,
The Autumnal, 1*

8 Whoever loves, if he do not propose
The right true end of love, he's one that goes
To sea for nothing but to make him sick.
Ib, No. 18, Love's Progress, 1

9 Licence my roving hands, and let them go,
Before, behind, between, above, below.

O my America! my new-found-land,
My Kingdom, safeliest when with one man man'd.
Elegies, No. 19, Going To Bed, 25

10 Death be not proud, though some have called thee
Mighty and dreadful, for, thou art not so,
For, those, whom thou think'st, thou dost overthrow,
Die not, poor death. *Holy Sonnets, 10*

11 Go, and catch a falling star,
Get with child a mandrake root,
Tell me, where all past years are,
Or who cleft the Devil's foot. *Song, Go and Catch a Falling
Star*

12 But I do nothing upon myself, and yet I am mine own Executioner. *Devotions, 12*

13 No man is an Island, entire of itself; every man is a piece of the
Continent, a part of the main. *Ib, 17*

14 Any man's death diminishes me, because I am involved in
Mankind; And therefore never send to know for whom the bell
tolls; it tolls for thee. *Ib, 17*

DONNELLY, Ignatius, 1831–1901

15 The Democratic Party is like a mule – without pride of ancestry
or hope of posterity. *Speech, Minnesota Legislature*

DOUGLAS, William, 1672–1748

16 And for bonnie Annie Laurie
I'll lay me down and dee. *Annie Laurie*

DOWSON, Ernest Christopher, 1867–1900

17 I have been faithful to thee, Cynara! in my fashion.
Non Sum Qualis Eram

DOYLE, Sir Arthur Conan, 1859–1930

18 It has long been an axiom of mine that the little things are
infinitely the most important.
The Adventures of Sherlock Holmes, A Case of Identity

19 It is quite a three-pipe problem. *Ib, The Red-Headed League*

20 You know my methods, Watson.
The Memoirs of Sherlock Holmes, The Crooked Man

21 'Excellent!' [*Dr Watson*] cried. 'Elementary,' said he [*Holmes*].
Ib

22 He [*Professor Moriarty*] is the Napoleon of crime.
The Memoirs of Sherlock Holmes, The Final Problem

23 'Is there any point to which you would wish to draw my attention?'
'To the curious incident of the dog in the night-time.'
'The dog did nothing in the night-time.'
'That was the curious incident,' remarked Sherlock Holmes.
Ib, Silver Blaze

24 An experience of women which extends over many nations and three continents.   *The Sign of Four*

25 When you have eliminated the impossible, whatever remains, however improbable, must be the truth.   *Ib*

26 The Baker Street irregulars.   *Ib*

27 London, that great cesspool into which all the loungers of the Empire are irresistibly drained.   *A Study in Scarlet*

28 The vocabulary of 'Bradshaw' is nervous and terse, but limited.
Ib

DRAKE, Sir Francis, 1540?–1596

29 I have singed the Spanish king's beard. *After destroying on 19 April 1587, a vast amount of shipping in the Harbour of Cadiz*

30 There is plenty of time to win this game, and to thrash the Spaniards too. *20 July 1588, while playing bowls, when the Armada was sighted*

DRAYTON, Michael, 1563–1631

31 Fair stood the wind for France
When we our sails advance.   *Agincourt*

32 Ill news hath wings, and with the wind doth go,
Comfort's a cripple and comes ever slow.
The Barrons' Wars, 2

33 Neat Marlowe, bathed in the Thespian springs,
Had in him those brave translunary things
That the first poets had.   *Of Poets and Poesy*

34 Since there's no help, come let us kiss and part –
Nay, I have done, you get no more of me;
And I am glad, yea glad with all my heart
That thus so cleanly I myself can free.
Sonnets, 61, The Parting

DRUMMOND, Thomas, 1797–1840

35 Property has its duties as well as its rights.   *Letter to the Earl of*
                                      Donoughmore, 22 May 1838

DRYDEN, John, 1631–1700

36 In pious times, e'r Priest-craft did begin,
    Before Polygamy was made a Sin.   *Absalom and Achitophel,*
                                            Part, 1, 1

37 What e'r he did was done with so much ease,
    In him alone, 'twas Natural to please.   *Ib, 1, 27*

38 Of these the false Achitophel was first,
    A Name to all succeeding Ages curst.
    For close Designs and crooked Counsels fit,
    Sagacious, Bold, and Turbulent of wit.   *Ib, 1, 150*

39 A fiery Soul, which working out its way,
    Fretted the Pigmy Body to decay:
    And o'r informed the Tenement of Clay.
    A daring Pilot in extremity;
    Pleas'd with the Danger, when the Waves went high
    He sought the Storms; but, for a Calm unfit,
    Would Steer too nigh the Sands to boast his Wit.
    Great Wits are sure to Madness near alli'd
    And thin Partitions do their Bounds divide.   *Ib, 1, 156*

40 Bankrupt of Life, yet Prodigal of Ease.   *Ib, 1, 168*

41 For Politicians neither love nor hate.   *Ib, 1, 223*

42 But far more numerous was the Herd of such,
    Who think too little, and who talk too much.   *Ib, 1, 533*

43 A man so various, that he seem'd to be
    Not one, but all Mankind's Epitome.
    Stiff in Opinions, always in the wrong;
    Was Everything by starts, and Nothing long:
    But, in the course of one revolving Moon,
    Was Chymist, Fidler, States-man, and Buffoon.   *Ib, 1, 545*

44 So over Violent, or over Civil,
    That every Man, with him, was God or Devil.
    In squandring Wealth was his peculiar Art:
    Nothing went unrewarded, but Desert.   *Ib, 1, 557*

45 Did wisely from Expensive Sins refrain,
    And never broke the Sabbath, but for Gain.   *Ib, 1, 587*

46 During his Office, Treason was no Crime.
    The Sons of Belial had a Glorious Time:
    For Shimei, though not prodigal of pelf,
    Yet lov'd his wicked Neighbour as himself.   *Ib, 1, 597*

47 Nor is the Peoples Judgment always true:
The Most may err as grosly as the Few.   *Absalom and*
                                             Achitophel, Part 1, 781

48 Beware the Fury of a Patient Man.   *Ib, 1, 1005*

49 The Midwife laid her hand on his Thick Skull,
With this Prophetick blessing – Be thou Dull.   *Ib, Part 2, 476*

50 The lovely Thais by his side,
Sate like a blooming Eastern Bride.   *Alexander's Feast, 9*

51 None but the Brave deserves the Fair.   *Ib, 15*

52 Sound the Trumpets; beat the Drums.   *Ib, 50*

53 Bacchus Blessings are a Treasure;
Drinking is the Soldiers Pleasure;
Rich the Treasure;
Sweet the Pleasure;
Sweet is Pleasure after Pain.   *Ib, 56*

54 Let old Timotheus yield the Prize,
Or both divide the Crown:
He rais'd a Mortal to the Skies;
She drew an Angel down.   *Ib, 167*

55 Errors, like Straws, upon the surface flow;
He who would search for Pearls must dive below.
                                             All for Love, Prologue

56 Men are but children of a larger growth.   DOLABELLA
                                             Ib, Act 4, Scene 1

57 Her Poverty was glad; her Heart content,
Nor knew she what the Spleen or Vapors meant.
                                             The Cock and the Fox, 29

58 He [*Shakespeare*] was the man who of all modern, and perhaps
ancient poets, had the largest and most comprehensive soul.
                                             Essay of Dramatic Poesy

59 He was naturally learned; he needed not the spectacles of books
to read nature; he looked inwards, and found her there. *Ib*

60 Here lies my wife: here let her lie!
Now she's at rest, and so am I.   *Epitaph intended for*
                                             Dryden's Wife

61 For truth has such a face and such a meen
As to be lov'd needs only to be seen.   *The Hind and the*
                                             Panther, 1, 33

62 Of all the Tyrannies on humane kind
The worst is that which Persecutes the mind.
Let us but weigh at what offence we strike,
'Tis but because we cannot think alike.   *Ib, 1, 239*

63 And love's the noblest frailty of the mind. CORTEZ
The Indian Emperor, Act 2, Scene 2

64 For all the happiness mankind can gain
Is not in pleasure, but in rest from pain. CORTEZ
Ib, Act 4, Scene 1

65 All heiresses are beautiful. ALBANACT *King Arthur, Act 1,*
Scene 2

66 Three Poets, in three distant Ages born,
Greece, Italy, and England did adorn.
The first in Loftiness of Thought surpass'd,
The next in Majesty, in both the last:
The Force of Nature could no farther go;
To make a third she join'd the former two. *Lines under*
Portrait of Milton

67 Cousin Swift, you will never be a poet. *Quoted in Johnson's*
Lives of the Poets, Swift

68 All humane things are subject to decay,
And, when Fate summons, Monarchs must obey:
This Fleckno found, who, like Augustus, young
Was call'd to Empire and had govern'd long:
In Prose and Verse was own'd, without dispute
Through all the realms of Non-sense, absolute.
Mac Flecknoe, 1

69 Shadwell alone my perfect image bears,
Mature in dullness from his tender years;
Shadwell alone of all my Sons is he
Who stands confirm'd in full stupidity.
The rest to some faint meaning make pretence,
But Shadwell never deviates into sense. *Ib, 15*

70 For I am young, a Novice in the Trade,
The Fool of Love, unpractis'd to persuade.
Palamon and Arcite, 3, 325

71 Happy the Man, and happy he alone,
He who can call to-day his own:
He who, secure within, can say,
Tomorrow do thy worst, for I have liv'd today.
Translation of Horace, 3, 65

72 Arms, and the man I sing, who, forced by fate,
And haughty Juno's unrelenting hate. *Translation of Virgil*
Aeneid, 1, 1

DUFFIELD, George, 1818–1888
73 Stand up! Stand up for Jesus! *Hymn*

DUMAS, Alexandre, 1803–1870

74 *Tous pour un, un pour tous.* All for one, and one for all.
The Three Musketeers

DUNBAR, William, 1460?–1520?

75 London, thou art the flower of Cities all!   *In honour of the*
City of London

76 *Timor mortis conturbat me.*   *Lament for the Makaris*

DYER, Sir Edward, 1540–1607

77 My mind to me a kingdom is.   *Title of poem*

DYER, John, 18th century

78 And he that will this health deny,
Down among the dead men let him lie!   *Here's a Health to*
the King

EDISON, Thomas Alva, 1847–1931

79 Genius is one per cent inspiration and ninety-nine per cent
perspiration.   *Newspaper interview*

EDWARD III of England, 1312–1377

80 Let the boy win his spurs.   *Of the Black Prince at Crécy, 1345*

EDWARD VIII of Great Britain (Duke of Windsor) 1894–1972

81 I have found it impossible to carry the heavy burden of responsibility and to discharge my duties as King as I would wish to do
without the help and support of the woman I love.
Broadcast, 11 Dec. 1936

EDWARDS, Oliver, 1711–1791

82 I have tried too in my time to be a philosopher; but, I don't
know how, cheerfulness was always breaking in.
Boswell's Johnson, 17 April 1778

EINSTEIN, Albert, 1879–1955

83 I never think of the future. It comes soon enough.
Interview, 1930

ELIOT, George (Mary Ann Evans), 1819–1880

84 A prophetess? Yea, I say unto you, and more than a prophetess
– a uncommon pretty young woman.   *Adam Bede, Ch. 1*

85 It's but little good you'll do a-watering the last year's crop.
Adam Bede, Ch. 18

86 The happiest women, like the happiest nations, have no history.
The Mill on the Floss, Book 6, Ch. 3

87 Animals are such agreeable friends – they ask no questions, they
pass no criticisms. *Scenes of Clerical Life, Mr Gilfil's
Love Story, Ch. 7*

ELIOT, Thomas Stearns, 1888–1965

88 Because I do not hope to turn again
Because I do not hope
Because I do not hope to turn. *Ash-Wednesday*

89 The readers of the Boston Evening Transcript
Sway in the wind like a field of ripe corn. *The Boston
Evening Transcript*

90 Time present and time past
Are both perhaps present in time future,
And time future contained in time past. *Burnt Norton*

91   Human kind
Cannot bear very much reality. *Ib*

92 Here I am, an old man in a dry month,
Being read to by a boy, waiting for rain. *Gerontion*

93 Thoughts of a dry brain in a dry season. *Ib*

94 We are the hollow men
We are the stuffed men
Leaning together
Headpiece filled with straw. *The Hollow Men*

95 Between the idea
And the reality
Between the motion
And the act
Falls the Shadow. *Ib*

96 This is the way the world ends
Not with a bang but a whimper. *Ib*

97 Ash on an old man's sleeve
Is all the ash the burnt roses leave.
Dust in the air suspended
Marks the place where a story ended. *Little Gidding*

98 Let us go then, you and I,
When the evening is spread out against the sky
Like a patient etherized upon a table. *The Love Song of
J. Alfred Prufrock*

99 In the room the women come and go
    Talking of Michelangelo. *The Love Song of J. Alfred Prufrock*

1 The yellow fog that rubs its back upon the window panes. *Ib*

2 I have measured out my life with coffee spoons. *Ib*

3 I grow old ... I grow old ...
    I shall wear the bottoms of my trousers rolled. *Ib*

4 Shall I part my hair behind? Do I dare to eat a peach?
    I shall wear white flannel trousers, and walk upon the beach.
    I have heard the mermaids singing, each to each. *Ib*

5 I do not think that they will sing to me. *Ib*

6 Macavity, Macavity, there's no one like Macavity.
    Macavity: The Mystery Cat

7 The winter evening settles down
    With smell of steaks in passageways. *Preludes, 1*

8 And the wind shall say 'Here were decent godless people;
    Their only monument the asphalt road
    And a thousand lost golf balls.' *The Rock*

9 Birth, and copulation, and death.
    That's all the facts when you come to brass tacks.
    Sweeney Agonistes, Fragment of an Agon

10 April is the cruellest month, breeding
    Lilacs out of the dead land, mixing
    Memory and desire, stirring
    Dull roots with spring rain. *The Waste Land, The Burial
    of the Dead, 1*

11 I read, much of the night, and go south in the winter. *Ib, 18*

12 When lovely woman stoops to folly and
    Paces about her room again, alone,
    She smoothes her hair with automatic hand,
    And puts a record on the gramophone. *Ib, The Fire Sermon,
    253*

13 Webster was much possessed by death
    And saw the skull beneath the skin. *Whispers of Immortality*

14 You've missed the point completely, Julia:
    There were no tigers. That was the point. ALEX
    The Cocktail Party, Act 1, Scene 1

15 You shouldn't interrupt my interruptions:
    That's really worse than interrupting. JULIA *Ib, Act 3*

16 Yet we have gone on living,
    Living and partly living. CHORUS *Murder in the Cathedral,
    Act 1*

17 The last temptation is the greatest treason:
   To do the right deed for the wrong reason.   THOMAS   *Murder*
   in the Cathedral, Act 1

18 However certain our expectation
   The moment foreseeen may be unexpected
   When it arrives.   THOMAS   *Ib, Act 2*

ELIZABETH I of England, 1533–1603

19 I will make you shorter by a head.   *Chamberlin, Sayings of*
   Queen Elizabeth

20 I know I have the body of a weak and feeble woman, but I
   have the heart and stomach of a King, and of a King of England
   too.   *Speech at Tilbury on the Approach of the Spanish Armada*

21 Though God hath raised me high, yet this I count the glory of
   my crown: that I have reigned with your loves.
   The Golden Speech, 1601

22 All my possessions for a moment of time.   *Last words*

ELLERTON, John, 1826–1893

23 Now the labourer's task is o'er;
   Now the battle day is past;
   Now upon the farther shore
   Lands the voyager at last.   *Now the Labourer's Task*

24 The day thou gavest, Lord, is ended,
   The darkness falls at thy behest.   *The Day Thou Gavest*

ELLIOTT, Ebenezer, 1781–1849

25 What is a communist? One who has yearnings
   For equal division of unequal earnings.   *Epigram*

EMERSON, Ralph Waldo, 1803–1882

26 Art is a jealous mistress.   *Conduct of Life, Wealth*

27 The louder he talked of his honour, the faster we counted our
   spoons.   *Ib, Worship*

28 Nothing great was ever achieved without enthusiasm.
   Essays, Circles

29 A Friend may well be reckoned the masterpiece of Nature.
   Ib, Friendship

30 The only reward of virtue is virtue; the only way to have a friend
   is to be one.   *Ib*

31 There is properly no history; only biography.   *Ib, History*

32 All mankind love a lover.   *Ib, Love*

33 The reward of a thing well done is to have done it.
Essays, New England Reformers

34 Every man is wanted, and no man is wanted much.
Ib, Nominalist and Realist

35 In skating over thin ice, our safety is in our speed.
Ib, Prudence

36 Whoso would be a man must be a nonconformist.
Ib, Self-Reliance

37 To be great is to be misunderstood.   *Ib*

38 Nothing can bring you peace but yourself.   *Ib*

39 Next to the originator of a good sentence is the first quoter of it.
Letters and Social Arms, Quotation and Originality

40 By necessity, by proclivity, and by delight, we all quote.   *Ib*

41 Every hero becomes a bore at last.   *Representative Men,*
Uses of Great Men

42 Never read any book that is not a year old.
Society and Solitude, Books

43 Hitch your wagon to a star.   *Ib, Civilization*

44 Poverty consists in feeling poor.   *Ib, Domestic Life*

45 We boil at different degrees.   *Ib, Eloquence*

46 America is a country of young men.   *Ib, Old Age*

47 Can anybody remember when the times were not hard, and
money not scarce?   *Ib, Works and Days*

48 If a man write a better book, preach a better sermon, or make
a better mouse-trap than his neighbour, though he build his
house in the woods, the world will make a beaten path to his
door.   *Attributed*

EMPSON, William, 1906–

49 Seven Types of Ambiguity.   *Title of book*

ESTIENNE, Henri, 1531–1598

50 *Si jeunesse savait; si vieillesse pouvait.* If only youth knew, if
only age could.   *Les Prémices*

EUCLID, c. 300 B.C.

51 *Quod erat demonstrandum.* Which was to be proved.
Translated from the Greek

52 There is no royal road to geometry.   *Said to Ptolemy 1*

EUWER, Anthony Henderson, 1877–

53 As a beauty I'm not a great star,
  There are others more handsome by far;
    But my face – I don't mind it
    Because I'm behind it;
  It's the folks out in front that I jar.   *Limerick*

EVELYN, John, 1620–1706

54 I saw Hamlet Prince of Denmark played, but now the old plays
  begin to disgust this refined age.   *Diary, 26 Nov. 1661*

FARQUHAR, George, 1678–1707

55 There's no scandal like rags, nor any crime so shameful as
  poverty. ARCHER   *The Beaux' Strategem, Act 1, Scene 1*

56 How a little love and good company improves a woman.
  MRS SULLEN   *Ib, Act 4, Scene 1*

57 Spare all I have, and take my life. SCRUB   *Ib, Act 5, Scene 2*

FERDINAND I, Holy Roman Emperor, 1503–1568

58 *Fiat justitia, et pereat mundus.* Let justice be done, though the
  world perish.   *Attributed*

FIELDING, Henry, 1707–1754

59 When widows exclaim loudly against second marriage, I would
  always lay a wager that the man, if not the wedding-day, is
  absolutely fixed on.   *Amelia, Book 6, Ch. 10*

60 I am as sober as a Judge.   *Don Quixote in England, 3, 14*

61 Oh! the roast beef of England,
  And old England's roast beef.   *The Grub Street Opera, 3, 3*

62 Public schools are the nurseries of all vice and immorality.
              Joseph Andrews, Book 3, Ch. 5

63 Thwackum was for doing justice, and leaving mercy to heaven.
              Tom Jones, Book 3, Ch. 10

FISHER, John Arbuthnot, 1st Baron, 1841–1920

64 Sack the lot!   *Letter to the Times, 2 Sept. 1919*

FITZGERALD, Edward, 1809–1883

65 Awake! for Morning in the Bowl of Night
  Has flung the Stone that puts the Stars to Flight:
    And Lo! the Hunter of the East has caught
  The Sultan's Turret in a Noose of Light.
          Rubáiyát of Omar Khayyám (1st ed.) Verse 1

66 Come, fill the Cup, and in the Fire of Spring
    The Winter Garment of Repentance fling:
        The Bird of Time has but a little way
    To fly – and Lo! the Bird is on the Wing.   *Rubáiyát of Omar*
                                       Khayyám (1st ed.) Verse 7

67 Here with a Loaf of Bread beneath the Bough,
    A Flask of Wine, a Book of Verse – and Thou
        Beside me singing in the Wilderness –
    And Wilderness is Paradise enow.   *Ib, 11*

68 The Worldly Hope men set their Hearts upon
    Turns Ashes – or it prospers; and anon,
        Like snow upon the Desert's dusty Face
    Lighting a little Hour or two – is gone.   *Ib, 14*

69 Ah, my Belovèd, fill the Cup that clears
    TODAY of past Regrets and future Fears:
        Tomorrow! – Why, Tomorrow I may be
    Myself with Yesterday's Sev'n Thousand Years.   *Ib, 20*

70 Ah, make the most of what we yet may spend,
    Before we too into the Dust descend;
        Dust into Dust, and under Dust, to lie,
    Sans Wine, sans Song, sans Singer, and – sans End!   *Ib, 23*

71   One thing is certain, that Life flies;
        One thing is certain, and the Rest is Lies;
    The Flower that once has blown for ever dies.   *Ib, 26*

72 I came like Water, and like Wind I go.   *Ib, 28*

73 There was a Door to which I found no key:
    There was a Veil past which I could not see.   *Ib, 32*

74 Ah, fill the Cup: – what boots it to repeat
    How Time is slipping underneath our Feet:
        Unborn TOMORROW, and dead YESTERDAY,
    Why fret about them if TODAY be sweet!   *Ib, 37*

75   Better be merry with the fruitful Grape
    Than sadden after none, or bitter, Fruit.   *Ib, 39*

76 You know, my Friends, how long since in my House
    For a new Marriage I did make Carouse:
        Divorced old barren Reason from my Bed,
    And took the Daughter of the Vine to Spouse.   *Ib, 40*

77 The Grape that can with Logic absolute
    The Two-and-Seventy jarring Sects confute.   *Ib, 43*

78 'Tis all a Chequer-board of Nights and Days
    Where Destiny with Men for Pieces plays:
        Hither and thither moves, and mates, and slays,
    And one by one back in the Closet lays.   *Ib, 49*

79 The Moving Finger writes; and, having writ,
Moves on: nor all thy Piety nor Wit
    Shall lure it back to cancel half a Line,
Nor all thy Tears wash out a Word of it.   *Rubáiyát of Omar*
Khayyám (1st ed.) Verse 51

80 And that inverted Bowl we call The Sky,
Whereunder crawling coop't we live and die,
    Lift not thy hands to *It* for help – for It
Rolls impotently on as Thou or I.   *Ib, 52*

81 Who *is* the Potter, pray, and who the Pot?   *Ib, 60*

82 Indeed the Idols I have loved so long
Have done my Credit in Men's Eye much wrong:
    Have drown'd my Honour in a shallow Cup,
And sold my Reputation for a Song.   *Ib, 69*

83 And when Thyself with shining Foot shall pass
Among the Guests Star-scattered on the Grass,
    And in thy joyous Errand reach the Spot
Where I made one – turn down an empty Glass!   *Ib, 75*

FLECKER, James Elroy, 1884–1915

84 For lust of knowing what should not be known,
We take the Golden Road to Samarkand.   *Hassan, 5, 2*

85 I have seen old ships sail like swans asleep,
Beyond the village which men still call Tyre.   *The Old Ships*

FLETCHER, John, see BEAUMONT, Francis

FLORIO, John, 1553?–1625

86 England is the paradise of women, the purgatory of men, and
the hell of horses.   *Second Fruits*

FOCH, Ferdinand, Marshal, 1851–1929

87 *Mon centre cède, ma droite recule, situation excellente. J'attaque.*
My centre is giving way, my right is retreating. Situation excellent. I shall attack.
    Message to Joffre, Sept. 1914

FONTAINE, Jean de la, 1621–1695

88 *Elle alla crier famine*
Chez la fourmi sa voisine.
She went to cry famine at her neighbour's the ant's.
    Fables, 1, 1, La Cigale et la Fourmi

89 *Aide-toi, le ciel t'aidera.*
Help yourself and heaven will help you. *Ib, 6, 18, Le Chartier*
Embourbé

FOOTE, Samuel, 1720–1777

90 He is not only dull in himself, but the cause of dullness in others.
Remark quoted in Boswell's Life of Johnson

FORD, Henry, 1863–1947

91 History is bunk. *In court, during libel action against Chicago Tribune, 1919*

FORD, John, 1586–1639?

92 He hath shook hands with time. BASSANES *The Broken Heart, Act 5, Scene 2*

93 'Tis Pity She's a Whore. *Title of Play*

FORD, Lena Guilbert, ?–1916?

94 Keep the home fires burning, while your hearts are yearning,
  Though your lads are far away they dream of home;
There's a silver lining through the dark cloud shining,
  Turn the dark cloud inside out, till the boys come home.
Keep the Home Fires Burning

FORGY, Howell Maurice, 1908–

95 Praise the Lord and pass the ammunition. *Said at Pearl Harbour, 7 Dec. 1941*

FORSTER, Edward Morgan, 1879–1970

96 Only connect. *Howard's End Motto on title-page*

97 It will be generally admitted that Beethoven's Fifth Symphony is the most sublime noise that has ever penetrated into the ear of man. *Ib, Ch. 5*

98 Two Cheers for Democracy. *Title of Book*

FOSTER, Sir George Eulas, 1847–1931

99 In these somewhat troublesome days when the great Mother Empire stands splendidly isolated in Europe.
Speech, Canadian House of Commons, 16 Jan. 1896

FOSTER, Stephen Collins, 1826–1864

1 Gwine to run all night!
  Gwine to run all day!
  I bet my money on de bob-tail nag,
  Somebody bet on de bay. *Camptown Races*

2 I dream of Jeanie with the light brown hair.
Jeanie with the Light Brown Hair

3 Down in de cornfield
Hear dat mournful sound!
All de darkies am a weeping
Massa's in de cold, cold ground.   *Massa's in de Cold, Cold
Ground*

4   Weep no more, my lady,
Oh! weep no more today!
We will sing one song for the old Kentucky Home,
For the old Kentucky Home far away.
My Old Kentucky Home

5 'Way down upon de Swanee Ribber.   *Old Folks at Home*

6 All de world am sad and dreary,
Ev'ry-where I roam.
O darkies, how my heart grows weary,
Far from de old folks at home.   *Ib*

7 Gone are the days when my heart was young and gay,
Gone are my friends from the cotton fields away,
Gone from the earth to a better land I know.   *Poor old Joe*

8 I'm coming, I'm coming,
For my head is bending low,
I hear the gentle voices calling
'Poor old Joe.'   *Ib*

9 Dere's no more hard work for poor old Ned,
He's gone whar de good niggers go.   *Uncle Ned*

FRANKLIN, Benjamin, 1706–1790

10 Remember that time is money.   *Advice to a Young Tradesman*

11 No nation was ever ruined by trade.   *Essays, Thoughts on
Commercial Subjects*

12 Be in general virtuous, and you will be happy.
Ib, On Early Marriages

13 Here Skugg lies snug
As a bug in a rug.   *Letter to Miss G. Shipley, 26 Sept. 1772*

14 We must indeed all hang together, or most assuredly, we shall
all hang separately.   *Remark at signing of Declaration of
Independence, 4 July 1776*

15 There never was a good war or a bad peace.   *Letter to Josiah
Quincy, 11 Sept. 1783*

16 Our Constitution is in actual operation; everything appears to promise that it will last; but in this world nothing is certain but death and taxes. *Letter to Jean-Baptiste Leroy, 13 Nov. 1789*

17 Man is a tool-making animal. *Boswell's Life of Johnson, 1778*

FREDERICK THE GREAT of Prussia, 1712–1786

18 You rogues, do you want to live for ever? *When the Guards hesitated at Kolin, 1757*

19 My people and I have come to an agreement which satisfies us both. They are to say what they please, and I am to do what I please. *Attributed*

FROHMAN, Charles, 1860–1915

20 Why fear death? It is the most beautiful adventure in life. *Last words before going down in the Lusitania*

FROST, Robert, 1875–1963

21   Earth's the right place for love:
I don't know where it's likely to go better. *Birches*

22 Most of the change we think we see in life
Is due to truths being in and out of favour. *The Black Cottage*

23 And nothing to look backward to with pride,
And nothing to look forward to with hope. *The Death of the Hired Man*

24 Home is the place where, when you have to go there,
They have to take you in. *Ib*

25 Some say the world will end in fire,
Some say in ice,
From what I've tasted of desire
I hold with those who favour fire. *Fire and Ice*

26 My apple trees will never get across
And eat the cones under his pines, I tell him.
He only says, 'Good fences make good neighbours.' *Mending Wall*

27 Something there is that doesn't love a wall,
That wants it down. *Ib*

28 Happiness makes up in Height for what it Lacks in Length. *Title of poem*

29 Like a piece of ice on a hot stove, a poem must ride on its own melting. A poem may be worked over once it is in being but may not be worried into being. *Preface, Collected Poems*

FRY, Christopher, 1907–

30 Why so shy, my pretty Thomasina?
Thomasin, O Thomasin,
Once you were so promising. 1ST GUARD, singing.
The Dark is Light Enough, Act 2

31   I travel light; as light
That is, as a man can travel who will
Still carry his body around because
Of its sentimental value. THOMAS   *The Lady's Not for*
Burning, Act 1

32   What after all
Is a halo? It's only one more thing to keep clean. THOMAS
Ib

33   What is official
Is incontestable. It undercuts
The problematical world and sells us life
At a discount. HUMPHREY   *Ib*

34 Where in this small-talking world can I find
A longitude with no platitude? THOMAS   *Ib, Act 3*

35   The best
Thing we can do is to make wherever we're lost in
Look as much like home as we can. NICHOLAS   *Ib*

36 Try thinking of love, or something.
Amor vincit insomnia. PRIVATE PETER ABLE
A Sleep of Prisoners

FULLER, Thomas, 1608–1661

37 There is a great difference between painting a face and not washing it.   *Church History, Book 7*

38 A proverb is much matter decorated into few words.
The History of the Worthies of England, Ch. 2

39 He knows little who will tell his wife all he knows. *The Holy*
and the Profane State, The Good Husband

40 Learning hath gained most by those books by which the printers
have lost.   *Ib, Of Books*

FYLEMAN, Rose, 1877–1957

41 There are fairies at the bottom of our garden.   *Fairies*

GALBRAITH, John Kenneth, 1908–

42 The Affluent Society.   *Title of Book*

43 Wealth is not without its advantages and the case to the contrary, although it has often been made, has never proved widely persuasive.   *The Affluent Society, Ch. 1*

GALILEO, 1564–1643
44 *Eppur si muove.* But it does move.   *Attributed*

GARBO, Greta, 1905–
45 I want to be alone.   *Attributed*

GARDNER, Augustus P., 1865–1918
46 Wake up, America.   *Speech, 16 Oct. 1916*

GARRICK, David, 1717–1779
47 For physic and farces
   His equal there scarce is;
   His farces are physic,
   His physic a farce is.   *Epigram, Written soon after Dr Hill's farce called 'The Rout' was acted*
48 Come, cheer up, my lads, 'tis to glory we steer,
   To add something more to this wonderful year;
   To honour we call you, as free-men, not slaves,
   For who are so free as the sons of the waves?
       Heart of oak are our ships,
       Jolly tars are our men.
       We always are ready,
       Steady, boys, steady;
   We'll fight and we'll conquer again and again.   *Heart of Oak*
49 Here lies Nolly Goldsmith, for shortness called Noll,
   Who wrote like an angel, but talked like poor Poll.
                        Impromptu Epitaph on Goldsmith

GAVARNI, Paul, 1801–1866
50 *Les enfants terribles.* The embarrassing young.   *Title of series of prints*

GAY, John, 1685–1732
51 O ruddier than the cherry
   O sweeter than the berry.   *Acis and Galatea, 2*
52 Do you think your mother and I should have liv'd comfortably so long together, if ever we had been married? PEACHUM
                        The Beggar's Opera, Act 1, Scene 8

53 MACHEATH: If with me you'd fondly stray
   POLLY PEACHUM: Over the hills and far away.   *The Beggar's*
   Opera, Act 1, Scene 13

54 How happy could I be with either,
   Were t'other dear charmer away!   MACHEATH   *Ib, Act 2,*
   Scene 13

55 She who has never loved has never lived.   ASTARBE   *The*
   Captives, 2, 2

56 Whence is thy learning? Hath thy toil
   O'er books consumed the midnight oil?   *Fables, Introduction*

57 Where yet was ever found a mother,
   Who'd give her booby for another?   *Ib, Part 1, No. 3*

58 Those who in quarrels interpose,
   Must often wipe a bloody nose.   *Ib, No. 34*

59 'Tis a gross error held in schools,
   That fortune always favours fools.   *Ib, Part 2, No. 12*

60 Life is a jest; and all things show it.
   I thought so once; but now I know it.   *My Own Epitaph*

GEORGE II of Great Britain, 1683–1760

61 Oh! he is mad, is he? Then I wish he would *bite* some other of
   my generals.   *Of General Wolfe*

GEORGE V of Great Britain, 1865–1936

62 Wake up, England.   *Title of reprinted speech*
63 How is the Empire?   *Last Words*

GIBBON, Edward, 1737–1794

64 To the University of Oxford I acknowledge no obligation; and
   she will as willingly renounce me for a son, as I am willing to
   disclaim her for a mother. I spent fourteen months at Magdalen
   College; they proved the fourteen months the most idle and
   unprofitable of my whole life.   *Autobiography*

65 Crowds without company, and dissipation without pleasure.
   [*London*]   *Ib*

66 History, which is, indeed, little more than the register of the
   crimes, follies, and misfortunes of mankind.   *Decline and Fall*
   of the Roman Empire, Ch. 3

67 All that is human must retrograde if it does not advance.   *Ib,*
   Ch. 71

GIBBONS, Stella, 1902–

68 Something nasty in the woodshed.   *Cold Comfort Farm*

GILBERT, Sir William Schwenk, 1836–1911

69 In enterprise of martial kind,
   When there was any fighting,
He led his regiment from behind –
   He found it less exciting. DUKE OF PLAZA-TORO
                                    The Gondoliers, Act 1

70   That celebrated,
      Cultivated,
      Underrated,
         Nobleman,
The Duke of Plaza-Toro! DUKE OF PLAZA-TORO   *Ib*

71 I stole the Prince, and I brought him here,
   And left him gaily prattling
With a highly respectable gondolier. DON ALHAMBRA etc.   *Ib*

72 Of that there is no manner of doubt –
No probable, possible shadow of doubt –
   No possible doubt whatever. DON ALHAMBRA etc.   *Ib*

73 A taste for drink, combined with gout,
   Had doubled him up for ever. DON ALHAMBRA etc.   *Ib*

74 When a merry maiden marries,
Sorrow goes and pleasure tarries. TESSA   *Ib*

75 Rising early in the morning,
   We proceed to light the fire,
Then our Majesty adorning
   In its workaday attire,
      We embark without delay
      On the duties of the day. GIUSEPPE   *Ib. Act 2*

76   But the privilege and pleasure
      That we treasure beyond measure
Is to run on little errands for the Ministers of State. GIUSEPPE
                                                         Ib

77 Take a pair of sparkling eyes. MARCO   *Ib*

78 When every one is somebodee,
   Then no one's anybody! DON ALHAMBRA   *Ib*

79 Tripping hither, tripping thither,
   Nobody knows why or whither. CHORUS OF FAIRIES *Iolanthe,*
                                                     Act 1

80 Bow, bow, ye lower middle classes!
   Bow, bow, ye tradesmen, bow, ye masses! CHORUS OF PEERS
                                                 Ib, Act 1

81 The Law is the true embodiment
   Of everything that's excellent.

It has no kind of fault or flaw,
And I, my lords, embody the Law. LORD CHANCELLOR
Iolanthe, Act 1

82 A pleasant occupation for
A rather susceptible Chancellor! LORD CHANCELLOR   *Ib*

83 When I went to the Bar as a very young man,
(Said I to myself – said I). LORD CHANCELLOR   *Ib*

84 My learned profession I'll never disgrace
By taking a fee with a grin on my face,
When I haven't been there to attend to the case.
LORD CHANCELLOR *Ib*

85 When all night long a chap remains
On sentry-go, to chase monotony
He exercises of his brains,
That is, assuming that he's got any. PRIVATE WILLIS
Ib, Act 2

86 I am an intellectual chap,
And think of things that would astonish you. PRIVATE WILLIS
Ib

87 I often think it's comical
How Nature always does contrive
That every boy and every gal
That's born into the world alive
Is either a little Liberal
Or else a little Conservative! PRIVATE WILLIS   *Ib*

88 When in that House M.P.'s divide,
If they've a brain and cerebellum, too,
They've got to leave that brain outside,
And vote just as their leaders tell 'em to. PRIVATE WILLIS *Ib*

89 Yet Britain won her proudest bays
In good Queen Bess's glorious days! LORD MOUNTARARAT *Ib*

90 The House of Peers, throughout the war,
Did nothing in particular,
And did it very well. LORD MOUNTARARAT   *Ib*

91 When you're lying awake with a dismal headache, and repose is
taboo'd by anxiety,
I conceive you may use any language you choose to indulge in,
without impropriety. LORD CHANCELLOR   *Ib*

92 For you dream you are crossing the Channel, and tossing about
in a steamer from Harwich –
Which is something between a large bathing machine and a very
small second-class carriage. LORD CHANCELLOR   *Ib*

93 Pooh-Bah (Lord High Everything Else) *The Mikado, Dramatis
Personae*

94 If you want to know who we are,
   We are gentlemen of Japan.   CHORUS OF NOBLES
                       The Mikado, Act 1

95 A wandering minstrel I –
   A thing of shreds and patches,
   Of ballads, songs and snatches,
And dreamy lullaby!   NANKI-POO   *Ib*

96 But if patriotic sentiment is wanted,
   I've patriotic ballads cut and dried.   NANKI-POO   *Ib, Act 1*

97 I can trace my ancestry back to a protoplasmal primordial
atomic globule.   POOH-BAH   *Ib*

98 Taken from the county jail
   By a set of curious chances.   KO-KO   *Ib*

99 As some day it may happen that a victim must be found,
   I've got a little list – I've got a little list
Of society offenders who might well be underground,
   And who never would be missed – who never would be
   missed!
There's the pestilential nuisances who write for autographs –
All people who have flabby hands and irritating laughs.   KO-KO
                                 Ib

 1 The idiot who praises, with enthusiastic tone,
   All centuries but this, and every country but his own.   KO-KO
                                 Ib

 2 Three little maids from school are we,
   Pert as a school-girl well can be,
   Filled to the brim with girlish glee.   YUM-YUM, PEEP-BO AND
                               PITTI-SING *Ib*

 3 To sit in solemn silence in a dull, dark dock,
   In a pestilential prison, with a life-long lock,
   Awaiting the sensation of a short sharp shock,
   From a cheap and chippy chopper on a big black block!
          KO-KO, POOH-BAH AND PISH-TUSH *Ib*

 4 Brightly dawns our wedding day;
   Joyous hour, we give thee greeting!   YUM-YUM, PITTI-SING,
                 NANKI-POO AND PISH-TUSH *Ib, Act 2*

 5   Here's a how-de-do!
     If I marry you,
  When your time has come to perish,
  Then the maiden whom you cherish
     Must be slaughtered, too!
  Here's a how-de-do!   YUM-YUM
                                  Ib

6   My object all sublime
    I shall achieve in time –
    To let the punishment fit the crime –
        The punishment fit the crime. MIKADO *The Mikado, Act 2*

7   A source of innocent merriment! MIKADO   *Ib*

8   On a cloth untrue,
        With a twisted cue
    And elliptical billiard balls! MIKADO   *Ib*

9   I have a left shoulder-blade that is a miracle of loveliness.
    People come miles to see it. My right elbow has a fascination
    that few can resist. KATISHA   *Ib*

10 Something lingering, with boiling oil in it, I fancy. MIKADO *Ib*

11 The flowers that bloom in the spring, -
                    Tra la,
    Have nothing to do with the case.
    I've got to take under my wing,
                    Tra la,
    A most unattractive old thing,
                    Tra la,
    With a caricature of a face. KO-KO   *Ib, Act 2*

12 On a tree by a river a little tom-tit
        Sang 'Willow, titwillow, titwillow!' KO-KO   *Ib*

13 Twenty love-sick maidens we,
        Love-sick all against our will. CHORUS   *Patience, Act 1*

14 Now is not this ridiculous – and is not this preposterous?
    A thorough-paced absurdity – explain it if you can.
                                    CHORUS OF DRAGOONS *Ib*

15 If this young man expresses himself in terms too deep for *me*,
    Why, what a very singularly deep young man this deep young
    man must be! BUNTHORNE   *Ib*

16 An attachment *à la* Plato for a bashful young potato, or a not-
    too-French French bean! BUNTHORNE   *Ib*

17 Prithee, pretty maiden, will you marry me?
        (Hey, but I'm hopeful, willow willow waly!) GROSVENOR *Ib*

18 A greenery-yallery, Grosvenor Gallery,
        Foot-in-the-grave young man! BUNTHORNE   *Ib, Act 2*

19 We sail the ocean blue,
    And our saucy ship's a beauty. CHORUS   *HMS Pinafore,
                                                        Act 1*

20 For I'm called Little Buttercup – dear Little Buttercup,
        Though I could never tell why,

But still I'm called Buttercup – poor Little Buttercup,
Sweet Little Buttercup I! LITTLE BUTTERCUP
HMS Pinafore, Act 1

21 CAPTAIN CORCORAN: I am the Captain of the *Pinafore*;
ALL: And a right good captain, too! *Ib*

22 CAPTAIN: I'm never, never sick at sea!
ALL: What, never?
CAPTAIN: No, never!
ALL: What, *never*?
CAPTAIN: Hardly ever! *Ib*

23 Though 'Bother it' I may
Occasionally say,
I never use a big, big D. CAPTAIN CORCORAN *Ib*

24 Then give three cheers, and one cheer more,
For the well-bred Captain of the *Pinafore*! CREW *Ib*

25 And so do his sisters, and his cousins, and his aunts! CHORUS
Ib

26 When I was a lad I served a term
As office boy to an Attorney's firm.
I cleaned the windows and I swept the floor,
And I polished up the handle of the big front door.
I polished up that handle so carefullee
That now I am the Ruler of the Queen's Navee!
SIR JOSEPH PORTER *Ib*

27 I grew so rich that I was sent
By a pocket borough into Parliament.
I always voted at my party's call,
And I never thought of thinking for myself at all.
I thought so little, they rewarded me
By making me the Ruler of the Queen's Navee!
SIR JOSEPH PORTER *Ib*

28 Never mind the why and wherefore. CAPTAIN CORCORAN
Ib, Act 2

29 For he himself has said it,
And it's greatly to his credit,
That he is an Englishman! BOATSWAIN *Ib*

30 For he might have been a Roosian,
A French, or Turk, or Proosian,
Or perhaps Itali-an! BOATSWAIN *Ib*

31 I am the very model of a modern Major-General,
I've information vegetable, animal and mineral,
I know the kings of England, and I quote the fights historical,
From Marathon to Waterloo, in order categorical.
MAJOR-GENERAL STANLEY *The Pirates of Penzance, Act 1*

32 When the foeman bares his steel,
   Tarantara! tarantara!
 We uncomfortable feel. SERGEANT *Pirates of Penzance, Act 2*

33 When constabulary duty's to be done –
 A policeman's lot is not a happy one. SERGEANT *Ib*

34 When the enterprising burglar's not a-burgling –
 When the cut-throat isn't occupied in crime –
 He loves to hear the little brook a-gurgling –
 And listen to the merry village chime. SERGEANT *Ib*

35 Politics we bar,
  They are not our bent;
 On the whole we are
  Not intelligent. ARAC   *Princess Ida, Act 1*

36 We will hang you, never fear,
  Most politely, most politely! HILDEBRAND *Ib*

37 Man's a ribald – Man's a rake,
 Man is Nature's sole mistake! LADY PSYCHE *Ib, Act 2*

38 While Darwinian Man, though well-behaved,
 At best is only a monkey shaved! LADY PSYCHE *Ib*

39 Hunger, I beg to state,
 Is highly indelicate. LADY BLANCHE *Ib*

40 Oh, don't the days seem lank and long
 When all goes right and nothing goes wrong,
 And isn't your life extremely flat
 With nothing whatever to grumble at! GAMA *Ib, Act 3*

41 Some word that teems with hidden meaning—like 'Basingstoke'.
    MAD MARGARET *Ruddigore, Act 2*

42 She may very well pass for forty-three
 In the dusk, with a light behind her! JUDGE *Trial by Jury*

43 The screw may twist and the rack may turn,
 And men may bleed and men may burn. DAME CARRUTHERS
    The Yeomen of the Guard, Act 1

44 Is life a boon?
   If so, it must befall
   That Death, whene'er he call,
 Must call too soon. FAIRFAX   *Ib*

45 POINT: I have a song to sing, O!
 ELSIE: Sing me your song, O!
 POINT: It is sung to the moon
   By a love-lorn loon.   *Ib, Act 1*

46 It's a song of a merryman, moping mum,
 Whose soul was sad, and whose glance was glum,

Who sipped no sup, and who craved no crumb,
As he sighed for the love of a ladye. POINT   *The Yeomen of*
                                                the Guard, Act 1

47 For he who'd make his fellow-creatures wise
     Should always gild the philosophic pill! POINT   *Ib*

48   Were I thy bride,
   Then all the world beside
       Were not too wide
           To hold my wealth of love—
           Were I thy bride! PHOEBE   *Ib*

49 Oh! a private buffoon is a light-hearted loon,
     If you listen to popular rumour. POINT   *Ib, Act 2*

50 It is purely a matter of skill,
   Which all may attain if they will:
       But every Jack,
       He must study the knack
   If he wants to make sure of his Jill!

                    ELSIE, PHOEBE AND FAIRFAX   *Ib*

GLADSTONE, William Ewart, 1809–1898

51 You cannot fight against the future. Time is on our side.
                            Speech on Reform Bill, 1866

52 [*The Turks*] one and all, bag and baggage, shall, I hope, clear
   out from the province they have desolated and profaned.
                    Speech, House of Commons, 7 May 1877

53 All the world over, I will back the masses against the classes.
                            Speech, Liverpool, 28 June 1886

54 We are part of the community of Europe, and we must do our
   duty as such.   *Speech, Caernarvon, 10 April 1888*

GLASSE, Hannah, 18th century

55 Take your hare when it is cased. *Art of Cookery (Often mis-*
              quoted as 'First catch your hare' and wrongly attributed to
                                                Mrs Beeton)

GLOUCESTER, William Henry, Duke of, 1743–1805

56 Another damned, thick, square book! Always scribble, scribble,
   scribble! Eh! Mr Gibbon?   *Attributed*

GLOVER-KIND, John A., ?–1918

57 I do Like to be Beside the Seaside.   *Title of Song*

GOERING, Hermann, 1893–1946

58 Guns will make us powerful; butter will only make us fat.
                                        Broadcast, 1936

GOETHE, Johann Wolfgang von, 1749–1832

59 *Ein unnütz Leben ist ein früher Tod.* A useless life is an early
 death. *Iphigenie, 1, 2*

60 *Mehr Licht!* More light! *Last words, attributed*

GOLDSMITH, Oliver, 1728?–1774

61 Sweet Auburn! loveliest village of the plain.
 The Deserted Village, 1

62 Ill fares the land, to hastening ills a prey
 Where wealth accumulates, and men decay. *Ib, 51*

63 A time there was, ere England's griefs began
 When every rood of ground maintained its man. *Ib, 57*

64 How happy he who crowns in shades like these,
 A youth of labour with an age of ease. *Ib, 99*

65 The watchdog's voice that bayed the whispering wind,
 And the loud laugh that spoke the vacant mind. *Ib, 121*

66 A man he was to all the country dear,
 And passing rich with forty pounds a year. *Ib, 141*

67 Truth from his lips prevailed with double sway,
 And fools, who came to scoff, remained to pray. *Ib, 179*

68 The village master taught his little school;
 A man severe he was, and stern to view;
 I knew him well, and every truant knew;
 Well had the boding tremblers learned to trace
 The day's disasters in his morning face. *Ib, 196*

69 And still they gazed, and still the wonder grew,
 That one small head could carry all he knew. *Ib, 215*

70 The chest contrived a double debt to pay,
 A bed by night, a chest of drawers by day. *Ib, 229*

71 In all the silent manliness of grief. *Ib, 384*

72 Man wants but little here below,
 Nor wants that little long. *Edwin and Angelina, 31*

73 The King himself has followed her, –
 When she has walked before. *Elegy on Mrs Mary Blaize, 19*

74 The doctors found, when she was dead, –
 Her last disorder mortal. *Ib, 23*

75 Good people all, of every sort,
 Give ear unto my song;
 And if you find it wond'rous short,
 It cannot hold you long.
 Elegy on the Death of a Mad Dog, 1

76 The dog, to gain some private ends,
    Went mad and bit the man.   *Elegy on the Death*
                                              of a Mad Dog, 19

77 The man recovered of the bite,
    The dog it was that died.   *Ib, 31*

78 Here lies our good Edmund, whose genius was such,
    We scarcely can praise it, or blame it too much;
    Who, born for the Universe, narrowed his mind,
    And to party gave up what was meant for mankind.
                        [*Edmund Burke*] *Retaliation, 29*

79 Too nice for a statesman, too proud for a wit:
    For a patriot, too cool; for a drudge, disobedient;
    And too fond of the *right* to pursue the *expedient*.
                              [*Edmund Burke*] *Ib, 38*

80 Here lies David Garrick, describe me, who can,
    An abridgement of all that was pleasant in man.   *Ib, 93*

81 As a wit, if not first, in the very first line.   [*Garrick*] *Ib, 96*

82 On the stage he was natural, simple, affecting;
    'Twas only that when he was off he was acting.
                                       [*Garrick*] *Ib, 101*

83 I love everything that's old: old friends, old times, old manners,
    old books, old wine.   HARDCASTLE   *She Stoops to Conquer,*
                                              Act 1, Scene 2

84 It's a damned long, dark, boggy, dirty, dangerous way.
                        TONY LUMPKIN   *Ib, Act 1, Scene 2*

85 This is Liberty Hall, gentlemen.   HARDCASTLE   *Ib, Act 2*

86 We are the boys
    That fear no noise
    Where the thundering cannons roar.   TONY LUMPKIN   *Ib*

87 Ask me no questions, and I'll tell you no fibs.   TONY LUMPKIN
                                                       Ib, Act 3

88 Women and music should never be dated.   MISS HARDCASTLE
                                                              Ib

89 Remote, unfriended, melancholy, slow.   *The Traveller, 1*

90 Where'er I roam, whatever realms to see,
    My heart untravelled fondly turns to thee.   *Ib, 7*

91 Such is the patriot's boast, where'er we roam,
    His first, best country ever is, at home.   *Ib, 73*

92 Where wealth and freedom reign, contentment fails,
    And honour sinks where commerce long prevails.   *Ib, 91*

93 Laws grind the poor, and rich men rule the law.   *Ib, 386*

94 Still to ourselves in every place consigned,
Our own felicity we make or find.   *The Traveller, 431*

95 A book may be amusing with numerous errors, or it may be
very dull without a single absurdity.
The Vicar of Wakefield, Preface

96 I was ever of opinion that the honest man who married and
brought up a large family, did more service than he who continued single and only talked of population.   *Ib, Ch. 1*

97 I . . . chose my wife, as she did her wedding gown, not for a
fine glossy surface, but such qualities as would wear well.
Ib, Ch. 1

98 Let us draw upon content for the deficiencies of fortune.
Ib, Ch. 3

99 I find you want me to furnish you with argument and intellects,
too.   *Ib, Ch. 7*

1 They would talk of nothing but high life, and high-lived company, with other fashionable topics, such as pictures, taste,
Shakespeare, and the musical glasses.   *Ib, Ch. 9*

2 When lovely woman stoops to folly,
  And finds too late that men betray,
What charm can soothe her melancholy,
  What art can wash her guilt away?   *Ib, Song, Ch. 9*

3 There is no arguing with Johnson: for if his pistol misses fire,
he knocks you down with the butt end of it.
1769, Boswell's Life of Johnson

4 [*To Dr Johnson*] If you were to make little fishes talk, they would
talk like whales.   *1773, Ib*

GOLDWYN, Samuel, 1882–1974

5 In two words: im - possible.   *Quoted in Alva Johnson,*
The Great Goldwyn

6 Include me out.   *Attributed*

GORDON, Adam Lindsay, 1833–1870

7 Life is mostly froth and bubble,
  Two things stand like stone,
Kindness in another's trouble,
  Courage in your own.   *Ye Wearie Wayfarer*

GOSCHEN, George Joachim, 1st Viscount, 1831–1907

8 We have stood alone in what is called isolation – our splendid

isolation, as one of our Colonial friends was good enough to
call it.   *Speech, Lewes, 26 Feb. 1896*
                                              (see Sir George Foster)

GRAHAM, Harry, 1874–1936

9 'There's been an accident,' they said,
  'Your servant's cut in half; he's dead!'
  ' Indeed!' said Mr Jones, 'and please,
  Send me the half that's got my keys.'
                                          Ruthless Rhymes, Mr Jones

10 I had written to Aunt Maud,
  Who was on a trip abroad,
  When I heard she'd died of cramp
  Just too late to save the stamp.   *Ib, Waste*

11 Billy, in one of his nice new sashes,
  Fell in the fire and was burned to ashes;
  Now, although the room grows chilly,
  I haven't the heart to poke poor Billy.   *Ib, Billy*

12 Weep not for little Leonie,
  Abducted by a French *Marquis*!
  Though loss of honour was a wrench,
  Just think how it's improved her French.   *Compensation*

GRAHAME, Kenneth, 1859–1932

13 There is nothing – absolutely nothing – half so much worth
doing as simply messing about in boats.   WATER RAT
                                    The Wind in the Willows, Ch. 1

14 The clever men at Oxford
    Know all that there is to be knowed.
  But they none of them know one half as much
    As intelligent Mr Toad.   TOAD   *Ib, Ch. 10*

GRANT, Ulysses Simpson, 1822–1885

15 No terms except an unconditional and immediate surrender can
be accepted.   *To General Buckner, 16 Feb. 1862*

16 I know no method to secure the repeal of bad or obnoxious laws
so effective as their stringent execution.
                                    Inaugural Address, 4 March 1869

GRANVILLE, George, 1st Baron Lansdowne, 1667–1735

17 Of all the plagues with which the world is curst,
  Of every ill, a woman is the worst.   AMADIS
                                    The British Enchanters, Act 2

GRAVES, Alfred Perceval, 1846–1931

18 Of priests we can offer a charmin' variety,
   Far renowned for larnin' and piety.   *Father O'Flynn*

19 Checkin' the crazy ones, coaxin' unaisy ones,
   Liftin' the lazy ones on wid the stick.   *Ib*

GRAVES, John Woodcock, 1795–1886

20 D'ye ken John Peel with his coat so gay,
   D'ye ken John Peel at the break of the day
   D'ye ken John Peel when he's far, far away
   With his hounds and his horn in the morning?

   For the sound of his horn brought me from my bed,
   And the cry of his hounds which he oft-times led;
   Peel's view halloo would a-waken the dead,
   Or a fox from his lair in the morning.   *John Peel*

GRAVES, Robert, 1895–

21 Goodbye to All That.   *Title of Book*

22 As you are woman, so be lovely:
   As you are lovely, so be various,
   Merciful as constant, constant as various,
   So be mine, as I yours for ever.   *Pygmalion to Galatea*

GRAY, Thomas, 1716–1771

23 'Twas on a lofty vase's side,
   Where China's gayest art had dy'd
     The azure flowers, that blow.
         Ode on the Death of a Favourite Cat, 1

24 What female heart can gold despise?
   What Cat's averse to fish?   *Ib, 23*

25 A Fav'rite has no friend!   *Ib, 36*

26 Not all that tempts your wand'ring eyes
   And heedless hearts, is lawful prize;
     Nor all, that glisters, gold.   *Ib, 40*

27 Where once my careless childhood stray'd,
   A stranger yet to pain!   *Ode on a Distant Prospect of*
                                   Eton College, 13

28 They hear a voice in every wind,
   And snatch a fearful joy.   *Ib, 39*

29   Where ignorance is bliss,
   'Tis folly to be wise.   *Ib, 99*

30 The Curfew tolls the knell of parting day,
    The lowing herd winds slowly o'er the lea,
    The plowman homeward plods his weary way,
    And leaves the world to darkness and to me.
                    Elegy written in a Country Church-Yard, 1

31 Now fades the glimmering landscape on the sight,
    And all the air a solemn stillness holds,
    Save where the beetle wheels his droning flight,
    And drowsy tinklings lull the distant folds.   *Ib. 5*

32 Save that from yonder ivy-mantled tow'r
    The moping owl does to the moon complain.   *Ib, 9*

33 The rude Forefathers of the hamlet sleep.   *Ib, 16*

34 Let not Ambition mock their useful toil,
    Their homely joys, and destiny obscure;
    Nor Grandeur hear with a disdainful smile,
    The short and simple annals of the poor.   *Ib, 29*

35 The boast of heraldry, the pomp of pow'r.   *Ib, 33*

36 The paths of glory lead but to the grave.   *Ib, 36*

37 Full many a gem of purest ray serene,
    The dark unfathom'd caves of ocean bear:
    Full many a flower is born to blush unseen,
    And waste its sweetness on the desert air.   *Ib, 53*

38 Some village-Hampden, that with dauntless breast
    The little Tyrant of his fields withstood;
    Some mute inglorious Milton here may rest,
    Some Cromwell guiltless of his country's blood.   *Ib 57*

39 Far from the madding crowd's ignoble strife.   *Ib, 73*

40 Here rests his head upon the lap of Earth
    A Youth to Fortune and to Fame unknown.
    Fair Science frown'd not on his humble birth,
    And Melancholy mark'd him for her own.
                              Ib, The Epitaph, 117

41 Large was his bounty, and his soul sincere,
    Heav'n did a recompense as largely send:
    He gave to Mis'ry all he had, a tear,
    He gain'd from Heav'n ('twas all he wish'd) a friend. *Ib, 121*

42 No farther seek his merits to disclose,
    Or draw his frailties from their dread abode,
    (There they alike in trembling hope repose,)
    The bosom of his Father and his God.   *Ib, 125*

43 Daughter of Jove, relentless Power,
    Thou Tamer of the human breast,

Whose iron scourge and tort'ring hour,
The Bad affright, afflict the Best! *Hymn to Adversity, 1*

44 Far from the sun and summer-gale,
In thy green lap was Nature's Darling laid. [*Shakespeare*]
The Progress of Poesy, 83

45 Yet shall he mount, and keep his distant way
Beyond the limits of a vulgar fate,
Beneath the Good how far – but far above the Great.
[*Milton*] *Ib, 121*

46 Too poor for a bribe, and too proud to importune,
He had not the method of making a fortune.
Sketch of his own Character

GREELEY, Horace, 1811–1872

47 Go West, young man, and grow up with the country.
Hints toward Reform

GREENE, Robert, 1560?–1592

48 Weep not, my wanton, smile upon my knee;
When thou art old there's grief enough for thee.
Sephestia's Song

49 For there is an upstart crow, beautified with our feathers, that
with his tiger's heart wrapped in a player's hide, supposes he is
as well able to bumbast out a blank verse as the best of you;
and being an absolute *Iohannes fac totum* is in his own conceit
the only shake-scene in a country. [*Reference probably to
Shakespeare*] *A Groatsworth of Wit*

GREGORY 1, Pope, 540–604

50 *Non Angli, sed Angeli.* Not Angles, but angels. *Attributed*
(*on seeing a group of English captives on sale at Rome*)

GREY OF FALLODON, Edward, 1st Viscount, 1862–1933

51 The lamps are going out all over Europe; we shall not see them
lit again in our lifetime. *On the eve of war, 3 Aug. 1914*

GROSSMITH, George, 1847–1912, and GROSSMITH, Walter Weedon, 1854–1919

52 What's the good of a home, if you are never in it?
The Diary of a Nobody, Ch. 1

GUINAN, Texas, 1884–1933

53 Fifty million Frenchmen can't be wrong. *Attributed*

GULBENKIAN, Nubar Sarkis, 1896–1972

54 The best number for a dinner party is two – myself and a dam' good head waiter. *Interviewed in Daily Telegraph, 14 Jan. 1965*

HALE, Sarah Josepha, 1788–1879

55 Mary had a little lamb,
Its fleece was white as snow;
And everywhere that Mary went
The lamb was sure to go. *Mary's Little Lamb*

HALIFAX, George Savile, 1st Marquis of, 1633–1695

56 Men are not hanged for stealing horses, but that horses may not be stolen. *Political Thoughts and Reflections of Punishment*

HALL, Charles Sprague, 19th century

57 John Brown's body lies a mould'ring in the grave,
His soul is marching on! *John Brown's Body*

HAMMERSTEIN, Oscar, 1895–1960

58 The last time I saw Paris, her heart was young and gay,
I heard the laughter of her heart in every street café. *The Last Time I saw Paris*

59 Ol' man river, dat ol' man river,
He must know sumpin', but don't say nothin',
He just keeps rollin', he keeps on rollin' along. *Ol' Man River*

HANDLEY, Thomas Reginald (Tommy), see KAVANAGH, Ted

HANFF, Minny Maud, c. 1900

60 Since then they called him Sunny Jim. *Advertisement for Force, a breakfast food*

HANKEY, Katherine, 1834–1911

61 Tell me the old, old story,
Of unseen things above. *Hymn*

HARCOURT, Sir William, 1827–1904

62 We are all Socialists now. *Speech*

HARDY, E. J., 1849–1910

63 How to be Happy though Married. *Title of book, 1910*

HARDY, Thomas, 1840–1928

64 My argument is that War makes rattling good history; but Peace
is poor reading. *The Dynasts, Part 1*

65 A lover without indiscretion is no lover at all.
The Hand of Ethelberta, Ch. 20

66 Good, but not religious-good. *Under the Greenwood Tree,
Ch. 2*

67 This is the weather the cuckoo likes,
And so do I. *Weathers*

HARE, Maurice Evan, 1886–

68 There once was a man who said, 'Damn!
It is borne in upon me I am
An engine that moves
In determinate grooves,
I'm not even a bus but a tram.' *Limerick*

HARGREAVES, William, 1846–1919

69 I'm Burlington Bertie:
I rise at ten-thirty. *Burlington Bertie*

HARINGTON, Sir John, 1561–1612

70 Treason doth never prosper: what's the reason?
For if it prosper, none dare call it treason.
Epigrams, Of Treason

HARRIS, Charles K., 1865–1930

71 Many a heart is aching, if you could read them all,
Many the hopes that have vanished, after the ball.
After the Ball

HARTE, Francis Bret, 1836–1902

72 And on that grave where English oak and holly
And laurel wreaths entwine
Deem it not all a too presumptuous folly, –
This spray of Western pine! *Dickens in Camp*

73 He smiled a kind of sickly smile, and curled up on the floor,
And the subsequent proceedings interested him no more.
The Society upon the Stanislaus

HAWKER, Robert Stephen, 1803–1875

74 And have they fixed the where and when?
And shall Trelawny die?

Here's twenty thousand Cornish men
   Will know the reason why!   *Song of the Western Men*

HAY, Ian (John Hay Beith), 1876–1952

75 Funny peculiar, or funny ha-ha?   "BUTTON' FARINGDON
                              Housemaster, Act 3

HAYES, J. Milton, 1884–1940

76 There's a one-eyed yellow idol to the north of Khatmandu,
   There's a little marble cross below the town,
   There's a broken-hearted woman tends the grave of Mad Carew,
   And the Yellow God forever gazes down.
                 The Green Eye of the Yellow God

HAZLITT, William, 1778–1830

77 His sayings are generally like women's letters; all the pith is in
   the postscript. [*Charles Lamb*]
         Conversations of Northcote, Boswell Redivivus

78 He [*Coleridge*] talked on for ever; and you wished him to talk
   on for ever.   *Lectures on the English Poets, 8*

79 The English (it must be owned) are rather a foul-mouthed
   nation.   *On Criticism*

80 No young man believes he shall ever die.
        On the Feeling of Immortality in Youth, 1

81 One of the pleasantest things in the world is going a journey;
   but I like to go by myself.   *On Going a Journey*

82 There is not a more mean, stupid, dastardly, pitiful, selfish,
   spiteful, envious, ungrateful animal than the public. It is the
   greatest of cowards, for it is afraid of itself.
                      On Living to Oneself

83 The art of pleasing consists in being pleased.   *On Manner*

84 A nickname is the heaviest stone that the devil can throw at a
   man.   *On Nicknames*

85 We never do anything well till we cease to think about the
   manner of doing it.   *On Prejudice*

HEBER, Bishop Reginald, 1783–1826

86 From Greenland's icy mountains,
    From India's coral strand,
  Where Afric's sunny fountains,
    Roll down their golden sand.
            From Greenland's Icy Mountains

87 Though every prospect pleases,
   And only man is vile.   *From Greenland's Icy Mountains*

88 Holy, Holy, Holy! all the Saints adore Thee.   *Holy, Holy, Holy!*

HEMANS, Felicia Dorothea, 1793–1835

89 The boy stood on the burning deck,
   Whence all but he had fled.   *Casabianca*

90 The stately homes of England!
   How beautiful they stand,
   Amidst their tall ancestral trees,
   O'er all the pleasant land.   *The Homes of England*

HEMINGWAY, Ernest, 1898–1961

91 A Farewell to Arms   *Title of novel*

92 Bullfighting is the only art in which the artist is in danger of
   death and in which the degree of brilliance in the performance
   is left to the fighter's honour.   *Death in the Afternoon, Ch. 9*

HENLEY, William Ernest, 1849–1903

93 Out of the night that covers me,
   Black as the pit from pole to pole,
   I thank whatever gods may be
   For my unconquerable soul.   *Invictus*

94 Under the bludgeonings of chance
   My head is bloody, but unbowed.   *Ib*

95 I am the master of my fate:
   I am the captain of my soul.   *Ib*

96 What have I done for you,
      England, my England?
   What is there I would not do,
      England, my own?
            Rhymes and Rhythms, 25, For England's Sake

HENRI IV of France, 1553–1610

97 *Paris vaut bien une messe*. Paris is well worth a mass.
                              Attributed

98 The wisest fool in Christendom. [*James 1*]   *Attributed*

HENRY II of England, 1133–1189

99 Will no one free me of this turbulent priest? [*Becket*]
                              Attributed

HENRY, Matthew, 1662–1714

1 They that die by famine die by inches.
Commentaries, Psalms, 59, 15

2 All this and heaven too.   *Life of Philip Henry*

HENRY, O. (William Sydney Porter), 1862–1910

3 Life is made up of sobs, sniffles, and smiles, with sniffles predominating.   *Gift of the Magi*

4 If men knew how women pass the time when they are alone,
they'd never marry.   *Memoirs of a Yellow Dog*

5 Turn up the lights; I don't want to go home in the dark.
Last words

HENRY, Patrick, 1736–1799

6 I know not what course others may take; but as for me, give
me liberty or give me death.
Speech in the Virginia Convention, 23 March 1775

HERBERT, Sir Alan Patrick, 1890–1971

7 Not huffy or stuffy, nor tiny or tall,
But fluffy, just fluffy, with no brains at all.   *I Like them Fluffy*

8 This high official, all allow,
Is grossly overpaid,
There wasn't any board; and now
There isn't any trade.   *On the President of the Board of Trade*

9 The Englishman never enjoys himself except for a noble purpose.
Uncommon Law

10 Holy Deadlock.   *Title of novel*

HERBERT, George, 1593–1633

11 Dare to be true: nothing can need a lie;
A fault, which needs it most, grows two thereby.
The Temple, The Church Porch

12 Love bade me welcome; yet my soul drew back,
Guilty of dust and sin.   *Ib, Love*

13 'You must sit down,' says Love, 'and taste My meat,'
So I did sit and eat.   *Ib*

14 Sweet day, so cool, so calm, so bright,
The bridal of the earth and sky.   *Ib, Virtue*

HERRICK, Robert, 1591–1674

15 Cherry ripe, ripe, ripe, I cry,
   Full and fair ones; come and buy:
   If so be, you ask me where
   They do grow? I answer, there
   Where my Julia's lips do smile;
   There's the land, or cherry-isle.   *Hesperides, Cherry Ripe*

16 A sweet disorder in the dress
   Kindles in clothes a wantonness.   *Ib, Delight in Disorder, 2*

17 A careless shoe-string, in whose tie
   I see a wild civility:
   Do more bewitch me, than when art
   Is too precise in every part.   *Ib*

18 Fair daffodils, we weep to see
     You haste away so soon:
   As yet the early-rising sun
     Has not attain'd his noon.   *Ib, To Daffodils*

19 I dare not ask a kiss;
     I dare not beg a smile;
   Lest having that, or this,
     I might grow proud the while.   *Ib, To Electra*

20 You say, to me-wards your affection's strong;
   Pray love me little so you love me long.
           Ib, Love me little, love me long

21 Night makes no difference 'twixt the Priest and Clerk;
   Joan as my Lady is as good i' th' dark.
           Ib, No difference i' th' dark

22 Attempt the end, and never stand to doubt;
   Nothing's so hard, but search will find it out. *Ib, Seek and find*

23 Whenas in silks my Julia goes,
   Then, then (methinks) how sweetly flows
   That liquefaction of her clothes.   *Ib, Upon Julia's Clothes*

24 Gather ye rosebuds while ye may,
     Old time is still a-flying:
   And this same flower that smiles today
     Tomorrow will be dying.
           Ib, To the Virgins, to make much of Time

25 Then be not coy, but use your time;
     And while ye may, go marry:
   For having lost but once your prime,
     You may for ever tarry.   *Ib*

HEYWOOD, Thomas, 1574?–1641

26 Seven cities warred for Homer, being dead,
Who, living, had no roof to shroud his head.
Hierarchy of the Blessed Angels

27 A Woman Killed with Kindness.   *Title of play*

HICKSON, William Edward, 1803–1870

28 If at first you don't succeed,
Try, try again.   *Try and Try Again*

HILL, Rowland, 1744–1833

29 He did not see any good reasons why the devil should have all
the good tunes.   *E. W. Broome, Rev. Rowland Hill*

HIPPOCRATES, 460?–377? B.C.

30 *Ars longa, vita brevis.* Art is long, but life is short.
The Latin version of the Greek original

HITLER, Adolf, 1889–1945

31 The Sudetenland is the last territorial claim I have to make in
Europe.   *Speech, 26 Sept. 1938*

32 Germany will be either a world power or will not be at all.
Mein Kampf

HOBBES, Thomas, 1588–1679

33 The condition of man . . . is a condition of war of everyone
against everyone.   *Leviathan, Part 1, Ch. 4*

34 No arts; no letters; no society; and which is worst of all, continual fear and danger of violent death; and the life of man,
solitary, poor, nasty, brutish, and short.   *Ib, Ch. 13*

35 I am about to take my last voyage, a great leap in the dark.
Last words

HOCH, Edward Wallis, 1849–1925

36 There is so much good in the worst of us,
And so much bad in the best of us,
That it hardly becomes any of us
To talk about the rest of us.   *Good and Bad*

HODGSON, Ralph, 1871–1962

37 Time, you old gypsy man,
Will you not stay,
Put up your caravan
Just for one day?   *Time, you old Gypsy Man*

HOFFMANN, August Heinrich, von Fallersleben, 1798–1874

38 *Deutschland, Deutschland, uber alles.* Germany, Germany above
all. *Song*

HOFFMANN, Heinrich, 1809–1874

39 But one day, one cold winter's day,
He screamed out, 'Take the soup away!'
Struwwelpeter, Augustus

40 Here is cruel Frederick, see!
A horrid wicked boy was he. *Ib, Cruel Frederick*

41 Look at little Johnny there,
Little Johnny Head-in-Air. *Ib, Johnny Head-In-Air*

42 Anything to me is sweeter
Than to see Shock-headed Peter. *Ib, Shock-headed Peter*

HOLMES, Oliver Wendell, 1809–1894

43 When the last reader reads no more. *The Last Reader*

44 And silence, like a poultice, comes
To heal the blows of sound. *The Music Grinders*

45 Wisdom has taught us to be calm and meek,
To take one blow, and turn the other cheek;
It is not written what a man shall do
If the rude caitiff smite the other too. *Non-Resistance*

46 Ay, tear her tattered ensign down!
Long has it waved on high,
And many an eye has danced to see
That banner in the sky. *Old Ironsides*

47 Man wants but little drink below,
But wants that little strong. *A Song of other Days*
(Parody on Goldsmith, see 150:72)

48 Man has his will, – but woman has her way.
The Autocrat of the Breakfast Table, Prologue

49 A thought is often original, though you have uttered it a hundred times. *Ib, Ch. 1*

50 Build thee more stately mansions, O my soul,
As the swift seasons roll!
Leave thy low-vaulted past! *Ib, Ch. 4,*
The Chambered Nautilus

51 The world's great men have not commonly been great scholars,
nor great scholars great men. *Ib, Ch. 6*

52 To be seventy years young is sometimes far more cheerful and
hopeful than to be forty years old.
On the Seventieth Birthday of Julia Ward Howe

HOME, Sir Alexander Frederick Douglas- (formerly 14th Earl of Home), 1903–

53 I suppose Mr Wilson, when you come to think of it, is the 14th Mr Wilson. *Television, 21 Oct. 1963*

HOMER, c. 900 B.C.

54 As the generation of leaves, so also is that of men.
Iliad, 6, 146

55 Always to be best and distinguished above others. *Ib, 6, 208*

HOOD, Thomas, 1799–1845

56 One more Unfortunate,
Weary of breath,
Rashly importunate,
Gone to her death!

Take her up tenderly,
Lift her with care;
Fashion'd so slenderly,
Young, and so fair! *The Bridge of Sighs*

57 Ben Battle was a soldier bold,
And used to war's alarms;
But a cannon-ball took off his legs,
So he laid down his arms! *Faithless Nelly Gray*

58 For here I leave my second leg,
And the Forty-second Foot! *Ib*

59 His death, which happen'd in his berth,
At forty-odd befell:
They went and told the sexton, and
The sexton toll'd the bell. *Faithless Sally Brown*

60 I remember, I remember,
The house where I was born,
The little window where the sun
Came peeping in at morn. *I Remember, I Remember*

61 I remember, I remember,
The fir trees dark and high;
I used to think their slender tops
Were close against the sky. *Ib*

62 But evil is wrought by want of Thought,
As well as want of Heart! *The Lady's Dream*

63 When Eve upon the first of Men
The apple press'd with specious cant
Oh! what a thousand pities then
That Adam was not Adamant! *A Reflection*

64 With fingers weary and worn,
    With eyelids heavy and red,
  A woman sat, in unwomanly rags,
    Plying her needle and thread –
      Stitch! stitch! stitch!
  In poverty, hunger, and dirt.   *The Song of the Shirt*

65 Oh! God! that bread should be so dear,
    And flesh and blood so cheap.   *Ib*

HOOVER, Herbert Clark, 1874–1964

66 The American system of rugged individualism.
               Speech, New York, 22 Oct. 1928

HOPKINS, Gerard Manley, 1844–1889

67 The world is charged with the grandeur of God.
               God's Grandeur

68 Glory be to God for dappled things –
  For skies of couple-colour as a brinded cow;
  For rose-moles all in stipple upon trout that swim.
               Pied Beauty

HORACE, Quintus Horatius Flaccus, 65–8 B.C.

69   *Brevis esse laboro,*
  Obscurus fio.
  I struggle to be brief, and become obscure.   *Ars Poetica, 25*

70 *Grammatici certant et adhuc sub iudice lis est.*
  Scholars dispute, and the case is still before the courts. *Ib, 78*

71 *Indignor, quandoque bonus dormitat Homerus.*
  I think it shame when the worthy Homer nods.   *Ib, 359*

72 *Si possis recte, si non, quocumque modo rem.*
  By honest means, if you can, but by any means make money.
               Epistles, 1, 1, 66

73 *Pallida Mors aequo pulsat pede pauperum tabernas Regumque turris.*
  Pale Death with impartial foot knocks at the doors of poor men's hovels and of King's palaces.   *Odes 1, 4, 13*

74 *Carpe diem, quam minimum credula postero.*
  Seize the present day, trusting the morrow as little as you can.
               Ib, 1, 11, 8

75 *Integer vitae scelerisque purus.*
  The man of upright life unstained by guilt.   *Ib, 1, 22, 1*

76 *Eheu fugaces, Postume, Postume,*
   Labuntur anni.
   Alas, Postumus, Postumus, the fleeting years are slipping by.
                                              Odes, 2, 14, 1

77 *Dulce et decorum est pro patria mori.*
   It is a sweet and seemly thing to die for one's country.
                                              Ib, 3, 2, 13

HORNE, Kenneth, see MURDOCH, Richard

HOUSMAN, Alfred Edward, 1859–1936

78 The Grizzly Bear is huge and wild;
   He has devoured the infant child.
   The infant child is not aware
   He has been eaten by the bear.   *Infant Innocence*

79 We'll to the woods no more,
   The laurels all are cut.   *Last Poems*

80 And naked to the hangman's noose
      The morning clocks will ring
   A neck God made for other use
      Than strangling in a string.   *A Shropshire Lad, 9*

81 When I was one-and-twenty
      I heard a wise man say,
   'Give crowns and pounds and guineas
      But not your heart away.'   *Ib, 13*

82 Here of a Sunday morning
      My love and I would lie,
   And see the coloured counties,
      And hear the larks so high
      About us in the sky.   *Ib, 21*

83 From far, from eve and morning
      And yon twelve-winded sky,
   The stuff of life to knit me
      Blew hither: here am I.   *Ib, 32*

84 With rue my heart is laden
      For golden friends I had,
   For many a rose-lipt maiden
      And many a lightfoot lad.   *Ib, 54*

85   Malt does more than Milton can
   To justify God's ways to man.   *Ib, 62*

HOWITT, Mary, 1799–1888

86 'Will you walk into my parlour?' said a spider to a fly;
' 'Tis the prettiest little parlour that ever you did spy.'
The Spider and the Fly

HOYLE, Edmond, 1672–1769

87 When in doubt, win the trick. *Hoyle's Games, Whist,*
Twenty-four Short Rules for Learners

HUBBARD, Elbert, 1856–1915

88 Life is just one damned thing after another.
A Thousand and One Epigrams

HUGHES, Thomas, 1822–1896

89 Life isn't all beer and skittles. *Tom Brown's Schooldays,*
Part 1, Ch. 2

HUME, David, 1711–1776

90 Avarice, the spur of industry. *Essays, Of Civil Liberty*
91 Custom, then, is the great guide of human life.
Inquiry Concerning Human Understanding, 5, 1

HUNGERFORD, Margaret, 1855?–1897

92 Beauty is altogether in the eye of the beholder. *Molly Bawn*

HUNT, George William, 1825–1904

93 We don't want to fight, but by jingo if we do,
We've got the ships, we've got the men, we've got the money too.
Music-Hall Song, 1878

HUNT, James Henry Leigh, 1784–1859

94 Abou Ben Adhem (may his tribe increase!)
Awoke one night from a deep dream of peace.
Abou Ben Adhem and the Angel

95 Write me as one that loves his fellow-men. *Ib*

96 Jenny kissed me when we met,
Jumping from the chair she sat in. *Rondeau*

HUXLEY, Aldous Leonard, 1894–1963

97 The time of our Ford. *Brave New World, Ch. 3*
98 Ending is better than mending. *Ib*
99 The Ideal man is the non-attached man.
Ends and Means, Ch. 1

1 I can sympathize with people's pains, but not with their pleasures. There is something curiously boring about somebody else's happiness.   *Limbo, Cynthia*

2 There are not enough *bons mots* in existence to provide any industrious conversationalist with a new stock for every social occasion.   *Point Counter Point, Ch. 7*

3 A bad book is as much a labour to write as a good one; it comes as sincerely from the author's soul.   *Ib, Ch. 13*

4 A million million spermatozoa,
   All of them alive:
   Out of their cataclysm but one poor Noah
   Dare hope to survive,
   And among that billion minus one
   Might have chanced to be
   Shakespeare, another Newton, a new Donne –
   But the One was Me.   *The Fifth Philosopher's Song*

5   But when the wearied Band
   Swoons to a waltz, I take her hand,
   And there we sit in peaceful calm,
   Quietly sweating palm to palm.   *Frascati's*

HUXLEY, Thomas Henry, 1825–1895

6 It is the customary fate of new truths to begin as heresies and to end as superstitions.
              The Coming of Age of the Origin of Species

IBSEN, Henrik, 1828–1906

7 In that moment it burst upon me that I had been living here these eight years with a strange man, and had borne him three children.   NORA HELMER   *A Doll's House, Act 3*

8 The majority never has right on its side. Never I say! That is one of the social lies that a free, thinking man is bound to rebel against. Who makes up the majority in any given country? Is it the wise men or the fools? I think we must agree that the fools are in a terrible, overwhelming majority, all the wide world over.   DR STOCKMANN   *An Enemy of the People, Act 4*

9 A man should never put on his best trousers when he goes out to battle for freedom and truth.   DR STOCKMANN   *Ib, Act 5*

10 Mother, give me the sun.   OSWALD ALVING   *Ghosts, Act 3*

11 What's a man's first duty? The answer's brief: To be himself.
          PEER GYNT *Peer Gynt, Act 4, Scene 1*

INGE, William Ralph, 1860–1954

12 Literature flourishes best when it is half a trade and half an art.
The Victorian Age

13 The nations which have put mankind and posterity most in their debt have been small states – Israel, Athens, Florence, Elizabethan England. *Marchant, Wit and Wisdom of Dean Inge*

INGERSOLL, Robert Green, 1833–1899

14 An honest God is the noblest work of man.
Gods, Part 1 (see also 250:16)

IRVING, Washington, 1783–1859

15 Whenever a man's friends begin to compliment him about looking young, he may be sure that they think he is growing old.
Bracebridge Hall, Bachelors

16 A woman's whole history is a history of the affections.
The Sketch Book, The Broken Heart

17 A sharp tongue is the only edged tool that grows keener with constant use. *Ib, Rip Van Winkle*

18 The almighty dollar, that great object of universal devotion throughout our land, seems to have no genuine devotees in these peculiar villages. *Wolfert's Roost, The Creole Village*

JAMES I of England, 1566–1625

19 A custom loathsome to the eye, hateful to the nose, harmful to the brain, dangerous to the lungs, and in the black, stinking fume thereof nearest resembling the horrible Stygian smoke of the pit that is bottomless. *A Counterblast to Tobacco*

20 Dr Donne's verses are like the peace of God: they pass all understanding. *Attributed*

21 No bishop, no King. *Attributed*

JAMES, Henry, 1843–1916

22 The deep well of unconscious cerebration.
The American, Preface

23 The only obligation to which in advance we may hold a novel without incurring the accusation of being arbitrary, is that it be interesting. *The Art of Fiction, Partial Portraits*

24 It takes a great deal of history to produce a little literature.
Life of Nathaniel Hawthorne, Ch. 1

25 He [*Thoreau*] was unperfect, unfinished, inartistic; he was worse than provincial – he was parochial. *Ib, Ch. 4*

JEFFERSON, Thomas, 1743–1826

26 We hold these truths to be self-evident: that all men are created
   equal; that they are endowed by their Creator with certain un-
   alienable rights; that among these are life, liberty, and the
   pursuit of happiness.
                       Declaration of American Independence, 4 July 1776

27 We mutually pledge to each other our lives, our fortunes, and
   our sacred honour.   *Ib*

28 Error of opinion may be tolerated when reason is left free to
   combat it.   *First Inaugural Address, 4 March 1801*

29 Peace, commerce, and honest friendship with all nations, entangling alliances with none.   *Ib*

30 The care of human life and happiness, and not their destruction,
   is the first and only legitimate object of good government.
                       To the Republican citizens of Washington County,
                                               Maryland, 1809

31 Resistance to tyrants is obedience to God.   *Epigrams*

32 Ignorance is preferable to error; and he is less remote from the
   truth who believes nothing, than he who believes what is wrong.
                               Notes on the state of Virginia

33 I tremble for my country when I reflect that God is just.   *Ib*

JEROME, Jerome Klapka, 1859–1927

34 Love is like the measles; we all have to go through with it.
                       Idle Thoughts of an Idle Fellow, On Being in Love

35 It always does seem to me that I am doing more work than I
   should do. It is not that I object to the work, mind you; I like
   work; it fascinates me. I can sit and look at it for hours. I love
   to keep it by me; the idea of getting rid of it nearly breaks my
   heart.   *Three Men in a Boat, Ch. 15*

36 The Passing of the Third Floor Back.   *Title of Play*

JERROLD, Douglas William, 1803–1857

37 Religion's in the heart, not in the knees.   *The Devil's Ducat, 1*

38 The best thing I know between France and England is the sea.
                           Wit and opinions of Douglas Jerrold

JOAD, Cyril Edwin Mitchinson, 1891–1953

39 It all depends what you mean by . . .
                               BBC Brains Trust, 1942–1948

JOHNSON, Samuel, 1709–1784

40 When I took the first survey of my undertaking, I found our
   speech copious without order, and energetic without rules.
   Dictionary of the English Language, Preface

41 I am not yet so lost in lexicography, as to forget that words are
   the daughters of earth, and that things are the sons of heaven.
   Ib

42 Every quotation contributes something to the stability or en-
   largement of the language.   *Ib*

43 I have protracted my work till most of those whom I wished to
   please have sunk into the grave, and success and miscarriage
   are empty sounds; I therefore dismiss it with frigid tranquillity,
   having little to fear or hope from censure or from praise.   *Ib*

44 *Cricket.* – A sport, at which the contenders drive a ball with
   sticks in opposition to each other.   *Ib, Definitions*

45 *Grubstreet.* – Originally the name of a street near Moorfields
   in London much inhabited by writers of small histories, dictionaries, and temporary poems.   *Ib*

46 *Lexicographer.* – A harmless drudge.   *Ib*

47 *Network.* – Any thing reticulated or decussated, at equal dis-
   tances, with interstices between the intersections.   *Ib*

48 *Oats.* – A grain, which in England is generally given to horses,
   but in Scotland supports the people.   *Ib*

49 *Patron.* – Commonly a wretch who supports with insolence, and
   is paid with flattery.   *Ib*

50 *Pension.* – An allowance made to any one without an equivalent.
   In England it is generally understood to mean pay given to a
   state hireling for treason to his country.   *Ib*

51 When two Englishmen meet, their first talk is of the weather.
   The Idler, 11

52 Condemned to hope's delusive mine.   *On the Death of Mr Levet*

53 Officious, innocent, sincere,
      Of every friendless name the friend.   *Ib*

54 Of all the griefs that harass the distressed,
   Sure the most bitter is a scornful jest.   *London*

55 This mournful truth is ev'rywhere confessed
   Slow rises worth, by poverty depressed.   *Ib*

56 If the man who turnips cries,
   Cry not when his father dies,
   'Tis a proof that he had rather
   Have a turnip than his father.
   Burlesque of lines by Lope De Vega

57 Long expected, one-and-twenty,
   Lingering year, at length is flown.   *One-and-twenty*

58 When learning's triumph o'er her barb'rous foes
   First rear'd the stage, immortal Shakspeare rose;
   Each change of many-colour'd life he drew,
   Exhausted worlds, and then imagin'd new:
   Existence saw him spurn her bounded reign,
   And panting time toil'd after him in vain.   *Prologue at the*
                   Opening of the Theatre in Drury Lane, 1747

59 For we that live to please, must please to live.   *Ib*

60 No place affords a more striking conviction of the vanity of
   human hopes, than a public library.
                                   The Rambler, 23 March 1751

61 Ye who listen with credulity to the whispers of fancy, and pursue
   with eagerness the phantoms of hope; who expect that age will
   perform the promises of youth, and that the deficiencies of the
   present day will be supplied by the morrow; attend to the
   history of Rasselas, prince of Abyssinia.   *Rasselas, Ch. 1*

62 Some desire is necessary to keep life in motion, and he whose
   real wants are supplied, must admit those of fancy.   *Ib, Ch. 8*

63 The business of a poet, said Imlac, is to examine, not the individual, but the species; to remark general properties and large
   appearances: he does not number the streaks of the tulip, or
   describe the different shades in the verdure of the forest.
                                                  Ib, Ch. 10

64 Human life is every where a state in which much is to be endured, and little to be enjoyed.   *Ib, Ch. 11*

65 The life of a solitary man will be certainly miserable, but not
   certainly devout.   *Ib. Ch. 21*

66 To live without feeling or exciting sympathy, to be fortunate
   without adding to the felicity of others, or afflicted without
   tasting the balm of pity, is a state more gloomy than solitude:
   it is not retreat but exclusion from mankind. Marriage has many
   pains, but celibacy has no pleasures.   *Ib, Ch. 26*

67 Let observation with extensive view,
   Survey mankind from China to Peru;
   Remark each anxious toil, each eager strife,
   And watch the busy scenes of crowded life.
                                   The Vanity of Human Wishes

68 There mark what ills the scholar's life assail,
   Toil, envy, want, the patron, and the jail.   *Ib*

69 He left the name, at which the world grew pale,
To point a moral, or adorn a tale. *The Vanity of Human Wishes*

70 Hides from himself his state, and shuns to know
That life protracted is protracted woe. *Ib*

71 Still raise for good the supplicating voice,
But leave to Heaven the measure and the choice. *Ib*

72 JOHNSON: I have no notion that I was wrong or irreverent to my
tutor.
BOSWELL: That, Sir, was great fortitude of mind.
JOHNSON: No, Sir, stark insensibility.
Boswell's Life of Johnson, 1728

73 If you call a dog Hervey, I shall love him. *Ib, 1737*

74 When asked how he felt upon the ill success of his tragedy
[*Irene*], he replied, 'Like the Monument'. *Ib, 1750*

75 Johnson scolded him [*Langton*] for 'leaving his social friends to
go and sit with a set of wretched un-idea'd girls'. *Ib, 1752*

76 This man [*Lord Chesterfield*] I thought had been a Lord among
wits; but, I find, he is only a wit among Lords! *Ib, 1754*

77 They teach the morals of a whore, and the manners of a dancing-
master. [*Lord Chesterfield's Letters*] *Ib*

78 Is not a Patron, my Lord, one who looks with unconcern on a
man struggling for life in the water, and, when he has reached
ground, encumbers him with help? The notice which you have
been pleased to take of my labours, had it been early, had been
kind; but it has been delayed till I am indifferent, and cannot
enjoy it; till I am solitary, and cannot impart it; till I am known,
and do not want it. *Ib, Letter to Lord Chesterfield, 7 Feb. 1755*

79 When the messenger who carried the last sheet [*of Johnson's
Dictionary*] to Millar returned, Johnson asked him, 'Well, what
did he say?' – 'Sir, (answered the messenger) he said, thank
God I have done with him.' 'I am glad (replied Johnson, with a
smile,) that he thanks God for any thing.' *Ib, 1755*

80 I respect Millar, Sir; he has raised the price of literature. *Ib*

81 Ignorance, Madam, pure ignorance. [*When asked why, in his
Dictionary, he defined 'Pastern' as the 'knee of a horse'*] *Ib*

82 If a man does not make new acquaintances as he advances
through life, he will soon find himself left alone. A man, Sir,
should keep his friendship in constant repair. *Ib*

83 BOSWELL: I do indeed come from Scotland, but I cannot help
it . . .
JOHNSON: That, Sir, I find, is what a very great many of your
countrymen cannot help. *Ib, 1763*

84 The morality of an action depends on the motive from which we act. If I fling half a crown to a beggar with intention to break his head, and he picks it up and buys victuals with it, the physical effect is good; but, with respect to me, the action is very wrong.
Boswell's Life of Johnson, 1763

85 The noblest prospect which a Scotchman ever sees, is the high road that leads him to England. *Ib*

86 A man ought to read just as inclination leads him; for what he reads as a task will do him little good. *Ib*

87 In civilized society, personal merit will not serve you so much as money will. Sir, you may make the experiment. Go into the street, and give one man a lecture on morality, and another a shilling, and see which will respect you most. *Ib*

88 It is a sad reflection but a true one, that I knew almost as much at eighteen as I do now. *Ib*

89 Your levellers wish to level down as far as themselves; but they cannot bear levelling up to themselves. They would all have some people under them; why not then have some people above them? *Ib*

90 A woman's preaching is like a dog's walking on his hind legs. It is not done well, but you are surprised to find it done at all. *Ib*

91 I mind my belly very studiously, and very carefully; for I look upon it, that he who does not mind his belly, will hardly mind any thing else. *Ib*

92 This was a good dinner enough, to be sure; but it was not a dinner to ask a man to. *Ib*

93 A very unclubbable man. [*Sir John Hawkins*] *Ib, 1764*

94 The longer we live, and the more we think, the higher value we learn to put on the friendship and tenderness of parents and of friends. Parents we can have but once; and he promises himself too much, who enters life with the expectation of finding many friends. *Ib, 1766*

95 I cannot see that lectures can do so much good as reading the books from which the lectures are taken. *Ib*

96 So far is it from being true that men are naturally equal, that no two people can be half an hour together, but one shall acquire an evident superiority over the other. *Ib*

97 JOHNSON: Well, we had good talk.
BOSWELL: Yes, Sir, you tossed and gored several persons.
Ib, 1768

98 It matters not how a man dies, but how he lives. *Ib, 1769*

99 Now that you are going to marry, do not expect more from life, than life will afford. *Boswell's Life of Johnson, 1769*

1 A gentleman who had been very unhappy in marriage, married immediately after his wife died: Johnson said, it was the triumph of hope over experience. *Ib, 1770*

2 I would not give half a guinea to live under one form of Government rather than another. It is of no moment to the happiness of an individual. *Ib, 1772*

3 The mass of every people must be barbarous where there is no printing. *Ib*

4 Much may be made of a Scotchman, if he be caught young. *Ib*

5 People seldom read a book which is given to them; and few are given. The way to spread a work is to sell it at a low price. No man will send to buy a thing that costs even sixpence, without an intention to read it. *Ib, 1773*

6 The Irish are not in a conspiracy to cheat the world by false representations of the merits of their countrymen. No, Sir; the Irish are a fair people; – they never speak well of one another. *Ib, 1775*

7 They [*the Americans*] are a race of convicts, and ought to be thankful for any thing we allow them short of hanging. *Ib*

8 There are few ways in which a man can be more innocently employed than in getting money. *Ib*

9 Fleet-street has a very animated appearance; but I think the full tide of human existence is at Charing-Cross. *Ib*

10 There may be other reasons for a man's not speaking in publick than want of resolution: he may have nothing to say. *Ib*

11 The greatest part of a writer's time is spent in reading, in order to write; a man will turn over half a library to make one book. *Ib*

12 Patriotism is the last refuge of a scoundrel. *Ib*

13 Being pressed upon this subject, and asked if he really was of opinion, that though, in general, happiness was very rare in human life, a man was not sometimes happy in the moment that was present, he answered, 'Never, but when he is drunk.' *Ib*

14 Knowledge is of two kinds. We know a subject ourselves, or we know where we can find information upon it. *Ib*

15 There is now less flogging in our great schools than formerly, but then less is learned there; so that what the boys get at one end they lose at the other. *Ib*

16 A ship is worse than a gaol. There is, in gaol, better air, better company, better conveniency of every kind; and a ship has the additional disadvantage of being in danger. When men come to like a sea-life, they are not fit to live on land.
Boswell's Life of Johnson, 1776

17 There is no private house, (said he) in which people can enjoy themselves so well, as at a capital tavern.   *Ib*

18 Marriage is the best state for a man in general; and every man is a worse man, in proportion as he is unfit for the married state.   *Ib*

19 It is commonly a weak man, who marries for love.   *Ib*

20 Melancholy, indeed, should be diverted by every means but drinking.   *Ib*

21 No man but a blockhead ever wrote, except for money.   *Ib*

22 A man who has not been in Italy, is always conscious of an inferiority.   *Ib*

23 If I had no duties, and no reference to futurity, I would spend my life in driving briskly in a post-chaise with a pretty woman.
Ib, 1777

24 Depend upon it, Sir, when a man knows he is to be hanged in a fortnight, it concentrates his mind wonderfully.   *Ib*

25 You find no man, at all intellectual, who is willing to leave London. No, Sir, when a man is tired of London, he is tired of life; for there is in London all that life can afford.   *Ib*

26 I am willing to love all mankind, except an American. *Ib, 1778*

27 It is better to live rich than to die rich.   *Ib*

28 I have always said, the first Whig was the Devil.   *Ib*

29 Wine gives great pleasure; and every pleasure is of itself a good. It is a good, unless counterbalanced by evil.   *Ib*

30 What I gained by being in France was, learning to be better satisfied with my own country.   *Ib*

31 Claret is the liquor for boys; port for men; but he who aspires to be a hero must drink brandy.   *Ib, 1779*

32 BOSWELL: Is not the Giant's-Causeway worth seeing?
JOHNSON: Worth seeing? Yes; but not worth going to see. *Ib*

33 Sir, I have two very cogent reasons for not printing any list of subscribers; – one, that I have lost all the names, – the other, that I have spent all the money.   *Ib, 1781*

34 Clear your mind of cant. You may talk as other people do: you may say to a man, 'Sir, I am your most humble servant.' You are *not* his most humble servant.   *Ib, 1783*

35 Let your imports be more than your exports, and you'll never
go far wrong. *Boswell's Life of Johnson, 1783*

36 No man is a hypocrite in his pleasures. *Ib, 1784*

37 I look upon every day to be lost, in which I do not make a new
acquaintance. *Ib*

38 *Nullum quod tetigit non ornavit* – He touched nothing that he
did not adorn. *Epitaph on Goldsmith*

39 There is no tracing the connection of ancient nations, but by
language; and therefore I am always sorry when any language
is lost, because languages are the pedigree of nations.
Boswell's Journal of a Tour to the Hebrides.

40 Difficult do you call it, Sir? I wish it were impossible. [*Of a
violinist's performance*] *Anecdotes by William Seward*

41 What is written without effort is in general read without pleasure.
Ib

42 The great source of pleasure is variety.
Lives of the English Poets, Butler

43 But what are the hopes of man! I am disappointed by that stroke
of death, which has eclipsed the gaiety of nations and im-
poverished the public stock of harmless pleasure. [*Garrick's
death*] *Ib, Edmund Smith*

44 I have heard him assert, that a tavern chair was the throne of
human felicity. *Hawkin's Life of Johnson*

45 A man is in general better pleased when he has a good dinner
upon his table, than when his wife talks Greek.
Johnsonian Miscellanies

46 You could not stand five minutes with that man [*Edmund Burke*]
beneath a shed, while it rained, but you must be convinced you
had been standing with the greatest man you had ever yet seen.
Attributed by Mrs Piozzi

JONSON, Ben, 1573–1637

47 Our scene is London, 'cause we would make known,
No country's mirth is better than our own.
The Alchemist, Prologue

48 Zeal-of-the-Land Busy. *Bartholomew Fair, name of character*

49 Drink to me only with thine eyes
And I will pledge with mine;
Or leave a kiss but in the cup
And I'll not look for wine. *To Celia*

50 Queen and Huntress, chaste and fair,
Now the sun is laid to sleep,

Seated in thy silver chair,
State in wonted manner keep:
    Hesperus entreats thy light,
    Goddess, excellently bright.   HESPERUS.
                        Cynthia's Revels, Act 5, Scene 3

51 Still to be neat, still to be drest,
   As you were going to a feast.   SONG   *Epicoene, Act 1, Scene 1*

52 Such sweet neglect more taketh me,
   Than all the adulteries of art;
   They strike mine eyes, but not my heart.   SONG   *Ib*

53   Soul of the Age!
   The applause! delight! the wonder of our Stage.
                        To the Memory of William Shakespeare

54 Thou art a monument, without a tomb.   *Ib*

55   How far thou didst our Lyly out-shine
   Or sporting Kyd, or Marlowe's mighty line.   *Ib*

56 Thou hadst small Latin, and less Greek.   *Ib*

57 He was not of an age, but for all time!   *Ib*

58 Sweet Swan of Avon!   *Ib*

59 Good morning to the day: and, next, my gold! –
   Open the shrine, that I may see my saint.   VOLPONE
                        Volpone, Act 1, Scene 1

60 O, health! health! the blessing of the rich! the riches of the poor!
   who can buy thee at too dear a rate, since there is no enjoying
   the world without thee?   VOLPONE   *Ib, Act 2, Scene 1*

61 Come, my Celia, let us prove,
   While we can, the sports of love,
   Time will not be ours for ever,
   He, at length, our good will sever.   VOLPONE
                        Ib, Act 3, Scene 6

62 O rare Ben Jonson.   *Epitaph in Westminster Abbey*

JORDAN, Dorothea, 1762–1816

63 'Oh! where, and Oh! where is your Highland Laddie gone?'
   'He's gone to fight the French, for King George upon the throne,
   And it's Oh! in my heart, how I wish him safe at home!'
                        The Blue Bells of Scotland

JOYCE, James, 1882–1941

64 A Portrait of the Artist as a Young Man.   *Title of Book*

JUDGE, Jack, see WILLIAMS, Harry

JUNIUS, 18th century

65 The Liberty of the press is the *Palladium* of all the civil, political and religious rights of an Englishman. *Letters, Dedication*

66 To be acquainted with the merit of a ministry, we need only observe the condition of the people. *Letter 1, 21 Jan. 1769*

67 There is a holy, mistaken zeal in politics, as well as religion. By persuading others we convince ourselves.
Letter 35, 19 Dec. 1769

JUVENAL, 60–130? A.D.

68 *Nemo repente fuit turpissimus.* No one ever became thoroughly bad in one step. *Satires, 2, 83*

69 *Quis custodiet ipsos Custodes?*
Who is to guard the guards themselves? *Ib, 6, 347*

70 *Tenet insanabile multos Scribendi cacoethes et aegro in corde senescit.*
An inveterate and incurable itch for writing besets many and grows old with their sick hearts. *Ib, 7, 51*

71 *Orandum est ut sit mens sana in corpore sano.*
Your prayer must be for a sound mind in a sound body.
Ib, 10, 356

KARR, Alphonse, 1808–1890

72 *Plus ça change, plus c'est la même chose.* The more things change, the more they are the same. *Les Guêpes, Jan. 1849*

KAVANAGH, Ted, 1892–1958

73 Can I do you now, sir? MRS MOP *Itma, BBC Radio Programme, 1939–1949, with Tommy Handley (1892–1949)*

74 Don't forget the diver. *Ib*

75 I don't mind if I do. COLONEL CHINSTRAP *Ib*

76 It's That Man Again. *Ib*

77 Wot, me? In my state of health? ATLAS *Ib*

KEATS, John, 1795–1821

78 Season of mists and mellow fruitfulness,
Close bosom-friend of the maturing sun;
Conspiring with him how to load and bless
With fruit the vines that round the thatch-eves run.
To Autumn

79   To set budding more,
And still more, later flowers for the bees,
Until they think warm days will never cease,
    For Summer has o'er-brimm'd their clammy cells.
                                                    To Autumn

80 Who hath not seen thee oft amid thy store?
    Sometimes whoever seeks abroad may find
Thee sitting careless on a granary floor.   *Ib*

81 Where are the songs of Spring? Ay, where are they?
    Think not of them, thou hast thy music too.   *Ib*

82 The red-breast whistles from a garden-croft;
And gathering swallows twitter in the skies.   *Ib*

83 Bards of Passion and of Mirth,
Ye have left your souls on earth!
Have ye souls in heaven too,
Double lived in regions new?
                    Ode, Written on the blank page before
            Beaumont and Fletcher's 'The Fair Maid of the Inn'

84 The imagination of a boy is healthy, and the mature imagination
    of a man is healthy; but there is a space of life between, in
    which the soul is in a ferment, the character undecided, the way
    of life uncertain, the ambition thick-sighted: thence proceeds
    mawkishness.   *Endymion, Preface*

85 A thing of beauty is a joy for ever:
    Its loveliness increases; it will never
    Pass into nothingness.   *Ib, Book 1, 1*

86 Pleasure is oft a visitant; but pain
    Clings cruelly to us.   *Ib, 906*

87   O Sorrow,
        Why dost borrow
Heart's lightness from the merriment of May? *Ib, Book 4, 164*

88   It is a flaw
In happiness, to see beyond our bourn, –
It forces us in summer skies to mourn,
It spoils the singing of the Nightingale.
                    Epistle to John Hamilton Reynolds, 82

89 St Agnes' Eve – Ah, bitter chill it was!
The owl, for all his feathers, was a-cold;
The hare limp'd trembling through the frozen grass,
And silent was the flock in woolly fold.   *The Eve of St Agnes, 1*

90 Upon the honey'd middle of the night.   *Ib, 6*

91 And they are gone: aye, ages long ago
These lovers fled away into the storm.   *Ib, 42*

92   The Beadsman, after thousand aves told,
      For aye unsought for slept among his ashes cold.
                                        The Eve of St Agnes, 42

93 Fanatics have their dreams, wherewith they weave
    A paradise for a sect.   *The Fall of Hyperion, Book 1, 1*

94 The poet and the dreamer are distinct,
    Diverse, sheer opposite, antipodes.
    The one pours out a balm upon the World,
    The other vexes it.   *Ib, 199*

95 Ever let the fancy roam,
    Pleasure never is at home.   *Fancy, 1*

96 Deep in the shady sadness of a vale
    Far sunken from the healthy breath of morn,
    Far from the fiery noon, and eve's one star,
    Sat gray-hair'd Saturn, quiet as a stone. *Hyperion, Book 1, 1*

97   No stir of air was there,
    Not so much life as on a summer's day
    Robs not one light seed from the feather'd grass,
    But where the dead leaf fell, there did it rest.   *Ib, 7*

98   As when, upon a tranced summer-night,
    Those green-rob'd senators of mighty woods,
    Tall oaks, branch-charmed by the earnest stars,
    Dream, and so dream all night without a stir.   *Ib, 72*

99 For as in theatres of crowded men
    Hubbub increases more they call out 'Hush!'   *Ib, 253*

1   For 'tis the eternal law
    That first in beauty should be first in might. *Ib, Book 2, 228*

2 Knowledge enormous makes a God of me.   *Ib, Book 3, 113*

3 Parting they seem'd to tread upon the air,
      Twin roses by the zephyr blown apart
    Only to meet again more close, and share
      The inward fragrance of each other's heart.   *Isabella, 10*

4 But, for the general award of love,
      The little sweet doth kill much bitterness.   *Ib, 13*

5 So the two brothers and their murder'd man
      Rode past fair Florence.   *Ib, 27*

6   O cruelty,
    To steal my Basil-pot away from me!   *Ib, 63*

7 Ah, what can ail thee, wretched wight,
      Alone and palely loitering;
    The sedge is wither'd from the lake,
      And no birds sing.   *La Belle Dame Sans Merci, 1*

8 I met a lady in the meads
  Full beautiful, a faery's child;
Her hair was long, her foot was light,
  And her eyes were wild.   *La Belle Dame Sans Merci, 4*

9 She look'd at me as she did love,
  And made sweet moan.   *Ib, 6*

10 And sure in language strange she said,
  I love thee true.   *Ib, 7*

11 Love in a hut, with water and a crust,
  Is – Love, forgive us! – cinders, ashes, dust;
Love in a palace is perhaps at last
More grievous torment than a hermit's fast.   *Lamia, Part 2, 1*

12   Do not all charms fly
At the mere touch of cold philosophy?   *Ib, 229*

13 Philosophy will clip an Angel's wings.   *Ib, 234*

14 Souls of Poets dead and gone,
What Elysium have ye known,
Happy field or mossy cavern,
Choicer than the Mermaid Tavern?
Have ye tippled drink more fine
Than mine host's Canary wine?
                          Lines on the Mermaid Tavern, 1

15 Ah! dearest love, sweet home of all my fears,
  And hopes, and joys, and panting miseries. *Ode to Fanny, 2*

16 Thou still unravish'd bride of quietness,
  Thou foster-child of silence and slow time.
                          Ode on a Grecian Urn, 1

17 Heard melodies are sweet, but those unheard
  Are sweeter; therefore, ye soft pipes, play on;
Not to the sensual ear, but, more endear'd,
Pipe to the spirit ditties of no tone.   *Ib, 2*

18 She cannot fade, though thou hast not thy bliss,
  For ever wilt thou love, and she be fair!   *Ib*

19 For ever piping songs for ever new.   *Ib, 3*

20 'Beauty is truth, truth beauty,' – that is all
  Ye know on earth, and all ye need to know.   *Ib, 5*

21 No, no, go not to Lethe, neither twist
  Wolf's-bane, tight-rooted, for its poisonous wine.
                          Ode on Melancholy, 1

22 She dwells with Beauty – Beauty that must die;
  And Joy, whose hand is ever at his lips
Bidding adieu.   *Ib, 3*

23 My heart aches, and a drowsy numbness pains
   My sense, as though of hemlock I had drunk.
                               Ode to a Nightingale, 1

24 O for a beaker full of the warm South,
      Full of the true, the blushful Hippocrene,
         With beaded bubbles winking at the brim,
            And purple-stained mouth;
   That I might drink, and leave the world unseen,
      And with thee fade away into the forest dim.   *Ib, 2*

25 Where youth grows pale, and spectre-thin, and dies
      Where but to think is to be full of sorrow
         And leaden-eyed despairs.   *Ib, 3*

26 Away! away! for I will fly to thee,
      Not charioted by Bacchus and his pards,
   But on the viewless wings of Poesy,
      Though the dull brain perplexes and retards:
   Already with thee! tender is the night,
      And haply the Queen-Moon is on her throne.   *Ib, 4*

27 I cannot see what flowers are at my feet,
      Nor what soft incense hangs upon the boughs.   *Ib, 5*

28 The murmurous haunt of flies on summer eves.   *Ib*

29 Darkling I listen; and, for many a time
      I have been half in love with easeful Death,
   Call'd him soft names in many a mused rhyme,
      To take into the air my quiet breath;
   Now more than ever seems it rich to die,
      To cease upon the midnight with no pain,
   While thou art pouring forth thy soul abroad
         In such an ecstasy!   *Ib, 6*

30 Thou wast not born for death, immortal Bird!
      No hungry generations tread thee down;
   The voice I hear this passing night was heard
      In ancient days by emperor and clown:
   Perhaps the self-same song that found a path
      Through the sad heart of Ruth, when, sick for home,
         She stood in tears amid the alien corn;
            The same that oft-times hath
   Charm'd magic casements, opening on the foam
      Of perilous seas, in faery lands forlorn.   *Ib, 7*

31 Forlorn! the very word is like a bell
      To toll me back from thee to my sole self!   *Ib, 8*

32 Was it a vision, or a waking dream?
      Fled is that music: – Do I wake or sleep?   *Ib*

33 A bright torch, and a casement ope at night,
   To let the warm Love in!   *Ode to Psyche, 66*

34 What is more gentle than a wind in summer?
                                              Sleep and Poetry, 1

35 Stop and consider! life is but a day;
   A fragile dew-drop on its perilous way
   From a tree's summit.   *Ib, 85*

36 O for ten years, that I may overwhelm
   Myself in poesy; so I may do the deed
   That my own soul has to itself decreed.   *Ib, 96*

37 And can I ever bid these joys farewell?
   Yes, I must pass them for a nobler life,
   Where I may find the agonies, the strife
   Of human hearts.   *Ib, 122*

38   A drainless shower
   Of light is poesy; 'tis the supreme of power;
   'Tis might half slumb'ring on its own right arm.   *Ib, 235*

39   The great end
   Of poesy, that it should be a friend
   To sooth the cares, and lift the thoughts of man.   *Ib, 245*

40 Much have I travell'd in the realms of gold,
   And many goodly states and kingdoms seen.
                    Sonnet, On First Looking into Chapman's Homer

41 Then felt I like some watcher of the skies
   When a new planet swims into his ken;
   Or like stout Cortez when with eagle eyes
   He star'd at the Pacific – and all his men
   Look'd at each other with a wild surmise –
   Silent, upon a peak in Darien.   *Ib*

42 The poetry of earth is never dead:
   When all the birds are faint with the hot sun,
   And hide in cooling trees, a voice will run
   From hedge to hedge about the new-mown mead.
                    Sonnet, On the Grasshopper and Cricket

43 Happy is England! I could be content
   To see no other verdure than its own.
                    Sonnet, Happy is England

44 Happy is England, sweet her artless daughters;
   Enough their simple loveliness for me.   *Ib*

45 Four seasons fill the measure of the year;
   There are four seasons in the mind of man.
                    Sonnet, The Human Seasons

46 Glory and loveliness have pass'd away.   *Sonnet, To Leigh Hunt*

47 To one who has been long in city pent,
　　'Tis very sweet to look into the fair
　　And open face of heaven.   *Sonnet, To one who has been*
　　　　　　　　　　　　　　　　　　　　　long in City pent

48 When I have fears that I may cease to be
　　Before my pen has glean'd my teeming brain.
　　　　　　　　　　　　　　　　Sonnet, When I have fears

49 　　　　　　　　　Then on the shore
　　Of the wide world I stand alone, and think
　　Till love and fame to nothingness do sink.   *Ib*

50 I am certain of nothing but of the holiness of the Heart's affec-
　　tions and the truth of Imagination – What the imagination
　　seizes as Beauty must be truth – whether it existed before or not.
　　　　　　　　　Letter to Benjamin Bailey, 22 Nov. 1817

51 O for a Life of Sensations rather than of Thoughts!   *Ib*

52 Negative Capability, that is, when a man is capable of being in
　　uncertainties, mysteries, doubts, without any irritable reaching
　　after fact and reason.
　　　　　　　Letter to George and Thomas Keats, 28 Dec. 1817

53 I am quite perplexed in a world of doubts and fancies – there
　　is nothing stable in the world; uproar's your only music.
　　　　　　　Letter to George and Thomas Keats, 13 Jan. 1818

54 Poetry should be great and unobtrusive, a thing which enters
　　into one's soul, and does not startle it or amaze it with itself,
　　but with its subject.   *Letter to J. H. Reynolds, 3 Feb. 1818*

55 Poetry should surprise by a fine excess and not by Singularity –
　　it should strike the Reader as a wording of his own highest
　　thoughts, and appear almost a Remembrance.
　　　　　　　　　Letter to John Taylor, 27 Feb. 1818

56 If Poetry comes not as naturally as the Leaves to a tree it had
　　better not come at all.   *Ib*

57 Scenery is fine – but human nature is finer.
　　　　　　　　　Letter to Benjamin Bailey, 13 March 1818

58 I have not the slightest feel of humility towards the Public – or
　　to anything in existence, – but the eternal Being, the Principle
　　of Beauty, and the Memory of great Men.
　　　　　　　　　Letter to J. H. Reynolds, 9 April 1818

59 I find that I can have no enjoyment in the World but continual
　　drinking of Knowledge.   *Letter to John Taylor, 24 April 1818*

60 I compare human life to a large Mansion of Many Apartments, two of which I can only describe, the doors of the rest being as yet shut upon me. *Letter to J. H. Reynolds, 3 May 1818*

61 I would sooner fail than not be among the greatest.
Letter to J. A. Hessey, 9 Oct. 1818

62 I think I shall be among the English Poets after my death.
Letter to George and Georgiana Keats, Oct. 1818

63 Though the most beautiful Creature were waiting for me at the end of a Journey or a Walk . . . my Happiness would not be so fine, as my Solitude is sublime. Then instead of what I have described, there is a Sublimity to welcome me home. The roaring of the wind is my wife and the Stars through the window pane are my children. The mighty abstract Idea I have of Beauty in all things stifles the more divided and minute domestic happiness. *Ib*

64 A Man's life of any worth is a continual allegory, and very few eyes can see the Mystery of his life – a life like the scriptures, figurative – which such people can no more make out than they can the hebrew Bible. Lord Byron cuts a figure – but he is not figurative – Shakespeare led a life of Allegory: his works are the comments on it. *Letter to George and Georgiana Keats, 14 Feb. 1819*

65 I have two luxuries to brood over in my walks, your Loveliness and the hour of my death. O that I could have possession of them both in the same minute. *Letter to Fanny Brawne, 25 July 1819*

66 I equally dislike the favour of the public with the love of a woman – they are both a cloying treacle to the wings of independence. *Letter to John Taylor, 24 Aug. 1819*

67 Love is my religion – I could die for that.
Letter to Fanny Brawne, 13 Oct. 1819

68 'If I should die,' said I to myself, 'I have left no immortal work behind me – nothing to make my friends proud of my memory – but I have lov'd the principle of beauty in all things, and if I had had time I would have made myself remember'd.'
Letter to Fanny Brawne, Feb. 1820

69 You, I am sure, will forgive me for sincerely remarking that you might curb your magnanimity, and be more of an artist, and load every rift of your subject with ore.
Letter to P. B. Shelley, Aug. 1820

70 Here lies one whose name was writ in water. *Epitaph*

KEMPIS, Thomas À, 1380-1471

71 Man proposes but God disposes. *The Imitation of Christ, 1, 19*

72 *Sic transit gloria mundi.* Thus the glory of the world passes away.
Ib, 3, 6

73 It is much safer to obey than to rule. *Ib, 9, 1*

KENNEDY, John Fitzgerald, 1917-1963

74 Let the word go forth from this time and place, to friend and
foe alike, that the torch has been passed to a new generation of
Americans – born in this century, tempered by war, disciplined
by a hard and bitter peace, proud of our ancient heritage.
Inaugural address, 20 Jan. 1961

75 My fellow Americans: ask not what your country can do for
you, ask what you can do for your country. My fellow citizens
of the world: ask not what America will do for you, but what
together we can do for the freedom of man. *Ib*

KESSELRING, Joseph, 1902-1967

76 Arsenic and Old Lace. *Title of play*

KETHE, William, ?-1608

77 All people that on earth do dwell
  Sing to the Lord with cheerful voice.
All People that on Earth do Dwell

78 For why, the Lord our God is good:
  His mercy is for ever sure;
  His truth at all times firmly stood,
  And shall from age to age endure. *Ib*

KEY, Francis Scott, 1780-1843

79 O! say can you see, by the dawn's early light,
  What so proudly we hailed at the twilight's last gleaming,
  Whose broad stripes and bright stars, through the perilous fight,
  O'er the ramparts we watched, were so gallantly streaming.
The Star-Spangled Banner

80 'Tis the star-spangled banner! O long may it wave,
  O'er the land of the free, and the home of the brave. *Ib*

KHAYYÁM, Omar, see FITZGERALD, Edward

KILMER, Joyce, 1886-1918

81 I think that I shall never see
  A poem lovely as a tree.

A tree whose hungry mouth is pressed
Against the earth's sweet flowing breast.   *Trees*

82 Poems are made by fools like me
But only God can make a tree.   *Ib*

KING, Benjamin Franklin, 1857–1894

83 Nothing to do but work,
Nothing to eat but food,
Nothing to wear but clothes,
To keep one from going nude.   *The Pessimist*

KING, Stoddard, 1889–1933

84 There's a long, long trail a-winding
Into the land of my dreams.   *The Long, Long Trail*

KINGSLEY, Charles, 1819–1875

85 Airly Beacon, Airly Beacon;
    Oh the pleasant sight to see
Shires and towns from Airly Beacon,
    While my love climbed up to me.   *Airly Beacon*

86 Be good, sweet maid, and let who will be clever;
    Do noble things, not dream them, all day long:
And so make life, death, and that vast for-ever
    One grand, sweet song.   *A Farewell, to C.E.G.*

87 For men must work, and women must weep,
And the sooner it's over, the sooner to sleep. *The Three Fishers*

88 When all the world is young, lad,
    And all the trees are green.
            Songs from the Water Babies, Young and Old

89 Young blood must have its course, lad,
    And every dog its day.   *Ib*

90 He did not know that a keeper is only a poacher turned outside
in, and a poacher is a keeper turned inside out.
                                    The Water Babies, Ch. 1

91 More ways of killing a cat than choking her with cream.
                                    Westward Ho! Ch. 20

KIPLING, Rudyard, 1865–1936

92 Oh, East is East, and West is West, and never the twain shall
meet.   *The Ballad of East and West*

93 Four things greater than all things are, –
Women and Horses and Power and War.
                                Ballad of the King's Jest

94 And a woman is only a woman, but a good cigar is a smoke.
The Betrothed

95 Boots – boots – boots – boots – movin' up an' down again!
Boots

96 But the Devil whoops, as he whooped of old:
'It's clever, but is it art?' *The Conundrum of the Workshops*

97 And what should they know of England who only England
know? *The English Flag*

98 For the female of the species is more deadly than the male.
The Female of the Species

99 Gentlemen-rankers out on the spree,
Damned from here to Eternity. *Gentlemen Rankers*

1 You're a better man than I am, Gunga Din. *Gunga Din*

2 If you can keep your head when all about you
Are losing theirs and blaming it on you. *If*

3 If you can dream – and not make dreams your master. *Ib*

4 If you can meet with Triumph and Disaster
And treat those two impostors just the same. *Ib*

5 If you can fill the unforgiving minute
With sixty seconds' worth of distance run,
Yours is the Earth and everything that's in it,
And – which is more – you'll be a Man, my son! *Ib*

6 Now this is the Law of the Jungle – as old and true as the sky.
The Law of the Jungle

7 On the road to Mandalay
Where the flyin'-fishes play. *Mandalay*

8 Ship me somewhere East of Suez, where the best is like the worst,
Where there aren't no Ten Commandments, an' a man can raise
a thirst. *Ib*

9 The tumult and the shouting dies –
The captains and the kings depart. *Recessional*

10 Lest we forget, lest we forget! *Ib*

11 Oh, it's Tommy this, an' Tommy that, an' 'Tommy, go away';
But it's 'Thank you, Mister Atkins,' when the band begins to
play. *Tommy*

12 Take up the White Man's Burden. *The White Man's Burden*

13 This is too butch for be. *Just-so Stories, The Elephant's Child*

14 Led go! You are hurtig be! *Ib*

15 The camel's hump is an ugly lump
Which well you may see at the Zoo;

But uglier yet is the hump we get
From having too little to do. *Ib, How the Camel got his Hump*

16 A man of infinite – resource – and – sagacity.
Ib, How the Whale got his Throat

17 The Light that Failed. *Title of novel*

KLINGER, Friedrich von, 1752–1831

18 *Sturm und Drang*. Storm and stress. *Title of play*

KNOX, John, 1505–1572

19 The First Blast of the Trumpet Against the Monstrous Regiment of Women. *Title of Pamphlet, 1558*

KNOX, Ronald Arbuthnot, 1888–1957

20 There once was a man who said, 'God
Must think it exceedingly odd
  If he finds that this tree
  Continues to be
When there's no one about in the Quad.' *Limerick*

21 A loud noise at one end and no sense of responsibility at the other. *Definition of a Baby*

KYD, Thomas, 1558?–1594?

22 In time the savage bull sustains the yoke,
In time all haggard hawks will stoop to lure,
In time small wedges cleave the hardest oak,
In time the flint is pierced with softest shower. LORENZO
The Spanish Tragedy, Act 2, Scene 1

LABOUCHERE, Henry, 1831–1912

23 He [*Labouchère*] did not object, he once said, to Gladstone's always having the ace of trumps up his sleeve, but only to his pretence that God had put it there.
Quoted in Dictionary of National Biography, 1912–1921

LAMB, Lady Caroline, 1785–1828

24 Mad, bad, and dangerous to know. [*Byron*] *Journal*

LAMB, Charles, 1775–1834

25 The human species, according to the best theory I can form of it, is composed of two distinct races, the men who borrow, and the men who lend. *Essays of Elia, The Two Races of Men*

26 Borrowers of books – those mutilators of collections, spoilers
   of the symmetry of shelves, and creators of odd volumes.
                         Essays of Elia, The Two Races of Men

27 'A clear fire, a clean hearth, and the rigour of the game.' This
   was the celebrated wish of old Sarah Battle (now with God)
   who, next to her devotions, loved a good game of whist.
                         Ib, Mrs Battle's Opinions on Whist

28 'Presents,' I often say, 'endear Absents.'
                         Ib, A Dissertation upon Roast Pig

29 I love to lose myself in other men's minds. When I am not
   walking, I am reading; I cannot sit and think. Books think
   for me.   *Last Essays of Elia,*
                         Detached Thoughts on Books and Reading

30 To be strong-backed and neat-bound is the desideratum of a
   volume. Magnificence comes after.   *Ib*

31 Newspapers always excite curiosity. No one ever lays one down
   without a feeling of disappointment.   *Ib*

32 I have had playmates, I have had companions,
   In my days of childhood, in my joyful schooldays –
   All, all are gone, the old familiar faces. *The Old Familiar Faces*

LANDOR, Walter Savage, 1775–1864

33 George the First was always reckoned
   Vile, but viler George the Second;
   And what mortal ever heard
   Any good of George the Third?
   When from earth the Fourth descended
   God be praised, the Georges ended.   *Epigram*

34 I strove with none; for none was worth my strife;
      Nature I loved and, next to Nature, Art:
   I warmed both hands before the fire of life;
      It sinks, and I am ready to depart.   *Finis*

35 I loved him not; and yet now he is gone,
      I feel I am alone.
   I check'd him while he spoke: yet, could he speak,
      Alas! I would not check.   *The Maid's Lament*

36 Ah, what avails the sceptred race!
      Ah, what the form divine!   *Rose Aylmer*

LANE, George Martin, 1823–1897

37 The waiter roars it through the hall:
   'We don't give bread with one fish-ball!'   *One Fish-ball*

LANGBRIDGE, Frederick, 1849–1923

38 Two men look out through the same bars:
   One sees the mud, and one the stars.

   A Cluster of Quiet Thoughts

LANGLAND, William, 1330?–1400?

39 In a somer seson, when soft was the sonne.

   A Vision of William concerning Piers the Plowman,
   B Text, Prologue, 1

LATIMER, Bishop Hugh, 1485?–1555

40 Be of good comfort, Master Ridley, and play the man; we shall
   this day light such a candle by God's grace in England, as I
   trust shall never be put out.   *16 Oct. 1555, while Latimer*
   and Ridley were being burned at the stake for heresy

LAUDER, Sir Harry, 1870–1950

41 I love a lassie.   *Song*

42 Just a wee doch-an'-dorris
   Before we gang awa' . . .
   If you can say, 'It's a braw, bricht, moonlicht nicht'
   Ye're a' richt.   *Song*

43 Keep right on to the end of the road,
   Keep right on to the end.
   'Though you're tired and weary still journey on.   *Song*

44 O! it's nice to get up in the mornin'
   But it's nicer to lie in bed.   *Song*

45 Roamin' in the gloamin'.   *Song*

LAWRENCE, David Herbert, 1885–1930

46 How beastly the bourgeois is
   especially the male of the species. *How beastly the Bourgeois is*

47 Nicely groomed, like a mushroom
   Standing there so sleek and erect and eyeable –
   and like a fungus, living on the remains of bygone life
   sucking his life out of the dead leaves of greater life than his
   own.   *Ib*

48 My love lies underground
   With her face upturned to mine,
   And her mouth unclosed in a last long kiss
   That ended her life and mine.   *Hymn to Priapus*

49 When I read Shakespeare I am struck with wonder
   That such trivial people should muse and thunder
   In such lovely language.   *When I Read Shakespeare, 1*

LEACOCK, Stephen Butler, 1869–1944

50 If every day in the life of a school could be the last day but one,
   there would be little fault to find with it.
                    College Days, Memories and Miseries of a Schoolmaster

51 Lord Ronald said nothing; he flung himself from the room,
   flung himself upon his horse and rode madly off in all directions.
                    Nonsense Novels, Gertrude the Governess

52 Golf may be played on Sunday, not being a game within the
   view of the law, but being a form of moral effort.
                    Other Fancies, Why I refuse to play Golf

53 The general idea, of course, in any first-class laundry is to see
   that no shirt or collar ever comes back twice.
                    Winnowed Wisdom, Ch. 6

LEAR, Edward, 1812–1888

54 Who, or why, or which, or *what*, is the Akond of Swat?
                    The Akond of Swat

55 On the Coast of Coromandel
          Where the early pumpkins blow,
   In the middle of the woods
          Lived the Yonghy-Bonghy-Bò.
                    The Courtship of the Yonghy-Bonghy-Bò

56   The Dong! – the Dong!
   The wandering Dong through the forest goes!
          The Dong! – the Dong!
   The Dong with a luminous Nose!
                    The Dong with a Luminous Nose

57 They went to sea in a sieve, they did
          In a sieve they went to sea.   *The Jumblies*

58 Far and few, far and few,
   Are the lands where the Jumblies live;
   Their heads are green, and their hands are blue,
   And they went to sea in a sieve.   *Ib*

59 'How pleasant to know Mr Lear!'
   Who has written such volumes of stuff!
   Some think him ill-tempered and queer,
   But a few think him pleasant enough.
                    Nonsense Songs, Preface

60 The Owl and the Pussy-Cat went to sea
    In a beautiful pea-green boat,
They took some honey, and plenty of money,
    Wrapped up in a five-pound note.
The Owl and the Pussy-Cat

61 They sailed away for a year and a day,
    To the land where the Bong-tree grows,
nd there in a wood a Piggy-wig stood,
    With a ring at the end of his nose.   *Ib*

62 They dined on mince and slices of quince,
    Which they ate with a runcible spoon;
And hand in hand, on the edge of the sand
    They danced by the light of the moon.   *Ib*

63 He has gone to fish, for his Aunt Jobiska's
Runcible Cat with crimson whiskers.
The Pobble who has no Toes

64 Two old Bachelors were living in one house;
One caught a Muffin, the other caught a Mouse.
The Two Old Bachelors

65 There was an Old Man who said, 'Hush!
I perceive a young bird in this bush!'
    When they said, 'Is it small?'
    He replied, 'Not at all!
It is four times as big as the bush!'
The Old Man Who said 'Hush!'

66 There was an Old Man with a beard,
Who said, 'It is just as I feared! –
    Two Owls and a Hen,
    Four Larks and a Wren,
Have all built their nests in my beard!'
The Old Man With a Beard

LEE, Nathaniel, 1655?–1692
67 When Greeks joined Greeks, then was the tug of war.   CLYTUS
The Rival Queens, Act 4, Scene 2

LELAND, Charles Godfrey, 1824–1903
68 Hans Breitmann gife a barty –
Where ish dat barty now?   *Hans Breitmann's Barty*

LENIN, Nikolai, 1870–1924
69 It is true that liberty is precious – so precious that it must be
rationed.   *Attributed*

LÉVIS, Duc de, 1764–1830

70 *Noblesse oblige.* Nobility imposes its own obligations. *Maximes et Réflexions*

LEYBOURNE, George, ?–1884

71 O, he flies through the air with the greatest of ease,
This daring young man on the flying trapeze.
The Man on the Flying Trapeze

LINCOLN, Abraham, 1809–1865

72 If the good people in their wisdom shall see fit to keep me in the background, I have been too familiar with disappointments to be very much chagrined. *Speech, 9 March 1832*

73 No man is good enough to govern another man without that other's consent. *Speech, 1854*

74 The ballot is stronger than the bullet. *Speech, 19 May, 1856*

75 We cannot be free men if this is, by our national choice, to be a land of slavery. Those who deny freedom to others, deserve it not for themselves. *Ib*

76 That is the issue that will continue in this country when these poor tongues of Judge Douglas and myself shall be silent. It is the eternal struggle between these two principles – right and wrong – throughout the world. They are the two principles that have stood face to face from the beginning of time, and will ever continue to struggle. *Speech, 15 Oct. 1858*

77 What is conservatism? Is it not adherence to the old and tried, against the new and untried? *Speech, 27 Feb. 1860*

78 I intend no modification of my oft-expressed personal wish that all men everywhere could be free.
Letter to Horace Greeley, 22 Aug. 1862

79 That this nation, under God, shall have a new birth of freedom; and that government of the people, by the people, and for the people, shall not perish from the earth. *Address at Dedication of National Cemetery, Gettysburg, 19 Nov. 1863*

80 An old Dutch farmer, who remarked to a companion once that it was not best to swap horses in mid-stream.
Speech, 9 June 1864

81 With malice toward none; with charity for all; with firmness in the right, as God gives us to see the right, – let us strive on to finish the work we are in: to bind up the nation's wounds; to care for him who shall have borne the battle, and for his widow

and his orphan; to do all which may achieve and cherish a just and lasting peace among ourselves, and with all nations.
Second Inaugural Address, 1865

82 You can fool some of the people all the time and all the people some of the time; but you can't fool all the people all the time.
Attributed

83 People who like this sort of thing will find this is the sort of thing they like. *Criticism of book*

LITVINOV, Maxim, 1876–1951

84 Peace is indivisible. *Speech, Geneva, 1 July 1936*

LIVY, 59 B.C.–A.D. 17

85 *Vae victis.* Woe to the vanquished. *History, 5, 48*

LLOYD, Marie, 1870–1922

86 A little of what you fancy does you good. *Song*
87 I'm one of the ruins that Cromwell knocked about a bit. *Song*
88 Oh, mister porter, what shall I do?
I wanted to go to Birmingham, but they've carried me on to Crewe. *Song, words by Thomas Le Brunn*

LLOYD, Robert, 1733–1764

89 Slow and steady wins the race. *The Hare and the Tortoise*

LLOYD GEORGE, David, 1st Earl, 1863–1945

90 What is our task? To make Britain a fit country for heroes to live in. *Speech, 24 Nov. 1918*

LONGFELLOW, Henry Wadsworth, 1807–1882

91 I shot an arrow into the air,
It fell to earth I knew not where. *The Arrow and the Song*

92 Thou, too, sail on, O Ship of State!
Sail on, O Union, strong and great!
Humanity with all its fears,
With all the hopes of future years
Is hanging breathless on thy fate! *The Building of the Ship*

93 The shades of night were falling fast,
As through an Alpine village passed
A youth, who bore, 'mid snow and ice,
A banner with the strange device,
Excelsior! *Excelsior*

94 A traveller, by the faithful hound,
   Half-buried in the snow was found.   *Excelsior*

95 Tell me not, in mournful numbers,
        Life is but an empty dream!
   For the soul is dead that slumbers,
        And things are not what they seem.

   Life is real! Life earnest!
        And the grave is not its goal;
   Dust thou art, to dust returnest,
        Was not spoken of the soul.   *A Psalm of Life*

96 Art is long, and Time is fleeting,
        And our hearts, though stout and brave,
   Still, like muffled drums, are beating
        Funeral marches to the grave.   *Ib*

97 Lives of great men all remind us
        We can make our lives sublime,
   And, departing, leave behind us
        Footprints on the sands of time.   *Ib*

98 Let us, then, be up and doing,
        With a heart for any fate,
   Still achieving, still pursuing,
        Learn to labour and to wait.   *Ib*

99 Though the mills of God grind slowly,
              yet they grind exceeding small;
   Though with patience He stands waiting,
              with exactness grinds He all.
                    Retribution (translation from von Logau)

1 'Wouldst thou' – so the helmsman answered, –
        'Learn the secret of the sea?
   Only those who brave its dangers
        Comprehend its mystery.'   *The Secret of the Sea*

2 From the waterfall he named her,
   Minnehaha, Laughing Water.   *The Song of Hiawatha, 4*

3 As unto the bow the cord is,
   So unto the man is woman,
   Though she bends him, she obeys him,
   Though she draws him, yet she follows,
   Useless each without the other!   *Ib, 10*

4 Ships that pass in the night, and speak each other in passing,
   Only a signal shown and a distant voice in the darkness;
   So on the ocean of life we pass and speak one another,
   Only a look and a voice, then darkness again and a silence.
        Tales of a Wayside Inn, 3, The Theologian's Tale

5 There was a little girl
  Who had a little curl
  Right in the middle of her forehead,
  And when she was good,
  She was very, very good,
  But when she was bad she was horrid.   *There was a Little Girl*

6 Under a spreading chestnut-tree
    The village smithy stands;
  The smith, a mighty man is he,
    With large and sinewy hands.   *The Village Blacksmith*

7   He earns whate'er he can,
  And looks the whole world in the face,
    For he owes not any man.   *Ib*

8 Something attempted, something done
    Has earned a night's repose.   *Ib*

9 It was the schooner Hesperus,
    That sailed the wintry sea;
  And the skipper had taken his little daughter,
    To bear him company.   *The Wreck of the Hesperus*

LOOS, Anita, 1893–

10 Gentlemen Prefer Blondes.   *Title of Book*

11 Kissing your hand may make you feel very very good but a
   diamond and safire bracelet lasts forever.   *Gentlemen Prefer
                                                   Blondes, Ch. 4*

LOUIS XIV of France, 1638–1715

12 *L'État c'est moi.* I am the State.   *Attributed*

13 *Il n'y a plus de Pyrénées.* The Pyrenees no longer exist.
                                                    Attributed

LOUIS XVIII of France, 1755–1824

14 *L'exactitude est la politesse des rois.* Punctuality is the politeness
   of kings.   *Attributed*

LOVELACE, Richard, 1618–1658

15 Stone walls do not a prison make,
     Nor iron bars a cage.   *To Althea, from Prison*

16 Tell me not, sweet, I am unkind,
     That from the nunnery
   Of thy chaste breast, and quiet mind,
     To war and arms I fly.   *To Lucasta, Going to the Wars*

17 I could not love thee, Dear, so much,
  Loved I not Honour more.   *To Lucasta, Going to the Wars*

LOVELL, Maria Anne, 1803–1877

18 Two souls with but a single thought,
  Two hearts that beat as one.   *Ingomar the Barbarian*
  (translated from German)

LOVER, Samuel, 1797–1868

19 When once the itch of literature comes over a man, nothing can
  cure it but the scratching of a pen.   *Handy Andy, Ch. 36*

LOWELL, James Russell, 1819–1891

20 An' you've got to get up airly
  Ef you want to take in God.   *The Biglow Papers, 1st*
  series, No. 1

21 I *don't* believe in princerple,
  But O, I *du* in interest.   *Ib, No. 6*

22 No man is born into the world, whose work
  Is not born with him; there is always work,
  And tools to work withal, for those who will:
  And blessed are the horny hands of toil!   *A Glance Behind*
  the Curtain, 201

23 The birch, most shy and ladylike of trees.   *An Indian Summer*
  Reverie

24 Once to every man and nation comes the moment to decide,
  In the strife of Truth with Falsehood, for the good or evil side.
      The Present Crisis

25 And what is so rare as a day in June?
  Then, if ever, come perfect days;
  Then Heaven tries earth if it be in tune,
  And over it softly her warm ear lays.   *The Vision of Sir*
  Launfal, Part 1, Prelude

26 A wise scepticism is the first attribute of a good critic.
      Among My Books, Shakespeare Once More

27 There is no good in arguing with the inevitable. The only argument available with an east wind is to put on your overcoat.
      Democracy and Addresses

LUTHER, Martin, 1483–1546

28 *Wer nicht liebt Wein, Weib und Gesang,*
  Der bleibt ein Narr sein Lebelang.
  Who loves not wine, woman and song,
  Remains a fool his whole life long.   *Attributed*

LYLY, John, 1554?–1606

29 Cupid and my Campaspe play'd
    At cards for kisses – Cupid paid.   *Campaspe, 3, 5*

30 O Love! has she done this to thee?
    What shall, alas! become of me?   *Ib*

LYTE, Henry Francis, 1793–1847

31 Abide with me; fast falls the eventide;
    The darkness deepens; Lord, with me abide!
    When other helpers fail, and comforts flee,
    Help of the helpless, O abide with me.   *Abide with Me*

32 Change and decay in all around I see;
    O thou who changest not, abide with me.   *Ib*

33 I fear no foe with thee at hand to bless;
    Ills have no weight, and tears no bitterness.
    Where is death's sting? where, grave, thy victory?
    I triumph still, if thou abide with me.   *Ib*

34 Praise my soul, the King of Heaven;
    To his feet thy tribute bring.   *Praise, my soul, the King of*
                                              Heaven

LYTTON, 1st Earl of, see MEREDITH, Owen

MACAULAY, Thomas Babington, 1st Baron, 1800–1859

35 Lars Porsena of Clusium
    By the Nine Gods he swore
    That the great house of Tarquin
    Would suffer wrong no more.   *Lays of Ancient Rome,*
                                          Horatius, 1

36 And how can man die better
    Than facing fearful odds,
    For the ashes of his fathers,
    And the temples of his Gods?   *Ib, 27*

37 Now who will stand on either hand,
    And keep the bridge with me?   *Ib, 29*

38 Then none was for a party;
    Then all were for the state.   *Ib, 32*

39 But those behind cried 'Forward!'
    And those before cried 'Back!'   *Ib, 50*

40 Oh, Tiber! father Tiber!
    To whom the Romans pray,
    A Roman's life, a Roman's arms,
    Take thou in charge this day!   *Ib, 59*

41 And even the ranks of Tuscany
Could scarce forbear to cheer. *Lays of Ancient Rome,*
Horatius, 60

42 Every schoolboy knows who imprisoned Montezuma, and who
strangled Atahualpa. *Essay in Edinburgh Review, Lord Clive*

43 The English Bible, a book which, if everything else in our
language should perish, would alone suffice to show the whole
extent of its beauty and power. *Ib, On John Dryden*

44 The gallery in which the reporters sit has become a fourth estate
of the realm. *Ib, Hallam's Constitutional History*

45 The history of England is emphatically the history of progress.
Ib, Sir J. Mackintosh's History of the Revolution

46 We know of no spectacle so ridiculous as the British public in
one of its periodical fits of morality. *Ib, Moore's Life of Lord*
Byron

47 The Puritan hated bear-baiting, not because it gave pain to the
bear, but because it gave pleasure to the spectators.
History of England, Ch. 2

McCRAE, John, 1872–1918

48 In Flanders fields the poppies blow
Between the crosses, row on row. *In Flanders Fields*

49 If ye break faith with us who die
We shall not sleep, though poppies grow
In Flanders fields. *Ib*

MACDONALD, George, 1824–1905

50 Here lie I, Martin Elginbrodde:
Hae mercy o' my soul, Lord God;
As I wad do, were I Lord God,
And ye were Martin Elginbrodde. *David Elginbrod, Book 1,*
Ch. 13

MACMAHON, Maurice de, 1808–1893

51 *J'y suis, j'y reste.* Here I am, and here I stay. *Attributed at*
taking of Malakoff, 1855

MACMILLAN, Harold, 1894–

52 Most of our people have never had it so good. Go around the
country – go to the industrial towns, go to the farms – and you
will see a state of prosperity such as we have never had in my
lifetime, or indeed ever in the history of this country.
Speech, Bedford Football Ground, 20 July 1957

53 The wind of change is blowing through the continent. Whether
we like it or not, this growth of national consciousness is a
political fact.   *Speech, South African
Parliament, Cape Town, 3 Feb. 1960*

MACNEICE, Louis, 1907–1963

54 It's no go the merrygoround, it's no go the rickshaw,
All we want is a limousine and a ticket for the peepshow.
                                        Bagpipe Music

55 It's no go my honey love, it's no go my poppet;
Work your hands from day to day, the winds will blow the
    profit.
The glass is falling hour by hour, the glass will fall for ever,
But if you break the bloody glass you won't hold up the weather.
                                                        Ib

56 Between the enormous fluted Ionic columns
There seeps from heavily jowled or hawk-like foreign faces
The guttural sorrow of the refugees.   *The British Museum
                                        Reading Room*

57 Time was away and somewhere else,
There were two glasses and two chairs
And two people with one pulse
(Somebody stopped the moving stairs):
Time was away and somewhere else.   *Meeting Point*

MAISTRE, Joseph de, 1754–1821

58 *Toute nation a le gouvernement qu'elle mérite.* Every nation has
the government it deserves.   *Letter about Russia, 1811*

MALLET, David, 1705?–1765

59 O grant me, Heaven, a middle state,
Neither too humble nor too great;
More than enough, for nature's ends,
With something left to treat my friends.   *Imitation of Horace*

MANDALE, W. R., 19th century

60 Up and down the City Road,
In and out the Eagle,
That's the way the money goes –
Pop goes the weasel!   *Pop Goes the Weasel*

MANNERS, Lord John, see RUTLAND, 7th Duke of

MARIE-ANTOINETTE, Queen of France, 1755–1793

61 *Qu'ils mangent de la brioche*. Let them eat cake.   *Attributed*
    (Similar phrases date back to thirteenth century)

MARLOWE, Christopher, 1564–1593

62 What doctrine call you this, *Che sera, sera,*
    What will be, shall be? FAUSTUS   *Doctor Faustus*

63 Was this the face that launch'd a thousand ships
    And burnt the topless towers of Ilium?
    Sweet Helen, make me immortal with a kiss.
    Her lips suck forth my soul: see, where it flies!
    Come, Helen, come, give me my soul again.
    Here will I dwell, for heaven is in these lips,
    And all is dross that is not Helena. FAUSTUS   *Ib*

64 O, thou art fairer than the evening air
    Clad in the beauty of a thousand stars. FAUSTUS   *Ib*

65 Now hast thou but one bare hour to live,
    And then thou must be damn'd perpetually!
    Stand still, you ever-moving spheres of heaven,
    That time may cease, and midnight never come. FAUSTUS *Ib*

66 Ugly hell, gape not! come not, Lucifer!
    I'll burn my books! FAUSTUS   *Ib*

67 Cut is the branch that might have grown full straight,
    And burned is Apollo's laurel-bough,
    That sometime grew within this learned man. CHORUS   *Ib*

68 My men, like satyrs grazing on the lawns,
    Shall with their goat-feet dance an antic hay. GAVESTON
    Edward the Second

69 I count religion but a childish toy,
    And hold there is no sin but ignorance. MACHIAVEL *The Jew*
    of Malta, Prologue

70 And, as their wealth increaseth, so inclose
    Infinite riches in a little room. BARABAS   *Ib, Act 1*

71 FRIAR BARNARDINE: Thou hast committed –
    BARABAS: Fornication: but that was in another
                      country;
                      And beside the wench is dead. *Ib, Act 4*

72 Jigging veins of rhyming mother-wits. *Tamburlaine the Great,*
    Part 1, Prologue

73 Zenocrate, lovelier than the love of Jove,
    Brighter than is the silver Rhodope,
    Fairer than whitest snow on Scythian hills. TAMBURLAINE
    Ib, Act 1, Scene 2

74 Accurs'd be he that first invented war. MYCETES
Tamburlaine the Great, Act 2, Scene 4

75 Is it not passing brave to be a king,
And ride in triumph through Persepolis? TAMBURLAINE
Ib, Act 2, Scene 5

76 Nature, that fram'd us of four elements
Warring within our breasts for regiment,
Doth teach us all to have aspiring minds:
Our souls, whose faculties can comprehend
The wondrous architecture of the world,
And measure every wandering planet's course,
Still climbing after knowledge infinite,
And always moving as the restless spheres,
Will us to wear ourselves, and never rest,
Until we reach the ripest fruit of all,
That perfect bliss and sole felicity,
The sweet fruition of an earthly crown. TAMBURLAINE
Ib, Act 2, Scene 7

77 Ah, fair Zenocrate! – divine Zenocrate!
Fair is too foul an epithet for thee. TAMBURLAINE *Ib, Act 5,*
Scene 1

78 Holla, ye pamper'd jades of Asia!
What, can ye draw but twenty miles a-day? TAMBURLAINE
Ib, Part 2, Act 4, Scene 3

79 Tamburlaine, the scourge of God, must die. TAMBURLAINE
Ib, Act 5, Scene 3

80 It lies not in our power to love or hate,
For will in us is over-rul'd by fate. *Hero and Leander*

81 Where both deliberate, the love is slight:
Who ever lov'd, that lov'd not at first sight? *Ib*

82 Come live with me, and be my love;
And we will all the pleasures prove
That hills and valleys, dales and fields,
Woods or steepy mountain yields. *The Passionate Shepherd*
to his Love

MARQUIS, Donald Robert, 1878–1937

83 its cheerio
my dearie that
pulls a lady through *archy and mehitabel, cheerio my deario*

84 toujours gai archy
toujours gai *Ib*

85   so unlucky
that he runs into accidents
which started out to happen
to somebody else   *archy's life of mehitabel, archy says*

MARRYAT, Frederick, 1792–1848

86 If you please, ma'am, it was a very little one. [*The Nurse: Of her illegitimate baby*]   *Midshipman Easy, Ch. 3*

87 I never knows the children. It's just six of one and half-a-dozen of the other.   *The Pirate, Ch. 4*

88 Every man paddle his own canoe.   *Settlers in Canada, Ch. 8*

MARVELL, Andrew, 1621–1678

89 Where the remote Bermudas ride,
In the ocean's bosom unespied.   *Bermudas, 1*

90 Echo beyond the Mexique Bay.   *Ib, 36*

91 And all the way, to guide their chime,
With falling oars they kept the time.   *Ib, 39*

92 Had we but world enough, and time,
This coyness, lady, were no crime.   *To his Coy Mistress, 1*

93 My vegetable love should grow
Vaster than empires and more slow.   *Ib, 11*

94 But at my back I always hear
Time's winged chariot hurrying near;
And yonder all before us lie
Deserts of vast eternity.   *Ib, 21*

95 The grave's a fine and private place,
But none, I think, do there embrace.   *Ib, 31*

96 Thus, though we cannot make our sun
Stand still, yet we will make him run.   *Ib, 45*

97 My love is of a birth as rare
As 'tis, for object, strange and high;
It was begotten by Despair
Upon Impossibility.   *The Definition of Love, 1*

98 Therefore the love which us doth bind,
But fate so enviously debars,
Is the conjunction of the mind,
And opposition of the stars.   *Ib, 29*

99 Annihilating all that's made
To a green thought in a green shade.   *The Garden, 47*

1 Casting the body's vest aside,
My soul into the boughs does glide.   *Ib, 51*

2 So restless Cromwell could not cease
In the inglorious arts of peace.   *An Horatian Ode upon*
     Cromwell's Return from Ireland, 9

3 He nothing common did or mean,
  Upon that memorable scene.
    But with his keener eye
    The axe's edge did try. [*Charles I*]   *Ib, 57*

4 Who can foretell for what high cause
This darling of the Gods was born?   *The Picture of Little*
    T.C. in a Prospect of Flowers, 9

5 Gather the flowers, but spare the buds.   *Ib, 35*

MARX, Karl, 1818–1883

6 From each according to his abilities, to each according to his
needs.   *Criticism of the Gotha Programme*

7 Religion . . . is the opium of the people.   *Criticism of the*
    Hegelian Philosophy of Right, Introduction

8 The ruling ideas of each age have ever been the ideas of its
ruling class.   *Manifesto of the Communist Party, 2*

9 The workers have nothing to lose but their chains. They have a
world to gain. Workers of the world, unite.   *Ib, 4*

MARY TUDOR, Queen of England, 1516–1558

10 When I am dead and opened, you shall find 'Calais' lying in my
heart.   *Holinshed's Chronicles, 3, 1160*

MASEFIELD, John, 1878–1967

11 But the loveliest things of beauty God ever has showed to me,
Are her voice, and her hair, and eyes, and the dear red curve of
her lips.   *Beauty*

12 Quinquireme of Nineveh from distant Ophir
Rowing home to haven in sunny Palestine,
With a cargo of ivory,
And apes and peacocks,
Sandalwood, cedarwood, and sweet white wine.   *Cargoes*

13 Dirty British coaster with a salt-caked smoke-stack
Butting through the Channel in the mad March days.   *Ib*

14 I must down to the seas again, to the lonely sea and the sky,
And all I ask is a tall ship and a star to steer her by.
    Sea Fever

15 I must down to the seas again, for the call of the running tide
Is a wild call and a clear call that may not be denied.   *Ib*

16 I must down to the seas again, to the vagrant gypsy life,
   To the gull's way and the whale's way where the wind's like a
      whetted knife;
   And all I ask is a merry yarn from a laughing fellow-rover,
   And quiet sleep and a sweet dream when the long trick's over.
                                                      Sea Fever

17 It is good to be out on the road, and going one knows not
      where,
   Going through meadow and village, one knows not whither nor
   why.   *Tewkesbury Road*

MASSINGER, Philip, 1583–1640

18 He that would govern others, first should be
   The master of himself.   *The Bondman, Act 1, Scene 3*

19 A New Way to Pay Old Debts.   *Title of Play*

MAUGHAM, William Somerset, 1874–1965

20 People ask you for criticism, but they only want praise.
                                        Of Human Bondage, Ch. 50

21 Impropriety is the soul of wit.   *The Moon and Sixpence, Ch. 4*

22 I would sooner read a time-table or a catalogue than nothing at
   all. They are much more entertaining than half the novels that
   are written.   *The Summing Up*

23 Life is too short to do anything for oneself that one can pay
   others to do for one.   *Ib*

MEARNS, Hughes, 1875–1965

24 As I was going up the stair
   I met a man who wasn't there.
   He wasn't there again today.
   I wish, I wish he'd stay away.   *The Psychoed*

MELBOURNE, William Lamb, 2nd Viscount, 1779–1848

25 I like the Garter; there is no damned merit in it.
                                    On the Order of the Garter

26 Things have come to a pretty pass when religion is allowed to
   invade the sphere of private life.   *Attributed*

27 I wish that I was as cocksure of anything as Tom Macaulay is of
   everything.   *Attributed*

MENCKEN, Henry Louis, 1880–1956

28 All successful newspapers are ceaselessly querulous and bellicose.
   They never defend anyone or anything if they can help it; if the

job is forced upon them, they tackle it by denouncing someone
or something else. *Prejudices, First Series*

29 The average schoolmaster is and always must be essentially an
ass, for how can one imagine an intelligent man engaging in so
puerile an avocation? *Ib, Third Series*

30 I've made it a rule never to drink by daylight and never to
refuse a drink after dark. *Quoted in New York Post,*
18 Sept. 1945

MEREDITH, George, 1828–1909

31 Cynicism is intellectual dandyism. *The Egoist, Ch. 7*

32 The actors are, it seems, the usual three:
Husband, and wife, and lover. *Modern Love, Stanza 25*

33   We'll sit contentedly
And eat our pot of honey on the grave. *Ib, Stanza 29*

34 Ah, what a dusty answer gets the soul
When hot for certainties in this our life! *Ib, Stanza 50*

35 I expect that Woman will be the last thing civilized by Man.
The Ordeal of Richard Feverel, Ch. 1

36 Kissing don't last: cookery do! *Ib, Ch. 28*

MEREDITH, Owen (Earl of Lytton), 1831–1891

37 Genius does what it must, and Talent does what it can.
Last Words of a Sensitive Second-rate Poet

MERRITT, Dixon Lanier, 1879–1954

38 A wonderful bird is the pelican,
His beak holds more than his belican.
   He can take in his beak
   Enough food for a week,
But I'm damned if I know how the helican! *The Pelican*

MIKES, George, 1912–

39 On the Continent people have good food; in England people
have good table manners. *How to be an Alien*

40 Continental people have sex life; the English have hot-water
bottles. *Ib*

41 An Englishman, even if he is alone, forms an orderly queue of
one. *Ib*

MILL, John Stuart, 1806–1873

42 All good things which exist are the fruits of originality.
On Liberty, Ch. 3

43 The worth of a State in the long run is the worth of the individuals composing it. *On Liberty, Ch. 3*

44 That so few now dare to be eccentric marks the chief danger of
the time. *Ib*

MILLAY, Edna St Vincent, 1892–1950

45 My candle burns at both ends;
    It will not last the night;
But, oh, my foes, and oh, my friends –
    It gives a lovely light. *Figs from Thistles, First Fig*

46 What lips my lips have kissed, and where, and why,
I have forgotten, and what arms have lain
Under my head till morning; but the rain
Is full of ghosts tonight, that tap and sigh
Upon the glass and listen for reply. *Sonnet, What Lips My
Lips Have Kissed*

47 I only know that summer sang in me
A little while, that in me sings no more. *Ib*

MILLIGAN, Spike, 1918–

48 'Do you come here often?'
'Only in the mating season.' *BBC programme, The Goon
Show, with Spike Milligan, Harry Secombe and
Peter Sellers*

MILNE, Alan Alexander, 1882–1956

49 The more it snows
    (Tiddely pom),
The more it goes
    (Tiddely pom),
The more it goes
    (Tiddely pom),
  On snowing.
And nobody knows
    (Tiddely pom),
How cold my toes
    (Tiddely pom),
How cold my toes
    (Tiddely pom),
Are growing. POOH *The House at Pooh Corner, Ch. 1*

50 Tiggers don't like honey. TIGGER *Ib, Ch. 2*

51 'Climbing trees is what they do best,' said Tigger. 'Much better
than Poohs.' *Ib, Ch. 4*

52 King John was not a good man –
   He had his little ways.   *Now We are Six, King John's*
                                                    Christmas

53 No one can tell me,
   Nobody knows,
Where the wind comes from,
   Where the wind goes.   *Ib, Wind on the Hill*

54 They're changing guard at Buckingham Palace –
Christopher Robin went down with Alice.
Alice is marrying one of the guard.
'A soldier's life is terrible hard,'
         Says Alice.   *When We Were Very*
                          Young, Buckingham Palace

55 'Do you think the King knows all about me?'
'Sure to, dear, but it's time for tea,'
         Says Alice.   *Ib*

56 James James
Morrison Morrison
Weatherby George Dupree
Took great
Care of his Mother,
Though he was only three.   *Ib, Disobedience*

57 You must never go down to the end of the town, if you don't go
down with me.   *Ib*

58 *What* is the matter with Mary Jane?
I've promised her sweets and a ride in the train,
And I've begged her to stop for a bit and explain –
What *is* the matter with Mary Jane?   *Ib, Rice Pudding*

59 The King asked
The Queen, and
The Queen asked
The Dairymaid:
'Could we have some butter for
The Royal slice of bread?'   *Ib, The King's Breakfast*

60 I do like a little bit of butter to my bread!   *Ib*

61 Little Boy kneels at the foot of the bed,
Droops on the little hands little gold head.
Hush! Hush! Whisper who dares!
Christopher Robin is saying his prayers,   *Ib, Vespers*

62 Isn't it funny
How a bear likes honey?

Buzz! Buzz! Buzz!

I wonder why he does?   *Winnie-the-Pooh, Ch. 1*

63 'Well', said Owl, 'the customary procedure in such cases is as
follows.'

'What does Crustimoney Proseedcake mean?' said Pooh. 'For I
am a Bear of Very Little Brain, and long words Bother me.'

Ib, Ch. 4

64 Eeyore, the old grey Donkey, stood by the side of the stream, and
looked at himself in the water.

'Pathetic,' he said. 'That's wat it is, Pathetic.'   *Ib, Ch. 6*

65 Cottleston, Cottleston, Cottleston Pie.

A fly can't bird, but a bird can fly.

Ask me a riddle and I reply:

'*Cottleston, Cottleston, Cottleston Pie*.'   POOH   *Ib*

66 Time for a little something.   POOH   *Ib*

67 My spelling is Wobbly. It's good spelling but it Wobbles, and
letters get in the wrong places.   POOH   *Ib*

68 A Useful Pot to put things in.   POOH   *Ib*

69 Sing Ho! for the life of a Bear.   POOH   *Ib, Ch. 8*

70 3 Cheers for Pooh!

(For Who?)

For Pooh –

(Why What did he do?)

I thought you knew;

He saved his friend from a wetting.   ANXIOUS POOH SONG

Ib, Ch. 10

MILTON, John, 1608–1674

71 Blest pair of Sirens, pledges of Heaven's joy,

Sphere-born harmonious sisters, Voice and Verse.

At a Solemn Music, 1

72 Before the starry threshold of Jove's court

My mansion is.   ATTENDANT SPIRIT.   *Comus: A Mask, 1*

73 Above the smoke and stir of this dim spot

Which men call Earth.   ATTENDANT SPIRIT   *Ib, 5*

74 What hath night to do with sleep?   COMUS   *Ib, 122*

75 Come, knit hands, and beat the ground

In a light fantastic round.   COMUS   *Ib, 143*

76 'Tis chastity, my brother, chastity:

She that has that, is clad in complete steel.   ELDER BROTHER

Ib, 420

77 How charming is divine Philosophy!
   Not harsh and crabbed, as dull fools suppose.
   But musical as is Apollo's lute,
   And a perpetual feast of nectared sweets,
   Where no crude surfeit reigns.   SECOND BROTHER
                                        Comus: A Mask, 476

78   That power
      Which erring men call Chance.   ELDER BROTHER   *Ib, 587*

79 Beauty is Nature's coin; must not be hoarded,
   But must be current.   COMUS   *Ib, 739*

80 Sabrina fair,
      Listen where thou art sitting
   Under the glassy, cool, translucent wave,
      In twisted braids of lilies knitting
   The loose train of thy amber-dropping hair.
                              ATTENDANT SPIRIT   *Ib, 859*

81   Mortals, that would follow me,
   Love Virtue, she alone is free.
   She can teach ye how to climb
   Higher than the sphery chime;
   Or, if Virtue feeble were,
   Heaven itself would stoop to her.   ATTENDANT SPIRIT   *Ib, 1018*

82 Hence, vain deluding Joys,
      The brood of Folly without father bred!   *Il Penseroso, 1*

83 But, hail! thou Goddess sage and holy
   Hail, divinest Melancholy!   *Ib, 11*

84 Thy rapt soul sitting in thine eyes.   *Ib, 40*

85 Sweet bird, that shunn'st the noise of folly,
   Most musical, most melancholy!   *Ib, 61*

86 Where glowing embers through the room
   Teach light to counterfeit a gloom,
   Far from all resort of mirth,
   Save the cricket on the hearth.   *Ib, 79*

87 Where more is meant than meets the ear.   *Ib, 120*

88 And storied windows richly dight,
   Casting a dim religious light.   *Ib, 159*

89 Till old experience do attain
   To something like prophetic strain.   *Ib, 173*

90 These pleasures, Melancholy, give;
   And I with thee will choose to live.   *Ib, 175*

91 Hence, loathed Melancholy,
      Of Cerberus and blackest Midnight born

In Stygian cave forlorn
'Mongst horrid shapes, and shrieks, and sights unholy!
L'Allegro, 1

92 So buxom, blithe, and debonair. *Ib, 24*

93 Haste thee, Nymph, and bring with thee
Jest, and youthful Jollity,
Quips and Cranks and wanton Wiles,
Nods and Becks and wreathed Smiles. *Ib, 25*

94 Sport that wrinkled Care derides,
And Laughter holding both his sides.
Come, and trip it as you go
On the light fantastic toe. *Ib, 31*

95 The mountain-nymph, sweet Liberty. *Ib, 36*

96 And, if I give thee honour due,
Mirth, admit me of thy crew,
To live with her, and live with thee,
In unreproved pleasures free. *Ib, 37*

97 To hear the lark begin his flight,
And, singing, startle the dull night,
From his watch-tower in the skies,
Till the dappled dawn doth rise;
Then to come, in spite of sorrow,
And at my window bid good morrow
Through the sweet-briar or the vine,
Or the twisted eglantine. *Ib, 41*

98 While the ploughman, near at hand,
Whistles o'er the furrowed land,
And the milkmaid singeth blithe,
And the mower whets his scythe,
And every shepherd tells his tale
Under the hawthorn in the dale. *Ib, 63*

99 Then to the spicy nut-brown ale. *Ib, 100*

1 Towered cities please us then,
And the busy hum of men. *Ib, 117*

2   Store of ladies, whose bright eyes
Rain influence, and judge the prize
Of wit or arms. *Ib, 121*

3 Such sights as youthful poets dream
On summer eves by haunted stream. *Ib, 129*

4 Or sweetest Shakespeare, Fancy's child,
Warble his native wood-notes wild. *Ib, 133*

5 Untwisting all the chains that tie
The hidden soul of harmony.   *L'Allegro, 143*

6 Such strains as would have won the ear
Of Pluto, to have quite set free
His half-regained Eurydice.   *Ib, 148*

7   These delights if thou canst give,
Mirth, with thee I mean to live.   *Ib, 151*

8 Yet once more, O ye laurels, and once more,
Ye myrtles brown, with ivy never sere,
I come to pluck your berries harsh and crude,
And with forced fingers rude
Shatter your leaves before the mellowing year.   *Lycidas, 1*

9   He knew
Himself to sing, and build the lofty rhyme.   *Ib, 10*

10   But, oh! the heavy change, now thou art gone,
Now thou art gone, and never must return!   *Ib, 37*

11   Alas! what boots it with incessant care
To tend the homely, slighted, shepherd's trade,
And strictly meditate the thankless Muse?   *Ib, 64*

12 To sport with Amaryllis in the shade,
Or with the tangles of Neaera's hair?   *Ib, 68*

13 Fame is the spur that the clear spirit doth raise
(That last infirmity of noble mind)
To scorn delights, and live laborious days.   *Ib, 70*

14 Fame is no plant that grows on mortal soil.   *Ib, 78*

15 Blind mouths! that scarce themselves know how to hold
A sheep-hook.   *Ib, 119*

16 And, when they list, their lean and flashy songs
Grate on their scrannel pipes of wretched straw;
The hungry sheep look up, and are not fed,
But, swoln with wind and the rank mist they draw,
Rot inwardly, and foul contagion spread.   *Ib, 123*

17 Bring the rathe primrose that forsaken dies.   *Ib, 142*

18 At last he rose, and twitched his mantle blue:
To-morrow to fresh woods, and pastures new.   *Ib, 192*

19 This is the month, and this the happy morn.   *On the Morning
of Christ's Nativity, 1*

20 It was the winter wild,
While the Heaven-born Child
All meanly wrapt in the rude manger lies.   *Ib, 29*

21 Time will run back and fetch the age of gold.   *Ib, 135*

22 So when the sun in bed,
  Curtained with cloudy red,
    Pillows his chin upon an orient wave.
        On the Morning of Christ's Nativity, 229

23 What needs my Shakespeare for his honoured bones,
  The labour of an age in piled stones?   *On Shakespeare, 1*

24 Dear son of memory, great heir of fame,
  What need'st thou such weak witness of thy name?   *Ib, 5*

25 Kings for such a tomb would wish to die.   *Ib, 16*

26 Rhyme being no necessary adjunct or true ornament of poems
  or good verse, in longer works especially, but the invention of a
  barbarous age, to set off wretched matter and lame metre.
        Paradise Lost, Preface, The Verse

27 Of Man's first disobedience, and the fruit
  Of that forbidden tree, whose mortal taste
  Brought death into the World, and all our woe,
  With loss of Eden, till one greater Man
  Restore us, and regain the blissful seat,
  Sing, Heavenly Muse.   *Ib, Book 1, 1*

28 Things unattempted yet in prose or rhyme.   *Ib, 1, 16*

29   What in me is dark
  Illumine, what is low raise and support;
  That, to the height of this great argument,
  I may assert Eternal Providence,
  And justify the ways of God to men.   *Ib, 1, 22*

30   What though the field be lost?
  All is not lost – the unconquerable will,
  And study of revenge, immortal hate,
  And courage never to submit or yield:
  And what is else not to be overcome?   *Ib, 1, 105*

31   To be weak is miserable,
  Doing or suffering.   *Ib, 1, 157*

32 And out of good still to find means of evil.   *Ib, 1, 165*

33 What reinforcement we may gain from hope,
  If not, what resolution from despair.   *Ib, 1, 190*

34   Farewell, happy fields,
  Where joy for ever dwells! Hail, horrors! hail.   *Ib, 1, 249*

35 A mind not to be changed by place or time.
  The mind is its own place, and in itself
  Can make a Heaven of Hell, a Hell of Heaven.   *Ib, 1, 253*

36 To reign is worth ambition, though in Hell:
  Better to reign in Hell than serve in Heaven.   *Ib, 1, 262*

37 Awake, arise, or be for ever fallen!   *Ib, 1, 330*

38   And when night
Darkens the streets, then wander forth the sons
Of Belial, flown with insolence and wine.   *Paradise Lost,*
                                                                       Book 1, 500

39 Th' imperial ensign; which, full high advanced,
Shone like a meteor streaming to the wind.   *Ib, 1, 536*

40 A shout that tore Hell's concave, and beyond
Frighted the reign of Chaos and old Night.   *Ib, 1, 542*

41   His form had yet not lost
All her original brightness, nor appeared
Less than Archangel ruined, and the excess
Of glory obscured.   *Ib, 1, 591*

42 Tears, such as Angels weep, burst forth.   *Ib, 1, 620*

43   Who overcomes
By force hath overcome but half his foe.   *Ib, 1, 648*

44   From morn
To noon he fell, from noon to dewy eve,
A summer's day, and with the setting sun
Dropped from the zenith, like a falling star.   *Ib, 1, 742*

45 High on a throne of royal state, which far
Outshone the wealth of Ormus and of Ind,
Or where the gorgeous East with richest hand
Showers on her kings barbaric pearl and gold,
Satan exalted sat, by merit raised
To that bad eminence.   *Ib, Book 2, 1*

46 My sentence is for open war. Of wiles,
More unexpert, I boast not.   *Ib, 2, 51*

47   In our proper motion we ascend
Up to our native seat; descent and fall
To us is adverse.   *Ib, 2, 75*

48   Though his tongue
Dropped manna, and could make the worse appear
The better reason.   *Ib, 2, 112*

49   For who would lose,
Though full of pain, this intellectual being,
Those thoughts that wander through eternity,
To perish rather, swallowed up and lost
In the wide womb of uncreated Night,
Devoid of sense and motion?   *Ib, 2, 146*

50 Unrespited, unpitied, unreprieved,
Ages of hopeless end.   *Ib, 2, 185*

51 Our torments also may, in length of time,
Become our elements.   *Ib, 2, 274*

52   With grave
Aspect he rose, and in his rising seemed
A pillar of state; deep on his front engraven
Deliberation sat, and public care;
And princely counsel in his face yet shone,
Majestic, though in ruin.   *Paradise Lost, Book 2, 300*

53   Another World, the happy seat
Of some new race, called Man, about this time
To be created like to us, though less
In power and excellence.   *Ib, 2, 347*

54   Long is the way
And hard that out of Hell leads up to light.   *Ib, 2, 432*

55 Others apart sat on a hill retired,
In thoughts more elevate, and reasoned high
Of Providence, Foreknowledge, Will, and Fate –
Fixed fate, free will, foreknowledge absolute –
And found no end, in wandering mazes lost.   *Ib, 2, 557*

56   The other Shape –
If shape it might be called that shape had none.   *Ib, 2, 666*

57 For Hot, Cold, Moist, and Dry, four champions fierce,
Strive here for mastery.   *Ib, 2, 898*

58 Hail, holy Light, Offspring of Heaven first-born! *Ib, Book 3, 1*

59   Thus with the year
Seasons return; but not to me returns
Day, or the sweet approach of even or morn,
Or sight of vernal bloom, or summer's rose,
Or flocks, or herds, or human face divine;
But clouds instead and ever-during dark
Surrounds me.   *Ib, 3, 40*

60 Into a Limbo large and broad, since called
The Paradise of Fools; to few unknown.   *Ib, 3, 495*

61   At whose sight all the stars
Hide their diminished heads.   *Ib, Book 4, 34*

62 Me miserable! which way shall I fly
Infinite wrath and infinite despair?
Which way I fly is Hell; myself am Hell;
And, in the lowest deep, a lower deep
Still threat'ning to devour me opens wide,
To which the Hell I suffer seems a Heaven.   *Ib, 4, 73*

63 So farewell hope, and, with hope, farewell fear,
Farewell remorse! All good to me is lost;
Evil, be thou my Good.   *Ib, 4, 180*

64 Thence up he flew, and on the Tree of Life
   The middle tree and highest there that grew,
   Sat like a cormorant.   *Paradise Lost, Book 4, 194*

65 A Heaven on Earth.   *Ib, 4, 208*

66 For contemplation he and valour formed,
   For softness she and sweet attractive grace;
   He for God only, she for God in him.   *Ib, 4, 297*

67 Adam, the goodliest man of men since born
   His sons; the fairest of her daughters Eve.   *Ib, 4, 323*

68 Imparadised in one another's arms.   *Ib, 4, 506*

69 Now came still Evening on, and Twilight grey
   Had in her sober livery all things clad.   *Ib, 4, 598*

70 God is thy law, thou mine: to know no more
   Is woman's happiest knowledge, and her praise.
   With thee conversing, I forget all time.   *Ib, 4, 637*

71 Hail, wedded Love, mysterious law, true source
   Of human offspring.   *Ib, 4, 750*

72 Not to know me argues yourselves unknown.   *Ib, 4, 830*

73   Abashed the Devil stood,
   And felt how awful goodness is, and saw
   Virtue in her shape how lovely.   *Ib, 4, 846*

74 But wherefore thou alone? Wherefore with thee
   Came not all Hell broke loose?   *Ib, 4, 917*

75 Now Morn, her rosy steps in th' eastern clime
   Advancing, sowed the earth with orient pearl. *Ib, Book 5, 1*

76   Good, the more
   Communicated, more abundant grows.   *Ib, 5, 71*

77 Best image of myself, and dearer half.   *Ib, 5, 95*

78 Him first, him last, him midst, and without end. *Ib, 5, 165*

79   Nor jealousy
   Was understood, the injured lover's hell.   *Ib, 5, 449*

80   Midnight brought on the dusky hour
   Friendliest to sleep and silence.   *Ib, 5, 667*

81 Among the faithless, faithful only he.   *Ib, 5, 897*

82 Servant of God, well done! Well hast thou fought
   The better fight, who single hast maintained
   Against revolted multitudes the cause
   Of truth, in word mightier than they in arms. *Ib, Book 6, 29*

83 More safe I sing with mortal voice, unchanged
   To hoarse or mute, though fallen on evil days,

On evil days though fallen, and evil tongues;
In darkness, and with dangers compassed round,
And solitude. *Paradise Lost, Book 7, 24*

84   God saw the light was good;
And light from darkness by the hemisphere
Divided: light the Day, and darkness Night,
He named. *Ib, 7, 249*

85 The Angel ended, and in Adam's ear
So charming left his voice that he a while
Thought him still speaking, still stood fixed to hear. *Ib, Book 8, 1*

86   To know
That which before us lies in daily life,
Is the prime wisdom. *Ib, 8, 192*

87   In solitude
What happiness? who can enjoy alone,
Or, all enjoying, what contentment find? *Ib, 8, 364*

88 Accuse not Nature! she hath done her part;
Do thou but thine. *Ib, 8, 561*

89 My unpremeditated verse. *Ib, Book 9, 24*

90 Since first this subject for heroic song
Pleased me, long choosing and beginning late. *Ib, 9, 25*

91   Revenge, at first though sweet,
Bitter ere long back on itself recoils. *Ib, 9, 171*

92 For solitude sometimes is best society,
And short retirement urges sweet return. *Ib, 9, 249*

93 As one who, long in populous city pent,
Where houses thick and sewers annoy the air. *Ib, 9, 445*

94 O fairest of creation, last and best
Of all God's works, creature in whom excelled
Whatever can to sight or thought be formed,
Holy, divine, good, amiable, or sweet!
How art thou lost! how on a sudden lost,
Defaced, deflowered, and now to death devote! *Ib, 9, 896*

95   Yet I shall temper so
Justice with mercy as may illustrate most
Them fully satisfied, and thee appease. *Ib, Book 10, 77*

96 A dismal universal hiss, the sound
Of public scorn. *Ib, 10, 508*

97 Demoniac frenzy, moping melancholy,
And moon-struck madness. *Ib, Book 11, 485*

98 Nor love thy life, nor hate; but what thou liv'st
Live well; how long or short permit to Heaven. *Ib, 11, 553*

99 A bevy of fair women, richly gay
   In gems and wanton dress.   *Paradise Lost, Book 11, 582*

 1 An olive-leaf he brings, pacific sign.   *Ib, 11, 860*

 2 In me is no delay; with thee to go
   Is to stay here; without thee here to stay
   Is to go hence unwilling; thou to me
   Art all things under Heaven, all places thou,
   Who for my wilful crime art banished hence. *Ib, Book 12, 615*

 3 The world was all before them, where to choose
   Their place of rest, and Providence their guide:
   They, hand in hand, with wandering steps and slow,
   Through Eden took their solitary way.   *Ib, 12, 646*

 4   Most men admire
   Virtue who follow not her lore. *Paradise Regained, Book 1*
                                    482

 5   Beauty stands
   In the admiration only of weak minds
   Led captive.   *Ib, Book 2, 220*

 6   The childhood shows the man,
   As morning shows the day.   *Ib, Book 4, 220*

 7 The first and wisest of them all professed
   To know this only, that he nothing knew.   *Ib, 4, 293*

 8 Deep-versed in books and shallow in himself.   *Ib, 4, 327*

 9   He, unobserved,
   Home to his mother's house private returned.   *Ib, 4, 638*

10 Let us with a gladsome mind,
   Praise the Lord, for He is kind,
     For His mercies ay endure,
     Ever faithful, ever sure.   *Paslm 136*

11 A little onward lend thy guiding hand
   To these dark steps, a little further on. SAMSON
                     Samson Agonistes, 1

12 Ask for this great deliverer now, and find him
   Eyeless in Gaza at the mill with slaves. SAMSON   *Ib, 40*

13 O dark, dark, dark, amid the blaze of noon,
   Irrecoverably dark, total eclipse,
   Without all hope of day! SAMSON   *Ib, 80*

14 The Sun to me is dark
   And silent as the Moon,
   When she deserts the night,
   Hid in her vacant interlunar cave. SAMSON   *Ib, 86*

15   Wisest men
Have erred, and by bad women been deceived. CHORUS
                    Samson Agonistes, 210

16 Just are the ways of God,
And justifiable to men,
Unless there be who think not God at all. CHORUS   *Ib, 293*

17   Let me here,
As I deserve, pay on my punishment,
And expiate, if possible, my crime,
Shameful garrulity. SAMSON   *Ib, 488*

18   But who is this, what thing of sea or land?
Female of sex it seems,
That, so bedecked, ornate, and gay,
Comes this way sailing,
Like a stately ship
Of Tarsus, bound for th' isles
Of Javan or Gadire,
With all her bravery on, and tackle trim,
Sails filled, and streamers waving,
Courted by all the winds that hold them play. CHORUS *Ib, 710*

19 Out, out, hyaena! These are thy wonted arts,
And arts of every woman false like thee. SAMSON   *Ib, 748*

20   Weakness is thy excuse,
And I believe it; weakness to resist
Philistian gold. SAMSON   *Ib, 829*

21   At length, that grounded maxim,
So rife and celebrated in the mouths
Of wisest men, that to the public good
Private respects must yield, with grave authority
Took full possession of me, and prevailed. DALILA   *Ib, 865*

22 In argument with men a woman ever
Goes by the worse, whatever be her cause. DALILA   *Ib, 903*

23 Fame, if not double-faced, is double-mouthed,
And with contrary blast proclaims most deeds. DALILA
          Ib, 971

24 Yet beauty, though injurious, hath strange power,
After offence returning, to regain
Love once possessed. CHORUS   *Ib, 1003*

25 He's gone, and who knows how he may report
Thy words by adding fuel to the flame? CHORUS   *Ib, 1350*

26 All is best, though we oft doubt
What th' unsearchable dispose
Of Highest Wisdom brings about. CHORUS   *Ib, 1745*

27 His servants he, with new acquist
   Of true experience from this great event,
   With peace and consolation hath dismissed,
   And calm of mind, all passion spent. CHORUS
                              Samson Agonistes, 1755

28 How soon hath Time, the subtle thief of youth,
      Stolen on his wing my three-and-twentieth year! *Sonnet, On*
                     being arrived at the age of twenty-three

29 When I consider how my light is spent
   Ere half my days in this dark world and wide,
   And that one talent which is death to hide
   Lodged with me useless.   *Sonnet, On his Blindness*

30   God doth not need
   Either man's work or his own gifts. Who best
   Bear his mild yoke, they serve him best: his state
   Is kingly: thousands at his bidding speed,
   And post o'er land and ocean without rest;
   They also serve who only stand and wait.   *Ib*

31 New Presbyter is but old Priest writ large. *Sonnet, On the new*
                  Forcers of Conscience under the Long Parliament

32   Peace hath her victories
   No less renowned than War.   *Sonnet, To the Lord General*
                                    Cromwell, May 1652

33 For what can war but endless war still breed? *Sonnet, On the*
                                    Lord General Fairfax

34 Fly envious Time, till thou run out thy race,
   Call on the lazy, leaden-stepping hours.   *Sonnet, On Time*

35 Methought I saw my late espoused saint.   *Sonnet, On his*
                                          deceased wife

36 He who would not be frustrate of his hope to write well hereafter in laudable things ought himself to be a true poem.
                              Apology for Smectymnuus

37 Who kills a man kills a reasonable creature, God's image; but he
   who destroys a good book, kills reason itself, kills the image of
   God, as it were in the eye.   *Areopagitica*

38 A good book is the precious life-blood of a master spirit,
   embalmed and treasured up on purpose to a life beyond life. *Ib*

39 I cannot praise a fugitive and cloistered virtue, unexercised and
   unbreathed, that never sallies out and sees her adversary, but
   slinks out of the race, where that immortal garland is to be run
   for, not without dust and heat.   *Ib*

40 Our sage and serious poet Spenser, whom I dare be known to
   think a better teacher than Scotus or Aquinas.   *Ib*

41 God sure esteems the growth and completing of one virtuous person more than the restraint of ten vicious. *Areopagitica*

42 God is decreeing to begin some new and great period in His Church, even to the reforming of Reformation itself: what does He then but reveal Himself to His servants, and as His manner is, first to His Englishmen? *Ib*

43 Methinks I see in my mind a noble and puissant nation rousing herself like a strong man after sleep, and shaking her invincible locks. Methinks I see her as an eagle mewing her mighty youth, and kindling her undazzled eyes at the full midday beam. *Ib*

44 Give me the liberty to know, to utter, and to argue freely according to conscience, above all liberties. *Ib*

45 Let her and Falsehood grapple; who ever knew Truth put to the worse, in a free and open encounter? *Ib*

46 None can love freedom heartily, but good men; the rest love not freedom, but licence. *Tenure of Kings and Magistrates*

MIRABEAU, Comte de, 1749–1791

47 *La guerre est l'industrie nationale de la Prusse.* War is the national industry of Prussia. *Attributed*

MOLIÈRE (Jean Baptiste Poquelin), 1622–1673

48 *Par ma foi! il y a plus de quarante ans que je dis de la prose sans que j'en susse rien.* M. JOURDAIN
Good heavens! I have been talking prose for over forty years without realizing it. *Le Bourgeois Gentilhomme, Act 2, Scene 4*

49 *C'est une folie à nulle autre seconde,*
De vouloir se mêler à corriger le monde. PHILINTE
It is a stupidity second to none, to want to busy oneself with the correction of the world. *Le Misanthrope, Act 1, Scène 1*

50 *Ah! pour être dévot, je n'en suis pas moins homme!* TARTUFFE
Oh, I may be devout, but I am human all the same. *Tartuffe, Act 3, Scene 3*

51 *La scandale du monde est ce qui fait l'offense,*
Et ce n'est pas pécher que pécher en silence. TARTUFFE
It is a public scandal that gives offence, and it is no sin to sin in secret. *Ib, Act 4, Scene 5*

MONKHOUSE, William Cosmo, 1840–1901

52 There was an old party of Lyme,
Who married three wives at one time.

When asked, 'Why the third?'
He replied, 'One's absurd,
And bigamy, sir, is a crime!'   *Limerick*

MONSELL, John Samuel Bewley, 1811–1875

53 Fight the good fight with all thy might,
Christ is thy strength, and Christ thy right;
Lay hold on life, and it shall be
Thy joy and crown eternally.   *Fight the Good Fight*

MONTAIGNE, Michel de, 1533–1592

54 The greatest thing in the world is to know how to be self-sufficient.   *Essays, 1, 39*

55 When I play with my cat, who knows whether she is not amusing herself with me more than I with her?   *Ib, 2, 12*

56 Marriage is like a cage; one sees the birds outside desperate to get in, and those inside equally desperate to get out.   *Ib, 3, 5*

57 It might well be said of me that here I have merely made up a bunch of other men's flowers, and provided nothing of my own but the string to tie them together.   *Ib, 3, 12*

MONTGOMERY OF ALAMEIN, Bernard Law, 1st Viscount, 1887–1976

58 Anyone who votes Labour ought to be locked up.   *Speech, Woodford, Essex, 1959*

MONTROSE, Percy, 19th century

59 In a cavern, in a canyon,
  Excavating for a mine,
Dwelt a miner, Forty-niner,
  And his daughter Clementine.
Oh my darling, oh my darling, oh my darling Clementine!
Thou art lost and gone for ever, dreadful sorry, Clementine.
                                             Clementine

60 Light she was and like a fairy,
  And her shoes were number nine;
Herring boxes, without topses,
  Sandals were for Clementine.   *Ib*

61 How I missed her, how I missed her.
  How I missed my Clementine!
But I kissed her little sister,
  And forgot my Clementine.   *Ib*

MOORE, Thomas, 1779–1852

62 The harp that once through Tara's halls
    The soul of music shed,
Now hangs as mute on Tara's walls,
    As if that soul were fled.   *Irish Melodies, The Harp that*
                                         once through Tara's Halls

63 'Tis the last rose of summer
    Left blooming alone;
All her lovely companions
    Are faded and gone.   *Ib, The Last Rose of Summer*

64 The Minstrel Boy to the war is gone,
    In the ranks of death you'll find him;
His father's sword he has girded on,
    And his wild harp slung behind him. *Ib, The Minstrel Boy*

65 'Come, Come,' said Tom's father, 'at your time of life,
    There's no longer excuse for thus playing the rake –
It is time you should think, boy, of taking a wife' –
    'Why, so it is, father – whose wife shall I take?'
                                       A Joke Versified

MORE, Sir Thomas, 1478–1535

66 I pray you, Master Lieutenant, see me safe up, and for coming
down let me shift for myself. [*On mounting the scaffold*]   *Roper,*
                                     Life of Sir Thomas More

67 Pluck up thy spirits, man, and be not afraid to do thine office;
my neck is very short; take heed therefore thou strike not awry,
for saving of thine honesty. [*To the executioner*]   *Ib*

MORELL, Thomas, 1703–1784

68 See, the conquering hero comes!
Sound the trumpets, beat the drums!   *Joshua, Part 3*

MORGAN, Augustus de, 1806–1871

69 Great fleas have little fleas upon their backs to bite 'em,
And little fleas have lesser fleas, and so *ad infinitum.*
                                   A Budget of Paradoxes

MORLEY, Christopher Darlington, 1890–1957

70 The man who never in his life
    Has washed the dishes with his wife
    Or polished up the silver plate –
    He still is largely celibate.   *Washing the Dishes*

MORRIS, William, 1834–1896

71 Dreamer of dreams, born out of my due time,
   Why should I strive to set the crooked straight?
                              The Earthly Paradise, An Apology

72 Love is enough: though the world be a-waning,
   And the woods have no voice but the voice of complaining.
                              Love is Enough, 1

MOTLEY, John Lothrop, 1814–1877

73 Give us the luxuries of life, and we will dispense with its necessities.   *O. W. Holmes, The Autocrat of the Breakfast Table,*
                                                       Ch. 6

MOTTEUX, Peter Anthony, 1660–1718

74 The devil was sick, the devil a monk wou'd be;
   The devil was well, and the devil a monk he'd be.   *Translation*
                   of Rabelais, Gargantua and Pantagruel, Book 4,
                                                       Ch. 24

MUNRO, Hector Hugh, see 'SAKI'

MUNSTER, Ernst Friedrich Herbert, 1766–1839

75 Absolutism tempered by assassination.
                              [The Russian Constitution] Letter

MURDOCH, Richard, 1907–, and HORNE, Kenneth, 1900–1969

76 Have you read any good books lately?   *Much Binding in the*
                   Marsh, BBC Radio Programme, 1945 to 1954

MURPHY, C. W., 19th century

77 Has anybody here seen Kelly?
   Kelly from the Isle of Man?   *Has Anybody Here seen Kelly?*

MUSSET, Alfred de, 1810–1857

78 *Il faut qu'une porte soit ouverte ou fermée.* A door must be either
   open or shut.   *Title of Play*

79 *On ne badine pas avec l'amour.* One must not trifle with love.
                                             Title of Play

NAIRNE, Lady Caroline, 1766–1845

80 Charlie is my darling, my darling, my darling,
   Charlie is my darling, the young Chevalier.   *Charlie is my*
                                                  Darling

81 Better lo'ed ye canna be,
   Will ye no come back again? *Will ye no come back again?*

NAPIER, Sir Charles James, 1782–1853

82 *Peccavi.* [I have Sind]. *Despatch after victory of Hyderabad
in Sind, 1843*

NAPOLEON, Bonaparte, 1769–1821

83 *Soldats, songez que, du haut de ces pyramides, quarante siècles vous
   contemplent.* – Think of it, soldiers, from the summit of these
   pyramids, forty centuries look down upon you. *Speech before
   Battle of the Pyramids, 1798*

84 *Du sublime au ridicule il n'y a qu'un pas.* – It is only a step from
   the sublime to the ridiculous. *After the retreat from Moscow,
   1812*

85 *L'Angleter unere est nation de boutiquiers.* – England is a nation
   of shopkeepers. *Attributed, See Adam Smith (374:98)*

86 *Tout soldat français porte dans sa giberne le bâton de maréchal
   de France.* – Every French soldier carries in his cartridge-
   pouch the baton of a marshal of France. *Attributed*

87 An army marches on its stomach. *Attributed*

NASH, Ogden, 1902–1971

88 A girl whose cheeks are covered with paint
   Has an advantage with me over one whose ain't.
   Biological Reflection

89 One would be in less danger
   From the wiles of the stranger
   If one's own kin and kith
   Were more fun to be with. *Family Court*

90 Home is heaven and orgies are vile
   But you need an orgy, once in a while. *Home, 99·44/100%
   Sweet Home*

91 Beneath this slab
   John Brown is stowed.
   He watched the ads
   And not the road. *Lather as You Go*

92 I have a bone to pick with fate,
   Come here and tell me, girlie,
   Do you think my mind is maturing late,
   Or simply rotted early? *Lines on Facing Forty*

93 Children aren't happy with nothing to ignore,
   And that's what parents were created for. *The Parent*

94 A bit of talcum
  Is always walcum.   *Reflection on Babies*

95 Candy
  is dandy
  But liquor
  is quicker.   *Reflection on Ice-breaking*

96 I test my bath before I sit,
  And I'm always moved to wonderment
  That what chills the finger not a bit
  Is so frigid upon the fundament.   *Samson Agonistes*

97 I think that I shall never see
  A billboard lovely as a tree.
  Perhaps unless the billboards fall,
  I'll never see a tree at all.   *Song of the Open Road*

98 The turtle lives 'twixt plated decks
  Which practically conceal its sex.
  I think it clever of the turtle
  In such a fix to be so fertile.   *The Turtle*

NASHE, Thomas, 1567–1601

99 Brightness falls from the air;
  Queens have died young and fair;
  Dust hath closed Helen's eye.   *In Times of Pestilence*

NEALE, John Mason, 1818–1866

1 Brief Life is here our portion;
  Brief sorrow, short-lived care.   *Brief Life is Here*

2 Good Christian men, rejoice
  With heart, and soul, and voice.   *Good Christian Men*

3 Good King Wenceslas looked out
  On the Feast of Stephen;
  When the snow lay round about,
  Deep and crisp and even.   *Good King Wenceslas*

4 Bring me flesh and bring me wine,
  Bring me pine logs hither.   *Ib*

5 In his master's steps he trod
  Where the snow lay dinted.   *Ib*

NELSON, Horatio, 1st Viscount, 1758–1805

6 Westminster Abbey or victory.   *Remark at Battle of Cape St*
Vincent

7 England expects every man will do his duty.
Battle of Trafalgar

8 Thank God, I have done my duty. *Battle of Trafalgar*

9 Kiss me, Hardy. *Ib*

NERO (Nero Claudius Caesar), A.D. 37–68

10 *Qualis artifex pereo!* What an artist dies with me! *Last words, attributed*

NEWBOLT, Sir Henry John, 1862–1938

11 Drake he's in his hammock till the great Armadas come.
(Capten, art tha sleepin' there below?)
Slung atween the round shot, listenin' for the drum,
An' dreamin' arl the time o' Plymouth Hoe. *Drake's Drum*

12 Where the old trade's plying an' the old flag flyin'
They shall find him ware an' wakin', as they found him long
ago! *Ib*

13 There's a breathless hush in the Close tonight –
Ten to make and the match to win –
A bumping pitch and a blinding light,
An hour to play and the last man in. *Vitai Lampada*

14 But his captain's hand on his shoulder smote –
'Play up! play up! and play the game!' *Ib*

NEWMAN, John Henry, Cardinal, 1801–1890

15 It is almost a definition of a gentleman to say that he is one who
never inflicts pain. *The Idea of a University, Knowledge and
Religious Duty*

16 Lead, Kindly Light, amid the encircling gloom,
Lead thou me on;
The night is dark, and I am far from home,
Lead thou me on. *Lead Kindly Light*

NICHOLAS I of Russia, 1796–1855

17 Russia has two generals in whom she can confide – Generals
Janvier and Février. *Punch, 10 March 1853*

NORTH, Christopher (John Wilson), 1785–1854

18 His Majesty's dominions, on which the sun never sets.
Noctes Ambrosianae, No. 20, April 1829

19 Laws were made to be broken. *Ib, No. 24, May 1830*

NOYES, Alfred, 1880–1958

20 Go down to Kew in lilac-time, in lilac-time, in lilac-time,
Go down to Kew in lilac-time (it isn't far from London!)

And you shall wander hand in hand with love in summer's
    wonderland;
Go down to Kew in lilac-time (it isn't far from London!)
The Barrel Organ

21   Look for me by moonlight;
        Watch for me by moonlight;
I'll come to thee by moonlight, though hell should bar the way!
The Highwayman

NURSERY RHYMES

The Oxford Dictionary of Nursery Rhymes, edited by Iona and Peter
Opie, gives the sources of over 500 nursery rhymes.
In many cases nursery rhymes have changed considerably since they
first appeared in print. It seemed most useful in the selection of
familiar nursery rhymes below, to give the version most commonly
in use today, together with title and date of the first known publication.

22 As I was going to St Ives,
    I met a man with seven wives.   *Mother Goose's Quarto,*
c. 1825

23 Baa, baa, black sheep,
    Have you any wool?
Yes, sir, yes, sir,
    Three bags full;
One for the master,
    And one for the dame,
And one for the little boy
    Who lives down the lane.   *Tommy Thumb's Pretty Song*
Book, c. 1744

24 Bobby Shafto's gone to sea,
    Silver buckles at his knee;
He'll come back and marry me,
    Bonny Bobby Shafto!   *Songs for the Nursery, 1805*

25 Boys and girls come out to play,
    The moon doth shine as bright as day.   *Useful Transactions*
in Philosophy, William King, 1708–1709

26 Cock a doodle doo!
    My dame has lost her shoe,
My master's lost his fiddlestick,
    And knows not what to do.   *The Most Cruel and Bloody*
Murder, 1606

27 Curly locks, Curly locks,
    Wilt thou be mine?

Thou shalt not wash dishes
  Nor yet feed the swine,
But sit on a cushion
  And sew a fine seam,
And feed upon strawberries,
  Sugar and cream. *Infant Institutes, 1797*

28 Ding dong, bell,
  Pussy's in the well.
Who put her in?
  Little Johnny Green.
Who pulled her out?
  Little Tommy Stout. *Mother Goose's Melody, c. 1765*

29 Eena, meena, mina, mo,
  Catch a nigger by his toe;
If he squeals, let him go,
  Eena, meena, mina, mo. *Games and Songs of American
Children, Newell, 1883*

30 A frog he would a-wooing go,
    Heigh ho! says Rowley,
  A frog he would a-wooing go,
  Whether his mother would let him or no.
    With a rowley, powley, gammon and spinach,
    Heigh ho! says Anthony Rowley. *Melismata,
Thomas Ravenscroft, 1611*

31 Georgie Porgie, pudding and pie,
  Kissed the girls and made them cry;
When the boys came out to play,
  Georgie Porgie ran away. *Nursery Rhymes, J. O. Halliwell,
1844*

32 Goosey, goosey gander,
    Whither shall I wander?
  Upstairs and downstairs
    And in my lady's chamber. *Gammer Gurton's Garland,
1784*

33 Hey diddle diddle,
  The cat and the fiddle,
  The cow jumped over the moon;
  The little dog laughed
  To see such sport,
  And the dish ran away with the spoon. *Mother Goose's
Melody, c. 1765*

34 Hickory, dickory, dock,
  The mouse ran up the clock.

The clock struck one,
The mouse ran down,
Hickory, dickory, dock.   *Tommy Thumb's Pretty Song Book,*
c. 1744

35 Hot cross buns!
Hot cross buns!
One a penny, two a penny,
Hot cross buns!   *Christmas Box, 1797*

36 How many miles to Babylon?
Three score miles and ten.
Can I get there by candle-light?
Yes, and back again.
If your heels are nimble and light,
You may get there by candle-light.   *Songs for the Nursery,*
1805

37 Humpty Dumpty sat on a wall,
Humpty Dumpty had a great fall.
   All the king's horses,
   And all the king's men,
Couldn't put Humpty together again.   *Gammer Gurton's*
Garland, 1810

38 Hush-a-bye, baby, on the tree top,
When the wind blows the cradle will rock;
When the bough breaks the cradle will fall,
Down will come baby, cradle, and all.   *Mother Goose's*
Melody, c. 1765

39 I had a little nut tree,
   Nothing would it bear
But a silver nutmeg
   And a golden pear;
The King of Spain's daughter
   Came to visit me,
And all for the sake
   Of my little nut tree.   *Newest Christmas Box, c. 1797*

40 I love sixpence, jolly little sixpence,
I love sixpence better than my life;
I spent a penny of it, I lent a penny of it,
   And I took fourpence home to my wife.   *Gammer Gurton's*
Garland, 1810

41 I'm the king of the castle,
Get down you dirty rascal.   *Brand's Popular Antiquities, 1870*

42 I saw three ships come sailing by,
   Come sailing by, come sailing by,

I saw three ships come sailing by,
   On Christmas day in the morning.   *Bishoprick Garland,*
                                         Sir Cuthbert Sharp, 1834

43 I see the moon,
   And the moon sees me;
God bless the moon,
   And God bless me.   *Gammer Gurton's Garland, 1784*

44 Jack and Jill went up the hill
   To fetch a pail of water;
Jack fell down and broke his crown,
   And Jill came tumbling after.   *Mother Goose's Melody,*
                                         c. 1765

45 Jack Sprat could eat no fat,
   His wife could eat no lean,
And so between them both you see,
   They licked the platter clean.   *Paroemiologia Anglo-Latina,*
                                         John Clark, 1639

46 Ladybird, ladybird,
   Fly away home,
Your house is on fire
   And your children all gone.   *Tommy Thumb's Pretty Song*
                                         Book, c. 1744

47 The lion and the unicorn
   Were fighting for the crown;
The lion beat the unicorn
   All round about the town.

Some gave them white bread,
   And some gave them brown;
Some gave them plum cake
   And drummed them out of town.   *Useful Transactions in*
                             Philosophy, William King, 1708–1709

48 Little Bo-peep has lost her sheep,
   And can't tell where to find them;
Leave them alone, and they'll come home,
   And bring their tails behind them.   *Gammer Gurton's*
                                       Garland, 1810

49 Little Boy Blue,
   Come blow your horn,
The sheep's in the meadow,
   The cow's in the corn.   *Famous Tommy Thumb's Little*
                                       Story Book, c. 1760

50 Little Jack Horner
    Sat in the corner,
    Eating a Christmas pie;
    He put in his thumb,
    And pulled out a plum,
    And said, What a good boy am I!   *Namby Pamby,*
                                              Henry Carey, 1725

51 Little Miss Muffet
    Sat on a tuffet,
    Eating her curds and whey;
    There came a big spider,
    Who sat down beside her
    And frightened Miss Muffet away.   *Songs for the Nursery,*
                                              1805

52 Little Tommy Tucker,
        Sings for his supper:
    What shall we give him?
        White bread and butter.
    How shall he cut it
        Without a knife?
    How will he be married
        Without a wife?   *Tommy Thumb's Pretty Song Book,*
                                 c. 1744

53 London Bridge is broken down,
        My fair lady.   *Namby Pamby, Henry Carey,*
                               1725

54   The man in the moon
        Came down too soon,
    And asked his way to Norwich;
        He went by the south,
        And burnt his mouth
    With supping cold plum porridge.   *Gammer Gurton's*
                                              Garland, 1784

55 Mary, Mary, quite contrary,
        How does your garden grow?
    With silver bells and cockle shells,
        And pretty maids all in a row.   *Tommy Thumb's Pretty*
                                                Song Book, c. 1744

56 Monday's child is fair of face,
    Tuesday's child is full of grace,
    Wednesday's child is full of woe,
    Thursday's child has far to go,
    Friday's child is loving and giving,

Saturday's child works hard for his living,
And the child that is born on the Sabbath day
Is bonny and blithe, and good and gay.   *Traditions of Devon-
shire, A. E. Bray, 1838*

57 My mother said that I never should
Play with the gypsies in the wood;
If I did, she would say,
Naughty girl to disobey.   *Come Hither, Walter de la Mare,
1922*

58   Old King Cole
        Was a merry old soul,
And a merry old soul was he;
        He called for his pipe,
        And he called for his bowl,
And he called for his fiddlers three.   *Useful Transactions in
Philosophy, William King, 1708–1709*

59   Old Mother Hubbard
        Went to the cupboard,
To fetch her poor dog a bone;
        But when she got there
        The cupboard was bare
And so the poor dog had none.   *The Comic Adventures of
Old Mother Hubbard and Her Dog, 1805*

60 One, two,
        Buckle my shoe;
        Three, four,
        Knock at the door.   *Songs for the Nursery, 1805*

61   Oranges and lemons,
        Say the bells of St Clement's.

        You owe me five farthings,
        Say the bells of St Martin's.

        When will you pay me?
        Say the bells of Old Bailey.

        When I grow rich,
        Say the bells of Shoreditch.

        When will that be?
        Say the bells of Stepney.

        I'm sure I don't know,
        Says the great bell at Bow.

Here comes a candle to light you to bed,
Here comes a chopper to chop off your head.
          Tommy Thumb's Pretty Song Book, c. 1744

62 Pat-a-cake, pat-a-cake, baker's man,
   Bake me a cake as fast as you can;
   Pat it and prick it, and mark it with B,
   Put it in the oven for baby and me.   *The Campaigners,*
                                 Tom D'Urfey, 1698

63 Peter Piper picked a peck of pickled pepper;
   A peck of pickled pepper Peter Piper picked;
   If Peter Piper picked a peck of pickled pepper,
   Where's the peck of pickled pepper Peter Piper picked?
     Peter Piper's Practical Principles of Plain and Perfect
                                 Pronunciation, 1819

64 Pussy cat, pussy cat, where have you been?
   I've been to London to look at the queen.
   Pussy cat, pussy cat, what did you there?
   I frightened a little mouse under her chair.   *Songs for the*
                                  Nursery, 1805

65 The Queen of Hearts
     She made some tarts,
  All on a summer's day;
     The Knave of Hearts
     He stole the tarts,
  And took them clean away.
                  The European Magazine, April 1782

66 Ride a cock-horse to Banbury Cross,
   To see a fine lady upon a white horse;
   Rings on her fingers and bells on her toes,
   And she shall have music wherever she goes.
                  Gammer Gurton's Garland, 1784

67 Ring-a-ring o' roses,
   A pocket full of posies,
     A-tishoo! A-tishoo!
  We all fall down.   *Mother Goose, Kate Greenway, 1881*

68 See-saw, Margery Daw,
   Jacky shall have a new master;
   Jacky shall have but a penny a day,
   Because he can't work any faster.
                  Mother Goose's Melody, c. 1765

69 Simple Simon met a pieman,
     Going to the fair;
  Says Simple Simon to the pieman,
     Let me taste your ware.
  Says the pieman to Simple Simon,
     Show me first your penny;

Says Simple Simon to the pieman,
Indeed I have not any.
                    Simple Simon (Chapbook Advertisement), 1764

70 Sing a song of sixpence,
    A pocket full of rye;
Four and twenty blackbirds,
    Baked in a pie.

When the pie was opened,
    The birds began to sing;
Was not that a dainty dish,
    To set before the king?

The king was in his counting-house,
    Counting out his money;
The queen was in the parlour,
    Eating bread and honey.

The maid was in the garden,
    Hanging out the clothes,
There came a little blackbird,
    And snapped off her nose.
                    Tommy Thumb's Pretty Song Book, c. 1744

71 Solomon Grundy,
   Born on a Monday,
   Christened on Tuesday,
   Married on Wednesday,
   Took ill on Thursday,
   Worse on Friday,
   Died on Saturday,
   Buried on Sunday.
   This is the end
   Of Solomon Grundy.   *Nursery Rhymes, J. O. Halliwell, 1842*

72 The first day of Christmas,
   My true love sent to me
   A partridge in a pear tree.   *Mirth without Mischief, c. 1780*

73 The twelfth day of Christmas,
   My true love sent to me
   Twelve lords a-leaping,
   Eleven ladies dancing,
   Ten pipers piping,
   Nine drummers drumming,
   Eight maids a-milking,
   Seven swans a-swimming,
   Six geese a-laying,
   Five gold rings,

Four colly birds,
Three French hens,
Two turtle doves, and
A partridge in a pear tree.   *Mirth without Mischief, c. 1780*

74 There was a crooked man, and he walked a crooked mile,
He found a crooked sixpence against a crooked stile:
He bought a crooked cat, which caught a crooked mouse,
And they all lived together in a little crooked house.
                              Nursery Rhymes, J. O. Halliwell, 1842

75 There was an old woman
      Lived under a hill,

And if she's not gone
      She lives there still.   *Academy of Complements, 1714*

76 There was an old woman who lived in a shoe,
She had so many children she didn't know what to do;
She gave them some broth without any bread;
She whipped them all soundly and put them to bed.
                              Gammer Gurton's Garland, 1784

77 Thirty days hath September,
April, June, and November;
All the rest have thirty-one,
Excepting February alone
And that has twenty-eight days clear
And twenty-nine in each leap year.   *Abridgement of the*
                              Chronicles of England, Richard Grafton, 1570

78 This little pig went to market,
This little pig stayed at home,
This little pig had roast beef,
This little pig had none,
And this little pig cried, Wee-wee-wee-wee-wee,
      I can't find my way home.   *The Famous Tommy Thumb's*
                              Little Story Book, c. 1760

79 This is the farmer sowing his corn,
That kept the cock that crowed in the morn,
That waked the priest all shaven and shorn,
That married the man all tattered and torn,
That kissed the maiden all forlorn,
That milked the cow with the crumpled horn,
That tossed the dog,
That worried the cat,
That killed the rat,
That ate the malt,
That lay in the house that Jack built.
                              Nurse Truelove's New-Year-Gift, 1755

80 Three blind mice, see how they run!
They all run after the farmer's wife,
Who cut off their tails with a carving knife,
Did you ever see such a thing in your life,
    As three blind mice?

Deuteromelia, Thomas Ravenscroft, 1609

81 Tinker,
    Tailor,
Soldier,
    Sailor,
Rich man,
    Poor man,
Beggarman,
    Thief. *Popular Rhymes and Nursery Tales,*
J. O. Halliwell, 1849

82 Tom, he was a piper's son,
He learnt to play when he was young,
And all the tune that he could play
Was 'Over the hills and far away'.

Tom, The Piper's Son, c. 1795

83 Tom, Tom, the piper's son,
Stole a pig and away he run;
    The pig was eat
    And Tom was beat,
And Tom went howling down the street. *Ib*

84 Two little dicky birds,
Sitting on a wall;
One named Peter,
The other named Paul.
Fly away, Peter!
Fly away, Paul!
Come back, Peter!
Come back, Paul! *Mother Goose's Melody, c. 1765*

85 What are little boys made of?
What are little boys made of?
    Frogs and snails
    And puppy-dogs' tails,
That's what little boys are made of.
What are little girls made of?
What are little girls made of?
    Sugar and spice
    And all that's nice,
That's what little girls are made of. *Nursery Rhymes,*
J. O. Halliwell, 1844

86 Where are you going to, my pretty maid?
   I'm going a-milking, sir, she said. *Archaeologia Cornu-*
                                          Britannica, William Pryce, 1790

87 What is your fortune, my pretty maid?
   My face is my fortune, sir, she said.

   Then I can't marry you, my pretty maid.
   Nobody asked you, sir, she said.   *Ib*

88 Who killed Cock Robin?
   I, said the Sparrow,
   With my bow and arrow,
   I killed Cock Robin.

   Who saw him die?
   I, said the Fly,
   With my little eye,
   I saw him die.   *Tommy Thumb's Pretty Song Book, c. 1744*

89 All the birds of the air
   Fell a-sighing and a-sobbing,
   When they heard the bell toll
   For poor Cock Robin.   *Ib*

90 Yankee Doodle came to town,
      Riding on a pony;
   He stuck a feather in his cap
      And called it macaroni.   *Gammer Gurton's Garland, 1810*

   For other nursery rhymes, see Thomas Ady (10 : 13), S. J. Hale
   (157 : 55) and Jane Taylor (384 : 36)

OAKELEY, Frederick, 1802–1880

91 O come, all ye faithful,
   Joyful and triumphant,
   O come ye, O come ye to Bethlehem.   *Hymn translated from*
                                          Latin, Adeste Fideles

92 Sing, choirs of Angels,
   Sing in exultation,
   Sing, all ye citizens of heaven above.   *Ib*

OATES, Lawrence Edward Grace, 1880–1912

93 I am just going outside, and may be some time.   *Last words.*
        Recorded in Captain R. F. Scott's Antarctic Diary,
                                          16 March 1912

O'CASEY, Sean, 1884–1964

94 The whole worl's in a state o' chassis. BOYLE
                                Juno and the Paycock, Act 1

OCHS, Adolph S., 1858–1935

95 All the news that's fit to print.   *Motto of New York Times*

O'KEEFE, Patrick, 1872–1934

96 Say it with flowers.   *Slogan for Society of American Florists*

OPIE, John, 1761–1807

97 I mix them with my brains, sir.   *When asked with what he mixed his colours. Quoted in Samuel Smiles, Self Help, Ch. 4*

ORWELL, George, (Eric Blair) 1903–1950

98 All animals are equal but some animals are more equal than others.   *Animal Farm, Ch. 10*

99 It was a bright cold day in April, and the clocks were striking thirteen.   *Nineteen Eighty-Four, Part 1, Ch. 1*

 1 Big Brother is watching you   *Ib*

 2 War is Peace, Freedom is Slavery, Ignorance is Strength.   *Ib*

 3 Down with Big Brother.   *Ib*

 4 Doublethink means the power of holding two contradictory beliefs in one's mind simultaneously, and accepting both of them.   *Ib, Part 2, Ch. 9*

OSBORNE, John, 1929–

 5 But I have a go, lady, don't I? I 'ave a go.   ARCHIE RICE
     The Entertainer, No. 7

 6 Don't clap too hard – it's a very old building.   ARCHIE RICE
     Ib

 7 Yes, thank God we're normal,
    Yes, this was our finest shower!   ARCHIE RICE   *Ib*

 8 How I long for a little ordinary human enthusiasm. Just enthusiasm – that's all. I want to hear a warm, thrilling voice cry out Hallelujah! Hallelujah! I'm alive!   JIMMY PORTER
     Look Back in Anger, Act 1

 9 His knowledge of life and ordinary human beings is so hazy, he really deserves some sort of decoration for it – a medal inscribed 'For Vaguery in the Field'.   JIMMY PORTER   *Ib*

10 I don't think one 'comes down' from Jimmy's university. According to him, it's not even red brick, but white tile.
    ALISON PORTER   *Ib, Act 2, Scene 1*

OTIS, James, 1725–1783

11 Taxation without representation is tyranny.
Watchword of the American Revolution

OVID (Publius Ovidius Naso), 43 B.C.–17 A.D.

12 *Quae dant, quaeque negant, gaudent tamen esse rogatae.* Whether they give or refuse, women are glad to have been asked.
Ars Amatoria, 1

13 *Inopem me copia fecit.* Plenty makes me poor.
Metamorphoses, 3

14 *Tempus edax rerum.* Time, the devourer of things.   *Ib, 15*

OWEN, Robert, 1771–1858

15 All the world is queer save thee and me, and even thou art a little queer.   *Of his business partner, William Allen, 1828*

OWEN, Wilfred, 1893–1918

16 What passing-bells for those who die as cattle?
Only the monstrous anger of the guns.
Anthem for Doomed Youth

17 Move him into the sun –
Gently its touch awoke him once,
At home, whispering of fields unsown.   *Futility*

18 Above all I am not concerned with Poetry.
My subject is War, and the pity of War.
The Poetry is in the pity.   *Preface to Poems*

PAINE, Thomas, 1737–1809

19 The sublime and the ridiculous are often so nearly related that it is difficult to class them separately. One step above the sublime makes the ridiculous; and one step above the ridiculous makes the sublime again.   *The Age of Reason, Part 2*

20 Government, even in its best state, is but a necessary evil; in its worst state, an intolerable one.   *Common Sense, Ch. 1*

PALMERSTON, Henry John Temple, 3rd Viscount, 1784–1865

21 Die, my dear Doctor, that's the last thing I shall do!
Last words, attributed

PARKER, Dorothy, 1893–1967

22 Men seldom make passes
At girls who wear glasses.   *News Item*

23 Guns aren't lawful;
Nooses give;

Gas smells awful;
You might as well live. *Résumé*

PARKER, Ross, 1914–, and CHARLES, Hughie, 1907–

24 There'll always be an England
While there's a country lane,
Wherever there's a cottage small
Beside a field of grain. *There'll Always be an England*

PARKINSON, Cyril Northcote, 1909–

25 Work expands so as to fill the time available for its completion. General recognition of this fact is shown in the proverbial phrase 'It is the busiest man who has time to spare.'
Parkinson's Law

26 The Law of Triviality. Briefly stated, it means that the time spent on any item of the agenda will be in inverse proportion to the sum involved.
Ib, High Finance or the Point of Vanishing Interest

PASCAL, Blaise, 1623–1662

27 *Le nez de Cléopâtre: s'il eût été plus court, toute la face de la terre aurait changé.* – Had Cleopatra's nose been shorter, the whole history of the world would have been different.
Pensées, 2, 162

28 *Le cœur a ses raisons que la raison ne connaît point.* – The heart has its reasons which reason does not know. *Ib, 4, 277*

PATER, Walter Horatio, 1839–1894

29 To burn always with this hard, gem-like flame, to maintain this ecstasy, is success in life. *The Renaissance, Conclusion*

PATERSON, Andrew, 1864–1941

30 Once a jolly swagman camped by a billabong,
Under the shade of a coolibah tree,
And he sang as he sat and waited till his billy boiled,
'You'll come a-waltzing, Matilda, with me.'
Waltzing Matilda

PATMORE, Coventry Kersey Dighton, 1823–1896

31 'I saw you take his kiss!' ''Tis true,'
'O, modesty!' ''Twas strictly kept:
He thought me asleep; at least, I knew
He thought I thought he thought I slept.'
The Angel in the House, Book 2, 8

32 A woman is a foreign land,
Of which, though there he settle young,
A man will ne'er quite understand
The customs, politics, and tongue.   *The Angel in the House,*
                                      Book 2, 9

PAUL, Leslie Allen, 1905–

33 Angry Young Man.   *Title of Book, 1951*

PAYNE, John Howard, 1791–1852

34 Mid pleasures and palaces though we may roam,
Be it ever so humble, there's no place like home.
                   Clari, The Maid of Milan, Home, Sweet Home

PEACOCK, Thomas Love, 1785–1866

35 Respectable means rich, and decent means poor. I should die if
I heard my family called decent.   LADY CLARINDA
                                      Crotchet Castle, Ch. 3

36 A book that furnishes no quotations is, *me judice*, no book – it
is a plaything.   *Ib, Ch. 9*

37 There are two reasons for drinking: one is, when you are thirsty,
to cure it; the other, when you are not thirsty, to prevent it . . .
Prevention is better than cure.   MR PORTPIPE
                                      Melincourt. Ch. 16

38 The mountain sheep are sweeter,
But the valley sheep are fatter;
We therefore deemed it meeter
To carry off the latter.   *The Misfortunes of Elphin, Ch. 11,*
                              The War Song of Dinas Vawr

PENN, William, 1644–1718

39 Men are generally more careful of the breed of their horses and
dogs than of their children.
                       Reflexions and Maxims, Part 1, 85

PEPYS, Samuel, 1633–1703

40 And so to bed.   *Diary, 6 May 1660 and passim*

41 A silk suit, which cost me much money, and I pray God to make
me able to pay for it.   *Ib, 1 July 1660*

42 Strange to say what delight we married people have to see these
poor fools decoyed into our condition.   *Ib, 25 Dec. 1665*

43 Music and women I cannot but give way to, whatever my
business is.   *Ib, 9 March 1666*

44 To church; and with my mourning, very handsome, and new periwig, make a great show.·   *Diary, 31 March 1667*

45 And so I betake myself to that course, which is almost as much as to see myself go into my grave; for which, and all the discomforts that will accompany my being blind, the good God prepare me!   *Ib, 31 May 1669 (final entry)*

PERRAULT, Charles, 1628–1703

46 She [*Cinderella*] was as good as she was beautiful.   *Histoires ou Contes du Temps Passé, 1697, First English Translation by Robert Samber*

47 Sister Anne, sister Anne, do you see anyone coming?   BLUE BEARD   *Ib*

PÉTAIN, Marshal Henri Phillipe, 1856–1951

48 *Ils ne passeront pas*. They shall not pass.   *Verdun, Feb. 1916*

PETRONIUS, ?–66? A.D.

49 *Cave canem.* – Beware of the dog.   *Satyricon, 29, 1*

PHELPS, Edward John, 1822–1900

50 The man who makes no mistakes does not usually make anything.   *Speech, Mansion House, London, 24 Jan. 1899*

PHILLIPS, Wendell, 1811–1884

51 One on God's side is a majority.
          Speech, Brooklyn, 1 Nov. 1859

52 Every man meets his Waterloo at last.   *Ib*

PINDAR, 522?–442? B.C.

53 Water is best.   *Olympian Odes, 1*

PITT, William, 1st Earl of Chatham, 1708–1778

54 The atrocious crime of being a young man . . . I shall neither attempt to palliate nor deny.   *Speech, House of Commons, 27 Jan. 1741*

55 Unlimited power is apt to corrupt the minds of those who possess it.   *Speech, House of Lords, 9 Jan. 1770*

PITT, William, 1759–1806

56 Necessity is the plea for every infringement of human freedom. It is the argument of tyrants; it is the creed of slaves.
          Speech, House of Commons, 18 Nov. 1783

57 England has saved herself by her exertions, and will, as I trust, save Europe by her example.   *Speech, Guildhall, 1805*

58 Roll up that map: it will not be wanted these ten years.
   On hearing of Napoleon's victory at the Battle of Austerlitz

59 I think I could eat one of Bellamy's veal pies.
                                              Last words, attributed

60 Oh, my country! How I leave my country! [Or 'love' for 'leave']
                                              Last words, attributed

PLATO, 429?–347? B.C.

61 The good is the beautiful.   *Lysis*

62 Our object in the construction of the state is the greatest happiness of the whole, and not that of any one class.   *Republic, 4*

PLAUTUS, 254–184 B.C.

63 *Miles gloriosus.* – The Boastful Soldier.   *Title of Play*

PLINY, The Elder, 23–79

64 *Ex Africa semper aliquid novi.* There is always something new out of Africa.   *Natural History, 2, 8, 42*

65 *In vino veritas.* Truth comes out in wine.   *Ib, 14, 141*

POE, Edgar Allan, 1809–1849

66   The glory that was Greece
   And the grandeur that was Rome.   *To Helen*

67 Take thy beak from out my heart, and take thy form from off my door!
   Quoth the Raven, 'Nevermore.'   *The Raven*

POMPADOUR, Madame de, 1721–1764

68 *Après nous le déluge.* After us the deluge.
                                    After Battle of Rossbach, 1757

POPE, Alexander, 1688–1744

69 A wit with dunces, and a dunce with wits.
                                          The Dunciad, 4, 90

70 The right divine of kings to govern wrong.   *Ib, 4, 188*

71 O Grave! where is thy Victory?
   O Death! where is thy Sting?
                              The Dying Christian to his Soul

72 What beckoning ghost along the moonlight shade
Invites my steps, and points to yonder glade. *Elegy to the*
Memory of an Unfortunate Lady, 1

73 Is it, in heav'n, a crime to love too well? *Ib, 6*

74 Ambition first sprung from your blest abodes,
The glorious fault of angels and of gods. *Ib, 13*

75 Love, free as air, at sight of human ties,
Spreads his light wings, and in a moment flies.
Eloisa to Abelard, 75

76 How happy is the blameless vestal's lot!
The world forgetting, by the world forgot. *Ib, 207*

77 Shut, shut the door, good John! fatigued, I said;
Tie up the knocker, say I'm sick, I'm dead.
Epistle to Dr Arbuthnot, 1

78 Is there a parson much bemused in beer,
A maudlin poetess, a rhyming peer,
A clerk, foredoom'd his father's soul to cross,
Who pens a stanza, when he should engross? *Ib, 15*

79 No creature smarts so little as a fool. *Ib, 84*

80 Why did I write? whose sin to me unknown
Dipt me in ink, my parents', or my own?
As yet a child, nor yet a fool to fame,
I lisp'd in numbers, for the numbers came. *Ib, 125*

81 The Muse but serv'd to ease some friend, not Wife,
To help me through this long disease, my Life. *Ib, 131*

82 And He, whose fustian's so sublimely bad,
It is not Poetry, but prose run mad. *Ib, 187*

83 Damn with faint praise, assent with civil leer,
And, without sneering, teach the rest to sneer. *Ib, 201*

84 Who but must laugh, if such a man there be?
Who would not weep, if Atticus were he? *Ib, 213*

85 Curst be the verse, how well so'er it flow,
That tends to make one worthy man my foe. *Ib, 283*

86 Wit that can creep, and pride that licks the dust. *Ib, 333*

87 Unlearn'd, he knew no schoolman's subtle art,
No language but the language of the heart. *Ib, 398*

88 Nature and Nature's Laws lay hid in Night:
God said, Let Newton be! and all was Light.
Epitaph, intended for Sir Isaac Newton

89 In wit a man: simplicity a child. *Epitaph on Mr Gay*

90 'Tis hard to say, if greater want of skill
Appear in writing or in judging ill. *An Essay on Criticism, 1*

91 'Tis with our judgments as our watches, none
Go just alike, yet each believes his own. *Ib, 9*

92 First follow Nature, and your judgment frame
By her just standard, which is still the same:
Unerring Nature, still divinely bright,
One clear, unchang'd, and universal light,
Life, force, and beauty, must to all impart,
At once the source, and end, and test of Art. *Ib, 58*

93 Of all the causes which conspire to blind
Man's erring judgment, and misguide the mind,
What the weak head with strongest bias rules,
Is Pride, the never-failing vice of fools. *Ib, 201*

94 A little learning is a dangerous thing;
Drink deep, or taste not the Pierian spring:
There shallow draughts intoxicate the brain,
And drinking largely sobers us again. *Ib, 215*

95 A perfect judge will read each work of Wit
With the same spirit that its author writ. *Ib, 233*

96 Whoever thinks a faultless piece to see,
Thinks what ne'er was, nor is, nor e'er shall be. *Ib, 253*

97 True wit is nature to advantage dress'd;
What oft was thought, but ne'er so well express'd. *Ib, 297*

98   As some to church repair,
Not for the doctrine, but the music there. *Ib, 342*

99 True ease in writing comes from art, not chance,
As those move easiest who have learn'd to dance.
'Tis not enough no harshness gives offence,
The sound must seem an echo to the sense. *Ib, 362*

1 Yet let not each gay turn thy rapture move,
For fools admire, but men of sense approve. *Ib, 390*

2 Some praise at morning what they blame at night,
But always think the last opinion right. *Ib, 430*

3 Fondly we think we honour merit then,
When we but praise ourselves in other men. *Ib, 454*

4 To err is human, to forgive, divine. *Ib, 525*

5 The bookful blockhead, ignorantly read,
With loads of learned lumber in his head. *Ib, 612*

6 For fools rush in where angels fear to tread. *Ib, 625*

7 Awake, my St John! leave all meaner things
   To low ambition, and the pride of kings.
   Let us (since life can little more supply
   Than just to look about us and to die)
   Expatiate free o'er all this scene of man;
   A mighty maze! but not without a plan.
                              An Essay on Man, Epistle 1, 1

8 Laugh where we must, be candid where we can;
   But vindicate the ways of God to Man.   *Ib, 1, 15*

9 Hope springs eternal in the human breast;
   Man never is, but always to be blest.   *Ib, 1, 95*

10 Why has not man a microscopic eye?
   For this plain reason, man is not a fly.   *Ib, 1, 193*

11 All are but parts of one stupendous whole,
   Whose body Nature is, and God the soul.   *Ib, 1, 267*

12 All nature is but art, unknown to thee;
   All chance, direction which thou canst not see;
   All discord, harmony not understood;
   All partial evil, universal good:
   And, spite of pride, in erring reason's spite,
   One truth is clear, whatever is, is right.   *Ib, 1, 289*

13 Know then thyself, presume not God to scan,
   The proper study of Mankind is Man.   *Ib, Epistle 2, 1*

14 Vice is a master of so frightful mien,
   As to be hated needs but to be seen;
   Yet seen too oft, familiar with her face,
   We first endure, then pity, then embrace.   *Ib, 2, 217*

15 O happiness! our being's end and aim!
   Good, pleasure, ease, content! whate'er thy name:
   That something still which prompts th' eternal sigh,
   For which we bear to live, or dare to die.   *Ib, Epistle 4, 1*

16 An honest Man's the noblest work of God.   *Ib, 4, 248*

17 If parts allure thee, think how Bacon shined,
   The wisest, brightest, meanest of mankind:
   Or, ravished with the whistling of a name,
   See Cromwell, damned to everlasting fame.   *Ib, 4, 281*

18 Formed by thy converse happily to steer
   From grave to gay, from lively to severe.   *Ib, 4, 379*

19 Thou wert my guide, philosopher, and friend.   *Ib, 4, 390*

20 That true self-love and social are the same;
   That virtue only makes our bliss below;
   And all our knowledge is, ourselves to know.   *Ib, 4, 396*

21 To observations which ourselves we make,
   We grow more partial for th' observer's sake.
                                    Moral Essays, Epistle 1, 11
22 'Tis education forms the common mind,
   Just as the twig is bent, the tree's inclined.   *Ib, 1, 149*
23 Men, some to business, some to pleasure take;
   But every woman is at heart a rake.   *Ib, Epistle 2, 215*
24 See how the world its veterans rewards!
   A youth of frolics, an old age of cards.   *Ib, 2, 243*
25 And mistress of herself, though China fall.   *Ib, 2, 268*
26 Woman's at best a contradiction still.   *Ib, 2, 270*
27 The ruling passion, be it what it will
   The ruling passion conquers reason still.   *Ib, Epistle 3, 153*
28 Happy the man, whose wish and care
   A few paternal acres bound,
   Content to breathe his native air,
     In his own ground.   *Ode on Solitude*
29 Thus let me live, unseen, unknown,
   Thus unlamented let me die,
   Steal from the world, and not a stone
     Tell where I lie.   *Ib*
30 I am His Highness' dog at Kew;
   Pray tell me sir, whose dog are you?   *On the collar of a dog
         given to His Royal Highness, Frederick, Prince of Wales*
31 I know the thing that's most uncommon;
   (Envy, be silent and attend!)
   I know a reasonable woman,
   Handsome and witty, yet a friend.
                                    On a Certain Lady at Court
32 Where'er you walk, cool gales shall fan the glade.
   Trees where you sit shall crowd into a shade:
   Where'er you tread, the blushing flowers shall rise,
   And all things flourish where you turn your eyes.
                                    Pastorals, Summer, 73
33 What dire offence from am'rous causes springs,
   What mighty contests rise from trivial things.
                                    The Rape of the Lock, Canto 1, 1
34 If to her share some female errors fall,
   Look on her face, and you'll forget 'em all.   *Ib, Canto 2, 17*
35 Fair tresses man's imperial race insnare,
   And beauty draws us with a single hair.   *Ib, 2, 27*
36 At ev'ry word a reputation dies.   *Ib, Canto 3, 16*

37 The hungry judges soon the sentence sign,
And wretches hang that jury-men may dine.
The Rape of the Lock, Canto 3, 21

38 Coffee, which makes the politician wise,
And see through all things with his half-shut eyes. *Ib, 3, 117*

39 Charms strike the sight, but merit wins the soul. *Ib, Canto 5, 34*

PORSON, Richard, 1759–1808

40 When Dido found Aeneas would not come,
She mourn'd in silence, and was Di-do-dum.
Epigram on Latin Gerunds

41 I went to Frankfort, and got drunk
With that most learned professor, Brunck;
I went to Worts, and got more drunken
With that more learn'd professor, Ruhnken.
Facetiae Cantabrigienses

PORTER, William Sydney, see HENRY, O.

POTTER, Beatrix, 1866–1943

42 They [*the rabbits*] did not awake because the lettuces had been
so soporific. *The Tale of the Flopsy Bunnies*

POTTER, Stephen, 1900–1969

43 Gamesmanship or The Art of Winning Games Without Actually
Cheating. *Title of book*

44 *How to be one up* – how to make the other man feel that something has gone wrong, however slightly.
Lifemanship, Introduction

45 We work from half a dozen centres co-ordinated, of course, from
our 'H.Q.' at Station Road, Yeovil. *Ib*

46 'Yes, but not in the South', with slight adjustments will do for
any argument about any place, if not about any person.
Ib, The Canterbury Block

POUND, Ezra Loomis, 1885–1972

47 Winter is icummen in,
Lhude sing Goddamm,
Raineth drop and staineth slop
And how the wind doth ramm!
Sing: Goddamm. *Ancient Music*

48 Bah! I have sung women in three cities,
But it is all the same;
And I will sing of the sun. *Cino*

PRESCOTT, William, 1726–1795

49 Don't fire until you see the whites of their eyes. *Bunker Hill, 1775 (Also attributed to Israel Putnam, 1718–1790)*

PRIOR, Matthew, 1664–1721

50 Be to her virtues very kind;
Be to her faults a little blind;
Let all her ways be unconfined;
And clap your padlock on her mind. *An English Padlock, 78*

51 The merchant to secure his treasure,
    Conveys it in a borrowed name;
Euphelia serves to grace my measure;
But Chloe is my real flame.
                    Ode, The Merchant to Secure his Treasure

52 From ignorance our comfort flows,
The only wretched are the wise. *To the Hon. C. Montague*

PROVERBS

In this selection of familiar proverbs mainly in the English language, the name and publication date of the Dictionary in which the proverb was first included has been given, or the century of the first recorded use of the proverb in literature. Most proverbs were obviously in common use for many years before they were included in a dictionary.

The abbreviations shown opposite proverbs refer to the following Dictionaries:

Bohn   *H. G. Bohn, A Handbook of Proverbs, 1855.*
Camden   *W. Camden, Remains Concerning Britain, 1614 or later edition.*
Clarke   *J. Clarke, Parœmiologia Anglo-Latina, 1639.*
Draxe   *T. Draxe, Bibliotheca Scholastica, 1616 or later edition.*
Fergusson   *D. Fergusson, Scottish Proverbs, 1641.*
Fuller   *T. Fuller, Gnomologia, 1732.*
Herbert   *G. Herbert, Outlandish Proverbs, 1640 or later edition.*
Heywood   *J. Heywood, A Dialogue containing . . . the Proverbs in the English Tongue, 1546 or later edition.*
Howell   *J. Howell, Proverbs, 1659.*
Kelly   *J. Kelly, A Complete Collection of Scottish Proverbs, 1721.*
Lean   *V. S. Lean, Collectanea, 1902–4.*
Ray   *J. Ray, A Collection of English Proverbs, 1670, 1678 or later edition.*

53 Absence sharpens love, presence strengthens it. *Fuller, 1732*
54 Absent are always in the wrong, The. *Herbert, 1640*
55 Abundance of money ruins youth, The, *Ray, 1670*
56 Accidents will happen in the best-regulated families. *19th c.*
57 Accounting for tastes, There is no. *Latin*
58 Actions speak louder than words. *20th c.*
59 Adversity makes a man wise, not rich. *Ray, 1678*
60 Adversity, Many can bear/ but few contempt. *Fuller, 1732*
61 Advise none to marry or go to war. *Herbert, 1640*
62 After a storm comes a calm. *16th c.*
63 Agree, for the law is costly. *Camden, 1623*
64 All in the day's work, It is. *18th c.*
65 All is fair in love and war. *17th c.*
66 All is not gold that glitters. *Latin*
67 All is over bar (but) the shouting. *19th c.*
68 All is well that ends well. *14th c.*
69 All my eye and Betty Martin. *18th c.*
70 All sorts to make a world, It takes. *17th c.*
71 Any port in a storm. *18th c.*
72 Anything for a quiet life. *17th c.*
73 Apple a day keeps the doctor away, An. *19th c.*
74 Apple-cart, To upset the. *18th c.*
75 Archer is not known by his arrows, but his aim, A good.
16th c.

76 Art has no enemy except ignorance. *Latin*
77 Art lies in concealing art. *Latin*
78 Ask no questions and you will be told no lies. *18th c.*
79 Ask thy purse what thou shouldst buy. *Fuller, 1732*
80 Ass of oneself, To make an. *19th c.*
81 *Audi alteram partem* – Hear the other side. *Latin*
82 Aunt had been a man, If my/ she'd have been my uncle.
Ray, 1813

83 *Autres temps, autres moeurs* – Other times, other manners.
French

84 Axe to grind, To have an. *19th c.*

85 Bachelors' fare: bread and cheese, and kisses. *18th c.*
86 Back again, like a bad penny. *19th c.*

87 Bad excuse is better than none, A.   *16th c.*
88 Bad workman quarrels with his tools, A.   *Herbert, 1640*
89 Bald as a coot, As.   *15th c.*
90 Bald heads are soon shaven.   *Ray, 1678*
91 Barber shaves so close but another finds work, No.
                                                     Herbert, 1640
92 Bark at the moon, To.   *15th c.*
93 Bark is worse than his bite, His.   *17th c.*
94 Bark up the wrong tree, To.   *19th c.*
95 Barking dogs seldom bite.   *16th c.*
96 Bats in the belfry, To have.   *20th c.*
97 Be sure before you marry of a house wherein to tarry. *Italian*
98 Bear wealth, poverty will bear itself.   *Fergusson, 1641*
99 Beat about the bush, To.   *16th c.*
 1 Beauty is but skin-deep.   *17th c.*
 2 Beauty is potent, but money is omnipotent.   *Ray, 1670*
 3 Beauty will buy no beef.   *Fuller, 1732*
 4 Bee in one's bonnet, To have a.   *19th c.*
 5 Before one can say Jack Robinson.   *18th c.*
 6 Beggar can never be bankrupt, A.   *Clarke, 1639*
 7 Beggars cannot be choosers.   *Heywood, 1546*
 8 Believe, He does not/ that does not live according to his belief.
                                                      Fuller, 1732
 9 Beloved, To be/ is above all bargains.   *Herbert, 1640*
10 Best foot forward, To put one's.   *16th c.*
11 Best of a bad job, To make the.   *16th c.*
12 Better a lean peace than a fat victory.   *17th c.*
13 Better an egg today than a hen tomorrow.   *Italian*
14 Better an open enemy than a false friend.   *17th c.*
15 Better be alone than in bad company.   *15th c.*
16 Better be born lucky than rich.   *Clarke, 1639*
17 Better be envied than pitied.   *Greek*
18 Better be happy than wise.   *Heywood, 1546*
19 Better be sure (safe) than sorry.   *19th c.*
20 Better be the head of a dog than the tail of a lion. *16th c.*
21 Better buy than borrow.   *Fergusson, 1641*
22 Better die a beggar than live a beggar.   *Ray, 1670*

23 Better give a shilling than lend a half-crown.   *Howell, 1659*

24 Better go to heaven in rags than to hell in embroidery.
Fuller, 1732

25 Better late than never.   *Latin*

26 Better luck next time.   *19th c.*

27 Better never begin than never make an end.   *16th c.*

28 Better some of a pudding than none of a pie.   *Ray, 1670*

29 Better suffer ill than do ill.   *Clarke, 1639*

30 Better the devil you know than the devil you don't know.
19th c.

31 Better untaught than ill-taught.   *Ray, 1678*

32 Better wear out shoes than sheets.   *17th c.*

33 Between Scylla and Charybdis.   *Greek*

34 Between two stools one falls to the ground.   *Latin*

35 Between you and me and the (gate) post.   *19th c.*

36 Bird in hand is worth two in the bush, A.   *Latin*

37 Birds of a feather flock together.   *16th c.*

38 Bitter to endure may be sweet to remember, That which was.
Latin

39 Black as ink.   *16th c.*

40 Black as soot.   *15th c.*

41 Black as the devil.   *14th c.*

42 Black sheep in every flock, There are.   *19th c.*

43 Blessings are not valued till they are gone.   *Fuller, 1732*

44 Blind as a bat, As.   *16th c.*

45 Blind as those who won't see, None so.   *Heywood, 1546*

46 Blind in their own cause, Men are.   *Heywood, 1546*

47 Blind man will not thank you for a looking-glass, A.
Fuller, 1732

48 Blind, In the land of the/ the one-eyed man is king.   *Greek*

49 Blood is thicker than water.   *17th c.*

50 Blow one's own trumpet, To.   *16th c.*

51 Bone in one's leg, To have a.   *Greek*

52 Book that is shut is but a block, A.   *Fuller, 1732*

53 Books and friends should be few and good.   *Spanish*

54 Books, To be in a person's good (or bad).   *19th c.*

55 Boot is on the other leg, The.   *19th c.*

56 Born on the wrong side of the blanket.   *18th c.*

57 Born to be hanged, He that is/ shall never be drowned.   *16th c.*
58 Born with a silver spoon in his mouth, He was.   *Clarke, 1639*
59 Born within the sound of Bow Bells, To be.   *16th c.*
60 Born yesterday, I was not.   *19th c.*
61 Both ends meet, To make.   *Clarke, 1639*
62 Bow at all, If you/ bow low.   *Chinese*
63 Boys will be boys.   *17th c.*
64 Boys will be men.   *17th c.*
65 Bread is buttered on both sides, His.   *Ray, 1678*
66 Bull in a china shop, A.   *19th c.*
67 Bulls the cow must keep the calf, He that.   *16th c.*
68 Bully is always a coward, A.   *19th c.*
69 Burn one's boats, To.   *19th c.*
70 Burn the candle at both ends, To.   *Ray, 1678*
71 Burn the midnight oil, To.   *17th c.*
72 Bury the hatchet, To.   *18th c.*
73 Busiest men have the most leisure, The.   *19th c.*
74 Business is business.   *18th c.*
75 Business before pleasure.   *19th c.*
76 Busy, Who is more/ than he that hath least to do?
    Draxe, 1616
77 Butter would not melt in his mouth.   *Heywood, 1546*
78 Buy a pig in a poke, To.   *Heywood, 1546*
79 Buy and sell, and live by the loss, To.   *Draxe, 1616*
80 Bygones be bygones, Let.   *Heywood, 1546*

81 Calf love, half love; old love, cold love.   *19th c.*
82 Call a spade a spade, To.   *Latin*
83 Cap fits, If the/wear it.   *18th c.*
84 Care killed a cat.   *16th c.*
85 Carry coals to Newcastle, To.   *16th c.*
86 Cart before the horse, To put the.   *Latin*
87 Cast ne'er a clout till May be out.   *Fuller, 1732*
88 Castles in Spain, To build.   *14th c.*
89 Castles in the air, To build.   *Latin*
90 Cat has nine lives, A.   *Heywood, 1546*
91 Cat jumps, To see which way the.   *19th c.*

92 Cat on hot bricks, Like a. *17th c.*

93 *Caveat emptor* – Let the buyer beware. *Latin*

94 Chalk and cheese. *14th c.*

95 Chanceth in an hour, It/ that happeneth not in seven years.
Heywood, 1546

96 Charity begins at home. *14th c.*

97 *Che sera, sera* – Whatever will be, will be. *Italian*

98 Children should be seen and not heard. *19th c.*

99 Chip of the old block, A. *17th c.*

1 Choose a horse made, and a wife to make. *Herbert, 1640*

2 Choose a wife rather by your ear than your eye. *Fuller, 1732*

3 Choose neither a woman nor linen by candle-light. *16th c.*

4 Chop and change, To. *16th c.*

5 Christmas comes but once a year
But when it comes it brings good cheer. *16th c.*

6 Circumstances alter cases. *19th c.*

7 Civility costs nothing. *19th c.*

8 Clean as a whistle, As. *19th c.*

9 Clean breast, To make a. *18th c.*

10 Cleanliness is next to godliness. *Hebrew*

11 Close mouth catcheth no flies, A. *Italian*

12 Cloud has a silver lining, Every. *19th c.*

13 Cloud, To be under a. *16th c.*

14 Coast is clear, The. *17th c.*

15 Cock-a-hoop, To be. *17th c.*

16 Cock-and-bull story, A. *17th c.*

17 Cold as charity. *14th c.*

18 Cold comfort. *16th c.*

19 Cold hand and a warm heart, A. *Lean, 1902*

20 Cold shoulder, To give the. *19th c.*

21 Company makes the feast. The. *17th c.*

22 Comparisons are odious. *15th c.*

23 Confession is good for the soul. *Kelly, 1721*

24 Constant guest is never welcome, A. *Fuller, 1732*

25 Cook one's goose, To. *19th c.*

26 Cook that cannot lick his own fingers, He is an ill.
Heywood, 1546

27 Cool one's heels, To.   *17th c.*
28 Costs more to do ill than to do well, It.   *Herbert, 1640*
29 Counsel be good, If the/ no matter who gave it.   *Fuller, 1732*
30 Count one's chickens before they are hatched, To.   *16th c.*
31 Couple is not a pair, Every.   *19th c.*
32 Courtesy on one side only lasts not long.   *Herbert, 1640*
33 Coventry, To send to.   *17th c.*
34 Creditors have better memories than debtors.   *Howell, 1659*
35 Crocodile tears.   *16th c.*
36 Crooked by nature is never made straight by education.
                                                        Fuller, 1732
37 Cross the bridge till you get to it, Don't.   *19th c.*
38 Crowd is not company, A.   *17th c.*
39 Cry for the moon, To.   *19th c.*
40 Cry 'Wolf', To.   *17th c.*
41 Crying over spilt milk, It is no use.   *Howell, 1659*
42 Cupboard love.   *17th c.*
43 Curate's egg, good in parts, Like the. (*See Punch, 285:86*)
                                                        19th c.
44 Curses are like chickens; they come home to roost.   *14th c.*
45 Custom without reason is but ancient error.   *16th c.*
46 Cut off one's nose to spite one's face, To.   *13th c.*
47 Cut off with a shilling, To.   *18th c.*
48 Cut the grass from under a person's feet, To.   *16th c.*
49 Cut your coat according to your cloth.   *Heywood, 1546*

50 Dally not with money or women.   *Herbert, 1640*
51 Daughter win, He that would the/ must with the mother first
   begin.   *Ray, 1670*
52 Day is short and the work is long, The.   *15th c.*
53 *De gustibus non est disputandum* – There is no disputing about
   tastes.   *Latin*
54 *De mortuis nil nisi bonum* – Concerning the dead (say) nothing
   but good.   *Latin*
55 Dead as a door-nail, As.   *14th c.*
56 Dead men don't bite.   *Greek*
57 Dead men tell no tales.   *17th c.*
58 Deaf as a post.   *16th c.*

59 Deaf as those who won't hear, None so. *Heywood, 1546*

60 Death devours lambs as well as sheep. *17th c.*

61 Death is the grand leveller. *Fuller, 1732*

62 Death pays all debts. *17th c.*

63 Debt is the worst poverty. *Fuller, 1732*

64 Deceives me once, If a man/ shame on him; if he deceives me twice, shame on me. *Italian*

65 Deceive oneself is very easy, To. *Herbert, 1640*

66 Deeds are males, and words are females. *16th c.*

67 Deepest water is the best fishing, In the. *Draxe, 1616*

68 Delays are dangerous. *14th c.*

69 Deserves not the sweet that will not taste the sour, He. *Latin*

70 Desires honour, He that/ is not worthy of honour. *17th c.*

71 Desperate diseases must have desperate remedies. *Latin*

72 Devil and the deep sea, Between the. *17th c.*

73 Devil is not so black as he is painted, The. *16th c.*

74 Devil take the hindmost, The. *17th c.*

75 Discreet women have neither eyes nor ears. *Herbert, 1640*

76 Discretion is the better part of valour. *16th c.*

77 *Divide et impera* – Divide and rule. *Latin*

78 Divine grace was never slow. *Herbert, 1640*

79 Do as you would be done by. *14th c.*

80 Do as you're bidden and you'll never bear blame. *Ray, 1678*

81 Dog does not eat dog. *18th c.*

82 Dog has his day, Every. *Heywood, 1546*

83 Dog will not howl if you beat him with a bone, A. *Howell, 1659*

84 Dogs that bark at a distance never bite. *Camden, 1623*

85 Done by night appears by day, What is. *14th c.*

86 Done cannot be undone, Things. *Heywood, 1546*

87 Door may be shut but death's door, Every. *Italian*

88 Draw the line somewhere, One must. *19th c.*

89 Drink wine, and have the gout; drink no wine, and have the gout too. *16th c.*

90 Drowning man will catch at a straw, A. *17th c.*

91 Drunk as a fish, As. *17th c.*

92 Drunk as a lord, As. *17th c.*

No.	Proverb	Source
93	Drunk as a mouse, As.	*14th c.*
94	Drunk as a wheelbarrow, As.	*Ray, 1678*
95	Drunken folks seldom take harm.	*17th c.*
96	Drunken night makes a cloudy morning, A.	*Fuller, 1732*
97	Dry as dust, As.	*16th c.*
98	Ducks and drakes of, To make.	*16th c.*
99	Dull as ditchwater, As.	*18th c.*
1	Dumb men get no lands.	*14th c.*
2	Dying duck in a thunderstorm, Like a.	*18th c.*
3	Ears burn, If your/ someone is talking about you.	*Heywood, 1546*
4	Early bird catches the worm, The.	*Camden, 1636*
5	Early to bed and early to rise, Makes a man healthy, wealthy and wise.	*Clarke, 1639*
6	Easier said than done.	*15th c.*
7	East or west, home is best.	*Bohn, 1855*
8	Easy come, easy go.	*19th c.*
9	Easy to be wise after the event, It is.	*17th c.*
10	Eat, and welcome; fast, and heartily welcome.	*Ray, 1678*
11	Eat one's words, To.	*16th c.*
12	Eat to live, but do not live to eat.	*Latin*
13	Eat your cake and have it, You cannot.	*Heywood, 1546*
14	Education begins a gentleman, conversation completes him.	*Fuller, 1732*
15	Eggs in one basket, Do not put all your.	*18th c.*
16	Eleventh Commandment: The/ thou shalt not be found out.	*19th c.*
17	Empty purse that is full of other men's money, That is but an.	*Ray, 1678*
18	Empty vessels make the most noise.	*16th c.*
19	End justifies the means, The.	*17th c.*
20	England is the paradise of women, the hell of horses, and the purgatory of servants.	*16th c.*
21	English never know when they are beaten, The.	*19th c.*
22	Englishman's house (home) is his castle, An.	*17th c.*
23	Enough is as good as a feast.	*15th c.*
24	Enough is enough.	*Heywood, 1546*

25 Evening crowns the day, The. *17th c.*

26 Every little helps. *18th c.*

27 Every man for himself, and God for us all. *Heywood, 1562*

28 Every man has his faults. *16th c.*

29 Every man is best known to himself. *Draxe, 1616*

30 Every man to his taste. *16th c.*

31 Everybody's business is nobody's business. *17th c.*

32 Everything comes to him who waits. *16th c.*

33 Everything hath an end, and a pudding hath two. *16th c.*

34 Everything is the worse for wearing. *Clarke, 1639*

35 Everything must have a beginning. *14th c.*

36 Evils, Of two/ choose the least. *14th c.*

37 Example is better than precept. *Latin*

38 Exception proves the rule, The. *17th c.*

39 Experience is good, if not bought too dear. *Kelly, 1721*

40 *Experientia docet* – Experience teaches. *Latin*

41 Extremes meet. *18th c.*

42 Eye sees not, What the/ the heart rues not. *Heywood, 1546*

43 Failing to trust everybody, It is an equal/ and to trust nobody.
Fuller, 1732

44 Faint heart never won fair lady. *16th c.*

45 Fair and softly goes far. *14th c.*

46 Fair exchange is no robbery, A. *16th c.*

47 Fair face and a foul heart, A. *Howell, 1659*

48 Fair face is half a fortune, A. *Draxe, 1616*

49 Fair play's a jewel. *19th c.*

50 Fairer the hostess, the fouler the reckoning, The.
Howell, 1659

51 Familiarity breeds contempt. *Latin*

52 Far from eye, far from heart. *14th c.*

53 Fast bind, fast find. *Heywood, 1546*

54 Fat in in the fire, The. *Heywood, 1546*

55 Faults are theirs that commit them, The first/ the second theirs
that permit them. *Fuller, 1732*

56 Faults are thick where love is thin. *Howell, 1659*

57 Few lawyers die well, few physicians live well. *16th c.*

58 Few words are best. *Ray, 1678*

59 *Fiat justitia, ruat coelum* – Let justice be done, though heaven
fall.   *Latin*

60 Fiddle while Rome is burning, To.   *17th c.*

61 Finding's keeping.   *19th c.*

62 Finger in the pie, To have a.   *17th c.*

63 Fire is a good servant but a bad master.   *17th c.*

64 First blow is half the battle, The.   *18th c.*

65 First catch your hare and then cook it.   *18th c.*

66 First come, first served.   *16th c.*

67 First impressions are most lasting.   *19th c.*

68 First think, and then speak.   *Clarke, 1639*

69 Fish out of water, Like a.   *Latin*

70 Fish to fry, I have other.   *17th c.*

71 Fit as a fiddle, As.   *17th c.*

72 Flat as a pancake, As.   *16th c.*

73 Fling dirt enough, and some will stick.   *Latin*

74 Flog a dead horse, To.   *19th c.*

75 Follow the river and you'll get to the sea.   *Fuller, 1732*

76 Fool and his money are soon parted, A.   *16th c.*

77 Fool like an old fool, No.   *Heywood, 1546*

78 Fool that forgets himself, He is a.   *14th c.*

79 Fool that is not melancholy once a day, He is a.   *Ray, 1678*

80 Fool to the market, Send a/ and a fool he'll return.   *16th c.*

81 Fool wanders, The/ the wise man travels.   *Fuller, 1732*

82 Fools went not to market, If/ bad wares would not be sold.
                                                       Herbert, 1640

83 Forewarned, forearmed.   *Latin*

84 Forgive and forget.   *Heywood, 1546*

85 Fortune favours fools.   *Latin*

86 Fortune is blind.   *16th c.*

87 Fortune knocks, When/ open the door.   *17th c.*

88 Foul water will quench fire.   *Heywood, 1546*

89 Four eyes see more than two.   *Latin*

90 Fox knows much, The/ but more he that catcheth him.
                                                       Herbert, 1640

91 Friend at court, A.   *17th c.*

92 Friend in need is a friend indeed, A.   *Latin*

93 Friend to thyself, Be a/ and others will befriend thee.
Kelly, 1721

94 Friend to everybody is a friend to nobody, A. *17th c.*

95 Friends are thieves of time. *17th c.*

96 Friends both in heaven and hell, It is good to have some.
Herbert, 1640

97 Friends (The best of friends) must part. *17th c.*

98 Friends, Have but few/ though many acquaintances.
Howell, 1659

99 Friendship should not be all on one side. *17th c.*

1 Frying-pan into the fire, Out of the. *Heywood, 1546*

2 Full of courtesy, full of craft. *16th c.*

3 Game is not worth the candle, The. *17th c.*

4 Geese are swans, All his. *16th c.*

5 Gift horse in the mouth, Look not a. *Latin*

6 Give a dog a bad name and hang him. *Kelly, 1721*

7 Give him an inch and he'll take an ell. *Heywood, 1546*

8 Give the devil his due. *16th c.*

9 Gives to all, denies all, Who. *Herbert, 1640*

10 Gives twice who gives quickly, He. *Latin*

11 Giving much to the poor doth increase a man's store.
Herbert, 1640

12 Glass houses, People who live in/ should never throw stones.
Herbert, 1640

13 Gluttony kills more than the sword. *16th c.*

14 Go down the ladder when thou marriest a wife; go up when thou choosest a friend. *Ray, 1678*

15 Go farther and fare worse. *Heywood, 1546*

16 Go to bed with the lamb, and rise with the lark. *16th c.*

17 God comes at last when we think he is furthest off. *Italian*

18 God defend me from my friends; from my enemies I can defend myself. *17th c.*

19 God heals, and the doctor takes the fee. *Herbert, 1640*

20 God help the poor, for the rich can help themselves.
Kelly, 1721

21 God help the rich, the poor can beg. *Howell, 1659*

22 God helps them that help themselves. *Herbert, 1640*

23 God send me a friend that will tell me of my faults.

Fuller, 1732

24 God send you joy, for sorrow will come fast enough.

Draxe, 1616

25 God sends fortune to fools.   *Heywood, 1546*

26 God tempers the wind to the shorn lamb.   *French*

27 God's mill grinds slow but sure.   *Greek*

28 Good against evil, Set.   *Herbert, 1640*

29 Good and quickly seldom meet.   *Herbert, 1640*

30 Good beginning makes a good ending, A.   *14th c.*

31 Good example is the best sermon, A.   *Fuller, 1732*

32 Good face needs no paint, A.   *Fuller, 1732*

33 Good judgement that relieth not wholly on his own, He hath a.

Fuller, 1732

34 Good life is the only religion, A.   *Fuller, 1732*

35 Good to want and to have, It is not.   *Fergusson, 1641*

36 Good turn deserves another, One.   *15th c.*

37 Good wife and health are a man's best wealth, A.

Fuller, 1732

38 Good wife makes a good husband, A.   *Heywood, 1546*

39 Good wine needs no bush.   *16th c.*

40 Good workmen are seldom rich.   *Herbert, 1640*

41 Grasp all, lose all.   *14th c.*

42 Great minds think alike.   *20th c.*

43 Great ones if there were no little ones, There would be no.

Herbert, 1640

44 Great talkers are great liars.   *French*

45 Great trees are good for nothing but shade.   *Herbert, 1640*

46 Greater the truth, The/ the greater the libel.   *18th c.*

47 Greatest hate springs from the greatest love, The.   *16th c.*

48 Greek to me, It is.   *16th c.*

49 Grist to the mill, To bring.   *16th c.*

50 Hail fellow well met, To be.   *16th c.*

51 Half a loaf is better than no bread.   *Heywood, 1546*

52 Half the world knows not how the other half lives.

Herbert, 1640

53 Half-seas over, To be.   *18th c.*

54 Halves, Never do things by. *18th c.*

55 Hand and glove. *17th c.*

· 56 Handful of good life is better than a bushel of learning, A.
Herbert, 1640

57 Hands, Many/ make light work. *Latin*

58 Handsome at twenty, He that is not/ nor strong at thirty, nor rich at forty, nor wise at fifty, will never be handsome, strong, rich or wise. *Herbert, 1640*

59 Handsome is that handsome does. *Ray, 1670*

60 Hanged for a sheep as a lamb, As good be. *Ray, 1678*

61 Hanging and wiving go by destiny. *Heywood, 1546*

62 Happiness takes no account of time. *18th c.*

63 Happy is he that is happy in his children. *Fuller, 1732*

64 Happy is the country which has no history. *19th c.*

65 Happy is the child whose father goes to the devil. *16th c.*

66 Hard as a Flint (stone), As. *14th c.*

67 Hard cases make bad law. *Lean, 1902*

68 Hard cheese. *19th c.*

69 Hard nut to crack, A. *16th c.*

70 Haste, The more/ the less speed. *Heywood, 1546*

71 Hatred is blind, as well as love. *Fuller, 1732*

72 Hatch, match and despatch. *19th c.*

73 Haul over the coals, To. *16th c.*

74 Head, He that hath no/ needs no hat. *Herbert, 1640*

75 Heads I win, tails you lose. *17th c.*

76 Health is better than wealth. *16th c.*

77 Health is not valued till sickness come. *Fuller, 1732*

78 Hear all parties. *15th c.*

79 Hear twice before you speak once. *19th c.*

80 Heard a pin drop, You might have. *19th c.*

81 Heart is in his mouth, His. *16th c.*

82 Heavy purse makes a light heart, A *17th c.*

83 Hell and Chancery are always open. *Fuller, 1732*

84 Hell is paved with good intentions. (The road to) *18th c.*

85 Hell, Hull and Halifax, From/ good Lord deliver us. *16th c.*

86 Higher up, The/the greater the fall. *16th c.*

87 History repeats itself. *19th c.*

88 Hit the nail on the head, To.   *16th c.*
89 Hobson's choice.   *17th c.*
90 Hoist with his own petard.   *17th c.*
91 Hold a candle to the devil, To.   *15th c.*
92 Honest man's word is as good as his bond, An.   *17th c.*
93 Honest men marry soon, wise ones not at all.   *Ray, 1670*
94 Honesty is the best policy.   *16th c.*
95 *Honi soit qui mal y pense* – Evil be to him who evil thinks.
                                                               French
96 Honour among thieves, There is.   *18th c.*
97 Hook or by crook, By.   *14th c.*
98 Hope for the best and prepare for the worst.   *16th c.*
99 Hope is as cheap as despair.   *Fuller, 1732*
 1 Hot love is soon cold.   *16th c.*
 2 Hour in the morning is worth two in the evening, An.   *19th c.*
 3 Hour of pain is as long as a day of pleasure, An.
                                                               Fuller, 1732
 4 Hour today, One/ is worth two tomorrow.   *Fuller, 1732*
 5 Hour's sleep before midnight, One/ is worth three after.
                                                               Herbert, 1640
 6 House on fire, Like a.   *19th c.*
 7 *Humanum est errare* – To err is human   *Latin*
 8 Hypocrisy is a homage that vice pays to virtue.   *Fuller, 1732*

 9 Idle that might be better employed, He is.   *Fuller, 1732*
10 If Ifs and Ans were pots and pans
    There'd be no trade for tinkers.   *19th c.*
11 *Il faut reculer pour mieux sauter* – One must draw back in order
    to leap better.   *French*
12 Ill doers are ill thinkers.   *16th c.*
13 Ill gotten, ill spent,   *Latin*
14 Ill news comes too soon.   *16th c.*
15 Ill wind that blows nobody good, It is an.   *Heywood, 1546*
16 In at one ear and out at the other.   *14th c.*
17 In for a penny, in for a pound.   *17th c.*
18 Insult to injury, To add.   *Latin*
19 Iron entered his soul, The.   *Latin*
20 Iron hand in a velvet glove, An.   *French*

21 Irons in the fire, To have many. *16th c.*

22 Jack has his Jill, Every. *17th c.*

23 Jack of all trades and master of none. *18th c.*

24 Joan is as good as my lady, in the dark. *17th c.*

25 Jolly (happy) as a sandboy, As. *19th c.*

26 Judge from appearances, Never. *16th c.*

27 Keep a dog and bark yourself, Do not. *16th c.*

28 Keep a thing seven years and you will find a use for it.
17th c.

29 Keep one's tongue between one's teeth, To. *17th c.*

30 Keep up with the Joneses, To. *20th c.*

31 Keep your eyes wide open before marriage and half shut afterwards. *18th c.*

32 Keep your mouth shut and your eyes open. *18th c.*

33 Kill not the goose that lays the golden eggs. *15th c.*

34 Kill two birds with one stone, To. *17th c.*

35 King can do no wrong, The. *17th c.*

36 King never dies, The. *Latin*

37 King's favour is no inheritance, The. *Fuller, 1732*

38 Kiss and be friends. *14th c.*

39 Kiss the mistress, If you can/ never kiss the maid. *Ray, 1670*

40 Knaves and fools divide the world. *Ray, 1670*

41 Knocked me down with a feather, You might have. *19th c.*

42 Know on which side one's bread is buttered, To.
Heywood, 1546

43 Know the ropes, To. *19th c.*

44 Know the worth of water till the well is dry, We never.
Kelly, 1721

45 Know which way the wind blows, To. *Heywood, 1546*

46 Knowledge is power. *17th c.*

47 Knows how many beans make nine, He. *19th c.*

48 Knows little, He that/ soon repeats it. *18th c.*

49 Knows nothing, He that/ doubts nothing. *Herbert, 1640*

50 *Laborare est orare* – To work is to pray. *Latin*

51 Large as life, As. *18th c.*

52 Last but not least. *16th c.*

53 Last legs, To be on one's.   *16th c.*
54 Last straw breaks the camel's back, The.   *17th c.*
55 Laughs best who laughs last, He.   *18th c.*
56 Law is a bottomless pit.   *18th c.*
57 Law for the rich, One/ and another for the poor.   *19th c.*
58 Law makers should not be law breakers.   *14th c.*
59 Laws, The more/ the more offenders.   *Latin*
60 Lawyers' houses are built on the heads of fools.
                                                    Herbert, 1640
61 Lay it on with a trowel, To.   *16th c.*
62 Lead a horse to the water, A man may/ but he cannot make him
   drink.   *Heywood, 1546*
63 Lean as a rake, As.   *14th c.*
64 Learning makes a good man better and an ill man worse.
                                                               17th c.
65 Least foolish is wise, The.   *Herbert, 1640*
66 Least said, soonest mended.   *15th c.*
67 Leave in the lurch, To.   *16th c.*
68 Leave no stone unturned, To.   *Greek*
69 Lend I am a friend, When I/ when I ask I am a foe.   *16th c.*
70 Lend your money and lose your friend.   *17th c.*
71 Let sleeping dogs lie.   *14th c.*
72 Let the cat out of the bag, To.   *18th c.*
73 Liar is not believed when he speaks the truth, A.   *Latin*
74 Liars should have good memories.   *Latin*
75 Lick into shape, To.   *15th c.*
76 Lie begets a lie, A.   *Fuller, 1732*
77 Lies upon the ground, He that/ can fall no lower.   *Latin*
78 Life is half spent before we know what it is.   *Herbert, 1640*
79 Life is sweet.   *14th c.*
80 Life, While there is/ there is hope.   *Latin*
81 Lifeless that is faultless, He is.   *Heywood, 1546*
82 Light cares speak, great ones are dumb.   *Latin*
83 Light purse makes a heavy heart, A.   *16th c.*
84 Lightly come, lightly go.   *16th c.*
85 Like father, like son.   *Latin*
86 Like it, If you don't/ you can (may) lump it.   *19th c.*

87 Like master, like man. *Latin*
88 Line one's pockets, To. *16th c.*
89 Lion is not so fierce as he is painted, The. *17th c.*
90 Listeners hear no good of themselves. *17th c.*
91 Little and often fills the purse. *17th c.*
92 Little things please little minds. *Latin*
93 Live and learn. *Clarke, 1639*
94 Live and let live. *Dutch*
95 Live without our friends, We can/ but not without our neighbours. *Kelly, 1721*
96 Lock, stock, and barrel. *19th c.*
97 Lombard Street to a China orange, All. *18th c.*
98 Long absent, soon forgotten. *Draxe, 1616*
99 Long spoon, He should have a/ that sups with the devil.
    14th c.
1 Longest day must have an end, The. *17th c.*
2 Look before you leap. *14th c.*
3 Look (at) on the bright side. *19th c.*
4 Lookers-on see most of the game. *16th c.*
5 Losers are always in the wrong. *Spanish*
6 Losers seekers, finders keepers. *19th c.*
7 Lost his taste, To him that has/ sweet is sour. *Draxe, 1616*
8 Love and a cough cannot be hid. *Latin*
9 Love and business teach eloquence. *Herbert, 1640*
10 Love begets love. *Latin*
11 Love best, Whom we/ to them we can say least. *16th c.*
12 Love comes in at the window and goes out at the door.
    Camden, 1614
13 Love is blind. *14th c.*
14 Love is sweet in the beginning but sour in the ending.
    Draxe, 1616
15 Love lives in cottages as well as in courts. *16th c.*
16 Love makes one fit for any work. *Herbert, 1640*
17 Love makes the world go round. *17th c.*
18 Love me little, love me long. *Heywood, 1546*
19 Love me, love my dog. *Latin*
20 Love of money and the love of learning rarely meet, The.
    Herbert, 1651

21 Love too much that die for love, They.　*17th c.*
22 Love will find a way.　*16th c.*

23 Mad as a hatter.　*19th c.*
24 Mad as a March hare, As.　*14th c.*
25 Maidens should be meek until they be married.
　Fergusson, 1641
26 Main chance, Have an eye to the,　*16th c.*
27 Make hay while the sun shines.　*Heywood, 1546*
28 Man can only die once, A.　*16th c.*
29 Man in the moon.　*14th c.*
30 Man in the street, The.　*19th c.*
31 Man loveth his fetters, No/ be they made of gold.
　- Heywood, 1546
32 Man is as old as he feels, and a woman as old as she looks, A.
　20th c.
33 Man is known by the company he keeps, A.　*17th c.*
34 Man lives, As a/ so shall he die.　*16th c.*
35 Man or mouse.　*16th c.*
36 Man proposes, God disposes.　*Latin*
37 Many a little makes a mickle.　*13th c.*
38 March comes in like a lion and goes out like a lamb.
　Ray, 1670
39 Mare's nest, To find a.　*16th c.*
40 Marriage is a lottery.　*17th c.*
41 Marriages are made in heaven.　*16th c.*
42 Marries for wealth, He that/ sells his liberty.　*Herbert, 1640*
43 Marries late, He that/ marries ill.　*16th c.*
44 Marrieth for love without money, Who/hath good nights and
sorry days.　*Ray, 1670*
45 Marry first and love will follow.　*17th c.*
46 Marry in haste and repent at leisure.　*16th c.*
47 Marry late or never, It is good to.　*Clarke, 1639*
48 Marry your daughters betimes, lest they marry themselves.
　16th c.
49 Marry your son when you will, your daughter when you can.
　Herbert, 1640
50 Measure in all things, There is a.　*14th c.*

51 Measure thrice before you cut once. *Italian*

52 Meat, One man's/ is another man's poison. *Latin*

53 Meet troubles half-way, Don't. *16th c.*

54 Men who make a city, It is the. *Greek*

55 Meekness of Moses is better than the strength of Samson, The.
Fuller, 1732

56 Merry as a cricket, As. *Heywood, 1546*

57 Might is right. *14th c.*

58 Mind your own business. *Clarke, 1639*

59 Mirror, The best/ is an old friend. *Herbert, 1640*

60 Misfortunes never come singly. *14th c.*

61 Miss is as good as a mile, A. *19th c.*

62 Mob has many heads, but no brains, The. *Fuller, 1732*

63 Money be not thy servant, If/ it will be thy master. *17th c.*

64 Money begets money. *Italian*

65 Money is a good servant, but a bad master. *17th c.*

66 Money makes marriage. *Fuller, 1732*

67 Money makes the man. *Greek*

68 Money or your life! Your. *19th c.*

69 Money talks. *17th c.*

70 More the merrier, The/ the fewer the better cheer.
Heywood, 1546

71 Mother, Like/ like daughter. *16th c.*

72 Mother-in-law remembers not that she was a daughter-in-law,
The. *Howell, 1659*

73 Mountain out of a molehill, To make a. *16th c.*

74 Much law, but little justice. *Fuller, 1732*

75 Murder will out. *14th c.*

76 Natural folly is bad enough, but learned folly is intolerable.
Fuller, 1732

77 Necessity hath no law. *Latin*

78 Necessity is the mother of invention. *16th c.*

79 Neck or nothing. *Ray, 1678*

80 Need makes the old wife trot. *15th c.*

81 Needle in a haystack, To look for a. *15th c.*

82 Needs must when the devil drives. *15th c.*

83 Never a bad day that hath a good night, It is. *17th c.*

84 Never ask pardon before you are accused.   *Bohn, 1855*

85 Never put off till tomorrow what may be done today.   *14th c.*

86 Never refuse a good offer.   *Ray, 1670*

87 Never say die.   *19th c.*

88 Never too late to mend, It is.   *17th c.*

89 Never too old to learn.   *17th c.*

90 Never trouble trouble till trouble troubles you.   *19th c.*

91 New broom sweeps clean, A.   *Heywood, 1546*

92 No fire without some smoke.   *Heywood, 1546*

93 No man's religion ever survives his morals.   *Fuller, 1722*

94 No mischief but a woman or a priest is at the bottom of it.
                                                        Latin

95 No money, no swiss.   *17th c.*

96 No names, no pack drill.   *20th c.*

97 No news is good news.   *Italian*

98 No pleasure without pain.   *16th c.*

99 No rose without a thorn.   *15th c.*

 1 No smoke without some fire.   *15th c.*

 2 No sunshine but has some shadow.   *Ray, 1678*

 3 No taxation without representation.   *18th c.*

 4 Nose to the grindstone, To keep one's.   *16th c.*

 5 Nothing costs so much as what is given us.   *Fuller, 1732*

 6 Nothing for nothing.   *18th c.*

 7 Nothing is certain but uncertainty.   *Latin*

 8 Nothing is ours, but time.   *Fuller, 1732*

 9 Nothing questioneth, He that/ nothing learneth.   *16th c.*

10 Nothing seek, nothing find.   *16th c.*

11 Nothing succeeds like success.   *French*

12 Nothing that is violent is permanent.   *16th c.*

13 Nothing venture, nothing win.   *15th c.*

14 Nowadays truth is the greatest news.   *Fuller, 1732*

15 Obedience is much more seen in little things than in great.
                                                   Fuller, 1732

16 Oil upon the waters, To pour.   *19th c.*

17 Old as the hills, As.   *19th c.*

18 Old friends and old wine are best.   *Herbert, 1640*

19 Old head on young shoulders, An. *Clarke, 1639*
20 Old poacher makes a good game-keeper, An. *14th c.*
21 Once bitten, twice shy. *19th c.*
22 One foot in the grave, To have *16th c.*
23 Opportunity makes the thief. *13th c.*
24 Ounce of discretion is worth a pound of learning, An. *17th c.*
25 Out of sight, out of mind. *13th c.*

26 P's and Q's, To mind one's. *17th c.*
27 Painters and poets have leave to lie. *16th c.*
28 Past cure, past care. *16th c.*
29 Patience is a flower that grows not in everyone's garden.
Ray, 1670
30 Patience, money and time bring all things to pass.
Herbert, 1640
31 Pay a person in his own coin, To. *16th c.*
32 Pay through the nose, To. *17th c.*
33 Pays the piper may call the tune, He who. *17th c.*
34 Peace makes plenty. *15th c.*
35 Penny and penny laid up will be many. *Clarke, 1639*
36 Penny for your thoughts, A. *Heywood, 1546*
37 Penny wise, pound foolish. *17th c.*
38 Pension never enriched a young man. *Herbert, 1640*
39 Pigs might fly, but they are very unlikely birds. *19th c.*
40 Pillar to post, From. *15th c.*
41 Plain as a pike-staff, As. *16th c.*
42 Play first (or second) fiddle, To. *19th c.*
43 Plays best (well) that wins, He. *Heywood, 1555*
44 Pleased as Punch, As. *19th c.*
45 Pleased ourselves, When we are/ we begin to please others.
Fuller, 1732
46 Pleasure, There is more/ in loving than in being loved.
Fuller, 1732
47 Pleasure, To overcome/ is the greatest pleasure. *Fuller, 1732*
48 Pleasure of what we enjoy is lost by coveting more, The.
Fuller, 1732
49 Poor as Job, As. *14th c.*
50 Poor heart that never rejoices, It is a. *19th c.*

51 Possession is nine points of the law. *Draxe, 1616*

52 Pot calls the kettle black, The. *17th c.*

53 Poverty breeds strife. *Ray, 1678*

54 Poverty is no sin. *Herbert, 1640*

55 Poverty is not a shame, but the being ashamed of it is.
Fuller, 1732

56 Practice makes perfect. *Latin*

57 Practise what you preach. *14th c.*

58 Praise makes good men better and bad men worse.
Fuller, 1732.

59 Preaches well that lives well, He. *17th c.*

60 Prevention is better than cure. *Latin*

61 Pride will have a fall. *16th c.*

62 Promises too much, He that/ means nothing. *Draxe, 1616*

63 Proof of the pudding is in the eating, The. *Camden, 1623*

64 Prospect is often better than possession. *Fuller, 1732*

65 Prosperity has damned more souls than all the devils together.
Fuller, 1732

66 Proud as Lucifer, As. *14th c.*

67 Proud as a peacock, As. *14th c.*

68 Put on one's thinking cap, To. *17th c.*

69 Pull down than to build, It is easier to. *16th c.*

70 Purse-strings are the most common ties of friendship, The.
Fuller, 1732

71 Put that in your pipe and smoke it. *19th c.*

72 Put your shoulder to the wheel. *17th c.*

73 Queen Anne is dead. *18th c.*

74 *Quos Deus vult perdere, prius dementat* – Whom God wishes to
destroy, he first makes mad. *Latin*

75 Rain before seven: fine before eleven. *19th c.*

76 Rain, rain, go to Spain: fair weather come again.
Howell, 1659

77 Rains but it pours, It never. *18th c.*

78 Rainy day, Lay it up for a. *16th c.*

79 Rats desert a sinking ship. *17th c.*

80 Red as a rose, As. *14th c.*

81 Red rag to a bull, Like a *16th c.*

82 Redemption from hell, There is no.   *17th c.*

83 Religion an ill man is of, It matters not what.   *Fuller, 1732*

84 Religion is the best armour in the world, but the worst cloak.
                                                           Fuller, 1732

85 Remedy for all things but death, There is a.   *16th c.*

86 Repentance comes too late.   *15th c.*

87 Resolves to deal with none but honest men, He that/ must leave
   off dealing.   *Fuller, 1732*

88 Respects not is not respected, He that.   *Herbert, 1640*

89 Revenge is sweet.   *16th c.*

90 Revenge never repairs an injury.   *Fuller, 1732*

91 Rich men have no faults.   *Fuller, 1732*

92 Rich that is satisfied, He is.   *Fuller, 1732*

93 Riches of the mind only that make a man rich and happy, It is.
                                                           Fuller, 1732

94 Ridicule than commend, It is easier to.   *Fuller, 1732*

95 Right as rain, As.   *19th c.*

96 Roads lead to Rome, All.   *14th c.*

97 Roar like a bull, To.   *16th c.*

98 Rob Peter to pay Paul, To.   *14th c.*

99 Rod for his own back, He makes a.   *14th c.*

 1 Rolling stone gathers no moss, A.   *Heywood, 1546*

 2 Rome was not built in a day.   *Latin*

 3 Room to swing a cat, Not.   *18th c.*

 4 Rope enough and he'll hang himself, Give a thief.   *Ray, 1670*

 5 Rough with the smooth, Take the.   *15th c.*

 6 Rule the roast (roost), To.   *15th c.*

 7 Rule youth well, for age will rule itself.   *Fergusson, 1641*

 8 Run with the hare and hunt with the hounds, To.
                                                         Heywood, 1546

 9 Sadness and gladness succeed each other.   *Clarke, 1639*

10 Sail near the wind, To.   *19th c.*

11 Same boat, To be all in the.   *16th c.*

12 Sauce for the goose is sauce for the gander, What is.
                                                           Ray, 1670

13 Save one's bacon, To.   *17th c.*

14 Say Bo(o) to a goose, He cannot.   *16th c.*

15 Say no ill of the year till it be past.   *Herbert, 1640*
16 Saying is one thing and doing another.   *Heywood, 1550*
17 Scot-free, To go.   *16th c.*
18 Scratch, To come up to (the).   *19th c.*
19 Scratch my back and I'll scratch yours, You.   *17th c.*
20 Screw loose somewhere, There is a.   *19th c.*
21 Second thoughts are best.   *Latin*
22 See Naples and die.   *Italian*
23 See the wood for the trees, You cannot.   *Heywood, 1546*
24 See what we shall see, We shall.   *19th c.*
25 Seeing is believing.   *Clarke, 1639*
26 Seeks trouble, He that/ never misses.   *Herbert, 1640*
27 Self-praise is no recommendation.   *17th c.*
28 Self-preservation is the first law of nature.   *17th c.*
29 Set the Thames on fire, To.   *18th c.*
30 Share and share alike.   *17th c.*
31 Shoe pinches, To know where the.   *14th c.*
32 Short and sweet.   *16th c.*
33 Shortest answer is doing, The.   *Herbert, 1640*
34 Short life and a merry one, A.   *17th c.*
35 Short pleasure, long lament.   *15th c.*
36 Sickness is better than sadness.   *Fuller, 1732*
37 Sight for sore eyes, A.   *19th c.*
38 Silence gives consent.   *14th c.*
39 Silk purse out of a sow's ear, You cannot make a   *16th c.*
40 Six hours' sleep for a man, seven for a woman, and eight for
   a fool.   *18th c.*
41 Six of one and half a dozen of the other.   *19th c.*
42 Sixes and sevens, To be at.   *14th c.*
43 Skin of one's teeth, By the.   *16th c.*
44 Slept well, He hath/ that remembers not he hath slept ill.
                                                                       Fuller, 1732.
45 Slippery as an eel, As.   *15th c.*
46 Slow but sure.   *Clarke, 1639*
47 Small profits and quick returns.   *19th c.*
48 Smell a rat, To.   *16th c.*
49 Snake in the grass, There is a.   *Latin*

50 Sneezed at, Not to be. *19th c.*

51 So far, so good. *Kelly, 1721*

52 Soberness conceals, What/ drunkenness reveals. *Latin*

53 Some are wise and some are otherwise. *Howell, 1659*

54 Soon as a man is born he begins to die, As. *Latin*

55 Soon got, soon spent. *Heywood, 1546*

56 Soon hot, soon cold. *15th c.*

57 Soon ripe, soon rotten. *Latin*

58 Sorrow comes unsent for. *Latin*

59 Soup and love, Of/ the first is the best. *Spanish*

60 Sour grapes can ne'er make sweet wine. *Fuller, 1732*

61 Speak not of my debts unless you mean to pay them.
Herbert, 1640

62 Speak well of your friend, of your enemy say nothing. *18th c.*

63 Speak when you are spoken to. *16th c.*

64 Speaks ill of his wife, He that/ dishonours himself. *Fuller, 1732*

65 Speech is silver, silence is golden. *Persian*

66 Spick and span. *16th c.*

67 Split hairs, To. *16th c.*

68 Spoke in one's wheel, To put a. *17th c.*

69 Sprat to catch a mackerel (whale), To throw a. *19th c.*

70 Spur a free horse, Do not. *Latin*

71 Spur of the moment, On the *19th c.*

72 Stepmother, Take heed of a/ the very name of her sufficeth.
Herbert, 1651

73 Stew (fry) in one's own juice (grease), To. *14th c.*

74 Sticks and stones may break my bones, but words will never
hurt me. *19th c.*

75 Stiff as a poker. *18th c.*

76 Stiff upper lip, To keep a. *19th c.*

77 Still waters run deep. *14th c.*

78 Sting is in the tail, The. *16th c.*

79 Sting of a reproach is the truth of it, The. *Fuller, 1732*

80 Stir up a hornets' nest, To. *Latin*

81 Stitch in time saves nine, A. *Fuller, 1732*

82 Stone that lieth not in your way need not offend you, The.
Fuller, 1732

83 Storm in a tea-cup, A. *19th c.*

84 Straight trees have crooked roots.   *16th c.*
85 Strike while the iron is hot.   *14th c.*
86 Subtlety is better than force.   *Draxe, 1616*
87 Sun shines upon all alike, The.   *16th c.*
88 Sure as eggs is eggs, As.   *17th c.*
89 Swallow, One/ does not make a summer.   *Greek*
90 Sweet discourse makes short days and nights.   *Herbert, 1640*
91 Sweet tooth, To have a.   *16th c.*
92 Swine, women, and bees cannot be turned.   *Ray, 1678*

93 Take a farthing away from a thousand pounds, it will be a
   thousand pounds no longer.   *18th c.*
94 Take a leaf out of one's book, To.   *19th c.*
95 Take away my good name and take away my life. *Ray, 1670*
96 Take care of the pence and the pounds will take care of themselves.   *18th c.*
97 Take one down a peg or two, To.   *16th c.*
98 Take the bull by the horns, To.   *19th c.*
99 Take the gilt off the gingerbread, To.   *19th c.*
 1 Take the law into one's own hands, To.   *17th c.*
 2 Take the wind out of one's sails, To.   *19th c.*
 3 Take things as you find them.   *Lean, 1902*
 4 Tales out of school, To tell.   *16th c.*
 5 Talk the hind leg off a donkey, To.   *19th c.*
 6 Talk of the devil, and he is sure to appear.   *17th c.*
 7 Talk without thinking, To/ is to shoot without aiming.
                                                    Fuller, 1732
 8 Talkers, The greatest/ are (always) the least doers. *16th c.*
 9 Talks to himself, He that/ speaks to a fool.   *Kelly, 1721*
10 Tarred with the same brush, All.   *19th c.*
11 Taste of the kitchen is better than the smell, The   *19th c.*
12 Teach an old dog tricks, It is hard to.   *16th c.*
13 Teach your grandmother to suck eggs.   *18th c.*
14 Teacheth ill, He/ who teacheth all.   *Howell, 1659*
15 Tell that to the Marines.   *19th c.*
16 Tell the truth and shame the devil.   *16th c.*
17 Tells his wife news, He that/is but newly married. *Herbert,*
                                                          1640

18 *Tempus fugit* – Time flies. *Latin*

19 Tenterhooks, To be on. *18th c.*

20 There's many a slip 'twixt the cup and the lip. *Greek*

21 Thick as thieves, As. *19th c.*

22 Thief to catch a thief, Set a. *Ray, 1670*

23 Thin end of the wedge is to be feared. The. *19th c.*

24 Things are difficult before they are easy, All. *Fuller, 1732*

25 Things at the worst will mend. *17th c.*

26 Think today and speak tomorrow. *Bohn, 1855*

27 Think well of all men. *Howell, 1659*

28 Think with the wise, but talk with the vulgar. *Greek*

29 Thinking is very far from knowing. *18th c.*

30 Though I say it that should not. *16th c.*

31 Thought is free. *14th c.*

32 Thousand pounds of law, In a/ there's not an ounce of love.
Ray, 1670

33 Threadneedle Street, The old lady of. *19th c.*

34 Threatened men live long. *16th c.*

35 Three may keep counsel if two be away. *Heywood, 1546*

36 Three women and a goose make a market. *Italian*

37 Throw good money after bad, To. *19th c.*

38 Time and thinking tame the strongest grief. *Ray, 1670*

39 Time and tide wait for no man. *16th c.*

40 Time for all things, There is a. *14th c.*

41 Time like the present, No. *18th c.*

42 Today, One/ is worth two tomorrows. *17th c.*

43 Tomorrow never comes. *Ray, 1678*

44 Tomorrow is a new day. *16th c.*

45 Tongue, One/ is enough for a woman. *Ray, 1678*

46 Tongue is not steel, yet it cuts, The. *Heywood, 1546*

47 Tongue of idle people is never idle, The. *Fuller, 1732*

48 Too big for one's boots, To be. *19th c.*

49 Too clever by half. *19th c.*

50 Too many cooks spoil the broth. *16th c.*

51 Touch him with a pair of tongs, I would not. *Ray, 1670*

52 Touch wood. *20th c.*

53 *Tout passe, tout casse, tout lasse.* Everything passes, everything perishes, everything palls. *French*

54 Translators, traitors. *Italian*

55 Travels far, He that/ knows much. *Clarke, 1639*

56 Tread on a worm and it will turn. *Heywood, 1546*

57 Tree is known by its fruit, A. *14th c.*

58 True blue will never stain. *Howell, 1659*

59 True word is spoken in jest, Many a. *14th c.*

60 Trust not a new friend nor an old enemy. *Kelly, 1721*

61 Truth fears no colours. *Ray, 1678*

62 Truth is stranger than fiction. *19th c.*

63 Truth is the daughter of God. *Fuller, 1732*

64 Truth never grows old. *Fuller, 1732*

65 Truth, The/ the whole truth, and nothing but the truth. *17th c.*

66 Turn an honest penny, To. *Heywood, 1546*

67 Turn in his grave, To make a person. *19th c.*

68 Turn over a new leaf, To. *Heywood, 1546*

69 Turn the tables, To. *17th c.*

70 Turn up one's nose, To. *16th c.*

71 Turn up trumps, To. *17th c.*

72 Twist round one's little finger, To. *19th c.*

73 Two bites of a cherry, To make. *French*

74 Two black dots do not make a white. *Kelly, 1721*

75 Two can play at that game. *19th c.*

76 Two dogs strive for a bone, and a third runs away with it. *16th c.*

77 Two heads are better than one. *Heywood, 1546*

78 Two is company, three is none. *19th c.*

79 Two negatives make an affirmative. *16th c.*

80 Two sides to every question, There are. *19th c.*

81 Two strings to one's bow, To have. *15th c.*

82 Two to make a quarrel, It takes. *19th c.*

83 Two wrongs don't make a right. *19th c.*

84 Ugly as sin, As. *19th c.*

85 Uncertainty of the law, The glorious. *19th c.*

86 Under the blanket the black one is as good as the white. *Fuller, 1732*

87 Unforeseen (unexpected) that always happens, It is the.   *Latin*

88 Unity is strength.   *French*

89 Variety is pleasing.   *Greek*

90 Vengeance, The noblest/ is to forgive.   *16th c.*

91 Venom to that of the tongue, There is no.   *Howell, 1659*

92 *Verbum sapienti sat est* – A word is enough to the wise.   *Latin*

93 Virtue dwells not in the tongue but in the heart.   *Fuller, 1732*

94 Virtue is its own reward.   *Latin*

95 Virtue never grows old.   *Herbert, 1640*

96 Virtue of necessity, Make a.   *Latin*

97 Vows made in storms are forgotten in calm.   *Fuller, 1732*

98 Wait and see.   *19th c.*

99 Walls have ears.   *17th c.*

 1 Want a thing well done, If you/ do it yourself.   *Draxe, 1616*

 2 Want of wit is worse than want of wealth.   *Kelly, 1721*

 3 War begins, When/ hell opens.   *Herbert, 1651*

 4 Wars bring scars.   *Clarke, 1639*

 5 Warm the cockles of the heart, To.   *17th c.*

 6 Wash dirty linen in public, To.   *19th c.*

 7 Wash your hands often, your feet seldom, and your head never.
                                                   Ray, 1670

 8 Waste not, want not.   *18th c.*

 9 Watched pot never boils, A.   *19th c.*

10 Water in a sieve, To carry.   *Latin*

11 Water off a duck's back, Like.   *19th c.*

12 Water (blood) out of a stone, To get.   *Latin*

13 Way to an Englishman's heart is through his stomach, The
                                                     19th c.

14 Way to be safe is never to be secure, The.   *Fuller, 1732*

15 Weakest goes to the wall, The.   *16th c.*

16 Wealth, The greatest/ is contentment with a little.   *Ray, 1670*

17 Wear one's heart on one's sleeve, To.   *17th c.*

18 Wear the breeches (pants), To.   *15th c.*

19 Wedlock is a padlock.   *Ray, 1678*

20 Welcome is the best cheer.   *Greek*

21 Well begun is half done.   *Latin*

22 Wet one's whistle, To.   *14th c.*
23 What can't be cured must be endured.   *14th c.*
24 What is worth doing is worth doing well.   *18th c.*
25 What's yours is mine, and what's mine is my own.   *18th c.*
26 Wheels within wheels, There are.   *17th c.*
27 When in doubt, leave out.   *20th c.*
28 When the cat is away the mice will play.   *16th c.*
29 Whispering, Where there is/ there is lying.   *Ray, 1678*
30 Widows are always rich.   *Ray, 1678*
31 Wife, He that has a/ has a master.   *Kelly, 1721*
32 Wild oats, To sow one's.   *16th c.*
33 Will, Where there's a/ there's a way.   *Herbert, 1640*
34 Will, Where there's a/ there's trouble.   *20th c.*
35 Wine and wenches empty men's purses.   *Clarke, 1639*
36 Wine in the bottle does not quench thirst, The. *Herbert, 1640*
37 Wine in, truth out.   *16th c.*
38 Wisdom like silence, No.   *Greek*
39 Wise child that knows its own father, It is a.   *16th c.*
40 Wise man, He is not a/ who cannot play the fool on occasion.
                                                            16th c.
41 Wise men learn by other men's mistakes; fools by their own.
                                                             Latin
42 Wish is father to the thought, The.   *Latin*
43 Wive and thrive both in a year, It is hard to.   *15th c.*
44 Wives must be had, be they good or bad.   *Clarke, 1639*
45 Wolf from the door, To keep the.   *Heywood, 1546*
46 Woman conceals what she knows not, A.   *16th c.*
47 Woman's work is never done, A.   *16th c.*
48 Women and geese, Where there are/ there wants no noise.
                                                        Draxe, 1616
49 Women are always in extremes.   *Clarke, 1639*
50 Women are necessary evils.   *16th c.*
51 Women look in their glass, The more/ the less they look to their
   house.   *Herbert, 1640*
52 Women must have their wills while they live, because they make
   none when they die.   *17th c.*
53 Women must have the last word.   *16th c.*
54 Wonders will never cease.   *18th c.*

55 Wool over a person's eyes, To pull the   *19th c.*
56 Work and no play makes Jack a dull boy, All.   *Ray, 1670*
57 World and his wife, All the   *18th c.*
58 Worse things happen at sea.   *19th c.*
59 Worth his weight in gold, He is.   *16th c.*
60 Worth of a thing is best known by the want, The.   *17th c.*
61 Wrong never comes right.   *19th c.*

62 Young man should not marry yet, A/an old man not at all.
    16th c.
63 Young men may die, old men must.   *16th c.*
64 Young men think old men fools, and old men know young men
   to be so.   *16th c.*
65 Young saint, old devil.   *15th c.*
66 Youth and age will never agree.   *16th c.*
67 Youth will be served.   *19th c.*
68 Youth will have its course (or swing, or fling).   *16th c.*

69 Zeal is fit only for wise men, but is found mostly in fools.
    Fuller, 1732
70 Zeal, when it is a virtue, is a dangerous one.   *Fuller, 1732*
71 Zeal without knowledge is fire without light.   *Fuller, 1732*

PUDNEY, John, 1908–
72 Do not despair
   For Johnny head-in-air;
   He sleeps as sound
   As Johnny underground.   *For Johnny*

PUNCH
73 Advice to persons about to marry. – 'Don't.'   *Vol. 8, Page 1,*
    1845

74 You pays your money and you takes your choice.   *Vol. 10,*
    16, 1846

75 What is better than Presence of Mind in a Railway accident? –
   Absence of Body.   *Vol. 16, 231, 1849*

76 Never do today what you can put off till tomorrow.   *Vol. 17,*
    241, 1849

77 What is Matter? – Never Mind.
   What is Mind? – No Matter.   *Vol. 29, 19, 1855*

78 Why are Trafalgar Square fountains like Government Clerks? –
   Because they play from 10 till 4.   *Vol. 35, 21, 1858*

79 Mun, a had no' been the-erre abune two hours when – bang –
   went saxpence!!!   *Vol. 55, 235, 1868*

80 Nothink for nothink 'ere, and precious little for sixpence.
                                              Vol. 57, 152, 1869

81 Go directly – see what she's doing, and tell her she mustn't.
                                              Vol. 63, 202, 1872

82 Here was an old owl liv'd in an oak,
   The more he heard the less he spoke:
   The less he spoke, the more he heard,
   O, if men were all like that wise bird.   *Vol. 68, 155, 1875*

83 I never read books – I *write* them.   *Vol. 74, 210, 1878*

84 I used your soap two years ago: since then I have used no other.
                                              Vol. 86, 197, 1884

85 Nearly all our best men are dead! Carlyle, Tennyson, Browning,
   George Eliot! I'm not feeling very well myself!   *Vol. 104, 210,*
                                                             1893

86 I'm afraid you've got a bad egg, Mr Jones.
   Oh no, my Lord, I assure you! Parts of it are excellent.
                                              Vol. 109, 222, 1895

87 Look here, Steward, if this is coffee, I want tea; but if this is tea,
   then I wish for coffee.   *Vol. 123, 44, 1902*

QUESNAY, François, 1694–1774

88 *Laissez faire, laissez passer.* – No interference, and complete
   freedom of movement.   [*Of Government interference*]
                                                       Attributed

RABELAIS, François, 1494?–1553?

89 *L'appétit vient en mangeant.* Appetite comes with eating.
                                              Gargantua, 1, 5

90 *Tirez le rideau, la farce est jouée.* Ring down the curtain, the
   farce is over.   *Last words, attributed*

91 *Je m'en vais chercher un grand peut-être.* I am going in search of a
   great perhaps.   *Last words, attributed*

RACINE, Jean, 1639–1699

92 *Elle flotte, elle hésite; en un mot, elle est femme.* She wavers, she
   hesitates; in a word, she is a woman. MATHAN   *Athalie,*
                                                      Act 3, Scene 3

RALEIGH, Sir Walter, 1552?-1618

93 Even such is Time, that takes in trust
    Our youth, our joys, our all we have,
  And pays us but with age and dust;
    Who in the dark and silent grave,
  When we have wandered all our ways,
  Shuts up the story of our days;
  But from this earth, this grave, this dust,
  My God shall raise me up, I trust. *Written the night before*
his death

94 Give me my scallop-shell of quiet,
  My staff of faith to walk upon,
  My scrip of joy, immortal diet,
  My bottle of salvation,
  My gown of glory, hope's true gage,
  And thus I'll take my pilgrimage. *The Passionate Man's*
Pilgrimage

95 So the heart be right, it is no matter which way the head lies.
On laying his head on the block

96 If all the world and love were young,
  And truth in every shepherd's tongue,
  These pretty pleasures might me move
  To live with thee, and be thy love. *The Nymph's Reply to*
the Passionate Shepherd

RALEIGH, Sir Walter Alexander, 1861-1922

97 I wish I loved the Human Race;
  I wish I loved its silly face;
  I wish I liked the way it walks;
  I wish I liked the way it talks;
  And when I'm introduced to one
  I wish I thought *What Jolly fun!* *The Wishes of an Elderly*
Man

RANKIN, Jeremiah Eames, 1828-1904

98 God be with you till we meet again. *Hymn*

RANSOME, Arthur, 1884-1967

99 Grab a chance and you won't be sorry for a might-have-been.
COMMANDER WALKER *We didn't Mean to Go to Sea*

READE, Charles, 1814-1884

1 *Courage, mon ami, le diable est mort.* Courage, my friend, the
  devil is dead. *The Cloister and the Hearth, Ch. 24*

2 Make 'em laugh; make 'em cry; make 'em wait.   *Advice to*
young author on writing novels

REED, Henry, 1914–

3 Today we have naming of parts. Yesterday,
We had daily cleaning. And tomorrow morning
We shall have what to do after firing. But today,
Today we have naming of parts.   *Naming of Parts*

REMARQUE, Erich Maria, 1898–1970

4 *Im Westen nichts Neues*. All Quiet on the Western Front.
Title of Novel

REYNOLDS, Frederic, 1764–1841

5 [*Taking out his watch*] How goes the enemy?   ENNUI
The Dramatist, Act 1

REYNOLDS, Sir Joshua, 1723–1792

6 If you have great talents, industry will improve them: if you have
but moderate abilities, industry will supply their deficiency.
Discourses, 2

RHODES, Cecil John, 1853–1902

7 So little done, so much to do.   *Last words*
8 Educational relations make the strongest tie.   *Will, endowing*
Rhodes Scholarships

RICE, Grantland, 1880–1954

9 For when the one Great Scorer comes
To write against your name,
He marks – not that you won or lost –
But how you played the game.   *Alumnus Football*

RIPLEY, Robert Leroy, 1893–1949

10 Believe it or not.   *Title of newspaper feature*

ROCHE, Sir Boyle, 1743–1807

11 My love for England and Ireland is so great that I would have
the two sisters embrace like one brother.   *Reported in Irish*
Parliamentary Register, 11, 294

12 What has posterity done for us?   *Speech in Irish Parliament,*
1780

13 Mr Speaker, I smell a rat; I see him forming in the air and darkening the sky; but I'll nip him in the bud. *Attributed*

ROCHEFOUCAULD, Duc de la, 1613–1680

14 We have all enough strength to bear the misfortunes of others.
Les Maximes, 19

15 Everyone complains of his memory, but no one complains of his judgment. *Ib, 89*

16 The intellect is always fooled by the heart. *Ib, 102*

17 Hypocrisy is the homage paid by vice to virtue. *Ib, 218*

18 The height of cleverness is to conceal one's cleverness. *Ib, 245*

19 In the misfortunes of our best friends, we find something that is not displeasing. *Maximes supprimées, 583*

ROCHEFOUCAULD-LIANCOURT, Duc de La, 1747–1827

20 LOUIS XVI: *C'est une révolte?* Is it a revolt?
THE DUKE: *Non, sire, c'est une révolution.* No, sire it is a revolution. *On hearing of the Fall of the Bastille, 1789*

ROCHESTER, John Wilmot, 2nd Earl of, 1647–1680

21 Here lies our sovereign lord the King,
    Whose word no man relies on;
He never said a foolish thing,
    Nor ever did a wise one. *Epitaph on Charles II*

ROGERS, E. W., 1864–1913

22 Ev'ry member of the force
Has a watch and chain, of course;
If you want to know the time,
Ask a P'liceman. *Ask a P'liceman*

ROGERS, Samuel, 1763–1855

23 When a new book is published, read an old one. *Attributed*

24 Think nothing done while aught remains to do. *Human Life, 49*

25 Sheridan was listened to with such attention that you might have heard a pin drop. *Table Talk*

ROLAND, Madame Marie Jeanne Philipon, 1754–1793

26 *O Liberté! O Liberté! que de crimes on commet en ton nom!* O liberty, liberty, what crimes are committed in your name!
Remark from the scaffold, on viewing the Statue of Liberty

ROOSEVELT, Franklin Delano, 1882–1945

27 I pledge you, I pledge myself, to a new deal for the American people.   *Speech accepting nomination for Presidency, Democratic National Convention, Chicago, 2 July 1932*

28 The only thing we have to fear is fear itself.   *First Inaugural Address, 4 March 1933*

29 In the field of world policy, I would dedicate this nation to the policy of a good neighbour.   *Ib*

30 I see one third of a nation ill-housed, ill-clad, ill-nourished.   *Second Inaugural Address, 20 Jan. 1937*

31 A radical is a man with both feet firmly planted in the air.   *Broadcast, 26 Oct. 1939*

32 We look forward to a world founded upon four essential human freedoms. The first is freedom of speech and expression – everywhere in the world. The second is freedom of every person to worship God in his own way – everywhere in the world. The third is freedom from want . . . everywhere in the world. The fourth is freedom from fear . . . anywhere in the world.   *Speech to Congress, 6 Jan. 1941*

33 We all know that books burn – yet we have the greater knowledge that books cannot be killed by fire. People die, but books never die. No man and no force can abolish memory . . . In this war, we know, books are weapons.   *Message to American Booksellers Association, 23 April 1942*

34 More than an end to war, we want an end to the beginnings of all wars.   *Speech written for broadcast, 13 April 1945 (the day after his death)*

ROOSEVELT, Theodore, 1858–1919

35 I wish to preach, not the doctrine of ignoble ease, but the doctrine of the strenuous life.   *Speech, Chicago, 10 April 1899*

36 The first requisite of a good citizen in this Republic of ours is that he shall be able and willing to pull his weight.   *Speech, New York, 11 Nov. 1902*

37 A man who is good enough to shed his blood for his country is good enough to be given a square deal afterwards. More than that no man is entitled to, and less than that no man shall have.   *Speech, Springfield, Illinois, 4 July 1903*

38 There is no room in this country for hyphenated Americanism.   *Speech, New York, 12 Oct. 1915*

39 No man is justified in doing evil on the ground of expediency.
The Strenuous Life

ROSEBERY, Archibald Philip Primrose, 5th Earl of, 1847–1929
40 The Empire is a Commonwealth of Nations.   *Speech,*
Adelaide, 18 Jan. 1884
41 It is beginning to be hinted that we are a nation of amateurs.
Rectorial Address, Glasgow, 16 Nov. 1900

ROSS, Alan Strode Campbell, 1907–
42 U and Non-U, An Essay in Sociological Linguistics.   *Title of*
Essay included in Noblesse Oblige, 1956

ROSSETTI, Christina Georgina, 1830–1894
43 In the bleak mid-winter
   Frosty wind made moan,
Earth stood hard as iron,
   Water like a stone;
Snow had fallen, snow on snow,
   Snow on snow,
In the bleak mid-winter,
   Long ago.   *Mid-Winter*
44 Remember me when I am gone away,
   Gone far away into the silent land.   *Remember*
45 Better by far you should forget and smile
   Than that you should remember and be sad.   *Ib*
46 'Does the road wind up-hill all the way?'
   'Yes, to the very end.'
   'Will the day's journey take the whole long day?'
   'From morn to night, my friend.'   *Up-Hill*
47 When I am dead, my dearest
   Sing no sad songs for me.   *When I am Dead*
48 And if thou wilt, remember,
   And if thou wilt, forget.   *Ib*

ROSSETTI, Dante Gabriel, 1828–1882
49 A sonnet is a moment's monument, –
   Memorial from the Soul's eternity
   To one dead deathless hour.   *The House of Life, Part 1,*
Introduction

50 The hour when you too learn that all is vain
   And that Hope sows what Love shall never reap.
Ib, 44, Cloud and Wind

51   My name is Might-Have-Been;
I am also called No-More, Too-Late, Farewell.   *The House of*
Life, Part 2, 97. A Superscription

52 Unto the man of yearning, thought
And aspiration, to do nought
Is in itself almost an act.   *Soothsay*

53 I have been here before.
But when or how I cannot tell:
I know the grass beyond the door,
The sweet keen smell,
The sighing sound, the lights around the shore.   *Sudden*
Light, 1

ROUGET DE LISLE, Claude Joseph, 1760–1836

54 *Allons, enfants, de la patrie,*
Le jour de gloire est arrivé.
Come, children of our native land, the day of glory has arrived.
La Marseillaise

ROUSSEAU, Jean Jacques, 1712–1778

55 *L'homme est né libre, et partout il est dans les fers.* Man was born
free and everywhere he is in chains.   *Du Contrat Social,*
Ch. 1

ROUTH, Martin Joseph, 1755–1854

56 Always verify your references.   *Attributed*

'RED ROWLEY', 20th century

57 Mademoiselle from Armenteers,
Hasn't been kissed for forty years,
Hinky dinky, parley-voo.   *Mademoiselle from Armentières*

RUNYON, Damon, 1884–1946

58 More than somewhat.   *Passim*

RUSKIN, John, 1819–1900

59 All travelling becomes dull in exact proportion to its rapidity.
Modern Painters

60 If a book is worth reading, it is worth buying.   *Sesame and*
Lilies

61 Remember that the most beautiful things in the world are the
most useless; peacocks and lilies for instance.   *The Stones of*
Venice

62 The purest and most thoughtful minds are those which love
colour the most. *The Stones of Venice*

63 Fine art is that in which the hand, the head, and the heart of
man go together. *The Two Paths*

64 There is no wealth but life. *Unto this Last*

RUSSELL, John, 1st Earl, 1792–1878

65 If peace cannot be maintained with honour, it is no longer
peace. *Speech, Greenock, 19 Sept.*
1853

RUSSELL, Bertrand Arthur William, 3rd Earl, 1872–1970

66 Men are capable, not only of fear and hate, but also of hope and
benevolence. If the populations of the world can be brought to
see and to realize in imagination the hell to which hate and fear
must condemn them on the one hand, and, on the other, the
comparative heaven which hope and benevolence can create by
means of new skills, the choice should not be difficult, and our
self-tormented species should allow itself a life of joy such as the
past has never known. *Common Sense and Nuclear Warfare,*
1959

67 Mathematics possesses not only truth, but supreme beauty – a
beauty cold and austere, like that of sculpture. *The Study of*
Mathematics

RUTLAND, John, 7th Duke of, 1818–1906

68 Let wealth and commerce, laws and learning die,
But leave us still our old nobility. *England's Trust, 3, 227*

'SAKI' (Hector Hugh Munro), 1870–1916

69 He's simply got the instinct for being unhappy highly developed.
Chronicles of Clovis, The Match-Maker

70 The cook was a good cook, as cooks go; and as cooks go she
went. *Reginald on Besetting Sins*

SALINGER, Jerome David, 1919–

71 If you really want to hear about it, the first thing you'll probably
want to know is where I was born, and what my lousy childhood
was like, and how my parents were occupied and all before they
had me, and all that David Copperfield kind of crap, but I don't
feel like going into it. *The Catcher in the Rye, opening words*

SALISBURY, Robert Cecil, 3rd Marquis of, 1830–1903

72 By office boys for office boys. *Remark about the Daily Mail*

SALLUST, 86–34 B.C.

73 *Idem velle atque idem nolle, ea demum firma amicitia est.* To like and dislike the same things, that is indeed true friendship.
Catiline, 20

74 *Pro patria, pro liberis, pro aris atque focis suis.* On behalf of their country, their children, their altars, and their hearths. *Ib, 59*

SAMUEL, Herbert Louis, 1st Viscount, 1870–1963

75 It takes two to make a marriage a success and only one a failure.
A Book of Quotations

76 A truism is on that account none the less true. *Ib*

SANDBURG, Carl, 1878–1967

77 The fog comes
on little cat feet.
It sits looking
over the harbor and city
on silent haunches
and then moves on. *Fog*

78 Pile the bodies high at Austerlitz and Waterloo.
Shovel them under and let me work –
I am the grass; I cover all. *Grass*

79 Look out how you use proud words,
When you let proud words go, it is not easy to call them back.
Primer Lesson

80 Homestead, Braddock, Birmingham, they make their steel with men,
Smoke and blood is the mix of steel. *Smoke and Steel*

SARGENT, Epes, 1813–1880

81 A life on the ocean wave,
A home on the rolling deep. *A Life on the Ocean Wave*

SASSOON, Siegfried, 1886–

82 And when the war is done and youth stone dead
I'd toddle safely home and die – in bed. *Base Details*

83 Everyone suddenly burst out singing. *Everyone Sang*

SAYERS, Henry, 1855–1932

84 Ta-ra-ra-boom-de-ay! *Title of song*

SCHILLER, Friedrich von, 1759–1805

85 *Alle Menschen werden Brüder Wo dein sanfter Flügel weilt.* In the
   shade of your soft wings, all men will be brothers.

An die Freude

86 *Die Weltgeschichte ist das Wetlgericht.* World history is the
   world's judgment. *Lecture, Jena, 26 May 1789*

SCHNECKENBURGER, Max, 1819–1849

87 *Die Wacht am Rhein.* The Watch on the Rhine. *Title of song*

SCOTT, Charles Prestwich, 1846–1932

88 Neither in what it gives, nor in what it does not give, nor in the
   mode of presentation, must the unclouded face of truth suffer
   wrong. Comment is free but facts are sacred. *Manchester
   Guardian, 6 May 1926*

SCOTT, Robert Falcon, 1868–1912

89 Great God! this is an awful place. *[The South Pole] Journal,
   17 Jan. 1912*

90 For God's sake look after our people. *Ib, 25 March 1912*

91 Had we lived, I should have had a tale to tell of the hardihood,
   endurance, and courage of my companions which would have
   stirred the hearts of every Englishman. These rough notes and
   our dead bodies must tell the tale. *Message to the Public*

SCOTT, Sir Walter, 1771–1832

92 Come fill up my cup, come fill up my can,
   Come saddle your horses, and call up your men;
   Come open the West Port, and let me gang free,
   And it's room for the bonnets of Bonny Dundee.

Bonny Dundee, The Doom of Devorgoil, 2, 3

93 But answer came there none. *Bridal of Triermain, 3, 10*

94 The stag at eve had drunk his fill,
   Where danced the moon on Monan's rill. *The Lady of the
   Lake, 1, 1*

95 Forward and frolic glee was there,
   The will to do, the soul to dare. *Ib, 1, 21*

96 Yet seem'd that tone, and gesture bland,
   Less used to sue than to command. *Ib*

97 Soldier, rest! thy warfare o'er,
   Sleep the sleep that knows not breaking;
   Dream of battled fields no more,
   Days of danger, nights of waking. *The Lady of the Lake, 1, 31*

98 Like the dew on the mountain,
   Like the foam on the river,
   Like the bubble on the fountain,
   Thou art gone, and for ever!   *Ib, 3, 16*

99 The way was long, the wind was cold,
   The Minstrel was infirm and old;
   His wither'd cheek, and tresses grey,
   Seem'd to have known a better day.
                The Lay of the Last Minstrel, Introduction, 1

1 If thou would'st view fair Melrose aright,
   Go visit it by the pale moonlight.   *Ib, 2, 1*

2 Love rules the court, the camp, the grove.
   And men below, and saints above;
   For love is heaven, and heaven is love.   *Ib, 3, 2*

3 Call it not vain; they do not err,
   Who say, that when the Poet dies,
   Mute Nature mourns her worshipper,
   And celebrates his obsequies.   *Ib, 5, 1*

4 True love's the gift which God has given
   To man alone beneath the heaven.   *Ib, 5, 13*

5 Breathes there the man, with soul so dead,
   Who never to himself hath said,
   This is my own, my native land!   *Ib, 6, 1*

6 The wretch, concentrated all in self,
   Living, shall forfeit fair renown,
   And, doubly dying, shall go down
   To the vile dust, from whence he sprung,
   Unwept, unhonour'd, and unsung.   *Ib, 6, 1*

7 That day of wrath, that dreadful day,
   When heaven and earth shall pass away.   *Ib, 6, 31, Hymn*
                                            for the Dead

8 November's sky is chill and drear,
   November's leaf is red and sear.   *Marmion, 1, Introduction*

9 And come he slow or come he fast,
   It is but Death who comes at last.   *Ib, 2, 30*

10 O, young Lochinvar is come out of the west,
   Through all the wide Border his steed was the best.   *Ib, 5, 12,*
                                                        Lochinvar

11 So faithful in love, and so dauntless in war,
There never was Knight like the young Lochinvar.
Marmion, 5, 12, Lochinvar

12 And dar'st thou then
To beard the lion in his den,
The Douglas in his hall? *Ib, 6, 14*

13 O what a tangled web we weave,
When first we practise to deceive! *Ib, 6, 17*

14 O Woman! in our hours of ease,
Uncertain, coy, and hard to please,
And variable as the shade,
By the light quivering aspen made;
When pain and anguish wring the brow,
A ministering angel thou! *Ib, 6, 30*

15 He shook the fragment of his blade,
And shouted 'Victory!
Charge, Chester, charge! On, Stanley, on!'
Were the last words of Marmion. *Ib, 6, 32*

16 MRS. BERTRAM: That sounds like nonsense, my dear.
MR BERTRAM: May be so, my dear; but it may be very good law
for all that. *Guy Mannering, Ch. 9*

17 The hour is come, but not the man. *The Heart of Midlothian,*
Ch. 4, Heading

SCOTT, William, 1st Baron Stowell, 1745–1836
18 A dinner lubricates business. *Boswell's Life of Johnson, 1781*

SEARS, Edmund Hamilton, 1810–1876
19 It came upon the midnight clear,
That glorious song of old. *That Glorious Song of Old*

SEEGER, Alan, 1888–1916
20 I have a rendezvous with Death
At some disputed barricade. *I have a Rendezvous with Death*

SELDEN, John, 1584–1654
21 Old friends are best. King James used to call for his old shoes;
they were easiest for his feet. *Table Talk*

22 There is not anything in the world so much abused as this
sentence, Salus populi suprema lex esto. *Ib*

23 Philosophy is nothing but discretion. *Ib*

24 Preachers say, Do as I say, not as I do. *Ib*

25 A king is a thing men have made for their own sakes, for quietness' sake. Just as if in a family one man is appointed to buy the meat.   *Table Talk*

26 Every law is a contract between the king and the people, and therefore to be kept.   *Ib*

SELLAR, Walter Carruthers, 1898–1951, and YEATMAN, Robert Julian, 1897–

27 1066 And All That.   *Title of Book*

28 The Roman Conquest was, however, a *Good Thing*, since the Britons were only natives at that time.   *1066 And All That, Ch. 1*

29 Has it never occurred to you that the Romans *counted backwards*? (Be honest.)   *Ib, Test Paper 1*

30 Finding, however, that he was not memorable, he very patriotically abdicated in favour of Henry IV, Part II.   *Ib, Ch. 26*

31 Shortly after this the cruel Queen died and a post-mortem examination revealed the word 'CALLOUS' engraved on her heart.   *Ib, Ch. 32*

32 Williamanmary: England Ruled by an Orange.   *Ib, Heading to Ch. 38*

33 Napoleon's armies used to march on their stomachs, shouting: 'Vive l'intérieur!'   *Ib, Ch. 48*

34 Do not on any account attempt to write on both sides of the paper at once.   *Ib, Test Paper 5*

SERVICE, Robert William, 1874–1958

35 This is the Law of the Yukon, that only the strong shall thrive; That surely the weak shall perish, and only the Fit survive.   *The Law of the Yukon*

36 When we, the Workers, all demand: 'What are we fighting for?' . . .
Then, then we'll end that stupid crime, that devil's madness – War.   *Michael*

SEWARD, William Henry, 1801–1872

37 There is a higher law than the Constitution.   *Speech, US Senate, 11 March 1850*

SHADWELL, Thomas, 1642?–1692

38 Words may be false and full of art,
Sighs are the natural language of the heart.   CUPID   *Psyche Act 3*

39 He's a wise man that marries a harlot; he's on the surest side.
Who but an ass would marry an uncertainty? SIR POSITIVE-
AT-ALL *The Sullen Lovers, Act 5*

40 I'll do't instantly, in the twinkling of a bed-staff. SIR SAMUEL
HEARTY *The Virtuoso, Act 1*

SHAKESPEARE, William, 1564–1616
All's Well that Ends Well

41   Love all, trust a few,
Do wrong to none; be able for thine enemy
Rather in power than use, and keep thy friend
Under thy own life's key; be check'd for silence,
But never tax'd for speech. COUNTESS OF ROUSILLON
Act 1, Scene 1, Line 57

42 Our remedies oft in ourselves do lie,
Which we ascribe to heaven. HELENA   *1, 1, 202*

43 My friends were poor, but honest. HELENA   *1, 3, 186*

44 A young man married is a man that's marr'd. PAROLLES
2, 3, 291

45 No legacy is so rich as honesty. MARIANA   *3, 5, 12*

46 The web of our life is of a mingled yarn, good and ill together.
2ND LORD   *4, 3, 67*

47   Praising what is lost
Makes the remembrance dear. KING OF FRANCE   *5, 3, 19*

48 Th' inaudible and noiseless foot of Time. KING OF FRANCE
5, 3, 41

Antony and Cleopatra

49 The triple pillar of the world transform'd
Into a strumpet's fool. PHILO   *1, 1, 12*

50 There's beggary in the love that can be reckon'd. ANTONY
1, 1, 15

51 The nature of bad news infects the teller. MESSENGER
1, 2, 92

52 Where's my serpent of old Nile? CLEOPATRA   *1, 5, 25*

53   My salad days,
When I was green in judgment. CLEOPATRA   *1, 5, 73*

54 The barge she sat in, like a burnish'd throne,
Burn'd on the water. The poop was beaten gold;
Purple the sails, and so perfumed that
The winds were love-sick with them; the oars were silver,

Which to the tune of flutes kept stroke and made
The water which they beat to follow faster,
As amorous of their strokes. For her own person,
It beggar'd all description. ENOBARBUS   *Antony and*
                                          Cleopatra, 2, 2, 195

55 Age cannot wither her, nor custom stale
Her infinite variety. Other women cloy
The appetites they feed, but she makes hungry
Where most she satisfies. ENOBARBUS   *2, 2, 239*

56 Though it be honest, it is never good
To bring bad news. CLEOPATRA   *2, 5, 85*

57 I will praise any man that will praise me. ENOBARBUS
                                          2, 6, 88

58 He will to his Egyptian dish again. ENOBARBUS   *2, 6, 121*

59 Celerity is never more admir'd
Than by the negligent. CLEOPATRA   *3, 7, 24*

60   He wears the rose
Of youth upon him. ANTONY   *3, 13, 20*

61 Let's have one other gaudy night. ANTONY   *3, 13, 183*

62 To business that we love we rise betime,
And go to't with delight. ANTONY   *4, 4, 20*

63 O infinite virtue, com'st thou smiling from
The world's great snare uncaught? CLEOPATRA   *4, 8, 18*

64 Unarm, Eros; the long day's task is done,
And we must sleep. ANTONY   *4, 14, 35*

65 I am dying, Egypt, dying; only
I here importune death awhile, until
Of many thousand kisses the poor last
I lay upon thy lips. ANTONY   *4, 15, 18*

66 O, wither'd is the garland of the war,
The soldier's pole is fall'n! Young boys and girls
Are level now with men. The odds is gone,
And there is nothing left remarkable
Beneath the visiting moon. CLEOPATRA   *4, 15, 64*

67   The bright day is done,
And we are for the dark. IRAS   *5, 2, 192*

68 His biting is immortal; those that do die of it do seldom or never
recover. CLOWN   *5, 2, 246*

69 I wish you joy o' th' worm. CLOWN   *5, 2, 277*

70   I have
Immortal longings in me. CLEOPATRA   *5, 2, 278*

71 Dost thou not see my baby at my breast
That sucks the nurse asleep? CLEOPATRA *Antony and*
Cleopatra, 5, 2, 307

As You Like It

72 Fleet the time carelessly, as they did in the golden world.
CHARLES *1, 1, 108*

73 Well said; that was laid on with a trowel. CELIA *1, 2, 94*

74 Beauty provoketh thieves sooner than gold. ROSALIND
1, 3, 106

75 Sweet are the uses of adversity;
Which, like the toad, ugly and venomous,
Wears yet a precious jewel in his head;
And this our life, exempt from public haunt,
Finds tongues in trees, books in the running brooks,
Sermons in stones, and good in everything. DUKE SENIOR
2, 1, 12

76 Sweep on, you fat and greasy citizens. 1ST LORD (quoting
Jaques) *2, 1, 55*

77 Unregarded age in corners thrown. ADAM *2, 3, 42*

78 Therefore my age is as a lusty winter,
Frosty, but kindly. ADAM *2, 3, 52*

79 O good old man, how well in thee appears
The constant service of the antique world,
When service sweat for duty, not for meed!
Thou art not for the fashion of these times,
Where none will sweat but for promotion. ORLANDO *2, 3, 56*

80 I had rather bear with you than bear you. TOUCHSTONE
2, 4, 9

81 Ay, now am I in Arden; the more fool I; when I was at home I
was in a better place; but travellers must be content.
TOUCHSTONE *2, 4, 13*

82 If thou rememb'rest not the slightest folly
That ever love did make thee run into,
Thou hast not lov'd. SILVIUS *2, 4, 31*

83 Under the greenwood tree
Who loves to lie with me,
And turn his merry note
Unto the sweet bird's throat,
Come hither, come hither, come hither.
Here shall he see
No enemy
But winter and rough weather. AMIENS *2, 5, 1*

84 I can suck melancholy out of a song, as a weasel sucks eggs.
                    JAQUES   *As You Like It, 2, 5, 12*

85 Who doth ambition shun,
   And loves to live i' th' sun,
   Seeking the food he eats,
   And pleas'd with what he gets.   AMIENS, ETC.   *2, 5, 34*

86 I'll rail against all the first-born of Egypt.   JAQUES   *2, 5, 56*

87 A fool! I met a fool i' th' forest,
   A motley fool.   JAQUES   *2, 7, 12*

88 And so, from hour to hour, we ripe and ripe,
   And then, from hour to hour, we rot and rot;
   And thereby hangs a tale.   JAQUES   *2, 7, 26*

89   Whate'er you are
   That in this desert inaccessible,
   Under the shade of melancholy boughs,
   Lose and neglect the creeping hours of time.   ORLANDO
                                                       2, 7, 109

90   All the world's a stage,
   And all the men and women merely players;
   They have their exits and their entrances;
   And one man in his time plays many parts,
   His acts being seven ages. At first the infant,
   Mewling and puking in the nurse's arms;
   Then the whining school-boy, with his satchel
   And shining morning face, creeping like snail
   Unwillingly to school. And then the lover,
   Sighing like furnace, with a woeful ballad
   Made to his mistress' eyebrow. Then a soldier,
   Full of strange oaths, and bearded like the pard,
   Jealous in honour, sudden and quick in quarrel,
   Seeking the bubble reputation
   Even in the cannon's mouth. And then the justice,
   In fair round belly with good capon lin'd,
   With eyes severe and beard of formal cut,
   Full of wise saws and modern instances;
   And so he plays his part. The sixth age shifts
   Into the lean and slipper'd pantaloon,
   With spectacles on nose and pouch on side,
   His youthful hose, well sav'd, a world too wide
   For his shrunk shank; and his big manly voice,
   Turning again toward childish treble, pipes
   And whistles in his sound. Last scene of all,
   That ends this strange eventful history,

Is second childishness and mere oblivion;
Sans teeth, sans eyes, sans taste, sans every thing. JAQUES
As You Like It, 2, 7, 139

91   Blow, blow, thou winter wind,
       Thou art not so unkind
         As man's ingratitude;
       Thy tooth is not so keen,
       Because thou art not seen,
         Although thy breath be rude.
Heigh-ho! sing heigh-ho! unto the green holly.
Most friendship is feigning, most loving mere folly. AMIENS
2, 7, 174

92 Run, run, Orlando; carve on every tree,
The fair, the chaste, and unexpressive she. ORLANDO   *3, 2, 9*

93 He that wants money, means, and content, is without three good
friends. CORIN   *3, 2, 23*

94 Let us make an honourable retreat; though not with bag and
baggage, yet with scrip and scrippage. TOUCHSTONE   *3, 2, 150*

95 O wonderful, wonderful, and most wonderful wonderful, and
yet again wonderful, and after that, out of all whooping!
CELIA   *3, 2, 177*

96 Do you not know I am a woman? When I think, I must speak.
ROSALIND   *3, 2, 234*

97 I do desire we may be better strangers. ORLANDO   *3, 2, 243*

98 Time travels in divers paces with divers persons. I'll tell you who
Time ambles withal, who Time trots withal, who Time gallops
withal, and who he stands still withal. ROSALIND   *3, 2, 290*

99 Truly, I would the gods had made thee poetical. TOUCHSTONE
3, 3, 13

1 The truest poetry is the most feigning. TOUCHSTONE   *3, 3, 16*

2 I am not a slut, though I thank the gods I am foul. AUDREY
3, 3, 34

3 Men have died from time to time, and worms have eaten them,
but not for love. ROSALIND   *4, 1, 94*

4 Men are April when they woo, December when they wed: maids
are May when they are maids, but the sky changes when they
are wives. ROSALIND   *4, 1, 130*

5 No sooner met but they look'd; no sooner look'd but they lov'd;
no sooner lov'd but they sigh'd; no sooner sigh'd but they ask'd
one another the reason; no sooner knew the reason but they
sought the remedy. ROSALIND   *5, 2, 29*

6 O, how bitter a thing it is to look into happiness through another man's eyes! ORLANDO   *As You Like It, 5, 2, 40*

7 It was a lover and his lass,
  With a hey, and a ho, and a hey nonino,
That o'er the green corn-field did pass
  In the spring time, the only pretty ring time,
When birds do sing, hey ding a ding, ding.
Sweet lovers love the spring. TWO PAGES   *5, 3, 14*

8 An ill-favour'd thing, sir, but mine own. TOUCHSTONE
                                            5, 4, 55

9 I will name you the degrees. The first, the Retort Courteous; the second, the Quip Modest; the third, the Reply Churlish; the fourth, the Reproof Valiant; the fifth, the Countercheck Quarrelsome; the sixth, the Lie with Circumstance; the seventh, the Lie Direct. TOUCHSTONE   *5, 4, 86*

10 Your If is the only peace-maker; much virtue in If.
                           TOUCHSTONE *5, 4, 97*

11 If it be true that good wine needs no bush, 'tis true that a good play needs no epilogue. ROSALIND   *Epilogue, 3*

The Comedy of Errors

12 They brought one Pinch, a hungry lean-fac'd villain,
A mere anatomy, a mountebank,
A threadbare juggler, and a fortune-teller,
A needy, hollow-ey'd, sharp-looking wretch,
A living dead man. ANTIPHOLUS OF EPHESUS   *5, 1, 237*

Coriolanus

13 My gracious silence, hail! CORIOLANUS   *2, 1, 166*

14   Bid them wash their faces
And keep their teeth clean. CORIOLANUS   *2, 3, 59*

15   Custom calls me to't.
What custom wills, in all things should we do't,
The dust on antique time would lie unswept,
And mountainous error be too highly heap'd
For truth to o'erpeer. CORIOLANUS   *2, 3, 114*

16 Hear you this Triton of the minnows? Mark you
His absolute 'shall'? CORIOLANUS   *3, 1, 89*

17 His nature is too noble for the world:
He would not flatter Neptune for his trident,

Or Jove for's power to thunder. His heart's his mouth;
What his breast forges, that his tongue must vent.
                                        MENENIUS *Coriolanus, 3, 1, 255*

18   Like a dull actor now
I have forgot my part and I am out,
Even to a full disgrace. CORIOLANUS   *5, 3, 40*

19 If you have writ your annals true, 'tis there
That, like an eagle in a dove-cote, I
Flutter'd your Volscians in Corioli.
Alone I did it. CORIOLANUS   *5, 6, 114*

Cymbeline

20 Hark, hark! the lark at heaven's gate sings,
    And Phoebus 'gins arise,
His steeds to water at those springs
    On chalic'd flow'rs that lies;
And winking Mary-buds begin
    To ope their golden eyes.
With everything that pretty bin,
    My lady sweet, arise;
        Arise, arise! SONG   *2, 3, 19*

21   There be many Caesars
Ere such another Julius. Britain is
A world by itself, and we will nothing pay
For wearing our own noses. CLOTEN   *3, 1, 11*

22 O for a horse with wings! IMOGEN   *3, 2, 47*

23   O, this life
Is nobler than attending for a check,
Richer than doing nothing for a bribe,
Prouder than rustling in unpaid-for silk. BELARIUS *3, 3, 21*

24 I have not slept one wink. PISANIO   *3, 4, 99*

25 Hath Britain all the sun that shines? IMOGEN   *3, 4, 135*

26   Society is no comfort
To one not sociable. IMOGEN   *4, 2, 12*

27   Though mean and mighty rotting
Together have one dust, yet reverence –
That angel of the world – doth make distinction
Of place 'tween high and low. BELARIUS   *4, 2, 247*

28 Thersites' body is as good as Ajax',
When neither are alive. GUIDERIUS   *4, 2, 253*

29 Fear no more the heat o' th' sun
    Nor the furious winter's rages;

Thou thy worldly task hast done,
  Home art gone, and ta'en thy wages.
Golden lads and girls all must,
As chimney-sweepers, come to dust. GUIDERIUS   *Cymbeline,*
                                                  4, 2, 259

30 All lovers young, all lovers must
   Consign to thee and come to dust. GUIDERIUS AND ARVIRAGUS
                                                  4, 2, 275

31 Quiet consummation have,
   And renowned be thy grave! GUIDERIUS AND ARVIRAGUS
                                                  4, 2, 281

32 He that sleeps feels not the toothache. GAOLER   *5, 4, 171*

Hamlet

33 For this relief much thanks. 'Tis bitter cold,
   And I am sick at heart. FRANCISCO   *1, 1, 8*

34 What, has this thing appear'd again to-night? HORATIO
                                                  1, 1, 21

35 We do it wrong, being so majestical,
   To offer it the show of violence. MARCELLUS   *1, 1, 143*

36 But look, the morn, in russet mantle clad,
   Walks o'er the dew of yon high eastward hill. HORATIO
                                                  1, 1, 166

37 The memory be green. CLAUDIUS   *1, 2, 2*

38 A little more than kin, and less than kind. HAMLET   *1, 2, 65*

39 Not so, my lord; I am too much in the sun. HAMLET *1, 2, 67*

40 Thou know'st 'tis common – all that lives must die,
   Passing through nature to eternity. GERTRUDE   *1, 2, 72*

41 But I have that within which passes show –
   These but the trappings and the suits of woe. HAMLET
                                                  1, 2, 85

42 O, that this too too solid flesh would melt,
   Thaw, and resolve itself into a dew!
   Or that the Everlasting had not fix'd
   His canon 'gainst self-slaughter! O God! God!
   How weary, stale, flat, and unprofitable,
   Seem to me all the uses of this world! HAMLET   *1, 2, 129*

43 So excellent a king that was to this
   Hyperion to a satyr. HAMLET   *1, 2, 139*

44   Why, she would hang on him
   As if increase of appetite had grown
   By what it fed on. HAMLET   *1, 2, 143*

45 Frailty, thy name is woman! HAMLET   *Hamlet*, *1, 2, 146*

46 It is not, nor it cannot come to good. HAMLET   *1, 2, 158*

47 A truant disposition, good my lord. HORATIO   *1, 2, 169*

48 Thrift, thrift, Horatio! The funeral bak'd-meats
Did coldly furnish forth the marriage tables. HAMLET

1, 2, 180

49 'A was a man, take him for all in all,
I shall not look upon his like again. HAMLET   *1, 2, 187*

50 A countenance more in sorrow than in anger. HORATIO

1, 2, 231

51 Give it an understanding, but no tongue. HAMLET   *1, 2, 249*

52   All is not well.
I doubt some foul play. HAMLET   *1, 2, 254*

53 The chariest maid is prodigal enough
If she unmask her beauty to the moon. LAERTES   *1, 3, 36*

54 Do not, as some ungracious pastors do,
Show me the steep and thorny way to heaven,
Whiles, like a puff'd and reckless libertine,
Himself the primrose path of dalliance treads
And recks not his own rede. OPHELIA   *1, 3, 47*

55 And these few precepts in thy memory
Look thou character. Give thy thoughts no tongue,
Nor any unproportion'd thought his act.
Be thou familiar, but by no means vulgar.
Those friends thou hast, and their adoption tried,
Grapple them to thy soul with hoops of steel. POLONIUS

1, 3, 58

56   Beware
Of entrance to a quarrel; but, being in,
Bear't that th' opposed may beware of thee.
Give every man thy ear, but few thy voice;
Take each man's censure, but reserve thy judgment.
Costly thy habit as thy purse can buy,
But not express'd in fancy; rich, not gaudy;
For the apparel oft proclaims the man. POLONIUS   *1, 3, 65*

57 Neither a borrower nor a lender be;
For loan oft loses both itself and friend,
And borrowing dulls the edge of husbandry.
This above all – to thine own self be true,
And it must follow, as the night the day,
Thou canst not then be false to any man. POLONIUS

1, 3, 75

58 Be something scanter of your maiden presence. POLONIUS
   Hamlet, 1, 3, 121

59 But to my mind, though I am native here
   And to the manner born, it is a custom
   More honour'd in the breach than the observance. HAMLET
   1, 4, 14

60 Angels and ministers of grace defend us!
   Be thou a spirit of health or goblin damn'd,
   Bring with thee airs from heaven or blasts from hell,
   Be thy intents wicked or charitable,
   Thou com'st in such a questionable shape
   That I will speak to thee. HAMLET   *1, 4, 39*

61 I do not set my life at a pin's fee;
   And for my soul, what can it do to that,
   Being a thing immortal as itself? HAMLET   *1, 4, 65*

62 Something is rotten in the state of Denmark. MARCELLUS
   1, 4, 90

63   I am thy father's spirit,
   Doom'd for a certain term to walk the night. GHOST   *1, 5, 9*

64   But that I am forbid
   To tell the secrets of my prison-house,
   I could a tale unfold whose lightest word
   Would harrow up thy soul, freeze thy young blood,
   Make thy two eyes, like stars, start from their spheres,
   Thy knotted and combined locks to part,
   And each particular hair to stand on end,
   Like quills upon the fretful porpentine.
   But this eternal blazon must not be
   To ears of flesh and blood. List, list, O, list! GHOST   *1, 5, 13*

65 Revenge his foul and most unnatural murder. GHOST *1, 5, 25*

66 Murder most foul, as in the best it is;
   But this most foul, strange, and unnatural. GHOST *1, 5, 27*

67 O my prophetic soul! My uncle! HAMLET   *1, 5, 40*

68 O Hamlet, what a falling off was there. GHOST   *1, 5, 47*

69 There are more things in heaven and earth, Horatio,
   Than are dreamt of in your philosophy. HAMLET   *1, 5, 166*

70 To put an antic disposition on. HAMLET   *1, 5, 172*

71 The time is out of joint. O cursed spite,
   That ever I was born to set it right! HAMLET   *1, 5, 189*

72 Brevity is the soul of wit. POLONIUS   *2, 2, 90*

73 More matter with less art. GERTRUDE   *2, 2, 95*

74 That he's mad, 'tis true: 'tis true 'tis pity;
And pity 'tis 'tis true. POLONIUS   *Hamlet*, 2, 2, 97

75 POLONIUS: Do you know me, my lord?
HAMLET: Excellent well; you are a fishmonger.   2, 2, 172

76 To be honest, as this world goes, is to be one man pick'd out
of ten thousand. HAMLET   2, 2, 177

77 POLONIUS: What do you read, my Lord?
HAMLET: Words, words, words.   2, 2, 190

78 Though this be madness, yet there is method in't. POLONIUS
                                                  2, 2, 204

79 HAMLET: What news?
ROSENCRANTZ: None, my lord, but that the world's grown
                honest.
HAMLET: Then is doomsday near.   2, 2, 235

80 There is nothing either good or bad, but thinking makes it so.
                                        HAMLET   2, 2, 248

81 What a piece of work is a man! How noble in reason! how
infinite in faculties! in form and moving, how express and
admirable! in action, how like an angel! in apprehension, how
like a god! the beauty of the world! the paragon of animals!
And yet, to me, what is this quintessence of dust? Man delights
not me – no, nor woman neither. HAMLET   2, 2, 303

82 He that plays the king shall be welcome. HAMLET   2, 2, 317

83 I am but mad north-north-west; when the wind is southerly I
know a hawk from a handsaw. HAMLET   2, 2, 374

84 The best actors in the world, either for tragedy, comedy, history,
pastoral, pastoral-comical, historical-pastoral, tragical-historical, tragical-comical-historical-pastoral, scene individable, or
poem unlimited. POLONIUS   2, 2, 392

85 The play, I remember, pleas'd not the million; 'twas caviare
to the general. HAMLET   2, 2, 429

86 The mobled queen. 1ST PLAYER   2, 2, 496

87 Let them be well used; for they are the abstract and brief
chronicles of the time. HAMLET   2, 2, 517

88 Use every man after his desert, and who shall scape whipping?
                                        HAMLET 2, 2, 523

89 O, what a rogue and peasant slave am I! HAMLET   2, 2, 543

90 What's Hecuba to him or he to Hecuba,
That he should weep for her? HAMLET   2, 2, 552

91 A dull and muddy-mettl'd rascal. HAMLET   2, 2, 561

92 But I am pigeon-liver'd and lack gall
   To make oppression bitter. HAMLET   *Hamlet, 2, 2, 572*

93   This is most brave,
  That I, the son of a dear father murder'd,
  Prompted to my revenge by heaven and hell,
  Must, like a whore, unpack my heart with words,
  And fall a-cursing like a very drab. HAMLET   *2, 2, 578*

94   The play's the thing
  Wherein I'll catch the conscience of the King. HAMLET
                                                  2, 2, 600

95 To be, or not to be – that is the question;
  Whether 'tis nobler in the mind to suffer
  The slings and arrows of outrageous fortune,
  Or to take arms against a sea of troubles,
  And by opposing end them? To die, to sleep –
  No more; and by a sleep to say we end
  The heart-ache and the thousand natural shocks
  That flesh is heir to. 'Tis a consummation
  Devoutly to be wish'd. To die, to sleep;
  To sleep, perchance to dream. Ay, there's the rub;
  For in that sleep of death what dreams may come,
  When we have shuffled off this mortal coil,
  Must give us pause. There's the respect
  That makes calamity of so long life;
  For who would bear the whips and scorns of time,
  Th' oppressor's wrong, the proud man's contumely,
  The pangs of despis'd love, the law's delay,
  The insolence of office, and the spurns
  That patient merit of th' unworthy takes,
  When he himself might his quietus make
  With a bare bodkin? Who would fardels bear,
  To grunt and sweat under a weary life,
  But that the dread of something after death –
  The undiscover'd country, from whose bourn
  No traveller returns – puzzles the will,
  And makes us rather bear those ills we have
  Than fly to others that we know not of?
  Thus conscience does make cowards of us all;
  And thus the native hue of resolution
  Is sicklied o'er with the pale cast of thought,
  And enterprises of great pith and moment,
  With this regard, their currents turn awry
  And lose the name of action. HAMLET   *3, 1, 56*

96   For to the noble mind
Rich gifts wax poor when givers prove unkind. OPHELIA
Hamlet, 3, 1, 100

97 Get thee to a nunnery. HAMLET   *3, 1, 121*

98 Be thou as chaste as ice, as pure as snow, thou shalt not escape calumny. HAMLET   *3, 1, 135*

99 I have heard of your paintings too, well enough; God hath given you one face, and you make yourselves another. HAMLET
3, 1, 142

1 O, what a noble mind is here o'erthrown!
The courtier's, soldier's, scholar's, eye, tongue, sword;
Th' expectancy and rose of the fair state,
The glass of fashion and the mould of form,
Th' observ'd of all observers – quite, quite down! OPHELIA
3, 1, 150

2 Madness in great ones must not unwatch'd go. CLAUDIUS
3, 1, 188

3 Speak the speech, I pray you, as I pronounc'd it to you, trippingly on the tongue; but if you mouth it, as many of our players do, I had as lief the town-crier spoke my lines. Nor do not saw the air too much with your hand, thus, but use all gently. HAMLET   *3, 2, 1*

4 It out-herods Herod. HAMLET   *3, 2, 14*

5 Suit the action to the word, the word to the action; with this specia observance, that you o'erstep not the modesty of nature.
    HAMLET *3, 2, 17*

6   Give me that man
That is not passion's slave, and I will wear him
In my heart's core, ay, in my heart of heart,
As I do thee. HAMLET   *3, 2, 69*

7 Here's metal more attractive. HAMLET   *3, 2, 106*

8 OPHELIA: 'Tis brief, my lord.
HAMLET: As woman's love.   *3, 2, 148*

9 The lady doth protest too much, methinks. GERTRUDE
3, 2, 225

10 We that have free souls, it touches us not. Let the galled jade wince, our withers are unwrung. HAMLET   *3, 2, 235*

11 The proverb is something musty. HAMLET   *3, 2, 334*

12 Very like a whale. POLONIUS   *3, 2, 372*

13 'Tis now the very witching time of night,
When churchyards yawn, and hell itself breathes out
Contagion to this world. HAMLET   *3, 2, 378*

14 Let me be cruel, not unnatural:
I will speak daggers to her, but use none.   HAMLET   *Hamlet,*
3, 2, 385

15 O, my offence is rank, it smells to heaven.   CLAUDIUS   *3, 3, 36*

16 My words fly up, my thoughts remain below.
Words without thoughts never to heaven go.   CLAUDIUS
3, 3, 97

17 How now! a rat? Dead, for a ducat, dead!   HAMLET   *3, 4, 23*

18 A king of shreds and patches.   HAMLET   *3, 4, 102*

19 Assume a virtue, if you have it not.   HAMLET   *3, 4, 160*

20 I must be cruel only to be kind.   HAMLET   *3, 4, 178*

21   Diseases desperate grown
By desperate appliance are reliev'd,
Or not at all.   CLAUDIUS   *4, 3, 9*

22 How all occasions do inform against me,
And spur my dull revenge! What is a man,
If his chief good and market of his time
Be but to sleep and feed? A beast, no more!   HAMLET
4, 4, 32

23   Some craven scruple
Of thinking too precisely on th' event.   HAMLET   *4, 4, 40*

24   Rightly to be great
Is not to stir without great argument,
But greatly to find quarrel in a straw,
When honour's at the stake.   HAMLET   *4, 4, 53*

25 Come, my coach! Good night, ladies; good night, sweet ladies,
good night, good night.   OPHELIA   *4, 5, 69*

26 When sorrows come, they come not single spies,
But in battalions!   CLAUDIUS   *4, 5, 75*

27 There's such divinity doth hedge a king
That treason can but peep to what it would.   CLAUDIUS
4, 5, 120

28 There's rosemary, that's for remembrance; pray you, love,
remember.
And there is pansies, that's for thoughts.   OPHELIA   *4, 5, 172*

29 A very riband in the cap of youth.   CLAUDIUS   *4, 7, 77*

30 There is a willow grows aslant the brook
That shows his hoar leaves in the glassy stream.   GERTRUDE
4, 7, 167

31 Alas, poor Yorick! I knew him, Horatio: a fellow of infinite jest,
of most excellent fancy.   HAMLET   *5, 1, 179*

32   Lay her i' th' earth;
And from her fair and unpolluted flesh
May violets spring! I tell thee, churlish priest,
A minist'ring angel shall my sister be
When thou liest howling. LAERTES   *Hamlet, 5, 1, 232*

33 Sweets to the sweet, farewell! GERTRUDE   *5, 1, 237*

34 Let Hercules himself do what he may,
The cat will mew, and dog will have his day. HAMLET *5, 1, 285*

35 There's a divinity that shapes our ends,
Rough-hew them how we will. HAMLET   *5, 2, 10*

36 A hit, a very palpable hit. OSRIC   *5, 2, 273*

37 Report me and my cause aright. HAMLET   *5, 2, 331*

38 If thou didst ever hold me in thy heart,
Absent thee from felicity awhile,
And in this harsh world draw thy breath in pain,
To tell my story. HAMLET   *5, 2, 338*

39 The rest is silence. HAMLET   *5, 2, 350*

40 Now cracks a noble heart. Good night, sweet prince,
And flights of angels sing thee to thy rest! HORATIO *5, 2, 351*

41 For he was likely, had he been put on,
To have prov'd most royal. FORTINBRAS   *5, 2, 389*

King Henry the Fourth, Part One

42 So shaken as we are, so wan with care. HENRY IV   *1, 1, 1*

43 To chase these pagans in those holy fields
Over whose acres walk'd those blessed feet
Which fourteen hundred years ago were nail'd
For our advantage on the bitter cross. HENRY IV   *1, 1, 24*

44 See riot and dishonour stain the brow
Of my young Harry. HENRY IV   *1, 1, 85*

45 Shall there be gallows standing in England when thou art king?
FALSTAFF *1, 2, 56*

46 O, thou hast damnable iteration, and art indeed able to corrupt
a saint. FALSTAFF   *1, 2, 88*

47 Why, Hal, 'tis my vocation, Hal; 'tis no sin for a man to labour
in his vocation. FALSTAFF   *1, 2, 101*

48 There's neither honesty, manhood, nor good fellowship in thee.
FALSTAFF *1, 2, 133*

49 I know you all, and will awhile uphold
The unyok'd humour of your idleness. PRINCE   *1, 2, 188*

50 If all the year were playing holidays,
To sport would be as tedious as to work. PRINCE
Henry the Fourth, Part One, 1, 2, 197

51   A certain lord, neat, and trimly dress'd,
Fresh as a bridegroom, and his chin new reap'd
Show'd like a stubble-land at harvest-home.
He was perfumed like a milliner,
And 'twixt his finger and his thumb he held
A pouncet-box, which ever and anon
He gave his nose and took't away again. HOTSPUR   *1, 3, 33*

52   He made me mad
To see him shine so brisk, and smell so sweet,
And talk so like a waiting-gentlewoman
Of guns, and drums, and wounds – God save the mark! --
And telling me the sovereignest thing on earth
Was parmaceti for an inward bruise. HOTSPUR   *1, 3, 53*

53   O, the blood more stirs
To rouse a lion than to start a hare! HOTSPUR   *1, 3, 197*

54 By heaven, methinks it were an easy leap
To pluck bright honour from the pale-fac'd moon;
Or dive into the bottom of the deep,
Where fathom-line could never touch the ground,
And pluck up drowned honour by the locks. HOTSPUR
1, 3, 201

55 I know a trick worth two of that. FIRST CARRIER   *2, 1, 36*

56 I am bewitch'd with the rogue's company. If the rascal have not
given me medicines to make me love him, I'll be hang'd.
FALSTAFF   *2, 2, 16*

57 Have you any levers to lift me up again, being down? FALSTAFF
2, 2, 33

58 It would be argument for a week, laughter for a month, and a
good jest for ever. PRINCE   *2, 2, 91*

59   Falstaff sweats to death
And lards the lean earth as he walks along. PRINCE   *2, 2, 104*

60 Out of this nettle, danger, we pluck this flower, safety.
HOTSPUR   *2, 3, 10*

61   Constant you are,
But yet a woman; and for secrecy,
No lady closer; for I well believe
Thou wilt not utter what thou dost not know. HOTSPUR
2, 3, 105

62 I am not yet of Percy's mind, the Hotspur of the north; he that kills me some six or seven dozen of Scots at a breakfast, washes his hands, and says to his wife 'Fie upon this quiet life! I want work'. PRINCE *Henry the Fourth, Part One, 2, 4, 97*

63 A plague of all cowards, I say. FALSTAFF *2, 4, 109*

64 There lives not three good men unhang'd in England, and one of them is fat and grows old. FALSTAFF *2, 4, 123*

65 I have pepper'd two of them; two I am sure I have paid – two rogues in buckram suits. I tell thee what, Hal, if I tell thee a lie, spit in my face, call me horse. Thou knowest my old ward: here I lay, and thus I bore my point. Four rogues in buckram let drive at me. FALSTAFF *2, 4, 183*

66 O monstrous! eleven buckram men grown out of two! PRINCE *2, 4, 212*

67 A plague of sighing and grief! it blows a man up like a bladder. FALSTAFF *2, 4, 322*

68 That reverend vice, that grey iniquity, that father ruffian, that vanity in years. PRINCE *2, 4, 437*

69 Banish plump Jack, and banish all the world. FALSTAFF *2, 4, 462*

70 O monstrous! but one halfpenny-worth of bread to this intolerable deal of sack! PRINCE *2, 4, 521*

71 I am not in the roll of common men. GLENDOWER *3, 1, 43*

72 GLENDOWER: I can call spirits from the vasty deep.
   HOTSPUR: Why, so can I, or so can any man;
           But will they come when you do call for them?
           3, 1, 53

73 I had rather be a kitten and cry mew
   Than one of these same metre ballad-mongers. HOTSPUR
           3, 1, 129

74   Mincing poetry.
   'Tis like the forc'd gait of a shuffling nag. HOTSPUR *3, 1, 134*

75 I understand thy kisses, and thou mine,
   And that's a feeling disputation. MORTIMER *3, 1, 204*

76 Swear me, Kate, like a lady as thou art,
   A good mouth-filling oath. HOTSPUR *3, 1, 254*

77 He was but as the cuckoo is in June,
   Heard, not regarded. HENRY IV *3, 2, 75*

78 Do I not bate? Do I not dwindle? Why, my skin hangs about me like an old lady's loose gown. FALSTAFF *3, 3, 2*

79 Company, villainous company, hath been the spoil of me.
FALSTAFF *Henry the Fourth, Part One, 3, 2, 10*

80 I have more flesh than another man, and therefore more frailty.
FALSTAFF *3, 3, 167*

81 Doomsday is near; die all, die merrily. HOTSPUR *4, 1, 134*

82 I have misused the King's press damnably. FALSTAFF *4, 2, 11*

83 The cankers of a calm world and a long peace. FALSTAFF
4, 2, 30

84 To the latter end of a fray and the beginning of a feast
Fits a dull fighter and a keen guest. FALSTAFF *4, 2, 77*

85 For nothing can seem foul to those that win. HENRY IV
5, 1, 8

86 Rebellion lay in his way, and he found it. FALSTAFF *5, 1, 28*

87 I would 'twere bed-time, Hal, and all well. FALSTAFF
5, 1, 125

88 Honour pricks me on. Yea, but how if honour prick me off when
I come on? How then? Can honour set to a leg? No. Or an arm?
No. Or take away the grief of a wound? No. Honour hath no
skill in surgery, then? No. What is honour? A word. What is in
that word? Honour. What is that honour? Air. A trim reckoning! Who hath it? He that died o' Wednesday. Doth he feel it?
No. Doth he hear it? No. 'Tis insensible then? Yea, to the dead.
But will it not live with the living? No. Why? Detraction will
not suffer it. Therefore I'll none of it. Honour is a mere scutcheon. And so ends my catechism. FALSTAFF *5, 1, 129*

89   The time of life is short!
To spend that shortness basely were too long. HOTSPUR
5, 2, 82

90 Two stars keep not their motion in one sphere. PRINCE
5, 4, 65

91 But thoughts, the slaves of life, and life, time's fool,
And time, that takes survey of all the world,
Must have a stop. HOTSPUR *5, 4, 81*

92 What, old acquaintance! Could not all this flesh
Keep in a little life? Poor Jack, farewell!
I could have better spar'd a better man. PRINCE *5, 4, 102*

93 The better part of valour is discretion; in the which better part
I have saved my life. FALSTAFF *5, 4, 120*

94 Lord, Lord, how this world is given to lying! FALSTAFF
5, 4, 143

95 I'll purge, and leave sack, and live cleanly, as a nobleman
should do. FALSTAFF *5, 4, 163*

King Henry the Fourth, Part Two

96 This man's brow, like to a title-leaf,
Foretells the nature of a tragic volume. NORTHUMBERLAND
1, 1, 60

97 Yet the first bringer of unwelcome news
Hath but a losing office, and his tongue
Sounds ever after as a sullen bell,
Rememb'red tolling a departing friend. NORTHUMBERLAND
1, 1, 100

98 The brain of this foolish-compounded clay, man, is not able to
invent anything that tends to laughter, more than I invent or is
invented on me. I am not only witty in myself, but the cause that
wit is in other men. I do here walk before thee like a sow that
hath overwhelm'd all her litter but one. FALSTAFF *1, 2, 7*

99 My lord, I was born about three of the clock in the afternoon,
with a white head and something a round belly. For my voice –
I have lost it with hallooing and singing of anthems. FALSTAFF
1, 2, 176

1 Well, I cannot last ever; but it was always yet the trick of our
English nation, if they have a good thing, to make it too common.
FALSTAFF *1, 2, 200*

2 I would to God my name were not so terrible to the enemy as
it is. FALSTAFF *1, 2, 204*

3 I can get no remedy against this consumption of the purse;
borrowing only lingers and lingers it out, but the disease is
incurable. FALSTAFF *1, 2, 223*

4 O thoughts of men accurs'd!
Past and to come seems best; things present, worst.
ARCHBISHOP *1, 3, 107*

5 Away, you scullion! you rampallian! you fustilarian! I'll tickle
your catastrophe. FALSTAFF *2, 1, 57*

6 He hath eaten me out of house and home. HOSTESS *2, 1, 71*

7 Now, the Lord lighten thee! Thou art a great fool.
CHIEF JUSTICE *2, 1, 187*

8 He was indeed the glass
Wherein the noble youth did dress themselves. LADY PERCY
2, 3, 21

9 Hollow pamper'd jades of Asia. PISTOL *2, 4, 155*

10 Is it not strange that desire should so many years outlive
performance? POINS *2, 4, 250*

11 Now comes in the sweetest morsel of the night, and we must
hence, and leave it unpick'd. FALSTAFF *2, 4, 354*

12 You see, my good wenches, how men of merit are sought after; the undeserver may sleep, when the man of action is call'd on.
FALSTAFF *Henry the Fourth, Part Two, 2, 4, 361*

13 How many thousands of my poorest subjects
Are at this hour asleep! O sleep, O gentle sleep,
Nature's soft nurse, how have I frighted thee,
That thou no more wilt weigh my eyelids down,
And steep my senses in forgetfulness? HENRY IV   *3, 1, 4*

14 Canst thou, O partial sleep, give thy repose
To the wet sea-boy in an hour so rude;
And in the calmest and most stillest night,
With all appliances and means to boot,
Deny it to a king? Then, happy low, lie down!
Uneasy lies the head that wears a crown. HENRY IV   *3, 1, 26*

15 O God! that one might read the book of fate. HENRY IV
3, 1, 45

16 There is a history in all men's lives,
Figuring the natures of the times deceas'd. WARWICK   *3, 1, 80*

17 Death, as the Psalmist saith, is certain to all; all shall die. How a good yoke of bullocks at Stamford fair? SHALLOW   *3, 2, 36*

18 We have heard the chimes at midnight. FALSTAFF   *3, 2, 210*

19 I care not; a man can die but once; we owe God a death.
FEEBLE   *3, 2, 228*

20 Care I for the limb, the thews, the stature, bulk, and big assemblance of a man! Give me the spirit. FALSTAFF   *3, 2, 251*

21 Lord, Lord, how subject we old men are to this vice of lying!
FALSTAFF   *3, 2, 294*

22 Against ill chances men are ever merry;
But heaviness foreruns the good event. ARCHBISHOP   *4, 2, 81*

23 A peace is of the nature of a conquest;
For then both parties nobly are subdu'd,
And neither party loser. ARCHBISHOP   *4, 2, 89*

24 I may justly say with the hook-nos'd fellow of Rome – I came, saw, and overcame. FALSTAFF   *4, 3, 40*

25 He hath a tear for pity and a hand
Open as day for melting charity. HENRY IV   *4, 4, 31*

26 Most subject is the fattest soil to weeds. HENRY IV   *4, 4, 54*

27 O polish'd perturbation! golden care!
That keep'st the ports of slumber open wide
To many a watchful night! PRINCE
4, 5, 23

28 This sleep is sound indeed; this is a sleep
That from this golden rigol hath divorc'd
So many English kings. PRINCE
Henry the Fourth, Part Two, 4, 5, 35

29 Thy wish was father, Harry, to that thought. HENRY IV
4, 5, 93

30   Commit
The oldest sins the newest kind of ways. HENRY IV   *4, 5, 126*

31 This is the English, not the Turkish court;
Not Amurath an Amurath succeeds,
But Harry Harry. HENRY V   *5, 2, 47*

32 Under which king, Bezonian?
Speak, or die. PISTOL   *5, 3, 112*

33 Let us take any man's horses: the laws of England are at my
commandment. FALSTAFF   *5, 3, 134*

34 I know thee not, old man. Fall to thy prayers.
How ill white hairs become a fool and jester!
I have long dreamt of such a kind of man,
So surfeit-swell'd, so old, and so profane. HENRY V   *5, 5, 48*

35 Master Shallow, I owe you a thousand pound. FALSTAFF
5, 5, 74

King Henry the Fifth

36 O for a Muse of fire, that would ascend
The brightest heaven of invention. CHORUS   *Prologue, 1*

37   Can this cockpit hold
The vasty fields of France? Or may we cram
Within this wooden O the very casques
That did affright the air at Agincourt? CHORUS *Prologue, 11*

38 Turn him to any cause of policy,
The Gordian knot of it he will unloose,
Familiar as his garter; that, when he speaks,
The air, a charter'd libertine, is still.
ARCHBISHOP OF CANTERBURY   *1, 1, 45*

39   For so work the honey bees,
Creatures that by a rule in nature teach
The act of order to a peopled kingdom.
They have a king, and officers of sorts,
Where some like magistrates correct at home;
Others like merchants venture trade abroad;
Others like soldiers, armed in their stings,
Make boot upon the summer's velvet buds,
Which pillage they with merry march bring home
To the tent-royal of their emperor;

Who, busied in his majesty, surveys
The singing masons building roofs of gold,
The civil citizens kneading up the honey,
The poor mechanic porters crowding in
Their heavy burdens at his narrow gate,
The sad-ey'd justice, with his surly hum,
Delivering o'er to executors pale
The lazy yawning drone. ARCHBISHOP OF CANTERBURY
Henry the Fifth, 1, 2, 187

40 Now all the youth of England are on fire,
And silken dalliance in the wardrobe lies;
Now thrive the armourers, and honour's thought
Reigns solely in the breast of every man;
They sell the pasture now to buy the horse,
Following the mirror of all Christian kings
With winged heels, as English Mercuries.
For now sits Expectation in the air. CHORUS
2, Prologue, 1

41 I dare not fight; but I will wink and hold out mine iron. NYM
2, 1, 6

42 Though patience be a tired mare, yet she will plod. NYM
2, 1, 24

43 He's in Arthur's bosom, if ever man went to Arthur's bosom.
'A made a finer end, and went away an it had been any christom
child; 'a parted ev'n just between twelve and one, ev'n at the
turning o' th' tide. HOSTESS *2, 3, 9*

44 His nose was as sharp as a pen, and 'a babbl'd of green fields.
HOSTESS *2, 3, 17*

45 Once more unto the breach, dear friends, once more;
Or close the wall up with our English dead.
In peace there's nothing so becomes a man
As modest stillness and humility;
But when the blast of war blows in our ears,
Then imitate the action of the tiger:
Stiffen the sinews, summon up the blood,
Disguise fair nature with hard-favour'd rage. HENRY V *3, 1, 1*

46   On, on, you noblest English,
Whose blood is fet from fathers of war-proof. HENRY V
3, 1, 17

47 I see you stand like greyhounds in the slips,
Straining upon the start. The game's afoot:
Follow your spirit; and upon this charge
Cry 'God for Harry, England, and Saint George!' HENRY V
3, 1, 31

48 Men of few words are the best men. BOY
                             Henry the Fifth, 3, 2, 36

49 I know the disciplines of war.   FLUELLEN   *3, 2, 132*

50 Now entertain conjecture of a time
   When creeping murmur and the poring dark
   Fills the wide vessel of the universe.
   From camp to camp, through the foul womb of night,
   The hum of either army stilly sounds,
   That the fix'd sentinels almost receive
   The secret whispers of each other's watch.   CHORUS
                             4, Prologue, 1

51 The King's a bawcock and a heart of gold,
   A lad of life, an imp of fame;
   Of parents good, of fist most valiant.
   I kiss his dirty shoe, and from heart-string
   I love the lovely bully.   PISTOL   *4, 1, 44*

52 I think the King is but a man as I am: the violet smells to him
   as it doth to me.   HENRY V   *4, 1, 101*

53 Every subject's duty is the King's; but every subject's soul is
   his own.   HENRY V   *4, 1, 175*

54   O that we now had here
   But one ten thousand of those men in England
   That do no work today!   WESTMORELAND   *4, 3, 16*

55 If we are mark'd to die, we are enow
   To do our country loss; and if to live,
   The fewer men, the greater share of honour.   HENRY V *4, 3, 20*

56 But if it be a sin to covet honour,
   I am the most offending soul alive.   HENRY V   *4, 3, 28*

57 This day is call'd the feast of Crispian.
   He that outlives this day, and comes safe home,
   Will stand a tip-toe when this day is nam'd,
   And rouse him at the name of Crispian.   HENRY V   *4, 3, 40*

58 Old men forget; yet all shall be forgot,
   But he'll remember, with advantages,
   What feats he did that day.   HENRY V   *4, 3, 49*

59 We few, we happy few, we band of brothers;
   For he to-day that sheds his blood with me
   Shall be my brother; be he ne'er so vile,
   This day shall gentle his condition;
   And gentlemen in England now a-bed
   Shall think themselves accurs'd they were not here,
   And hold their manhoods cheap whiles any speaks

That fought with us upon Saint Crispin's day.   HENRY V
Henry the Fifth, 4, 3, 60

60 There is occasions and causes why and wherefore in all things.
FLUELLEN   *5, 1, 3*

61 For these fellows of infinite tongue, that can rhyme themselves
into ladies' favours, they do always reason themselves out again.
HENRY V   *5, 2, 157*

King Henry the Sixth, Part One

62 Hung be the heavens with black, yield day to night!   BEDFORD
1, 1, 1

63   Unbidden guests
Are often welcomest when they are gone.   BEDFORD   *2, 2, 55*

64 She's beautiful, and therefore to be woo'd;
She is a woman, therefore to be won.   SUFFOLK   *5, 3, 78*

King Henry the Sixth, Part Two

65 Smooth runs the water where the brook is deep.   SUFFOLK
3, 1, 53

66 I will make it felony to drink small beer.   JACK CADE
4, 2, 64

67 The first thing we do, let's kill all the lawyers.   DICK   *4, 2, 73*

68 Thou hast most traitorously corrupted the youth of the realm
in erecting a grammar school; and whereas, before, our forefathers had no other books but the score and the tally, thou hast
caused printing to be us'd, and, contrary to the King, his crown,
and dignity, thou hast built a paper-mill. It will be proved to thy
face that thou hast men about thee that usually talk of a noun
and a verb, and such abominable words as no Christian ear
can endure to hear.   JACK CADE   *4, 7, 30*

69 Away with him, away with him! He speaks Latin.   JACK CADE
4, 7, 54

King Henry the Sixth, Part Three

70 O God! methinks it were a happy life
To be no better than a homely swain;
To sit upon a hill, as I do now,
To carve out dials quaintly, point by point,
Thereby to see the minutes how they run –
How many makes the hour full complete,
How many hours brings about the day,
How many days will finish up the year,
How many years a mortal man may live.   HENRY VI   *2, 5, 21*

71 Gives not the hawthorn bush a sweeter shade
    To shepherds looking on their silly sheep,
    Than doth a rich embroider'd canopy
    To kings that fear their subjects' treachery? HENRY VI
                    Henry the Sixth, Part Three, 2, 5, 42

72 Suspicion always haunts the guilty mind:
    The thief doth fear each bush an officer. GLOUCESTER
                                                    5, 6, 11

73 Down, down to hell; and say I sent thee thither. GLOUCESTER
                                                    5, 6, 67

King Henry the Eighth

74 Heat not a furnace for your foe so hot
    That it do singe yourself. We may outrun
    By violent swiftness that which we run at,
    And lose by over-running. NORFOLK   *1, 1, 140*

75 I swear 'tis better to be lowly born
    And range with humble livers in content
    Than to be perk'd up in a glist'ring grief
    And wear a golden sorrow. ANNE   *2, 3, 19*

76   I would not be a queen
    For all the world. ANNE   *2, 3, 45*

77 Orpheus with his lute made trees,
    And the mountain tops that freeze,
        Bow themselves when he did sing. SONG   *3, 1, 3*

78 Heaven is above all yet: there sits a Judge
    That no king can corrupt. QUEEN KATHARINE   *3, 1, 100*

79 I have touch'd the highest point of all my greatness,
    And from that full meridian of my glory
    I haste now to my setting. I shall fall
    Like a bright exhalation in the evening,
    And no man see me more. WOLSEY   *3, 2, 223*

80 Farewell, a long farewell, to all my greatness!
    This is the state of man: to-day he puts forth
    The tender leaves of hopes; to-morrow blossoms
    And bears his blushing honours thick upon him;
    The third day comes a frost, a killing frost,
    And when he thinks, good easy man, full surely
    His greatness is a-ripening, nips his root,
    And then he falls, as I do. WOLSEY   *3, 2, 351*

81 Vain pomp and glory of this world, I hate ye;
    I feel my heart new open'd. O, how wretched
    Is that poor man that hangs on princes' favours!

There is betwixt that smile we would aspire to,
That sweet aspect of princes, and their ruin
More pangs and fears than wars or women have;
And when he falls, he falls like Lucifer,
Never to hope again. WOLSEY *Henry the Eighth, 3, 2, 365*

82 A peace above all earthly dignities,
A still and quiet conscience. WOLSEY *3, 2, 379*

83 Love thyself last; cherish those hearts that hate thee;
Corruption wins not more than honesty. WOLSEY *3, 2, 443*

84 Had I but serv'd my God with half the zeal
I serv'd my King, he would not in mine age
Have left me naked to mine enemies. WOLSEY *3, 2, 455*

85 So may he rest; his faults lie gently on him! KATHARINE
4, 2, 31

86 Men's evil manners live in brass: their virtues
We write in water. GRIFFITH *4, 2, 45*

87 He was a scholar, and a ripe and good one;
Exceeding wise, fair-spoken, and persuading;
Lofty and sour to them that lov'd him not,
But to those men that sought him sweet as summer. GRIFFITH
4, 2, 51

88   Love and meekness, lord,
Become a churchman better than ambition. CRANMER
5, 3, 62

Julius Caesar

89 You blocks, you stones, you worse than senseless things!
MARULLUS *1, 1, 36*

90 Beware the ides of March. SOOTHSAYER *1, 2, 18*

91 Well, honour is the subject of my story.
I cannot tell what you and other men
Think of this life; but, for my single self
I had as lief not be as live to be
In awe of such a thing as I myself. CASSIUS *1, 2, 92*

92   Ye gods! it doth amaze me
A man of such a feeble temper should
So get the start of the majestic world,
And bear the palm alone. CASSIUS *1, 2, 128*

93 Why, man, he doth bestride the narrow world
Like a Colossus, and we petty men
Walk under his huge legs, and peep about
To find ourselves dishonourable graves.

Men at some time are masters of their fates:
The fault, dear Brutus, is not in our stars,
But in ourselves, that we are underlings. CASSIUS
Julius Caesar, 1, 2, 135

94 Let me have men about me that are fat;
Sleek-headed men, and such as sleep o' nights.
Yond Cassius has a lean and hungry look;
He thinks too much. Such men are dangerous. CAESAR
1, 2, 192

95 'Tis very like. He hath the falling sickness. BRUTUS *1, 2, 253*

96 For mine own part, it was Greek to me. CASCA *1, 2, 283*

97 And yesterday the bird of night did sit,
Even at noon-day, upon the market-place,
Hooting and shrieking. CASCA *1, 3, 26*

98 Between the acting of a dreadful thing
And the first motion, all the interim is
Like a phantasma or a hideous dream.
The Genius and the mortal instruments
Are then in council; and the state of man,
Like to a little kingdom, suffers then
The nature of an insurrection. BRUTUS *2, 1, 63*

99 Let's carve him as a dish fit for the gods. BRUTUS *2, 1, 173*

1 Cowards die many times before their deaths:
The valiant never taste of death but once. CAESAR *2, 2, 32*

2 How hard it is for women to keep counsel! PORTIA *2, 4, 9*

3 Et tu, Brute? CAESAR *3, 1, 77*

4 Why, he that cuts off twenty years of life
Cuts off so many years of fearing death. CASSIUS *3, 1, 102*

5   How many ages hence
Shall this our lofty scene be acted over
In states unborn and accents yet unknown! CASSIUS *3, 1, 112*

6 O mighty Caesar! dost thou lie so low?
Are all thy conquests, glories, triumphs, spoils,
Shrunk to this little measure? MARK ANTONY *3, 1, 149*

7 The choice and master spirits of this age. MARK ANTONY
3, 1, 164

8 O, pardon me, thou bleeding piece of earth,
That I am meek and gentle with these butchers!
Thou art the ruins of the noblest man
That ever lived in the tide of times. MARK ANTONY *3, 1, 255*

9 Cry 'Havoc!' and let slip the dogs of war. MARK ANTONY
3, 1, 274

10 Not that I lov'd Caesar less, but that I lov'd Rome more.
BRUTUS *Julius Caesar, 3, 2, 20*

11 As Caesar lov'd me, I weep for him; as he was fortunate, I
rejoice at it; as he was valiant, I honour him; but – as he was
ambitious, I slew him. There is tears for his love; joy for his
fortune; honour for his valour; and death for his ambition.
Who is here so base that would be a bondman? If any, speak;
for him have I offended. BRUTUS   *3, 2, 24*

12 Friends, Romans, countrymen, lend me your ears;
I come to bury Caesar, not to praise him.
The evil that men do lives after them;
The good is oft interred with their bones. MARK ANTONY
3, 2, 73

13 For Brutus is an honourable man;
So are they all, all honourable men. MARK ANTONY   *3, 2, 82*

14 Ambition should be made of sterner stuff. MARK ANTONY
3, 2, 92

15 But yesterday the word of Caesar might
Have stood against the world: now lies he there,
And none so poor to do him reverence. MARK ANTONY
3, 2, 118

16 The will, the will! We will hear Caesar's will. PLEBEIANS
3, 2, 139

17 If you have tears, prepare to shed them now. MARK ANTONY
3, 2, 169

18 See what a rent the envious Casca made. MARK ANTONY
3, 2, 175

19 This was the most unkindest cut of all. MARK ANTONY
3, 2, 183

20 O, what a fall was there, my countrymen! MARK ANTONY
3, 2, 190

21 For I have neither wit, nor words, nor worth,
Action, nor utterance, nor the power of speech,
To stir men's blood; I only speak right on. MARK ANTONY
3, 2, 221

22 Tear him for his bad verses, tear him for his bad verses!
4TH PLEBEIAN *3, 3, 30*

23   You yourself
Are much condemn'd to have an itching palm. BRUTUS
4, 3, 9

24 I had rather be a dog and bay the moon
Than such a Roman. BRUTUS   *4, 3, 27*

25 Away, slight man! BRUTUS *Julius Caesar, 4, 3, 37*

26 A friend should bear his friend's infirmities,
But Brutus makes mine greater than they are. CASSIUS
4, 3, 85

27 There is a tide in the affairs of men
Which, taken at the flood, leads on to fortune;
Omitted, all the voyage of their life
Is bound in shallows and in miseries.
On such a full sea are we now afloat,
And we must take the current when it serves,
Or lose our ventures. BRUTUS *4, 3, 216*

28 For ever and for ever farewell, Cassius!
If we do meet again, why, we shall smile;
If not, why then this parting was well made. BRUTUS
5, 1, 116

29   O that a man might know
The end of this day's business ere it come! BRUTUS *5, 1, 122*

30 This was the noblest Roman of them all.
All the conspirators save only he
Did that they did in envy of great Caesar. MARK ANTONY
5, 5, 68

31 His life was gentle; and the elements
So mix'd in him that Nature might stand up
And say to all the world 'This was a man!' MARK ANTONY
5, 5, 73

King John

32 A strange beginning – 'borrowed majesty'! ELINOR *1, 1, 5*

33 Lord of thy presence and no land beside. ELINOR *1, 1, 137*

34 For courage mounteth with occasion. AUSTRIA *2, 1, 82*

35 Saint George, that swing'd the dragon, and e'er since
Sits on's horse back at mine hostess' door. BASTARD *2, 1, 288*

36 Mad world! mad kings! mad composition! BASTARD *2, 1, 561*

37 That smooth-fac'd gentleman, tickling commodity,
Commodity, the bias of the world. BASTARD *2, 1, 573*

38 Well, whiles I am a beggar, I will rail
And say there is no sin but to be rich;
And being rich, my virtue then shall be
To say there is no vice but beggary. BASTARD *2, 1, 593*

39   Here I and sorrows sit;
Here is my throne, bid kings come bow to it. CONSTANCE
3, 1, 73

40 Bell, book, and candle, shall not drive me back,
When gold and silver becks me to come on. BASTARD
King John, 3, 3, 12

41 Life is as tedious as a twice-told tale
Vexing the dull ear of a drowsy man. LEWIS   *3, 4, 108*

42 Heat me these irons hot. HUBERT   *4, 1, 1*

43 To gild refined gold, to paint the lily,
To throw a perfume on the violet,
To smooth the ice, or add another hue
Unto the rainbow, or with taper-light
To seek the beauteous eye of heaven to garnish,
Is wasteful and ridiculous excess. SALISBURY   *4, 2, 11*

44 And oftentimes excusing of a fault
Doth make the fault the worse by th' excuse. PEMBROKE
4, 2, 30

45 How oft the sight of means to do ill deeds
Make deeds ill done! KING JOHN   *4, 2, 219*

46 I beg cold comfort. KING JOHN   *5, 7, 42*

47 This England never did, nor never shall,
Lie at the proud foot of a conqueror,
But when it first did help to wound itself. BASTARD   *5, 7, 112*

48   Nought shall make us rue,
If England to itself do rest but true. BASTARD   *5, 7 117*

King Lear

49 Nothing will come of nothing. Speak again. LEAR   *1, 1, 89*

50 LEAR: So young and so untender?
CORDELIA: So young, my lord, and true.   *1, 1, 105*

51 A still-soliciting eye. CORDELIA   *1, 1, 231*

52 These late eclipses in the sun and moon portend no good to us.
GLOUCESTER   *1, 2, 99*

53 This is the excellent foppery of the world, that, when we are
sick in fortune, often the surfeits of our own behaviour, we make
guilty of our disasters the sun, the moon, and stars. EDMUND
1, 2, 112

54 My cue is villainous melancholy, with a sigh like Tom o' Bedlam.
EDMUND   *1, 2, 129*

55 KENT: You have that in your countenance which I would fain
call master.
LEAR: What's that?
KENT: Authority.   *1, 4, 28*

56 LEAR: Dost thou call me fool, boy?
   FOOL: All thy other titles thou hast given away; that thou wast
   born with.   *King Lear, 1, 4, 147*

57 Ingratitude, thou marble-hearted fiend,
   More hideous when thou show'st thee in a child
   Than the sea-monster! LEAR   *1, 4, 259*

58 How sharper than a serpent's tooth it is
   To have a thankless child. LEAR   *1, 4, 288*

59 Striving to better, oft we mar what's well. ALBANY *1, 4, 347*

60 O, let me not be mad, not mad, sweet heaven!
   Keep me in temper; I would not be mad! LEAR   *1, 5, 43*

61 Thou whoreson zed! thou unnecessary letter! KENT *2, 2, 58*

62 I have seen better faces in my time
   Than stands on any shoulder that I see
   Before me at this instant. KENT   *2, 2, 88*

63 Fortune, good night; smile once more; turn thy wheel. KENT
                                                  2, 2, 168

64 Hysterica passio – down, thou climbing sorrow,
   Thy element's below. LEAR   *2, 4, 56*

65   You are old;
   Nature in you stands on the very verge
   Of her confine. REGAN   *2, 4, 144*

66 LEAR: I gave you all.
   REGAN: And in good time you gave it.   *2, 4, 248*

67 O, reason not the need! Our basest beggars
   Are in the poorest thing superfluous.
   Allow not nature more than nature needs,
   Man's life is cheap as beast's. LEAR   *2, 4, 263*

68 And let not women's weapons, water-drops,
   Stain my man's cheeks! LEAR   *2, 4, 276*

69 No, I'll not weep.
   I have full cause of weeping; but this heart
   Shall break into a hundred thousand flaws
   Or ere I'll weep. O fool, I shall go mad! LEAR *2, 4, 282*

70 Who's there, besides foul weather? KENT   *3, 1, 1*

71 Blow, winds, and crack your cheeks; rage, blow.
   You cataracts and hurricanoes, spout
   Till you have drench'd our steeples, drown'd the cocks. LEAR
                                                  3, 2, 1

72 Rumble thy bellyful. Spit, fire; spout, rain.
   Nor rain, wind, thunder, fire, are my daughters.
   I tax not you, you elements, with unkindness. LEAR *3, 2, 14*

73   Here I stand, you slave,
A poor, infirm, weak and despis'd old man. LEAR
King Lear, 3, 2, 19

74 For there was never yet fair woman but she made mouths in a
glass. FOOL   *3, 2, 35*

75   Things that love night
Love not such nights as these. KENT   *3, 2, 42*

76   I am a man
More sinn'd against than sinning. LEAR   *3, 2, 59*

77 O, that way madness lies; let me shun that. LEAR   *3, 4, 21*

78 Poor naked wretches, wheresoe'er you are,
That bide the pelting of this pitiless storm,
How shall your houseless heads and unfed sides,
Your loop'd and window'd raggedness, defend you
From seasons such as these? LEAR   *3, 4, 28*

79   Take physic, pomp;
Expose thyself to feel what wretches feel. LEAR   *3, 4, 33*

80 'Tis a naughty night to swim in. FOOL   *3, 4, 109*

81 Poor Tom's a-cold. EDGAR   *3, 4, 143*

82 Child Rowland to the dark tower came,
His word was still 'Fie, foh, and fum,
I smell the blood of a British man'. EDGAR   *3, 4, 178*

83   Out vile jelly!
Where is thy lustre now? CORNWALL   *3, 7, 82*

84   The worst is not
So long as we can say 'This is the worst'. EDGAR   *4, 1, 28*

85 As flies to wanton boys are we to th' gods –
They kill us for their sport. GLOUCESTER   *4, 1, 37*

86 Wisdom and goodness to the vile seem vile;
Filths savour but themselves. ALBANY   *4, 2, 38*

87   It is the stars,
The stars above us, govern our conditions. KENT   *4, 3, 32*

88   How fearful
And dizzy 'tis to cast one's eyes so low!
The crows and choughs that wing the mid-way air
Show scarce so gross as beetles. EDGAR   *4, 6, 11*

89 Ay, every inch a king. LEAR   *4, 6, 107*

90 The wren goes to't, and the small gilded fly
Does lecher in my sight. LEAR   *4, 6, 112*

91 Give me an ounce of civet, good apothecary, to sweeten my
imagination. LEAR   *4, 6, 129*

92 Through tatter'd clothes small vices do appear;
Robes and furr'd gowns hide all.   LEAR   *King Lear, 4, 6, 164*

93   Get thee glass eyes,
And, like a scurvy politician, seem
To see the things thou dost not.   LEAR   *4, 6, 170*

94 When we are born, we cry that we are come
To this great stage of fools.   LEAR   *4, 6, 183*

95   Mine enemy's dog,
Though he had bit me, should have stood that night
Against my fire.   CORDELIA   *4, 7, 36*

96 Thou art a soul in bliss; but I am bound
Upon a wheel of fire, that mine own tears
Do scald like molten lead.   LEAR   *4, 7, 46*

97 I am a very foolish fond old man,
Fourscore and upward, not an hour more nor less;
And, to deal plainly,
I fear I am not in my perfect mind.   LEAR   *4, 7, 60*

98   Men must endure
Their going hence, even as their coming hither:
Ripeness is all.   EDGAR   *5, 2, 9*

99   Come, let's away to prison.
We two alone will sing like birds i' th' cage;
When thou dost ask me blessing, I'll kneel down
And ask of thee forgiveness; so we'll live,
And pray, and sing, and tell old tales, and laugh
At gilded butterflies, and hear poor rogues
Talk of court news; and we'll talk with them too –
Who loses and who wins; who's in, who's out –
And take upon's the mystery of things
As if we were God's spies.   LEAR   *5, 3, 8*

1 The gods are just, and of our pleasant vices
Make instruments to plague us:
The dark and vicious place where thee he got
Cost him his eyes.   EDGAR   *5, 3, 170*

2 The wheel is come full circle.   EDMUND   *5, 3, 174*

3   But his flaw'd heart –
Alack, too weak the conflict to support! –
'Twixt two extremes of passion, joy and grief,
Burst smilingly.   EDGAR   *5, 3, 196*

4 How, howl, howl, howl! O, you are men of stones!
Had I your tongues and eyes, I'd use them so
That heaven's vault should crack.   LEAR   *5, 3, 257*

5   Her voice was ever soft,
Gentle, and low – an excellent thing in woman. LEAR
                                        King Lear, *5, 3, 272*

6 And my poor fool is hang'd! No, no, no life!
  Why should a dog, a horse, a rat have life,
  And thou no breath at all? Thou'lt come no more,
  Never, never, never, never, never.
  Pray you undo this button. LEAR   *5, 3, 305*

7 Vex not his ghost. O, let him pass! He hates him
  That would upon the rack of this tough world
  Stretch him out longer. KENT   *5, 3, 313*

Love's Labour's Lost

8 Spite of cormorant devouring Time. KING   *1, 1, 4*

9 Why, all delights are vain; but that most vain
  Which, with pain purchas'd, doth inherit pain. BEROWNE
                                                  1, 1, 72

10 Small have continual plodders ever won,
   Save base authority from others' books. BEROWNE *1, 1, 86*

11 At Christmas I no more desire a rose
   Than wish a snow in May's new-fangled shows. BEROWNE
                                                  1, 1, 105

12 Remuneration! O, that's the Latin word for three farthings.
                                      COSTARD *3, 1, 129*

13 He hath never fed of the dainties that are bred in a book; he
   hath not eat paper, as it were; he hath not drunk ink; his intellect
   is not replenished. SIR NATHANIEL   *4, 2, 22*

14 For where is any author in the world
   Teaches such beauty as a woman's eye?
   Learning is but an adjunct to ourself. BEROWNE *4, 3, 308*

15 And when Love speaks, the voice of all the gods
   Make heaven drowsy with the harmony. BEROWNE *4, 3, 340*

16 From women's eyes this doctrine I derive.
   They sparkle still the right Promethean fire;
   They are the books, the arts, the academes,
   That show, contain, and nourish, all the world. ROSALINE
                                                  4, 3, 346

17 A world-without-end bargain. PRINCESS   *5, 2, 777*

18 A jest's prosperity lies in the ear
   Of him that hears it, never in the tongue
   Of him that makes it. BEROWNE   *5, 2, 849*

19 When daisies pied and violets blue
   And lady-smocks all silver-white
   And cuckoo-buds of yellow hue
   Do paint the meadows with delight,
   The cuckoo then on every tree
   Mocks married men, for thus sings he:
   'Cuckoo;
   Cuckoo, cuckoo' – O word of fear,
   Unpleasing to a married ear! SPRING
                           Love's Labour's Lost, 5, 2, 881

20 When icicles hang by the wall,
   And Dick the shepherd blows his nail,
   And Tom bears logs into the hall,
   And milk comes frozen home in pail,
   When blood is nipp'd, and ways be foul,
   Then nightly sings the staring owl:
   'Tu-who;
   Tu-whit, Tu-who' – A merry note,
   While greasy Joan doth keel the pot.

   When all aloud the wind doth blow,
   And coughing drowns the parson's saw,
   And birds sit brooding in the snow,
   And Marian's nose looks red and raw,
   When roasted crabs hiss in the bowl. WINTER   *5, 2, 899*

21 The words of Mercury are harsh after the songs of Apollo.
                      ARMADO *5, 2, 917*

Macbeth

22 1ST WITCH: When shall we three meet again?
           In thunder, lightning, or in rain?
   2ND WITCH: When the hurlyburly's done,
           When the battle's lost and won.   *1, 1, 1*

23 Fair is foul, and foul is fair:
   Hover through the fog and filthy air. THREE WITCHES
                           1, 1, 10

24 What bloody man is that? DUNCAN   *1, 2, 1*

25 So foul and fair a day I have not seen. MACBETH   *1, 3, 38*

26 What are these,
   So wither'd, and so wild in their attire,
   That look not like th' inhabitants o' th' earth,
   And yet are on't? BANQUO
                            1, 3, 39

27 If you can look into the seeds of time
   And say which grain will grow and which will not,
   Speak then to me, who neither beg nor fear
   Your favours nor your hate. BANQUO   *Macbeth, 1, 3, 58*

28 This supernatural soliciting
   Cannot be ill; cannot be good. MACBETH   *1, 3, 130*

29 Come what come may,
   Time and the hour runs through the roughest day. MACBETH
                                                    1, 3, 146

30 Nothing in his life
   Became him like the leaving it: he died
   As one that had been studied in his death
   To throw away the dearest thing he ow'd
   As 'twere a careless trifle. MALCOLM   *1, 4, 7*

31 Stars, hide your fires. MACBETH   *1, 4, 50*

32 Yet do I fear thy nature;
   It is too full o' th' milk of human kindness
   To catch the nearest way. LADY MACBETH   *1, 5, 13*

33 Come, thick night,
   And pall thee in the dunnest smoke of hell. LADY MACBETH
                                                    1, 5, 47

34 O, never
   Shall sun that morrow see!
   Your face, my thane, is as a book where men
   May read strange matters. LADY MACBETH   *1, 5, 57*

35 If it were done when 'tis done, then 'twere well
   It were done quickly. MACBETH   *1, 7, 1*

36 That but this blow
   Might be the be-all and the end-all here –
   But here upon this bank and shoal of time –
   We'd jump the life to come. MACBETH   *1, 7, 4*

37 I have no spur
   To prick the sides of my intent, but only
   Vaulting ambition, which o'er-leaps itself,
   And falls on th' other. MACBETH   *1, 7, 25*

38 MACBETH: If we should fail?
   LADY MACBETH: We fail!
                    But screw your courage to the sticking place,
                    And we'll not fail.   *1, 7, 59*

39 False face must hide what the false heart doth know. MACBETH
                                                    1, 7, 82

40 Is this a dagger which I see before me,
The handle toward my hand? MACBETH *Macbeth, 2, 1, 33*

41   The bell invites me.
Hear it not, Duncan, for it is a knell
That summons thee to heaven or to hell. MACBETH *2, 1, 62*

42 Methought I heard a voice cry 'Sleep no more;
Macbeth does murder sleep' – the innocent sleep,
Sleep that knits up the ravell'd sleave of care,
The death of each day's life, sore labour's bath,
Balm of hurt minds, great nature's second course,
Chief nourisher in life's feast. MACBETH *2, 2, 35*

43 Will all great Neptune's ocean wash this blood
Clean from my hand? No; this my hand will rather
The multitudinous seas incarnadine,
Making the green one red. MACBETH *2, 2, 60*

44 I had thought to have let in some of all professions that go the
primrose way to th' everlasting bonfire. PORTER *2, 3, 18*

45 It provokes the desire, but it takes away the performance. Therefore much drink may be said to be an equivocator with lechery.
PORTER *2, 3, 28*

46 Had I but died an hour before this chance,
I had liv'd a blessed time; for, from this instant,
There's nothing serious in mortality –
All is but toys. MACBETH *2, 3, 89*

47   Where we are,
There's daggers in men's smiles; the near in blood,
The nearer bloody. DONALBAIN *2, 3, 138*

48 Ay, in the catalogue ye go for men;
As hounds, and greyhounds, mongrels, spaniels, curs,
Shoughs, water-rugs, and demi-wolves, are clept
All by the name of dogs. MACBETH *3, 1, 91*

49 I am one, my liege,
Whom the vile blows and buffets of the world
Hath so incens'd that I am reckless what
I do to spite the world. 2ND MURDERER *3, 1, 107*

50 Nought's had, all's spent,
Where our desire is got without content.
'Tis safer to be that which we destroy,
Than by destruction dwell in doubtful joy. LADY MACBETH
3, 2, 4

51   Duncan is in his grave;
After life's fitful fever he sleeps well. MACBETH *3, 2, 22*

52 Things bad begun make strong themselves by ill. MACBETH
Macbeth, 3, 2, 55

53 I had else been perfect,
Whole as the marble, founded as the rock,
As broad and general as the casing air,
But now I am cabin'd, cribb'd, confin'd, bound in
To saucy doubts and fears. MACBETH   *3, 4, 21*

54 Now good digestion wait on appetite,
And health on both! MACBETH   *3, 4, 38*

55   The time has been
That when the brains were out the man would die,
And there an end. MACBETH   *3, 4, 78*

56 Stand not upon the order of your going,
But go at once. LADY MACBETH   *3, 4, 119*

57   I am in blood
Stepp'd in so far that, should I wade no more,
Returning were as tedious as go o'er. MACBETH   *3, 4, 136*

58 Double, double toil and trouble;
Fire burn, and cauldron bubble. THREE WITCHES   *4, 1, 10*

59 Ditch-deliver'd by a drab. 3RD WITCH   *4, 1, 31*

60 How now, you secret, black, and midnight hags! MACBETH
4, 1, 47

61 A deed without a name. THREE WITCHES   *4, 1, 49*

62 Be bloody, bold, and resolute; laugh to scorn
The pow'r of man, for none of woman born
Shall harm Macbeth. SECOND APPARITION   *4, 1, 79*

63 But yet I'll make assurance double sure,
And take a bond of fate. MACBETH   *4, 1, 83*

64 What, will the line stretch out to th' crack of doom? MACBETH
4, 1, 117

65 I think our country sinks beneath the yoke;
It weeps, it bleeds; and each new day a gash
Is added to her wounds. MALCOLM   *4, 3 39*

66 Stands Scotland where it did? MACDUFF   *4, 3, 164*

67 The night is long that never finds the day. MALCOLM *4, 3, 240*

68 Out, damned spot! out, I say! LADY MACBETH   *5, 1, 33*

69 Here's the smell of the blood still. All the perfumes of Arabia
will not sweeten this little hand. LADY MACBETH   *5, 1, 48*

70 To bed, to bed; there's knocking at the gate. Come, come, come,
come, give me your hand. What's done cannot be undone.
LADY MACBETH   *5, 1, 64*

71 I have liv'd long enough. My way of life
Is fall'n into the sear, the yellow leaf;
And that which should accompany old age,
As honour, love, obedience, troops of friends,
I must not look to have. MACBETH *Macbeth, 5, 3, 22*

72 Canst thou not minister to a mind diseas'd,
Pluck from the memory a rooted sorrow,
Raze out the written troubles of the brain,
And with some sweet oblivious antidote
Cleanse the stuff'd bosom of that perilous stuff
Which weighs upon the heart? MACBETH *5, 3, 40*

73 I will not be afraid of death and bane
Till Birnam Forest come to Dunsinane. MACBETH *5, 3, 59*

74 Hang out our banners on the outward walls;
The cry is still 'They come'. MACBETH *5, 5, 1*

75 I have supp'd full with horrors. MACBETH *5, 5, 13*

76 She should have died hereafter;
There would have been a time for such a word.
Tomorrow, and tomorrow, and tomorrow,
Creeps in this petty pace from day to day
To the last syllable of recorded time,
And all our yesterdays have lighted fools
The way to dusty death. Out, out, brief candle!
Life's but a walking shadow, a poor player,
That struts and frets his hour upon the stage,
And then is heard no more; it is a tale
Told by an idiot, full of sound and fury,
Signifying nothing. MACBETH *5, 5, 17*

77 I gin to be aweary of the sun,
And wish th' estate o' th' world were now undone.
Ring the alarum bell. Blow wind, come wrack;
At least we'll die with harness on our back. MACBETH *5, 5, 49*

78 MACBETH: I bear a charmed life, which must not yield
      To one of woman born.
   MACDUFF: Despair thy charm;
      And let the angel whom thou still hast serv'd
      Tell thee Macduff was from his mother's womb
      Untimely ripp'd.   *5, 8, 12*

79 Live to be the show and gaze o' th' time. MACDUFF *5, 8, 24*

80   Lay on, Macduff;
   And damn'd be him that first cries 'Hold, enough!'
                                        MACBETH *5, 8, 33*

Measure for Measure

81 'Tis one thing to be tempted, Escalus,
    Another thing to fall. I not deny
    The jury, passing on the prisoner's life,
    May in the sworn twelve have a thief or two
    Guiltier than him they try. ANGELO   *2, 1, 17*

82 Some rise by sin, and some by virtue fall. ESCALUS   *2, 1, 38*

83 This will last out a night in Russia,
    When nights are longest there. ANGELO   *2, 1, 128*

84 No ceremony that to great ones longs,
    Not the king's crown nor the deputed sword,
    The marshal's truncheon nor the judge's robe,
    Become them with one half so good a grace
    As mercy does. ISABELLA   *2, 2, 59*

85 The law hath not been dead, though it hath slept. ANGELO
                                                          2, 2, 90

86   O, it is excellent
    To have a giant's strength! But it is tyrannous
    To use it like a giant. ISABELLA   *2, 2, 107*

87   But man, proud man,
    Dress'd in a little brief authority,
    Most ignorant of what he's most assur'd,
    His glassy essence, like an angry ape,
    Plays such fantastic tricks before high heaven
    As makes the angels weep. ISABELLA   *2, 2, 117*

88 That in the captain's but a choleric word
    Which in the soldier is flat blasphemy. ISABELLA   *2, 2, 130*

89 The miserable have no other medicine
    But only hope. CLAUDIO   *3, 1, 2*

90 Ay, but to die, and go we know not where;
    To lie in cold obstruction, and to rot;
    This sensible warm motion to become
    A kneaded clod; and the delighted spirit
    To bathe in fiery floods or to reside
    In thrilling region of thick-ribbed ice. CLAUDIO   *3, 1, 119*

91 The weariest and most loathed worldly life
    That age, ache, penury, and imprisonment,
    Can lay on nature is a paradise
    To what we fear of death. CLAUDIO   *3, 1, 130*

92 Take, O, take those lips away,
    That so sweetly were forsworn;

And those eyes, the break of day,
  Lights that do mislead the morn;
But my kisses bring again, bring again;
Seals of love, but seal'd in vain, seal'd in vain. SONG
Measure for Measure, 4, 1, 1

93 I am a kind of burr; I shall stick. LUCIO   *4, 3, 173*

94 Haste still pays haste, and leisure answers leisure;
  Like doth quit like, and Measure still for Measure. DUKE
5, 1, 408

95 What's mine is yours, and what is yours is mine. DUKE
5, 1, 535

The Merchant of Venice

96 I hold the world but as the world, Gratiano –
  A stage, where every man must play a part,
  And mine a sad one. ANTONIO   *1, 1, 77*

97 There are a sort of men whose visages
  Do cream and mantle like a standing pond. GRATIANO
1, 1, 88

98 As who should say 'I am Sir Oracle,
  And when I ope my lips let no dog bark'. GRATIANO *1, 1, 93*

99 In Belmont is a lady richly left,
  And she is fair and, fairer than that word,
  Of wondrous virtues. BASSANIO   *1, 1, 161*

1 By my troth, Nerissa, my little body is aweary of this great
  world. PORTIA   *1, 2, 1*

2 If to do were as easy as to know what were good to do, chapels
  had been churches, and poor men's cottages princes' palaces.
  PORTIA *1. 2, 11*

3 How like a fawning publican he looks!
  I hate him for he is a Christian;
  But more for that in low simplicity
  He lends out money gratis, and brings down
  The rate of usance here with us in Venice.
  If I can catch him once upon the hip,
  I will feed fat the ancient grudge I bear him. SHYLOCK *1, 3, 36*

4 The devil can cite Scripture for his purpose. ANTONIO *1, 3, 93*

5   Many a time and oft
  In the Rialto you have rated me. SHYLOCK   *1, 3, 101*

6 Still have I borne it with a patient shrug,
  For suff'rance is the badge of all our tribe;
  You call me misbeliever, cut-throat dog,
  And spit upon my Jewish gaberdine. SHYLOCK   *1, 3, 104*

7 I like not fair terms and a villain's mind. BASSANIO
The Merchant of Venice, 1, 3, 174

8 It is a wise father that knows his own child. LAUNCELOT GOBBO
2, 2, 69

9 There is some ill a-brewing towards my rest,
For I did dream of money-bags tonight. SHYLOCK   *2, 5, 17*

10 But love is blind, and lovers cannot see
The pretty follies that themselves commit. JESSICA   *2, 6, 36*

11 The ancient saying is no heresy:
Hanging and wiving goes by destiny. NERISSA   *2, 9, 82*

12 Let him look to his bond. SHYLOCK   *3, 1, 39*

13 Hath not a Jew eyes? Hath not a Jew hands, organs, dimensions,
senses, affections, passions, fed with the same food, hurt with
the same weapons, subject to the same diseases, healed by the
same means, warmed and cooled by the same winter and
summer, as a Christian is? If you prick us, do we not bleed?
If you tickle us, do we not laugh? If you poison us, do we not
die? And if you wrong us, shall we not revenge? SHYLOCK
3, 1, 49

14 Tell me where is fancy bred,
Or in the heart or in the head,
How begot, how nourished? SONG   *3, 2, 63*

15 The quality of mercy is not strain'd;
It droppeth as the gentle rain from heaven
Upon the place beneath. It is twice blest:
It blesseth him that gives and him that takes.
'Tis mightiest in the mightiest; it becomes
The throned monarch better than his crown;
His sceptre shows the force of temporal power,
The attribute to awe and majesty,
Wherein doth sit the dread and fear of kings;
But mercy is above this sceptred sway,
It is enthroned in the hearts of kings,
It is an attribute to God himself;
And earthly power doth then show likest God's
When mercy seasons justice. Therefore, Jew,
Though justice be thy plea, consider this —
That in the course of justice none of us
Should see salvation; we do pray for mercy,
And that same prayer doth teach us all to render
The deeds of mercy. PORTIA   *4, 1, 179*

16 Wrest once the law to your authority;
To do a great right do a little wrong. BASSANIO   *4, 1, 210*

17 A Daniel come to judgment! Yea, a Daniel! SHYLOCK
The Merchant of Venice, *4, 1, 218*

18 'Tis not in the bond. SHYLOCK   *4, 1, 257*

19 A pound of that same merchant's flesh is thine.
The court awards it and the law doth give it. PORTIA
4, 1, 294

20 You take my house when you do take the prop
That doth sustain my house; you take my life
When you do take the means whereby I live. SHYLOCK
4, 1, 370

21 He is well paid that is well satisfied. PORTIA *4, 1, 410*

22 How sweet the moonlight sleeps upon this bank!
Here will we sit and let the sounds of music
Creep in our ears; soft stillness and the night
Become the touches of sweet harmony.
Sit, Jessica. Look how the floor of heaven
Is thick inlaid with patines of bright gold;
There's not the smallest orb which thou behold'st
But in his motion like an angel sings,
Still quiring to the young-ey'd cherubins;
Such harmony is in immortal souls,
But whilst this muddy vesture of decay
Doth grossly close it in, we cannot hear it. LORENZO *5, 1, 54*

23 I am never merry when I hear sweet music. JESSICA *5, 1, 69*

24 The man that hath no music in himself,
Nor is not mov'd with concord of sweet sounds,
Is fit for treasons, stratagems, and spoils. LORENZO *5, 1, 83*

25 How far that little candle throws his beams!
So shines a good deed in a naughty world. PORTIA *5, 1, 90*

26 For a light wife doth make a heavy husband. PORTIA
5, 1, 130

The Merry Wives of Windsor

27 I will make a Star Chamber matter of it. SHALLOW *1, 1, 1*

28 I had rather than forty shillings I had my Book of Songs and
Sonnets here. SLENDER   *1, 1, 179*

29 Here will be an old abusing of God's patience and the King's
English. MISTRESS QUICKLY   *1, 4, 5*

30 Why, then the world's mine oyster,
Which I with sword will open. PISTOL   *2, 2, 4*

31 I cannot tell what the dickens his name is. MRS PAGE *3, 2, 15*

32 O, what a world of vile ill-favour'd faults
Looks handsome in three hundred pounds a year! ANNE PAGE
The Merry Wives of Windsor, 3, 4, 32

33 I'll no pullet-sperm in my brewage. FALSTAFF   *3, 5, 27*

34 They say there is divinity in odd numbers, either in nativity,
chance, or death. FALSTAFF   *5, 1, 3*

A Midsummer Night's Dream

35 To live a barren sister all your life,
Chanting faint hymns to the cold fruitless moon. THESEUS
1, 1, 72

36   For aught that I could ever read,
Could ever hear by tale or history,
The course of true love never did run smooth. LYSANDER
1, 1, 132

37 O hell! to choose love by another's eyes. HERMIA   *1, 1, 140*

38 Love looks not with the eyes, but with the mind;
And therefore is wing'd Cupid painted blind. HELENA
1, 1, 234

39 'The most Lamentable Comedy and most Cruel Death of
Pyramus and Thisby.' QUINCE   *1, 2, 10*

40 A part to tear a cat in, to make all split. BOTTOM   *1, 2, 24*

41 I am slow of study. SNUG   *1, 2, 59*

42 Over hill, over dale,
Thorough bush, thorough brier,
Over park, over pale,
Thorough flood, thorough fire. FAIRY   *2, 1, 2*

43 Ill met by moonlight, proud Titania. OBERON   *2, 1, 60*

44 Since once I sat upon a promontory,
And heard a mermaid on a dolphin's back
Uttering such dulcet and harmonious breath
That the rude sea grew civil at her song,
And certain stars shot madly from their spheres
To hear the sea-maid's music. OBERON   *2, 1, 149*

45 I'll put a girdle round about the earth
In forty minutes. PUCK   *2, 1, 175*

46 I know a bank whereon the wild thyme blows,
Where oxlips and the nodding violet grows,
Quite over-canopied with luscious woodbine,
With sweet musk-roses, and with eglantine. OBERON *2, 1, 249*

47 A lion among ladies is a most dreadful thing; for there is not a
more fearful wild-fowl than your lion living. BOTTOM *3, 1, 27*

48 A calendar, a calendar! Look in the almanack; find out moonshine, find out moonshine. BOTTOM
A Midsummer Night's Dream, 3, 1, 46

49 Bless thee, Bottom, bless thee! Thou art translated. QUINCE
3, 1, 109

50 Lord, what fools these mortals be! PUCK *3, 2, 115*

51 I have a reasonable good ear in music. Let's have the tongs and
the bones. BOTTOM *4, 1, 26*

52 The lunatic, the lover, and the poet,
Are of imagination all compact. THESEUS *5, 1, 7*

53 The poet's eye, in a fine frenzy rolling,
Doth glance from heaven to earth, from earth to heaven;
And as imagination bodies forth
The forms of things unknown, the poet's pen
Turns them to shapes, and gives to airy nothing
A local habitation and a name. THESEUS *5, 1, 12*

54 Very tragical mirth. THESEUS *5, 1, 57*

55 The iron tongue of midnight hath told twelve.
Lovers, to bed; 'tis almost fairy time. THESEUS *5, 1, 352*

Much Ado About Nothing

56 A victory is twice itself when the achiever brings home full
numbers. LEONATO *1, 1, 7*

57 He wears his faith but as the fashion of his hat. BEATRICE
1, 1, 62

58 BEATRICE: I wonder that you will still be talking, Signior Benedick; nobody marks you.
BENEDICK: What, my dear Lady Disdain! Are you yet living?
1, 1, 99

59 Would you have me speak after my custom, as being a professed
tyrant to their sex? BENEDICK *1, 1, 144*

60 Benedick the married man. BENEDICK *1, 1, 232*

61 What need the bridge much broader than the flood?
DON PEDRO *1, 1, 278*

62 Friendship is constant in all other things
Save in the office and affairs of love. CLAUDIO *2, 1, 154*

63 She speaks poniards, and every word stabs. BENEDICK
2, 1, 220

64 Silence is the perfectest herald of joy: I were but little happy if I
could say how much. CLAUDIO *2, 1, 275*

65 DON PEDRO: Will you have me, lady?
  BEATRICE: No, my lord, unless I might have another for work-
    ing-days; your Grace is too costly to wear every
    day. *Much Ado About Nothing, 2, 1, 293*

66 I was born to speak all mirth and no matter. BEATRICE
  2, 1, 297

67 There was a star danc'd, and under that was I born. BEATRICE
  2, 1, 302

68 Sigh no more, ladies, sigh no more,
    Men were deceivers ever,
  One foot in sea and one on shore,
    To one thing constant never. BALTHASAR *2, 3, 57*

69 Doth not the appetite alter? A man loves the meat in his youth
  that he cannot endure in his age. BENEDICK *2, 3, 215*

70 The world must be peopled. When I said I would die a bachelor
  I did not think I should live till I were married. BENEDICK
  2, 3, 219

71 Disdain and scorn ride sparkling in her eyes. HERO *3, 1, 51*

72 Are you good men and true? DOGBERRY *3, 3, 1*

73 To be a well-favoured man is the gift of fortune; but to write
  and read comes by nature. DOGBERRY *3, 3, 13*

74 You are thought here to be the most senseless and fit man for
  the constable of the watch. DOGBERRY *3, 3, 19*

75 For the watch to babble and to talk is most tolerable and not
  to be endured. DOGBERRY *3, 3, 32*

76 I thank God I am as honest as any man living that is an old
  man and no honester than I. VERGES *3, 5, 13*

77 Comparisons are odorous. DOGBERRY *3, 5, 16*

78 A good old man, sir, he will be talking; as they say 'When the
  age is in the wit is out'. DOGBERRY *3, 5, 32*

79 Our watch, sir, have indeed comprehended two aspicious persons. DOGBERRY *3, 5, 42*

80 O, what men dare do! What men may do! What men daily do,
  not knowing what they do! CLAUDIO *4, 1, 18*

81   For it so falls out
  That what we have we prize not to the worth
  Whiles we enjoy it, but being lack'd and lost,
  Why, then we rack the value, then we find
  The virtue that possession would not show us
  Whiles it was ours. FRIAR FRANCIS *4, 1, 217*

82 Write down that they hope they serve God; and write God first; for God defend but God should go before such villains!
DOGBERRY *Much Ado About Nothing, 4, 2, 17*

83 Flat burglary as ever was committed. DOGBERRY 4, 2, 46

84 O villain! thou wilt be condemn'd into everlasting redemption for this. DOGBERRY 4, 2, 52

85 O that he were here to write me down an ass! DOGBERRY
4, 2, 70

86 For there was never yet philosopher
That could endure the toothache patiently. LEONATO 5, 1, 35

87 They have committed false report; moreover, they have spoken untruths; secondarily, they are slanders; sixth and lastly, they have belied a lady; thirdly, they have verified unjust things; and to conclude, they are lying knaves. DOGBERRY 5, 1, 204

88 Done to death by slanderous tongues. CLAUDIO 5, 3, 3

Othello

89 But I will wear my heart upon my sleeve
For daws to peck at. IAGO 1, 1, 65

90   Rude am I in my speech,
And little blest with the soft phrase of peace;
For since these arms of mine had seven years' pith,
Till now some nine moons wasted, they have us'd
Their dearest action in the tented field. OTHELLO 1, 3, 81

91 I will a round unvarnish'd tale deliver
Of my whole course of love. OTHELLO 1, 3, 90

92   My story being done,
She gave me for my pains a world of sighs;
She swore, in faith, 'twas strange, 'twas passing strange;
'Twas pitiful, 'twas wondrous pitiful.
She wish'd she had not heard it; yet she wish'd
That heaven had made her such a man. She thank'd me;
And bade me, if I had a friend that lov'd her,
I should but teach him how to tell my story,
And that would woo her. Upon this hint I spake;
She lov'd me for the dangers I had pass'd;
And I lov'd her that she did pity them.
This only is the witchcraft I have us'd. OTHELLO 1, 3, 158

93 To mourn a mischief that is past and gone
Is the next way to draw new mischief on. DUKE 1, 3, 204

94 The robb'd that smiles steals something from the thief. DUKE
1, 3, 208

95 Look to her, Moor, if thou hast eyes to see:
She has deceiv'd her father, and may thee.   BRABANTIO
Othello, 1, 3, 292

96 Put money in thy purse.   IAGO   *1, 3, 338*

97 For I am nothing if not critical.   IAGO   *2, 1, 119*

98 To suckle fools and chronicle small beer.   IAGO   *2, 1, 159*

99 But men are men; the best sometimes forget.   IAGO   *2, 3, 233*

1 Reputation, reputation, reputation! O, I have lost my reputation! I have lost the immortal part of myself, and what remains
is bestial.   CASSIO   *2, 3, 254*

2 Good wine is a good familiar creature if it be well us'd.   IAGO
2, 3, 299

3 How poor are they that have not patience!
What wound did ever heal but by degrees?   IAGO   *2, 3, 358*

4 Thereby hangs a tail.   CLOWN   *3, 1, 8*

5 Excellent wretch! Perdition catch my soul
But I do love thee; and when I love thee not
Chaos is come again.   OTHELLO   *3, 3, 91*

6 Good name in man and woman, dear my lord,
Is the immediate jewel of their souls:
Who steals my purse steals trash; 'tis something, nothing;
'Twas mine, 'tis his, and has been slave to thousands;
But he that filches from me my good name
Robs me of that which not enriches him
And makes me poor indeed.   IAGO   *3, 3, 159*

7 O, beware, my lord, of jealousy;
It is the green-ey'd monster which doth mock
The meat it feeds on.   IAGO   *3, 3, 169*

8   O curse of marriage,
That we can call these delicate creatures ours,
And not their appetites! I had rather be a toad,
And live upon the vapour of a dungeon,
Than keep a corner in the thing I love
For others' uses.   OTHELLO   *3, 3, 272*

9 He that is robb'd, not wanting what is stol'n,
Let him not know't, and he's not robb'd at all.   OTHELLO
3, 3, 346

10   O, now for ever
Farewell the tranquil mind! farewell content!
Farewell the plumed troops, and the big wars
That make ambition virtue! O, farewell!
Farewell the neighing steed and the shrill trump,
The spirit-stirring drum, th' ear-piercing fife,

The royal banner, and all quality,
Pride, pomp, and circumstance, of glorious war! OTHELLO
Othello, 3, 3, 351

11 They are not ever jealous for the cause,
But jealous for they are jealous. EMILIA　　　*3, 4, 161*

12 But yet the pity of it, Iago! O, Iago, the pity of it, Iago!
OTHELLO　*4, 1, 191*

13　　　　　　But, alas, to make me
The fixed figure for the time of scorn
To point his slow unmoving finger at. OTHELLO　　*4, 2, 54*

14　　　　　　O thou weed
Who are so lovely fair and smell'st so sweet
That the sense aches at thee!
Would thou had'st never been born! OTHELLO　*4, 2, 67*

15 'Tis neither here nor there. EMILIA　　　*4, 3, 57*

16　　　　If Cassio do remain,
He hath a daily beauty in his life
That makes me ugly. IAGO　　　*5, 1, 18*

17　　　　This is the night
That either makes me or fordoes me quite. IAGO　*5, 1, 128*

18 It is the cause, it is the cause, my soul –
Let me not name it to you, you chaste stars –
It is the cause. OTHELLO　　　*5, 2, 1*

19 Put out the light, and then put out the light.
If I quench thee, thou flaming minister,
I can again thy former light restore,
Should I repent me; but once put out thy light,
Thou cunning'st pattern of excelling nature,
I know not where is that Promethean heat
That can thy light relume. When I have pluck'd thy rose,
I cannot give it vital growth again. OTHELLO　　*5, 2, 7*

20 Not Cassio kill'd! Then murder's out of tune,
And sweet revenge grows harsh. OTHELLO　*5, 2, 118*

21 Here is my journey's end, here is my butt,
And very sea-mark of my utmost sail. OTHELLO　*5, 2, 270*

22 Soft you; a word or two before you go.
I have done the state some service, and they know't –
No more of that. I pray you, in your letters,
When you shall these unlucky deeds relate,
Speak of me as I am; nothing extenuate,
Nor set down aught in malice. Then must you speak
Of one that lov'd not wisely, but too well;

Of one not easily jealous, but, being wrought,
Perplexed in the extreme; of one whose hand,
Like the base Indian, threw a pearl away
Richer than all his tribe; of one whose subdu'd eyes,
Albeit unused to the melting mood,
Drop tears as fast as the Arabian trees
Their med'cinable gum. Set you down this:
And say besides that in Aleppo once,
Where a malignant and a turban'd Turk
Beat a Venetian and traduc'd the state,
I took by th' throat the circumcised dog,
And smote him – thus. OTHELLO   *Othello, 5, 2, 341*

23 I kiss'd thee ere I kill'd thee. No way but this –
Killing my self, to die upon a kiss. OTHELLO   *5, 2, 361*

Pericles

24 See where she comes, apparell'd like the spring. PERICLES
1, 1, 12

25 Few love to hear the sins they love to act. PERICLES   *1, 1, 92*

26 Kings are earth's gods; in vice their law's their will. PERICLES
1, 1, 103

27 3RD FISHERMAN: Master, I marvel how the fishes live in the sea.
  1ST FISHERMAN: Why, as men do a-land – the great ones eat up
                the little ones.   *2, 1, 27*

King Richard the Second

28 Old John of Gaunt, time-honoured Lancaster. RICHARD II
1, 1, 1

29 Let's purge this choler without letting blood. RICHARD II
1, 1, 153

30 The purest treasure mortal times afford
Is spotless reputation; that away,
Men are but gilded loam or painted clay.
A jewel in a ten-times barr'd-up chest
Is a bold spirit in a loyal breast.
Mine honour is my life; both grow in one;
Take honour from me, and my life is done. MOWBRAY
1, 1, 177

31 We were not born to sue, but to command. RICHARD II
1, 1, 196

32 That which in mean men we entitle patience
Is pale cold cowardice in noble breasts.
                    DUCHESS OF GLOUCESTER *1, 2, 33*

33   This must my comfort be –
That sun that warms you here shall shine on me.
           BOLINGBROKE *Richard the Second, 1, 3, 144*

34 How long a time lies in one little word!
Four lagging winters and four wanton springs
End in a word: such is the breath of Kings. BOLINGBROKE
                                   1, 3, 213

35 Things sweet to taste prove in digestion sour. GAUNT
                                   1, 3, 236

36 All places that the eye of heaven visits
Are to a wise man ports and happy havens.
Teach thy necessity to reason thus:
There is no virtue like necessity. GAUNT   *1, 3, 275*

37 O, who can hold a fire in his hand
By thinking on the frosty Caucasus?
Or cloy the hungry edge of appetite
By bare imagination of a feast?
Or wallow naked in December snow
By thinking on fantastic summer's heat?
O, no! the apprehension of the good
Gives but the greater feeling to the worse. BOLINGBROKE
                                   1, 3, 295

38 Pray God we may make haste, and come too late!
                    RICHARD II *1, 4, 64*

39 More are men's ends mark'd than their lives before.
The setting sun, and music at the close,
As the last taste of sweets, is sweetest last,
Writ in remembrance more than things lost past. GAUNT
                                   2, 1, 11

40 Methinks I am a prophet new inspir'd,
And thus expiring do foretell of him:
His rash fierce blaze of riot cannot last,
For violent fires soon burn out themselves;
Small showers last long, but sudden storms are short;
He tires betimes that spurs too fast betimes. GAUNT *2, 1, 31*

41 This royal throne of kings, this sceptred isle,
This earth of majesty, this seat of Mars,
This other Eden, demi-paradise,
This fortress built by Nature for herself
Against infection and the hand of war,
This happy breed of men, this little world,
This precious stone set in the silver sea,
Which serves it in the office of a wall,

Or as a moat defensive to a house;
Against the envy of less happier lands;
This blessed plot, this earth, this realm, this England,
This nurse, this teeming womb of royal kings,
Fear'd by their breed, and famous by their birth. GAUNT
Richard the Second, 2, 1, 40

42 England, bound in with the triumphant sea,
Whose rocky shore beats back the envious siege
Of wat'ry Neptune, is now bound in with shame,
With inky blots and rotten parchment bonds;
That England, that was wont to conquer others,
Hath made a shameful conquest of itself.
Ah, would the scandal vanish with my life,
How happy then were my ensuing death! GAUNT   *2, 1, 61*

43 Can sick men play so nicely with their names? RICHARD II
2, 1, 84

44 I count myself in nothing else so happy
As in a soul rememb'ring my good friends. BOLINGBROKE
2, 3, 46

45 Grace me no grace, nor uncle me no uncle. YORK   *2, 3, 87*

46 The caterpillars of the commonwealth. BOLINGBROKE
2, 3, 166

47 Things past redress are now with me past care. YORK
2, 3, 171

48 Eating the bitter bread of banishment. BOLINGBROKE *3, 1, 21*

49   I weep for joy
To stand upon my kingdom once again.
Dear earth, I do salute thee with my hand,
Though rebels wound thee with their horses' hoofs.
RICHARD II   *3, 2, 4*

50 Not all the water in the rough rude sea
Can wash the balm from an anointed king;
The breath of worldly men cannot depose
The deputy elected by the Lord. RICHARD II   *3, 2, 54*

51 O, call back yesterday, bid time return. SALISBURY   *3, 2, 69*

52 Cry woe, destruction, ruin, and decay —
The worst is death, and death will have his day. RICHARD II
3, 2, 102

53   Of comfort no man speak.
Let's talk of graves, of worms, and epitaphs;
Make dust our paper, and with rainy eyes
Write sorrow on the bosom of the earth.
Let's choose executors and talk of wills. RICHARD II *3, 2, 144*

54 For God's sake let us sit upon the ground
And tell sad stories of the death of kings:
How some have been depos'd, some slain in war,
Some haunted by the ghosts they have depos'd,
Some poison'd by their wives, some sleeping kill'd,
All murder'd – for within the hollow crown
That rounds the mortal temples of a king
Keeps Death his court; and there the antic sits,
Scoffing his state and grinning at his pomp;
Allowing him a breath, a little scene,
To monarchize, be fear'd, and kill with looks;
Infusing him with self and vain conceit,
As if this flesh which walls about our life
Were brass impregnable; and, humour'd thus,
Comes at the last, and with a little pin
Bores through his castle wall, and farewell, king!   RICHARD II
Richard the Second, 3, 2, 155

55 What must the King do now? Must he submit?
The King shall do it. Must he be depos'd?
The King shall be contented. Must he lose
The name of king? A God's name, let it go.
I'll give my jewels for a set of beads,
My gorgeous palace for a hermitage,
My gay apparel for an almsman's gown,
My figur'd goblets for a dish of wood,
My sceptre for a palmer's walking staff,
My subjects for a pair of carved saints,
And my large kingdom for a little grave,
A little little grave, an obscure grave.   RICHARD II   *3, 3, 143*

56 And if you crown him, let me prophesy –
The blood of English shall manure the ground
And future ages groan for this foul act;
Peace shall go sleep with Turks and infidels.   CARLISLE
4, 1, 136

57 Did they not sometime cry 'All hail!' to me?
So Judas did to Christ; but he, in twelve,
Found truth in all but one; I, in twelve thousand, none.
God save the King! Will no man say amen?
Am I both priest and clerk? Well then, amen.   RICHARD II
4, 1, 169

58 I give this heavy weight from off my head,
And this unwieldy sceptre from my hand,
The pride of kingly sway from out my heart;

With mine own tears I wash away my balm,
With mine own hands I give away my crown.   RICHARD II
Richard the Second, 4, 1, 204

59 The woe's to come; the children yet unborn
Shall feel this day as sharp to them as thorn.   CARLISLE
4, 1, 322

60   I am sworn brother, sweet,
To grim Necessity; and he and I
Will keep a league till death.   RICHARD II   *5, 1, 19*

61 As in a theatre the eyes of men
After a well-grac'd actor leaves the stage
Are idly bent on him that enters next,
Thinking his prattle to be tedious.   YORK   *5, 2, 23*

62 I have been studying how I may compare
This prison where I live unto the world.   RICHARD II   *5, 5, 1*

63   How sour sweet music is
When time is broke and no proportion kept!
So is it in the music of men's lives.   RICHARD II   *5, 5, 42*

King Richard the Third

64 Now is the winter of our discontent
Made glorious summer by this sun of York.   GLOUCESTER
1, 1, 1

65 Our stern alarums chang'd to merry meetings,
Our dreadful marches to delightful measures.   GLOUCESTER
1, 1, 7

66 Deform'd, unfinish'd, sent before my time
Into this breathing world scarce half made up,
And that so lamely and unfashionable
That dogs bark at me as I halt by them.   GLOUCESTER   *1, 1, 20*

67 In this weak piping time of peace.   GLOUCESTER   *1, 1, 24*

68 I am determined to prove a villain.   GLOUCESTER   *1, 1, 30*

69 Was ever woman in this humour woo'd?
Was ever woman in this humour won?   GLOUCESTER
1, 2, 227

70 And thus I clothe my naked villainy
With odd old ends stol'n forth of holy writ,
And seem a saint when most I play the devil.   GLOUCESTER
1, 3, 336

71 O, I have pass'd a miserable night,
So full of fearful dreams, of ugly sights,
That, as I am a Christian faithful man,

I would not spend another such a night
Though 'twere to buy a world of happy days –
So full of dismal terror was the time!   CLARENCE
Richard the Third, 1, 4, 2

72 O Lord, methought what pain it was to drown,
What dreadful noise of waters in my ears,
What sights of ugly death within my eyes!
Methought I saw a thousand fearful wrecks,
A thousand men that fishes gnaw'd upon,
Wedges of gold, great anchors, heaps of pearl,
Inestimable stones, unvalued jewels,
All scatt'red in the bottom of the sea;
Some lay in dead men's skulls, and in the holes
Where eyes did once inhabit there were crept,
As 'twere in scorn of eyes, reflecting gems,
That woo'd the slimy bottom of the deep
And mock'd the dead bones that lay scatt'red by.   CLARENCE
1, 4, 21

73 So wise so young, they say, do never live long.   GLOUCESTER
3, 1, 79

74 My lord of Ely, when I was last in Holborn
I saw good strawberries in your garden there.   GLOUCESTER
3, 4, 32

75 Talk'st thou to me of ifs? Thou art a traitor.
Off with his head!   GLOUCESTER   *3, 4, 77*

76 High-reaching Buckingham grows circumspect.   RICHARD III
4, 2, 31

77   But I am in
So far in blood that sin will pluck on sin.   RICHARD III
4, 2, 65

78 I am not in the giving vein today.   RICHARD III   *4, 2, 120*

79 Their lips were four red roses on a stalk,
And in their summer beauty kiss'd each other.   TYRREL
4, 3, 12

80 An honest tale speeds best being plainly told.
QUEEN ELIZABETH   *4, 4, 358*

81 Harp not on that string.   RICHARD III   *4, 4, 364*

82 Is the chair empty? Is the sword unsway'd?
Is the King dead, the empire unpossess'd?   RICHARD III
4, 4, 470

83 True hope is swift and flies with swallow's wings;
Kings it makes gods, and meaner creatures kings.   RICHMOND
5, 2, 23

84 The King's name is a tower of strength. RICHARD III
Richard the Third, 5, 3, 12

85 I have not that alacrity of spirit
Nor cheer of mind that I was wont to have. RICHARD III
5, 3, 73

86 My conscience hath a thousand several tongues,
And every tongue brings in a several tale,
And every tale condemns me for a villain. RICHARD III
5, 3, 193

87 A horse! a horse! my kingdom for a horse! RICHARD III
5, 4, 7

Romeo and Juliet

88 A pair of star-cross'd lovers. CHORUS *Prologue, 6*

89 The two hours' traffic of our stage. CHORUS *Ib, 12*

90 Saint-seducing gold. ROMEO *1, 1, 213*

91 For I am proverb'd with a grandsire phrase;
I'll be a candle-holder and look on. ROMEO *1, 4, 37*

92 O, then I see Queen Mab hath been with you.
She is the fairies' widwife, and she comes
In shape no bigger than an agate stone
On the fore-finger of an alderman,
Drawn with a team of little atomies
Athwart men's noses as they lie asleep. MERCUTIO *1, 4, 53*

93 For you and I are past our dancing days. CAPULET *1, 5, 29*

94 O, she doth teach the torches to burn bright!
It seems she hangs upon the cheek of night
As a rich jewel in an Ethiop's ear –
Beauty too rich for use, for earth too dear! ROMEO *1, 5, 42*

95 For I ne'er saw true beauty till this night. ROMEO *1, 5, 51*

96 My only love sprung from my only hate! JULIET *1, 5, 136*

97 He jests at scars that never felt a wound.
But, soft! What light through yonder window breaks?
It is the east, and Juliet is the sun. ROMEO *2, 2, 1*

98 See how she leans her cheek upon her hand!
O that I were a glove upon that hand,
That I might touch that cheek! ROMEO *2, 2, 23*

99 O Romeo, Romeo! wherefore art thou Romeo? JULIET
2, 2, 33

1 What's in a name? That which we call a rose
By any other name would smell as sweet. JULIET *2, 2, 43*

2 O, swear not by the moon, th' inconstant moon,
That monthly changes in her circled orb,
Lest that thy love prove likewise variable. JULIET
Romeo and Juliet, 2, 2, 109

3 This bud of love, by summer's ripening breath,
May prove a beauteous flow'r when next we meet. JULIET
2, 2, 121

4 Love goes toward love as school-boys from their books;
But love from love, toward school with heavy looks. ROMEO
2, 2, 156

5 How silver-sweet sound lovers' tongues by night,
Like softest music to attending ears! ROMEO   *2, 2, 166*

6 Good night, good night! Parting is such sweet sorrow
That I shall say good night till it be morrow. JULIET   *2, 2, 185*

7 Wisely and slow; they stumble that run fast. FRIAR LAWRENCE
2, 3, 94

8 O flesh, flesh, how art thou fishified! MERCUTIO   *2, 4, 37*

9 I am the very pink of courtesy. MERCUTIO   *2, 4, 56*

10 Therefore love moderately: long love doth so;
Too swift arrives as tardy as too slow. FRIAR LAWRENCE
2, 6, 14

11 A plague o' both your houses!
They have made worms' meat of me. MERCUTIO   *3, 1, 103*

12 O, I am fortune's fool! ROMEO   *3, 1, 133*

13   Come, civil night,
Thou sober-suited matron, all in black. JULIET   *3, 2, 10*

14 Night's candles are burnt out, and jocund day
Stands tiptoe on the misty mountain tops. ROMEO   *3, 5, 9*

15 Thank me no thankings, nor proud me no prouds. CAPULET
3, 5, 152

16 'Tis an ill cook that cannot lick his own fingers. SERVINGMAN
4, 2, 6

17   Beauty's ensign yet
Is crimson in thy lips and in thy cheeks,
And death's pale flag is not advanced there. ROMEO *5, 3, 94*

18   O, here
Will I set up my everlasting rest,
And shake the yoke of inauspicious stars
From this world-wearied flesh. Eyes, look your last.
Arms, take your last embrace. ROMEO   *5, 3, 109*

The Taming of the Shrew

19 Look in the chronicles: we came in with Richard Conqueror.
CHRISTOPHER SLY *Induction, 1, 4*

20 No profit grows where is no pleasure ta'en;
In brief, sir, study what you most affect. TRANIO *1, 1, 39*

21 There's small choice in rotten apples. HORTENSIO *1, 1, 131*

22 Kiss me, Kate. PETRUCHIO *2, 1, 316*

23 Thereby hangs a tale. GRUMIO *4, 1, 50*

24 This is a way to kill a wife with kindness. PETRUCHIO
4, 1, 192

25 Our purses shall be proud, our garments poor;
For 'tis the mind that makes the body rich;
And as the sun breaks through the darkest clouds,
So honour peereth in the meanest habit. PETRUCHIO *4, 3, 167*

26 A woman mov'd is like a fountain troubled –
Muddy, ill-seeming, thick, bereft of beauty. KATHERINA
5, 2, 142

The Tempest

27 He hath no drowning mark upon him; his complexion is perfect
gallows. GONZALO *1, 1, 28*

28 The wills above be done, but I would fain die a dry death.
GONZALO *1, 1, 63*

29   What seest thou else
In the dark backward and abysm of time? PROSPERO *1, 2, 49*

30 Your tale, sir, would cure deafness. MIRANDA *1, 2, 106*

31   My library
Was dukedom large enough. PROSPERO *1, 2, 109*

32 From the still-vex'd Bermoothes. ARIEL *1, 2, 229*

33 You taught me language, and my profit on't
Is, I know how to curse. The red plague rid you
For learning me your language! CALIBAN *1, 2, 363*

34 Come unto these yellow sands,
And then take hands. ARIEL *1, 2, 375*

35 Full fathom five thy father lies;
Of his bones are coral made;
Those are pearls that were his eyes;
Nothing of him that doth fade
But doth suffer a sea-change
Into something rich and strange. ARIEL *1, 2, 396*

36   This swift business
I must uneasy make, lest too light winning
Make the prize light.   PROSPERO   *The Tempest*, *1, 2, 450*

37 He receives comfort like cold porridge.   SEBASTIAN   *2, 1, 10*

38 I' th' commonwealth I would by contraries
Execute all things.   GONZALO   *2, 1, 141*

39 While you here do snoring lie,
Open-ey'd conspiracy
  His time doth take.   ARIEL   *2, 1, 291*

40 When they will not give a doit to relieve a lame beggar, they will
lay out ten to see a dead Indian.   TRINCULO   *2, 2, 29*

41 Misery acquaints a man with strange bedfellows.   TRINCULO
                                                2, 2, 38

42 Well, here's my comfort. (*Drinks*)   STEPHANO   *2, 2, 43*

43 The master, the swabber, the boatswain, and I,
The gunner, and his mate,
Lov'd Mall, Meg, and Marian, and Margery,
But none of us car'd for Kate.   STEPHANO   *2, 2, 44*

44 'Ban 'Ban, Ca – Caliban,
Has a new master – Get a new man.   CALIBAN   *2, 2, 173*

45 They say there's but five upon this isle: we are three of them;
if th' other two be brain'd like us, the state totters.   TRINCULO
                                               3, 2, 4

46 He that dies pays all debts.   STEPHANO   *3, 2, 126*

47 Be not afeard.   The isle is full of noises,
Sounds, and sweet airs, that give delight, and hurt not.   CALIBAN
                                              3, 2, 130

48   Travellers ne'er did lie,
 Though fools at home condemn 'em.   ANTONIO   *3, 3, 26*

49   You fools! I and my fellows
Are ministers of Fate; the elements
Of whom your swords are temper'd may as well
Wound the loud winds, or with bemock'd-at stabs
Kill the still-closing waters, as diminish
One dowle that's in my plume.   ARIEL   *3, 3, 60*

50 Our revels now are ended. These our actors,
As I foretold you, were all spirits, and
Are melted into air, into thin air;
And, like the baseless fabric of this vision,
The cloud-capp'd towers, the gorgeous palaces,
The solemn temples, the great globe itself,
Yea, all which it inherit, shall dissolve,

And, like this insubstantial pageant faded,
Leave not a rack behind. We are such stuff
As dreams are made on; and our little life
Is rounded with a sleep. PROSPERO   *The Tempest, 4, 1, 148*

51 Wit shall not go unrewarded while I am king of this country.
STEPHANO *4, 1, 240*

52 With foreheads villainous low. CALIBAN   *4, 1, 248*

53   The rarer action is
In virtue than in vengeance. PROSPERO   *5, 1, 27*

54 Ye elves of hills, brooks, standing lakes, and groves;
And ye that on the sands with printless foot
Do chase the ebbing Neptune, and do fly him
When he comes back. PROSPERO   *5, 1, 33*

55   I'll break my staff,
Bury it certain fathoms in the earth,
And deeper than did ever plummet sound
I'll drown my book. PROSPERO   *5, 1, 54*

56   Where the bee sucks, there suck I;
In a cowslip's bell I lie;
There I couch when owls do cry.
On the bat's back I do fly
After summer merrily.
Merrily, merrily shall I live now
Under the blossom that hangs on the bough. ARIEL *5, 1, 88*

57 How beauteous mankind is! O brave new world
That has such people in't! MIRANDA   *5, 1, 183*

58   Retire me to my Milan, where
Every third thought shall be my grave. PROSPERO *5, 1, 310*

Timon of Athens

59 'Tis not enough to help the feeble up
But to support him after. TIMON   *1, 1, 110*

60 I wonder men dare trust themselves with men. APEMANTUS
1, 2, 42

61 Uncover, dogs, and lap. TIMON   *3, 6, 85*

Titus Andronicus

62 Sweet mercy is nobility's true badge. TAMORA   *1, 1, 119*

63 She is a woman, therefore may be woo'd;
She is a woman, therefore may be won;
She is Lavinia, therefore must be lov'd.

What, man! more water glideth by the mill
Than wots the miller of; and easy it is
Of a cut loaf to steal a shive, we know.   DEMETRIUS
Titus Andronicus, 2, 1, 82

64 If one good deed in all my life I did,
I do repent it from my very soul.   AARON   *5, 3, 189*

Troilus and Cressida

65   Women are angels, wooing:
Things won are done; joy's soul lies in the doing.
That she belov'd knows nought that knows not this:
Men prize the thing ungain'd more than it is.   CRESSIDA
1, 2, 278

66 The heavens themselves, the planets, and this centre,
Observe degree, priority, and place,
Insisture, course, proportion, season, form,
Office, and custom, in all line of order.   ULYSSES   *1, 3, 85*

67   O, when degree is shak'd,
Which is the ladder of all high designs,
The enterprise is sick!   ULYSSES   *1, 3, 101*

68 Take but degree away, untune that string,
And hark what discord follows!   ULYSSES   *1, 3, 109*

69 I would thou didst itch from head to foot and I had the
scratching of thee.   THERSITES   *2, 1, 26*

70 To be wise and love
Exceeds man's might.   CRESSIDA   *3, 2, 152*

71 Time hath, my lord, a wallet at his back,
Wherein he puts alms for oblivion,
A great-siz'd monster of ingratitudes.   ULYSSES   *3, 3, 145*

72 One touch of nature makes the whole world kin.   ULYSSES
3, 3, 175

73 There's language in her eye, her cheek, her lip,
Nay, her foot speaks; her wanton spirits look out
At every joint and motive of her body.   ULYSSES   *4, 5, 55*

74 Lechery, lechery! Still wars and lechery! Nothing else holds
fashion.   THERSITES   *5, 2, 193*

Twelfth Night

75 If music be the food of love, play on,
Give me excess of it, that, surfeiting,
The appetite may sicken and so die.
That strain again! It had a dying fall;
O, it came o'er my ear like the sweet sound

That breathes upon a bank of violets,
Stealing and giving odour! Enough, no more;
'Tis not so sweet now as it was before. DUKE ORSINO
Twelfth Night, 1, 1, 1

76 Speaks three or four languages word for word without book.
SIR TOBY BELCH *1, 3, 24*

77 Is it a world to hide virtues in? SIR TOBY BELCH *1, 3, 123*

78 Many a good hanging prevents a bad marriage. FESTE
1, 5, 18

79 A plague o' these pickle-herring! SIR TOBY BELCH *1, 5, 114*

80 Make me a willow cabin at your gate,
And call upon my soul within the house;
Write loyal cantons of contemned love
And sing them loud even in the dead of night;
Halloo your name to the reverberate hills,
And make the babbling gossip of the air
Cry out 'Olivia!' VIOLA *1, 5, 252*

81 Farewell, fair cruelty. VIOLA *1, 5, 272*

82 Not to be abed after midnight is to be up betimes.
SIR TOBY BELCH *2, 3, 1*

83 O mistress mine, where are you roaming?
O, stay and hear; your true love's coming,
That can sing both high and low,
Trip no further, pretty sweeting;
Journeys end in lovers meeting,
Every wise man's son doth know. FESTE *2, 3, 38*

84 What is love? 'Tis not hereafter;
Present mirth hath present laughter;
What's to come is still unsure.
In delay there lies no plenty,
Then come kiss me, sweet and twenty;
Youth's a stuff will not endure. FESTE *2, 3, 46*

85 He does it with a better grace, but I do it more natural.
SIR ANDREW AGUECHEEK *2, 3, 79*

86 Is there no respect of place, persons, nor time, in you?
MALVOLIO *2, 3, 89*

87 Dost thou think, because thou art virtuous, there shall be no
more cakes and ale? SIR TOBY BELCH *2, 3, 109*

88 Come away, come away, death;
And in sad cypress let me be laid;
Fly away, fly away, breath,
I am slain by a fair cruel maid.

My shroud of white, stuck all with yew,
    O, prepare it!
My part of death no one so true
    Did share it.   FESTE   *Twelfth Night, 2, 4, 50*

89   She never told her love,
But let concealment, like a worm i' th' bud,
Feed on her damask cheek. She pin'd in thought;
And with a green and yellow melancholy
She sat like Patience on a monument,
Smiling at grief.   VIOLA   *2, 4, 109*

90 I am all the daughters of my father's house,
And all the brothers too.   VIOLA   *2, 4, 119*

91 Some are born great, some achieve greatness, and some have
greatness thrust upon 'em.   MALVOLIO (reading letter)
                                                  2, 5, 129

92 Remember who commended thy yellow stockings, and wish'd
to see thee ever cross-garter'd.   MALVOLIO (reading letter)
                                                  2, 5, 135

93 O world, how apt the poor are to be proud!   OLIVIA *3, 1, 124*

94 Love sought is good, but given unsought is better.   OLIVIA
                                                  3, 1, 153

95 Why, this is very midsummer madness.   OLIVIA   *3, 4, 53*

96 If this were play'd upon a stage now, I could condemn it as an
improbable fiction.   FABIAN   *3, 4, 121*

97 More matter for a May morning.   FABIAN   *3, 4, 136*

98 Still you keep o' th' windy side of the law.   FABIAN *3, 4, 156*

99 Out of my lean and low ability
I'll lend you something.   VIOLA   *3, 4, 328*

1 I hate ingratitude more in a man
Than lying, vainness, babbling drunkenness,
Or any taint of vice whose strong corruption
Inhabits our frail blood.   VIOLA   *3, 4, 338*

2 And thus the whirligig of time brings in his revenges.   FESTE
                                                5, 1, 363

3 When that I was and a little tiny boy,
    With hey, ho, the wind and the rain,
A foolish thing was but a toy,
For the rain it raineth every day.   FESTE   *5, 1, 375*

The Two Gentlemen of Verona

4 Home-keeping youth have ever homely wits.   VALENTINE
                                                  1, 1, 2

5 I have no other but a woman's reason:
I think him so, because I think him so. LUCETTA
The Two Gentlemen of Verona, 1, 2, 23

6 O, how this spring of love resembleth
The uncertain glory of an April day. PROTEUS   *1, 3, 84*

7 Dumb jewels often in their silent kind
More than quick words do move a woman's mind. VALENTINE
3, 1, 90

8 Who is Silvia? What is she,
That all our swains commend her?
Holy, fair, and wise is she. SONG   *4, 2, 38*

9 Is she kind as she is fair?
For beauty lives with kindness. SONG   *4, 2, 43*

10 How use doth breed a habit in a man! VALENTINE   *5, 4, 1*

11   O, heaven, were man
But constant, he were perfect! PROTEUS   *5, 4, 110*

The Winter's Tale

12 Two lads that thought there was no more behind
But such a day tomorrow as to-day,
And to be boy eternal. POLIXENES   *1, 2, 63*

13 A sad tale's best for winter. I have one
Of sprites and goblins. MAMILLIUS   *2, 1, 25*

14   What's gone and what's past help
Should be past grief. PAULINA   *3, 2, 219*

15 *Exit, pursued by a bear.* STAGE DIRECTION   *3, 3, 58*

16 I would there were no age between ten and three and twenty, or
that youth would sleep out the rest; for there is nothing in the
between but getting wenches with child, wronging the ancientry,
stealing, fighting. SHEPHERD   *3, 3, 59*

17 When daffodils begin to peer,
With heigh! the doxy over the dale,
Why, then comes in the sweet o' the year,
For the red blood reigns in the winter's pale. AUTOLYCUS
4, 3, 1

18 A snapper-up of unconsidered trifles. AUTOLYCUS   *4, 3, 26*

19 Jog on, jog on, the footpath way,
And merrily hent the stile-a;
A merry heart goes all the day,
Your sad tires in a mile-a. AUTOLYCUS   *4, 3, 118*

20 For you there's rosemary and rue; these keep
Seeming and savour all the winter long. PERDITA   *4, 4, 74*

21   What you do
   Still betters what is done. When you speak, sweet,
   I'd have you do it ever. When you sing,
   I'd have you buy and sell so; so give alms;
   Pray so; and, for the ord'ring your affairs,
   To sing them too.   FLORIZEL   *The Winter's Tale*, *4, 4, 135*
22 Lawn as white as driven snow.   AUTOLYCUS   *4, 4, 215*
23 The self-same sun that shines upon his court.   PERDITA
                                                  4, 4, 436

24 Prosperity's the very bond of love,
   Whose fresh complexion and whose heart together
   Affliction alters.   CAMILLO   *4, 4, 565*
25 Though I am not naturally honest, I am so sometimes by chance.
                                   AUTOLYCUS   *4, 4, 701*
26 Let me have no lying; it becomes none but tradesmen.
                                   AUTOLYCUS   *4, 4, 711*
27 Though authority be a stubborn bear, yet he is oft led by the
   nose with gold.   CLOWN   *4, 4, 790*

Sonnets
28 To the onlie begetter of these insuing sonnets.   *Dedication*
29 From fairest creatures we desire increase,
   That thereby beauty's rose might never die.   *Sonnet 1*
30 Look in thy glass, and tell the face thou viewest.   *Sonnet 3*
31 But wherefore do not you a mightier way
   Make war upon this bloody tyrant Time?   *Sonnet 16*
32 Shall I compare thee to a summer's day?
   Thou art more lovely and more temperate.
   Rough winds do shake the darling buds of May,
   And summer's lease hath all too short a date.   *Sonnet 18*
33 But thy eternal summer shall not fade.   *Sonnet 18*
34 So long as men can breathe or eyes can see,
   So long lives this, and this gives life to thee.   *Sonnet 18*
35 A woman's face, with Nature's own hand painted,
   Hast thou, the Master Mistress of my passion.   *Sonnet 20*
36 For thy sweet love rememb'red such wealth brings
   That then I scorn to change my state with kings.   *Sonnet 29*
37 When to the sessions of sweet silent thought
   I summon up remembrance of things past,
   I sigh the lack of many a thing I sought,
   And with old woes new wail my dear time's waste.   *Sonnet 30*

38 But if the while I think on thee, dear friend,
   All losses are restored, and sorrows end.   *Sonnet 30*

39 So true a fool is love that in your will,
   Though you do anything, he thinks no ill.   *Sonnet 57*

40 Like as the waves make towards the pebbled shore,
   So do our minutes hasten to their end.   *Sonnet 60*

41 Some glory in their birth, some in their skill,
   Some in their wealth, some in their body's force;
   Some in their garments, though new-fangled ill;
   Some in their hawks and hounds, some in their horse.
                                                      Sonnet 91

42 For sweetest things turn sourest by their deeds:
   Lilies that fester smell far worse than weeds.   *Sonnet 94*

43 How like a winter hath my absence been
   From thee, the pleasure of the fleeting year!
   What freezings have I felt, what dark days seen!   *Sonnet 97*

44 From you have I been absent in the spring,
   When proud-pied April, dress'd in all his trim,
   Hath put a spirit of youth in every thing.   *Sonnet 98*

45 When in the chronicle of wasted time
   I see descriptions of the fairest weights.   *Sonnet 106*

46 For we, which now behold these present days,
   Have eyes to wonder, but lack tongues to praise.   *Sonnet 106*

47 Let me not to the marriage of true minds
   Admit impediments. Love is not love
   Which alters when it alteration finds,
   Or bends with the remover to remove.
   O, no! it is an ever-fixed mark,
   That looks on tempests and is never shaken.   *Sonnet 116*

48 Love alters not with his brief hours and weeks,
   But bears it out even to the edge of doom.
   If this be error, and upon me prov'd,
   I never writ, nor no man ever lov'd.   *Sonnet 116*

49 'Tis better to be vile than vile esteemed,
   When not to be receives reproach of being.   *Sonnet 121*

50 Th' expense of spirit in a waste of shame
   Is lust in action; and till action, lust
   Is perjur'd, murd'rous, bloody, full of blame,
   Savage, extreme, rude, cruel, not to trust;
   Enjoy'd no sooner but despised straight.   *Sonnet 129*

51 All this the world well knows; yet none knows well
   To shun the heaven that leads men to this hell.   *Sonnet 129*

52 My mistress' eyes are nothing like the sun;
Coral is far more red than her lips' red. *Sonnet 130*

53 And yet, by heaven, I think my love as rare
As any she belied with false compare. *Sonnet 130*

54 When my love swears that she is made of truth,
I do believe her, though I know she lies. *Sonnet 138*

55 Two loves I have, of comfort and despair,
Which like two spirits do suggest me still;
The better angel is a man right fair,
The worser spirit a woman colour'd ill. *Sonnet 144*

Poems

56 Crabbed age and youth cannot live together:
Youth is full of pleasance, age is full of care;
Youth like summer morn, age like winter weather;
Youth like summer brave, age like winter bare.
The Passionate Pilgrim, 12

57 Age, I do abhor thee; youth, I do adore thee. *Ib*

58 The first heire of my invention. *Venus and Adonis, Dedication*

59 Hunting he lov'd, but love he laugh'd to scorn. *Ib, 1, 4*

60 Beauty itself doth of itself persuade
The eyes of men without an orator. *The Rape of Lucrece,*
1, 29

SHAW, George Bernard, 1856–1950

61 Breakages, Limited, the biggest industrial corporation in the
country. BALBUS *The Apple Cart, Act 1*

62 You can always tell an old soldier by the inside of his holsters
and cartridge boxes. The young ones carry pistols and cartridges:
the old ones grub. BLUNTSCHLI *Arms and the Man, Act 1*

63 You are a very poor soldier: a chocolate cream soldier!
RAINA *Ib, Act 1*

64 It is enough that there *is* a beyond. LILITH *Back to*
Methuselah, Part 5, Last words

65 When a stupid man is doing something he is ashamed of, he
always declares that it is his duty. APOLLODORUS
Caesar and Cleopatra, Act 3

66 We have no more right to consume happiness without producing
it than to consume wealth without producing it. MORELL
Candida, Act 1

67 The overpaying instinct is a generous one: better than the underpaying instinct, and not so common. MORELL *Ib, Act 1*

68 I'm only a beer teetotaller, not a champagne teetotaller.
PROSERPINE *Candida, Act 3*

69 Martyrdom . . . is the only way in which a man can become
famous without ability. BURGOYNE   *The Devil's Disciple,*
Act 3

70 SWINDON: What will History say?
BURGOYNE: History, sir, will tell lies, as usual.   *Ib, Act 3*

71 Stimulate the phagocytes. B. B. *The Doctor's Dilemma, Act 1*

72 Go anywhere in England where there are natural, wholesome,
contented, and really nice English people; and what do you
always find? That the stables are the real centre of the household. LADY UTTERWORD   *Heartbreak House, Act 3*

73 Tell me all me faults as man to man, I can stand anything but
flattery. TIM   *John Bull's Other Island, Act 1*

74 The more a man knows, and the further he travels, the more
likely he is to marry a country girl afterwards. KEEGAN
Ib, Act 2

75 My way of joking is to tell the truth. Its the funniest joke in the
world. KEEGAN   *Ib*

76 I am a Millionaire. That is my religion. UNDERSHAFT
Major Barbara, Act 2

77 Wot prawce selvytion nah? BILL WALKER   *Ib*

78 A lifetime of happiness! No man alive could bear it: it would be
hell on earth. TANNER   *Man and Superman, Act 1*

79 There is no love sincerer than the love of food. TANNER   *Ib*

80 The true artist will let his wife starve, his children go barefoot,
his mother drudge for his living at seventy, sooner than work
at anything but his art. TANNER   *Ib*

81 It is a womans business to get married as soon as possible, and a
mans to keep unmarried as long as he can. TANNER *Ib, Act 2*

82 An Englishman thinks he is moral when he is only uncomfortable. THE DEVIL   *Ib, Act 3*

83 There are two tragedies in life. One is to lose your hearts desire.
The other is to gain it. MENDOZA   *Ib, Act 4*

84 Any person under the age of thirty, who, having any knowledge
of the existing social order, is not a revolutionist, is an inferior.
Ib, The Revolutionist's Handbook, Foreword

85 We learn from history that we learn nothing from history. *Ib*

86 The golden rule is that there are no golden rules. *Ib, Maxims*
for Revolutionists

87 Liberty means responsibility. That is why most men dread it.
Man and Superman, Maxims for Revolutionists

88 He who can, does. He who cannot, teaches. *Ib*

89 Marriage is popular because it combines the maximum of temptation with the maximum of opportunity. *Ib*

90 Ladies and gentlemen are permitted to have friends in the kennel, but not in the kitchen. *Ib*

91 Every man over forty is a scoundrel. *Ib*

92 There is only one religion, though there are a hundred versions of it. *Plays Pleasant, Preface*

93 Remember that you are a human being with a soul and the divine gift of articulate speech: that your native language is the language of Shakespear and Milton and The Bible; and dont sit there crooning like a bilious pigeon. HIGGINS *Pygmalion, Act 1*

94 I don't want to talk grammar. I want to talk like a lady.
ELIZA *Ib, Act 2*

95 Time enough to think of the future when you haven't any future to think of. HIGGINS *Ib*

96 Im one of the undeserving poor: thats what I am. Think of what that means to a man. It means that he's up agen middle class morality all the time. DOOLITTLE *Ib*

97 My aunt died of influenza: so they said . . . But its my belief they done the old woman in. ELIZA *Ib, Act 3*

98 Walk! Not bloody likely. ELIZA *Ib*

99 No eggs! No eggs!! Thousand thunders, man, what do you mean by no eggs? ROBERT *Saint Joan, Scene 1*

1 We want a few mad people now. See where the sane ones have landed us! POULENGEY *Ib*

2 I hear voices telling me what to do. They come from God.
JOAN *Ib*

3 A miracle, my friend, is an event which creates faith. That is the purpose and nature of miracles. ARCHBISHOP *Ib, Scene 2*

4 Do not think you can frighten me by telling me that I am alone. France is alone; and God is alone; and what is my loneliness before the loneliness of my country and my God? JOAN
Ib, Scene 5

5 THE EXECUTIONER: You have heard the last of her.
WARWICK: The last of her? Hm! I wonder! *Ib, Scene 6*

6 All dress is fancy dress, is it not, except our natural skins?
DUNOIS *Ib, Epilogue*

7 Well, sir, you never can tell. Thats a principle in life with me,
sir, if youll excuse my having such a thing, sir.   WAITER
You Never Can Tell, Act 2

8 With the single exception of Homer, there is no eminent writer,
not even Sir Walter Scott, whom I can despise so entirely as I
despise Shakespeare when I measure my mind against his.
Dramatic Opinions and Essays, Vol. 2, 52

SHELLEY, Percy Bysshe, 1792–1822

9 I weep for Adonais – he is dead!
O, weep for Adonais! though our tears
Thaw not the frost which binds so dear a head!   *Adonais, 1*

10 Ah, woe is me! Winter is come and gone,
But grief returns with the revolving year.   *Ib, 154*

11 Through wood and stream and field and hill and Ocean
A quickening life from the Earth's heart has burst
As it has ever done, with change and motion,
From the great morning of the world when first
God dawned on Chaos.   *Ib, 163*

12 Alas! that all we loved of him should be,
But for our grief, as if it had not been,
And grief itself be mortal!   *Ib, 181*

13 The Pilgrim of Eternity, whose fame
Over his living head like Heaven is bent,
An early but enduring monument.   *Ib, 264*

14 A pardlike Spirit beautiful and swift.   *Ib, 280*

15 Live thou, whose infamy is not thy fame!
Live! fear no heavier chastisement from me,
Thou noteless blot on a remembered name!   *Ib, 325*

16 He has outsoared the shadow of our night;
Envy and calumny and hate and pain,
And that unrest which men miscall delight,
Can touch him not and torture not again;
From the contagion of the world's slow stain
He is secure, and now can never mourn
A heart grown cold, a head grown gray in vain.   *Ib, 352*

17 He lives, he wakes – 'tis Death is dead, not he.   *Ib, 361*

18 He is a portion of the loveliness
Which once he made more lovely.   *Ib, 379*

19 The One remains, the many change and pass;
Heaven's light forever shines, Earth's shadows fly;
Life, like a dome of many-coloured glass,
Stains the white radiance of Eternity.   *Ib, 460*

20 The soul of Adonais, like a star,
   Beacons from the abode where the Eternal are. *Adonais, 494*

21 I bring fresh showers for the thirsting flowers,
   From the seas and the streams. *The Cloud, 1*

22 I wield the flail of the lashing tail,
   And whiten the green plains under,
   And then again I dissolve it in rain,
   And laugh as I pass in thunder. *Ib, 9*

23 I am the daughter of Earth and Water,
   And the nursling of the Sky;
   I pass through the pores of the ocean and shores;
   I change, but I cannot die. *Ib, 73*

24 How wonderful is Death,
   Death and his brother Sleep! *The Daemon of the World, 1, 1*

25 I never was attached to that great sect,
   Whose doctrine is, that each one should select
   Out of the crowd a mistress or a friend,
   And all the rest, though fair and wise, commend
   To cold oblivion. *Epipsychidion, 149*

26 True Love in this differs from gold and clay,
   That to divide is not to take away. *Ib, 160*

27 Good-night? ah! no; the hour is ill
   Which severs those it should unite;
   Let us remain together still,
   Then it will be good night. *Good-Night, 1*

28 The world's great age begins anew,
   The golden years return,
   The earth doth like a snake renew
   Her winter weeds outworn:
   Heaven smiles, and faiths and empires gleam,
   Like wrecks of a dissolving dream. *Hellas, 1060*

29 Thou Paradise of exiles, Italy! *Julian and Maddalo, 57*

30 I met Murder on the way —
   He had a mask like Castlereagh. *The Mask of Anarchy, 5*

31 Shake your chains to earth like dew
   Which in sleep had fallen on you —
   Ye are many — they are few. *Ib, 153*

32 Swiftly walk o'er the western wave,
   Spirit of Night!
   Out of the misty eastern cave,
   Where, all the long and lone daylight,
   Thou wovest dreams of joy and fear. *To Night, 1*

33 I ask of thee, belovèd Night –
Swift be thine approaching flight,
  Come soon, soon!   *To Night, 33*

34 A glorious people vibrated again
  The lightning of the nations.   *Ode to Liberty, 1*

35 O Wild West Wind, thou breath of Autumn's being,
Thou, from whose unseen presence the leaves dead
Are driven, like ghosts from an enchanter fleeing,
Yellow, and black, and pale, and hectic red,
Pestilence-stricken multitudes.   *Ode to the West Wind, 1*

36 Wild Spirit, which art moving everywhere;
Destroyer and preserver; hear, oh, hear!   *Ib, 13*

37 Oh, lift me as a wave, a leaf, a cloud!
I fall upon the thorns of life! I bleed!
A heavy weight of hours has chained and bowed
One too like thee: tameless, and swift, and proud.   *Ib, 53*

38 Scatter, as from an unextinguished hearth
Ashes and sparks, my words among mankind!
Be through my lips to unawakened earth
The trumpet of a prophecy! O, Wind,
If Winter comes, can Spring be far behind?   *Ib, 66*

39 I met a traveller from antique land
Who said: Two vast and trunkless legs of stone
Stand in the desert.   *Ozymandias, 1*

40 And on the pedestal these words appear:
'My name is Ozymandias, king of kings:
Look on my works, ye Mighty, and despair!'
Nothing beside remains. Round the decay
Of that colossal wreck, boundless and bare
The lone and level sands stretch far away.   *Ib, 9*

41 Hell is a city much like London –
  A populous and a smoky city.   *Peter Bell the Third,*
                                     Part 3, Hell, 1

42 Crucified 'twixt a smile and whimper.   *Ib, 196*

43 But from these create he can
Forms more real than living man,
Nurslings of immortality!   *Prometheus Unbound, 1, 747*

44   Yet all love is sweet,
Given or returned. Common as light is love,
And its familiar voice wearies not ever.   *Ib, 2, 5, 39*

45 Familiar acts are beautiful through love.   *Ib, 4, 403*

46 A Sensitive Plant in a garden grew,
   And the young winds fed it with silver dew,
   And it opened its fan-like leaves to the light,
   And closed them beneath the kisses of Night.   *The Sensitive
                                                        Plant, 1, 1*

47 It is a modest creed, and yet
   Pleasant if one considers it,
   To own that death itself must be,
   Like all the rest, a mockery.   *Ib, Conclusion, 126*

48 For love, and beauty, and delight,
   There is no death nor change.   *Ib, Ib, 134*

49   Hail to thee, blithe Spirit!
         Bird thou never wert,
      That from Heaven, or near it,
         Pourest thy full heart
   In profuse strains of unpremeditated art.   *To a Skylark, 1*

50   We look before and after,
         And pine for what is not:
      Our sincerest laughter
         With some pain is fraught;
   Our sweetest songs are those that tell of saddest thought. *Ib, 86*

51   Teach me half the gladness
         That thy brain must know,
      Such harmonious madness
         From my lips would flow
   The world should listen then – as I am listening now.   *Ib, 101*

52 Rarely, rarely, comest thou,
      Spirit of Delight!   *Song, Rarely, Rarely, Comest Thou*

53 An old, mad, blind, despised, and dying king.   *Sonnet,
                                                     England in 1819*

54 Music, when soft voices die,
      Vibrates in the memory –
   Odours, when sweet violets sicken,
   Live within the sense they quicken.
   Rose leaves, when the rose is dead,
   Are heaped for the belovèd's bed;
   And so thy thoughts, when thou art gone,
   Love itself shall slumber on.   *To —, Music, When Soft
                                                 Voices Die*

55 I fear thy kisses, gentle maiden,
      Thou needst not fear mine;
   My spirit is too deeply laden
      Ever to burthen thine.   *To —, I Fear Thy Kisses*

56 The desire of the moth for the star,
　 Of the night for the morrow,
　 The devotion to something afar
　　 From the sphere of our sorrow. *To —, One Word is too
often Profaned*

57 Poetry lifts the veil from the hidden beauty of the world, and
makes familiar objects be as if they were not familiar.
A Defence of Poetry

58 Poetry is the record of the best and happiest moments of the
happiest and best minds. *Ib*

59 Poets are the unacknowledged legislators of the world. *Ib*

SHENSTONE, William, 1714–1763

60 Whoe'er has travell'd life's dull round,
　 Where'er his stages may have been,
　 May sigh to think he still has found
　 The warmest welcome, at an inn. *Written at an Inn at
Henley*

SHERIDAN, Philip Henry, 1831–1888

61 The only good Indian is a dead Indian. *Attributed*

SHERIDAN, Richard Brinsley, 1751–1816

62 Yes, sir, puffing is of various sorts; the principal are, the puff
direct, the puff preliminary, the puff collateral, the puff collusive,
and the puff oblique, or puff by implication. PUFF *The Critic,
Act, 1, Scene 2*

63 No scandal about Queen Elizabeth I hope. SNEER *Ib, Act 2,
Scene 1*

64 An oyster may be crossed in love. TILBURINA *Ib, Act 3,
Scene 1*

65 Thought does not become a young woman. MRS MALAPROP
The Rivals, Act 1, Scene 2

66 Illiterate him, I say, quite from your memory.
MRS MALAPROP *Ib*

67 'Tis safest in matrimony to begin with a little aversion.
MRS MALAPROP *Ib*

68 A circulating library in a town is as an ever-green tree of
diabolical knowledge! It blossoms through the year.
SIR ANTHONY ABSOLUTE *Ib*

69 A progeny of learning. MRS MALAPROP *Ib*

70 A supercilious knowledge in accounts. MRS MALAPROP *Ib*

71 If I reprehend any thing in this world it is the use of my oracular tongue and a nice derangement of epitaphs. MRS MALAPROP
The Rivals, Act 3, Scene 3

72 As headstrong as an allegory on the banks of the Nile.
MRS MALAPROP *Ib*

73 Too civil by half. ACRES *Ib, Act 3, Scene 4*

74 You shall see them on a beautiful quarto page, where a neat rivulet of text shall meander through a meadow of margin.
SIR BENJAMIN BACKBITE *School for Scandal, Act 1, Scene 1*

75 Though I can't make her love me, there is great satisfaction in quarrelling with her. SIR PETER TEAZLE *Ib, Act 2, Scene 1*

76 There is the whole set! a character dead at every word.
SIR PETER TEAZLE *Ib, Act 2, Scene 2*

77 I'm called away by particular business. But I leave my character behind me. SIR PETER TEAZLE *Ib*

78 Here's to the maiden of bashful fifteen;
    Here's to the widow of fifty;
Here's to the flaunting extravagant quean,
    And here's to the housewife that's thrifty.
        Let the toast pass, –
        Drink to the lass,
I'll warrant she'll prove an excuse for a glass.
SIR HARRY BUMPER *Ib, Act 3, Scene 3*

79 What is principle against the flattery of a handsome, lively young fellow? SIR PETER TEAZLE *Ib, Act, 4, Scene 2*

80 The Right Honourable gentleman is indebted to his memory for his jests, and to his imagination for his facts. *Reply to Mr Dundas, House of Commons*

SHERMAN, General William Tecumseh, 1820–1891

81 There is many a boy here today who looks on war as all glory, but, boys, it is all hell. *Speech, 1880*

SIDNEY, Algernon, 1622–1683

82 Liars ought to have good memories. *Discourses on Government, Ch. 2, 15*

SIDNEY, Sir Philip, 1554–1586

83 My true love hath my heart, and I have his,
By just exchange one for another given:
I hold his dear, and mine he cannot miss,
There never was a better bargain driven. *The Arcadia, 3*

84 Biting my truant pen, beating myself for spite:
   'Fool!' said my Muse to me, 'look in thy heart and write.'
                               Astrophel and Stella, Sonnet 1

85 With how sad steps, O Moon, thou climb'st the skies!
   How silently, and with how wan a face!   *Ib, Sonnet 31*

86 With a tale forsooth he cometh unto you, with a tale which
   holdeth children from play, and old men from the chimney
   corner.   *The Defence of Poesy*

87 Certainly, I must confess mine own barbarousness, I never heard
   the old song of Percy and Douglas, that I found not my heart
   moved more than with a trumpet.   *Ib*

88 Thy necessity is greater than mine.   *On giving his water-*
             bottle to a dying soldier at Zutphen, 1586

SIMS, George Robert, 1847–1922

89 It was Christmas Day in the Workhouse.   *Christmas Day*
                              in the Workhouse

SITWELL, Edith, 1887–1964

90 Still falls the Rain –
   Dark as the world of man, black as our loss –
   Blind as the nineteen hundred and forty nails
   Upon the Cross.   *Still Falls the Rain*

SITWELL, Sir Osbert, 1892–1969

91 The British Bourgeoisie
   Is not born,
   And does not die,
   But, if it is ill,
   It has a frightened look in its eyes.   *At the House of*
                             Mrs Kinfoot

SKELTON, John, 1460?–1529

92 For though my ryme be ragged,
   Tattered and jagged,
   Rudely rayne beaten,
   Rusty and mothe eaten;
   If ye take well therwith,
   It hath in it some pyth.   *Colyn Cloute, 2, 53*

93 With solace and gladness,
   Much mirth and no madness,
   All good and no badness.   *To Mistress Margaret Hussey*

SMART, Christopher, 1722–1771

94 Glorious the northern lights astream;
   Glorious the song, when God's the theme;
   Glorious the thunder's roar. *Song to David, 85*

95 And now the matchless deed's achieved,
   Determined, dared, and done! *Ib, 86*

SMEDLEY, Francis Edward, 1818–1864

96 You are looking as fresh as paint. *Frank Fairleigh, Ch. 41*

SMITH, Adam, 1723–1790

97 No society can surely be flourishing and happy, of which the far
   greater part of the members are poor and miserable.
   The Wealth of Nations, 1, 8

98 To found a great empire for the sole purpose of raising up a
   people of customers, may at first sight appear a project fit only
   for a nation of shopkeepers. It is, however, a project altogether
   unfit for a nation of shopkeepers; but extremely fit for a nation
   that is governed by shopkeepers. *Ib, 2, 4*

SMITH, Logan Pearsall, 1865–1946

99 Happiness is a wine of the rarest vintage, and seems insipid to
   a vulgar taste. *Afterthoughts, 1, Life and Human Nature*

 1 There are few sorrows, however poignant, in which a good
   income is of no avail. *Ib*

 2 The wretchedness of being rich is that you live with rich people.
   Ib, 4, In the World

 3 People say that Life is the thing, but I prefer Reading.
   Ib, 6, Myself

 4 Thank heavens, the sun has gone in, and I don't have to go out
   and enjoy it. *Last words*

SMITH, Samuel Francis, 1808–1895

 5 My country, 'tis of thee,
   Sweet land of liberty,
      Of thee I sing. *America*

SMITH, Sydney, 1771–1845

 6 Poverty is no disgrace to a man, but it is confoundedly inconvenient. *His Wit and Wisdom*

 7 No furniture so charming as books. *Lady Holland, Memoir,
   Vol. 1, Ch. 9*

8 How can a bishop marry? How can he flirt? The most he can say is, 'I will see you in the vestry after the service.'
Lady Holland, Memoir, Vol. 1, Ch. 9

9 As the French say, there are three sexes, – men, women, and clergymen. *Ib*

10 Praise is the best diet for us, after all. *Ib*

11 I never read a book before reviewing it; it prejudices a man so.
H. Pearson, The Smith of Smiths, Ch. 3

12 I am convinced digestion is the great secret of life. *Letter to Arthur Kinglake, 30 Sept. 1837*

13 I have no relish for the country; it is a kind of healthy grave.
Letter to Miss G. Harcourt, 1838

SMOLLETT, Tobias George, 1721–1771

14 Hark ye, Clinker, you are a most notorious offender. You stand convicted of sickness, hunger, wretchedness, and want.
Humphrey Clinker

15 Some folk are wise, and some are otherwise.
Roderick Random, Ch. 6

16 I consider the world as made for me, not me for the world. It is my maxim therefore to enjoy it while I can, and let futurity shift for itself. *Ib, Ch. 45*

17 True patriotism is of no party. *Sir Launcelote Greavers*

18 That great Cham of literature, Samuel Johnson. *Letter to John Wilkes, 16 March 1759, quoted in Boswell's Life of Johnson*

SNAGGE, John, 1904–

19 I can't see who's ahead – it's either Oxford or Cambridge.
BBC Commentary on Boat Race, 1949

SOCRATES, 469–399 B.C.

20 I am a citizen, not of Athens or Greece, but of the world.
Plutarch, De Exilio

21 Other men live to eat, whereas I eat to live. *Plutarch, Moralia*

SOLON, 640?–558? B.C.

22 Call no man happy until he dies; he is at best fortunate.
Herodotus, Histories, 1, 32

SOMERVILLE, William, 1675–1742

23   The chase, the sport of kings;
Image of war, without its guilt. *The Chase, 1, 13*

SOULE, John Babsone Lane, 1815–1891

24 Go west, young man. *Terre Haute Express, Indiana, 1851*

SOUTHEY, Robert, 1774–1843

25 My days among the Dead are past:
 Around me I behold,
 Where'er these casual eyes are cast,
 The mighty minds of old. *My Days among the Dead*

26 Yet leaving here a name, I trust,
 That will not perish in the dust.

27 It was a summer's evening,
 Old Kaspar's work was done. *The Battle of Blenheim*

28 And by him sported on the green
 His little grandchild Wilhelmine. *Ib*

29 But what they fought each other for,
 I could not well make out. *Ib*

30 'And everybody praised the Duke
 Who this great fight did win.'
 'But what good came of it at last?'
 Quoth little Peterkin.
 'Why that I cannot tell,' said he,
 'But 'twas a famous victory.' *Ib*

SPENCER, Herbert, 1820–1903

31 Time: that which man is always trying to kill, but which
 ends in killing him. *Definitions*

32 Science is organized knowledge. *Education, Ch. 2*

33 The Republican form of Government is the highest form of
 government; but because of this it requires the highest type of
 human nature – a type nowhere at present existing. *Essays,
 The Americans*

34 Survival of the fittest. *Principles of Biology*

35 We all decry prejudice, yet are all prejudiced. *Social Statics,
 Part 2*

36 Education has for its object the formation of character. *Ib*

37 Hero-worship is strongest where there is least regard for human
 freedom. *Ib, Part 3*

SPENSER, Edmund, 1552?–1599

38 The woods shall to me answer and my Echo ring.
 Epithalamion, 18

39 Ah! when will this long weary day have end,
And lend me leave to come unto my love? *Epithalamion, 278*

40 Fierce wars and faithful loves shall moralize my song. *The
Fairie Queen, Book 1, Introduction, Stanza 1*

41 A gentle knight was pricking on the plain. *Ib, Book 1,
Canto, 1, 1*

42 Sleep after toil, port after stormy seas,
Ease after war, death after life does greatly please. *Ib, Book, 1,
Canto 9, 40*

43 And as she looked about, she did behold,
How over that same door was likewise writ,
Be bold, be bold, and everywhere Be bold. *Ib, Book 3,
Canto 11, 54*

44 Dan Chaucer, well of English undefiled,
On Fame's eternal beadroll worthy to be filed. *Ib, Book 4,
Canto 2, 32*

45 The gentle mind by gentle deeds is known,
For a man by nothing is so well bewrayed
As by his manners. *Ib, Book 6, Canto, 3, 1*

46 Calm was the day, and through the trembling air,
Sweet breathing Zephyrus did softly play. *Prothalamion, 1*

47 Sweet Thames! run softly, till I end my Song. *Ib, 18*

48 So now they have made our English tongue a gallimaufry or
hodgepodge of all other speeches. *The Shepherd's Calendar,
Letter to Gabriel Harvey*

SPOONER, Rev. William Archibald, 1844–1930

49 Kinquering Congs their titles take. *Announcing the hymn in
New College Chapel, Oxford, 1879 (See 95:18)*

50 Sir, you have tasted two whole worms; you have hissed all my
mystery lectures and been caught fighting a liar in the quad;
you will leave by the next town drain. *Attributed*

51 Let us drink to the queer old Dean. *Attributed*

52 I remember your name perfectly, but I just can't think of your
face. *Attributed*

SPRING-RICE, Sir Cecil Arthur, 1858–1918

53 I vow to thee, my country – all earthly things above –
Entire and whole and perfect, the service of my love.
I Vow to Thee, My Country

54 I am the Dean of Christ Church, Sir,
This is my wife – look well at her.
She is the Broad: I am the High:
We are the University. *The Masque of Balliol*

SQUIRE, Sir John Collings, 1884–1958

55 It did not last: the Devil howling 'Ho,
Let Einstein be,' restored the status quo. *In Continuation of*
Pope on Newton (see 248 : 88)

56 But I'm not so think as you drunk I am. *Ballade of Soporific*
Absorption

STANLEY, Sir Henry Morton, 1841–1904

57 Dr Livingstone, I presume? *On meeting Livingstone in Ujiji,*
Central Africa, 10 Nov. 1871

STANTON, Frank Lebby, 1857–1927

58 Sweetest li'l feller, everybody knows;
Dunno what to call him, but he's mighty lak' a rose.
Mighty Lak' a Rose

STEELE, Sir Richard, 1672–1729

59 Among all the diseases of the mind there is not one more
epidemical or more pernicious than the love of flattery.
The Spectator, No. 238

60 There are so few who can grow old with a good grace.
Ib, No. 263

61 Reading is to the mind what exercise is to the body.
The Tatler, No. 147

STEPHEN, James Kenneth, 1859–1892

62 Two voices are there: one is of the deep . . .
And one is of an old half-witted sheep
Which bleats articulate monotony
And indicates that two and one are three. *Lapsus Calami,*
Sonnet (Parody of Wordsworth, see 412 : 1)

63 When the Rudyards cease from kipling
And the Haggards ride no more. *Ib, To R.K.*

STERNE, Laurence, 1713–1768

64 They order, said I, this matter better in France. *A Sentimental*
Journey, Opening words

65 As an Englishman does not travel to see Englishmen, I retired
   to my room.   *A Sentimental Journey, Preface*

66 I pity the man who can travel from Dan to Beersheba, and cry,
   'tis all barren.   *Ib, In the Street, Calais*

67 There are worse occupations in the world than feeling a woman's
   pulse.   *Ib, The Pulse*

68 'God tempers the wind,' said Maria, 'to the shorn lamb.'
   Ib, Maria

69 So that when I stretched out my hand, I caught hold of the fille
   de chambre's—.   *Ib, Last words*

70 'Our armies swore terribly in Flanders,' cried my Uncle Toby,
   'but nothing to this.'   *Tristram Shandy, Book 3, Ch. 11*

71 Love, 'an please your honour, is exactly like war in this; that a
   soldier, though he has escaped three weeks complete o' Saturday
   night, – may nevertheless be shot through his heart on Sunday
   morning.   *Ib, Book, 8 Ch. 21*

72 'L—d!' said my mother, 'what is all this story about?'
   'A Cock and a Bull,' said Yorick.   *Ib, Last words*

STEVENSON, Robert Louis, 1850–1894

73 Sing me a song of a lad that is gone,
   Say, could that lad be I?
   Merry of soul he sailed on a day
   Over the sea to Skye.   *Songs of Travel, 42*

74 Fifteen men on the dead man's chest –
   Yo-ho-ho and a bottle of rum!
   Drink and the devil had done for the rest. SONG
   Treasure Island, Ch. 1

75 Many's the long night I've dreamed of cheese – toasted, mostly.
   BEN GUNN *Ib, Ch. 15*

76 This be the verse you grave for me:
   'Here he lies where he longed to be;
   Home is the sailor, home from sea,
   And the hunter home from the hill.'   *Underwoods, Book 1,
   21, Requiem*

77 Even if we take matrimony at its lowest, even if we regard it as
   no more than a sort of friendship recognised by the police.
   Virginibus Puerisque, Part 1

78 Extreme busyness, whether at school or college, kirk or market,
   is a symptom of deficient vitality.   *Ib, An Apology for Idlers*

79 There is no duty we so much underrate as the duty of being
   happy.   *Ib*

80 To travel hopefully is a better thing than to arrive, and the true
  success is to labour.   *Virginibus Puerisque, El Dorado*

STEVENSON, William, 1530?–1575

81 I cannot eat but little meat
    My stomach is not good;
  But sure I think that I can drink
    With him that wears a hood. SONG   *Gammer Gurton's*
                                           Needle, Act 2

82 I stuff my skin, so full within,
    Of jolly good ale and old. SONG

STONE, Samuel John, 1839–1900

83 The Church's one foundation
    Is Jesus Christ her Lord;
  She is His new creation
    By water and the Word.   *The Church's One Foundation*

STOWE, Harriet Elizabeth Beecher, 1811–1896

84 'Never had any mother? What do you mean? Where were you
  born?' 'Never was born!' persisted Topsy; 'never had no father,
  nor mother, nor nothin'. I was raised by a speculator.'
                                    Uncle Tom's Cabin, Ch. 20

85 'Do you know who made you?' 'Nobody, as I knows on,' said
  the child, [*Topsy*] with a short laugh ... 'I 'spect I grow'd. Don't
  think nobody never made me.'   *Ib*

SUCKLING, Sir John, 1609–1642

86 Out upon it, I have loved
    Three whole days together;
  And am like to love three more,
    If it prove fair weather.   *A Poem with the Answer*

SUETONIUS, 75?–150? A.D.

87 *Festina lente*. Hasten slowly.   *Augustus, 25*

88 *Ave, Imperator, morituri te salutant*. Hail, Emperor, those about
  to die salute you.   *Claudius, 21*

SURTEES, Robert Smith, 1803–1864

89 The only infallible rule we know is, that the man who is always
  talking about being a gentleman never is one.   *Ask Mamma,*
                                                      Ch. 1

90 Hellish dark, and smells of cheese!   *Handley Cross, Ch. 50*

91 Three things I never lends – my 'oss, my wife, and my name.
Hillingdon Hall, Ch. 33

92 Women never look so well as when one comes in wet and dirty from hunting. *Mr Sponge's Sporting Tour, Ch. 21*

93 He was a gentleman who was generally spoken of as having nothing a-year, paid quarterly. *Ib, Ch. 24*

94 There is no secret so close as that between a rider and his horse.
Ib, Ch. 31

SWIFT, Jonathan, 1667–1745

95 The two noblest of things, which are sweetness and light.
The Battle of the Books, Preface

96 'Tis an old maxim in the schools,
That flattery's the food of fools;
Yet now and then your men of wit
Will condescend to take a bit. *Cadenus and Vanessa*

97 Yet malice never was his aim;
He lash'd the vice, but spared the name;
No individual could resent,
Where thousands equally were meant. *On the Death of
Dr Swift, 512*

98 He put this engine [*a watch*] to our ears, which made an incessant noise like that of a water-mill; and we conjecture it is either some unknown animal, or the god that he worships. *Gulliver's Travels,
Voyage to Lilliput, Ch. 2*

99 Big-endians and small-endians. *Ib, Ch. 4*

1 I cannot but conclude the bulk of your natives to be the most pernicious race of little odious vermin that nature ever suffered to crawl upon the surface of the earth. *Ib, Voyage to
Brobdingnag, Ch. 6*

2 Whoever could make two ears of corn or two blades of grass to grow upon a spot of ground where only one grew before would deserve better of mankind and do more essential service to his country than the whole race of politicians put together.
Ib Ch. 7

3 Proper words in proper places make the true definition of a style.
Letter to a young clergyman, 9 Jan. 1720

4 Hail fellow, well met,
All dirty and wet;
Find out, if you can,
Who's master, who's man. *My Lady's Lamentation*

5 So, naturalists observe, a flea
  Hath smaller fleas that on him prey,
  And these have smaller fleas to bite 'em,
  And so proceed *ad infinitum*.   *On Poetry, 337*

6 Promises and pie-crust are made to be broken.
                                    Polite Conversation, 1

7 The sight of you is good for sore eyes.   *Ib*

8 What though his head be empty, provided his common-place
  book be full.   *A Tale of a Tub, Digression in Praise of
                                                    Digression*

9 We have just enough religion to make us hate, but not enough to
  make us love one another.   *Thoughts on Various Subjects*

10 Few are qualified to shine in company; but it is in most men's
   power to be agreeable.   *Ib*

11 A nice man is a man of nasty ideas.   *Ib*

12 *Ubi saeva indignatio ulterius cor lacerare nequit* – Where burning
   indignation no longer lacerates his heart.   *Swift's Epitaph*

13 I shall be like that tree, I shall die at the top.   *Attributed*

14 Good God! What a genius I had when I wrote that book.
                                    [*A Tale of a Tub*] *Attributed*

SWINBURNE, Algernon Charles, 1837–1909

15 When the hounds of spring are on winter's traces,
       The mother of months in meadow or plain
   Fills the shadows and windy places
       With lisp of leaves and ripple of rain.   *Atalanta in
                                                         Calydon*

16 Before the beginning of years
       There came to the making of man
   Time, with a gift of tears,
       Grief, with a glass that ran.   *Ib*

17 Shall I strew on thee rose or rue or laurel,
       Brother, on this that was the veil of thee? *Ave Atque Vale*

18 Could you hurt me, sweet lips, though I hurt you?
       Men touch them, and change in a trice
   The lilies and languors of virtue
       For the raptures and roses of vice.   *Dolores*

19 I am tired of tears and laughter,
       And men that laugh and weep;
   Of what may come hereafter
       For men that sow to reap.   *The Garden of Proserpine*

20 From too much love of living,
    From hope and fear set free,
We thank with brief thanksgiving
    Whatever gods may be
That no life lives for ever;
That dead men rise up never;
That even the weariest river
    Winds somewhere safe to sea.   *The Garden of Proserpine*

21 Glory to Man in the Highest! for Man is the master of things.
                                        Hymn of Man

22 I have lived long enough, having seen one thing, that love hath
   an end;
Goddess and maiden and queen, be near me now and befriend.
                                Hymn to Proserpine

23 Laurel is green for a season, and love is sweet for a day;
But love grows bitter with treason, and laurel outlives not May.
                                              Ib

24 Rise ere the dawn be risen;
    Come, and be all souls fed;
From field and street and prison
    Come, for the feast is spread;
Live, for the truth is living; wake, for night is dead.
                               A Marching Song

25 I will go back to the great sweet mother,
    Mother and lover of men, the sea.
I will go down to her, I and no other,
    Close with her, kiss her and mix her with me.   *The Triumph*
                                                    of Time

SYNGE, John Millington, 1871–1909

26 When I was writing 'The Shadow of the Glen' I got more aid
than any learning could have given me from a chink in the
floor of the old Wicklow house where I was staying, that let me
hear what was being said by the servant girls in the kitchen.
                   The Playboy of the Western World, Preface

TACITUS, 55?–117? A.D.

27 *Ubi solitudinem faciunt pacem appellant.* – They create desolation
and call it peace.   *Agricola, 30*

28 *Proprium humani ingenii est odisse quem laeseris.* – It is human
nature to hate the man whom you have hurt.   *Ib*

TALLEYRAND, Charles Maurice de, 1754-1838

29 *C'est le commencement de la fin.* – It is the beginning of the end.
Remark to Napoleon, 1813

30 *Noir comme le diable,*
Chaud comme l'enfer,
Pur comme un ange,
Doux comme l'amour.

Black as the devil,
Hot as hell,
Pure as an angel,
Sweet as love. *Recipe for coffee*

31 *Ils n'ont rien appris, ni rien oublié.* – They have learnt nothing,
and forgotten nothing. *Attributed*

32 *La parole a été donnée à l'homme pour déguiser sa pensée.* –
Speech was given to man to disguise his thoughts. *Attributed*

33 *Pas trop de zèle.* – Not too much zeal. *Attributed*

34 War is much too serious a thing to be left to military men.
Attributed

TATE, Nahum, 1652-1715

35 While shepherds watched their flocks by night,
All seated on the ground,
The Angel of the Lord came down,
And glory shone around.

'Fear not,' said he, for mighty dread
Had seized their troubled mind;
'Glad tidings of great joy I bring
To you and all mankind'. *While Shepherds Watched*

TAYLOR, Jane, 1783-1827

36 Twinkle, twinkle, little star,
How I wonder what you are!
Up above the world so high,
Like a diamond in the sky. *The Star*

TENNYSON, Alfred, 1st Baron, 1809-1892

37 O for the touch of a vanish'd hand,
And the sound of a voice that is still! *Break, Break, Break*

38 A happy bridesmaid makes a happy bride. *The Bridesmaid, 4*

39 For men may come and men may go
But I go on for ever. *The Brook, 33*

40 Half a league, half a league,
     Half a league onward,
   All in the valley of Death
     Rode the six hundred.   *The Charge of the Light Brigade, 1*

41 'Forward the Light Brigade!'
     Was there a man dismay'd?   *Ib, 2*

42 Their's not to make reply,
     Their's not to reason why,
     Their's but to do and die.   *Ib, 2*

43 Into the jaws of Death
     Into the mouth of Hell.   *Ib, 3*

44 Sunset and evening star,
     And one clear call for me!
   And may there be no moaning of the bar
     When I put out to sea.   *Crossing the Bar*

45 The spacious times of great Elizabeth
     With sounds that echo still.   *A Dream of Fair Women, 7*

46 A daughter of the gods, divinely tall,
     And most divinely fair.   *Ib, 87*

47 He clasps the crag with crooked hands;
   Close to the sun in lonely lands,
   Ring'd with the azure world, he stands.

   The wrinkled sea beneath him crawls;
   He watches from his mountain walls,
   And like a thunderbolt he falls.   *The Eagle*

48 God made the woman for the man,
     And for the good and increase of the world. *Edwin Morris, 43*

49 Then she rode forth, clothed on with chastity.   *Godiva, 53*

50 His honour rooted in dishonour stood,
     And faith unfaithful kept him falsely true.   *Idylls of the King,*
                                          Lancelot and Elaine, 871

51 He makes no friend who never made a foe.   *Ib, 1082*

52 For men at most differ as Heaven and Earth,
     But women, worst and best, as Heaven and Hell.   *Ib, Merlin*
                                               and Vivien, 812

53 The days darken round me, and the years,
     Among new men, strange faces, other minds.   *Ib, The Passing*
                                               of Arthur, 405

54   And slowly answer'd Arthur from the barge:
   'The old order changeth, yielding place to new,
   And God fulfils himself in many ways.'   *Ib, 407*

55 Pray for my soul. More things are wrought by prayer
  Than this world dreams of.   *Idylls of the King,*
                           The Passing of Arthur, 415

56 Our little systems have their day;
  They have their day and cease to be.   *In Memoriam*
                             A.H.H., Prologue

57   Men may rise on stepping-stones
  Of their dead selves to higher things.   *Ib, 1*

58   For words, like Nature, half reveal
  And half conceal the Soul within.   *Ib, 5*

59 I hold it true, whate'er befall;
    I feel it, when I sorrow most;
    'Tis better to have loved and lost
  Than never to have loved at all.   *Ib, 27*

60 Be near me when my light is low,
    When the blood creeps, and the nerves prick
    And tingle; and the heart is sick,
  And all the wheels of Being slow.   *Ib, 50*

61 Oh yet we trust that somehow good
  Will be the final goal of ill.   *Ib, 54*

62 Are God and Nature then at strife
    That Nature lends such evil dreams?
    So careful of the type she seems,
  So careless of the single life.   *Ib, 55*

63 Nature, red in tooth and claw.   *Ib, 56*

64   Fresh from brawling courts
  And dusty purlieus of the law.   *Ib, 89*

65   There lives more faith in honest doubt,
  Believe me, than in half the creeds.   *Ib, 96*

66 He seems so near and yet so far.   *Ib, 97*

67 Ring out, wild bells, to the wild sky.   *Ib, 106*

68 Ring out the old, ring in the new,
    Ring, happy bells, across the snow:
    The year is going, let him go;
  Ring out the false, ring in the true.   *Ib, 106*

69 Ring out a slowly dying cause,
    And ancient forms of party strife;
    Ring in the nobler modes of life,
  With sweeter manners, purer laws.   *Ib, 106*

70   Ring out the thousand wars of old,
  Ring in the thousand years of peace.   *Ib, 106*

71 Ring in the valiant man and free,
  The larger heart, the kindlier hand;
    Ring out the darkness of the land,
  Ring in the Christ that is to be.   *In Memoriam A.H.H., 106*

72 And thus he bore without abuse
  The grand old name of gentleman,
  Defamed by every charlatan,
  And soil'd with all ignoble use.   *Ib, 111*

73   One God, one law, one element,
    And one far-off divine event,
  To which the whole creation moves.   *Ib, 131*

74 Kind hearts are more than coronets,
  And simple faith than Norman blood.   *Lady Clara Vere*
                                                     de Vere

75 On either side the river lie
  Long fields of barley and of rye,
  That clothe the wold and meet the sky;
  And thro' the field the road runs by
    To many-tower'd Camelot.   *The Lady of Shalott, 1*

76 Willows whiten, aspens quiver,
  Little breezes dusk and shiver.   *Ib*

77 'The curse is come upon me,' cried
  The Lady of Shalott.   *Ib, 3*

78 Comrades, leave me here a little, while as yet 'tis early morn:
  Leave me here, and when you want me, sound upon the bugle-
  horn.   *Locksley Hall, 1*

79 In the Spring a young man's fancy lightly turns to thoughts of
  love.   *Ib, 20*

80 For I dipt into the future, far as human eye could see,
  Saw the Vision of the world, and all the wonder that would be.
                                                     Ib, 116

81 Till the war-drum throbb'd no longer, and the battle-flags were
  furl'd
  In the Parliament of man, the Federation of the world. *Ib, 127*

82 Knowledge comes, but wisdom lingers.   *Ib, 141*

83 Woman is the lesser man, and all thy passions, match'd with
  mine
  Are as moonlight unto sunlight, and as water unto wine.
                                                     Ib, 151

84   They came upon a land
  In which it seemed always afternoon.   *The Lotos-Eaters*

85 Music that gentlier on the spirit lies,
    Than tir'd eyelids upon tir'd eyes.   *The Lotos Eaters*

86 Come into the garden, Maud,
    For the black bat, night, has flown,
Come into the garden, Maud,
    I am here at the gate alone.   *Maud, Part 1, 22*

87 There has fallen a splendid tear
    From the passion-flower at the gate.
She is coming, my dove, my dear;
    She is coming, my life, my fate.   *Ib, 22*

88 O that 'twere possible
After long grief and pain
To find the arms of my true love
Round me once again!   *Ib, Part 2, 4*

89 You must wake and call me early, call me early, mother dear.
    The May Queen

90 For I'm to be Queen of the May.   *Ib*

91 Follow the Gleam.   *Merlin and the Gleam*

92 The last great Englishman is low.   *Ode on the Death of the
Duke of Wellington, 3*

93 O fall'n at length that tower of strength
    Which stood four-square to all the winds that blew!   *Ib*

94 Not once or twice in our rough island-story,
    The path of duty was the way to glory.   *Ib, 8*

95 With prudes for proctors, dowagers for deans,
    And sweet girl-graduates in their golden hair.   *The Princess,
Prologue, 141*

96 Sweet and low, sweet and low,
    Wind of the Western Sea.   *Ib, 3, Song*

97 The splendour falls on castle walls
    And snowy summits old in story.   *Ib, 4, Song*

98 Blow, bugle, blow, set the wild echoes flying,
    Blow, bugle; answer, echoes, dying, dying, dying.   *Ib*

99 Tears, idle tears, I know not what they mean,
    Tears from the depth of some divine despair.   *Ib, 2nd Song*

1 Man is the hunter; woman is his game:
    The sleek and shining creatures of the chase,
    We hunt them for the beauty of their skins.   *Ib, 5, 147*

2 Man for the field and woman for the hearth:
  Man for the sword and for the needle she:
  Man with the head and woman with the heart:
  Man to command and woman to obey:
  All else confusion.   *The Princess, 2nd Song, 5, 427*

3 My strength is as the strength of ten,
      Because my heart is pure.   *Sir Galahad*

TERENCE, 190?–159? B.C.

4 *Hinc illae lacrimae.* – Hence these tears.   *Andria, 126*

5 *Amantium irae amoris integratio est.* – Lovers' quarrels are the
  renewal of love.   *Ib, 555*

6 *Fortis fortuna adiuvat.* – Fortune favours the brave.   *Phormio,
                                                  203*

7 *Quot homines tot sententiae.* – So many men, so many opinions.
                                              Ib, 454

THACKERAY, William Makepeace, 1811–1863

8 It is impossible, in our condition of society, not to be sometimes
  a Snob.   *The Book of Snobs, Ch. 3*

9 'Tis not the dying for a faith that's so hard, Master Harry –
  every man of every nation has done that – 'tis the living up to it
  that is difficult. RICHARD STEELE *Henry Esmond, Bk. 1, Ch. 6*

10 'Tis strange what a man may do, and a woman yet think him an
   angel.   *Ib, Ch. 7*

11 The *Pall Mall Gazette* is written by gentlemen for gentlemen.
                                          Pendennis, Ch. 32

12 A woman with fair opportunities and without a positive hump,
   may marry whom she likes.   *Vanity Fair, Ch. 4*

13 Whenever he met a great man he grovelled before him and my-
   lorded him as only a free-born Englishman can do.   *Ib, Ch. 13*

14 Them's my sentiments. FRED BULLOCK   *Ib, Ch. 21*

15 I think I could be a good woman if I had five thousand a year.
                               BECKY SHARP   *Ib, Ch. 36*

THOMAS, Brandon, 1857–1914

16 I'm Charley's aunt from Brazil, where the nuts come from.
           LORD FANCOURT BABERLEY   *Charley's Aunt, Act 1*

THOMAS, Dylan, 1914–1953

17 And death shall have no dominion.
Dead men naked they shall be one
With the man in the wind and the west moon.
And Death shall have no Dominion

18 Do not go gentle into that good night,
Old age should burn and rave at close of day;
Rage, rage, against the dying of the light.
Do not go gentle into that good night

19 The force that through the green fuse drives the flower
Drives my green age. *The Force that through the green
Fuse drives the Flower*

20 The hand that signed the treaty bred a fever,
And famine grew, and locusts came;
Great is the hand that holds dominion over
Man by a scribbled name. *The Hand that Signed the Paper*

21 Light breaks where no sun shines;
Where no sea runs, the waters of the heart
Push in their tides. *Light Breaks where no Sun Shines*

22 After the first death, there is no other. *A Refusal to Mourn
the Death, by Fire, of a Child in London*

23 It is spring, moonless night in the small town, starless and
bible-black. FIRST VOICE *Under Milk Wood*

24 It is night neddying among the snuggeries of babies.
FIRST VOICE *Ib*

25 You're thinking, you're no better than you should be, Polly, and
that's good enough for me. Oh, isn't life a terrible thing,
thank God? POLLY GARTER *Ib*

26 Praise the Lord! We are a musical nation. REV. ELI JENKINS *Ib*

27 Organ Morgan, you haven't been listening to a word I said. It's
organ organ all the time with you. MRS ORGAN MORGAN *Ib*

THOMPSON, Francis, 1859–1907

28 For the field is full of shades as I near the shadowy coast,
And a ghostly batsman plays to the bowling of a ghost;
And I look through my tears on a soundless-clapping host
As the run-stealers flicker to and fro,
To and fro: –
O my Hornby and my Barlow long ago! *At Lord's*

29 Nothing begins, and nothing ends,
That is not paid with moan;
For we are born in other's pain,
And perish in our own. *Daisy*

30 I fled Him, down the nights and down the days;
I fled Him, down the arches of the years. *The Hound of*
Heaven

31 'Tis ye, 'tis your estrangèd faces,
That miss the many-splendour'd thing. *The Kingdom of God*

32 Look for me in the nurseries of Heaven. *To my Godchild*

THOMSON, James, 1700–1748

33 When Britain first, at Heaven's command,
Arose from out the azure main,
This was the charter of the land,
And guardian angels sung this strain:
'Rule, Britannia, rule the waves;
Britons never will be slaves.' *Alfred: A Masque, Act 2,*
Scene 5

34 An elegant sufficiency, content,
Retirement, rural quiet, friendship, books,
Ease and alternate labour, useful life,
Progressive virtue, and approving Heaven! *The Seasons,*
Spring, 1161

THOMSON, Roy Herbert, 1st Lord, 1894–

35 It is as good as having a Government licence to print money.
Remark on the profitability of commercial television
in Great Britain, made during an interview in Canada

THOREAU, Henry David, 1817–1862

36 The mass of men lead lives of quiet desperation.
Walden, Economy

37 Our life is frittered away by detail . . . Simplify, simplify.
Walden, Where I Lived and What I Lived For

38 The government of the world I live in was not framed, like that
of Britain, in after-dinner conversations over the wine.
Ib, Conclusion

39 It takes two to speak the truth – one to speak, and another to
hear. *A Week on the Concord and Merrimack Rivers,*
Wednesday

40 Not that the story need be long, but it will take a long while to
make it short. *Letter*

THUCYDIDES, c. 471–c. 400 B.C.

41 It is great glory in a woman to show no more weakness than is
natural to her sex, and not to be talked of, either for good or
evil by men.   *History, 2, 45, 2*

THURBER, James, 1894–1961

42 Early to rise and early to bed makes a male healthy and wealthy
and dead.   *Fables for Our Time, The Shrike and the*
Chipmunks

43 All right, have it your way – you heard a seal bark.   *Title of*
Cartoon

44 Well, if I called the wrong number, why did you answer the
phone?   *Title of cartoon*

45 The War between Men and Women. *Title of series of cartoons*

TILZER, Harry, 1878–1956

46 Come, Come, Come and have a drink with me
Down at the old 'Bull and Bush'.   *Song*

47 Come, Come, Come and make eyes at me.   *Ib*

TOBIN, John, 1770–1804

48 The man that lays his hand upon a woman,
Save in the way of kindness is a wretch
Whom 'twere gross flattery to name a coward.
The Honeymoon, Act 2, Scene 1

TOLSTOY, Leo, 1828–1910

49 All happy families resemble one another, each unhappy family
is unhappy in its own way.   *Anna Karenina, 1, Ch. 1*

50 Pure and complete sorrow is as impossible as pure and complete
joy.   *War and Peace, 15, Ch. 1*

TOPLADY, Augustus Montague, 1740–1778

51 Rock of Ages, cleft for me,
Let me hide myself in Thee.   *Rock of Ages*

TRAHERNE, Thomas, 1637?–1674

52 You will never enjoy the world aright, till the sea itself floweth
in your veins, till you are clothed with the heavens, and crowned
with the stars.   *Centuries of Meditation, 1, 29*

53 The corn was orient and immortal wheat, which never should
be reaped, nor was ever sown. I thought it had stood from
everlasting to everlasting.   *Ib, 3, 3*

TRAPP, Joseph, 1679–1747

54 The King, observing with judicious eyes,
 The state of both his universities,
 To Oxford sent a troop of horse, and why?
 That learned body wanted loyalty;
 To Cambridge books, as very well discerning,
 How much that loyal body wanted learning.   *On George I's*
donation of a library to Cambridge University
(For reply, see 72–3:8)

TROLLOPE, Anthony, 1815–1882

55 It's dogged as does it. It ain't thinking about it.   *Last Chronicle*
of Barset, Ch. 61

56 Three hours a day will produce as much as a man ought to write.
Autobiography, Ch. 15

TUER, Andrew White, 1838–1900

57 English as she is Spoke.   *Title of Portuguese-English*
Conversation Guide

TUSSER, Thomas, 1524?–1580

58 At Christmas play and make good cheer,
 For Christmas comes but once a year.   *Five Hundred Points of*
Good Husbandry, Ch. 12

TWAIN, Mark (Samuel Langhorne Clemens), 1835–1910

59 There was things which he stretched, but mainly he told the
 truth.   *The Adventures of Huckleberry Finn, Ch. 1*

60 *Pilgrim's Progress*, about a man that left his family, it didn't say
 why. I read considerable in it now and then. The statements was
 interesting but tough.   *Ib, Ch. 17*

61 Deep down in me I knowed it was a lie, and He knowed it. You
 can't pray a lie – I found that out.   *Ib, Ch. 21*

62 All Kings is mostly rapscallions.   *Ib, Ch. 23*

63 There are three kinds of lies: lies, damned lies, and statistics.
Autobiography

64 Soap and education are not as sudden as a massacre, but they
 are more deadly in the long run.   *The Facts concerning the*
Recent Resignation

65 I must have a prodigious quantity of mind; it takes me as much
 as a week, sometimes, to make it up.   *The Innocents Abroad,*
Ch. 7

66 They spell it Vinci and pronounce it Vinchy; foreigners always spell better than they pronounce. *The Innocents Abroad, Ch. 19*

67 Familiarity breeds contempt – and children. *Notebooks*

68 Adam was but human – this explains it all. He did not want the apple for the apple's sake, he wanted it only because it was forbidden. *Pudd'nhead Wilson's Calendar, Ch. 2*

69 Training is everything. The peach was once a bitter almond; cauliflower is nothing but cabbage with a college education. *Ib, Ch. 5*

70 One of the most striking differences between a cat and a lie is that a cat has nine lives. *Ib, Ch. 7*

71 When angry, count four; when very angry, swear. *Ib, Ch. 10*

72 Nothing so needs reforming as other people's habits. *Ib, Ch. 15*

73 A classic is something that everybody wants to have read and nobody wants to read. *Speech, The Disappearance of Literature*

74 There ain't-a-going to *be* no core. *Tom Sawyer Abroad, Ch. 1*

75 Reports of my death are greatly exaggerated. *Cable to the Associated Press*

UNITED NATIONS

76 WE THE PEOPLES OF THE UNITED NATIONS DETERMINED

to save succeeding generations from the scourge of war, which twice in our lifetime has brought untold sorrow to mankind, and

to reaffirm faith in fundamental human rights, in the dignity and worth of the human person, in the equal rights of men and women and of nations large and small, and

to establish conditions under which justice and respect for the obligations arising from treaties and other sources of international law can be maintained, and

to promote social progress and better standards of life in larger freedom,

AND FOR THESE ENDS

to practise tolerance and live together in peace with one another as good neighbours and

to unite our strength to maintain international peace and security, and to ensure, by the acceptance of principles and the institution of methods, that armed force shall not be used, save in the common interest, and

to employ international machinery for the promotion of
the economic and social advancement of all peoples,
HAVE RESOLVED TO COMBINE OUR EFFORTS TO ACCOMPLISH THESE
AIMS.
Preamble to United Nations Charter, 1945

UNWIN, Sir Stanley, 1884–1968

77 Much is written of the power of the Press, a power which may
last but a day; by comparison, little is heard of the power of
books, which may endure for generations.   *The Truth about*
Publishing

UPTON, Ralph R., 20th century

78 Stop; look; listen.   *Notice at American railway crossings,*
1912

USTINOV, Peter, 1921–

79 THE PHOTOGRAPHER: The prisoners have been brought in, Your
Excellency.
THE MARSHALL: Question them, promise them life, and then kill
them. Let us have the honour of honourable
men. Give them hope before you blacken their
world. Lift them high in the air before you drop
them.   *The Moment of Truth, Act 3*

80 You will find us only on the very best atlases, because we are
the smallest country left in Europe . . . a self-respecting country
which deserves and sometimes achieves a colour of its own on
the map – usually a dyspeptic mint green, which misses the outline
of the frontier by a fraction of an inch, so that one can almost
hear the printer saying damn. THE GENERAL
Romanoff and Juliet, Act 1

81 As for being a General, well, at the age of four with paper hats
and wooden swords we're all Generals. Only some of us never
grow out of it. THE GENERAL   *Ib*

82 A diplomat these days is nothing but a head-waiter who's
allowed to sit down occasionally. THE GENERAL   *Ib*

VANBRUGH, Sir John, 1664–1726

83 The want of a thing is perplexing enough, but the possession of
it is intolerable. CLARISSA   *The Confederacy, Act 1, Scene 3*

84 Much of a muchness. JOHN MOODY   *The Provok'd Husband,*
Act 1

VAUGHAN, Henry, 1622–1695

85 They are all gone into the world of light,
And I alone sit lingering here. *Ascension Hymn*

86 Man is the shuttle, to whose winding quest
And passage through these looms
God order'd motion, but ordain'd no rest. *Man*

87 My soul, there is a country
Far beyond the stars. *Peace*

VEGETIUS, 4th century

88 *Qui desiderat pacem, praeparet bellum.* – Let him who desires
peace, prepare for war. *De re mil., 3, Prologue*

VERLAINE, Paul, 1844–1896

89 *Et tout le reste est littérature.* – All the rest is just literature.
L'Art Poétique

90 *Il pleure dans mon cœur
Comme il pleut sur la ville.* – Tears fall in my heart like rain
on the town. *Romances sans paroles, 3*

VICTORIA, Queen, 1819–1901

91 We are not amused. *Notebooks of a Spinster Lady, 2 Jan.
1900*

92 He [*Gladstone*] speaks to Me as If I was a public meeting.
Russell, Collections and Recollections, Ch. 14

VIGNY, Alfred de, 1797–1863

93 *Hélas je suis, Seigneur, puissant et solitaire.* – Alas, Lord, I am
powerful but alone. *Moïse*

94 *Seul le silence est grand; tout le reste est faiblesse.* – Only silence
is great; all else is weakness. *La Mort du Loup*

VILLON, François, 1431–1485

95 *Mais où sont les neiges d'antan?* – But where are the snows of
yesteryear? *Ballade des Dames du Temps Jadis*

VIRGIL, 70–19 B.C.

96 *Arma virumque cano.* Arms and the man I sing. *Aeneid, 1, 1*

97 *Furor arma ministrat.* Anger supplies the arms. *Ib, 1, 150*

98 *Forsan et haec olim meminisse iuvabit.* Perhaps even these things
will some day be pleasant to remember. *Ib, 1, 203*

99 *Timeo Danaos et dona ferentes.* I fear the Greeks, even when they bring gifts. *Aeneid, 2, 49*

1 *Varium et mutabile semper Femina.*
Woman is always fickle and changing. *Ib, 4, 569*

2 *Facilis descensus Averni.* The way down to Hell is easy. *Ib, 6, 126*

3 *Omnia vincit amor, et nos cedamus amori.* Love conquers all, and we too succumb to love. *Ib, 10, 69*

4 *Labor omnia vicit Improbus et duris urgens in rebus egestas.*
Persistent labour overcame all things, and the stress of need in a hard life. *Georgics, 1, 145*

5 *Felix qui potuit rerum cognoscere causas.* Happy is he who has been able to learn the causes of things. *Ib, 2, 490*

6 *Sed fugit interea, fugit inreparabile tempus.* Meanwhile, time is flying – flying, never to return. *Ib, 3, 284*

VOLTAIRE, François Marie Arouet, 1694–1778

7 *Tout est pour le mieux dans le meilleur des mondes possibles.* All is for the best in the best of possible worlds. *Candide, Ch. 1*

8 *Dans ce pays-ci il est bon de tuer de temps en temps un amiral pour encourager les autres.* In this country [*England*] it is good to kill an admiral from time to time, to encourage the others. *Ib, Ch. 23*

9 *Cela est bien dit, répondit Candide, mais il faut cultiver notre jardin.* 'That is well said,' replied Candide, 'but we must cultivate our garden.' *Ib, Ch. 30*

10 *Ils ne se servent de la pensée que pour autoriser leurs injustices, et n'emploient les paroles que pour déguiser leurs pensées.* Men use thought only to justify their wrong-doing, and words only to conceal their thoughts. *Dialogue 14, Le Chapon et la Poularde*

11 *Le mieux est l'ennemi du bien.* The best is the enemy of the good. *Dictionnaire Philosophique, Art Dramatique*

12 *Si Dieu n'existait pas, il faudrait l'inventer.* If God did not exist, it would be necessary to invent Him. *Épîtres, 96, A L'Auteur du livre des Trois Imposteurs*

13 *L'histoire des grandes événements de ce monde n'est guère que l'histoire des crimes.* The history of the great events of this world is scarcely more than the history of crimes. *Essai sur les Mœurs et L'Esprit des Nations, 23*

14 *Ce corps qui s'appelait et qui s'appelle encore le saint empire romain n'était en aucune manière ni saint, ni romain, ni empire.* This agglomeration which was called and which still calls itself the Holy Roman Empire was neither holy, nor Roman, nor an empire. *Essai sur les Mœurs et L'Esprit des Nations, 70*

15 *On dit que Dieu est toujours pour les gros bataillons.* It is said that God is always for the big battalions.
Letter to M. le Riche, 1770

16 I disapprove of what you say, but I will defend to the death your right to say it. *Attributed*

WALLER, Edmund, 1606–1687

17 Go, lovely Rose!
Tell her that wastes her time and me,
That now she knows
When I resemble her to thee,
How sweet and fair she seems to be. *Go, Lovely Rose*

18 Poets that lasting marble seek
Must carve in Latin or in Greek. *Of English Verse*

WALPOLE, Sir Robert, 1st Earl of Orford, 1676–1745

19 The balance of power. *Speech, House of Commons, 1741*

20 All those men have their price. *W. Coxe, Memoirs of Walpole*

21 Anything but history, for history must be false. *Walpoliana*

WALPOLE, Horace, 4th Earl of Orford, 1717–1797

22 It is charming to totter into vogue. *Letter to G. A. Selwyn, 1765*

23 The world is a comedy to those who think, a tragedy to those who feel. *Letter to Sir Horace Mann 1769*

24 Prognostics do not always prove prophecies, – at least the wisest prophets make sure of the event first.
Letter to Thomas Walpole, 1785

WALTON, Izaak, 1593–1683

25 We may say of angling as Dr Boteler said of strawberries, 'Doubtless God could have made a better berry, but doubtless God never did.' *The Compleat Angler, Ch. 5*

WARD, Artemus (Charles Farrar Browne), 1834–1867

26 My pollertics, like my religion, being of an exceedin' accommodatin' character. *Artemus Ward His Book, The Crisis*

27 Did you ever have the measels, and if so how many?
Artemus Ward His Book, The Census

28 I prefer temperance hotels – although they sell worse kinds of liquor than any other kind of hotels. *Artemus Ward's Lecture*

29 Why is this thus? What is the reason of this thusness? *Ib*

30 I am happiest when I am idle. I could live for months without performing any kind of labour, and at the expiration of that time I should feel fresh and vigorous enough to go right on in the same way for numerous more months. *Pyrotechny*

31 Let us all be happy and live within our means, even if we have to borrer the money to do it with. *Science and Natural History*

WASHINGTON, George, 1732–1799

32 It is our true policy to steer clear of permanent alliances with any portion of the foreign world.
Farewell Address, 17 Sept. 1796

33 Associate yourself with men of good quality if you esteem your own reputation; for 'tis better to be alone than in bad company.
Rules of Civility

34 Father, I cannot tell a lie. I did it with my little hatchet.
Attributed

WATTS, Isaac, 1674–1748

35 How doth the little busy bee
Improve each shining hour,
And gather honey all the day
From every opening flower. *Against Idleness*

36 For Satan finds some mischief still
For idle hands to do. *Ib*

37 Birds in their little nests agree;
And 'tis a shameful sight,
When children of one family
Fall out, and chide, and fight.
Love between Brothers and Sisters

38 O God, our help in ages past,
Our hope for years to come,
Our shelter from the stormy blast,
And our eternal home. *O God, our help in ages past*

39 A thousand ages in thy sight
Are like an evening gone,
Short as the watch that ends the night
Before the rising sun. *Ib*

40 Time, like an ever-rolling stream,
    Bears all its sons away;
  They fly forgotten, as a dream
    Dies at the opening day.   *O God, our help in ages past*

41 'Tis the voice of the sluggard, I heard him complain:
  'You have waked me too soon, I must slumber again.'
                                                  The Sluggard

WEBB, Sidney, 1st Baron Passfield, 1859-1947

42 The inevitability of gradualness.   *Presidential Address to*
                                       Labour Party Conference, 1923

WEBSTER, Daniel, 1782-1852

43 Let our object be our country, our whole country and nothing
  but our country.   *Speech, Bunker Hill, 17 June 1825*

44 Liberty and Union, now and for ever, one and inseparable.
                                             Speech, 26 Jan. 1830

45 I was born an American; I will live an American; I shall die an
  American.   *Speech, 17 July 1850*

46 There is always room at the top.   *When advised not to become*
                             a lawyer, as there were already too many

WEBSTER, John, 1580?-1625?

47 I am Duchess of Malfi still.
                           The Duchess of Malfi, Act 4, Scene 2

48 Glories, like glow-worms, afar off shine bright,
    But looked to near, have neither heat nor light.   BOSOLA   *Ib*

49 Other sins only speak; murder shrieks out.   BOSOLA   *Ib*

50 Cover her face: mine eyes dazzle: she died young.
                                             FERDINAND   *Ib*

51 We are merely the stars' tennis balls, struck and bandied
  Which way please them.   BOSOLA   *Ib, Act 5, Scene 4*

52 Is not old wine wholesomest, old pippins toothsomest, old wood
  burn brightest, old linen wash whitest? Old soldiers, sweethearts are surest, and old lovers are soundest.   BIRDLIME
                                 Westward Hoe, Act 2, Scene 2

53 I saw him even now going the way of all flesh, that is to say
  towards the kitchen.   BIRDLIME   *Ib*

54 Call for the robin redbreast, and the wren,
  Since o'er shady groves they hover,
  And with leaves and flowers do cover
  The friendless bodies of unburied men.   CORNELIA
                               The White Devil, Act 5, Scene 4

55 My soul, like to a ship in a black storm,
Is driven, I know not whither.   VITTORIA   *The White Devil,
Act 5, Scene 6*

56   I have caught
An everlasting cold; I have lost my voice
Most irrecoverably.   FLAMINEO   *Ib*

WELLINGTON, Arthur Wellesley, 1st Duke of, 1769–1852

57 Nothing except a battle lost can be half so melancholy as a battle
won.   *Dispatch, 1815*

58 I used to say of him [*Napoleon*] that his presence on the field
made the difference of forty thousand men.   *Stanhope, Notes
of Conversations with the Duke of Wellington, 2 Nov. 1831*

59 Ours [*our army*] is composed of the scum of the earth.
Ib, 4 Nov. 1831

60 Up, Guards, and at 'em.   *Waterloo, 18 June 1815, Attributed*

61 The battle of Waterloo was won on the playing fields of Eton.
Attributed

62 Publish and be damned.   *Attributed*

WELLS, Herbert George, 1866–1946

63 He [*Mr Polly*] broke into a quavering song: Roöötten Beëëastly
Silly Hole!   *The History of Mr Polly, Ch. 1, 2*

64 'Sesquippledan,' he would say. 'Sesquippledan verboojuice.'
Ib, Ch. 1, 5

65 I was thinking jest what a Rum Go everything is.
Kipps, Book 2, Ch. 3, 8

66 In England we have come to rely upon a comfortable time-lag
of fifty years or a century intervening between the perception
that something ought to be done and a serious attempt to do it.
The Work, Wealth and Happiness of Mankind, Ch. 11

67 The Shape of Things to Come.   *Title of Book*

WESKER, Arnold, 1932–

68 God in heaven, Mother, you live in the country but you got no
– no – no majesty. You spend your time among green fields, you
grow flowers and you breathe fresh air and you got no majesty.
You go on and you go on talking and talking so your mind's
cluttered up with nothing and you shut out the world. What
kind of life did you give me?   BEATIE BRYANT
Roots, Act 2, Scene 2

69 Education ent only books and music – it's asking questions, all
the time. There are millions of us, all over the country and no

one, not one of us, is asking questions, we're all taking the easiest way out. Everyone I ever worked with took the easiest way out. We don't fight for anything, we're so mentally lazy we might as well be dead!   BEATIE BRYANT   *Roots, Act 3*

WESLEY, Charles, 1707–1788

70 Gentle Jesus, meek and mild,
   Look upon a little child;
   Pity my simplicity,
   Suffer me to come to thee.   *Gentle Jesus, Meek and Mild*

71 Hark! the herald Angels sing
   Glory to the new-born King;
   Peace on earth and mercy mild,
   God and sinners reconciled.   *Hark! the Herald Angels sing*

72 Love Divine, all loves excelling,
      Joy of heaven, to earth come down,
   Fix in us thy humble dwelling,
      All thy faithful mercies crown.
   Jesu, thou art all compassion,
      Pure unbounded love thou art;
   Visit us with thy salvation,
      Enter every trembling heart.
                         Love Divine, All Loves Excelling

WESLEY, John, 1703–1791

73 I look upon all the world as my parish.   *Journal, 11 June 1739*

WEST, Mae, 1893–

74 Come up and see me sometime.   *Diamond Lil*

WHISTLER, James Abbott McNeill, 1834–1903

75 I am not arguing with you – I am telling you.
                         The Gentle Art of Making Enemies

76 OSCAR WILDE: I wish I had said that.
   WHISTLER: You will, Oscar, you will.
                         L. C. Ingleby, Oscar Wilde

WHITE, E. B., 1899–

77 Commuter – one who spends his life
   In riding to and from his wife;
   A man who shaves and takes a train,
   And then rides back to shave again.   *The Commuter*

WHITMAN, Walt, 1819–1892

78 Women sit or move to and fro, some old, some young,
The young are beautiful – but the old are more beautiful than
the young.   *Beautiful Women*

79 I hear it was charged against me that I sought to destroy
institutions,
But really I am neither for nor against institutions.
I Hear it was Charged Against Me

80 If anything is sacred the human body is sacred.
I Sing the Body Electric, 8

81 O Captain! my Captain! our fearful trip is done,
The ship has weather'd every rack, the prize we sought is won,
The port is near, the bells I hear, the people all exulting.
O Captain! My Captain!

82 I celebrate myself, and sing myself,
And what I assume you shall assume.   *Song of Myself, 1*

83 I loafe and invite my soul.   *Ib, 1*

84 I think I could turn and live with animals, they're so placid
and self-contain'd,
I stand and look at them long and long.   *Ib, 32*

85 Behold, I do not give lectures or a little charity,
When I give I give myself.   *Ib, 40*

86 I have said that the soul is not more than the body,
And I have said that the body is not more than the soul,
And nothing, not God, is greater to one than one's self is.
Ib, 48

87 Do I contradict myself?
Very well then I contradict myself,
(I am large, I contain multitudes).   *Ib, 51*

WHITTIER, John Greenleaf, 1807–1892

88 Oh, rank is good, and gold is fair,
And high and low mate ill;
But love has never known a law
Beyond its own sweet will!   *Amy Wentworth*

89 'Shoot, if you must, this old gray head,
But spare your country's flag,' she said.   *Barbara Frietchie*

90 For all sad words of tongue or pen,
The saddest are these: 'It might have been!'   *Maud Muller*

WILCOX, Ella Wheeler, 1850–1919

91 Laugh, and the world laughs with you;
  Weep, and you weep alone,
 For the sad old earth must borrow its mirth,
  But has trouble enough of its own.   *Solitude*

92 Feast, and your halls are crowded;
  Fast, and the world goes by.   *Ib*

93 So many gods, so many creeds,
 So many paths that wind and wind,
 When just the art of being kind
 Is all this sad world needs.   *The World's Need*

WILDE, Oscar Fingall O'Flahertie Wills, 1856–1900

94 Yet each man kills the thing he loves,
  By each let this be heard,
 Some do it with a bitter look,
  Some with a flattering word.
 The coward does it with a kiss,
  The brave man with a sword!
             The Ballad of Reading Gaol, 1, 7

95 Something was dead in each of us,
  And what was dead was Hope.   *Ib, 3, 31*

96 For he who lives more lives than one
  More deaths than one must die.   *Ib, 3, 37*

97 I know not whether Laws be right
  Or whether Laws be wrong;
 All that we know who live in gaol
  Is that the wall is strong;
 And that each day is like a year,
  A year whose days are long.   *Ib, 5, 1*

98 The man who sees both sides of a question is a man who sees
 absolutely nothing at all.   *The Critic as Artist, Part 2*

99 A little sincerity is a dangerous thing, and a great deal of it is
 absolutely fatal.   *Ib*

1 Ah! don't say you agree with me. When people agree with me I
 always feel that I must be wrong.   *Ib*

2 There is no sin except stupidity.   *Ib*

3 To love oneself is the beginning of a lifelong romance.
             LORD GORING *An Ideal Husband, Act 3*

4 Really, if the lower orders don't set us a good example, what
 on earth is the use of them? ALGERNON
             The Importance of Being Earnest, Act 1

5 The truth is rarely pure and never simple. Modern life would be very tedious if it were either, and modern literature a complete impossibility! ALGERNON *The Importance of Being Earnest, 1*

6 I have invented an invaluable permanent invalid called Bunbury, in order that I may be able to go down into the country whenever I choose. ALGERNON *Ib, 1*

7 The amount of women in London who flirt with their own husbands is perfectly scandalous. It looks so bad. It is simply washing one's clean linen in public. ALGERNON *Ib, 1*

8 In married life three is company and two is none. ALGERNON *Ib, 1*

9 I do not approve of anything that tampers with natural ignorance. Ignorance is like a delicate exotic fruit; touch it, and the bloom is gone. LADY BRACKNELL *Ib, 1*

10 To lose one parent, Mr Worthing, may be regarded as a misfortune; to lose both looks like carelessness. LADY BRACKNELL *Ib, 1*

11 JACK: In a hand-bag.
LADY BRACKNELL: A hand-bag?
JACK: Yes, Lady Bracknell. It was in a hand-bag – a somewhat large, black leather hand-bag, with handles to it – an ordinary hand-bag in fact. *Ib, 1*

12 LADY BRACKNELL: The cloak-room at Victoria Station?
JACK: Yes. The Brighton line.
LADY BRACKNELL: The line is immaterial. *Ib, 1*

13 Memory, my dear Cecily, is the diary we all carry about with us.
MISS PRISM *Ib, Act 2*

14 I never travel without my diary. One should always have something sensational to read in the train. GWENDOLEN FAIRFAX *Ib, 2*

15 No woman should ever be quite accurate about her age. It looks so calculating. LADY BRACKNELL *Ib, Act 3*

16 It is a terrible thing for a man to find out suddenly that all his life he has been speaking nothing but the truth. JACK *Ib, 3*

17 Please do not shoot the pianist. He is doing his best.
Impressions of America, Leadville

18 It is absurd to divide people into good and bad. People are either charming or tedious. LORD DARLINGTON
Lady Windermere's Fan, Act 1

19 I can resist everything except temptation. LORD DARLINGTON *Ib, 1*

20 Scandal is gossip made tedious by morality. CECIL GRAHAM
Lady Windermere's Fan, Act 3

21 CECIL GRAHAM: What is a cynic?
LORD DARLINGTON: A man who knows the price of everything
and the value of nothing. *Ib, 3*

22 All Art is quite useless. *The Picture of Dorian Gray, Preface*

23 There is only one thing in the world worse than being talked
about, and that is not being talked about. *Ib, 1*

24 The only way to get rid of a temptation is to yield to it. *Ib, 2*

25 MRS ALLONBY: They say, Lady Hunstanton, that when good
Americans die they go to Paris.
LADY HUNSTANTON: Indeed? And when bad Americans die
where do they go?
LORD ILLINGWORTH: Oh, they go to America.
A Woman of No Importance, Act 1

26 The youth of America is their oldest tradition. It has been going
on now for three hundred years. LORD ILLINGWORTH *Ib, 1*

27 One knows so well the popular idea of health. The English
country gentleman galloping after a fox – the unspeakable in
full pursuit of the uneatable. LORD ILLINGWORTH *Ib, 1*

28 We in the House of Lords are never in touch with public opinion.
That makes us a civilized body. LORD ILLINGWORTH *Ib, 1*

29 One should never trust a woman who tells one her real age. A
woman who would tell one that, would tell one anything.
LORD ILLINGWORTH *Ib, 1*

30 LORD ILLINGWORTH: People's mothers always bore me to death.
All women become like their mothers. That
is their tragedy.
MRS ALLONBY: No man does. That is his. *Ib, 2*

31 Moderation is a fatal thing, Lady Hunstanton. Nothing succeeds like excess. LORD ILLINGWORTH *Ib, 3*

32 No woman should have a memory. Memory in a woman is the
beginning of dowdiness. LORD ILLINGWORTH *Ib, 3*

33 I have nothing to declare except my genius.
At New York Custom House

34 I suppose that I shall have to die beyond my means. [*When asked
a large fee for an operation*] *Sherard, Life of Wilde*

35 Work is the curse of the drinking classes. *Attributed*

WILLIAM III of England, 1650–1702
36 I will die in the last ditch.
Quoted in Hume's History of England

37 Every bullet has its billet.   *John Wesley, Journal, 6 June 1765*

WILLIAM OF WYKEHAM, 1324–1404
38 Manners maketh man.   *Motto of his foundations, Winchester College and New College, Oxford*

WILLIAMS, Harry, 1874–1924, and JUDGE, Jack, 1878–1938
39 It's a long way to Tipperary, it's a long way to go;
It's a long way to Tipperary, to the sweetest girl I know!
Good-bye, Piccadilly, farewell, Leicester Square,
It's a long, long way to Tipperary, but my heart's right there!
   Tipperary

WILLIAMS, W., 1717–1791
40 Guide me, O thou great Redeemer,
  Pilgrim through this barren land;
I am weak, but thou art mighty,
  Hold me with thy powerful hand:
    Bread of heaven,
Feed me till I want no more.   *Guide me, O thou great Redeemer*

WILLS, William Gorman, 1828–1891
41 I'll sing thee songs of Araby,
  And Tales of fair Cashmere.   *Lalla Rookh*

WILSON, Charles Erwin, 1890–1961
42 I thought what was good for the country was good for General Motors and vice versa.   *Statement to U.S. Congressional Committee, 23 Jan. 1953*

WILSON, Harriette, 1789–1846
43 I shall not say why and how I became, at the age of fifteen, the mistress of the Earl of Craven.   *Memoirs, Opening words*

WILSON, John, see NORTH, Christopher

WILSON, Sandy, 1924–
44 I could be happy with you.   *The Boy Friend, Title of Song*

WILSON, Thomas Woodrow, 1856–1924
45 There is such a thing as a man being too proud to fight.
   Speech, 10 May 1915

46 America cannot be an ostrich with its head in the sand.
Speech, 1 Feb. 1916

47 The world must be made safe for democracy.
Speech, 2 April 1917

WITHER, George, 1588–1667

48 I loved a lass, a fair one,
    As fair as e'er was seen;
She was indeed a rare one,
Another Sheba Queen.   *I Loved a Lass*

49 Shall I, wasting in despair,
    Die because a woman's fair?
Or make pale my cheeks with care,
'Cause another's rosy are?   *The Lover's Resolution*

50 If she love me, this believe,
I will die ere she shall grieve;
If she slight me when I woo;
I can scorn and let her go;
    For if she be not for me,
What care I for whom she be?   *Ib*

WODEHOUSE, Pelham Grenville, 1881–1975

51 He spoke with a certain what-is-it in his voice, and I could see
that, if not actually disgruntled, he was far from being gruntled.
The Code of the Woosters

WOLFE, Charles, 1791–1823

52 Not a drum was heard, not a funeral note,
    As his corse to the rampart we hurried;
Not a soldier discharged his farewell shot
    O'er the grave where our hero we buried.
The Burial of Sir John Moore at Corunna, 1

53 We carved not a line, and we raised not a stone,
    But we left him alone with his glory.   *Ib, 31*

WOLFE, James, 1727–1759

54 I would rather have written that poem, [*Gray's Elegy*], gentlemen, than take Quebec.
The night before he was killed in battle in Quebec

WOLSEY, Thomas, Cardinal, 1475?–1530

55 Had I but served God as diligently as I have served the king, he
would not have given me over in my gray hairs.
To Sir William Kingston

WOOD, Mrs Henry, 1814–1887

56 Dead! and . . . never called me mother.

East Lynne, dramatized version

WOOLCOTT, Alexander, 1887–1943

57 I must get out of these wet clothes and into a dry Martini.

Attributed

(*Also attributed to Robert Benchley and Billy Wilder*)

WOOLF, Virginia, 1882–1941

58 A Room of One's Own.   *Title of Book*

WORDSWORTH, Elizabeth, 1840–1932

59 If all the good people were clever,
   And all clever people were good,
The world would be wiser than ever
   We thought that it possibly could.
But somehow 'tis seldom or never
   The two hit it off as they should;
The good are so harsh to the clever,
   The clever so rude to the good!   *Good and Clever*

WORDSWORTH, William, 1770–1850

60 Give all thou canst; high Heaven rejects the lore
Of nicely-calculated less or more.   *Ecclesiastical Sonnets,*
Part 3, 43, King's College Chapel

61 The light that never was, on sea or land,
The consecration, and the Poet's dream.   *Elegiac Stanzas*
suggested by a Picture of Peele Castle in a storm, 15

62 A deep distress hath humanized my Soul.   *Ib, 39*

63 On Man, on Nature, and on Human Life,
Musing in solitude.   *The Excursion, Preface, 1*

64   Oh, Sir! the good die first,
And they whose hearts are dry as summer dust
Burn to the socket.   *Ib, 1, 500*

65 Think you, 'mid all this mighty sum
Of things for ever speaking,
That nothing of itself will come,
But we must still be seeking?   *Expostulation and Reply, 25*

66 I travelled among unknown men,
   In lands beyond the sea;
Nor, England! did I know till then
   What love I bore to thee.   *I travelled among unknown men*

67 I wandered lonely as a cloud
   That floats on high o'er vales and hills,
   When all at once I saw a crowd,
   A host, of golden daffodils;
   Beside the lake, beneath the trees,
   Fluttering and dancing in the breeze.
I wandered lonely as a Cloud, 1

68 Continuous as the stars that shine
   And twinkle on the milky way.
Ib, 7

69 Ten thousand saw I at a glance,
   Tossing their heads in sprightly dance.
Ib, 11

70 A poet could not but be gay,
   In such a jocund company.
Ib, 15

71 For oft, when on my couch I lie
   In vacant or in pensive mood,
   They flash upon that inward eye
   Which is the bliss of solitude.
Ib, 19

72 There was a time when meadow, grove, and stream,
   The earth, and every common sight,
      To me did seem
    Apparelled in celestial light,
   The glory and the freshness of a dream.
*Ode, Intimations of
Immortality from Recollections of Early Childhood,
Stanza 1*

73 The Rainbow comes and goes,
   And lovely is the Rose.
Ib, Stanza 2

74   The sunshine is a glorious birth;
    But yet I know, where'er I go,
   That there hath past away a glory from the earth.
Ib

75   While the young lambs bound
   As to the tabor's sound
Ib, Stanza 3

76 Whither is fled the visionary gleam?
   Where is it now, the glory and the dream?
Ib, Stanza 4

77 Our birth is but a sleep and a forgetting:
   The Soul that rises with us, our life's Star,
    Hath had elsewhere its setting,
      And cometh from afar:
    Not in entire forgetfulness,
    And not in utter nakedness,
   But trailing clouds of glory do we come
    From God, who is our home:
   Heaven lies about us in our infancy!

Shades of the prison-house begin to close
    Upon the growing Boy. *Ode, Intimations of Immortality*
        from Recollections of Early Childhood, Stanza 5

78 The Youth, who daily farther from the east
    Must travel, still is Nature's Priest,
    And by the vision splendid
    Is on his way attended;
  At length the Man perceives it die away,
  And fade into the light of common day.   *Ib*

79 Behold the Child among his new-born blisses,
  A six years' Darling of a pigmy size!   *Ib, Stanza 7*

80 O joy! that in our embers
  Is something that doth live,
  That nature yet remembers
  What was so fugitive!   *Ib, Stanza 9*

81 And O, ye Fountains, Meadows, Hills, and Groves,
  Forebode not any severing of our loves!   *Ib, Stanza 11*

82 To me the meanest flower that blows can give
  Thoughts that do often lie too deep for tears.   *Ib*

83 I heard a thousand blended notes,
  While in a grove I sate reclined,
  In that sweet mood when pleasant thoughts
  Bring sad thoughts to the mind *Lines written in early Spring, 1*

84 Have I not reason to lament
  What man has made of man?   *Ib, 23*

85 I chanced to see at break of day
  The solitary child.   *Lucy Gray, 3*

86 The sweetest thing that ever grew
  Beside a human door!   *Ib, 7*

87   Meantime Luke began
  To slacken in his duty; and, at length,
  He in the dissolute city gave himself
  To evil courses.   *Michael, 442*

88 There is a comfort in the strength of love;
  'Twill make a thing endurable, which else
  Would overset the brain, or break the heart.   *Ib, 448*

89 Nuns fret not at their convent's narrow room;
  And hermits are contented with their cells.
        Miscellaneous Sonnets, Part 1, 1

90   'Twas pastime to be bound
  Within the Sonnet's scanty plot of ground.   *Ib*

91 Surprised by joy – impatient as the Wind
  I turned to share the transport.   *Ib, 1, 27*

92 It is a beauteous evening, calm and free,
The holy time is quiet as a Nun
Breathless with adoration. *Miscellaneous Sonnets, Part 1, 30*

93 The world is too much with us; late and soon,
Getting and spending, we lay waste our powers:
Little we see in Nature that is ours. *Ib, 1, 33*

94 Great God! I'd rather be
A Pagan suckled in a creed outworn;
So might I, standing on this pleasant lea,
Have glimpses that would make me less forlorn;
Have sight of Proteus rising from the sea;
Or hear old Triton blow his wreathèd horn. *Ib*

95 Scorn not the Sonnet; Critic, you have frowned,
Mindless of its just honours; with this key
Shakespeare unlocked his heart. *Ib, Part 2, 1*

96 Earth has not anything to show more fair:
Dull would he be of soul who could pass by
A sight so touching in its majesty:
This City now doth, like a garment, wear
The beauty of the morning; silent, bare,
Ships, towers, domes, theatres, and temples lie
Open unto the fields, and to the sky;
All bright and glittering in the smokeless air. *Ib, 2, 36*

97 Dear God! the very houses seem asleep;
And all that mighty heart is lying still! *Ib*

98 My heart leaps up when I behold
A rainbow in the sky. *My Heart leaps up*

99 The Child is father of the Man;
And I could wish my days to be
Bound each to each by natural piety. *Ib*

1 Two Voices are there; one is of the sea,
One of the mountains; each a mighty Voice:
In both from age to age thou didst rejoice,
They were thy chosen music, Liberty! *National Independence*
and Liberty, Part 1, 12, Thoughts of a Briton
on the Subjugation of Switzerland

2 Plain living and high thinking are no more:
The homely beauty of the good old cause
Is gone; our peace, our fearful innocence,
And pure religion breathing household laws.
Ib, 1, 13, Written in London, Sept. 1802

3 Milton! thou shouldst be living at this hour:
England hath need of thee: she is a fen
Of stagnant waters.   *National Independence and Liberty,*
                              Part 1, 14, London, 1802

4 Thy soul was like a Star, and dwelt apart;
Thou hadst a voice whose sound was like the sea:
Pure as the naked heavens, majestic, free,
So didst thou travel on life's common way,
In cheerful godliness; and yet thy heart
The lowliest duties on herself did lay,   *Ib*

5 We must be free or die, who speak the tongue
That Shakespeare spake; the faith and morals hold
Which Milton held.   *Ib, Pt. 1, 16*

6 Another year! – another deadly blow!
Another mighty Empire overthrown!
And We are left, or shall be left, alone.   *Ib, 1, 27*

7 Stern Daughter of the Voice of God!
O Duty! if that name thou love
Who art a light to guide, a rod
To check the erring, and reprove.   *Ode to Duty, 1*

8 Give unto me, made lowly wise,
The spirit of self-sacrifice.   *Ib, 54*

9 Bliss was it in that dawn to be alive,
But to be young was very Heaven!   *The Prelude, 11, 108*

10   There is
One great society alone on earth:
The noble Living and the noble Dead.   *Ib, 11, 393*

11 There was a roaring in the wind all night;
The rain came heavily and fell in floods.
                          Resolution and Independence, 1

12 I thought of Chatterton, the marvellous Boy,
The sleepless Soul that perished in his pride.   *Ib, 7*

13 Still glides the Stream, and shall for ever glide;
The Form remains, the Function never dies.
                          The River Duddon, 34, After-Thought

14 Through love, through hope, and faith's transcendent dower,
We feel that we are greater than we know.   *Ib*

15 She dwelt among the untrodden ways
Beside the springs of Dove,
A Maid whom there were none to praise
   And very few to love.
                          She Dwelt among the Untrodden Ways

16 She was a Phantom of delight
   When first she gleamed upon my sight.

She was a Phantom of Delight, 1

17 I saw her upon nearer view,
   A Spirit, yet a Woman too!

Ib, 11

18 A perfect Woman, nobly planned,
   To warn, to comfort, and command;
   And yet a Spirit still, and bright
   With something of angelic light.

Ib, 27

19 No motion has she now, no force;
   She neither hears nor sees;
   Rolled round in earth's diurnal course,
   With rocks, and stones, and trees.

A Slumber did my Spirit seal

20 Behold her, single in the field,
   Yon solitary Highland Lass!   *The Solitary Reaper, 1*

21 Will no one tell me what she sings? –
   Perhaps the plaintive numbers flow
   For old, unhappy, far-off things,
   And battles long ago.

Ib, 17

22 I listened, motionless and still;
   And, as I mounted up the hill,
   The music in my heart I bore,
   Long after it was heard no more.

Ib, 29

23 Strange fits of passion have I known:
   And I will dare to tell.   *Strange Fits of Passion, 1*

24 What fond and wayward thoughts will slide
   Into a Lover's head!
   'O mercy!' to myself I cried,
   'If Lucy should be dead!'

Ib, 25

25 Up! up! my Friend, and quit your books;
   Or surely you'll grow double.   *The Tables Turned, 1*

26 Books! 'tis a dull and endless strife:
   Come, hear the woodland linnet,
   How sweet his music! on my life,
   There's more of wisdom in it.

Ib, 9

27 Come forth into the light of things,
   Let Nature be your Teacher.

Ib, 15

28 One impulse from a vernal wood
   May teach you more of man,
   Of moral evil and of good,
   Than all the sages can.

Ib, 21

29 Come forth, and bring with you a heart
   That watches and receives.   *The Tables Turned, 31*

30 Three years she grew in sun and shower,
   Then Nature said, 'A lovelier flower
   On earth was never sown;
   This Child I to myself will take;
   She shall be mine, and I will make
   A Lady of my own.'   *Three Years she Grew, 1*

31   That best portion of a good man's life,
   His little, nameless, unremembered, acts
   Of kindness and of love.   *Lines composed a few miles above*
                               Tintern Abbey, 33

32   That blessed mood,
   In which the burthen of the mystery,
   In which the heavy and the weary weight
   Of all this unintelligible world,
   Is lightened.   *Ib, 37*

33   We are laid asleep
   In body, and become a living soul:
   While with an eye made quiet by the power
   Of harmony, and the deep power of joy,
   We see into the life of things,   *Ib, 45*

34 How oft, in spirit, have I turned to thee,
   O sylvan Wye!   *Ib, 55*

35   I have learned
   To look on nature, not as in the hour
   Of thoughtless youth; but hearing often-times
   The still, sad music of humanity.   *Ib, 88*

36   Nature never did betray
   The heart that loved her.   *Ib, 122*

37 O Blithe New-comer! I have heard,
   I hear thee and rejoice.
   O Cuckoo! shall I call thee Bird,
   Or but a wandering Voice?   *To the Cuckoo, 1*

38 Thrice welcome, darling of the Spring!   *Ib, 13*

39 O blessèd Bird! the earth we pace
   Again appears to be
   An unsubstantial, faery place;
   That is fit home for Thee!   *Ib, 29*

40 'And where are they? I pray you tell.'
   She answered, 'Seven are we;
   And two of us at Conway dwell,
   And two are gone to sea.'   *We are Seven, 17*

41 'You run about, my little Maid,
Your limbs they are alive;
If two are in the church-yard laid,
Then ye are only five.'   *We are Seven, 33*

42 Poetry is the spontaneous overflow of powerful feelings: it takes
its origin from emotion recollected in tranquillity.
Lyrical Ballads, Preface

WORK, Henry Clay, 1832–1884

43 But it stopped short – never to go again –
When the old man died.   *Grandfather's Clock*

44 Bring the good old bugle, boys, we'll sing another song:
Sing it with a spirit that will start the world along,
Sing it as we used to sing it – fifty thousand strong,
As we were marching through Georgia.
Marching through Georgia

45 'Hurrah! hurrah! we bring the Jubilee!
Hurrah! hurrah! the flag that makes you free!'
So they sang the chorus from Atlanta to the sea
As we were marching through Georgia.   *Ib, Chorus*

WOTTON, Sir Henry, 1568–1639

46 An Ambassador is an honest man sent to lie abroad for his
country.   *Written in Mr Christopher Fleckamore's Album*

47 He first deceased; she for a little tried
To live without him, liked it not, and died.
Upon the Death of Sir Albertus Morton's wife

48 How happy is he born and taught,
That serveth not another's will;
Whose armour is his honest thought,
And simple truth his utmost skill!
The Character of a Happy Life

WREN, Sir Christopher, 1632–1723

49 *Si monumentum requiris, circumspice.* If you seek my monument,
look around you.   *Inscription in St Paul's Cathedral,*
London, written by his son

WYKEHAM, William of, see WILLIAM OF WYKEHAM

XENOPHON, 435?–354? B.C.
50 The sea! the sea!   *Anabasis, 4, 7*

YEATMAN, Robert Julian, see SELLAR, Walter Carruthers

YEATS, William Butler, 1865–1939
51   When I was young,
    I had not given a penny for a song
    Did not the poet sing it with such airs
    That one believed he had a sword upstairs.
                                            All Things can Tempt Me

52 I will arise and go now, and go to Innisfree,
    And a small cabin build there, of clay and wattles made;
    Nine bean rows will I have there, a hive for the honey bee,
    And live alone in the bee-loud glade.   *The Lake Isle of Innisfree*

53 And I shall have some peace there, for peace comes dropping
        slow,
    Dropping from the veils of the morning to where the cricket
        sings.   *Ib*

54   The land of faery,
    Where nobody gets old and godly and grave,
    Where nobody gets old and crafty and wise,
    Where nobody gets old and bitter of tongue.
                                            The Land of Heart's Desire

55 All things uncomely and broken, all things worn out and old,
    The cry of a child by the roadway, the creak of a lumbering cart,
    The heavy steps of the ploughman, splashing the wintry mould,
    Are wronging your image that blossoms a rose in the deeps of
        my heart.   *The Lover Tells of the Rose in his Heart*

56 When I was a boy with never a crack in my heart.
                            The Meditation of the Old Fisherman

57 A pity beyond all telling
    Is hid in the heart of love.   *The Pity of Love*

58 When you are old and grey and full of sleep
    And, nodding by the fire, take down this book,
    And slowly read, and dream of the soft look
    Your eyes had once, and of their shadows deep.
                                            When You are Old

YOUNG, Edward, 1683–1765
59 Some for renown, on scraps of learning dote,
    And think they grow immortal as they quote.
                                            Love of Fame, 1 89

60   Be wise with speed,
    A fool at forty is a fool indeed,   *Ib, 2, 281*

61 Be wise today; 'tis madness to defer.
Night Thoughts, Night 1, 390

62 Procrastination is the thief of time. *Ib, 393*

63 At thirty man suspects himself a fool;
Knows it at forty, and reforms his plan;
At fifty chides his infamous delay,
Pushes his prudent purpose to resolve:
In all the magnanimity of thought
Resolves; and re-resolves; then dies the same. *Ib, 417*

64 Man wants but little, nor that little, long. *Ib, Night 4, 118*

ZOLA, Émile, 1840–1902

65 *J'accuse.* I accuse. *Title of open letter to French President about Dreyfus Case, 1898*

Index

NOTE TO INDEX

The overriding aims in compiling the index have been to refresh memories by providing fingerposts to half-remembered quotations, and to furnish useful quotations related to given subjects. This being so, in many cases brief and pregnant passages have received particularly thorough analysis.

'A' and 'the' have frequently been omitted from the beginnings of quoted phrases when their presence did not seem essential. The object has been to quote what are, in each case, the most informative words in a phrase. 'Your', 'yours', 'would', 'could', 'should' are the principal abbreviated words; any other isolated abbreviations have been made only when they are unmistakable.

References in the index after a quotation are to the page and to the place on the page. Thus 95:6 after a quotation refers to page 95, quotation 6.

Index

Ace of trumps up [Gladstone's] sleeve
191:23

Ache, penury and imprisonment
337:91

Aches: the sense a. at thee 346:14

Achieve: my object ... shall a. in time
146:6

Achieving: still a., still pursuing
198:98

Aching: an a. void 113:62

Achitophel: of these the false A. was
first 126:38

A-cold: owl, for all his feathers, was a.
181:89

Acquaintance: day ... lost ... do not
make a new a. 178:37

hope our a. ... a long 'un 121:69

shd. auld a., be forgot 79:99

what, old a.!... all this flesh! 315:92

Acquaintances: few friends though
many a. 264:98

if a man does not make new a.
174:82

Acquist: he with new a. 223:27

Acres: a few paternal a. 251:28

over whose a. walked those blessed
feet 312:43

three a. and a cow 107:85

Act: between the motion and the a.
130:95

every prudent a. ... barter 78:74

future ages groan for this foul a.
350:56

hear the sins they love to a. 347:25

is in itself almost an a. 291:52

unproportion'd thought his a.
306:55

Acting: only ... when ... off he was a.
151:82

Action: a. nor utterance 325:21

dearest a. in the tented field 344:90

I cannot forecast ... the a. of Russia
100:91

in a., how like an angel! 308:81

lose the name of a. 309:95

lust in a., and till a., lust 363:50

man of a. is called on 317:12

rarer a. is in virtue 357:53

suit the a. to the word 310:5

Actions speak louder than words
254:58

Actor: after a well-graced a. leaves
351:61

like a dull a. ... I have forgot 304:18

Actors: best a. ... for tragedy, comedy
308:84

our a. ... were all spirits 356:50

the a. are ... the usual three 209:32

Acts: desires but a. not 69:59

familiar a. are beautiful 369:45

his a. being seven ages 301:90

little, nameless, unremembered a.
415:31

Ad infinitum: and so proceed *a.* 382:5

Adam: A. the goodliest man 219:67

A. was but human 394:68

A. was not Adamant! 165:63

in A.'s ear so charming ... his voice
220:85

the old A. in this child 64:94

when A. and Eve were dispossessed
69:68

when A. delved and Eve span 27:50

Adamant: Adam was not A. 165:63

Add: a. insult to injury 267:18

God shall a. ... the plagues 61:35

Adder: deaf a. that stoppeth her ear
42:11

Addington: Pitt is to A. 88:28

Adieu: a. a.! my native shore 83:57

joy ... is ever ... bidding a. 183:22

Adjunct: learning is but an a. to ourself
331:14

Admiral: kill an a. from time to time
397:8

Admiration only of weak minds 221:5

Admire: fools a., but men of sense
approve 249:1

Admiring: an a. bog 122:81

Admittance: no a. till ... week after
next 94:97

Adonais: O, weep for A.! 367:9

the soul of A. like a star 368:20

Adoption: friends ... and their a. tried
306:55

Adoration: breathless with a. 412:92

Adore: Youth, I do a. thee 364:57

Adorn: nothing that he did not a.
178:38

Adriatic: in the A., an iron curtain
102:8

Adullam: David ... escaped to the cave
A. 39:45

Adulteries: all the a. of art 179:52

Adultery: men call gallantry and gods
a. 84:66

thou shalt not commit a. 37:89

Advance: retrograde if it does not a.
142:67

Advancement: economic and social a.
of all peoples 394–5:76

Advantage: a. of doing one's praising
83:48

for our a. on the bitter cross 312:43

Advantages: remember, with a., what
feats 320:58

All (*continued*)
a. knowledge... my province 27:39
a. she loves is love 84:73
a. things are artificial 72:1
a. were for the state 201:38
a. ye know on earth 183:20
gives to a., denies a. 264:9
Goodbye to A. That 154:21
grasp a., lose a. 265:41
Lord God made them a. 10:17
made and loveth a. 106:64
nor a. that glisters, gold 154:26
ripeness is a. 330:98
teacheth ill, who teacheth a. 279:14
1066 and A. That 297:27
we are a. Socialists now 157:62
Allegory: an a. on the banks of the Nile 372:72
life ... a continual a. 187:64
Shakespeare led a life of a. 187:64
Alliances: entangling a. with none 171:29
steer clear of permanent a. 399:32
Alluring: nothing is more a. than a levee 109:15
Almanack: look in the a.; find out moonshine 342:48
Almighty: an arrow from the A.'s bow 66-7:35
the a. dollar, that great object 170:18
Almond: peach was ... a bitter a. 394:69
Alms: a. for oblivion 358:71
if thou hast abundance, give a. 62:39
so give a.; pray so 362:21
Almsman: gay apparel for an a.'s gown 350:55
Alone: all we ask is to be let a. 117:13
a., a., all, all a. 105:54
a. and palely loitering 182:7
a. I did it 304:19
as I was walking all a. 12:40
bear the palm a. 323:92
better be a. than in bad company 255:15, 399:33
but wherefore thou a.? 219:74
France is a.; and God is a. 366:4
here at the gate a. 388:86
how women pass the time when ... a. 161:4
I a. sit lingering here 396:85
I am powerful but a. 396:93
I feel I am a. 192:35
I want to be a. 141:45
leave them a., and they'll come home 234:48

Alone (*continued*)
left him a. with his glory 408:53
not good that the man shd. be a. 35:32
we are left, or shall be left a. 413:6
we two a. will sing like birds 330:99
weep and you weep a. 404:91
who can enjoy a.? 220:87
Alph the sacred river ran 106:71
Alpha: I am A. and Omega 60:19
Alphabet: got to the end of the a. 121:70
Alpine: through an A. village passed 197:93
Altars: on behalf of ... their a. ... their hearths 293:74
Alteration: alters when it a. finds 363:47
Alternative: prefer old age to the a. 99:81
Alters: a. when it alteration finds 363:47
love a. not 363:48
Always (Alway): I am with you a. 53:52
it seemed a. afternoon 387:84
Am: by the grace of God I a. what I a. 57:59
here I a., and here I stay 202:51
I a. that I a. 36:71
I think, therefore I a. 119:31
Amami: Friday night is A. night 11:27
Amaryllis: sport with A. in the shade 215:12
Amateurs: hinted that we are a nation of a. 290:41
Amaze: Ye gods! it doth a. me 323:92
Ambassador: an a. is an honest man sent to lie 416:46
Ambiguity: Seven Types of A. 133:49
Ambition: a. first sprung from yr. blest abodes 248:74
a. shd. be made of sterner stuff 325:14
a. thick-sighted 181:84
become a churchman better than a. 323:88
death for his a. 325:11
let not a. mock 155:34
love ... not with a. join'd 109:14
meaner things to low a. 250:7
to reign is worth a. 216:36
vaulting a. which o'erleaps itself 333:37
wars that makes a. virtue 345:10
who doth a. shun 301:85
Ambitious: as he was a. I slew him 325:11

Amen: will no man say a.? 350:57
America: A. cannot be an ostrich
    408:46
    A. ... country of young men 133:46
    A.! God shed His grace 29:67
    ask not what A. will do for you
        188:75
    O my A.!, my new-found-land
        123–4:9
    Oh, they go to A. 406:25
    the youth of A. 406:26
    wake up, A. 141:46
American: a new deal for the A. people
        289:27
    A. system of rugged individualism
        166:66
    born an A.; I will live an A. 400:45
    love all mankind, except an A.
        177:26
    retreat of the A. Army to our line
        102:7
Americanism: no room ... for hyphen-
        ated A. 289:38
Americans: a new generation of A.
        188:74
    my fellow A., ask not 188:75
    when good A. die 406:25
Amiral: tuer de temps en temps un a.
        397:8
Ammunition: Praise the Lord and pass
        the a. 137:95
Amor: a. che muove il sole 117:4
    a. vincit insomnia 140:36
    omnia vincit a. 397:3
Amoris: amantium irae a. integratio est
        389:5
Amorous: water ... a. of their strokes
        298–9:54
Amour: absence est à l'a. 82:34
    doux comme l'a. 384:30
    on ne badine pas avec l'a. 227:79
Amurath: not A. an A. succeeds
        318:31
Amused: we are not a. 396:91
Amusing herself [my cat] more with me
        225:55
Anatomy: a mere a., a mountebank
        303:12
Ancestral voices prophesying war
        107:74
Ancestry: I can trace my a. back
        145:97
    mule without pride of a. 124:15
Anchors: great a., heaps of pearl
        352:72
Ancient: a. nobility ... act of time
        25:6
    a. of days 50:73

Ancient (*continued*)
    did those feet in a. time 67:38
    fear thee, a. Mariner 105:53
    from a. melody have ceased 68:54
    have you left the a. love 68:55
    it is an a. mariner 104:42
Ancientry: wronging the a., stealing
        361:16
Anderson: John A. my jo 80:11
Ange: pur comme un a. 384:30
Angel: a beautiful and ineffectual a.
        21:51
    a minist'ring a. ... my sister be
        312:32
    a ministering a. thou 296:14
    A. of the Lord came down 384:35
    a. whom thou still hast serv'd
        336:78
    clip an A.'s wings 183:13
    in action, how like an a.! 308:81
    is man an ape or an a.? 122:91
    like an a. sings 340:22
    reverence—that a. of the world
        304:27
    she drew an a. down 127:54
    sword of an a. king 66–7:35
    the A. ended 220:85
    the A. of Death has been abroad
        70:80
    the better a. is a man 364:55
    who wrote like an a. 141:49
    woman yet think him an a. 389:10
Angelic: something of a. light 414:18
Angels: a. and ministers of grace defend
        us 307:60
    a band of a. coming 18:8
    fantastic tricks ... as makes the a.
        weep 337:87
    flights of a. sing thee to thy rest
        312:40
    guardian a. sung this strain 391:33
    I ... am on the side of the a.
        122:91
    made him a little lower than the a.
        41:83
    sing, choirs of A. 241:92
    tears, such as A. weep 217:42
    the glorious fault of a. 248:74
    the herald a. sing 402:71
    where a. fear to tread 249:6
    women are a., wooing 358:65
Anger: a. supplies the arms 396:97
    monstrous a. of the guns 243:16
    more in sorrow than in a. 306:50
Angles: not A. but Angels 156:50
Angleterre est une nation de boutiquiers
        228:85
Angli: non A. sed Angeli 156:50

Apparelled in celestial light 410:72

Appeal: I a. unto Caesar 56:25

Appearance: judge not according to the
a. 55:2
man looketh on the outward a.
39:42
never judge from a. 268:26

Appears: done by night a. by day
260:85
God a., and God is light 66:31

Appétit vient en mangeant 285:89

Appetite: a. comes with eating 285:89
as if increase of a. had grown
305:44
cloy the hungry edge of a. 348:37
doth not the a. alter? 343:69
now good digestion wait on a.
335:54
surfeiting the a. may sicken 358:75

Appetites: cloy the a. they feed 299:55
creatures ours, and not their a.!
345:8

Applause: the a.! delight! ... of our
Stage 179:53

Apple: an a. a day ... doctor away
254:73
a. for the a.'s sake 394:68
kept him as the a. of his eye 38:14
my a. trees will never get across
139:26
the a. press'd with specious cant
165:63

Apple-cart: upset the a. 254:74

Apples: comfort me with a. 47:19
Kent ... a., cherries, hops and women
120:61
small choice in rotten a. 355:21

Appliance: by desperate a. are reliev'd
311:21

Appliances: all a. and means to boot
317:14

Apprehension: a. of the good gives ...
feeling 348:37
in a., how like a god! 308:81

Approach: sweet a. of even or morn
218:59

Approve: let age a. of youth 76:47

Approves all forms of competition
103:30

April: a bright cold day in A. 242:99
and after A. 74:22
A. is the cruellest month 131:10
A., June and November 239:77
A. with his shoures sote 96:25
men are A. when they woo 302:4
now that A.'s there 74:21
proud-pied A. 363:44
uncertain glory of an A. day 361:6

Aprons: made themselves a. 35:37

Aquinas: better teacher than ... A.
223:40

Arabia: all the perfumes of A. 335:69

Arabian trees their med'cinable gum
346–7:22

Araby: I'll sing thee songs of A.
407:41

Aram: how Eugene A.. though a thief
87:14

Ararat: upon the mountains of A.
35:46

Arbitrary: accusation of being a.
170:23

Arcadia: et in A. ego 19:19
I too am in A. 19:19

Archangel: nor appeared less than A.
ruined 217:41

Arches: fled Him down the a. of the
years 391:30

Architecture: the wondrous a. of the
world 205:76

Arden: am in A.; the more fool I
300:81

Arguing: I am not a. ... I am telling
402:75
no a. with Johnson 152:3
no good in a. with the inevitable
200:27

Argument: any a. about any place
252:46
a. for a week 313:58
furnish ... a. and intellects 152:99
height of this great a. 216:29
in a. with men a woman 222:22
not to stir without great a. 311:24
Tories ... no a. but force 72:8
Whigs ... no force but a. 72:8

Arise: I will a. and go now 417:52
my lady sweet, a. 304:20

Aristotle: bokes ... of A. and his
philosophye 96:33

Arithmetic: branches of A. – Ambition,
Distraction 91:60

Ark: a. rested in the seventh month
35:46
unto Noah into the a. 35:45

Arm: human on my faithless a. 22:60
I bit my a., I sucked the blood
105:51

Arma: a. virumque cano 396:96
cedant a. togae ... laurea laudi
102:17

Armadas: till the great A. come
230:11

Armageddon: a place called ... A.
61:31

Armies: our a. swore terribly 379:70

Armour: put on ... a. of God 58:73
  religion is the best a. 276:84
  whose a. is his honest thought
    416:48
Armourers: now thrive the a. 319:40
Arms: anger supplies the a. 396:97
  a. against a sea of troubles 309:95
  a. and the man I sing 128:72, 396:96
  a. of mine had seven years' pith
    344:90
  a., take your last embrace 354:18
  imparadised in one another's a.
    219:68
  so he laid down his a. 165:57
  the a. of my true love 388:88
  underneath are the everlasting a.
    38:17
  what a. ... under my head 210:46
Army: an a. marches on its stomach
    228:87
  hum of either a. stilly sounds
    320:50
noble a. of Martyrs 63:69
  terrible as an a. with banners 47:26
Arrive: a better thing than to a.
    380:80
Arrow: an a. from the Almighty's bow
    66–7:35
  I shot an a. into the air 197:91
  the a. that flieth by day 43:20
Arrows: my a. of desire 67:38
Ars longa, vita brevis 163:30
Arse upon which everyone has sat
    115:93
Arsenic and Old Lace 188:76
Art: all a. is quite useless 406:22
  all nature is but a. 250:12
  all the adulteries of a. 179:52
  a. for a.'s sake 111:38
  a. has no enemy except ignorance
    254:76
  a. is a jealous mistress 132:26
  A. is long, and Time is fleeting
    198:96
  a. is long, but life is short 163:30
  a. is too precise in every part 162:17
  a. lies in concealing a. 254:77
  a. of being kind 404:93
  a. of drawing sufficient conclusions
    82:44
  a. pour l'a. 111:38
  aspires ... to the condition of a.
    110:25
  China's gayest a. had dyed 154:23
  clever, but is it a.? 190:96
  fine a. ... hand ... head ... heart
    292:63
  half a trade and half an a. 170:12

Art (continued)
  more matter with less a. 307:73
  nature is the a. of God 72:1
  next to Nature, A. 192:34
  source, and end, and test, of A.
    249:92
  squandring ... his peculiar a.
    126:44
  strains of unpremeditated a. 370:49
  true ease in writing ... a., not
    chance 249:99
  what a. can wash her guilt 152:2
Arthur: he's in A.'s bosom 319:43
  slowly answered A. from the barge
    385:54
Article: snuff'd out by an a. 85:83
  these a. subscribed ... I may ...
    dwindle into a wife 109:18
Artifex: qualis a. pereo! 230:10
Artificial: all things are a. 72:1
Artisan: merchant, and a., without
    ... meddling 9:6
  to give employment to the a. 31:94
Artist: a. is in danger of death 160:92
  be more of an a. 187:69
  true a. will let his wife starve
    365:80
  what an a. dies with me! 230:10
Arts: a. of every woman false 222:19
  in the inglorious a. of peace 207:2
  the books, the a., the academes
    331:16
Ash on an old man's sleeve 130:97
Ashamed: naked ... and were not a.
    35:35
  she that maketh a. 45:65
Ashes: a. and sparks, my words
    among mankind 369:38
  a. to a., dust to dust 65:15
  for the a. of his fathers 201:36
  man ... splendid in a. 72:7
  slept among his a. cold 182:92
  to give ... beauty for a. 49:53
Asia: hollow pamper'd jades of A.
    316:9
  ye pamper'd jades of A.! 205:78
Ask: we a. and a. 21:44
Asked: nobody a. you, sir, she said
    241:87
  women are glad to have been a.
    243:12
Askelon: in the streets of A. 40:47
Asleep: he thought me a. 244:31
  old ships sail like swans a. 136:85
  the very houses seem a. 412:97
  we are laid a. in body 415:33
Aspect: meet in her a. and her eyes
    86:96

Aspect (*continued*)
  sweet a. of princes   322–3:81
  with grave a. he rose   218:52
Aspen: shade ... light quivering a.
  made   296:14
Aspens: willows whiten, a. quiver
  387:76
Aspicious: comprehended two a. persons   343:79
Ass: an a. wd. marry an uncertainty
  298:39
  a. [knoweth] his master's crib   48:29
  average schoolmaster ... essentially
  an a.   209:29
  bridle for ... a., a rod for the fool's
  back   46:83
  make an a. of oneself   254:80
  write me down an a.   344:85
Assassination: absolutism tempered by
  a.   227:75
Assay: th' a. so hard   97:50
Assert: I may a. Eternal Providence
  216:29
Asset: healthy citizens are the greatest
  a.   101:6
Assume: a. a virtue, if you have it not
  311:91
  what I a. you shall a.   403:82
Assuming that he's got any [brains]
  144:85
Assurance: I'll make a. double sure
  335:63
Assured: most ignorant of what he's
  most a.   337:87
Astonish: things that wd a. you   144:86
Astonished: a. at my own moderation
  103:24
  a. Mayor and Corporation   75:39
Asunder: let no man put a.   65:10
Atahualpa: knows ... who strangled A.
  202:42
Atheism: a little philosophy inclineth ...
  to a.   25:10
Athens: a citizen, not of A.   375:20
  Israel, A., Florence   170:13
  maid of A.   86:95
Atkins: it's Thank You, Mr. A.   190:11
Atlanta: from A. to the sea   416:45
Atlases: only on the very best a.
  395:80
Atomies: drawn with a team of little a.
  353:92
Attached: decidedly and conscien-
  tiously a.   115:87
Attachment à la Plato   146:16
Attack: dared a. my Chesterton   32:1
  situation excellent. I shall a.   136:87
Attempt: serious a. to do it   401:66

Attempted: something a., something
  done   199:8
Attentions: these pleasing a.   23:78
Attic: beauty crieth in an a.   82:47
  mellow glory of the A. stage   20:35
Atticus: if A. were he!   248:84
Attire: in its workaday a.   143:75
  so wild in their a.   332:26
Attitudes: Anglo-Saxon a.   94:92
Attorney: office boy to an A.'s firm
  147:26
Attraction and repulsion   68:56
Attribute: an a. to God himself
  339:15
  a. to awe and majesty   339:15
  grandest moral a. of a Scotsman
  28:64
Auburn: sweet A.! loveliest village
  150:61
Audace: de l'a., ... toujours de l'a.
  117:5
Audi alteram partem   254:81
Audible: illiberal ... ill-bred as a.
  laughter   98:59
August: to recommence [winter] in A.
  85:85
Augustus: Fleckno ... like A., young
  was called   128:68
Auld: a. acquaintance   79:99
  a. lang syne   79:1
  the a. wife sat   87:11
Aunt: if my a. had been a man   254:82
  I'm Charley's a. from Brazil   389:16
  my a. died of influenza   366:97
  written to A. Maud   153:10
Aunts: his cousins and his a.   147:25
Austerlitz: pile the bodies high at A.
  293:78
Austin: laboure, as A. bit   96:30
  let A. have his swink   96:30
Austria: Don John of A. is going to the
  war   99:71
Author: as sincerely from the a.'s soul
  169:3
  a. ... of all good things   64:90
  a. who speaks about his own books
  122:92
  where is any a. in the world   331:14
Authority: a man under a.   52:28
  a. be a stubborn bear   362:27
  base a. from others' books   331:10
  dress'd in a little brief a.   337:87
  in your countenance ... a.   327:55
  nothing destroys a. so much   25:14
  wrest ... the law to your a.   339:16
Autographs: nuisances who write for a.
  145:99
Autres temps, autres moeurs   254:83

Autumn: thou breath of A.'s being 369:35

Autumnal: grace ... in one a. face 123:7

Availeth: say not the struggle naught a. 103:32

Avails: what a. the sceptred race! 192:36

Avarice, the spur of industry 168:90

Ave: a. in perpetuum ... a. atque vale 94:6

Averni: facilis descensus A. 397:2

Aversion: in matrimony to begin with a little a. 371:67

Aves: after thousand a. told 182:92

Avocation: engaging in so puerile an a. 209:29

Avon: sweet Swan of A. 179:58

Awake: a.! for Morning in the Bowl of Night 134:65

a. my heart, to be loved 70:75

a., my St. John! 250:7

lying a. with a dismal headache 144:91

smiles a. you 118:20

Award: general a. of love 182:4

Aware: England bore, shaped, made a. 71:93

Away: a.! a.! for I will fly to thee 184:26

a. with him! He speaks Latin 321:69

a., you rolling river 18:1

come, dear children, let us a. 20:32

I wish, I wish he'd stay a. 208:24

spotless reputation; that a. 347:30

the little more, and what worlds a. 73:19

to bear my soul a. 10:13

were t'other dear charmer a. 142:54

Awe: attribute to a. and majesty 339:15

in a. of such a thing as I 323:91

Awful: felt how a. goodness is 219:73

nothing ... nobody ... it's a.! 30:74

that men might shun the a. shops 99:76

Awoke: I a. ... and found myself famous 86:2

so I a., and behold ... a dream 77:63

Awry: their currents turn a. 309:95

Axe: an a. to grind 254:84

Lizzie Borden took an a. 15:67

the a.'s edge did try 207:3

Axiom: long been an a. of mine 124:18

Axis: soft under-belly of the A. 101:4

Azure: arose from out the a. main 391:33

ring'd with the a. world 385:47

Azure (*continued*)

robes the mountain in ... a. hue 88:20

the a. flowers that blow 154:23

Baa, b., black sheep 231:23

Babble: watch to b. and to talk 343:75

Babbled: a' b. of green fields 319:44

Babe: find the b. ... in a manger 54:69

Babel: name of it called B. 35:52

Babes: out of the mouth of b. 41:81

Babies: bit the b. in the cradles 75:37

putting milk into b. 101:6

the snuggeries of b. 390:24

Baby: a Mother laid her B. 10:19

b., cradle, and all 233:38

every b. born ... finer than the last 120:53

hush-a-bye b., on the tree top 233:38

in the oven for b. and me 237:62

see my b. at my breast? 300:71

when the first b. laughed 28:59

Babylon: by the rivers of B. ... we sat 44:44

how many miles to B.? 233:36

king of B. ... at the parting 49:64

Bacchus: not chariotted by B. 184:26

Bachelor: I wd. die a b. 343:70

now I am a b. 17:95

Bachelors: two old b. ... in one house 194:64

Back: at my b. I always hear 206:94

die with harness on our b. 336:77

his wife looked b. from behind 36:56

mermaid on a dolphin's b. 341:44

one who never turned his b. 73:16

rod for his own b. 276:99

those before cried 'B.!' 201:39

Background: see fit to keep me in the b. 196:72

Backward: dark b. and abysm of time 355:29

I b. cast my e'e 80:19

look b. to with pride 139:23

Bacon: think how B. shined 250:17

to save one's b. 276:13

when their lordships asked B. 34:20

Bad: altogether irreclaimably b. 89:39

became ... b. in one step 180:68

hope ... good breakfast ... b. supper 26:38

how sad and b. and mad 73:20

mad, b., and dangerous 191:24

so much b. in the best of us 163:36

swans sing ... 'twere no b. thing 106:70

Bad (*continued*)
the b. affright 155:43
things b. begun make strong themselves 335:52
truth told with b. intent 66:29
when she was b. she was horrid 199:5
Badine: on ne b. pas avec l'amour 227:79
Badness: all good and no b. 373:93
Baffled to fight better 73:16
Bag: cat out of the b. 269:72
not with b. and baggage 302:94
one and all, b. and baggage, ... clear out 149:52
Bags: three b. full 231:23
Baked: you have b. me too brown 91:64
Baker Street: the B. irregulars 125:26
Balance: redress the b. of the Old 88:26
the b. of power 398:19
Bald: b. as a coot 255:89
b. heads are soon shaven 255:90
go up thou b. head 40:60
Ball: after the b. 158:71
contenders drive a b. with sticks 172:44
Ballad: woeful b. made to ... eyebrow 301:90
Ballad-mongers: these same metre b. 314:73
Ballads: of b., songs and snatches 145:95
patriotic b. cut and dried 145:96
Ballot is stronger than the bullet 196:74
Balls: the stars' tennis b. 400:51
Balm: a b. upon the world 182:94
b. of hurt minds 334:42
is there no b. in Gilead? 49:55
wash the b. off ... anointed king 349:50
with ... tears I wash away my b. 350:58
without tasting the b. of pity 173:66
Baltic: from Stettin in the B. 102:8
Banbury: cock-horse to B. Cross 237:66
to B. came I 70:74
Band: wearied b. swoons to a waltz 169:5
when the b. begins to play 190:11
Bands: with b. of love 50:77
Bane: I will not be afraid of death and b. 336:73
Bang: b. went saxpence! 285:79
not with a b. but a whimper 130:96

Banish plump Jack and b. all the world 314:69
Banishing: worst effect is b. for hours 112:53
Banishment: the bitter bread of b. 349:48
Bank: as I sat on a sunny b. 15:74
b. and shoal of time 333:36
b. whereon the wild thyme blows 341:46
moonlight sleeps upon this b. 340:22
Bankrupt: b. of life yet prodigal of ease 126:40
beggar can never be b. 255:6
Banks: bonnie b. o' Loch Lomon' 18:2
ye b. and braes 81:26
Banner: b. with the strange device 197:93
his b. over me was love 47:18
that b. in the sky 164:46
the royal b. and all quality 345:10
thy b., torn, but flying 84:63
Banners: hang out our b. on the outward walls 336:74
Bar: no moaning at the b. 385:44
when I went to the B. 144:83
Barabbas was a publisher 88:22
Barbara Allen 12:36
Barbarian: dancing ?... certainly a B. exercise 79:91
Barbarians, Philistines, Populace 21:48
Barbarous: mass of ... people must be b. 176:3
Barbarousness: I must confess my own b. 373:87
Barber: no b. shaves so close but 255:91
Bards: ancient love that b. of old enjoy'd 68:55
B. of Passion and of Mirth 181:83
Bare: the cupboard was b. 236:59
Bargain: a world-without-end b. 331:17
never was a better b. driven 372:83
Bargains: be beloved is above all b. 255:9
here's the rule for b. 120:49
Barge: answer'd Arthur from the b. 385:54
the b. she sat in, like a ... throne 298:54
Bark: all right ... you heard a seal b. 392:43
b. at a distance never bite 260:84
b. at the moon 255:92
b. up the wrong tree 255:94

Bark (*continued*)
 b. ... worse than his bite 255:93
 keep a dog and b. yourself 268:27
 when I ope my lips let no dog b.
  338:98
Barkis: 'as true,' said Mr. B., 'as taxes
 is' 120:43
 B. is willin' 119:38
Barley: long fields of b. and of rye
  387:75
Barlow: Councillor B. 33:10
Barrel: lock, stock and b. 270:96
Barren: a b. sister all your life 341:35
 and cry, 'tis all b. 379:66
 nature is b. 69:63
Barricade: at some disputed b. 296:20
Bars: look out through the same b.
  193:38
 nor iron b. a cage 199:15
Barter: founded on compromise and b.
  78:74
Base: so b. that wd. be a bondman
  325:11
Bashful: maiden of b. fifteen 372:78
Basia: da mi b. mille 94:4
Basil: steal my B.-pot 182:6
Basingstoke: word ... like B. 148:41
Basket: all yr. eggs in one b. 261:15
Bat: black b., night, has flown 388:86
 blind as a b. 256:44
 twinkle, twinkle, little b. 90:53
Bataillons: Dieu est ... pour les gros b.
  398:15
Bate: do I not b.? ... dwindle? 314:78
Bath: I test my b. before I sit 229:96
 sore labour's b. 334:42
Bathe: spirit to b. in fiery floods
  337:90
Bathing: caught the Whigs b. 122:89
Bathing machine: between a large b.
  144:92
Baton of a marshal of France 228:86
Bats: have b. in the belfry 255:96
 suspicions ... like b. amongst birds
  26:23
Batsman: a ghostly b. plays 390:28
Battalions: God is ... for the big b.
  398:15
 not single spies, but in b. 311:26
Battle: agreed to have a b. 92:74
 b. [is not] to the strong 47:8
 b. of Waterloo was won 401:61
 Ben B. was a soldier bold 165:57
 care for him who shall have borne the
  b. 196:81
 first blow is half the b. 263:64
 melancholy as a b. won 401:57
 nothing except a b. lost 401:57

Battle (*continued*)
 the b. and the breeze 88:21
 the b. day is past 132:23
 to b. for freedom and truth 169:9
 when the b.'s lost and won 332:22
Battle-flags: till ... the b. were furl'd
  387:81
Battles long ago 414:21
Bauble: what shall we do with this b.?
  115:89
Bays: Britain won her proudest b.
  144:89
Bay-tree: flourishing like a green b.
  42:4
Be: ain't-a-going to b. no core 394:74
 b. not solitary, b. not idle 82:33
 b. strong and of a good courage
  38:18
 fears that I may cease to b. 186:48
 Germany ... will not b. at all 163:32
 God said, Let Newton b.! 248:88
 Ho, let Einstein b.! 378:55
 lest we shd. b. by and by 10:16
 ne'er was, nor is, nor e'er shall b.
  249:96
 nobody is healthy ... nobody can b.
  23:66
 this tree continues to b. 191:20
 to b. or not to b. 309:95
 what will b., shall b. 204:62
 whatever will b., will b. 258:97
 when will that b.? say the bells
  236:61
 ye shall b. as gods 35:36
Be-all and the end-all 333:36
Beach: I shall ... walk upon the b.
  131:4
Beaches: we shall fight on the b.
  100:94
Beachy Head: to Birmingham by way
 of B. 99:73
Beacons from the abode ... Eternal are
  368:20
Beadle: a b. on boxin' day 121:72
Beads: jewels for a set of b. 350:55
Beadsman: the B., after thousand aves
  182:92
Beak: b. holds more than his belican
  209:38
 take thy b. from out my heart
  247:67
Beaker full of the warm South
  184:24
Beale: Miss B. and Miss Buss 15:68
Beam: at the full midday b. 224:43
Beamish: my b. boy! 92:71
Beams: little candle throws his b.!
  340:25

Bean: home of the b. and the cod 69:67

nine b. rows 417:52

not-too-French French b. 146:16

Beans: how many b. make nine 268:47

Bear: a B. of Very Little Brain 212:63

authority be a stubborn b. 362:27

b. those ills we have 309:95

because it gave pain to the b. 202:47

exit, *pursued by a b.* 361:15

funny how a b. likes honey? 211:62

grizzly b is huge and wild 167:78

he has been eaten by the b. 167:78

nothing wd. it b. 233:39

rather b. with you than b. you 300:80

sing Ho! for the life of a b. 212:69

Bear-baiting: the Puritan hated b. 202:47

Beard: b. of formal cut 301:90

b. the lion in his den 296:12

by thy long grey b. 104:42

Old Man with a b. 195:66

singed the Spanish king's b. 125:29

Bearded like the pard 301:90

Bears it out ... to the edge of doom 363:48

Beast: a b., but a just b. 14:59

a b., no more! 311:22

a wild b. or a god 26:20

both man and bird and b. 106:63

man's life is cheap as b.'s 328:67

wee ... cow'rin', tim'rous [beastie] 80:16

when people call this b. to mind 31:89

Beastly: don't let's be B. to the Germans 112:43

how b. the bourgeois is 193:46

Beasts: brute b. that have no understanding 64:4

Beat: b. him when he sneezes 90:51, 52

lion b. the unicorn 234:47

shall b. ... swords into plowshares 48:31

to b. about the bush 255:99

Tom was b. 240:83

ye b. my people to pieces 48:32

Beaten: English never know when ... b. 261:21

Beating: almost hear the b. of his wings 70:80

b. myself for spite 373:84

Beats: truth ... with bad intent b. all the lies 66:29

Beauteous: a b. evening, calm and free 412:92

Beautified with our feathers 156:49

Beautiful: all heiresses are b. 128:65

as good as she was b. 246:46

b. Soup! 91:65

full b., a faery's child 183:8

how b. upon the mountains 48:46

most b. things ... are the most useless 291:61

old are more b. than the young 403:78

see, not feel, how b. 106:68

she's b. and ... to be woo'd 321:64

stately homes ... how b. they stand 160:90

the good is the b. 247:61

the many men, so b. 105:55

Beauty: a b. cold and austere 292:67

a daily b. in his life 346:16

a thing of b. is a joy for ever 181:85

abstract Idea ... of B. 187:63

as a b. I'm not a ... star 134:53

as b. must be truth 186:50

b. crieth in an attic 82:47

b. draws us with a single hair 251:35

b. is but skin-deep 255:1

b. is ... in the eye of the beholder 168:92

b. is nature's coin; must not be hoarded 213:79

b. is potent 255:2

b. is truth, truth b. 183:20

b. itself doth of itself persuade 364:60

b. lives with kindness 361:9

b. of a thousand stars 204:64

b. provoketh thieves 300:74

b. stands in the admiration 221:5

b. though injurious, hath strange power 222:24

b. too rich for use 353:94

b. will buy no beef 255:3

b.'s ensign ... crimson in thy lips 354:17

dress her b. at yr. eyes 117:10

dwells with B.—B. that must die 183:22

extent of its b. and power 202:43

exuberance is b. 69:62

first in b. ... first in might 182:1

have loved the principle of b. 187:68

her B. and her Chivalry 83:59

hidden b. of the world 371:57

homely b. of the good old cause 412:2

humility towards ... Principle of B. 186:58

in their summer b. kiss'd 352:79

Isle of B., fare thee well 29:68

Beauty (*continued*)
  like a garment wear the b.   412:96
  love built on b., soon as b. dies
    123:6
  more inviting than b. unadorn'd
    31:87
  muddy, ill-seeming ... bereft of b.
    355:26
  needs not June for b.'s heightening
    21:46
  ne'er saw true b. till this night
    353:95
  no Spring, nor Summer b. hath such
    grace   123:7
  our saucy ship's a b.   146:19
  she walks in b., like the night   86:96
  teaches such b. as a woman's eye
    331:14
  that ... b.'s rose might never die
    362:29
  the b. of the world!   308:81
  to give unto them b. for ashes
    49:53
  unmask her b. to the moon   306:53
Because: b. he knows, a frightful fiend
    106:60
  b. I do not hope to turn   130:88
  b. we're here b. we're here b.   19:13
  we cannot do it, Sir, b.   93:90
Bechstein: if ... we pawn the B. Grand
    111:40
Becomes: in peace ... nothing so b. a
    man   319:45
  it hardly b. any of us   163:36
Bed: a b. by night, a chest ... by day
    150:70
  a manger for His b.   10:19
  and so to b.   245:40
  b. be blest that I lie on   10:13
  candle to light you to b.   236:61
  early to b. and early to rise   261:5
  early to b. makes a male ... dead
    392:42
  four angels to my b.   10:13
  nicer to lie in b.   193:44
  she whipped them ... put them to b.
    239:76
  to b., to b., there's knocking   335:70
  took her into b. and covered up her
    head   17:96
  welcome to yr. gory b.   81:22
Bedecked, ornate and gay   222:18
Bedfellows: misery acquaints ... with
    strange b.   356:41
Bed-time, Hal, and all well   315:87
Bee: a b. in one's bonnet   255:4
  the little busy b.   399:35
  where the b. sucks   357:56

Beef: beauty will buy no b.   255:3
  roast b. of England   134:61
  this little pig had roast b.   239:78
Been: shd. be ... as if it had not b.
    367:12
Beer: felony to drink small b.   321:66
  life isn't all b. and skittles   168:89
  parson, much bemused in b.   248:78
  suckle fools and chronicle small b.
    345:98
Beer-sheba: from Dan even to B.
    39:31
  travel from Dan to B.   379:66
Bees: late flowers for the b.   181:79
  so work the honey b.   318:39
  swine, women and b. cannot be
    turned   279:92
Beethoven's Fifth Symphony ... most
    sublime noise   137:97
Beetle wheels his droning flight   155:31
Beetles: scarce so gross as b.   329:88
Before: b., behind, between   123:9
  b. you are on with the new   17:93
  I have been here b.   291:53
  those b. cried 'Back!'   201:39
Befriend: be near me now and b.
    383:22
Beg: the poor can b.   264:21
  to b. I am ashamed   55:83
Begetter: onlie b. of these ... sonnets
    362:28
Beggar: b. can never be bankrupt
    255:6
  better die a b. than live a b.   255:22
  made a b. by banqueting   62:54
  not ... a doit to relieve a ... b.   356:40
  whiles I am a b. I will rail   326:38
Beggared: her own person it b. all
    description   298:54
Beggars: basest b. are in ... thing
    superfluous   328:67
  b. cannot be choosers   255:7
Beggary: b. in the love   298:50
  no vice but b.   326:38
Begin: b. with certainties ... end in
    doubts   26:37
  content to do b. with doubts   26:37
Beginning: as it was in the b.   63:68
  before the b. of years   382:16
  b. of a feast fits ... keen guest   315:84
  b. of a lifelong romance   404:3
  everything must have a b.   262:35
  good b. makes a good ending   265:30
  I am ... the b. and the ending   60:19
  in the b. God created   34:26
  in the b. was the Word   55:92
  it is the b. of the end   384:29
  long choosing and b. late   220:90

Beginning (*continued*)
  memory ... the b. of dowdiness
    406:32
  strange b.—'borrowed majesty'
    326:32
  that was the b. of fairies 28:59
Beginnings: end to the b. of all wars
  259:34
Begins: charity b. at home 258:96
  nothing b. and nothing ends 390:29
Begone dull care ... b. from me 16:75
Begot: how b., how nourished? 339:14
Begun: well b. is half done 282:21
Behaviour: often the surfeits of our
  own b. 327:53
Behest: darkness falls at thy b. 132:24
Behind: and, departing, leave b. us
  198:97
  bring their tails b. them 234:48
  fiend doth close b. him tread 106:60
  get thee b. me, Satan 53:36
  lads that thought there was no more
    b. 361:12
  led his regiment from b. 143:69
  my work is left b. 32:5
  those b. cried 'Forward!' 201:39
Behold: as she looked ... she did b.
  377:43
  b. her, single in the field 414:20
  b., this dreamer cometh 36:63
  mortality, b. and fear 29:71
Being: all the wheels of B. slow
  386:60
  eternal B., the Principle of Beauty
    186:58
  live and move and have our b. 56:20
  receives reproach of b. 363:49
  who wd. lose ... this intellectual b.?
    217:49
Belfry: bats in the b. 255:96
Belgium's capital had gathered then
  83:59
Belial: sons of B., flown with insolence
  217:38
  sons of B. had a Glorious Time
    126:46
Belied: they have b. a lady 344:87
Belief: does not live according to his b.
  255:8
Beliefs: holding two contradictory b.
  242:4
  home of ... forsaken b. 21:49
Believe: b. a woman or an epitaph
  85:91
  b. it or not 287:10
  I do b. her ... know she lies 364:54
  I don't b. in fairies 28:60
  say quick that you b. 28:62

Believe (*continued*)
  some b. they've none [soul] 82:40
Believed: have not seen, yet have b.
  56:14
  liar is not b. ... speaks the truth
    269:73
Believes: he who b. what is wrong
  171:32
  less remote ... who b. nothing
    171:32
  none go ... alike, yet each b. his
    own 249:91
Believing: seeing is b. 277:25
Bell: b. book and candle shall not drive
  327:40
  b. toll for poor Cock Robin 241:89
  for whom the b. tolls 124:14
  in a cowslip's b. I lie 357:56
  ring the alarum b. Blow wind, come
    wrack 336:77
  says the great b. at Bow 236:61
  sexton toll'd the b. 165:59
  the B. at Edmonton 113:55
  the b. invites me. Hear it not, Duncan
    334:41
  tongue sounds ... as a sullen b.
    316:97
  very word is like a b. 184:31
  why people ... do not ring the b.
    27:46
Bells: ring, happy b., across the snow
  386:68
  ring out, wild b. 386:67
  say the b. of St. Clement's 236:61
  silver b. and cockle shells 235:55
  the b. of hell go ting-a-ling-a-ling
    16:76
  the port is near, the b. I hear 403:81
  up so floating many b. down 116:94
Belly: b. (*see also* Under-belly): born
  ... with something a round b.
    316:99
  fair round b. with good capon lin'd
    301:90
  I mind my b. very studiously 175:91
  whose God is their b. 58:76
  wd. fain have filled his b. 55:81
Bellyful: rumble thy b. 328:72
Belmont: In B. is a lady richly left
  338:99
Beloved: be b. ... is above all bargains
  255:9
  heaped for the b.'s bed 370:54
  Oh sleep! ... b. from pole to pole!
    105:57
Below: down and away b. 20:32
Bends: he who b. himself a joy 66:34
  though she b. him, she obeys 198:3

Bitter: and shed a b. tear　92:79
　b. groan of a martyr's woe　66–7:35
　b. ... on itself [revenge] recoils
　　220:91
　b. to endure ... sweet to remember
　　256:38
　children ... make misfortunes more
　　b.　24:95
　eating the b. bread of banishment
　　349:48
　lack gall to make oppression b.
　　309:92
　love grows b. with treason　383:23
　old and b. of tongue　417:54
　peach was once a b. almond　394:69
　sadden after none or b. fruit　135:75
Bitterness: ills have no weight, and tears
　　no b.　201:33
　little sweet doth kill much b.　182:4
　no hatred or b. towards anyone　95:7
Black: b. as ink　256:39
　b. as soot　256:40
　b. as the devil　256:41
　b. as the devil, hot as hell　384:30
　b. as the pit from pole to pole　160:93
　b. one ... good as the white　281:86
　b. sheep in every flock　256:42
　dark as the world ... b. as our loss
　　373:90
　hung be the heavens with b.　321:62
　I am b. but comely　47:16
　I am b. ... my soul is white　68:51
　not so b. as he is painted　260:73
　one b., and one white, and two khaki
　　14:55
　pot calls the kettle b.　275:52
　ravens ... as b. as they might
　　be　12:39
　secret, b., and midnight hags!
　　335:60
　ship in a b. storm　401:55
　sober-suited matron all in b.　354:13
　two lovely b. eyes　104:37
Blackbird: there came a little b.　238:70
Blackbirds: four-and-twenty b.　238:70
Bladder: blows a man up like a b.
　　314:67
Blade: shook the fragment of his b.
　　296:15
　vorpal b. went snicker-snack!　92:70
Blame: murd'rous, bloody, full of b.
　　363:50
　poor wot gets the b.　18:5
　scarcely can ... b. it too much
　　151:78
　what they b. at night　249:2
Blanket: under the b. the black ... as
　　good　281:86

Blanket (*continued*)
　wrong side of the b.　256:56
Blasphemy: in the soldier is flat b.
　　337:88
Blast: our shelter from the stormy b.
　　399:38
　with contrary b. proclaims most deeds
　　222:23
Blaze: his rash fierce b. of riot cannot
　　last　348:40
Blazon: this eternal b. must not be
　　307:64
Bleats articulate monotony　378:62
Bleed: if you prick us, do we not b.?
　　339:13
　upon the thorns of life! I b.!　369:37
Bleeding: thou b. piece of earth　324:8
Bleeds: our country ... weeps it b.
　　335:65
Bless: b. the turf that wraps their clay
　　107–8:90
　God b. the moon and God b. me
　　234:43
　'God b. us every one!' said Tiny Tim
　　119:36
　with thee at hand to b.　201:33
Blessed: b. are the horny hands of toil
　　200:22
　judge none b. before his death　62:52
　more b. to give　56:22
Blesseth: it b. him that gives ... that
　　takes　339:15
Blessing: a boon and a b. to men　11:32
　b. of the Old Testament　24:90
　God bless—no harm in b.　83:53
　prophetick b. – Be thou dull　127:49
　set before you ... b. and cursing
　　38:13
　when thou dost ask me b.　330:99
Blessings: all the b. of this life　64:85
　b. are not valued till ... gone　256:43
Blest: always to be b.　250:9
　thou art b. compared with me　80:19
Blind: be to her faults a little b.　253:50
　b. as a bat　256:44
　b. as the nineteen hundred and forty
　　nails　373:90
　b., despised, and dying king　370:53
　b. man will not thank you　256:47
　b. mouths! that scarce ... know how
　　215:15
　Cupid painted b.　341:38
　discomforts ... accompany my being
　　b.　246:45
　hatred is b.　266:71
　if the b. lead the b.　52:33
　in the land of the b.　256:48
　love is b.　270:13, 339:10

Blind (*continued*)
 men are b. in their own cause
 256:46
 none so b. as those who won't see
 256:45
 the maimed, and the halt, and the b.
 54:79
 three b. mice 240:80
Blindly: never lov'd so b. 79:97
Bliss: b. was it in that dawn to be alive
 413:9
 inward eye ... the b. of solitude
 410:71
 perfect b. and sole felicity 205:76
 thou art a soul in b. 330:96
 though thou hast not thy b. 183:18
 virtue only makes our b. below
 250:20
 where ignorance is b. 154:29
Blisses: child among his new-born b.
 411:79
Blithe: no lark more b. than he 65:16
 O b. Newcomer ... O Cuckoo!
 415:37
Block: a chip of the old b. 258:99
 big black b. 145:3
 he was ... the old b. itself 78:76
Blockhead: bookful b., ignorantly read
 249:5
 no man but a b. ever wrote 177:21
Blockheads of all ages 109:8
Blocks: you b., you stones! 323:89
Blood: all great Neptune's ocean wash
 this b. 334:43
 b. and iron 66:23
 b. is fet from fathers of war-proof
 319:46
 b. is nipp'd and ways be foul
 332:20
 b. is thicker than water 25:49
 b. of English shall manure the ground
 350:56
 b. of this just person 53:51
 b. out of a stone 282:12
 by man shall his b. be shed 35:49
 corruption inhabits our frail b.
 360:1
 freeze thy young b. 307:64
 guiltless of his country's b. 155:38
 here's the smell of the b. still 335:69
 he today that sheds his b. with me
 320:59
 I am in b. stepp'd in so far 335:57
 I smell the b. of a British man
 329:82
 I sucked the b. 105:51
 in so far in b. that sin will pluck
 352:77

Blood (*continued*)
 nothing to offer but b., toil, tears and
 sweat 100:92
 O, the b. more stirs 313:53
 purge this cholar without letting b.
 347:29
 red b. reigns ... winter's pale 361:17
 simple faith than Norman b. 387:74
 smoke and b. is the mix of steel
 293:80
 some moment when the moon was b.
 98:67
 speech to stir men's b. 325:21
 summon up the b. 319:45
 sunset ran one glorious b.-red 74:24
 the b. of Jesus whispers peace 65:19
 the near in b. the nearer bloody
 334:47
 who thicks man's b. with cold
 105:52
 whoso sheddeth man's b. 35:49
 young b. must have its course
 189:89
Bloody: be b., bold and resolute
 335:62
 if you break the b. glass 203:55
 my head is b. but unbowed 160:94
 often wipe a b. nose 142:58
 walk! not b. likely 366:98
 what b. man is that? 332:24
 wrong with our b. ships 29:69
Bloom: how can ye b. sae fresh and
 fair? 81:26
 you seize the flow'r, its b. is shed
 81:25
Blooming: last rose ... left b. alone
 226:63
 like a b. Eastern bride 127:50
Blossom that hangs on the bough
 357:56
Blot: noteless b. on a remembered
 name 367:15
Blots: inky b. and rotten parchment
 bonds 349:42
Blow: another deadly b.! 413:6
 b., b., thou winter wind 302:91
 b., bugle, b., set ... echoes flying
 388:98
 b. out, you bugles, over the rich
 Dead 71:88
 b. wind, come wrack 336:77
 b. your pipe ... till you burst 75:42
 hear old Triton b. his wreathed horn
 412:94
 liberty's in every b. 81:23
 that but this b. might be the be-all
 333:36
 to take one b. and turn 164:45

Blows: heal the b. of sound   164:44
  the wild thyme b.   341:46
Bludgeonings: under the b. of chance
  160:94
Blue: Little Boy B.   234:49
  their hands are b.   194:58
  true b. will never stain   281:58
Blunder: wonder at so grotesque a b.
  33–4:19
  youth is a b.   123:95
Blunders: one of Nature's agreeable b.
  112:48
Blush: wd. it bring a b.?   120:59
Blushing: bears his b. honours   322:80
Blut und Eisen   66:23
Board: wasn't any b. ... isn't any
  trade   161:8
Boards: all the b. did shrink   105:50
Boast of heraldry ... pomp of power
  155:34
Boasts two soul-sides   74:34
Boat: all in the same b.   276:11
  beautiful pea-green b.   195:60
Boatman do not tarry   88:19
Boats: burn one's b.   257:69
  messing about in b.   153:13
Boatswain and I, the gunner and his
  mate   356:43
Bobby Shafto: bonny B.   231:24
Bodies: friendless b. of unburied men
  400:54
  pile the b. high   293:78
  rough notes and our dead b.   294:91
  their b. are buried in peace   62:62
Bodkin: quietus make with a bare b.
  309:95
Body: absent in b., ... present in spirit
  57:47
  asleep in b., ... become a living soul
  415:33
  b. is not more than the soul   403:86
  b. of a feeble woman   132:20
  carry ... b. around ... its sentimental
  value   140:31
  every joint and motive of her b.
  358:73
  fretted the pigmy b. to decay   126:39
  gin a b. meet a b.   79:3
  mind that makes the b. rich   355:25
  my little b. is aweary   338:1
  need a b. cry?   79:3
  perfect little b., without fault   70:78
  Presence of Mind ... Absence of B.
  284:75
  reading is to ... mind what exercise
  ... to the b.   378:61
  some in their b.'s force   363:41
  soul not more than the b.   403:86

Body (*continued*)
  sound mind in a sound b.   180:71
  that learned b. wanted loyalty
  393:54
  the corruptible b.   62:44
  Thersites' b. is as good as Ajax'
  304:28
  we ... are one b. in Christ   57:36
  we therefore commit his b.   65:15
  with my b. I thee worship   65:9
Bog: tell your name ... to an admiring
  b.   122:81
Boil: we b. at different degrees   133:45
Bold: he bloody, b. and resolute
  335:62
  be b., be b. ... everywhere Be b.
  377:43
Boldness, and again b., and always b.
  117:5
Bond: let him look to his b.   339:12
  take a b. of fate   335:63
  'tis not in the b.   340:18
  the very b. of love   362:24
  word is as good as his b.   267:92
Bondage: out of the house of b.   37:81
Bondman: so base that wd. be a b.?
  325:11
Bonds: inky blots and rotten parchment
  b.   349:42
Bone: a b. to pick with fate   228:92
  beat him with a b.   260:83
  b. of my bones   35:34
  fetch her poor dog a b.   236:59
  have a b. in one's leg   256:51
  two dogs strive for a b.   281:76
Bones: as rottenness in his b.   45:65
  good ... interred with their b.
  325:12
  let's have the tongs and the b.
  342:51
  mock'd the dead b. ... scatt'red by
  352:72
  my Shakespeare for his honoured b.
  216:23
  o ye dry b., hear the word   49:65
  of his b. are coral made   355:35
Bonfire: primrose way to th' everlasting
  b.   334:44
Bong-tree: land where the B. grows
  195:61
Bonnet: a bee in one's b.   255:4
Bonnets: the b. of Bonny Dundee
  294:92
Bonnie (Bonny): b., b. banks o' Loch
  Lomon'   18:2
  braes o' b. Doon   81:26
  bring back my B.   17:94
  for b. Annie Laurie   124:16

Bonnie (*continued*)
  is b. and blithe and good 235–6:56
  my B. is over the ocean 17:94
Bons mots: not enough b. in existence 169:2
Bonum: Summum b. 102:16
Bo(o): cannot say B. to a goose 276:14
Booby: give her b. for another 142:57
Book: a bad b. is as much labour 169:3
  a b. ... amusing with numerous errors 152:95
  a b.'s a b. although 85:89
  a good b. is the precious life-blood 223:38
  a leaf out of one's b. 279:94
  bell, b. and candle shall not drive me back 327:40
  b. ... shut is but a block 256:52
  b. that furnishes no quotations 245:36
  but where's the b.? 100:84
  dainties ... bred in a b. 331:13
  damned, thick, square b.! 149:56
  do not throw this b. about 31:88
  go, litel b. 98:52
  half a library to make one b. 176:11
  he who destroys a good b. 223:37
  his common-place b. ... full 382:8
  if a b. is worth reading ... worth buying 291:60
  I'll drown my b. 357:55
  is no b. – it is a plaything 245:36
  my B. of Songs and Sonnets 340:28
  never read a b. before reviewing 375:11
  never read ... b. ... not a year old 133:42
  seldom read a b. ... given to them 176:5
  take down this b. 417:58
  that one might read the b. of fate! 317:15
  upon a b. in cloistre ... to poure 96:30
  use of a b. without pictures? 89:42
  what genius ... when I wrote that b. 382:14
  when a new b. is published 288:23
  word for word without b. 359:76
  write a better b. 133:48
  your face, my thane, is as a b. 333:34
Books: as school-boys from their b. 354:4
  at his beddes heed twenty b. 96:33

Books (*continued*)
  author who speaks about his own b. 122:92
  base authority from others' b. 331:10
  b. and friends ... few and good 256:53
  b. cannot always please 114:80
  b. cannot be killed by fire 289:33
  b. from which the lectures are taken 175:95
  b. in the running brooks 300:75
  b. think for me 192:29
  b.! 'tis a dull and endless strife 414:26
  borrowers of b. 192:26
  deep-versed in b. and shallow 221:8
  his sins ... scarlet ... his b. ... read 31:93
  I keep my b. at the British Museum 82:42
  I never read b.—I *write* them 285:83
  I'll burn my b.! 204:66
  in a person's bad [good] b. 256:54
  in this war ... b. are weapons 289:33
  learning ... gained most by those b. 140:40
  needed not the spectacles of b. 127:59
  no furniture so charming as b. 374:7
  of making many b. ... is no end 47:13
  old b. maken us memorie 97:47
  old b., old wine 151:83
  quit your b. 414:25
  read any good b. lately? 227:76
  read of in b., or dreamt of 28:53
  rural quiet, friendship, b. 391:34
  some b. are to be tasted 26:32
  the b., the arts, the academes 331:16
  to Cambridge b. 393:54
  to Cambridge b. he sent 72–3:8
  true University ... collection of b. 89:37
  we all know that b. burn 289:33
Boom: strong gongs groaning ... guns b. far 99:71
Boon: a b. and a blessing to men 11:32
  is life a b.? 148:44
Boot: b. is on the other leg 256:55
  make b. upon the summer's ... buds 318:39
Boots: b., b., b. 190:95
  too big for one's b. 280:48

Bow (*continued*)

b., b., ye lower middle classes!
143:80

b. themselves when he did sing
322:76

bring me my b. of burning gold
67:38

if you b. ... b. low 257:62

my throne, bid kings come b. 326:39

says the great bell at B. 236:61

set my b. in the cloud 35:50

two strings to one's b. 281:81

with my b. and arrow 241:88

Bow Bells: within the sound of B.
257:59

Bowed: b. himself with all his might
39:30

I have not ... b. to its idolatries
83:61

Bowels: beseech you, in the b. of
Christ 115:88

his b. of compassion 60:15

Bower: Lime-tree B. my prison 107:77

Bowl: crabs hiss in the b. 332:20

fill the flowing b. 16:78

he called for his b. 236:58

inverted b. we call the sky 136:80

love in a golden b. 66:32

Box: worth a guinea a b. 11:34

Boy: a horrid, wicked b. was he 164:40

and to be b. eternal 361:12

being read to by a b. 130:92

b. stood on the burning deck 160:89

b. who lives down the lane 231:23

b. with never a crack in my heart
417:56

boys when I was a b. 32:7

Chatterton, the marvellous b.
413:12

every b. and every gal 144:87

imagination of a b. is healthy 181:84

let the b. win his spurs 129:80

little B. Blue 234:49

my beamish b.! 92:71

said, what a good b. am I 235:50

shades ... close upon the growing b.
410–11:77

speak roughly to your little b. 90:51

was and a little tiny b. 360:3

Boys: all the little b. and girls 75:43

as flies to wanton b. 329:85

b. and girls come out to play 231:25

b. will be b. 257:63

b. will be men 257:64

by office b. for office b. 293:72

Christian b. I can scarcely ... make
22:55

claret is the liquor for b. 177:31

Boys (*continued*)

guns with b., are never valued
114:82

mealy b., and beef-faced b. 120:57

men that were b. when I was 32:7

only know two sorts of b. 120:57

till the b. come home 137:94

we are the b. that fear no noise
151:86

what are little b. made of? 240:85

when the b. came out to play
232:31

young b. ... are level now with men
299:66

Brace: let us ... b. ourselves to our
duties 101:95

Braces: damn b. Bless relaxes 69:61

Bradshaw: the vocabulary of B. is
nervous 125:28

Brain: b. [begins] to think again 71:87

b. of ... man is not able 316:98

dull b. perplexes and retards 184:26

gladness ... thy b. must know
370:51

glean'd my teeming b. 186:48

got to leave my b. outside 144:88

I feared it might injure the b. 90:48

let my b. lie also 74:33

like madness in the b. 106:67

overset the b. or break the heart
411:88

shallow draughts intoxicate the b.
249:94

written troubles of the b. 336:72

Brains: fluffy, with no b. at all 161:7

he exercises of his b. 144:85

I mix them with my b., sir 242:97

mob has ... heads but no b. 272:62

when the b. were out the man would
die 335:55

Brand plucked out of the fire 51:95

Brandy: some are fou o' b. 80:10

to be a hero must drink b. 177:31

Brass: as if this flesh ... were b. impregnable 350:54

asked ... where he carried his b.
33:12

men's evil manners live in b. 323:86

Brave: b. that are no more 113:64

b. who sink to rest 107:89

fortune favours the b. 389:6

is it not passing b. to be a king?
205:75

none but the b. deserves the fair
127:51

O b. new world! 369:39

sons of the prophet were b. 18:7

toll for the b. 113:64

Bravery: all her b. on and tackle trim 222:18

Bravest: the b. by far in the ranks 18:7

Bray: I will be the Vicar of B. 17:92

Brazil, where the nuts come from 389:16

Breach: more honoured in the b. 307:59

once more unto the b. 319:45

Bread: a Loaf of B. beneath the Bough 135:67

bitter b. of banishment 349:48

b. and cheese and kisses 254:85

b. eaten in secret is pleasant 45:60

b. is buttered on both sides 257:65

b. of heaven, feed me 407:40

b. which the Lord hath given 37:80

b. with one fish-ball 192:37

but one halfpenny-worth of b. 314:70

cast thy b. upon the waters 47:9

did eat b. to the full 36:79

God! that b. shd. be so dear 166:65

in the sweat ... shalt thou eat b. 35:38

looked to government for b. 78:83

man doth not live by b. only 38:7

neither yet b. to the wise 47:8

nor his seed begging b. 42:3

not live by b. alone 51:7

some gave them white b. 234:47

thine enemy ... give him b. 45:81

this day our daily b. 52:18

to eat the b. of sorrows 44:42

trees were b. and cheese 15:65

which side one's b. is buttered 268:42

white b. and butter 235:52

Break: never doubted clouds wd. b. 73:16

Breakages Ltd., the biggest ... corporation 364:61

Breakfast: b., dinner, lunch and tea 31:92

b., supper, dinner, luncheon 75:41

hope is a good b. 26:38

kills me ... Scots at a b. 314:62

where shall we our b. take? 12:39

Breaking: sleep that knows not b. 295:97

Breast: bold spirit in a loyal b. 347:30

charms to soothe a savage b. 108:5

earth's sweet flowing b. 188–9:81

make a clean b. 258:9

nunnery of thy chaste b. 199:16

one who ... marched b. forward 73:16

panic's in thy b. [breastie] 80:16

Breast (continued)

safe ... on Abraham's b. 13:48

Tamer of the human b. 155:43

that with dauntless b. 155:38

what his b. forges ... tongue must vent 303–4:17

Breasts: cowardice in noble b. 347:32

Breath: allowing him a b., a little scene 350:54

although thy b. be rude 302:91

and thou no b. at all? 331:6

b. of worldly men 349:50

draw thy b. in pain 312:38

fly away, b. 359:88

not flatter'd its rank b. 83:61

such dulcet and harmonious b. 341:44

such is the b. of kings 348:34

summer's ripening b. 354:3

take into the air my quiet b. 184:29

thou b. of Autumn's being 369:35

Breathe: so long as men can b. or eyes can see 362:34

Breathes: b. ... man, with soul so dead 295:5

b. upon a bank of violets 358–9:75

Breathing: rifle all the b. spring 107:87

Breathless: a nun b. with adoration 412:92

hanging b. on thy fate! 197:92

Bred: where is fancy b. 339:14

Breeches: to wear the b. 282:18

Breed: b. of their horses and dogs 245:39

fear'd by their b. 348–9:41

this happy b. of men, this little world 348:41

Breeding lilacs out of the dead land 131:10

Breeze: fair b. blew, the white foam flew 105:48

fluttering and dancing in the b. 410:67

the battle and the b. 88:21

Breezes: little b. dusk and shiver 387:76

Brent: yr. bonnie brow was b. 80:11

Brethren: b. to dwell together in unity 44:43

least of these my b. 53:48

Brevis esse laboro, obscurus fio 166:69

Brevity is the soul of wit 307:72

Brewage: no pullet-sperm in my b. 341:33

Brewery: O take me to a b. 17:88

Bribe: doing nothing for a b. 304:23

too poor for a b. 156:46

Bribes: how many b. he had taken 34:20

Brick: straw to make b. 36:72

Bricks: a cat on hot b. 258:92

Bridal: the b. of the earth and sky 161:14

Bride: b. hath paced into the hall 104:45

happy bridesmaid ... happy b. 384:38

Jerusalem ... as a b. adorned 61:33

sate like a blooming Eastern b. 127:50

still unravish'd b. of quietness 183:16

were I thy b.! 149:48

Bridegroom: fresh as a b. 313:51

Bridesmaid: happy b., happy bride 384:38

Bridge: don't cross the b. till you get to it 259:37

keep the b. with me 201:37

on the b. at midnight 18:4

on the B. of Sighs 84:62

what need the b. much broader? 342:61

women, and champagne and b. 31:95

Brief: b. life is here our portion 229:1

b., my lord, as woman's love 310:8

dress'd in a little b. authority 337:87

I struggle to be b., and become obscure 166:69

out, out, b. candle! 336:76

Brigands demand ... women require 83:51

Bright: all things b. and beautiful 10:17

best of dark and b. 86:96

goddess, excellently b. 178–9:50

look, the land is b. 104:34

moon be still as b. 86:97

Sun came up ... and he shone b. 104:44

young lady named B. 76:52

Brightness: all her original b. 217:41

b. falls from the air 229:99

Brighton: yes, the B. line 405:12

Brilliance: degree of b. ... left to fighter's honour 160:92

Brillig: 'twas b. and the slithy toves 91:69

Bring: b. back my Bonnie to me 17:94

b. me flesh and b. me wine 229:4

b. me my bow ... arrows ... spear 67:38

b. the good old bugle, boys 416:44

Bringer: first b. of unwelcome news 316:97

Broche: qu'ils mangent de la b. 204:61

Britain: B. a fit country for heroes 197:90

B. is a world by itself 304:21

B. won her proudest bays 144:89

government ... framed, like that of B. 391:38

hath B. all the sun? 304:25

that B. would fight on alone 101:1

when B. first, at Heaven's command 391:33

British: B. Bourgeoisie ... if it is ill 373:91

B. Empire ... last for a thousand years 101:95

dirty B. coaster 207:13

I keep my books at the B. Museum 82:42

liquidation of the B. Empire 101:3

maxim of the B. ... 'Business as usual' 100:89

no spectacle so ridiculous as the B. 202:46

smell the blood of a B. man 329:82

tow, ... row, row, for the B. Grenadier 18:6

Britons: B. never will be slaves 391:33

B. were only natives 297:28

Broad: she is the B.: I am the High 378:54

Broken: a b. spirit: a b. ... contrite heart 42:9

laws were made to be b. 230:19

Broken-hearted: half b. to sever for years 86:99

we had ne'er been b. 79:97

Brood of Folly without father bred 213:82

Brook: a willow grows aslant the b. 311:30

hear the little b. a-gurgling 148:34

where the b. is deep 321:65

Brooks: books in the running b. 300:75

golden sands, and crystal b. 123:4

Broom: new b. sweeps clean 273:91

Broth: gave them ... b. without any bread 239:76

too many cooks spoil the b. 280:50

Brother: am I my b.'s keeper? 35:41

be my b.; he be ne'er so vile 320:59

Big B. is watching you 242:1

Death and his b. Sleep 368:24

down with Big B. 242:3

sworn b. ... to grim Necessity 351:60

Brother (*continued*)
two sisters embrace like one b. 287:11
Brotherhood: crown thy good with b. 29:67
Brotherly: let b. love continue 60:2
Brothers: all men will be b. 294:85
and all the b. too 360:90
two b. and their murder'd man 182:5
Brow: b. like to a title-leaf 316:96
on Ida's shady b. 68:54
yr. bonnie b. was brent 80:11
Brown: baked me too b. 91:64
Bruce: Scots whom B. has ... led 81:22
Brüder: alle Menschen werden B. 294:85
Bruise: parmaceti for an inward b. 313:52
Brunck: most learned professor, B. 252:41
Brush: all tarred with the same b. 279:10
Brute beasts that have no understanding 64:4
Brute: et tu, B.? 87:9, 324:3
Brutish: life ... nasty, b., and short 163:34
Brutus: for B. is an honourable man 325:13
the fault, dear B. 323–4:93
you too, B.? 87:9
Bubble: fire burn and cauldron b. 335:58
like the b. on the fountain 295:98
seeking the b. reputation 301:90
Bubbles: beaded b. winking 184:24
Bucket: nations are as a drop of a b. 48:43
Buckingham: Palace, changing the guard at B. 211:54
high-reaching B. grows circumspect 352:76
Buckram: rogues in b. 314:65
Bud: concealment, like a worm i' th' b. 360:89
this b. of love 354:3
Buds: gather the flowers, but spare the b. 207:5
shake the darling b. of May 362:32
Buffets: blows and b. of the world 334:49
Buffoon: a private b. 149:49
statesman and b. 126:43
Bugle: blow, b.; answer, echoes 388:98
bring the good old b., boys 416:44

Bugles: blow out, you b., over the rich Dead 71:88
Build: easier to pull down than to b. 275:69
except the Lord b. the house 44:41
on this rock ... b. my church 53:34
Building: don't clap too hard ... very old b. 242:6
Built: houses are b. to live in 26:28
Rome was not b. in a day 276:2
Bulbul: Abdul the B. Amir 18:7
Bull: b. in a china shop 257:66
in time the savage b. 191:22
red rag to a b. 275:81
roar like a b. 276:97
take the b. by the horns 279:98
Bull and Bush: down at the old B. 392:46
Bullet: ballot is stronger than the b. 196:75
every b. has its billet 407:37
Bullfighting is the only art in which 160:92
Bullocks: good yoke of b. at Stamford 317:17
he ... whose talk is of b. 62:58
Bulls the cow must keep the calf 257:67
Bully: I love the lovely b. 320:51
Bumbast out a blank verse 156:49
Bunbury: a ... permanent invalid called B. 405:6
Bunk: Gert's poems are b. 14:57
history is b. 137:91
Buns: hot cross b.! 233:35
Burden: take up the White Man's B. 190:12
Burdens: bear ye one another's b. 58:69
heavy b. at his narrow gate 318–9:39
Burglar: enterprising b.'s not a-burgling 148:34
Burglary: flat b. as ever was committed 344:83
Buried: half-b. in the snow was found 198:94
the old Adam ... so b. 64:94
Burlington: I'm B. Bertie 158:69
Burn: better to marry than to b. 57:50
b. ... candle at both ends 257:70
b. one's boats 257:69
b. the midnight oil 257:71
hearts are dry ... b. to the socket 409:64
I'll b. my books! 204:66
old age shd. b. and rave 390:18
violent fires soon b. out 348:40
we all know that books b. 289:33

Candle-light (*continued*)
  choose ... woman nor linen by c.
    258:3
Candles: night's c. are burnt out
    354:14
Candy is dandy 229:95
Cankered: heart ... grief hath c. 87:12
Cankers: the c. of a calm world 315:83
Cannon: even in the c.'s mouth 301:90
Cannon-ball: a c. took off his legs
    165:57
Cannons: where the thundering c. roar
    151:86
Canoe: paddle his own c. 206:88
Canon: his c. 'gainst self-slaughter
    305:42
Canopy: rich embroider'd c. to kings
    322:71
Canossa: nach C. gehen wir nicht 65:22
  We will not go to C. 65:22
Cant: apple press'd with specious c.
    165:63
  clear yr. mind of c. 177:34
Cantons: loyal c. of contemned love
    359:80
Cap: if the c. fits 257:83
  put on one's thinking c. 275:68
  riband in the c. of youth 311:29
  stuck a feather in his c. 241:90
Capability: Negative C. 186:52
Capon: belly with good c. lined 301:90
Captain! a right good c., too! 147:21
  a train-band c. eke was he 112:54
  C., art tha sleepin' there below?
    230:11
  c.'s hand on his shoulder smote
    230:14
  in the c.'s but a choleric word
    337:88
  O C.! my C.! 403:81
  the c. of my soul 160:95
Captains: the c. and the kings depart
    190:9
Captive: weak minds led c. 221:5
Caravan: put up yr. c. just for one day
    163:37
Cardinal: C. Lord Archbishop of
    Rheims 28:53
  jackdaw sat on the C.'s chair 28:52
Cards: an old age of c. 251:24
  can pack the c. ... cannot play
    25:15
  played at c. for kisses 201:29
Care: begone, dull c. 16:75
  c. killed a cat 257:84
  I c. for nobody 65:17
  I c. not whether a man is good 67:37
  nor for itself hath any c. 67:43

Care (*continued*)
  past my help is past my c. 29:72
  past redress ... with me past c.
    349:47
  polish'd perturbation! golden c.!
    317:27
  ravell'd sleave of c. 334:42
  sae weary, fu' o' c. 81:26
  so shaken ... wan with c. 312:42
  sport that wrinkled C. derides
    214:94
  this life if full of c. 117:11
  what boots it with incessant c.
    215:11
  what c. I for whom she be? 408:50
Career: which might damage his c.
    28:64
Careful: be very c. o' vidders ... Sammy
    121:67
Careless: first fine c. rapture 74:23
  sitting c. on a granary floor 181:80
  so c. of the single life 386:62
Cares: if no one c. for me 65:17
  light c. speak, great ones are dumb
    269:82
Carew: the grave of Mad C. 159:76
Cargo of ivory and apes 207:12
Caricature of a face 146:11
Carlyle, Tennyson, Browning 285:85
Carouse: for ... marriage I did make c.
    135:76
Carpe diem, quam minimum ... postero
    166:74
Carpenter: Walrus and the C.
    92–3:78–82
Carriage: a very small second-class c.
    144:92
  I can't afford a c. 116:99
  the c. held but just ourselves 122:84
Cart: creak of a lumbering c. 417:55
  put the c. before the horse 257:86
Carthago: delenda est C. 94:2
Carve: c. on every tree the fair ... she
    302:92
  c. out dials quaintly 321:70
  let's c. him as a dish 324:99
  must c. in Latin or in Greek 398:18
Carved: we c. not a line 408:53
Casca: the envious C. 325:18
Case: c. is still before the courts 166:70
  nothing to do with the c. 146:11
  there to attend to the c. 144:84
Cased: yr. hare when it is c. 149:55
Casement ope at night 185:33
Casements: magic c. opening on the
    foam 184:30
Cases: circumstances alter c. 258:6
  hard c. make bad law 266:67

Cash: he takes yr c., but where's the book? 100:84

Cashmere: tales of fair C. 407:41

Casques: within this wooden O the very c. 318:37

Cassio: if C. do remain 346:16
not C. kill'd! 346:20

Cassius: for ever ... farewell, C.! 326:28
yond C. has a lean and hungry look 324:94

Cast: I backward c. my e'e 80:19
pale c. of thought 309:95
the die is c. 87:7

Castle: a c. called Doubting C. 77:62
a man's house is his c. 104:39
Englishman's house is his c. 261:22
I'm the king of the c. 233:41
splendour falls on c. walls 388:97
the rich man in his c. 10:18

Castlereagh: a mask like C. 368:30

Castles: build c. in Spain 257:88
c. in the air 257:89

Cat: a c. and a lie 394:70
care killed a c. 257:84
c. has nine lives 257:90
c. is away the mice will play 283:28
c. out of the bag 269:72
c. will mew, and dog will have his day 312:34
fog comes on little c. feet 293:77
hanging of his c. 70:74
he bought a crooked c. 239:74
like a c. on hot bricks 258:92
more ways of killing a c. 189:91
part to tear a c. in 341:40
room to swing a c. 276:3
runcible c. with crimson whiskers 195:63
the c. and the fiddle 232:33
what c.'s averse to fish? 154:24
when I play with my c. 225:55
which way the c. jumps 257:91

Cataclysm: out of their c. but one poor Noah 169:4

Catalogue: in the c. ye go for men 334:48

Cataracts: you c. and hurricanoes, spout 328:71

Catastrophe: I'll tickle yr. c. 316:5

Catch: c. a falling star 124:11
c. a nigger by his toe 232:29
c. him once upon the hip 338:3
perdition c. my soul 345:5
set a thief to c. a thief 280:22

Catechism: and so ends my c. 315:88

Categorical: in order c. 147:31

Caterpillars of the commonwealth 349:46

Cats: killed the c. and bit the babies 75:37

Caucasus: thinking on the frosty C. 348:37

Caught: maidens ... are ever c. by glare 83:56
one c. a Muffin, the other c. a Mouse 195:64

Cauldron: fire burn and c. bubble 335:58

Causas: felix qui potuit rerum cognoscere c. 397:5

Cause: an effect whose c. is God 114:74
beauty of the good old c. 412:2
blind in their own c. 256:46
great c. of cheering us all up 33:10
it is the c., it is the c., my soul 346:18
jealous for the c. 346:11
know c., or just impediment 64:3
report me and my c. aright 312:37
ring out a slowly dying c. 386:69
'what great c. ... identified with?' 33:10

Causes: able to learn the c. of things 397:5
c. why and wherefore in all 321:60
home of lost c. ... beliefs 21:49
of all the c. which conspire 249:93

Cavaliero: he was a perfect c. 83:54

Cave canem 246:49

Cave: her vacant interlunar c. 221:14
Idols of the C. 27:41
in Stygian c. forlorn 213–14:91
out of the misty eastern c. 368:32

Cave (of) Adullam: escaped to the C. 39:45
retired into ... his political C. 71:82

Caveat emptor 258:93

Cavern: happy field or mossy c. 183:14
in a c. in a canyon 225:59

Caverns measureless to man 106:71

Caves: dark unfathom'd c. of ocean 155:37
pleasure-dome with c. of ice 107:75

Caviare to the general 308:85

Cavity: filling his last c. 13:49

Cease: I will not c. from mental fight 67:38
poor shall never c. 38:11
seedtime ... harvest ... shall not c. 35:48
warm days will never c. 181:79

Ceases: love c. to be a pleasure 30:85

Ceiling: stood up and spat on the c. 14:56

Celebrate: I c. myself 403:82

Celerity ... admir'd ... by the negligent 299:59
Celia: come, my C. 179:61
Celibacy has no pleasures 173:66
Celibate: he still is largely c. 226:70
Cells: hermits ... contented with their c. 411:89
  o'er-brimm'd their clammy c. 181:79
Censure: every trade save c. 85:90
  little to fear ... from c. ... praise 172:43
  no man can ... c. or condemn 72:4
  take each man's c. 306:56
Centre: mon c. cède, ma droite recule 136:87
Centuries: forty c. look down upon you 228:83
  praises ... all c. but this 145:1
Cerberus: of C. and ... Midnight born 213:91
Cerebration: deep well of unconscious c. 170:22
Ceremony: no c. that to great ones longs 337:84
Certain: death ... is c. to all 317:17
  however c. our expectation 132:18
  I am c. of nothing but 186:50
  nothing is c. but death and taxes 139:16
  nothing is c. but uncertainty 273:7
  of a 'c. age' ... certainly aged 85:81
  one thing is c. ... Rest is Lies 135:71
Certainly miserable, but not c. devout 173:65
Certainties: if a man will begin with c. 26:37
  when hot for c. 209:34
Certainty: the c. of power 117:15
Cesspool: London, that great c. 125:27
Chaffinch sings on the orchard bough 74:21
Chain: flesh to feel the c. 71:87
Chains: c. that tie ... soul of harmony 215:5
  nothing to lose but their c. 207:9
  shake yr. c. to earth 368:31
Chair: give Dayrolles a c. 98:65
  is the c. empty? 352:82
  little mouse under her c. 237:64
  seated in thy silver c. 178–9:50
  tavern c. ... throne of ... felicity 178:44
Chaise: all in a c. and pair 113:55
Chalk and cheese 258:94
Cham: that great C. of literature 375:18

Chamber: and in my lady's c. 232:32
Chambers: in the c. of the East 68:54
  the c. of the sun 68:54
Champagne: goes with women, and c., and bridge 31:95
  I'm ... not a c. teetotaller 365:68
Champions: four c. ... strive ... for mastery 218:57
Chance: all c., direction ... thou canst not see 250:12
  an hour before this c. 334:46
  eye to the main c. 271:26
  grab a c. 286:99
  happiness in marriage ... matter of c. 23:76
  I am ... [honest] sometimes by c. 362:22
  in nativity, c. or death 341:34
  power which erring men call C. 213:78
  time and c. happeneth to ... all 47:8
  under the bludgeonings of c. 160:94
Chancellor: a rather susceptible C.! 144:82
Chancery: hell and C. are always open 266:83
Chances: a set of curious c. 145:98
  against ill c. men are ... merry 317:22
Change: c. and decay in all around 201:32
  c. we think we see in life 139:22
  doth suffer a sea-c. 355:35
  heavy c., now thou art gone 215:10
  I c. but I cannot die 368:23
  plus ça c., plus ... même chose 180:72
  the more things c. the more ... the same 180:72
  the wind of c. is blowing 203:53
  what a c. of flesh is here 29:71
Changes: monthly c. in her circled orb 354:2
Changest: O thou who c. not 201:32
Channel: butting through the C. 207:13
  dream you are crossing the C. 144:92
Chant: how can ye c., ye little birds? 81:26
Chaos: reign of C. and old Night 217:40
  when first God dawned on C. 367:11
  when I love thee not C. is come 345:5
Chapel: Devil ... builds a c. there 118:18

Chapels had been churches ... cottages ... palaces 338:2
Chaps: biography is about c. 33:15
Character: a c. dead at every word 372:76
  education ... formation of c. 376:36
  I leave my c. behind me 372:77
  precepts ... look thou c. 306:55
  she gave me a good c. 91:67
Characteristics: vanity and love; ... their universal c. 98:62
Charge: c. Chester, c.! 296:15
  take thou in c this day 201:40
Charged with the grandeur of God 166:67
Charing-Cross: full tide of ... existence is at C. 176:9
Chariot: bring me my c. of fire 67:38
  swing low, sweet c. 18:8
  Time's winged c. hurrying near 206:94
Charioted: not c. by Bacchus 183:16
Chariots: some trust in c., and some in horses 42:90
Charity: c. begins at home 258:96
  c. shall cover ... sins 60:11
  cold as c. 258:17
  doings without c. are nothing worth 64:87
  greatest of these is c. 57:55
  hand open as day for melting c. 317:25
  I do not give ... c., ... I give myself 403:85
  in c. there is no excess 25:4
  living need c. more than the dead 20:29
  with c. for all 196:81
Charity-boy: as the c. said 121:70
Charlatan: defamed by every c. 387:72
Charles the First: King C. walked and talked 15:66
Charm: despair thy c. 336:78
  what c. can soothe her melancholy? 152:2
Charmed: I bear a c. life, which must not yield 336:78
Charmer: were t'other dear c. away 142:54
Charming: c. to totter into vogue 398:22
  how c. is divine Philosophy! 213:77
  people are either c. or tedious 405:18
  the rabbit has a c. face 15:70
Charms: c. strike the sight, but merit wins 252:39
  do not all c. fly? 183:12
  music has c. to soothe 108:5

Charms (continued)
  solitude! Where are the c.? 114:78
Charter: this was the c. of the land 391:33
Charybdis: between Scylla and C. 256:33
Chase: the c., the sport of kings 375:23
Chasing the wild deer 81:20
Chassis: whole worl's in a state of c. 241:94
Chaste: be thou as c. as ice 310:98
Chasteneth: c. his son, so the Lord ... c. thee 38:8
  loveth him c. him betimes 45:67
  whom the Lord loveth he c. 60:1
Chastisement: fear no heavier c. from me 367:15
Chastity: c. and continence, but not yet 22:63
  clothed on with c. 385:49
  'tis c., my brother, c. 212:76
Chatterton, the marvellous Boy 413:12
Chaucer: Dan C., well of English undefiled 377:44
Che sera sera 258:97
Che sera sera: what doctrine ... C.? 204:62
Cheap: flesh and blood so c. 166:65
  man's life is c. as beast's 328:67
Cheating: Winning Games Without Actually C. 252:43
Check: alas! I wd. not c. 192:35
  O dreadful is the c. 71:87
Checked: I c. him while he spoke 192:35
Cheek: bring a blush to the c. 120:59
  feed on her damask c. 360:89
  leans her c. upon her hand 353:98
  pale grew thy c. and cold 86:99
  she hangs upon the c. of night 353:94
  smite thee on thy right c. 52:13
  take one blow and turn the other c. 164:45
  that I might touch that c.! 353:98
  there's language in her eye, her c. 358:73
  wither'd c. and tresses grey 295:99
Cheeks: beauty's ensign ... crimson ... in thy c. 354:17
  blow winds, and crack yr. c. 328:71
  make pale my c. with care 408:49
  rosy c. and flaxen curls 75:43
  stain my man's c. 328:68
Cheer: Christmas ... brings good c. 258:5
  cd. scarce forbear to c. 202:41
  cups that c. 114:73

Cheer (*continued*)
  so I piped with merry c. 68:49
  the fewer the better c. 272:70
  welcome is the best c. 282:20
Cheerful: God loveth a c. giver 58:63
  merry heart ... c. countenance 45:70
  more c. ... than to be forty 164:52
Cheerfully: how c. he seems to grin
  89–90:45
Cheerfulness was always breaking in
  129:82
Cheering: great cause of c. us all up
  33:10
Cheerio my deario 205:83
Cheers: three c. and one cheer more
  147:24
Cheese: chalk and c. 258:94
  dreamed of c.—toasted mostly
  379:75
  hard c. 266:68
  hellish dark, and smells of c.!
  380:90
Cheltenham: killed by drinking C.
  waters 12:41
Chemist (Chymist): was c., fiddler,
  statesman 126:43
Chequer-board: a c. of Nights and
  Days 135:78
Cherish: c. those hearts that hate thee
  323:83
  to love and to c., till death 64:7
  to love, c., and to obey 64:8
Cherries: c. ... which none may buy
  88:25
  Kent ... apples, c., hops 120:61
Cherry: c. ripe, ripe ... I cry 162:15
  make two bites of a c. 281:73
  ruddier than the c. 141:51
  there's the land, or c.-isle 162:15
  till 'C. Ripe' themselves do cry
  88:25
Cherubins: quiring to the young-ey'd c.
  340:22
Chess: life's too short for c. 86:3
Chest: a c. of drawers by day 150:70
  on the dead man's c. 379:74
  ten-times barred-up c. 347:30
Chester: charge, C., charge! 296:15
Chesterton: dared attack my C. 32:1
Chestnut-tree: under a spreading c.
  199:6
Chevalier: the young C. 227:80
Chewing little bits of string 31:90
Chicken: Some c.! Some neck 101:1
Chickens: count one's c. before ...
  hatched 259:30
  curses are like c. ... home to roost
  259:44

Chides: at fifty c. his infamous delay
  418:63
Chief: brilliant c., irregularly great
  76:53
Child: a little c. shall lead them 48:37
  an it had been any christom c.
  319:43
  at break of day the solitary c. 411:85
  C. among his new-born blisses
  411:79
  C.! do not throw this book 31:88
  C. Rowland to the dark tower came
  329:82
  c. says 'I don't believe in fairies'
  28:60
  c. whose father goes to the devil
  266:65
  divide the ... c. in two 40:50
  even a c. is known by his doings
  45:76
  get with c. a mandrake root 124:11
  has devoured the infant c. 167:78
  Heaven-born C. all meanly wrapt
  215:20
  Jesus Christ her little c. 10:19
  Monday's c. is fair of face 235:56
  more hideous ... in a c. 328:57
  on a cloud I saw a c. 68:48
  the cry of a c. by the roadway
  417:55
  the old Adam in this c. 64:94
  this c. I to myself will take 415:30
  to have a thankless c. 328:58
  train up a c. in the way 45:80
  unto us a c. is born 48:36
  wise c. ... knows its own father
  283:39
  wise father ... knows his own c.
  339:8
  with that the wretched c. expires
  31:92
Childhood: companions, in my days of
  c. 192:32
  my careless c. stray'd 154:27
  the c. shows the man 221:6
  what my lousy c. was like 292:71
Childishness: second c. and mere
  oblivion 301–2:90
Children: artist will let ... his c. go
  barefoot 365:80
  as c. fear ... the dark 24:86
  become as little c. 53:37
  c., dear, was it yesterday? 20:33
  c. of one family fall out 399:37
  c. of this world ... wiser ... c. of light
  55:84
  c. shd. be seen and not heard 258:98
  c.'s teeth are set on edge 49:58

Children (*continued*)
c. sweeten labours 24:95
c. ... with nothing to ignore 228:93
c. yet unborn shall feel this day
    351:59
come, c. of our native land 291:54
come, dear c., let us away 20:32
do you hear the c. weeping? 73:11
familiarity breeds ... c. 394:67
father pitieth his c. 43:22
had borne him three c. 169:7
happy ... that is happy in his c.
    266:63
he that hath wife and c. 24:96
men ... c. of a larger growth 127:56
more careful of ... dogs than ... c.
    245:39
Rachel weepeth for her c. 51:3
she had so many c. 239:76
stars ... are my c. 187:63
tale which holdeth c. from play
    373:86
voices of c. are heard on the green
    68:52
your c. all gone 234:46
Chill: Ah, bitter c. it was 181:89
Chills the finger not a bit 229:96
Chilly: although the room grows c.
    153:11
Chime: higher than the sphery c.
    213:81
merry village c. 148:34
Chimes: heard the c. at midnight
    317:18
Chimney: old men from the c. corner
    373:86
Chimney-sweepers: as c., come to dust
    304–5:29
Chin: his c. new reap'd 313:51
his c. upon an orient wave 216:22
China: bull in a c. shop 257:66
C.'s gayest art had dyed 154:23
mistress of herself, though C. fall
    251:25
China orange: Lombard Street to a C.
    270:97
Chinamen: birds in ... nests agree with
    C. 32:99
Chink: aid ... from a c. in the floor
    383:26
Chip: a c. of the old block 258:99
not merely a c. of the old block
    78:76
Chirche-dore: housbondes at c. 97:39
Chivalry: age of c. is gone 78:73
her Beauty and her C. 83:59
Chloe: but C. is my real flame 253:51
Chocolate cream soldier 364:63

Choice: Hobson's c. 267:89
pays yr. money ... takes yr. c.
    284:74
small c. in rotten apples 355:21
Choir: sweet singing in the c. 16–17:87
Choler: purge ... c. without letting
    blood 347:29
Choleric: in the captain's but a c.
    word 337:88
Choose: c. life, that ... thy seed may
    live 38:13
to c. love by another's eyes 341:37
to c. time is to save time 26:18
where to c. their place of rest
    221:3
Choosing: subject for ... song ... long c.
    220:90
Chop and change 258:4
Chopper: cheap and chippy c. 145:3
here comes a c. 236:61
Chops and Tomata sauce ... Pickwick
    121:74
Chortled in his joy 92:71
Chorus: a c.-ending from Euripides
    73:17
Chosen: many are called, but few are c.
    53:42
Choughs: the crows and c. that wing
    329:88
Christ: beseech you, in the bowels of
    C. 115:88
C. is thy strength ... thy right
    225:53
so Judas did to C. 350:57
the C. that is to be 387:71
we ... are one body in C. 57:36
Christ Church: I am the Dean of C.,
    Sir 378:54
Christendom: the wisest fool in C.
    160:98
Christian: a C. faithful man 351:71
assume the honourable style of C.
    72:99
good C. men, rejoice 229:2
hate him for he is a C. 338:3
if possible ... C. men for C. boys
    22:55
in what peace a C. can die 10:12
mirror of all C. kings 319:40
persuadest me to be a C. 56:28
warmed and cooled ... as a C. is
    339:13
words ... no C. ear can endure
    321:68
Christians: C. awake, salute 83:52
profess and call themselves C. 63:82
Christmas: at C. I no more desire a
    rose 331:11

Christmas (*continued*)
C. comes but once a year 258:5, 393:58
C. Day in the Workhouse 373:89
eating a C. pie 235:50
on C. Day in the morning 15:74, 233–4:42
the first day of C. 238:72
the twelfth day of C. 238:73
Christopher Robin: C. is saying his prayers 211:61
C. went down with Alice 211:54
Chronicle: in the c. of wasted time 363:45
suckle fools and c. small beer 345:98
Chronicles: abstract and brief c. 308:87
look in the c.: we came in 355:19
Church: if at the C. ... give us some ale 68:45
new and great period in His C. 224:42
some to c. repair, ... for ... the music 249:98
the C.'s one foundation 380:83
the C.'s Restoration in 1883 34:24
wish from the C. to stray 68:45
Churches: chapels had been c. 338:2
let yr. women keep silence in the c. 57:56
Churchman: become a c. better than ambition 323:88
Church-yard: if two are in the c. laid 416:41
Churchyards: when c. yawn 310:13
Cigar: a good cigar is a smoke 190:94
Circle: weave a c. round him thrice 107:76
wheel is come full c. 330:2
Circumcised: took by th' throat the c. dog 346–7:22
Circumlocution office was beforehand 120:47
Circumspect: high-reaching Buckingham grows c. 352:76
Circumstances alter cases 258:6
Cities: sung women in three c. 252:48
towered c. please us then 214:1
Citizen: c. of no mean city 56:23
first requisite of a good c. 289:36
I am a c. ... of the world 375:20
John Gilpin was a c. 112:54
Citizens: civil c. kneading up the honey 318–19:39
healthy c. are the greatest asset 101:6
my fellow c. of the world 188:75

Citizens (*continued*)
sing, all ye c. of heaven 241:92
you fat and greasy c. 300:76
City: a populous and a smoky c. 369:41
c. now doth like a garment wear 412:96
c. with her dreaming spires 21:46
her in the dissolute c. 411:87
in Dublin's fair c. 17:89
it is the men who make a c. 272:54
long in c. pent 186:47
once in royal David's c. 10:19
one ... in populous c. pent 220:93
rose-red c. half as old as time 77:70
the first c. Cain [made] 112:46
without a c. wall 11:20
City Road: up and down the C. 203:60
Civet: an ounce of c. 329:91
Civil: over violent or over c. 126:44
too c. by half 372:73
Civilises: the sex whose presence c. ours 112:53
Civility: C. costs nothing 258:7
I see a wild c. 162:17
Civilized: woman will be the last thing c. 209:35
Civis Romanus sum 102:20
Clad: she that has [chastity] is c. in ... steel 212:76
Clap: don't c. too hard 242:6
if you believe, c. yr. hands 28:62
Claret is the liquor for boys 177:31
Class: not [happiness] of any one c. 247:62
Classes: the masses against the c. 149:53
the three great c. ... our society 21:48
to prove the upper c. 111:39
Classic: a c. ... nobody wants to read 394:73
Clay: as the c. is in the potter's hand 49:57
cabin ... of c. and wattles made 417:52
men ... gilded loam or painted c. 347:30
tenement of c. 126:39
turf that wraps their c. 107–8:90
Clean: as c. as a whistle 258:8
halo? ... one more thing to keep c. 140:32
make a c. breast 258:9
Cleaning: yesterday, we had daily c. 287:3
Cleanliness is next to godliness 258:10

Cleanly: thus so c. I myself can free
125:34
Cleanse the stuff'd bosom 336:72
Cleared: if this were only c. away
92:78
Clearing-house of the world 95:13
Clementine: oh my darling C. 225:59
Cleopatra: had C.'s nose been shorter
244:27
Cléopâtre: le nez de C. 244:27
Clergy: as the c. are, or are not 23:69
Clergymen: three sexes—men, women,
and c. 375:9
Clerk: am I both priest and c.? 350:57
c. foredoom'd his father's soul to
cross 248:78
Clerks: fountains like Government C.?
285:78
Clever: c. of the turtle 229:98
c. so rude to the good 409:59
if all the good people were c.
409:59
it's c., but is it art? 190:96
let who will be c. 189:86
our c. young poets 107:82
too c. by half 280:49
Cleverness: height of c. ... to conceal
one's c. 288:18
Climate: common where the c.'s sultry
84:66
Climax: that c. of all human ills
84:76
Climb: teach you how to c. 213:81
Climbing after knowledge infinite
205:76
Climbs: sun c. slow, how slowly
104:34
Clive: what I like about C. 33:17
Cloak: religion is ... the worst c.
276:84
Cloakroom: the c. at Victoria Station
405:12
Clock: mouse ran up the c. 232:34
stand the church c. at ten to three?
71:91
Clocks: morning c. will ring 167:80
the c. were striking thirteen 242:99
Clod: warm motion to become a
kneaded c. 337:90
Cloke: Knyf under the c. 97:44
Close: breathless hush in the C. tonight
230:13
c. yr. eyes with holy dread 107:76
fiend doth c. behind him tread
106:60
no barber shaves so c. but 255:91
now ... c. the shutters fast 114:73
porpoise c. behind us 91:62

Close (*continued*)
the setting sun, and music at the c.
348:39
Closet: one by one back in the c. lays
135:78
Cloth: cut yr. coat according to ... c.
259:49
on a c. untrue 146:8
Clothe: long fields ... that c. the wold
387:75
Clothed: she rode ... c. on with chastity
385:49
Clothes: fine c., rich furniture 31:87
hanging out the c. 238:70
kindles in c. a wantonness 162:16
out of ... wet c. and into a dry
Martini 409:57
that liquefaction of her c. 162:23
through tatter'd c. small vices
330:92
walked away with their c. 122:89
Clothing: false prophets ... in sheep's
c. 52:27
Cloud: a fiend hid in a c. 67–8:44
but c. instead ... surrounds me
218:59
every c. has a silver lining 258:12
I wandered lonely as a c. 410:67
on a c. I saw a child 68:48
set my bow in the c. 35:50
there ariseth a little c. 40:57
through the dark c. shining 137:94
to be under a c. 258:13
turn the dark c. inside out 137:94
Clouds: never doubted c. wd. break
73:16
O c., unfold! 67:38
sun breaks through the darkest c.
355:25
trailing c. of glory do we come
410:77
Clout: cast ne'er a c. 257:87
Clown: heard ... by emperor and c.
184:30
Cloy the hungry edge of appetite
348:37
Clutching the inviolable shade
21:43
Coals: carry c. to Newcastle 257:85
haul over the c. 266:73
heap c. of fire 45:81
Coarse: one of them is rather c. 15:64
Coast: the c. is clear 258:14
Coaster: dirty British c. 207:13
Coat: a riband to stick in his c. 74:28
c. of many colours 36:62
cut yr. c. according to yr. cloth
259:49

Cock: a C. and a Bull, said Yorick 379:72
  before the c. crow twice 54:65
  C. a doodle doo! 231:26
  c. that crowed in the morn 239:79
Cock Robin: heard the bell toll for poor C. 241:89
  I killed C. 241:88
Cock-a-hoop: to be c. 258:15
Cock-and-bull story 258:16
Cockles: c. and mussels ... alive O! 17:89
  warm the c. of the heart 282:5
Cockpit: can this c. hold ... fields of France? 318:37
Cocks: drench'd our steeples, drown'd the c. 328:71
Cocksure ... as Tom Macaulay 208:27
Cod: home of the bean and the c. 69:67
Coeur: le c. a ses raisons 244:28
Coffee: c. which makes the politicians wise 252:38
  if this is c., I want tea 285:87
Cogito ergo sum 119:31
Coil: shuffled off this mortal c. 309:95
Coin: beauty is nature's c. 213:79
  pay ... in his own c. 274:31
Cold: caught an everlasting c. 401:56
  c. comfort 258:18
  comfort like c. porridge 356:37
  I beg c. comfort 327:46
  pale grew thy cheek and c. 86:99
  poor Tom's a-c. 329:81
  seedtime ... harvest ... c. and heat 35:48
  slept among his ashes c. 182:92
  'tis bitter c. and I am sick at heart 305:33
  to lie in c. obstruction 337:90
  to shelter me from the c. 32:6
  we called a c. a c. 32:9
  who thicks man's blood with c. 105:52
Colder thy kiss 86:99
Coliseum: when falls the C. 84:64
  while stands the C. 84:64
College: I am Master of this C. 30:80
Colossus: bestride the ... world like a C. 323:93
Colour: a c. of its own on the map 395:80
  purest ... minds ... love c. the most 292:62
Coloured: see the c. counties 167:82
  worser spirit a woman c. ill 364:55
Colours: all c. will agree in the dark 24:88

Colours (*continued*)
  coat of many c. 36:62
  truth fears no c. 281:61
Column: urn throws up a steamy c. 114:73
Columns: enormous fluted Ionic c. 203:56
Combine: love and marriage rarely can c. 84:74
Come: but will they c. when you do call? 314:72
  c. and trip it as you go 214:94
  c. back, Peter! C. back, Paul! 240:84
  c., c. and have a drink 392:46
  c., c. and make eyes at me 392:47
  c., c., give me yr. hand 335:70
  c. forth into the light of things 414:27
  c., he slow or c. he fast 295:9
  c., Helen, give me my soul 204:63
  c. here often? ... in the mating season 210:48
  c., into the garden, Maud 388:86
  c., knit hands 212:75
  c., landlord, fill the flowing bowl 16:78
  c., lasses and lads 16:79
  c., let's away to prison 330:99
  c., my coach! 311:25
  c. not, Lucifer! 204:66
  c. up and see me sometime 402:74
  easy c., easy go 261:8
  lightly c., lightly go 269:84
  nothing of itself will c. 409:65
  O c., all ye faithful ... c. ye 241:91
  rise up, my love ... c. away 47:20
  suffer me to c. to thee 402:70
  the cry is still 'They c.' 336:74
  thou'lt c. no more 331:6
  will ye no c. back again? 228:81
Comedies: all c. are ended by a marriage 84:75
Comedy: most Lamentable C. ... of Pyramus 341:39
  world is a c. to those who think 398:23
Comes: c. from the heart, goes to the heart 107:84
  c. silent, flooding in, the main 103:33
  here she c. ... full sail ... fan spread 109:10
  knowledge c. but wisdom lingers 387:82
  nobody c., nobody goes 30:74
  repentance c. too late 276:86
  tomorrow never c. 280:43

Comes (*continued*)
  when daylight c., ·c. in the light
  104:34
Cometh: behold, this ·dreamer c.
  36:63
Comfort: cold c. 258:18
  c. in the strength of love 411:88
  c. me with apples 47:19
  c.'s a cripple and comes ... slow
  125:32
  from ignorance our c. flows 253:52
  here's my c. 356:42
  I beg cold c. 327:46
  no c. to one not sociable 304:26
  of c., no man speak 349:53
  receives c. like cold porridge 356:37
  this must my c. be 348:33
  to warm, to c., and command
  414:18
  two loves ... of c. and despair
  364:55
Comfortably: liv'd c. so long together
  141:52
Comforters: miserable c. are ye all
  41:70
Comforts: not without c. and hopes
  24:91
Comical: I often think it's c. 144:87
Coming: Campbells are c. 16:77
  c. through the rye 79:3
  I'm c., I'm c. 138:8
  she is c. my dove, my dear 388:87
  their going ... even as their c.
  330:98
  thy going out and thy c. in 44:39
Command: less used to sue than to c.
  294:96
  man to c. and woman to obey 389:2
  not born to sue but to c. 347:31
  not in mortals to c. success 9:4
  to warn, to comfort, and c.
  414:18
Commanded: nature, to be c., must be
  obeyed 27:42
Commandment: laws of England are
  at my c. 318:33
Commandments: aren't no Ten C.
  190:8
  fear God, and keep his c. 47:14
Commencement de la fin 384:29
Commend: all our swains c. her 361:8
  easier to ridicule than c. 276:94
Commended: who c. thy yellow stockings 360:92
Comment is free but facts are sacred
  294:88
Commerce: honour sinks where c. ...
  prevails 151:92

Commit: c. his body to the ground
  65:15
  pretty follies that themselves c.
  339:10
Committed: they have c. false report
  344:87
Commodity, the bias of the world
  326:37
Common: earth and every c. sight
  410:72
  fade into the light of c. day
  411:78
  have a good thing to make it too c.
  316:1
  more c. where the climate's sultry
  84:66
  nothing c. did or mean 207:3
Common-place: his c. book be full
  382:8
Commonwealth: caterpillars of the c.
  349:46
  if the ... C. last for a thousand years
  101:95
  i' th' c. I wd., ... execute 356:38
  The Empire is a C. of Nations
  290:40
Communicated: good, the more c.,
  more abundant 219:76
Communist: a c. ? One who has yearnings 132:25
Community: no finer investment for
  any c. 101:6
  part of the c. of Europe 149:54
Commuter—one who spends his life
  402:77
Compact: of imagination all c. 342:52
Companions: I have had c. 192:32
  lovely c. are faded and gone 226:63
  wives ... c. for middle age 24:97
Company: better ... alone than in bad
  c. 255:15
  c. makes the feast 258:21
  c., villainous c. 315:79
  crowd is not c. 259:38
  crowds without c. 142:65
  his little daughter, to bear him c.
  199:9
  in married life three is c. 405:8
  in such a jocund c. 410:70
  known by the c. he keeps 271:33
  qualified to shine in c. 382:10
  take the tone of the c. 98:57
  tell me what c. thou keepest 95:12
  two is c., three is none 281:78
  withouten other c. in youthe 97:39
Compare: belied with false c. 364:53
  c. thee to a summer's day? 362:32
  how I may c. this prison 351:62

Comparisons: c. are odious 258:22
c. are odorous 343:77
Compassion: shutteth up his bowls of
c. 60:15
thou art all c. 402:72
Compassions: his c. fall not ... new
every morning 49:61
Competition: tradition approves all
forms of c. 103:30
Complain: moping owl ... to the
moon c. 155:32
sluggard, I heard him c. 400:41
Complaining: woods have no voice
but ... c. 227:72
Complete: let ... death c. the same
76:47
Complexion: his c. is perfect gallows
355:27
that schoolgirl c. 11:30
whose fresh c. and whose heart
362:24
Complies against his will 82:39
Comprehended: our watch ... have
indeed c. 343:79
Compromise: All ... founded on c. and
barter 78:74
Comrades, leave me here a little
387:78
Conceal: cleverness is to c. one's
cleverness 288:18
knowing anything, shd. c. it 23:73
use ... words ... to c. ... thoughts
397:10
Concealment, like a worm i' th' bud
360:89
Conceit: infusing him with self and
vain c. 350:54
Conceits: wise in yr. own c. 57:39
Concentrates: it c. his mind wonderfully 177:24
Concessions of the weak, ... c. ... of
fear 77:71
Conclusions: life ... art of drawing ...
c. 82:44
Condemn: age shall not weary ...
years c. 65:20
travellers ... fools at home c. 'em
356:48
Condemned: much c. to have an itching palm 325:23
Condemns: Johnson c. whatever he
disapproves 79:93
Condescend: your men of wit will c.
381:96
Condition: the c. of man ... c. of war
163:33
Conditions: stars above us, govern
our c. 329:87

Cones: eat the c. under his pines
139:26
Conference [maketh] a ready man
26:33
Confession is good for the soul 258:23
Confidence: we shall fight with growing c. 100:94
Confident: never glad c. morning
again 74:29
Conflict: never in the field of human c.
101:96
too weak the c. to support 330:3
Confound: Lord did ... c. the language
35:52
Confusion: all else, c. 389:2
c. to his enemies 16:85
levee from a couch in some c.
109:15
Congregation: latter has the largest c.
118:18
Conjecture: now entertain c. of a time
320:50
we c. ... animal or ... god 381:98
Conjunction: is the c. of the mind
206:98
Connect: only c. 137:96
Conquer: England ... wont to c.
others 349:42
we'll c. again and again 141:48
Conquered: I came, I saw, I c. 87:8
nation ... perpetually to be c. 78:72
Conquering: see the c. hero comes
226:68
so sharp the c. 97:50
went forth c., and to conquer 61:25
Conqueror: came in with Richard C.
355:19
lie at the proud foot of a c. 327:47
Conquers: love c. all and we too succumb 397:3
Conquest: a shameful c. of itself
349:42
peace is of the nature of a c. 317:23
Conquests: all thy c., glories, triumphs,
spoils 324:6
Conscience: a still and quiet c. 323:82
argue freely according to c. 224:44
catch the c. of the king 309:94
c. does make cowards of us all
309:95
my c. hath a thousand ... tongues
353:86
Consciousness: this growth of national
c. 203:53
Consecration: the c. and the poet's
dream 409:61
Consent: govern another man without
... c. 196:73

Consent (*continued*)
  'I will ne'er c.' – consented 84:67
  silence gives c. 277:38
Consented: whispering 'I will ne'er
  consent – c. 84:67
Consequence: business of c., *do it yourself* 27:51
Conservatism: what is c.? 196:77
Conservative: a c. government ...
  organised hypocrisy 122:90
  or else a little C. 144:87
  with more propriety be called the C.
  115:87
Consider: though justice be thy plea, c.
  339:15
Considereth: blessed is he that c. the
  poor 42:6
Consign to thee and come to dust
  305:30
Consolation: with peace and c. ... dismissed 223:27
Consorts: constitution ... c. ... with
  all things 72:2
Conspiracy: a c. to cheat the world
  176:6
  open-ey'd c. his time doth take
  356:39
Conspirators: all the c. save only he
  326:30
Conspiring ... how to load and bless
  with fruit 180:78
Constable: fit man for the c. of the
  watch 343:74
Constabulary duty's to be done
  148:33
Constancy: c. lives in realms above
  106:67
  hope c. in wind 85:91
  in c. follow the Master 77:64
Constant: a woman c. ... argues a
  decay 109:9
  c. you are, but yet a woman 313:61
  friendship is c. in all ... things
  342:62
  merciful as c., c. as various 154:22
  to one thing c. never 343:68
  were man but c. 361:11
Constitution: higher law than the C.
  297:37
  I am of a c. so general 72:2
  our C. is in ... operation 139:16
  principle of the English c. 66:25
Consul: Rome, born when I was c.
  103:21
Consults: neither c. ... nor trusts
  [women] 98:60
Consume: no more right to c. happiness 364:66

Consumed: bush burned ... was not c.
  36:69
Consummation: a c. devoutly to be
  wish'd 309:95
  quiet c. have 305:31
Consumption: remedy against ... c. of
  the purse 316:3
Contagion: breathes out c. to this
  world 310:13
  c. of the world's slow stain 367:16
  rot inwardly, and foul c. spread
  215:16
Contemplate: let us c. existence
  120:48
Contemplation: for c. he 219:66
  left for c. not what ... used to be
  34:24
Contempt: familiarity breeds c. 262:51
  familiarity breeds c. ... children
  394:67
  few [can bear] c. 254:60
  means ... for c. too high 112:47
Content: be c. with yr. wages 54:73
  but if I'm c. with a little 65:18
  c. to breathe his native air 251:28
  c. to have them ... course by course
  100:90
  farewell c.! 345:10
  in whatsoever state ... to be c.
  58:80
  let us draw upon c. 152:98
  where our desire is got without c.
  334:50
Consented: hermits are c. with their
  cells 411:89
Contentment: all enjoying, what c.
  find? 220:87
  where wealth and freedom ... c. fails
  151:92
Contests: what mighty c. rise from
  trivial things 251:33
Continence: chastity and c., but not
  yet 22:63
Continent: every man ... a piece of
  the c. 124:13
Continued: how long so ever ... c. ...
  no force in law 104:38
Continuous as the stars that shine
  410:68
Contract between the king and the
  people 297:26
Contradict: very well, ... I c. myself
  403:87
Contradiction: woman's at best a c.
  still 251:26
Contraries: without c. is no progression 68:56
  wd. by c. execute all things 356:38

'Contrariwise', continued Tweedledee 92:75

Contrary (Contrairy): everything goes c. with me 119:37
Mary, Mary, quite c. 235:55

Contrive to write so even 23:77

Contumely: the proud man's c. 309:95

Convent's narrow room 411:89

Conversation: our c. is in heaven 58:77

Conversationalist: to provide any industrious c. 169:2

Conversations: after-dinner c. over the wine 391:38

Converse: formed by thy c. 250:18

Conversing: with thee c. I forget all time 219:70

Converted: except ye be c. 53:37

Convicted of sickness, hunger 375:14

Convicts: they [Americans] are a race of c. 176:7

Convince: persuading others we c. ourselves 180:67

Cook: ill c. ... cannot lick his own fingers 258:26, 354:16
to c. one's goose 258:25

Cookery: kissing don't last: c. do! 209:36

Cooking: no c., or washing, or sewing 12:43

Cooks: as c. go she went 292:70
too many c. spoil the broth. 280:50

Coolibah: shade of a c. tree 244:30

Coot: bald as a c. 255:89

Copulation: birth, and c., and death 131:9

Coral: c. is far more red 364:52
of his bones are c. made 355:35

Corbies: twa c. making a mane 12:40

Cord: a threefold c. is not quickly broken 46:99

Cords of a man, with bands of love 50:77

Corioli: flutter'd yr. Volscians in C. 304:19

Cormorant: c. devouring Time 331:8
sat like a c. 219:64

Corn: as soon ... hope ... c. in chaff 85:91
c. in Egypt 36:64
c. was orient and immortal wheat 392:53
cow's in the c. 234:49
farmer sowing his c. 239:79
in tears amid the alien c. 184:30
readers ... sway ... like ... ripe c. 130:89
when he treadeth out the c. 38:12

Corner: Jack Horner sat in the c. 235:50
keep a c. in the thing I love 345:8
some c. of a foreign field 71:92

Corners: unregarded age in c. thrown 300:77

Cornfield: down in de c. 138:3
o'er the green c. did pass 303:7

Cornish men: here's twenty thousand C. 158–9:74

Coromandel: on the Coast of C. 194:55

Coronets: kind hearts are more than c. 387:74

Corpse : he'd make a lovely c. 120:50

Correct: like magistrates, c. at home 318:39

Correcteth: whom the Lord loveth he c. 44:55

Corrupt: a people generally c. 78:86
art ... able to c. a saint 312:46
judge that no king can c. 322:78
power tends to c. 9:11
unlimited power is apt to c. 246:55

Corrupted the youth of the realm 321:68

Corrupteth: wanton love c. 25:99

Corruption: c. wins not more than honesty 323:83
vice whose ... c. inhabits 360:1

Corse: his c. to the rampart we hurried 408:52

Cortez: like stout C. 185:41

Cost: defend our island, whatever the c. may be 100–1:94

Costly: c. thy habit 306:56
Your Grace is too c. 343:65

Costs: nothing c. so much as what is given 273:5
victory at all c. 100:93

Cottage: wherever there's a c. small 244:24

Cottages: love lives in c. ... courts 270:15
poor men's c. princes' palaces 338:2

Cottleston, C. Pie 212:65

Cotton: from the c. fields away 138:7

Couch: a levee from a c. 109:15
oft, when on my c. I lie 410:71
there I c. when owls do fly 357:56

Cough cannot be hid 270:8

Coughing drowns the parson's saw 332:20

Counsel: hard ... for women to keep c. 324:2
if the c. be good 259:29
justice, c., and treasure 25:7

Counsel (*continued*)
  princely c. in his face yet shone
    218:52
  three may keep c. if two be away
    280:35
Counsellers: in the multitude of c. ...
    safety 45:63
Counsels: close designs and crooked c.
    126:38
Count one's chickens before ... hatched
    259:30
Countenance: knight of the sorrowful
    c. 95:8
  the Lord lift up his c. 38:2
  you have that in yr. c. 327:55
Countercheck: filth, the C. Quarrel-
    some 303:9
Counties: and see the coloured c.
    167:82
Counting-house: the king was in his c.
    238:70
Country: better satisfied with my own
    c. 177:30
  but spare yr. c.'s flag, she said
    403:89
  by all their c.'s wishes blest! 107:89
  fit c. for heroes to live in 197:90
  go West ... grow up with the c.
    156:47
  God made the c. 113:68
  good for the c. ... good for General
    Motors 407:42
  happy is the c. ... has no history
    266:64
  his first, best c. ever is at home
    151:91
  I have no relish for the c. 375:13
  I loathe the c. 109:16
  I love thee still, my c. 114:70
  I tremble for my c. 171:33
  I vow to thee, my c. 377:53
  left our c. for our c.'s good 29:65
  Mother, you live in the c. 401:68
  my c.! How I leave [love] my c.!
    247:60
  my c., 'tis of thee 374:5
  my soul, there is a c. 396:87
  not what yr. c. can do for you
    188:75
  not without honour save ... own c.
    52:32
  on behalf of ... c., ... children, ...
    altars 293:74
  our c., right or wrong 118:16
  our c. sinks beneath the yoke 335:65
  our c., ... whole c. and nothing but
    our c. 400:43
  [praises] every c. but his own 145:1

Country (*continued*)
  she is my c. still 100:82
  some Cromwell, guiltless of his c.'s
    blood 155:38
  sweet and seemly ... to die for one's
    c. 167:77
  the loneliness of my c. 366:4
  undiscover'd country from whose
    bourn 309:95
  walking ... 'tis a c. diversion 109:16
Countrymen: friends, Romans, c.
    325:12
  the merits of their c. 176:6
  what a fall ... my c. 325:20
Couple: every c. is not a pair
    259:31
Courage: be strong and of a good c.
    38:18
  c. in yr. own [trouble] 152:7
  c. mounteth with occasion 326:34
  c. never to submit or yield 216:30
  endurance and c. of my companions
    294:91
  screw yr. c. to the sticking place
    333:38
Course: content to have them ... c. by
    c. only 100:90
  c. of true love never ... smooth
    341:36
  c., proportion, season 358:66
  earth's diurnal c. 414:19
Courses: gave himself to evil c. 411:87
  stars in their c. fought 39:22
Court: c. awards it ... law doth give it
    340:19
  friend at c. 263:91
  starry threshold of Jove's c. 212:72
  sun that shines upon his c. 362:23
  the English, not the Turkish c.
    318:31
  within the ... crown ... keeps Death
    his c. 350:54
Courted by all the winds 222:18
Courteous: gracious and c. to strangers
    25:5
Courtesy: by c. a man 24:82
  c. on one side only 259:32
  full of c., full of craft 264:2
  I am the very pink of c. 354:9
Courtier's, soldier's, scholar's 310:1
Courting: I heard a linnet c. 70:76
Courts: brawling c. and dusty purlieus
    386:64
  white founts ... in the C. of the sun
    99:70
Cousins: his sisters, and his c., and his
    aunts! 147:25
Coventry: send to C. 259:33

Cover: c. her face: mine eyes dazzle
400:50
c. thee with his feathers 43:19
with leaves and flowers do c. 400:54
Covet: thou shalt not c.; but tradition
103:30
Coveting: pleasure ... is lost by c.
274:48
Cow: couple-colour as a brindled c.
166:68
c. jumped over the moon 232:33
c.'s in the corn 234:49
c. with the cumpled horn 239:79
c., proportion, season 358:66
I never saw a Purple C. 77:68
I wrote the 'Purple C.' 77:69
three acres and a c. 107:85
Coward: bully is always a c. 257:68
c. does it with a kiss 404:94
gross flattery to name a c. 392:48
no c. soul is mine 71:84
Cowardice: pale cold c. in noble
breasts 347:32
Cowards: a plague of all c. 314:63
conscience does make c. of us all
309:95
c. die many times before ... deaths
324:1
it [public] is the greatest of c. 159:82
though c. flinch, and traitors jeer
109–10:21
Cowslip: in a c.'s bell I lie 357:56
Coy: be not c. but use yr. time 162:25
Coyness: this c., lady, were no crime
206:92
Crabs: roasted c. hiss in the bowl
332:20
Crack: stretch out to th' c. of doom?
335:64
that heaven's vault shd. c. 330:4
winds ... c. yr. cheeks 328:71
Cracked: it c. and growled and roared
105:46
Crackling of thorns under a pot 46:4
Cracks: now c. a noble heart 312:40
Cradle: the c. will rock 233:38
Cradles: bit the babies in the c. 75:37
Craft: c. so long to lerne 97:50
gentlemen of the gentle c. 118:21
Cramp: when I heard she'd died of c.
153:10
Cravat: the one [robin] in red c.
122:85
Crawling: whereunder c. coop't we
live 136:80
Crazy: checkin' the c. ones 154:19
I'm half c. 116:99
Creak of a lumbering cart 417:55

Cream: choking her with c. 189:91
visages do c. and mantle 338:97
Created: about ... to be c. like to us
218:53
c. man in his own image 34:28
God c. the heaven 34:26
Creation: O fairest of c. 220:94
our c. preservation 64:85
she is His new c. 380:83
to which the whole c. moves 387:73
Creature: God's first c., which was
light 27:40
lone lorn c. 119:37
she is an excellent c., but 123:1
though the most beautiful C. ...
waiting 187:63
wine is a good familiar c. 345:2
Creatures: all c. great and small
10:17
call these delicate c. ours 345:8
from fairest c. we desire 362:29
the meanest of his c. 74:34
true hope ... makes ... meaner c.
kings 352:83
Credit: citizen of c. and renown
112:54
my c. in men's eyes 136:82
stories ... not to thy c. 87:15
to his c. ... is an Englishman!
147:29
Creditors have better memories 259:34
Creed: a modest c. and yet 370:47
Creeds: honest doubt ... than in half
the c. 386:65
so many gods, so many c. 404:93
vain are the thousand c. 71:85
Creeks: far back through c. and inlets
103:33
Creep: let the sounds of music c.
340:22
Creeping like snail ... to school
301:90
Creeps: when the blood c. ... nerves
prick 386:60
Crew: Mirth, admit me of thy c.
214:96
we were a ghastly c. 105:58
Cricket: c. – a sport at which the contenders 172:44
merry as a c. 272:56
save the c. on the hearth 213:86
to where the c. sings 417:53
Crime: atrocious c. of being ... young
246:54
bigamy, sir, is a c.! 224–5:52
cut-throat isn't occupied in c.
148:34
for my wilful c. art banished 221:2

Crime (*continued*)
  in heaven, a c. to love too well? 248:73
  no c.'s so great as ... to excel 100:83
  nor any c. so shameful as poverty 134:55
  the Napoleon of c. 125:22
  the punishment fit the c. 146:6
  this coyness, lady, were no c. 206:92
  treason was no c. 126:46
Crimes: c., follies and misfortunes of mankind 142:66
  history of the great events ... history of c. 397:13
  l'histoire des c. 397:13
  liberté, que de c. ... en ton nom 288:26
  liberty, what c. ... in yr. name 288:26
Crimson in thy lips and in thy cheeks 354:17
Cripple: comfort's a c. 125:32
Crispian: this day is call'd the feast of Crispian 320:57
Critic: first attribute of a good c. 200:26
  scorn not the sonnet; C., you have frowned 412:95
Critical: I am nothing if not c. 345:97
Criticism: ask ... for c. ... only want praise 208:20
  my own definition of c. 21:50
Criticisms: animals ... pass no c. 130:87
Critics: before you trust in c. 85:91
  c. all are ready made 85:90
Crocodile: c. tears 259:35
  how doth the little c. 89:45
Cromek: O! Mr. C., how do ye do? 67:42
Cromwell: restless C. cd. not cease 207:2
  ruins that C. knocked about 197:87
  see C., damned to everlasting fame 250:17
  some C. guiltless 155:38
Crooked: c. by nature is never ... straight 259:36
  straight trees have c. roots 279:84
  strive to set the c. straight? 227:71
  there was a c. man 239:74
Crop: a-watering the last year's c. 130:85
Cross: a little marble c. below the town 159:76
  blind as the ... nails upon the C. 373:90
  c. the bridge ... get to it 259:37

Cross (*continued*)
  e'en though it be a c. 9:3
  for our advantage on the bitter c. 312:43
  one more river to c. 15:73
  with the C. of Jesus 28:57
Cross-bow: with my c. I shot the albatross 105:47
Crosses: between the c., row on row 202:48
Cross-gartered: wishes to see thee ever c. 360:92
Crow: there is an upstart c. 156:49
Crowd: all at once I saw a c. 410:67
  c. is not company 259:38
  madding c.'s ignoble strife 155:39
  out of the c. a mistress or a friend 368:25
  trees ... shall c. into a shade 251:32
Crowded: feast, and yr. halls are c. 404:92
Crowds without company 142:65
Crowed: cock that c. in the morn 239:79
Crown: all thy faithful mercies c. 402:72
  c. thy good with brotherhood 29:67
  fighting for the c. 234:47
  I give away my c. 350–1:58
  I will give thee a c. of life 60:20
  if you c. him, let me prophesy 350:56
  let us c. ourselves with rosebuds 62:41
  not the king's c. ... deputed sword 337:84
  sweet fruition of an earthly c. 205:76
  the holly bears the c. 16–17:87
  this I count the glory of my c. 132:21
  throned monarch better than his c. 339:15
  uneasy ... head that wears a c. 317:14
  virtuous woman ... c. to her husband 45:65
  with the ... c. ... keeps Death his court 350:54
Crowns: evening c. the day 262:25
  give c. and pounds and guineas 167:81
  who c. ... a youth of labour 150:64
Crows: the c. and choughs that wing 329:88
Crucified: c. 'twixt a smile and a whimper 369:42
  the dear Lord was c. 11:20
Crucify him 54:66

Cruel: I must be c. only to be kind 311:20

let me be c., not unnatural 311:14

more c. the pen is than the sword 81:30

Cruelly: I am c. used 23:79

Cruelty: farewell, fair c. 359:81

O c., to steal my Basil-pot 182:6

Crumb: a memorial c. 122:85

who craved no c. 148–9:46

Crumbs ... from the rich man's table 55:86

Cruse: neither shall the c. of oil fail 40:55

Crustimoney Proseedcake: what does C. mean? 212:63

Cry: c. for the moon 259:39

c. 'Havoc!' 324:9

c. not when his father dies 172:56

c. out 'Olivia!' 359:80

c. woe, destruction, ruin 349:52

c. 'Wolf' 259:40

did they not sometime c. 'All hail'? 350:57

kissed the girls and made them c. 232:31

need a body c.? 79:3

the c. is still 'They come' 336:74

Crying over spilt milk 259:41

Cuckoo: but as the c. is in June 314:77

c., c. – O word of fear 332:19

lhude sing c. 15:71

O C., shall I call thee bird? 415:37

the c. then on every tree 332:19

the weather the c. likes 158:67

Cuckoo-buds of yellow hue 332:19

Cue: my c. is villainous melancholy 327:54

with a twisted c. 146:8

Cultivate: we must c. our garden 397:9

Cultiver: il faut c. notre jardin 397:9

Culture, the acquainting ourselves with the best 21:53

Cunning: my right hand forget her c. 44:48

Cup: ah, fill the C. 135:74

C. that clears TO-DAY of past Regrets 135:69

kiss but in the c. 178:49

'twixt the c. and the lip 280:20

we'll tak' a c. o' kindness 79:1

Cupboard: c. love 259:42

Mother Hubbard went to the c. 236:59

Cupid: C. and my Campaspe 201:29

C. painted blind 341:38

C.'s darts do not feel 15:68

Cups that cheer but not inebriate 114:73

Curate: like the C.'s egg 259:43

Curb: you might c. yr. magnanimity 187:69

Curds: eating her c. and whey 235:51

Cure: past c., past care 274:28

prevention is better than c. 275:60

there is no c. for this disease 31:91

Cured: can't be c. must be endured 283:23

Curfew tolls the knell of parting day 155:30

Curiosity: newspapers always excite c. 192:31

Curious: that was the c. incident 125:23

'Curiouser and c.!' cried Alice 89:44

Curled: he ... c. up on the floor 158:73

Curls: rosy cheeks and flaxen c. 75:43

Curly locks, c. 231:27

Current: take the c. when it serves 326:27

Currents: their c. turn awry 309:95

Curs: mongrels, spaniels, c. 334:48

Curse: I know how to c. 355:33

O c. of marriage 345:8

the c. is come upon me! 387:77

work ... c. of the drinking classes 406:35

Curses are like chickens 259:44

Cursing: fall a-c. like a very drab 309:93

Curst be the verse 248:85

Curtain: ring down the c., the farce is over 285:90

Curtained with cloudy red 216:22

Curtains: let fall the c., wheel the sofa 114:73

Curve: dear red c. of her lips 207:11

Custodiet: quis c. ipsos custodes? 180:69

Custom: a c. loathsome ... hateful ... harmful 170:19

c. calls me to't 303:15

c. without reason ... ancient error 259:45

what c. wills ... shd. we do 303:15

Customary: said Owl, the c. procedure 212:63

Customers: a people of c. 374:98

Customs: the c., politics, and tongue 245:32

Cut: c. is the branch that might have grown 204:67

c. it without a knife? 235:52

easy ... of a c. loaf to steal 357–8:63

Cut (*continued*)
  most unkindest c. of all   325:19
  the flash c. him   12:42
Cuts: he that c. off twenty years   324:4
  tongue is not steel yet it c.   280:46
Cut-throat: call me misbeliever, c. dog
  338:6
Cutting all the pictures out   31:88
Cynara: faithful to thee, C!   124:17
Cynic: what is a c.?   406:21
Cynicism is intellectual dandyism
  209:31
Cypress: in sad c. let me be laid   359:88

D: never use a big, big D.   147:23
Dads: get leave of yr. d.   16:79
Daffodils: a host of golden d.   410:67
  fair d., we weep to see   162:18
  when d. begin to peer   361:17
Dagger: is this a d. ... I see before me?
  334:40
Daggers: I will speak d. to her   311:14
  there's d. in men's smiles   334:47
Daisies pied and violets blue   332:19
Daisy, Daisy, give me yr. answer, do
  116:99
Dale: heigh! the doxy over the d.
  361:17
  over hill, over d.   341:42
  through wood and d. the sacred
  river   106:73
Dalliance: primrose path of d.   306:54
  silken d. in the wardrobe lies   319:40
Damage: which might d. his career
  28:64
Dame: my d. has lost her shoe   231:26
  one for the d.   231:23
Damn: a man who said 'D.!'   158:68
  almost hear the printer saying d.
  395:80
  d. with faint praise   248:83
Damned: and d. be him that first cries
  'Hold!'   336:80
  another d., thick ... book!   149:56
  d. from here to Eternity   190:99
  d. if I know how the helican   209:38
  d. to everlasting fame   250:17
  life ... one d. thing after another
  168:88
  out, d. spot!   335:68
  prosperity has d. more ... than ...
  devils   275:65
  publish, and be d.   401:62
  she cried, she d. near died   17:96
  thou must be d. perpetually   204:65
  what those d. dots meant   100:87
Damsel: to every man a d. or two
  39:24

Dan: can travel from D. to Beersheba
  379:66
  from D. even to Beer-sheba   39:31
Danaos: timeo D. et dona ferentes
  397:99
Dance: each d. the others wd. off the
  ground   118:26
  move easiest who have learn'd to d.
  249:99
  on with the d.!   83:60
  will you join the d.?   91:63
Danced: d. by the light of the moon
  195:62
  sang his didn't he d. his did   116:94
Dancing: d.? Oh, dreadful!   79:91
  you and I are past our d. days
  353:93
Dancing-master: teach ... the manners
  of a d.   174:77
Danger: continual ... d. of violent
  death   163:34
  d. from the wiles of a stranger 228:89
  out of this nettle d.   313:60
  pleas'd with the d.   126:39
  the chief d. of the time   210:44
  when we conquer without d.   110:32
Dangerous: a little learning is a d.
  thing   249:94
  boggy, dirty, d. way   151:84
  greater the power, the more d. the
  abuse   78:87
  he thinks too much; such men are d.
  324:94
Dangers: brave its d. comprehend its
  mystery   198:1
  lov'd me for the d. I had passed
  344:92
  with d. compassed round   219–20:83
Daniel: a D. come to judgment! Yea,
  a D.!   340:17
  brought D., ... cast him into the den
  50:72
  O. D., ... greatly beloved   50:74
*Dant: quae d. ... negant gaudent ... esse
  rogatae*   243:12
Dante, who loved ... hated   74:32
Dappled: glory be to God for d. things
  166:68
Dare: d. to be true   161:11
  I d. ... assume ... style of Christian
  72:99
  I d. not ask a kiss   162:19
  O, what men d. do! ... may do!
  343:80
  we d. n't go a-hunting   11:22
Dared attack my Chesterton   32:1
Darien: silent, upon a peak in D.
  185:41

Darjeeling: there was an old man from
D. 14:56
Dark: a great leap in the d. 163:35
all colours will agree in the d. 24:88
all that's best of d. and bright 86:96
as children fear to go in the d. 24:86
creeping murmur and the poring d.
320:50
d. as the world of man 373:90
d. backward and abysm of time
355:29
don't want to go home in the d.
161:5
ever-during d. 218:59
good as my lady in the d. 268:24
hellish d. and smells of cheese
380:90
in the morning's d. 117:14
Joan as my Lady is as good i' th' d.
162:21
never to refuse a drink after d.
209:30
O d., d., d., amid the blaze 221:13
the sun to me is d. 221:14
we are for the d. 299:67
what in me is d. illumine 216:29
Darken: the days d. round me
385:53
Darkeneth: who is this that d. counsel?
41:76
Darkling I listen 184:29
Darkly: see through a glass, d. 57:54
Darkness: a distant voice in the d.
198:4
and d. Night be named 220:84
and light from d. ... divided 220:84
d. again and a silence 198:4
d. falls at they behest 132:24
d. which may be felt 36:75
in d. and with dangers compassed
219-20:83
leaves the world to d. and to me
155:30
lighten our d. 63:74
men loved d. rather than light 55:1
pestilence that walketh in d. 43:21
ring out the d. of the land 387:71
rulers of the d. of this world 58:74
the d. deepens; Lord, with me abide!
201:31
the d. silvers away 70:75
the people that walked in d. 48:35
Darling: Charlie is my d. 227:80
d. buds of May 362:32
d. of the Spring 415:38
in thy green lap was Nature's d.
156:44
oh my d. Clementine 225:59

Darling (*continued*)
Six years' d. of a pigmy size 411:69
the d. of my heart 89:31
Darts: Cupid's d. do not feel 15:68
Dated: women and music shd. never
be d. 151:88
Daughter: d. of Earth and Water
368:23
d. of Jove, relentless Power 155:43
d. of the gods divinely tall 385:46
D. of the Vine to Spouse 135:76
don't put your d. on the stage
112.44
he that wd. the d. win 259:51
like mother, like d. 272:71
marry ... yr. d. ... when you can
270:18
skipper had taken his little d. 199:9
stern D. of the Voice of God 413:7
the King of Spain's d. 233:39
truth is the d. of God 281:63
Daughter-in-law: remembers not ...
she was a d. 272:72
Daughters: all the d. of my father's
house 360:90
d. of the Philistines rejoice 40:47
d. of the uncircumcised triumph
40:47
here lie I and my four d. 12:41
marry yr. d. betimes 271:48
nor rain, wind ... are my d. 328:72
sweet her artless d. 185:44
the fairest of her d. Eve 219:67
words are the d. of earth 172:41
David: D. ... escaped to the cave
Adullam 39:45
D. [hath slain] his ten thousands
39:44
D. took an harp and played 39:43
once in royal D.'s city 10:19
D. Copperfield kind of crap 292:71
Davy: Sir Humphrey D. detested gravy
33:18
Dawn: till the dappled d. doth rise
214:97
Daws: heart ... for d. to peck at
344:89
Day: a thousand years as one d. 60:14
a tip-toe when this d. is named
320:57
ah! when will this long weary d.
377:39
and those eyes, the break of d.
337-8:92
arrow that flieth by d. 43:20
as morning shows the d. 221:6
calm was the d. 377:46
chanced to see at break of d. 411:85

Day (*continued*)

compare thee to a summer's d. 362:32

d. and night shall not cease 35:48

d. as sharp to them as thorn 351:59

d. for a man to afflict his soul 49:52

d. is short and the work is long 259:52

d. of death ... d. of ... birth 64:3

d. of Empires has come 95:14

d. of wrath, that dreadful d. 295:7

d. returns too soon 86:98

d.'s at the morn 75:44

d.'s journey take the whole long d.? 290:46

d.'s out and the labour done 73:9

d. thou gavest, Lord, is ended 132:24

d. unto d. uttereth speech 41:87

death of each d.'s life 334:42

death will have his d. 349:52

deficiencies of the present d. 173:61

dies at the opening d. 400:40

dog will have his d. 312:34

drinka pinta milka d. 11:26

dwell in realms of d. 66:31

each d. is like a year 404:97

eclipse without all hope of d.! 221:13

every d., in every way ... better 111:37

every d. to be lost 178:37

every dog has his d. 260:82

every dog its d. 189:89

from this d. forward, for better for worse 64:7

good morning to the d. ... my gold! 179:59

he that outlives this d. 320:57

how many hours bring about the d. 321:70

if every d. ... last d. but one 194:50

in the d. of judgement 63:79

in the shade on a fine d. 23:70

jocund d. stands tiptoe 354:14

known a better d. 295:99

lay it up for a rainy d. 275:78

light the D. ... He named 220:84

live to fight another d. 14:61

longest d. ... have an end 270:1

merry heart goes all the d. 361:19

murmur of a summer's d. 21:40

never a bad d. ... hath a good night 272:83

night is long that never finds the d. 335:67

not to me returns d. 218:59

now the d. is over 28:56

Day (*continued*)

O frabjous d.! 92:71

old age ... at close of d. 390:18

one d. is with the Lord as a thousand years 60:14

our little systems have their d. 386:56

power of the press ... last but a d. 395:77

rain it raineth every d. 360:3

remember the sabbath d. 37:86

Rome was not built in a d. 276:2

sailed ... for a year and a d. 195:61

seize the present d. 166:74

sing ... pray all the livelong d. 68:45

so foul and fair a d. 332:25

so rare as a d. in June? 200:25

sufficient unto the d. ... evil thereof 52:22

sweet d., so cool, so calm 161:14

the bright d. is done 299:67

the d. of small things 51:96

the light of common d. 411:78

this d. our daily bread 52:18

time ... runs through the roughest d. 333:29

uncertain glory of an April d. 361:6

until the d. break, ... shadows flee 47:24

yield d. to night! 321:62

Daylight: all the long and lone d. 368:31

when d. comes, comes in the light 104:34

Days: all the d. of Methuselah 35:43

Ancient of d. 50:73

as thy d. ... thy strength 38:16

chequer-board of nights and d. 135:78

d. of danger, nights of waking 295:97

d. seem lank and long 148:40

ere half my d. in this dark world 223:29

former d. ... better than these 46:5

good nights and sorry d. 271:44

how many d. will finish ... year 321:70

in good Queen Bess's glorious d. 144:89

in the belly of the fish three d. 50:86

in the mad March d. 207:13

King Charles's golden d. 17:91

loved three whole d. 380:86

my d. among the dead 376:25

my salad d. 298:53

now behold these present d. 363:46

of few d. and full of trouble 41:69

Days (continued)
past our dancing d. 353:93
shalt find it after many d. 47:9
six d. shalt thou labour 37:86
teach us to number our d. 43:18
that has twenty-eight d. clear 239:77
that thy d. may be long 37:87
the d. of our years 43:17
then, if ever, come perfect d. 200:25
think warm d. will never cease 181:79
though fallen on evil d. 219–20:83
what dark d. seen! 363:43
while the evil d. come not 47:11
world of happy d. 351–2:71
year whose d. are long 404:97
Dazzle: mine eyes d.: she died young 400:50
Dead: a character d. at every word 372:76
and they all d. did lie 105:55
beside the wench is d. 204:71
blow ... bugles, over the rich D. 71:88
concerning the d. [say] ... good 259:54
courage ... the devil is d. 286:1
d.! and never called me mother! 409:56
d. as a door-nail 259:55
d. for a ducat, d.! 311:17
dew on the face of the d. 30:84
doctors found when she was d. 150:74
down among the d. men 129:78
faith without works is d. 60:4
great deal to be said for being d. 33:17
healthy and wealthy and d. 392:42
it struck him d.: and serve him right 31:94
just as d. as if he'd been wrong 13:50
little fairy ... falls down d. 28:60
my days among the d. 376:25
nearly all our best men are d.! 285:85
need charity more than the d. 20:29
on stepping-stones of their d. selves 386:57
Queen Anne is d. 275:73
say I'm sick, I'm d. 248:78
something ... d. in each of us 404:95
soul is d. that slumbers 198:95
that d. men rise up never 383:20
the law hath not been d. 337:85
the noble D. 413:10
'tis Death is d., not he 367:17
to see a d. Indian 356:40

Dead (continued)
two worlds, one d. 20:36
view halloo wd. awaken the d. 154:20
wake, for night is d. 383:24
we might as well be d. 401–2:69
weep for Adonais, he is d. 367:9
when I am d. and opened 207:10
when I am d., my dearest 290:47
Deadener: habit is a great d. 30:76
Deadlock: Holy D. 161:10
Deadly: soap ... more d. in the long run 393:64
Deaf: d. as a post 259:58
none so d. as those who won't hear 260:59
Deafness: your tale ... wd. cure d. 355:30
Deal: a new d. for the American people 289:27
d. with none but honest men 276:87
good enough to be given a square d. 289:37
Dean: I am the D. of Christ Church 378:54
queer old D. 377:51
Deans: with ... dowagers for d. 388:95
Dear: a man ... to all the country d. 150:66
beauty ... for earth too d. 353:94
d. to me as light and life 80:9
God! that bread shd. be so d.! 166:65
Plato is d. to me 20:28
the d. God who loveth us 106:64
Dearie: flew o'er me and my d. 80:9
Deario: its cheerio my d. 205:83
Death: a rendezvous with D. 296:20
a sunset-touch, a fancy ... some one's d. 73:17
after the first d. ... no other 390:22
all in the valley of D. 385:40
all tragedies are finished by a d. 84:75
and d. complete the same 76:47
and d. shall have no dominion 390:17
and now to d. devote 220:94
Angel of D. has been abroad 70:80
any man's d. diminishes me 124:14
as one that had been studied in his d. 333:30
be thou faithful unto d. 60:20
because I cd. not stop for D. 122:84
birth, and copulation, and d. 131:9
brood over ... the hour of my d. 187:65
come away, d. 359:88

Death (*continued*)
day of d. [is better] 46:3
d. after life does greatly please 377:42
d., as the Psalmist saith, is certain 317:17
d., be not proud 124:10
d. devours lambs as well 260:60
d. for his ambition 325:11
d. hath no more dominion 56:31
d. is an ende of every ... sore 97:45
d. is the grand leveller 260:61
d. ... like all the rest, a mockery 370:47
d. of each day's life 334:42
d. pays all debts 260:62
d.'s pale flag is not advanced 354:17
D., whene'er he call ... too soon 148:44
die not, poor d. 124:10
die the d. of the righteous 38:4
disappointed by that stroke of d. 178:43
dread of something after d. 309:95
every door ... shut but d.'s door 260:87
fear and danger of violent d. 163:34
for love, and beauty ... no d. 370:48
give me liberty or give me d. 161:6
half in love with easeful D. 184:29
happy ... were my ensuing d. 349:42
his d., which happened in his berth 165:59
how wonderful ... D. and ... Sleep! 368:24
I have set before you life and d. 38:13
I here importune d. awhile 299:65
I will not be afraid of d. and bane 336:73
I'll ... condemn you to d. 90:46
if ought but d. part 39:34
in nativity, chance, or d. 341:34
in that sleep of d. what dreams? 309:95
in the hour of d. 63:79
in the ranks of d. 226:64
in their d. ... not divided 40:48
into the jaws of D. 385:43
it is but D. who comes at last 295:9
judge none blessed before his d. 62:52
keep a league till d. 351:60
love is strong as d. 47:27
men fear d., as children ... dark 24:86
midst of life we are in d. 65:14
most cruel d. of Pyramus 341:39

Death (*continued*)
my part of d. no one so true 359–60:88
never taste of d. but once 324:1
no one till his d. ... unhappy 73:9
nothing is certain but d. and taxes 139:16
O D., where is thy sting? 57:60, 247:71
pale D. with impartial foot 166:73
pale horse ... that sat on him was D. 61:26
paradise to what we fear of d. 337:91
precious ... the d. of his saints 43:33
rashly importunate, gone to her d. 165:56
remedy for all ... but d. 276:85
reports of my d. ... exaggerated 394:75
sad stories of the d. of kings 350:54
so many years of fearing d. 324:4
the way to dusty d. 336:76
there is d. in the pot 40:61
there shall be no more d. 61:34
thou wast not born for d. 184:30
through envy of the devil came d. 62:42
till d. us do part 64:7
'tis D. is dead, not he 367:17
useless life is an early d. 150:59
valley of the shadow of d. 42:93
vasty Hall of D. 21:38
wages of sin is d. 56:32
we owe God a d. 317:19
Webster ... much possessed by d. 131:13
what sights of ugly d. 352:72
when d. to either shall come 70:79
where is d.'s sting? 201:33
whose mortal taste brought d. 216:27
within the hollow crown keeps D. his court 350:54
worst is d. and d. will have his day 349:52
wd. fain die a dry d. 355:28
Deaths: cowards die many times before ... d. 324:1
more d. than one must die 404:96
Debate: Rupert of D. 76:53
Debonair: so buxom, blithe and d. 214:92
Debt: contrived a double d. to pay 150:70
d. is the worst poverty 260:63
the d. which cancels all others 108:1

Debts: and forgive us our d. 52:18
  death pays all d. 260:62
  he that dies pays all d. 356:46
  speak not of my d. unless 278:61
Decay: be sincere ... argues a d. 109:9
  d. of that colossal wreck 369:40
  energies of our system will d. 27:48
  fretted the ... body to d. 126:39
  this muddy vesture of d. 340:22
  wealth accumulates, and men d.
    150:62
Deceased: he first d.; she for a little
    tried 416:47
Deceive: Oh, don't d. me 16:80
  to d. oneself is very easy 260:65
  when first we practise to d. 296:13
Deceived: by bad women been d.
    222:15
  d. her father, and may thee 345:95
Deceivers: men were d. ever 343:68
Deceives me once ... d. me twice
    260:64
December: as soon seek roses in D.
    85:91
  D. when they are wed 302:4
  wallow naked in D. snow 348:37
Decent: d. godless people 131:8
  d. means poor 245:35
Decently: things done d. and in order
    57:57
Deck: boy stood on the burning d.
    160:89
Declare: nothing to d. except my
    genius 406:33
Decoration: deserves some sort of d.
    242:9
Decoyed into our condition 245:42
Decreed: soul has to itself d. 185:36
Dee: lived on the river D. 65:16
Deed: a d. without a name 335:61
  a good d. in a naughty world 340:25
  if one good d. ... I did 358:64
  now the matchless d.'s achieved
    374:95
  so I may do the d. ... my soul ...
    decreed 185:36
Deeds: d. are males, and words are
    females 260:66
  means to do ill d. ... d. ill done
    327:45
  these unlucky d. relate 346:22
  turn sourest by their d. 363:42
Deep: call spirits from the vasty d.
    314:72
  d. and crisp and even 229:3
  in the lowest d., a lower d. 218:62
  thoughts ... too d. for tears 411:82
  two voices ... one is of the d. 378:62

Deep (continued)
  very singularly d. young man 146:15
Deeper than did ever plummet sound
    357:55
Deer: in the Highlands, a-chasing the
    d. 81:20
  the running of the d. 16-17:87
Defaced, deflowered 220:94
Defamed by every charlatan 387:72
Defeat: in D.: Defiance 102:10
  the problems of victory ... of d.
    101:5
Defect: chief d. of Henry King 31:90
Defence or apology before ... accused
    95:19
Defend: d. ... yr. right to say it 398:16
  from my enemies ... d. myself
    264:18
  they [newspapers] never d. anyone
    208:28
  we shall d. our island 100-1:94
Defender: I mean the Faith's D. 83:53
Defiance: in Defeat: D. 102:10
Defied: age will not be d. 26:22
Definition: true d. of a style 381:3
Definitions: homely d. of prose and
    poetry 107:82
Deflowered: defaced, d. 220:94
Deformed, unfinish'd, sent before my
    time 351:66
Degree: a d. of delight ... in ... mis-
    fortunes 78:88
  O, when d. is shak'd 358:67
  observe d., priority and place 358:66
  people ... a d. or two lower 23:64
  take but d. away 358:68
Degrees: did ever heal but by d.?
    345:3
  we boil at different d. 133:45
Delay: in d. ... lies no plenty 359:84
  in me is no d. 221:2
Delayed till ... I cannot enjoy ...
    impart it 174:78
Delays are dangerous 260:68
Deliberate: where both d., the love is
    slight 205:81
Deliberates: woman that d. 9:5
Deliberation: deep on his front en-
    graven d. sat 218:52
Delicate: we can call these d. creatures
    ours 345:8
Delicately: Agag came ... d. 39:41
Delight: a Phantom of d. 414:16
  d. in ... misfortunes ... of others
    78:88
  d. ... ornament ... ability 26:30
  energy is eternal d. 68:57
  go to't with d. 299:62

Delight (*continued*)
I sing this song for your d. 93:87
my d. on a shining night 18:98
paint the meadows with d. 332:19
rarely comest ... Spirit of D. 370:52
sounds ... give d. and hurt not
356:47
unrest which men miscall d. 367:16
Delights: man d. not me 308:81
scorn d. and live laborious days
215:13
these d. if thou canst give 215:7
Deliver: d. me from myself 72:6
from ... ghosties ... beasties ... d. us
14:60
Delos: where D. rose 84:77
Deluge: after us, the d. 247:68
Déluge: après nous le d. 247:68
Delusion: a d., a mockery, and a snare
119:28
Delved: when Adam d. 27:50
Dementat: quos Deus vult perdere ... d.
275:74
de Mille: Cecil B. d. ... was persuaded
34:21
Democracy: d. resumed her reign
31:95
two cheers for D. 137:98
world ... made safe for d. 408:47
Democratic Party is like a mule 124:15
Demon-lover: wailing for her d.
106:72
Den: ye have made it a d. of thieves
54:62
Denmark: something is rotten in the
state of D. 307:62
Denouncing someone or something
else 208-9:28
Deny: he that will this health d. 129:78
those who d. freedom to others
196:75
thou shalt d. me thrice 54:65
Departed: minds me o' d. joys 81:27
Depends: it all d. what you mean by
171:39
Depth in philosophy bringeth ... to
religion 25:10
Deputy elected by the Lord 349:50
Derangement: a nice d. of epitaphs
372:71
Descent and fall to us is adverse
217:47
Descriptions of the fairest wights
363:45
Desert: in this d. inaccessible 301:89
legs of stone stand in the d. 369:39
nothing ... unrewarded but d.
126:44

Desert (*continued*)
rats d. a sinking ship 275:79
use every man after his d. 308:88
waste its sweetness on the d. air
155:37
Deserts: d. of vast eternity 206:94
moon when she d. the night 221:14
Deserve: d. not [freedom] for themselves 196:75
Sempronius, we'll d. it 9:4
wd. d. better of mankind 381:2
Deserves: has the government it d.
203:58
Designs: close d. and crooked counsels
126:38
Desire: d. of the moth for the star
371:56
d. shd. so ... outlive performance?
316:10
few things to d. 25:13
from what I've tasted of d. 139:25
provokes the d. ... takes away the
performance 334:45
she is the antidote to d. 109:20
some d. is necessary 173:62
universal ... d. ... to live beyond ...
income 82:45
where our d. is got without content
334:50
Desired: more to be d. ... than gold
41:88
Desires: he who d. but acts not 69:59
Desolation: create d. and call it peace
383:27
Despair: a heaven in hell's d. 67:43
begotten by D. upon Impossibility
206:97
hope is as cheap as d. 267:99
look on my works ... and d. 369:40
loves ... of comfort and d. 364:55
owner whereof was Giant D. 77:62
shall I, wasting in d. 408:49
some divine d. 388:99
what resolution from d. 216:33
where Seraphs might d. 83:56
Despairs: leaden-eyed d. 184:25
Desperate: diseases d. grown 311:21
Desperation: lives of quiet d. 391:36
Despise ... as I d. Shakespeare 367:8
Despised: d. and rejected of men 48:47
enjoy'd no sooner by d. 363:50
Despond: name of the slough was D.
77:58
Destiny: d. with Men for Pieces plays
135:78
hanging and wiving goes by d.
339:11
homely joys and d. obscure 155:34

Destroy: doth the wingèd life d. 66:34
I sought to d. institutions 403:79
'tis safer to be that which we d. 334:50
whom God wishes to d. 275:74
Destroyer and preserver; hear, oh, hear! 369:36
Destruction: by d. dwell in doubtful joy 334:50
d. that wasteth at noonday 43:21
pride goeth before d. 45:72
Detail: our life is frittered away by d. 391:37
Determined, dared and done! 374:95
Detest: but they d. at leisure 85:84
Detraction will not suffer it 315:88
Deutschland über alles 164:38
Device: banner with the strange d. 197:93
miracle of rare d. 107:75
Devil: abashed the D. stood 219:73
better the d. you know 256:30
between the d. and the deep sea 260:72
black as the d. 256:41, 384:30
courage ... the d. is dead 286:1
d. ... builds a chapel 118:18
d. can cite Scripture 338:4
d., having nothing else to do 31:96
d. is not so black 260:73
d. shd. have all the good tunes 163:29
d.'s walking parody 99:68
d. take the hindmost 260:74
d. was sick ... a monk wd. be 227:74
d. was well ... a monk he'd be 227:74
d. whoops, as he whooped 190:96
drink and the d. had done for 379:74
every man ... god or d. 126:44
first Whig was the D. 177:28
give the d. his due 264:8
he ... that sups with the d. 270:99
heaviest stone ... d. can throw 159:84
hold a candle to the d. 267:91
needs must when the d. drives 272:82
renounce the d. ... his works 64:95
resist the d. and he will flee 60:6
saint when most I play the d. 351:70
shame the d. 279:16
talk of the d. ... sure to appear 279:6
the D., howling Ho! 378:55
the world, the flesh, and the d. 63:78
through envy of the d. came death 62:42
who cleft the d.'s foot 124:11

Devil (*continued*)
young saint, old d. 284:65
your adversary the d., as a roaring lion 60:12
Devils: prosperity has damned more ... than ... d. 275:65
Devoir: faites votre d. et laissez faire aux dieux 111:33
Devon, glorious D. 69:68
Dévot: pour être d. ... pas moins homme! 224:50
Devotion: dollar ... object of universal d. 170:18
the d. to something afar 371:56
Devour: threat'ning to d. me opens wide 218:62
Devout: d. but ... human 224:50
miserable, but not ... d. 173:65
Dew: d. on the face of the dead 30:84
foggy, foggy d. 17:96
hill-side's d.-pearled 75:44
like the d. on the mountain 295:98
resolve itself into a d. 305:42
walks o'er the d. of yon ... hill 305:36
Dew-drop: fragile d. on its perilous way 185:35
Diable: courage ... le d. est mort 286:1
noir comme le d. 384:30
Dials: carve out d. quaintly 321:70
Diamond: d. and safire bracelet lasts 199:11
like a d. in the sky 384:36
Diana of the Ephesians 56:21
Diary: I never travel without my d. 405:14
memory ... is the d. 405:13
Dick the shepherd blows his nail 332:20
Dickens: what the d. his name is 340:31
Dictate: not presume to d., but broiled fowl 120:60
Dictator: the German d., instead of snatching 100:90
Did: d. nothing ... d. it very well 144:90
d. that they d. in envy of great Caesar 326:30
nor ever d. a wiser one 288:21
sang his didn't he danced his d. 116:94
Dido found Aeneas wd. not come 252:40
Di-do-dum: Dido ... was D. 252:40
Die: a man can d. but once 317:19
and shall Trelawny d.? 158:74
appointed unto men once to d. 59:97

Die (*continued*)
as a man lives, so shall he d.   271:34
as natural to d.   24:87
beauty's rose might never d.   362:29
beauty that must d.   183:22
beneath its shade we'll live and d.
   109:21
break faith with us who d.   202:49
cowards d. many times   324:1
crawling coop't we live and d.
   136:80
d. a dry death   355:28
d. all, d. merrily   315:81
d. and go we know not where   337:90
d. because a woman's fair   408:49
d. beyond my means   406:34
d. in the last ditch   79:90
d. not, poor death   124:10
d. ... the last thing I shall do!   243:21
do d. of it do seldom ... recover
   299:68
how can man d. better?   201:36
I shall d. at the top   382:13
I will d. ere she shall grieve   408:50
I will d. in the last ditch   406:36
if I shd. d. think only this   71:92
if we are mark'd to d.   320:55
in what peace a Christian can d.
   10:12
lay me down and d.   124:16
leave me there to d.   17:88
let me d. the death of the righteous
   38:4
let us do or d.   81:23
look about us and to d.   250:7
love her till I d.   18:9
love too much ... d. for love   271:21
lovers ... d. as soon as one pleases
   109:13
man can only d. once   271:28
more deaths than one must d.
   404:96
never say d.   273:87
no young man believes he shall ... d.
   159:80
Oh, Sir! the good d. first   409:64
people d., but books never d.   289:33
said I wd. d. a bachelor   343:70
see Naples and d.   277:22
seemly ... to d. for one's country
   167:77
seems it rich to d.   184:29
shd. certain persons d. before they
   sing   106:70
soon as ... born, he begins to d.
   278:54
swans sing before they d.   106:70
Tamburlaine ... must d.   205:79

Die (*continued*)
the d. is cast   87:7
the Man perceives it d. away   411:78
theirs but to do and d.   385:42
they ... d. by famine, d. by inches
   161:1
those about to d. salute you   380:88
to d. ... awfully big adventure   28:61
to d., to sleep   309:95
to d. upon a kiss   347:23
toddle ... home and d. in bed   293:82
we must be free or d.   413:5
when good ... bad ... Americans d.
   406:25
who wd. wish to d.?   69:65
with my little eye, I saw him d.
   241:88
you asked this man to d.   22:58
young men may d., old men must
   284:63
Died: d. maintaining his right of way
   13:49
d. when his prospects ... brightening
   12:42
in the odour of sanctity d.   28:54
laugh! I thought I shd. have d.   99:79
liked it not, and d.   416:47
men have d. ... but not for love
   302:3
queens have d. young and fair
   229:99
she damned near d.   17:96
she had d. of cramp   153:10
she shd. have d. hereafter   336:76
since Maurice d.   70:77
stopped short ... when the old man
   d.   416:43
the dog it was that d.   151:77
to the North-west d. away   74:24
who d. to save us all   11:20
wd. God I had d. for thee   40:51
wd. to God we had d. ... in ...
   Egypt   36:79
Dies: flower ... once has blown for
   ever d.   135:71
he that d. pays all debts   356:46
light of the bright world d.   69:70
love ... soon as beauty d.   123:6
no man happy until he d.   375:22
not how a man d., but how he lives
   175:98
person who either marries or d.
   23:67
say that when the Poet d.   295:3
the king never d.   66:24, 268:36
what an artist d. with me!   230:10
Diet: all necessaries ... d. unparalleled
   120:52

Diet (*continued*)
  no ... idiosyncrasy in d. 72:2
  praise is the best d. 375:10
Dieu: D. est ... pour les gros bataillons
  398:15
  si D. n'existait pas 397:12
Differ: men ... d. as Heaven and Earth
  385:52
Different: how d. from us, Miss Beale
  15:68
Difficult: all things are d. before ...
  easy 280:24
  d. ..., Sir? I wish it were impossible
  178:40
  problems of victory ... no less d.
  101:5
Dig: I cannot d.; to beg I am ashamed
  55:83
Digest: mark, learn, and inwardly d.
  64:86
Digestion: d. ... great secret of life
  375:12
  now good d. wait on appetite 335:54
  things sweet ... prove in d. sour
  348:35
Diggeth: whoso d. a pit shall fall 46:85
Dignities: peace above all earthly d.
  323:82
Dignity and worth of the human
  person 394:76
Diminish one dowle ... in my plume
  356:49
Diminished: stars hide their d. heads
  218:61
Diminishes: any man's death d. me
  124:14
Dimmed: glory of the sun will be d.
  27:48
Dine: and go to inns to d. 99:76
  I shd. d. at Ware 113:59
  if wife shd. d. at Edmonton 113:59
  Noah ... when he sat down to d.
  99:77
  'whar shall we ... d. the day?
  12:40
Dined on mince and ... quince 195:62
Ding: d. dong, bell 232:28
  sing hey d. a d. d. 303:7
Dinner: a d. lubricates business 296:18
  best number for a d. party 157:54
  d. of herbs where love is 45:71
  good d. enough to be sure 175:92
  good d. upon his table 178:45
  people who want d. do not ring
  27:46
Diplomat these days ... a head-waiter
  395:82
Direction: all chance, d. 250:12

Directions: rode madly off in all d.
  194:51
Dirge: by forms unseen their d. is sung
  107:90
Dirt: fling d. enough ... will stick
  263:73
Dirty: hail fellow ... all d. and wet
  381:4
Disadvantage: ship has ... d. of ...
  danger 177:16
Disappointments: I have been too
  familiar with d. 196:72
Disapprove: I d. ... but will defend ...
  yr. right 398:16
Disapproves: condemns whatever he d.
  79:93
Disaster: meet with Triumph and D.
  190:4
  valiant ... 'gainst all d. 77:64
Disasters: day's d. in his morning face
  150:68
  we make guilty of our d. 327:53
Disbelief: willing suspension of d.
  107:79
Disciplines: I know the d. of war
  320:49
Discobolus: the D. standeth ... dusty
  ... maimed 82:47
Discommendeth: he who d. others
  72:98
Discontent: winter of our d. 351:64
Discord: all d., harmony not understood 250:12
  hark what d. follows! 358:68
Discount: sells us life at a d. 140:33
Discouragement: no d. shall make him
  ... relent 77:64
Discover: doth ... d. vice ... d. virtue
  24:92
Discretion: an ounce of d. is worth
  274:24
  being now come to the years of d.
  64:2
  better part of valour is d. 315:93
  d. is the better part of valour 260:76
  fair woman ... without d. 45:64
  philosophy ... nothing but d. 296:33
Disdain: d. and scorn ride sparkling
  343:71
  what, my dear Lady D.! 342:58
Disease: d. [consumption of purse] is
  incurable 316:3
  remedy ... worse than the d. 25:9
  strange d. of modern life 21:42
  'There is no cure for this d.' 31:91
  this long d., my Life 248:81
  when age, d., or sorrows strike him
  103:27

Do (*continued*)
we never d. anything well till   159:85
what men dare d. ... daily d.   343:80
what you can d. for yr. country
188:75
Doch-an'-dorris   193:42
Dock: in a dull, dark d.   145:3
Doctor: God heals ... d. takes the fee
264:19
Doctrine: d. is that each one shd.
select   368:25
d. of a strenuous life   289:35
from women's eyes this d. I derive
331:16
not for the d., but the music   249:98
Doctrines: makes all d. plain and clear
82:38
Dodger: sobriquet of 'The artful D.'
120:56
Dog: as a d. returneth to his vomit
46:84
beware of the d.   246:49
d. did nothing in the night-time
125:23
d. does not eat d.   260:81
d. is turned to his own vomit   60:13
d. it was that died   151:77
d.'s walking on his hind legs   175:90
d., to gain some private ends   151:76
d. will have his day   312:34
d. will not howl if you beat   260:83
every d. has his d.   260:82
every d. its day   189:89
fetch her poor d. a bone   236:59
give a d. a bad name   264:6
I am His Highness' d. at Kew   251:30
if you call a d. Hervey   174:73
keep a d. and bark yourself   268:27
let no d. bark   338:98
love me, love my d.   270:19
mine enemy's d., though he had bit
me   330:95
misbeliever, cut-throat d.   338:6
pray tell me sir, whose d. are you?
251:30
rather be a d. and bay the moon
325:24
teach an old d. tricks   279:12
the little d. laughed   232:33
the young man's d. with them   62:40
they grin like a d., and run   42:12
took by th' throat the circumcised d.
346-7:22
when a d. bites a man   116:1
why should a d. ... have life?   331:6
Dogged: it's d. as does it   393:55
Dogs: barking d. seldom bite   255:95
clept all by the name of d.   334:48

Dogs (*continued*)
d. bark at me as I halt   351:66
fought the d. and killed the cats
75:37
let sleeping d. lie   269:71
let slip the d. of war   324:9
mad d. and Englishmen   112:42
two d. strive ... a third runs ... with
[bone]   281:76
uncover, d., and lap   357:61
Doing: joy's soul lies in the d.   358:65
let us then be up and d.   198:98
nothing – half so much worth d.
153:13
saying is one thing and d. another
277:16
see what she's d. and tell her she
mustn't   285:81
shortest answer is d.   277:33
what was he d. ... god Pan?   73:13
worth d. at all is worth d. well   98:55
worth d. is worth d. well   283:24
Doings: all our d. without charity
64:87
even a child is known by his d.   45:76
Doit: a d. to relieve a lame beggar
356:40
Dollar: almighty d. ... object of ...
devotion   170:18
Dollars: however plenty ... d. may
become   103:23
Dolore: nessun maggior d. che ricor-
darsi   116:3
Dolphin: a mermaid on a d.,s back
341:44
Dome: a d. of many-coloured glass
367:19
Dominion: death hath no more d.
56:31
death shall have no d.   390:17
hand that holds d. over man   390:20
I'm truly sorry man's d.   80:17
Dominions on which the sun never sets
230:18
Don: remote and ineffectual d.   32:1
Done: do as you wd. be d. by   260:79
d. those things ... we ought not
63:67
easier said than d.   261:6
nothing d. while aught remains to do
288:24
put off ... what may be d. today
273:85
so little d., so much to do   287:7
something ought to be d.   401:66
surprised to find it d.   175:90
thank God I have d. with him
174:79

Done (*continued*)
they d. the old woman in   366:97
things d. cannot be undone   260:86
to have loved ... thought ... d.   20:31
'twere well it were d. quickly   333:35
well begun is half d.   282:21
what have I d. for you, England?
  160:96
what's d. cannot be undone   335:70
Dong with a luminous Nose   194:56
Donkey: talk the hind leg off a d.
  279:5
Donne: another Newton, a new D.
  169:4
  D.'s verses ... the peace of God
  170:20
Doom: even to the edge of d.   363:48
  stretch out to th' crack of d.   335:64
Doomed for a ... term to walk the
  night   307:63
Doomsday: d. is near; die ... merrily
  315:81
  then is d. near   308:79
Doon: banks and braes o' bonnie D.
  81:26
Door: a beaten path to his d.   133:48
  a d. must be ... open or shut   227:78
  a D. to which ... no key   135:73
  at her ivied d.   87:11
  every d. ... shut but death's d.
  260:87
  fortune knocks, open the d.   263:87
  keep the d. of my lips   44:51
  keep the wolf from the d.   283:45
  knocking at Preferment's d.   21:41
  knocking on the moonlit d.   118:23
  love ... goes out at the d.   270:12
  stand at the d., and knock   61:24
  three, four, knock at the d.   236:60
  thy form from off my d.   247:67
Doorkeeper: I had rather be a d.   43:15
Doors: d. ... being as yet shut upon me
  187:60
  pale Death ... knocks at the d.
  166:73
Dotheboys Hall: at ... D. Youth are
  boarded   120:52
Dots: what those damned d. meant
  100:87
Double: d., d., toil and trouble   335:58
  surely you'll grow d.   414:25
Double entendre: the horrible d.   13:53
Doubled him up for ever   143:73
Doublethink means ... two contradictory beliefs   242:4
Doubt: 'I d. it,' said the Carpenter
  92:79
  more faith in honest d.   386:65

Doubt (*continued*)
new philosophy calls all in d.   123:3
no probable ... possible d. whatever
  143:72
when in d., leave out   283:27
when in d., win the trick   168:87
Doubted: never d. clouds wd. break
  73:16
Doubtful: by destruction dwell in d.
  joy   334:50
Doubting: a castle called D. Castle
  77:62
Doubts: begin with d., ... end in
  certainties   26:37
  he shall end in d.   26:37
  knows nothing, d. nothing   268:49
  saucy d. and fears   335:53
Douglas: Judge D. and myself   196:76
  old song of Percy and D.   373:87
  the D. in his hall   296:12
Dove: beside the springs of D.   413:15
  d. came ... in the evening   35:47
  my d., my dear ... my life   388:87
  Oh that I had wings like a d.!   42:10
Dove-cote: like an eagle in a d.   304:19
Doves: grass is as soft as the breast of
  d.   111:34
Dowagers: with ... d. for deans   388:95
Dowdiness: memory ... beginning of d.
  406:32
Dower: faith's transcendent d.   413:14
Down: d., d. to hell   322:73
  d. will come baby, cradle   233:38
  easier to pull d. than to build   275:69
  get d. you dirty rascal   233:41
  he that is d. ... fear no fall   77:66
  I don't think one 'comes d.'   242:10
  levers to lift me ... being d.   313:57
  never go d. to the end of the town
  211:57
  quite, quite d.   310:1
Downstairs: be off, or I'll kick you d.
  90:49
Doxy over the dale   361:17
Drab: a-cursing like a very d.   309:93
  ditch-deliver'd by a d.   335:59
Dragon: Saint George, that swing'd
  the d.   326:35
Drain: leave by the next town d.
  377:50
Drake he's in his hammock   230:11
Draughts: shallow d. intoxicate the
  brain   249:94
Draw: d. back ... to leap better   267:11
  d. but twenty miles a-day?   205:78
  must d. the line somewhere   260:88
Drawers: hewers of wood and d. of
  water   38:19

Dread: close your eyes with holy d. 107:76
doth walk in fear and d. 106:60
d. and fear of kings 339:15
d. of something after death 309:95
Dreadful: dancing? Oh, d. 79:91
death ... mighty and d. 124:10
O! d. is the check 71:87
the acting of a d. thing 324:98
Dream: a sight to d. of 106:66
a vision or a waking d.? 184:32
and slowly read, and d. 417:58
awoke ... from a deep d. of peace 168:94
behold it was a d. 77:63
consecration, and the poet's d. 409:61
d. of battled fields no more 295:97
d. of money-bags to-night 339:9
d. you are crossing the Channel 144:92
fly, forgotten, as a d. dies 400:40
glory and the freshness of a d. 410:72
if you can d. 190:3
life is but an empty d. 198:95
lust of fame was but a d. 71:86
not d. them, all day long 189:86
oaks ... d., and so d. all night 182:98
old men shall d. dreams 50:80
perchance to d. Ay, there's the rub 309:95
phantasma or a hideous d. 324:98
the glory and the d. 410:76
they d. of home 137:94
wrecks of a dissolving d. 368:28
Dreamed: d. of cheese—toasted, mostly 379:75
I d. that Greece might ... be free 84–5:78
Dreamer: behold, this d. cometh 36:63
d. of dreams 227:71
poet and the d. 182:94
Dreaming: city with her d. spires 21:46
d. arl the time o' Plymouth Hoe 230:11
Dreams: fanatics have their d. 182:93
into the land of my d. 189:84
more things ... than this world d. 386:55
nature lends such evil d. 386:62
not make d. yr. master 190:3
read of ... or dreamt of in d. 28:53
so full of fearful d. 351:71
such stuff as d. are made on 356–7:50
wovest d. of joy and fear 368:32

Dreamt: d. of in yr. philosophy 307:69
d. that I dwelt in marble halls 76:55
I have long d. of such a ... man 318:34
read of ... or d. of 28:53
Dreary: how d. to be somebody 122:81
world am sad and d. 138:6
Drenched with dew, Old Nod the shepherd 118:25
Dress: a sweet disorder in the d. 162:16
all d. is fancy d. 366:6
noble youths did d. themselves 316:8
Drill: no names, no pack d. 273:96
Drink: a rule never to d. by daylight 209:30
d. and the devil had done for the rest 379:74
d. 'a pinta milka day 11:26
d. deep, or taste not the Pierian spring 249:94
'D. ME' beautifully printed 89:43
d. no longer water 59:90
d. to me only with thine eyes 178:49
d. with him that wears a hood 380:81
five reasons we shd. d. 10:16
lead a horse ... cannot make him d. 269:62
man wants but little d. 164:47
much d. ... equivocator with lechery 334:45
nor any drop to d. 105:50
shall sit and d. with me 32:7
taste for d., combined with gout 143:73
that I might d., and leave the world 184:24
what shd. we do for d.? 15:65
Drinking: continual d. of Knowledge 186:59
diverted by every means but d. 177:20
d. Cheltenham waters 12:41
d. is the soldier's pleasure 127:53
d. largely sobers us again 249:94
d. the blude red wine 12:37
there are two reasons for d. 245:37
Drinks his wine 'mid laughter free 19:10
Driven: soul ... d., I know not whither 401:55
Drives the flower ... d. my green age 390:19
Driving: d. of Jehu ... he driveth furiously 40:62

Driving (*continued*)
spend my life in d. briskly 177:23
Drone: the lazy, yawning d. 318–19:39
Drop: every d. of the Thames 79:94
nor any d. to drink 105:50
raineth d. and staineth slop 252:47
Drops: little d. of water 89:41
women's weapons, water-d. 328:68
Dross: all is d. that is not Helena 204:63
Drought of March hath perced 96:25
Drown: I'll d. my book 357:55
what paid … to d. 352:72
Drowned: drench'd our steeples, d. the cocks 328:71
d. in the depth of the sea 53:38
d. my Honour in a shallow Cup 136:82
pluck up d. honour by the locks 313:54
Drowning: d. man … catch at a straw 260:90
no d. mark upon him 355:27
Drowns things weighty and solid 26:35
Drudge: for a d., disobedient 151:79
lexicographer—a harmless d. 172:46
Drum: listenin' for the d. 230:11
not a d. was heard 408:52
the spirit-stirring d. 345:10
war-d. throbbed no longer 387:81
Drummed them out of town 234:47
Drummers: nine d. drumming 238:73
Drums: hearts … like muffled d. are beating 198:96
sound the trumpets, beat the d. 127:52
Drunk: d. as a fish 260:91
d. as a lord 260:92
d. as a mouse 260:93
d. as a wheelbarrow 260:94
d. the milk of Paradise 107:76
man … must get d. 84:71
never [happy] but when he is d. 176:13
not so think as you d. 378:56
stag at eve had d. his fill 294:94
this meeting is d. 121:73
Drunkard: the rolling English d. made the rolling English road 99:72
Drunken: do with the d. sailor 19:14
d. folks seldom take harm 260:95
d. night … cloudy morning 261:96
went to Worts and got more d. 252:41
Drunkenness: babbling d. 360:1
Dry: a d. brain in a d. season 130:93
as d. as dust 261:97

Dry (*continued*)
but oh, I am so d. 17:88
die a d. death 355:28
hearts … d. as summer dust 409:64
old man in a d. month 130:92
Dublin: in D.'s fair city 17:89
Duchess: I am D. of Malfi still 400:47
the D.! Oh, my dear paws! 90:47
the D. said, in a hoarse growl 90:50
Duck: dying d. in a thunderstorm 261:2
water off a d.'s back 282:11
Duckling: The Ugly D. 11:24
Ducks and drakes: to made d. of 261:98
Due: to give the devil his d. 264:8
one born out of d. time 57:58
Duke: became a most important d. 32:4
everybody praised the D. 376:30
Dukedom: library was d. large enough 355:31
Dulce et decorum est pro patria mori 167:77
Dull: as d. as ditchwater 261:99
d. in himself, … cause of dullness 11:12
d. wd. he be of soul 412:96
prophetick blessing – Be thou d. 127:49
Dullness: Shadwell … mature in d. 128:69
Dumb: d. men get no lands 261:1
great [cares] are d. 269:82
Duncan is in his grave 334:51
Dunce: a d. … kept at home 113:65
a d. … sent to roam 113:65
a d. with wits 247:69
Dundee: bonnets of Bonny D. 294:92
Dunfermline: king sits in D. town 12:37
Dungeon: live upon the vapour of a d. 345:8
Dunsinane: till Birnam Forest come to D. 336:73
Dusk: in the d. … light behind her 148:42
little breezes d. and shiver 387:76
Dust: a d. whom England bore 71:93
all lovers must … come to d. 305:30
as chimney-sweepers, come to d. 304–5:29
as dry as d. 261:97
ashes to ashes, d. to d. 65:15
before we too into the D. descend 135:70
cinders, ashes, d. 183:11
d. hath closed Helen's eye 229:99

Ears: e. burn, someone is talking 261:3
have e., but they hear not 43:31
he that hath e. to hear 54:56
lend me your e. 325:12
make two e. of corn ... to grow
381:2
music creep in our e. 340:22
noise of waters in my e. 352:72
put this engine to our e. 381:98
softest music to attending e. 354:5
there was a shout about my e. 99:69
to e. of flesh and blood 307:64
walls have e. 282:99
Earth: a girdle round about the e.
341:45
a Heaven on E. 219:65
a ladder set up on the e. 36:61
a new heaven and a new e. 61:32
all people that on e. do dwell 188:77
created the heaven and the e. 34:26
daughter of E. and Water 368:23
dear e., I do salute thee 349:49
differ as Heaven and E. 385:52
dim spot which men call E. 212:73
e. has not anything ... more fair
412:96
e. is the Lord's, and the fulness
42:94
e.'s diurnal course 414:19
e.'s sweet flowing breast 188–9:81
e.'s the right place for love 139:21
e. to e., ashes to ashes 65:15
e. was without form, and void 34:26
firm place ... I will move the e. 20:24
from this e., this grave, this dust
286:93
heaven to e., from e. to heaven
342:53
Heaven tries e. if it be in tune 200:25
Judge of all the e. 35:54
kings are e.'s gods 347:26
lards the lean e. as he walks 313:59
lay her i' th' e. 312:32
multiply and replenish the e. 34:29
old sad e. must borrow its mirth
404:91
past away a glory from the e. 410:74
poetry of e. is never dead 185:42
shall not perish from the e. 196:79
the e. abideth for ever 46:95
the e. and every common sight
410:72
the e. ... appear ... [a] faery place
415:39
the e. doth like a snake renew 368:28
the e., tideless and inert 27:48
the meek shall inherit the e. 42:2
there were giants in the e. 35:44

Earth (*continued*)
this e. of majesty, this seat of Mars
348:41
this e., this realm, this England
348–9:41
thou bleeding piece of e. 324:8
through my lips to unawakened e.
369:38
while the e. remaineth, seedtime
35:48
write sorrow on the bosom of the e.
349:53
yours is the E. and everything 190:5
Ease: bankrupt of life, ... prodigal of e.
126:40
done with so much e. 126:37
for another gives its e. 67:43
not the doctrine of ignoble e.
289:35
O Woman! in our hours of e. 296:14
through the air with the greatest of e.
196:71
true e. in writing comes from art
249:99
youth of labour ... age of e. 150:64
Easiest: the e. way out 401–2:69
Easy come, e. go 261:8
East: a long way e. of Camberwell
32:4
E. is E., and West is West 189:92
gorgeous E. with richest hand
217:45
in the chambers of the E. 68:54
it is the e. and Juliet is the sun
353:97
somewhere E. of Suez 190:8
we have seen his star in the e. 51:2
Eastern: like a blooming E. bride
127:50
not by e. windows only 104:34
Eat: dare to e. a peach 131:4
did e. bread to the full 36:79
dog does not e. dog 260:81
e. and welcome 261:10
e. one's words 261:11
e. to live ... not live to e. 261:12
e. yr. cake and have it 261:13
great ones e. up the little ones
347:27
I always e. peas with honey 15:63
I cannot e. but little meat 380:81
let us e. and drink; for tomorrow
we ... die 48:40
my apple trees will never ... e.
139:26
so I did sit and e. 161:13
some ... canna e., ... some wad e.
81:24

'Elementary,' said he [Holmes]   124:21

Elements: e. of whom yr. swords are temper'd   356:49

framed us of four e.   205:76

I tax not you, you e.   328:72

our torments also may ... become our e.   217:51

the e. so mix'd in him   326:31

Eleven: e. buckram men ... out of two   314:66

rain before seven, fine before e.   275:75

Eleventh Commandment ... not be found out   261:16

Elf: a servant's ... an impudent e.   27:51

Elijah ... cast his mantle   40:59

Eliminated: when you have e. the impossible   125:25

Elinor: 'I am afraid,' replied E.   23:80

Elizabeth: no scandal about Queen E.   371:63

spacious times of great E.   385:45

Eloquence: love and business teach e.   270:9

Elsewhere: when e., live as they live e.   11:23

Elves of hills, brooks, ... groves   357:54

Ely: my Lord of E., when I was ... in Holborn   352:74

Elysium: what E. have ye known?   183:14

Embarras des richesses   11:21

Embarrassing: the e. young   141:50

Embers: glowing e. through the room   213:86

O joy! that in our e. ... doth live   411:80

Embodiment: the Law is the true e.   143:81

Embody: I, my Lords, e. the Law   143–4:81

Embrace: arms, take your last e.   354:18

none, I think, do there e.   206:95

Eminence: by merit raised to that bad e.   217:45

Emotion recollected in tranquillity   416:42

Emperor: heard ... by e. and clown   184:30

to the tent-royal of their e.   318:39

Empire: all the loungers of the E.   125:27

another mighty E. overthrown!   413:6

how is the E.?   142:63

Empire (*continued*)

if the British E. ... last for a thousand years   101:95

King dead, the e. unpossess'd?   352:82

Mother E. stands splendidly isolated   137:99

neither holy, nor Roman, nor an e.   398:14

preside over the liquidation of the British E.   101:3

the E. is a Commonwealth of Nations   290:40

to found a great e.   374:98

young was called to E.   128:68

Empires: day of E. has come   95:14

vaster than e. and more slow   206:93

Employment: give e. to the artisan   31:94

the pleasantness of an e.   23:80

Empty vessels make the most noise   261:18

Enchanted: as holy and e.   106:72

Enchanter: ghosts from an e. fleeing   369:35

Enchantment: lends e. to the view   88:20

Encourage: kill an admiral ... to e. the others   397:8

Encourager: pour e. les autres   397:8

Encumbers: Patron ... e. him with help   174:78

End: a loud noise at one e.   191:21

'a made a finer e.   319:43

ages of hopeless e.   217:50

attempt the e.   162:22

beginning of the e.   384:29

big e.-ians and small e.-ians   381:99

boys get at one e. ... lose at the other   176:15

e. justifies the means   261:19

everything hath an e.   262:33

found no e., in wandering mazes lost   218:55

four ... winters ... springs e. in a word   348:34

he shall e. in certainties   26:37

long weary day have e.   377:39

longest day must have an e.   270:1

Lord, make me to know mine e.   42:5

more than an e. to war, we want   289:34

my last e. be like his!   38:4

not even the beginning of the e. ... but ... the e. of the beginning   101:2

End (*continued*)

our minutes hasten to their e. 363:40

seen one thing, that love hath an e. 383:22

the e. of this day's business 326:29

the man would die ... and there an e. 335:55

the right true e. of love 123:8

Sans Wine ... Song ... E.! 135:70

vegetate and wish ... an e. 79:92

yes, to the very e. 290:46

Endeavour: a disinterested e. to learn 21:50

Ending: e. is better than mending 168:98

love is ... sour in the e. 270:14

Endowed by their Creator with ... rights 171:26

Ends: divinity that shapes our e. 312:35

dog, to gain some private e. 151:76

make both e. meet 257:61

odd old e. stol'n forth of holy writ 351:70

to serve our private e. 100:84

Endurable: love [will] make a thing e. 411:88

Endure: cannot e. in his age 343:69

cd. e. the toothache patiently 344:86

first e., then pity, then embrace 250:14

from age to age e. 188:78

youth's a stuff will not e. 359:84

Endured: can't be cured, must be e. 283:23

much is to be e. 173:64

tolerable and not to be e. 343:75

Enemies: confusion to his e. 16:85

left me naked to mine e. 323:84

love your e. 52:14

Enemy: best ... e. of the good 397:11

better an open e. 255:14

here shall he see no e. 300:83

how goes the e.? 287:5

if thine e. be hungry 45:81

mine e.'s dog 330:95

my name ... terrible to the e. 316:2

of yr. e. say nothing 278:62

the e. faints not 103:32

trust not ... an old e. 281:60

Energetic: our speech ... e. without rules 172:40

Energies of our system will decay 27:48

Energy: e. is eternal delight 68:57

reason and e., love and hate 68:56

Enfants: les e. terribles 141:50

Enfer: chaud comme l'e. 384:30

Engine: e. that moves in determinate grooves 158:68

put this e. to our ears 381:98

England: a body of E.'s, breathing English air 71:93

a dust whom E. bore 71:93

a time there was, ere E.'s griefs 150:63

be E. what she will 100:82

between France and E. is the sea 171:38

E., bound in with the triumphant sea 349:42

E. expects every man 229:7

E. has saved herself ... save Europe 247:57

E. hath need of thee 413:3

E. ... hell for horses 81:31, 261:20

E. is a nation of shop-keepers 228:85

E. is the mother of parliaments 71:81

E. is the paradise of women 81:31, 136:86, 261:20

E., my E.? E. my own 160:96

E.'s green and pleasant land 67:38

E. will have her neck wrung 101:1

E., with all thy faults 114:70

E. ... wont to conquer others 349:42

Florence, Elizabethan E. 170:13

for E.'s the one land 71:90

foreign field ... forever E. 71:92

gallows standing in E. when thou art king? 312:45

gentlemen in E., now abed 320:59

Happy is E.! I cd. be content 185:43

heart and stomach of ... King of E. 132:20

high road that leads him to E. 175:85

history of E. is ... history of progress 202:45

I know the kings of E. 147:31

if E. to itself do rest but true 327:48

in E. – now! 74:21

in E. we ... rely on ... time-lag 401:66

know of E. who only E. know? 190:97

laws of E. are at my commandment 318:33

light such a candle ... in E. 193:40

men in E. that do no work today 320:54

my love for E. and Ireland 287:11

nor, E., did I know till then 409:66

not three good men unhang'd in E. 314:64

England (*continued*)

> *Oats. –* ... in E. ... given to horses 172:48
> Oh, to be in E. 74:21
> on E.'s pleasant pastures seen 67:38
> people of E. that never have spoken yet 99:75
> roast beef of E. 134:61
> Stately Homes of E. 111:39, 40
> stately homes of E.! 160:90
> there'll always be an E. 244:24
> this earth, this realm, this E. 348–9:41
> this E. never did ... lie at the ... foot 327:47
> 'Tis for the honour of E. 109:8
> wake up, E. 142:62
> walk upon E.'s mountains 67:38
> ye mariners of E. 88:21
> youth of E. are on fire 319:40

English: a body of England's, breathing E. air 71:93

> be among the E. Poets after my death 187:62
> blood of E. shall manure the ground 350:56
> Chaucer, well of E. undefiled 377:44
> E. are ... the least ... pure philosophers 27:45
> E. as she is Spoke 393:57
> E. never know when ... beaten 261:21
> E. winter—ending in July 85:85
> grave where E. oak and holly 158:72
> on, on, you noblest E. 319:46
> our E. tongue a gallimaufry 377:48
> principle of the E. constitution 66:25
> the E. ... a foul-mouthed nation 159:79
> the E. country gentleman 406:27
> the E. have hot-water bottles 209:40
> the rolling E. drunkard made the rolling E. road 99:72
> the sort of E. up with which 102:9
> trick of our E. nation 316:1
> under an E. heaven 71:94
> wholesome ... really nice E. people 365:72
> winged heels, as E. Mercuries 319:40
> with our E. dead 319:45

Englishman: an E., even ... alone, forms a ... queue 209:41

> an E. thinks he is moral 365:82
> E. does not travel to see Englishmen 379:65

Englishman (*continued*)

> E. ... enjoys himself ... for a noble purpose 161:9
> E.'s home is his castle 261:22
> my-lorded as only a free-born E. can 389:13
> rights of an E. 180:65
> stirred the hearts of every E. 294:91
> the last great E. is low 388:92
> to his credit ... an E.! 147:29
> way to an E.'s heart 282:13

Englishmen: mad dogs and E. 112:42

> reveal Himself ... first to his E. 224:42
> when two E. meet ... talk of the weather 172:51

Engross: pens a stanza when he shd. e. 248:78

Enigma: a riddle wrapped in a mystery inside an e. 100:91

Enjoy: can thoroughly e. the pepper 90:52

> e. themselves so well, as at ... tavern 177:17
> prize not ... whiles we e. it 343:81
> who can e. alone? 220:87
> you will never e. the world 392:52

Enjoyed: e. no sooner but despised 363:50

> human life ... little to be e. 173:64
> that bards of old e. 68:55
> to have e. the sun 20:31
> what peaceful hours I once e. 113:62

Enjoyment: variety is the mother of e. 123:99

Enjoys: the Englishman never e. himself 161:9

Enough: e. is as good as a feast 65:18, 261:23

> e. is e. 261:24
> e. that there *is* a beyond 364:64
> grant me ... more than e. 203:59
> wore e. for modesty 76:15

Enriched: pension never e. a young man 274:38

Enriches: robs me ... not e. him 345:6

Ense: calamus saevior e. patet 81:30

Ensign: beauty's e. yet is crimson 354:17

> tear her tattered e. down 164:46
> th' imperial e. ... high advanced 217:39

Enter: abandon hope all ye who e. 116:2

> e. ye in at ... strait gate 52:26
> ye shall not e. into ... Kingdom 53:37

Enterprise: the e. is sick 358:67

Enterprises: e. of great pith and moment 309:95

impediments to great e. 24:96

Entertaining: more e. than half the novels 208:22

Enthroned in the hearts of kings 339:15

Enthusiasm: considering that e. moves the world 27:49

long for a little ordinary e. 242:8

nothing great ... without e. 132:28

Enthusiasts: so few e. ... speak the truth 27:49

Entire and whole and perfect 377:53

Entrance: beware of e. to a quarrel 306:56

Entrances: have their exits and their e. 301:90

Envied: better be e. than pitied 255:17

Envious: rent the e. Casca made 325:18

Envy: e. and calumny and hate and pain 367:16

e., hatred, and malice 63:77

in e. of great Caesar 326:30

means ... too low for e. 112:47

the e. of less happier lands 348–9:41

Ephesians: Diana of the E. 56:21

Epilogue: a good play needs no e. 303:11

Epitaph: believe a woman or an e. 85:91

Epitaphs: a nice derangement of e. 372:71

graves and worms and e. 349:53

Epithet: fair is too foul an e. for thee 205:77

Epitome: all mankind's e. 126:43

Eppur si muove 141:44

Epsom Salts: had we but stuck to E. 12:41

Equal: all animals are e. but some are more e. 242:98

e. division of unequal earnings 132:25

far from ... true ... naturally e. 175:96

inferiors revolt ... be e. 20:27

that all men are created e. 171:26

Equals [revolt] that they may be superior 20:27

Eros: unarm, E.; the ... task is done 299:64

Err: better to e. with Pope 85:92

not e., who say ... when the Poet dies 295:3

the most may e. as grossly 127:47

to e. is human 267:7

Err (*continued*)

to e. is human, to forgive divine 249:4

Errand: in thy joyous e. reach the spot 136:83

Errands for the Ministers of State 143:76

Erred: we have e. and strayed 63:66

Erring: a rod to check the e. 413:7

Error: custom without reason ... ancient e. 259:45

e. of opinion may be tolerated 171:28

gross e. held in schools 142:59

if this be e. and upon me prov'd 363:48

ignorance is preferable to e. 171:32

mountainous e. ... highly heap'd 303:15

Errors: amusing with numerous e. [book] 152:95

e., like straws, upon the surface 127:55

if to her share some female e. 251:34

Esau: E. my brother ... a hairy man 36:59

the hands of E. 36:60

Escape: e. me?—never 74:27

thou shalt not e. calumny 310:98

who shall e. whipping? 308:88

Essence: his glassy e., like an angry ape 337:87

Estate: become a fourth e. of the realm 202:44

ordered their e. 10:18

Esteem: riches I hold in light e. 71:86

Esteemed: better to be vile than vile e. 363:49

Esther: loved E. above all ... women 40:64

État: l'É. c'est moi 199:12

Eternal: abode where the E. are 368:20

condition ... liberty ... e. vigilance 116:98

energy is e. delight 68:57

e. summer gilds them yet 84:77

on Fame's e. beadroll 377:44

thought ... to be boy e. 361:12

Eternity: damned from here to E. 190:99

deserts of vast e. 206:94

e. in an hour 66:27

lives in e.'s sunrise 66:34

make the mighty ages of e. 89:41

memorial from the soul's e. 290:49

passing through nature to e. 305:40

stains the white radiance of E. 367:19

Eternity (*continued*)
thoughts that wander through e. 217:49

Etherised: evening is spread out ... like a patient e. 130:98

Ethiop: a rich jewel in an E.'s ear 353:94

Ethiopian: can the E. change his skin? 49:56

Eton: Waterloo ... won on the playing fields of E. 401:61

Euphelia serves to grace my measure 253:51

Euripides: a chorus-ending from E. 73:17

Europe: all E. shd. know that we have blockheads 109:8
glory of E. is extinguished 78:78
lamps are going out all over E. 156:51
last territorial claim ... in E. 163:31
part of the community of E. 149:54
save E. by her example 247:57
Soviet power into heart of Western E. 102:7
splendidly isolated in E. 137:99
we are ... smallest country left in E. 395:80

Eurydice: half-regained E. 215:6

Eve: fairest of her daughters E. 219:67
from noon to dewy e. 217:44
when Adam delved and E. span 27:50
when E. upon the first of Men 165:63

Even: contrive to write so e. 23:77

Événements: l'histoire des grands é. 397:13

Evening: bright exhalation in the e. 322:79
e. crowns the day 262:25
e. is spread out against the sky 130:98
I light my lamp in the e. 32:5
it is a beauteous e. 412:92
It was a summer's e. 376:27
like an e. gone 399:39
now came still e. on 219:69
shadows of the e. steal 28:56
the winter e. settles down 131:7
whoso turns as I, this e. 74:25

Event: heaviness foreruns the good e. 317:22
one far-off divine e. 387:73
wise after the e. 261:9
wisest prophets make sure of the e. 398:44

Ever: but I go on for e. 384:39

Ever (*continued*)
do nothing for e. and e. 12:43
for e. and for e. farewell, Cassius! 326:28
for e. hold his peace 64:5
if for e., still for e. 85:93
left lonely for e. 20:34
that no life lives for e. 383:20
thou art gone, and for e. 295:98
what, *never*? Hardly e.! 147:22
wished him to talk on for e. 159:78

Everlasting: caught an e. cold 401:56
condemn'd into e. redemption 344:84
had stood [wheat] from e. to e. 392:53
primrose way to th' e. bonfire 334:44
that the E. had not fix'd 305:42

Everybody: e. praised the Duke 376:30
e. wants to have read 394:73
friend to e. ... friend to nobody 264:94

Everyman, I will go with thee 14:58

Everyone: e. ... put his whole wit 29:70
e. suddenly burst out singing 293:83
war of e. against e. 163:33

Everything: a smattering of e. 121:78
can resist e. except temptation 405:19
e. by starts and nothing long 126:43
e.'s got a moral 91:57
God saw e. ... he had made 35:30
sans taste, sans e. 301–2:90
sermons in stones, and good in e. 300:75
with e. that pretty bin 304:20

Everywhere: e. be bold 377:43
e. that Mary went 157:55
water, water e. 105:50

Eves: on summer e. by haunted stream 214:3

Evidence of things not seen 59:99

Evil: abhor that which is e. 57:37
all partial e., universal good 250:12
be not overcome of e. 57:41
care not whether ... good or e. 67:37
decide ... for the good or e. side 200:24
deliver us from e. 52:18
doing e. on the ground of expediency 290:39
E., be thou my Good 218:63
e. be to him who e. thinks 267:95
e. is wrought by want of Thought 165:62

Evil (*continued*)

e. that men do lives after them 325:12

e. which I wd. not, that I do 56:33

government ... a necessary e. 243:20

I will fear no e. 42:93

knowing good and e. 35:36

love of money ... root of all e. 59:92

loved darkness ... their deeds were e. 55:1

Luke ... gave himself to e. courses 411:87

maketh ... sun to rise on the e. 52:15

nature lends such e. dreams 386:62

of moral e. and of good 414:28

on e. days ... fallen, and e. tongues 219–20:83

out of good ... find means of e. 216:32

overcome e. with good 57:41

purer eyes than to behold e. 51:92

resist not e. 52:13

root of all e. The want of money 82:41

set good against e. 265:28

supernatural source of e. 110:27

the tongue ... is an unruly e. 60:5

them that call e. good 48:33

Evils: he ... must expect new e. 26:17

of two e. choose the least 262:36

women are necessary e. 283:50

Exact: an e. man 26:33

Exactitude ... politesse des rois 199:14

Exactness: with e. grinds he all 198:99

Exaggerated: reports of my death ... e. 394:75

Exalteth: righteousness e. a nation 45:68

Examination: post-mortem e. revealed ... 'Callous' 297:31

Examinations are formidable even to the best 108:99

Example: e. is better than precept 262:37

e. is the school of mankind 78:82

good e. is the best sermon 265:31

Excavating for a mine 225:59

Exceed: reach shd. e. his grasp 73:15

Excel: daring to e. 100:83

unstable ... thou shalt not e. 36:66

Excellent: an e. thing in woman 331:5

embodiment of everything ... e. 143:81

e. to have a giant's strength 337:86

Excels: how much a dunce ... e. 113:65

Excelsior: the strange device, E.! 197:93

Exception proves the rule 262:38

Excess: e. leads to wisdom 69:58

e. of glory obscured 217:41

give me e. of it 358:75

in charity there is no e. 25:4

nothing in e. 19:17

nothing succeeds like e. 406:31

surprise by a fine e. 186:55

wasteful and ridiculous e. 327:43

Exchange: by just e. one for another given 372:83

fair e. is no robbery 262:46

novels gain by the e. 85:87

Exciting: he found it less e. 143:69

Exclamation: 'fifty thousand!' was the e. 75:39

Excommunicate: unbaptized, or e. 65:12

Excuse: a bad e. is better than none 255:87

make the fault the worse by the e. 327:44

no longer e. for ... playing the rake 226:65

she'll prove an e. for a glass 372:78

Execution: their [of laws] stringent e. 153:16

Executioner: I am mine own e. 124:12

Executors: delivering o'er to e. pale 318–19:39

let's choose e. and talk of wills 349:53

Exercise: dancing? ... a barbarian e. 79:91

what e. is to the body 378:61

Exhalation: I shall fall like some bright e. 322:79

Exhausted worlds ... imagin'd new 173:58

Exiles: thou Paradise of e., Italy 368:29

Exist: if God did not e. 397:12

Existence: contraries ... are necessary to ... e. 68:56

E. saw him spurn her ... reign 173:58

love ... 'tis woman's whole e. 84:70

Exits: they have their e. and their entrances 301:90

Expands: work e. ... to fill the time available 244:25

Expatiate free o'er all this scene of man 250:7

Expectancy and rose of the fair state 310:1

Expectation: however certain our e. 132:18

now sits E. in the air 319:40

Expediency: doing evil on the ground
of e. 290:39

Expedient: all things ... lawful ... but
... not e. 57:49

too fond of the *right* to pursue the *e.*
151:79

Expense: at the e. of two [Gods]
103:28

Expensive: did ... from e. sins refrain
126:45

Experience: an e. of women which
extends 125:24

e. ... if not bought too dear 262:39

e. teaches 262:40

till old e. do attain ... prophetic
213:89

travel ... part of e. 25:12

triumph of hope over e. 176:1

true e. from this great event 223:27

Experientia docet 262:40

Expires: with that the Wretched Child
e. 31:92

Expiring: thus e. do foretell of him
348:40

Expose thyself to feel what wretches
feel 329:79

Expressed: oft was thought, but ne'er
so well e. 249:97

Expresses himself in terms too deep
146:15

Extensive: knowledge of London ... e.
and peculiar 121:66

Extent of [our language's] beauty and
power 202:43

Extenuate: speak ... as I am; nothing e.
346:22

Extinguished: glory of Europe is e.
78:78

nature is ... seldom e. 26:25

Extinguishes the small, ... inflames the
great 82:34

Extremes: e. meet 262:41

two e. of passion, joy and grief
330:3

women are always in e. 283:49

Extremity: a daring pilot in e. 126:39

Exuberance: e. is beauty 69:62

e. of his own verbosity 123:94

Exulting: the people all e. 403:81

Eye: a custom loathsome to the e.
170:19

a still-soliciting e. 327:51

all my e. and Betty Martin 254:69

all places that the e. of heaven visits
348:36

an e. for an e. 52:12

an e. made quiet by ... harmony
415:33

Eye (*continued*)

as the apple of his e. 38:14

camel ... through the e. of a needle
53:41

courtier's, soldier's, scholar's e.
310:1

e. for e., tooth for tooth 37:93

e. sees not, ... heart rues not 262:42

e. to the main chance 271:26

far from e., far from heart
262:52

flash upon that inward e. 410:71

has not man a microscopic e.?
250:10

holds him with his glittering e.
104:43

I backward cast my e. 80:19

if thine e. offend thee 53:39

in the e. of the beholder 168:92

keep me as the apple of the e.
41:85

long grey beard and glittering e.
104:42

many an e. has danced to see
164:46

my credit in men's e. 136:82

now mine e. seeth thee 41:79

poet's e. in a fine frenzy rolling
342:53

teaches such beauty as a woman's e.
331:14

the e. begins to see 71:87

the ... e. of heaven to garnish 327:43

there's language in her e. 358:73

what immortal hand or e. 68:46

with his keener e. the axe's edge
207:3

with my little e., I saw him die
241:88

Eyebrow: ballad ... to his mistress' e.
301:90

Eyeless in Gaza 221:12

Eyelids: no more wilt weigh my e.
down 317:13

tir'd e. upon tir'd eyes 388:85

with e. heavy and red 166:64

Eyes: and her e. were wild 183:8

and those e., the break of day
337–8:92

as in a theatre the e. of men 351:61

as 'twere in scorn of e. 352:72

choose love by another's e. 341:37

close yr. e. with holy dread 107:76

cost him his e. 330:1

discreet women ... neither e. nor ears
260:75

disdain and scorn ride ... in her e.
343:71

Eyes (*continued*)

dress her beauty at yr. e. 117:10

drink to me only with thine e. 178:49

e. have they but they see not 43:30

e., look your last 354:18

e. of all wait upon thee 44:52

e. wide open before marriage 268:31

flourish where you turn yr. e. 251:32

four e. see more than two 263:89

from women's e. this doctrine 331:16

get thee glass e. 330:93

golden slumbers kiss your e. 118:20

had I your tongues and e. 330:4

handkerchief before his streaming e. 93:81

happiness through another man's e. 303:6

have e. to wonder but lack tongues 363:46

her aspect and her e. 86:96

holes where e. did once inhabit 352:72

how fearful ... to cast one's e. so low 329:88

I was e. to the blind 41:74

if thou hast e. to see 345:95

justice ... with e. severe 301:90

kindling her undazzled e. 224:43

love looks not with the e. 341:38

make thy two e. ... start from ... spheres 307:64

mine e. dazzle 400:50

my mistress' e. ... nothing like the sun 364:52

night has a thousand e. 69:70

not all that tempts yr. wand'ring e. 154:26

one whose subdu'd e. ... drops tears 346-7:22

pearls that were his e. 355:35

pull the wool over ... e. 284:55

rapt soul sitting in thine e. 213:84

right in his own e. 39:32

see through all things with his half-shut e. 252:38

set my e. on sweet Molly Malone 17:89

sight for sore e. 277:37

sight ... good for sore e. 382:7

sights of ... death within my e. 352:72

so long as ... e. can see 362:34

soft look your e. had once 417:58

sparkling e., ... teeth like pearls 75:43

Eyes (*continued*)

stout Cortez ... with eagle e. 185:41

strike mine e. but not my heart 179:52

take a pair of sparkling e. 143:77

thou art of purer e. 51:92

tired eyelids upon tired e. 388:85

to ope their golden e. 304:20

two lovely black e. 104:37

until you see the whites of their e. 253:49

very few e. can see the Mystery 187:64

where'er these casual e. are cast 376:25

whose bright e. rain influence 214:2

with e. up-rais'd, as one inspired 108:92

with rainy e. write sorrow 349:53

yr. mouth shut and yr. e. open 268:32

Fabric: baseless f. of this vision 356:50

Face: a caricature of a f. 146:11

a garden in her f. 88:24

and with how wan a f.! 373:85

but then f. to f. 57:54

cover her f.: mine eyes dazzle 400:50

dew on the f. of the dead 30:84

disasters in his morning f. 150:68

Discobolus ... turneth his f. to the wall 82:47

f. that launch'd a thousand ships 204:63

f. with nature's own hand painted 362:35

fair and open f. of heaven 186:47

fair f. ... foul heart 262:47

fair f. half a fortune 262:48

false f. must hide 333:39

God hath given you one f. 310:99

good f. needs no paint 265:32

grace,... seen in one autumnal f. 123:7

grace to get ... red in the f. 34:20

honour the f. of the old man 38:1

human f. divine 218:59

I wish I loved its silly f. 286:97

in the sweat of thy f. 35:38

just can't think of yr. f. 377:52

look on her f. and you'll forget 251:34

looks the whole world in the f. 199:7

Monday's child is fair of f. 235:56

my f.—I don't mind it 134:53

my f. is my fortune, sir 241:87

Face (*continued*)
never f. so pleased my mind 18:9
painting a f. and not washing 140:37
princely counsel in his f. yet shone
  218:52
principles ... f. to f. from ... beginning 196:76
satchel and shining morning f.
  301:90
seen too oft, familiar with her f.
  250:14
smile on the f. of the tiger 13:52
tell the f. thou viewest 362:30
the air on his f. unkind 117:14
the unclouded f. of truth 294:88
with her f. upturned 193:48
your f., my thane ... a book 333:34
Faces: grind the f. of the poor 48:32
heavily jowled or hawk-like ... f.
  203:56
seen better f. in my time 328:62
so many millions of f. ... none alike
  72:3
strange f., other minds 385:53
the old familiar f. 192:32
'tis ye, 'tis yr. estranged f. 391:31
Facilis descensus Averni 397:2
Facing: Mr. F.-both-ways 77:61
Facts: all the f. when ... brass tacks
  131:9
,f. are sacred 294:88
indebted to ... imagination for his f.
  372:80
irritable reaching after f. 186:52
Faculties: our souls, whose f. can comprehend 205:76
Fade: f. away into the forest dim
  184:24
f. into the light of common day
  411:78
old soldiers ... only f. away 18:99
she cannot f. 183:18
thy eternal summer shall not f.
  362:33
Faded: like this insubstantial pageant
  f. 356–7:50
Fades: now f. the glimmering landscape 155:31
Faery: full beautiful, a f.'s child 183:8
in f. lands forlorn 184:30
the land of f. 417:54
Faiblesse: tout le reste est f. 396:94
Fail: if we shd. f.? We f.! 333:38
neither shall ... cruse of oil f. 40:55
sooner f. than not be among the
  greatest 187:61
we shall not flag or f. 100:94
Failed: The Light that F. 191:17

Faileth: enemy faints not, nor f.
  103:32
Failing: f. to trust everybody ... nobody 262:43
true ... she had one f. 80:12
Failure: only one [to make a marriage]
  a f. 293:75
Faint, yet pursuing 39:25
Faints: the enemy f. not 103:32
Fair: all is f. in love and war 254:65
brave deserves the f. 127:51
f. is foul and foul is f. 332:23
f. is too foul an epithet for thee
  205:77
f. stood the wind for France 125:31
for ever shalt thou love and she be f.
  183:18
holy, f. and wise is she 361:8
how sweet and f. she seems to be
  398:17
is she kind as she is f.? 361:9
like not f. terms and a villain's mind
  339:7
most divinely f. 385:46
pernicious weed! ... the f. annoys
  112:53
she is f. and, fairer 338:99
she is not f. to outward view 104:41
so foul and f. a day 332:25
Fair play's a jewel 262:49
Fairer: and f. than that word 338:99
I can't say no f. than that 120:45
thou art f. than the evening air
  204:64
Fairest: O, f. of creation 220:94
Fairies: do you believe in f.? 28:62
f. at the bottom of our garden
  140:41
I don't believe in f. 28:60
She is the f. midwife 353:92
that was the beginning of f. 28:59
Fair-spoken and persuading 323:87
Fairy: a little f. ... falls down dead
  28:60
by f. hands their knell is rung 107:90
light she was and like a f. 225:60
'tis almost f. time 342:55
Faith: an event which creates f. 366:3
break f. with us who die 202:49
f. and morals ... Milton held 413:5
f. ... as the fashion of his hat
  342:57
f. is ... substance of things 59:99
f. shines equal, arming me 71:84
f.'s transcendent dower 413:14
f. unfaithful kept him falsely true
  385:50
f. without works is dead 60:4

Faith (*continued*)

fight the good fight of f. 59:93
I have kept the f. 59:95
I mean the F.'s Defender 83:53
just shall live by f. 56:29
more f. in honest doubt 386:65
my staff of f. to walk upon 286:94
reaffirm f. in ... human rights 394:76
reason ... soul's left hand, f. her
    right 123:5
remembering ... yr. work of f. 59:83
simple f. than Norman blood 387:74
'tis not the dying for a f. 389:9
we walk by f., not by sight 58:62
which constitutes poetic f. 107:79
Faithful: be thou f. unto death 60:20
ever f., ever sure 221:10
f. are the wounds of a friend 46:87
f. only he 219:81
f. to thee, Cynara! 124:17
O come, all ye f. 241:91
so f. in love ... dauntless in war
    296:11
Faith-healer of Deal 13:51
Faithless: among the f., faithful only he
    219:81
yr. sleeping head ... on my f. arm
    22:60
Faiths: heaven smiles and f. and em-
    pires gleam 368:28
Fall: another thing to f. 337:81
A-tishoo! We all f. down 237:67
f. out, and chide, and fight 399:37
haughty spirit [goeth] before a f.
    45:72
he that is down need fear no f. 77:66
held we f. to rise 73:16
higher ... the greater the f. 266:86
Humpty Dumpty had a great f.
    93:84, 233:37
pride will have a f. 275:61
some by virtue f. 337:82
that strain ...! It had a dying f.
    358:75
the cradle will f. 233:38
the glass will f. for ever 203:55
unless the billboards f. 229:97
upon the ground, can f. no lower
    269:77
what a f. was there, my countrymen!
    325:20
Fallen: awake, ... or be for ever f.
    216:37
f. out of heigh degree 97:47
f. ... that tower of strength 388:93
there has f. a splendid tear 388:87
though f. on evil days 219:83
you are f. from grace 58:68

Falling: he hath the f. sickness 324:95
what a f. off was there 307:68
Falls: between two stools one f. 256:34
like a thunderbolt he f. 385:47
nips his root, and then he f. 322:80
when f. the Coliseum, Rome shall
    fall 84:64
when he f., he f. like Lucifer
    322–3:81
False: any other thing that's f.
    85:91
canst not then be f. to any man
    306:57
history must be f. 398:21
prov'd true ... prove f. again 82:38
ring out the f., ring in the true
    386:68
thou shalt not bear f. witness 37:91
true to thyself, as ... not f. to others
    25:16
what the f. heart doth know 333:39
Falsehood: let her and F. grapple
    224:45
Falstaff sweats to death 313:59
Fame: all the family of F. 107:78
an imp of f. 320:51
Cromwell, damned to everlasting f.
    250:17
f. ... is double-mouthed 222:23
f. is like a river 26:35
f. is no plant ... on mortal soil
    215:14
f. is the spur 215:13
his f. soon spread around 113:57
lust of f. 71:86
nor yet a fool to f. 248:80
on F.'s eternal beadroll 377:44
physicians of the utmost f. 31:91
servants of f. 25:1
son of memory, great heir of f.
    216:24
thou, whose infamy is not thy f.
    367:15
Familiar: f. acts are beautiful 369:45
f as his garter 318:38
f. but by no means vulgar 306:55
f. objects as if ... not f. 371:57
the old f. faces 192:32
too f. with disappointments 196:72
wine ... a good f. creature 345:2
Familiarity: f. breeds contempt 262:51
f. breeds contempt and children
    394:67
Families: accidents ... in best-regulated
    f. 120:44
all happy f. resemble one another
    392:49
I might ... be useful to their f. 23:64

Fate (*continued*)

f. so enviously debars 206:98

fixed f., free will 218:55

Foreknowledge, Will, and F. 218:55

hanging breathless on thy f.! 197:92

I am the master of my f. 160:95

J and my fellows are ministers of F. 356:49

limits of a vulgar f. 156:45

my dear ... my life, my f. 388:87

take a bond of f. 335:63

that one might read the book of f.! 317:15

when F. summons, Monarchs must obey 128:68

will in us is over-rul'd by f. 205:80

with a heart for any f. 198:98

Fates: masters of their f. 323–4:93

Father: as a f. pitieth his children 43:22

child whose f. goes to the devil 266:65

cry not when his f. dies 172:56

foredoom'd his f.'s soul to cross 248:78

full fathom five thy f. lies 355:35

gave her f. forty-one 15:67

hath the rain a f.? 41:77

have we not all one f.? 51:98

honour thy f. and thy mother 37:87

like f., like son 269:85

my mother groan'd, my f. wept 67:44

shall a man leave his f.? 58:72

she has deceived her f. 345:95

so were her f. and mother before 17:90

son of a dear f. murder'd 309:93

take example by your f. 121:67

wise child that knows its own f. 283:39

wise f. that knows his own child 339:8

wise son maketh a glad f. 45:61

wish is f. to the thought 283:42

Fathers: blood is fet from f. of war-proof 319:46

f. have eaten a sour grape 49:58

iniquity of the f. upon the children 37:84

Fathom: full f. five thy father lies 355:35

Fathom-line cd. never touch the ground 313:54

Fathoms: bury it certain f. in the earth 357:55

Fatigued ... tie up the knocker 248:77

Fatter: valley sheep are f. 245:38

Fault: a f. ... grows two thereby 161:11

body without f. or stain 70:78

excusing of a f. ... make f. worse 327:44

f., dear Brutus, is not in our stars 323–4:93

glorious f. of angels and of gods 248:74

Faultless: lifeless that is f. 269:81

Faults: be to her f. a little blind 253:50

England, with all thy f. 114:70

Every man has his f. 262:28

f. are theirs that commit ... permit 262:55

f. are thick ... love is thin 262:56

friend that will tell me ... f. 265:23

his f. lie gently on him! 323:85

rich men have no f. 276:91

tell me all my f. 365:73

with all her f., ... my country 100:82

Favour: I hold with those who f. fire 139:25

king's f. is no inheritance 268:37

truths in and out of f. 139:22

Favourite: a f. has no friend 154:25

Favours: hangs on princes' f. 322:81

neither beg ... your f. 333:27

Fawning: how like a f. publican he looks! 338:3

Fear: capable not only of f. and hate 292:66

concessions of the weak are ... of f. 77:71

doth walk in f. and dread 106:60

faith ... arming me from f. 71:84

f. ... God, ... walk in ... his ways 38:9

f. no more the heat o' th' sun 304:29

f. not, said he, for mighty dread 384:35

for f. of little men 11:22

freedom from f. ... anywhere 289:32

from hope and f. set free 383:20

having little to f. ... from censure 172:43

I f. the Greeks, even when 397:99

I f. thee, ancient Mariner 105:53

I f. thy kisses, gentle maiden 370:55

I guess an' f. 80–1:19

I'll f. not what men say 77:65

irrational f. of life 110:22

many things to f. 25:13

men f. death, as children f. dark 24:86

mortality, behold and f. 29:71

needs f. no fall ... no pride 77:66

no f. in love 60:17

Fear (*continued*)
O word of f.   332:19
only thing ... to f. is f. itself   289:28
perfect love casteth out f.   60:17
quite unaccustomed to f.   18:7
who neither beg not f.   333:27
wise f. ... forbids the robbing   100:84
with f. and trembling   58:75
with hope, farewell f.   218:63
yet do I f. thy nature   333:32
Fearful: a lovely and a f. thing   84:72
our f. innocence   412:2
our f. trip is done   403:81
snatch a f. joy   154:28
thy f. symmetry   68:46
'tis melancholy and a f. sign   84:74
Fears: bound in to saucy doubts and f.   335:53
enough for fifty hopes and f.   73:17
have f. that I may cease to be   186:48
humanity with all its f.   197:92
not without ... f. and distastes   24:91
past Regrets and future F.   135:69
so are their griefs and f.   24:94
Feast: as good as a f.   65:18
as you were going to a f.   179:51
bare imagination of a f.   348:37
chief nourisher in life's f.   334:42
company makes the f.   258:21
enough is as good as a f.   261:23
f., and yr. halls are crowded   404:92
perpetual f. of nectared sweets   213:17
Feather: birds of a f.   256:37
he stuck a f. in his cap   241:90
knocked me down with a f.   268:41
Feathers: cover thee with his f.   43:19
crow, beautified with our f.   156:49
Feats: 'twas one of my f.   86:94
February: excepting F. alone   239:77
Fed: appetite ... grown by what it f. on   305:44
bite the hand that f. them   78:83
f. with the same food   339:13
he on honey-dew hath f.   107:76
hungry sheep look up and are not f.   215:16
Federation: the F. of the world   387:81
Fee: taking a f. with a grin   144:84
Feeble: not enough to help the f. up   357:59
Feed: f. fat the ancient grudge   338:3
f. me till I want no more   407:40
f. me with food convenient   46:90
f. upon strawberries, sugar and cream   231–2:27
Feel: I f. it when I sorrow most   386:59
I f. no pain, dear mother   17:88

Feel (*continued*)
see, not f., how beautiful   106:68
to f. what wretches f.   329:79
we uncomfortable f.   148:32
what I fancy I f.   13:51
world ... a tragedy to those who f.   398:23
Feels: man is as old as he f.   271:32
Fees: as they took their f.   31:91
Feet: at the f. of Gamaliel   56:24
chase the ... Hours with flying f.   83:60
did those f. in ancient time   67:38
f. of him that bringeth good tidings   48:46
f. was I to the lame   41:74
palms before my f.   99:69
walked those blessed f.   312:43
what flowers are at my f.   184:27
Feigning: most friendship is f.   302:91
truest poetry ... most f.   302:1
Felicity: absent thee from f. awhile   312:38
our own f. we make or find   152:94
perfect bliss and sole f.   205:76
tavern chair ... throne of human f.   178:44
Felix qui potuit ... cognoscere causas   397:5
Fell: bowed himself ... and the house f.   39:30
I do not love thee, Dr F.   72:96
it f. to earth, I know not where   197:91
Fellow: hail f., well met   381:4
you're a f. Sir ..., you're another   121:65
you threaten us, f.?   75:42
Fellow-creatures: make his f. wise   149:47
Fellow-men: one that loves his f.   168:95
Fellowship: manhood, nor good f. in thee   312:48
right hands of f.   58:67
Felony: make it a f. to drink ... beer   321:66
Felt: darkness which may be f.   36:75
Female: f. of sex it seems   222:18
f. of the species is more deadly   190:98
into the ark the male and the f.   35:45
male and f. created he them   34:28
what f. heart can gold despise?   154:24
Femina: varium et mutabile semper f.   397:1

Fight (*continued*)
we don't want to f., but by jingo 168:93
we'll f. and we'll conquer 141:48
when the f. begins within himself 73:18
you cannot f. against the future 149:51
Fighter: fits a dull f. 315:84
Fighting: f. a liar in the quad 377:50
not conquering but f. well 111:36
were f. for the crown 234:47
Fights: he that f. and runs away 14:61
I quote the f. historical 147:31
Figs grew upon thorn 98:67
Figurative: cuts a figure – but he is not f. 187:64
Figure: fixed f. for the time of scorn 346:13
Filches from me my good name 345:6
Fill the unforgiving minute 190:5
Fille de chambre: caught hold of the f.'s 379:69
Filling: is f. his last cavity 13:49
Filths savour but themselves 329:86
Filthy lucre 59:87
Finchley: Lord F. tried to mend the ... light 31:94
Find: can't tell where to f. them 234:48
nothing seek, nothing f. 273:10
take things as you f. them 279:3
they shall f. him ware and wakin' 230:12
Finding's keeping 232:61
Finds too late that men betray 152:2
Fine arts: murder ... as one of the F. 119:30
Finer: no f. investment than ... milk in babies 101:6
Finest: men will still say, 'This was their f. hour' 101:95
this was our f. shower 242:7
Finger: have a f. in the pie 263:62
Moving F. writes: and, having writ 136:79
point his slow unmoving f. at 346:13
this is the f. of God 36:74
twist round one's little f. 281:72
Fingers: and with forced f. rude 215:8
ill cook ... cannot lick his own f. 258:26, 354:16
with f. weary and worn 166:64
Finish: tools and we will f. the job 101:98
Finished: I have f. my course 59:95
Fire: a clear f., a clean hearth 192:27
brand plucked out of ... f. 51:95
bring me my chariot of f. 67:38

Fire (*continued*)
element of f. is ... put out 123:3
fat is in the f. 262:54
fell in the f. ... burned to ashes 153:11
f. burn and cauldron bubble 335:58
f. is a good servant ... bad master 263:63
f. our souls to regale 68:45
foul water will quench f. 263:88
frying-pan into the f. 264:1
heap coals of f. upon his head 45:81
in the F. of Spring 135:66
like a house on f. 267:6
many irons in the f. 268:21
no f. without some smoke 273:92
no smoke without some f. 273:1
nor rain, wind, thunder, f. 328:72
now stir the f., ... close ... shutters 114:73
shd. have stood that night against my f. 330:95
spit f., spout rain 328:72
the right Promethean f. 331:16
upon a wheel of f. 330:96
warmed ... hands before the f. of life 192:34
we proceed to light the f. 143:75
what wind is to f. 82:34
who can hold a f. in his hand? 348:37
world will end in f. 139:25
Fires: keep the home f. burning 137:94
stars, hide your f. 333:31
violent f. soon burn out themselves 348:40
Firing: we shall have what to do after f. 287:3
Firmament: f. showeth his handywork 41:86
the spacious f. on high 9:9
Firmness: with f. in the right 196:81
First: f. baby laughed ... f. time 28:59
f. come, f. served 263:66
f. fine careless rapture 74:23
God's f. creature ... light 27:40
last of life, for which the f. was made 75:46
the f. that ever burst into ... sea 105:48
there is no last nor f. 75:45
when f. we practice to deceive 296:13
First-born: I'll rail against all the f. 301:86
the Lord smote all the f. 36:77
Fish: he has gone to f. 195:63
I sent a message to the f. 93:89

Fish (*continued*)
  in the belly of the f.   50:86
  like a f. out of water   263:69
  other f. to fry   263:70
  what cat's averse to f.?   154:24
Fish-ball: no bread with one f.   192:37
Fishers of men   51:8
Fishes: if you were to make little f.
  talk   152:4
  men that f. gnaw'd upon   352:72
  the little f. of the sea   93:90
  waiting for ... invasion. So are the f.
  101:97
  welcome little f. in   89–90:45
  when f. flew and forests walked
  98:67
Fishified: flesh, flesh, how art thou f.!
  354:8
Fishing: deepest water ... best f.
  260:67
Fishmonger: she was a f. ... 'twas no
  wonder   17:90
  you are a f.   308:75
Fit: all the news that's f. to print
  242:95
  f. for the kingdom of God   54:74
  f. for treasons, stratagems   340:24
  love makes one f. for any work
  270:16
  men ... not f. to live on land   177:16
  not f. that you shd. sit ... longer
  115:90
Fits: if the cap f., wear it   257:83
  strange f. of passion have I known
  414:23
Fittest: survival of the f.   376:34
Five: but f. upon this isle   356:45
  f. reasons why we shd. drink   10:16
  full fathom f. thy father lies   355:35
  stand f. minutes with that man
  178:46
  then ye are only f.   416:41
Five-pound note: as the gen'l'm'n said
  to the f.   121:69
  wrapped up in a f.   195:60
Fix: f. in us thy humble dwelling
  402:72
  in such a f. to be so fertile   229:98
Fixed the where and when   158:74
Flag: death's pale f. is not advanced
  354:17
  f. has braved a thousand years
  88:21
  keep the Red F. flying here!
  109–10:21
  spare yr. country's f.   403:89
  the old f. flyin'   230:12
  we shall not f. or fail   100:94

Flagons: stay me with f.   47:19
Flail: the f. of the lashing hail   368:22
Flame: adding fuel to the f.   222:25
  burn always with ... gem-like f.
  244:29
  Chloe is my real f.   253:51
  words ... full of subtle f.   29:70
Flanders: armies swore terribly in F.
  379:70
  in F. fields the poppies blow   202:48
Flash: he might have cut a f.   12:42
  they f. upon that inward eye   410:71
Flask: a F. of Wine, a Book of Verse
  137:67
Flat: your life extremely f.   148:40
Flatter: Mr Lely, f. me not   115:91
Flattered: I have not f. its rank breath
  83:61
Flatterer: scoundrel, hypocrite, and f.
  67:36
Flattering: talent for f. with delicacy
  23:78
Flattery: f.'s the food for fools   381:96
  gained by every sort of f.   98:63
  gross f. to name a coward   392:48
  I can stand anything but f.   365:73
  imitation ... sincerest form of f.
  108:98
  pernicious ... love of f.   378:59
  supports with insolence ... paid with
  f.   172:49
  what is principle against ... f.   372:79
Flavour: gives it [life] all its f.   114:71
Flaw: it is a f. in happiness   181:88
Flaws: break into a hundred thousand
  f.   328:69
Flax: smoking f. shall he not quench
  48:44
Flea: a f. hath smaller fleas   382:5
Fleas: great f. have little f.   226:69
  little f. have lesser f.   226:69
Fleckno(e) ... who like Augustus
  128:68
Fled: I f. Him down the nights   391:30
  whence all but he had f.   160:89
Flee from the wrath to come   51:6
Fleece was white as snow   157:55
Fleet-Street ... very animated appearance   176:9
Flesh: a pound of that same merchant's
  f.   340:19
  a thorn in the f.   58:65
  all f. is as grass   60:8
  all f. is grass   48:42
  all this f. keep in a little life   315:92
  and f. and blood so cheap   166:65
  bring me f. and bring me wine   229:4
  f., f., how art thou fishified   354:8

Flesh (*continued*)
 f. is weak 53:50
 f. of my f. 35:34
 f. which walls about our life 350:54
 from her fair and unpolluted f. 312:32
 going the way of all f. 400:53
 I have more f. ... more frailty 315:80
 I wants to make yr. 'f. creep 120:62
 shocks that f. is heir to 309:95
 study a weariness of the f. 47:13
 the f. to feel the chain 71:87
 the soul to feel the f. 71:87
 the Word was made f. 55:95
 the world, the f., and the devil 63:78
 this too too solid f. wd. melt 305:42
 this world-wearied f. 354:18
 two shall be one f. 58:72
 we wrestle not against f. 58:74
 what a change of f. 29:71
Fleshly School of Poetry 76:49
Fleshpots: when we sat by the f. 36:79
Flew: the white foam f. 105:48
Flies: as f. to wanton boys are we 329:85
 close mouth catcheth no f. 258:11
 he f. through the air 196:71
 murmurous haunt of f. 184:28
Flight: beetle wheels his droning f. 155:31
 swift be thy approaching f. 369:33
Flint: f. is pierced with ... shower 191:22
 hard as a f. 266:66
Flirt: how can [a bishop] f.? 375:8
Floats on high o'er vales and hills 410:67
Flock: keeping watch over their f. 54:68
 silent was the f. in woolly fold 181:89
Flocks: watched their f. by night 384:35
Flog a dead horse 263:74
Flogging: less f. in our great schools 176:15
Flood: bridge much broader than the f. 342:61
 taken at the f., leads – God knows where 85:50
 taken at the f., leads on to fortune 326:27
Flooding: comes silent f. in the main 103:33
Floods: spirit to bathe in fiery f. 337:90
Floor of heaven is thick inlaid 340:22

Florence: F., Elizabethan England 170:13
 rode past fair F. 182:5
Flotte: elle f., elle hésite 285:92
Flourish: all things f. where you turn 251:32
Flourishing like a green bay-tree 42:4
Flow gently, sweet Afton 79:98
Flower: a fancy from a f.-bell 73:17
 a Heaven in a wild f. 66:27
 a lovelier f. ... was never sown 415:30
 as a f. of the field ... he flourisheth 43:23
 force that ... drives the f. 390:19
 honey ... from every opening f. 399:35
 London ... f. of Cities 129:75
 many a f. is born to blush unseen 155:37
 may prove a beauteous f. 354:3
 patience is a f. 274:29
 pluck this f., safety 313:60
 the f. ... once has blown for ever dies 135:71
 this same f. that smiles today 162:24
 to me the meanest f. ... can bring 411:82
Flowers: a bunch of other men's f. 225:57
 f. that bloom in the spring, Tra la 146:11
 fresh showers for the thirsting f. 368:21
 gather the f., but spare the buds 207:5
 gave, once, her f. of love 71:93
 grow f. and ... got no majesty 401:68
 I cannot see what f. 184:27
 late f. for the bees 181:79
 on chalic'd f. that lies 304:20
 say it with f. 242:96
 the azure f. that blow 154:23
 the blushing f. shall rise 251:32
 the f. appear on the earth 47:22
 with leaves and f. do cover 400:54
Flowing with milk and honey 36:70
Flown with insolence and wine 217:38
Fluffy, with no brains at all 161:7
Flügel: wo dein sanfter F. weilt 294:85
Fluttered yr. Volscians in Corioli 304:19
Fluttering and dancing in the breeze 410:67
Fly: a f. can't bird, but a bird can f. 212:65
 f. away Peter ... come back Paul 240:84

Fool (*continued*)
  transform'd into a strumpet's f. 298:49
Foolish: a very f., fond old man 330:97
  f. thing was but a toy 360:3
  he never said a f. thing 288:21
  penny wise, pound f. 274:37
Fools: a shoal of f. for tenders 109:10
  all our yesterdays have lighted f. 336:76
  flattery ... food for f. 381:96
  f. admire, but men of sense approve 249:1
  f. are in a terrible ... majority 169:8
  f. are my theme 85:88
  f.! for I also had my hour 99:69
  f. rush in ... angels fear to tread 249:6
  f., who came to scoff 150:67
  fortune always favours f. 142:59
  fortune favours f. 263:85
  God sends fortune to f. 265:25
  if f. went not to market 263:82
  knaves and f. divide the world 268:40
  lawyers' houses ... on the heads of f. 269:60
  never-failing vice of f. 249:93
  not harsh [philosophy] as ... f. suppose 213:77
  Paradise of F. 218:60
  poems are made by f. like me 189:82
  poor f. decoyed into our condition 245:42
  suckle f. and chronicle small beer 345:98
  this great stage of f. 330:94
  travellers ... f. at home condemn 356:48
  what f. these mortals be? 342:50
  ye suffer f. gladly 58:64
  you f.! I and my fellows 356:49
  young men think old men f. 284:64
  zeal ... is found mostly in f. 284:70
Foot: and the Forty-second F. 165:58
  Feeble of f., and rheumatic 70:72
  her f. was light 183:8
  nay, her f. speaks 358:73
  noiseless f. of Time 298:48
  one f. in sea, and one on shore 343:68
  one f. in the grave 274:22
  put one's best f. forward 255:10
  thou shalt give ... f. for f. 37:93
  Thyself with shining F. shall pass 136:83
  who cleft the devil's f. 124:11

Foot (*continued*)
  ye that on the sands with printless f. 357:54
Footpath: jog on, the f. way 361:19
Footprint: looking for a man's f. 30:82
Footprints in the sands of time 198:97
Foppery: an excellent f. of the world 327:53
Forbearance ceases to be a virtue 78:77
Forbidden: wanted ... because f. 394:68
Forbids f. the cheating of our friends 100:84
  f. the robbing of a foe 100:84
Force: admit no f. but argument 72–3:8
  f. is not a remedy 71:83
  f. that through the green fuse 390:19
  own no argument but f. 72:8
  subtlety is better than f. 279:86
  that armed f. shall not be used 394:76
  use of f. alone ... *temporary* 78:82
  who overcomes by f. 217:43
Ford: the time of our F. 168:97
Fordoes: either makes me or f. me 346:17
Forebode not any severing of our loves 411:81
Forecast: I cannot f. to you the action of Russia 100:91
Forefathers: rude f. of the hamlet 155:33
  think of yr. f.! 9:2
Fore-finger: on the f. of an alderman 353:92
Forehead: curl ... in the middle of her f. 199:5
Foreheads: with f. villainous low 357:52
Foreign: some corner of a f. field 71:92
Foreigners always spell better 394:66
Foreknowledge absolute 218:55
Forest: a fool i' th' f. 301:87
  fade away into the f. dim 184:24
  Till Birnam F. come to Dunsinane 336:73
Forests: when fishes flew and f. walked 98:67
Foretell: expiring do f. of him 348:40
  who can f. for what high cause 207:4
Forever: pickets off duty f. 30:84
  that is f. England 71:92
  that vast f. 189:86
Forewarned, forearmed 263:83
Forget: and if thou wilt, f. 290:48

Forget (*continued*)
    better ... you shd. f. and smile
        290:45
    don't f. the diver 180:74
    forgive and f. 263:84
    lest we f. 190:10
    look on her face and you'll f. 251:34
    old men f., yet all shall be forgot
        320:58
    smile at us, pay us, pass us, but do
        not quite f. 99:75
    the best sometimes f. 345:99
Forgetfulness: sleep my senses in f.
    317:13
Forgets: is a fool that f. himself 263:78
Forgetting: our birth is but a sleep and
    a f. 410:77
    world f., by the world forgot 248:76
Forgive: Father, f. them 55:91
    f. and forget 263:84
    noblest vengeance is to f. 282:90
    to err is human, to f. divine 249:4
Forgiveness: and ask of thee f.; so we'll
    live 330:99
    mutual f. of each vice 66:33
Forgot: shd. auld acquaintance be f.?
    79:99
Forgotten: learnt nothing, f. nothing
    384:31
    long absent, soon f. 270:98
    they fly, f., as a dream 400:40
Forlorn: f.! the very word is like a bell
    184:31
    glimpses that wd. make me less f.
        412:94
Form: ah, what the f. divine! 192:36
    earth was without f. 34:26
    his f. had not yet lost ... brightness
        217:41
    in f. and moving, how ... admirable!
        308:81
    the F. remains 413:13
    thy f. from off my door! 247:67
Forms: by f. unseen ... dirge is sung
    107:90
    f. more real than living man 369:43
    f. of things unknown 342:53
    hope from outward f. to win 106:69
Fornication: but ... in another
    country 204:71
Forsake not an old friend 62:51
Fortitude: that was great f. of mind
    174:72
Fortress: this f. built by Nature for
    herself 348:41
Fortuna: fortis f. adiuvat 389:6
Fortunate: as he was f., I rejoice
    325:11

Fortunate (*continued*)
    be f. without adding ... felicity
        173:66
Fortune: a youth to f. and to fame
        unknown 155:40
    children ... hostages to f. 24:96
    fair face is half a f. 262:48
    f. always favours fools 142:59
    f. favours fools 263:85
    f. favours the brave 389:6
    f., good night; smile once more
        328:63
    f. is blind 263:86
    God sends f. to fools 265:25
    I am f.'s fool 354:12
    method of making a f. 156:46
    my face is my f., sir 241:87
    of f.'s sharp adversity 97:51
    possession of f. ... in want of a wife
        23:75
    slings and arrows of outrageous f.
        309:95
    taken at the flood, leads on to f.
        326:27
    well-favoured ... the gift of f. 343:73
    when f. knocks, open 263:87
    when we are sick in f. 327:53
Fortune-teller: threadbare juggler and
    a f. 303:12
Forty: every man over f. is a scoundrel
    366:91
    fool at f. is a fool indeed 417:60
    f. centuries look down on you
        228:83
    f. years on, growing older 70:72
    gave her mother f. whacks 15:67
    girdle round ... earth in f. minutes
        341:45
    he that is ... not rich at f. 266:58
    his death ... at f. odd befell
        165:59
    I had rather than f. shillings 340:28
    passing rich with f. pounds 150:66
    together now for f. years 99:80
Forty-niner: dwelt a miner, f. 225:59
Forward: f. the Light Brigade! 385:41
    f. tho' I canna see 80–1:19
    look f. to with hope 139:23
    those behind cried 'F.!' 201:39
Foster-child: thou f. of silence 183:16
Fought: better to have f. and lost
    103:31
    but what they f. each other for
        376:29
    f. with us upon St Crispin's day
        320–21:59
Foul: blood is nipp'd and ways be f.
    332:20

Foul (*continued*)
  fair is f. and f. is fair 332:23
  I doubt some f. play 306:52
  nothing can seem f. to those that win
    315:85
  so f. and fair a day 332:25
  thank the gods I am f. 202:2
Foul-mouthed: the English ... a f.
  nation 159:79
Found: half-buried in the snow was f.
  198:94
  I have f. it! (Eureka!) 20:25
  thou shalt not be f. out 261:16
  when f., make a note of 120:46
Foundation of morals and legislation
  33:14
Fountain: a woman mov'd is like a f.
  troubled 355:26
Fountains: and O, ye F., Meadows,
  Hills 411:81
  passion ... life, whose f. are within
    106:69
Founts: white f. falling in the Courts
  of the sun 99:70
Four: founded upon f. essential human
  freedoms 289:32
  f. angels round my head 10:13
  f. elements warring within our
    breasts 205:76
  f. lagging winters and f. wanton
    springs 348:34
  f. seasons in the mind 185:45
  f. times as big as the bush 195:65
  the f. pillars of government 25:7
  there are f. classes of Idols 27:41
  they f. had one likeness 49:63
  when angry, count f. 394:71
Four-footed: devil's walking parody
  on all f. things 99:68
Fourpence: took f. home to my wife
  233:40
Fourscore and upward, not an hour
  more 330:97
Fourteen months ... idle and unprofitable 142:64
Fowl: broiled f. and mushrooms –
  capital! 120:60
Fox: f. from his lair in the morning
  154:20
  gentlemen galloping after a f.
    406:27
Frabjous day! Callooh! Callay! 92:71
Fragrance: inward f. of each other's
  heart 182:3
Frailties: draw his f. from their dread
  abode 155:42
Frailty: f. folly, also crime 84:74
  f., thy name is woman 306:45

Frailty (*continued*)
  love's but the f. of the mind 109:14
  love's the noblest f. 128:63
  more flesh ... and therefore more f.
    315:80
Frame: all the human f. requires 31:92
  man ... bears in his bodily f. 117:6
  spangled heavens, a shining f. 9:9
France: bâton de maréchal de F. 228:86
  best thing between F. and England
    171:38
  fair stood the wind for F. 125:31
  F. is alone; and God is alone 366:4
  order ... this matter better in F.
    378:64
  the vasty fields of F.? 318:37
  we shall fight in F., we shall fight on
    the seas 100:94
  what I gained by being in F. 177:30
Frank, haughty, rash—the Rupert
  76:53
Frankfort: I went to F. and got drunk
  252:41
Frankie and Johnny 16:81
Fraternity: liberty, equality, f. 19:15
Fray: latter end of a f. 315:84
Frederick: cruel F. 164:40
Free: all men everywhere cd. be f.
  196:78
  beauteous evening, calm and f.
    412:92
  flag that makes you f. 416:45
  her looks were f. 105:52
  love Virtue, she alone is f. 213:81
  man ... born f. ... is in chains 291:55
  mother of the f. 33:13
  o'er the land of the f. 188:80
  others abide our question. Thou art
    f. 21:44
  pure ..., majestic, f. 413:4
  quite set f. ... Eurydice 215:6
  so cleanly I myself can f. 125:34
  so f. we seem, so fettered ... are
    73:14
  that Greece might still be f. 84-5:78
  the furrow followed f. 105:48
  the valiant man and f. 387:71
  thought is f. 280:31
  we cannot be f. men if 196:75
  we must be f. or die 413:5
  what a f. government is 78:84
Freed: from the thousands He hath f.
  95:18
Freedom: a new birth of f. 196:79
  battle for f. and truth 169:9
  can do for the f. of man 188:75
  every infringement of human f.
    246:56

Freedom (*continued*)
f. and Whisky 79:2
f. from fear ... anywhere 289:32
f. from want—everywhere 289:32
F. is Slavery 242:2
f. of speech and expression 289:32
F. shall a-while repair 107–8:90
f. ... to worship God 289:32
f. with which Dr Johnson condemns 79:93
least regard for human f. 376:37
love not f., but licence 224:46
none can love f. ... but good men 224:46
those who deny f. to others 196:75
whose service is perfect f. 63:71
yet, F.! yet thy banner 84:63
Freedoms: world ... upon four essential human f. 289:32
Freezings: what f. have I felt 363:43
French: F. are wiser than they seem 26:19
F. of Paris was to hir unknowe 96:28
F., or Turk, or Proosian 147:30
F. say, there are three sexes 375:9
F. she spak ful faire 96:28
he's gone to fight the F. 179:63
how it's improved her F. 153:12
not too F. F. bean 146:16
Frenchmen: fifty million F. can't be wrong 156:53
Frenzy: demonic f., moping melancholy 220:97
poet's eye in a fine f. rolling 342:53
Fresh: bloom sae f. and fair 81:26
f. as in the month of May 96:27
I shd. feel f. and vigorous 309:30
looking as f. as paint 374:96
Freshness: glory and ... f. of a dream 410:72
Fret: nuns f. not 411:89
Frets: that struts and f. his hour 336:76
Fretted the ... body to decay 126:39
Friday: F. night is Amami night 11:27
F.'s child is loving and giving 235:56
worse on F. 238:71
Friend: a faithful f. is ... medicine 62:47
a fav'rite has no f.! 154:25
a f. ... the masterpeice of Nature 132:29
(all he wished) a f. 155:41
best mirror ... old f. 272:59
faithful are the wounds of a f. 46:87
forsake not an old f. 62:51
f. at court 263:91

Friend (*continued*)
f., go up higher 54:78
f. in need ... f. indeed 263:92
f. shd. bear his f.'s infirmities 326:26
f. that will tell ... my faults 265:23
f. to everybody ... f. to nobody 264:94
f. to thyself ... others will befriend 264:93
good wine – a f. – or being dry 10:16
handsome and witty, yet a f. 251:31
if I had a f. that loved her 344:92
keep thy f. under ... life's key 298:41
keep wel thy tonge ... keep thy f. 97:49
lend yr. money and lose yr. f. 269:70
loan ... loses ... itself and f. 306:57
makes no f. who never made a foe 385:51
my guide, philosopher and f. 250:19
of every friendless name the f. 172:53
only way to have a f. 132:30
open enemy than a false f. 255:14
save me from the candid f. 88:27
speak well of your f. 278:62
tolling a departed f. 316:97
trust not a new f. 281:60
up the ladder ... choosest a f. 264:14
when I lend I am a f. 269:69
Friends: a soul remembering my good f. 349:44
animals are such agreeable f. 130:87
best of f. must part 19:11, 264:97
can live without our f. 270:95
expectation of finding many f. 175:94
f. are thieves of time 264:95
f. begin to compliment him 170:15
f. in heaven and in hell 264:96
f. of the mammon of unrighteousness 55:85
f., Romans, countrymen 325:12
f. shd. be few and good 256:53
God defend me from my f. 264:18
golden f. I had 167:84
have but few f. 264:98
How to Win F. and Influence People 89:40
I love ... old f., old times 151:83
in the misfortunes of our best f. 288:19
judge ... man by his foes as well as ... f. 110:24
kiss and be f. 268:38
laughter learnt of f. 71:94
lay down his life for his f. 56:10

Fury (*continued*)
civil f. first grew high 82:35
cunning old F. 90:46
nor hell a f. like a woman scorned 108:6
tale ... full of sound and f. 336:76
Fuse: through the green f. drives the flower 390:19
Fustian: whose f.'s so sublimely bad 248:82
Fustilarian: you f.! 316:5
Future: for I dipt into the f. 387:80
haven't any f. to think of 366:95
I never think of the f. 129:83
if you wd. divine the f. 108:3
you cannot fight ... the f. 149:51
Futurity: let f. shift for itself 375:16

Gaiety: eclipsed the g. of nations 178:43
Gain: broke the Sabbath but for g. 126:45
no painful inch to g. 103:33
Gales: cool g. shall fan the glade 251:32
Gallantly streaming 188:79
Gallantry: what men call g. 84:66
Gallery in which the reporters sit 202:44
Gallia ... in partes tres 87:6
Gallimaufry: made our English tongue a g. 377:48
Galloped: I g., Dirck g., we g. 74:26
Galloping after a fox 406:27
Gallows: his complexion is perfect g. 355:27
shall there be g. standing 312:45
Galumphing: he went g. back 92:70
Gamaliel: brought up ... at the feet of G. 56:24
Game: a rich man's g. 18:3
but how you played the g. 287:9
g. is not worth the candle 264:3
golf ... not being a g. 194:52
lookers-on see most of the g. 270:4
rigour of the g. 192:27
the g.'s afoot 319:47
win this g. ... thrash the Spaniards too 125:30
woman is his g. 388:1
Game-keeper: old poacher ... good g. 274:20
Gamesmanship or ... Winning Games Without ... Cheating 252:43
Gang: the old g. 100:85
Gaol: all ... we know who live in g. 404:97

Gaol (*continued*)
in a g. better air, better company 177:16
Garden: a g. in her face 88:24
a g. is a lovesome thing 72:97
come into the g., Maud 388:56
dispossessed of the g. hard by Heaven 69:68
fairies at the bottom of our g. 140:41
g. ... purest of human pleasures 26:29
God Almighty first planted a g. 26:29
God the first g. made 112:46
good strawberries in yr. g. 352:74
how does your g. grow 235:55
patience ... not in everyone's g. 274:29
put him into the g. of Eden 35:31
redbreast whistles from a g. croft 181:82
we must cultivate our g. 397:9
Garland: immortal g. is to be run for 223:39
wither'd is the g. of the war 299:66
Garment: City now doth like a g. wear 412:96
Winter G. of Repentance 135:66
Garments: g. though new-fangled ill 363:41
our purses ... proud, our g. poor 355:25
Garnish: the ... eye of heaven to g. 327:43
Garrick: here lies David G. 151:80
Garrulity: my crime, shameful g. 222:17
Garter: he will unloose, familiar as his g. 318:38
I like the G. ... no damned merit 208:25
Gas smells awful 243-4:23
Gash: each new day a g. is added 335:65
Gasp: at the last g. 63:64
Gate: aged man, a-sitting on a g. 94:95
at the strait g. 52:26
heavy burdens at his narrow g. 318-19:39
I am here at the g. alone 388:86
lark at heaven's g. sings 304:20
passion-flower at the g. 388:87
the poor man at his g. 10:18
there's knocking at the g. 335:70
willow cabin at your g. 359:80
Gatepost: you and me and the g. 256:35

Georgie Porgie, pudding and pie 232:31

German: I speak ... G. to my horse 96:24

the G. dictator, instead of snatching 100:90

Germans: Don't let's be Beastly to the G. 112:43

Germany: G. G. above all 164:38

G. will be ... world power or will not be 163:32

Gert and ... Epp and ... Ein 14:57

Get: g. thee glass eyes 330:93

g. thee to a nunnery 310:97

Getting and spending, we lay waste 412:93

Ghastly: we were a g. crew 105:58

Ghost: plays to the bowling of a g. 390:28

vex not his g. 331:7

what beckoning g. ... invites my steps? 248:72

Ghosts: g. from an enchanter fleeing 369:35

haunted by the g. they have depos'd 350:54

rain is full of g. tonight 210:46

Ghoulies: from g. and ghosties and ... beasties 14:60

Giant: g.'s strength ... use it like a g. 337:86

owner whereof was G. Despair 77:62

Giants: there were g. ... in those days 35:44

Giant's-Causeway worth seeing? 177:32

Gibbon: scribble ! Eh, Mr G.? 149:56

Gibeon: sun, stand thou still upon G. 38:20

Gift: time with a g. of tears 382:16

Gifts, even when they bring g. 397:99

man's work or his own g. 223:30

rich g. wax poor 310:96

Gilded: men are but g. loam 347:30

Gilead: is there no balm in G. ? 49:55

Gilpin: and G. long live he 113:61

away went G. – who but he ? 113:57

John G. was a citizen 112:54

said G., so am I 113:58

Gilt off the gingerbread 279:99

Gimble: gyre and g. in the wabe 91:69

Gingerbread: gilt off the g. 279:99

Girdle: I'll put a g. round ... the earth 341:45

Girl: a g. ... cheeks are covered with paint 228:88

Girl (*continued*)

little g. who had a little curl 199:5

marry a country g. afterwards 365:74

naughty g. to disobey 236:57

Poor Little Rich G. 112:45

sweet g.-graduates 388:95

to the sweetest g. I know 407:39

Girlish: filled ... with g. glee 145:2

Girls: a set of wretched un-idea'd g. 174:75

all the g. ... so smart 89:31

passes at g. who wore glasses 243:22

secrets with g. ... guns with boys 114:82

servant g. in the kitchen 383:26

what are little g. made of? 240:85

where the g. are so pretty 17:89

Give: better g. a shilling 256:23

g. all thou canst 409:60

g. me an ounce of civet 329:91

g. me back my legions 86:4

g. me my soul again 204:63

g. not thy soul unto a woman 62:50

g., oh g. me back my heart 86:95

g. one man a lecture ... another a shilling 175:87

g. us the luxuries of life 227:73

it is more blessed to g. 56:22

Mother, g. me the sun 169:10

no more g. the people straw 36:72

such as I have g. I thee 56:15

these pleasures, Melancholy, g. 213:90

when I g., I g. myself 403:85

Given: costs so much as what is g. 273:5

unto ... one that hath shall be g. 53:46

Giver; a cheerful g. 58:63

Givers: when g. prove unkind 310:96

Gives: blesseth him that g. 339:15

g. twice who g. quickly 264:10

who g. to all, denies all 264:9

Giving: g. much to the poor 264:11

not in the g. vein today 352:78

Glad: and I am g., yea g. 125:34

never g. confident morning 74:29

Glade: alone in the bee-loud g. 417:52

Gladly wolde he lerne ... teche 97:34

Gladness: sadness and g. succeed each other 276:9

teach me half the g. 370:51

Gladsome: let us with a g. mind 221:10

Gladstone's always having the ace of trumps 191:23

Glance: ten thousand saw I at a g. 410:69
  whose g. was glum 148:46
Glare; maidens ... moths ... caught by g. 83:56
Glass: double g. o' the inwariable 121:71
  get thee g. eyes 330:93
  ghosts ... tap and sigh upon the g. 210:46
  g. is falling hour by hour 203:55
  g. of fashion ... mould of form 310:1
  g. wherein the noble youths 316:8
  grief with a g. that ran 382:16
  look in thy g., and tell 362:30
  made mouths in a g. 329:74
  people who live in g. houses 264:12
  prove an excuse for a g. 372:78
  see through a g. darkly 57:54
  the more women look in their g. 283:51
  turn down an empty g.! 136:83
Glasses: taste, Shakespeare, and the musical g. 152:1
  there were two g. and two chairs 203:57
Gleam: faiths and empires g. 368:28
  follow the G. 388:91
  the visionary g. 410:76
Gleamed: she g. upon my sight 414:16
Glean: thou shalt not g. thy vineyard 37:98
Gleaned ... after the reapers 39:35
Glee: filled with girlish g. 145:2
  forward and frolic g. was there 294:95
  piping songs of pleasant g. 68:48
Glen: down the rushy g. 11:22
Glides: still g. the Stream 413:13
Glimpses that wd. make me less forlorn 412:94
Glittering: holds him with his g. eye 104:43
  long grey beard and g. eye 104:42
Globe: the great g. itself 356:50
  the race dwelling all round the g. 102:11
Globule: protoplasmal ... atomic g. 145:97
Gloire: le jour de g. est arrivé 291:54
Gloom: amid the encircling g. 230:16
  light to counterfeit a g. 213:86
Gloria: sic transit g. mundi 188:72
Gloriam: ad majorem Dei g. 19:18
Glories: g. like glow-worms ... shine bright 400:48
  I see Heaven's g. shine 71:84

Glorious: g. the northern lights astream 374:94
  Queen Bess's g. days 144:89
  sons of Belial had a g. time 126:46
  sunset ran, one g. blood-red 74:24
Glory: excess of g. obscured 217:41
  for the greater g. of God 19:18
  full meridian of my g. 322:79
  g. and loveliness have pass'd 186:46
  g. of Europe extinguished 78:78
  g. of the sun ... dimmed 27:48
  g. of the world passes away 188:72
  g. shone around 384:35
  g. to Man in the highest ! 383:21
  g. to the new-born King 402:71
  great g. in a woman 392:41
  land of hope and g. 33:13
  left him alone with his g. 408:53
  long hair ... a g. to her 57:52
  the g. of this latter house 51:94
  the g. that was Greece 247:66
  thine is ... power and the g. 52:18
  this I count the g. of my crown 132:21
  'tis to g. we steer 141:48
  trailing clouds of g. do we come 410:77
  triumph without g. ... without danger 110:32
  uncertain g. of an April day 361:6
  whose g. is in their shame 58:76
Glove: hand and g. 266:55
  iron hand in a velvet g. 267:20
  O that I were a g. upon that hand 353:98
Gloves: walk through the fields in g. 111:34
Glow-worms: glories, like g., afar off shine bright 400:48
Gluttony kills more than the sword 264:13
Go: g. and catch a falling star 124:11
  g. around the country – g. to ... towns ... farms 202:52
  as cooks g.; and as cooks g. 292:70
  better 'ole, g. to it 27:47
  g. farther and fare worse 264:15
  g. litel book, g. ... myn tregedie 98:52
  g., put off Holiness 67:37
  g. west, young man 376:24
  g. West, young man 156:47
  gone whar de good niggers g. 138:9
  he would not let them g. 36:76
  I have a g., lady, don't I ? 242:5
  is to g. hence unwilling 221:2
  its no g. my poppet 203:55
  it's no g. the merrygoround 203:54

Go (*continued*)

let him g. for a scapegoat   37:96
let my people g.   36:73
the lamb was sure to g.   157:55
train ... child in the way he shd. g.
    45:80
what a Rum G. everything is   401:65
whither thou goest I will g.   39:33
with thee to g. is to stay here
    221:2
year is going, let him g.   386:68
Goal: good ... the final g. of ill   386:61
grave is not its g.   198:95
Goat: with their g.-feet dance an antic
    hay   204:68
Goblets: my figur'd g. for a dish of
    wood   350:55
Goblin: spirit of health or g. damn'd
    307:60
Goblins: tales ... of sprites and g.
    361:13
God: a contrite heart, O G.   42:9
a lovesome thing, G. wot   72:97
a wild beast or a g.   26:20
all scripture ... inspiration of G.
    59:94
all service is the same with G.
    75:35
an old abusing of G.'s patience
    340:29
and G. said, Let there be light   34:27
and G. said to Jonah   50:87
and G. saw everything ... he had
    made   35:30
and the Word was G.   55:92
are G. and Nature ... at strife ?
    356:62
as G. gives us to see the right   196:81
as if we were G.'s spies   330:99
being blind, the good G. prepare me
    246:45
better to have no opinion of G.
    25:11
Cabots talk only to G.   69:67
cannot serve G. and mammon   52:20
charged with the grandeur of G.
    166:67
cry, G. for Harry, England!   319:47
destroys ... book, kills the image of
    G.   223:37
doorkeeper in the house of my G.
    43:15
doubtless G. could have made a
    better berry   398:25
earthly power doth then show likest
    G.'s   339:15
eternal G. is thy refuge   38:17
every man ... g. or devil   126:44

God (*continued*)

fear G. and keep his commandments
    47:14
fear G. Honour the king   60:9
fit for the kingdom of G.   54:74
fool hath said ... There is no G.
    41:84
for the greater glory of G.   19:18
freedom ... to worship G.   289:32
got up airly ... to take in G.   200:20
glorious the song, when G.'s the
    theme   374:94
glory be to G. for dappled things
    166:68
glory to G. in the highest   54:70
G. Almighty first planted a garden
    26:29
G. and sinners reconciled   402:71
G. appears, and G. is light   66:31
G. be praised, the Georges ended
    192:33
G. be thanked ... two soul-sides
    74:34
G. be with you till we meet again
    286:98
G. bless ... Faith's Defender   83:53
G. bless the moon and G. bless me
    234:43
G. chasteneth thee   38:8
G. comes at last   264:17
G. defend me from my friends
    264:18
G. disposes   188:71
G. doth not need ... man's work
    223:30
G. erects a house of prayer   118:18
G. ... esteems the growth ... of one
    virtuous person   224:41
G. for us all   262:27
G. fulfils himself in many ways
    385:54
G. gave the increase   57:46
G. hath given liberty   116:98
G. hath given you one face   310:99
G. heals ... doctor takes the fee
    264:19
G. help the poor   264:20
G. help the rich   264:21
G. helps them that help themselves
    264:22
G. is alone   366:4
G. is decreeing to begin   224:42
G. is ... for the big battalions   398:15
G. is in heaven and thou upon earth
    46:1
G. is love   60:16
G. is no respecter of persons   56:19
G. is not mocked   58:70

God (continued)

G. is our refuge and our strength 42:7

G. is thy law, thou mine   219:70

G. loveth a cheerful giver   58:63

G. made the country   114:69

G. made the wicked Grocer   99:76

G. made the woman for the man 385:48

G. made them, high or lowly   10:18

G. make me able to pay   245:41

G. moves in a mysterious way 113:63

G. must think it ... odd   191:20

g. of our idolatry, the press   113:66

G. order'd motion but ordain'd no rest   396:86

G. our help in ages past   399:38

G. ... put him into ... Eden   35:31

G. rest you merry   16:82

G. said, Let Newton be!   248:88

G. save our Gracious King   88:29

G. save the mark!   313:52

G. saw the light was good   220:84

G. send you joy   265:24

G.'s first creature ... light   27:40

G. shall add unto him   61:35

G. shall wipe away all tears   61:34

G. shed his grace on thee   29:67

G. shd. go before such villains 344:82

G.'s in his heaven   75:44

G.'s mill grinds slow   265:27

'G. tempers the wind,' said Maria 379:68

G. tempers the wind ... shorn lambs 265:26

G. the first garden made   112:46

G. who is our home   410:77

G. who made thee mighty   33:13

hath not one G. created us?   51:98

he for G. only, she for G. in him 219:66

heavens declare the glory of G. 41:86

honest G. ... noblest work of man 170:14

honest Man's the noblest work of G.   250:16

I am the Lord thy G.   37:81

I reflect that G. is just   171:33

I speak Spanish to G.   96:24

I the Lord your G. am holy   37:97

I ... thy G. am a jealous G.   37:84

if G. be for us   57:35

if G. did not exist   397:12

in apprehension, how like a g.! 308:81

God (continued)

in the beginning G. created   34:26

in the image of G. created He him 34:28

inclines to think there is a G.   103:27

into the hands of the living G. 59:98

isn't life ... terrible ... thank G.? 390:25

it shall please G. to call me   64:99

just are the ways of G.   222:16

justify the ways of G. to men   216:29

knowledge ... make a G. of me 182:2

knowledge of G. ... burnt offerings 50:75

land which the Lord thy G. giveth 37:87

last and best of all G.'s works 220:94

Lord G. made them all   10:17

love, we are in G.'s hands   73:14

make a joyful noise unto G.   43:13

malt ... to justify G.'s ways to man 167:85

man proposes, G. disposes   271:36

name of the Lord thy G. in vain 37:85

nature is the art of G.   72:1

nearer, my G., to thee   9:3

new Jerusalem, coming ... from G. 61:33

not G. is greater ... than ... self 403:86

O G., O Montreal!   82:47

of such is the kingdom of G.   54:61

Oh! G.! that bread shd. be so dear 166:65

one G., one law, one element   387:73

one on G.'s side is a majority   246:51

only G. can make a tree   189:82

out of the mouth of G.   51:7

peace of G., which passeth   58:78

powers ... ordained of G.   57:42

pray G. we may make haste   348:38

prepare to meet thy G.   50:83

presume not G. to scan   250:13

pretence that G. had put it [ace] there   191:23

pure in heart ... shall see G.   52:10

remember the name of the Lord our G.   42:90

resistance ... is obedience to G. 171:31

rib which ... G. had taken   35:33

rich man ... into the kingdom of G. 53:41

sabbath of the Lord thy G.   37:86

God (*continued*)

Sarah Battle, now with G.   192:27

servant of G., well done!   219:82

serv'd my G. with half the zeal 323:84

shall ... man be more just than G.? 41:66

shalt love the Lord thy G.   38:6

so G. created man   34:28

so lonely 'twas, that G. himself 106:62

souls ... in the hand of G.   62:43

stern daughter of the voice of G. 413:7

taken at the flood, leads – G. knows 85:80

thank G. we're normal   242:7

the dear G. who loveth us   106:64

the Lord our G. is one Lord   38:5

the Lord thy G. chasteneth thee 38:8

the sacrifices of G. are   42:9

there, but for the grace of G.   70:73

they [voices] come from G.   366:2

this is the finger of G.   36:74

those whom G. hath joined   65:10

thou shalt have one G. only   103:28

though G. hath raised me high 132:21

though the mills of G. grind slowly 198:99

thy G. my G.   39:33

to walk humbly with thy G.   51:91

true love's the gift which G.   295:4

turn to G. to praise   74:25

unto G. the things that are G.'s 53:43

vindicate the ways of G. to Man 250:8

voice of the people is the voice of G. 10:15

was the holy Lamb of G.   67:38

we owe G. a death   317:19

what therefore G. hath joined   54:60

when first G. dawned on Chaos 367:11

who think not G. at all   222:16

whole armour of G.   58:73

whom G. wishes to destroy   275:74

whose G. is their belly   58:76

Wonderful, Counsellor, The mighty G.   48:36

wd. G. I had died ... O Absalom 40:51

would to G. we had died   36:79

yellow g. forever gazes down   159:76

youth shows but half; trust G. 75–6:46

Goddess: g. and maiden and queen 383:22

g. excellently bright   178–9:50

Godliness: in cheerful g.   413:4

Gods: a daughter of the g.   385:46

as flies ... are we to th' g.   329:85

as g., knowing good and evil   35:36

by the Nine G. he swore   201:35

carve him as a dish for the g.   324:99

for the ... temples of his G.   201:36

I thank whatever g. may be   160:93

kings are earth's g.   347:26

kings it makes g.   352:83

leave the rest to G.   111:33

men call gallantry and g. adultery 84:66

no other g. before me   37:82

so many g., so many creeds 404:93

thank the g. I am foul   302:2

the darling of the G. was born   207:4

the g. are just   330:1

voice of all the g. make heaven drowsy   331:15

we thank ... whatever g. may be 383:20

wd. the g. had made thee poetical 302:99

Goest: whither thou g. I will go   39:33

Gog, the land of Magog   49:66

Going: as I was g. to St. Ives   231:22

at the g. down of the sun   65:20

Cross of Jesus g. on before   28:57

g. one knows not where   208:17

I am just g. outside   241:93

I don't feel like g. into it   292:71

men must endure their g. hence 330:98

the Lord shall preserve thy g.   44:39

where are you g. to, my pretty maid? 241:86

Gold: all is not g. that glitters   254:66

beauty provoketh ... sooner than g. 300:74

building roofs of g.   318–19:39

fetters, be they made of g.   271:31

floor of heaven ... with patines of bright g.   340:22

g. in phisik is a cordial   97:38

hadde he but litel g. in cofre   96:33

her locks were yellow as g.   105:52

if g. ruste, what shall iren do?   97:41

king's ... a heart of g.   320:51

led by the nose with g.   362:27

my bow of burning g.   67:38

my g.!—open the shrine   179:59

nor all, that glisters, g.   154:26

rank is good, and g. is fair   403:88

Gold (*continued*)
run back and fetch the age of g.
215:21
saint-seducing g. 353:90
showers ... barbaric pearl and g.
217:45
the poop was beaten g. 298:54
to gild refined g. 327:43
travell'd in the realms of g. 185:40
true love ... differs from g. 368:26
weakness to resist Philistian g.
222:20
wedges of g., great anchors 352:72
what female heart can g. despise?
154:24
when g. and silver becks me 327:40
worth his weight in g. 284:59
Golden: as they did in the g. world
300:72
from this g. rigol 318:28
girl-graduates in their g. hair 388:95
g. friends I had 167:84
g. lads and girls 304–5:29
g. rule ... there are no g. rules 365:86
g. slumbers kiss yr. eyes 118:20
love in a g. bowl 66:32
O polished perturbation! g. care!
317:27
silver nutmeg and a g. pear 233:39
the g. years return 368:28
waters of the Nile on every g. scale
89–90:45
wear a g. sorrow 322:75
Goldsmith: here lies Nolly G. ... called
Noll 141:49
Golf may be played on Sunday 194:52
Golf-balls: a thousand lost g. 131:8
Gondolier: a highly respectable g.
143:71
Gone: if she's not g. ... there still 239:75
now thou art g., and never must
return 215:10
thou art g., and for ever 295:98
thy thoughts, when thou art g. 370:54
what's g. ... shd. be past grief 361:14
Gongs: strong g. groaning as the guns
boom far 99:71
Good: a g., unless counterbalanced by
evil 177:29
all g. and no badness 373:93
all g. to me is lost 218:63
all partial evil, universal g. 250:12
all things work together for g. 56:34
and for the g. and increase 385:48
any g. of George the Third? 192:33
apprehension of the g. gives ... feeling 348:37
are you g. men and true? 343:72

Good (*continued*)
as gods, knowing g. and evil 35:36
as g. as she was beautiful 246:46
as g. be out of the world 102:12
be g., sweet maid 189:86
behold, it was very g. 35:30
beneath the g. how far 156:45
best is the enemy of the g. 397:11
but what g. came of it? 376:30
care not whether man is g. or evil
67:37
chief g. and market of his time
311:22
cleave to that which is good 57:37
Continent ... g. food ... England ...
g. table manners 209:39
crown thy g. with brotherhood
29:67
curate's egg, g. in parts 259:43
enough is as g. as a feast 65:18
Evil, be thou my G. 218:63
general g. ... plea of the scoundrel
67:36
giver of all g. things 64:90
go about doing g. 115:85
gone whar de g. niggers go 138:9
g. are so harsh to the clever 409:59
g., but not religious-g. 158:66
g. enough to govern another 196:73
g. enough to shed his blood 289:37
g. fences make g. neighbours 139:26
g. for the country was g. for General
Motors 407:42
g. is oft interred with their bones
325:12
g. that I wd. I do not 56:33
g. ... the final goal of Ill 386:61
g., the more communicated 219:76
g. to be merry ... honest and true
17:93
g. to be out on the road 208:17
Guinness is g. for you 11:28
he [Time] ... our g. will sever 179:61
he who wd. do g. to another 67:36
hear no g. of themselves 270:90
hold fast that which is g. 59:85
if all the g. people were clever 409:59
ill wind that blows nobody g. 267:15
it is not, nor it cannot come to g.
306:46
Joan is as g. as my lady 268:24
let him do what seemeth him g.
39:37
little of what you fancy does you g.
197:86
money ... not g. unless ... spread 25:8
never g. to bring bad news 299:56
never had it so g. 202:52

Good (*continued*)
not g. that man shd. be alone 35:32
nothing ... g. or bad, but thinking makes 308:80
Oh, Sir! the g. die first 409:64
only g. Indian is a dead Indian 371:61
out of g. still to find means of evil 216:32
sermons in stones, and g. in everything 300:75
she was very, very g. 199:5
so much g. in the worst of us 163:36
some said it might do g. 76:56
the g. is the beautiful 247:61
the greatest g. 102:16
to the public g. private respects must yield 222:21
wives must be had, ... g. or bad 283:44
Good night: fortune, g. 328:63
g.? ah! no; the hour is ill 368:27
g. g.! Parting is such sweet sorrow 354:6
say g. till it be morrow 354:6
sweet ladies, g. 311:25
Goodbye to All That 154:21
Goodness: felt how awful g. is 219:73
g., what is she a-doin' of? 18:4
Goods: with all my worldly g. 65:9
Goose: g. that lays the golden eggs 268:33
sauce for the g. ... the gander 276:12
say Bo(o) to a g. 276:14
three women and a g. 280:36
Goosey, goosey gander 232:32
Gordian: the G. knot ... he will unloose 318:38
Gormed: I'm G. – I can't say no fairer 120:45
Gossip, babbling g. of the air 359:80
scandal is g. made tedious 406:20
Got: vicious place where thee he g. 330:1
Gourd: to be angry for the g. 50:87
Gout: drink, combined with g. 143:73
wine ... the g.; ... no wine ... the g. too 260:89
Gouvernement: le g. qu'elle mérite 203:58
Govern: g. another man without that other's consent 196:73
he that wd. g. others 208:18
Governed: a nation is not g. 78:72
Government: all g. ... founded on compromise 78:74
every nation has the g. it deserves 203:58

Government (*continued*)
g. ... a necessary evil 243:20
g. ... framed ... in after-dinner conversations 391:38
g. of the people, by the people 196:79
g. shall be upon his shoulder 48:36
having looked to g. for bread 78:83
if any ask me what a free g. is 78:84
one form of G. rather than another 176:2
only legitimate object of good g. 171:31
Gower: O moral G. 98:53
Gown: g. of glory, hope's true gage 286:94
like an old lady's loose g. 314:78
Gowns: robes and furr'd g. hide all 330:92
Grace: an inward and spiritual g. 64:1
divine g. was never slow 260:78
God shed his g. 29:67
g. me no g. 349:45
grow old with a good g. 378:60
he does it with a better g. 359:85
he had at least the g. 34:20
my g. is sufficient for thee 58:66
no ... beauty hath such g. 123:7
sweet attractive g. 219:66
Tuesday's child is full of g. 235:56
with one half so good a g. 337:84
ye are fallen from g. 58:68
Graced with polished manners 114:75
Gradualness: the inevitability of g. 400:42
Graduates, sweet girl-g. in their golden hair 388:95
Grain: which g. will grow ... will not 333:27
Grammar: erecting a g. school 321:68
Grammatici certant ... sub iudice lis est 166:70
Gramophone: puts a record on the g. 131:12
Granary: sitting careless on a g. floor 181:80
Grand: they said, 'it wd. be g.' 92:78
Grandchild: his little g. Wilhelmine 376:28
Grandeur: g. hear with a disdainful smile 155:34
g. that was Rome 247:66
Grandmother: teach yr. g. to suck eggs 279:13
Grandsire: proverb'd with a g. phrase 353:91
Grape: fathers have eaten a sour g. 49:58

Grape (*continued*)
  merry with the fruitful g. 135:75
  neither shalt thou gather every g.
   37:98
  the g. that can with Logic absolute
   135:77
Grapes: our vines have tender g. 47:23
  sour g. can ne'er make sweet wine
   278:60
Grapeshot: a whiff of g. 89:34
Grapple them to thy soul 306:55
Grasp: a man's reach shd. exceed his g.
   73:15
Grass: a snake in the g. 277:49
  all flesh is as g. 60:8
  all flesh is g. 48:42
  cut the g. from under ... feet 259:48
  g. ... as soft as ... breast of doves
   111:34
  Guests star-scattered on the G.
   136:83
  hare limp'd trembling through the
   frozen g. 181:89
  his days are as g. 43:23
  I am the g.; I cover all 293:78
  I know the g. beyond the door
   291:53
  seed from the feather'd g. 182:97
  two blades of g. to grow 381:2
Grate on their scrannel pipes 215:16
Gratis: he lends out money g. 338:3
Grave: a little g., an obscure g. 350:55
  body lies a mould'ring in the g.
   157:57
  country ... a kind of healthy g.
   375:13
  Duncan is in his g. 334:51
  eat our pot of honey on the g.
   209:33
  every third thought ... my g. 357:58
  from g. to gay, from lively to severe
   250:18
  funeral marches to the g. 198:96
  g. is not its goal 198:95
  g. of Mike O'Day 13:50
  g. where English oak and holly
   158:72
  g. where our hero we buried 408:52
  g.'s a fine and private place 206:95
  in the dark and silent g. 286:93
  lead but to the g. 155:36
  make ... turn in his g. 281:67
  man ... pompous in the g. 72:7
  my large kingdom for a little g.
   350:55
  O g., where is thy victory? 57:60
  O G., where is thy Victory? 247:71
  one foot in the g. 274:22

Grave (*continued*)
  renowned be thy g.! 305:31
  see myself go into my g. 246:45
  where, g., thy victory? 201:33
Graves: find ourselves dishonourable
   g. 323:93
  talk of g., of ... epitaphs 349:53
Gravity: approach this spot with g.!
   13:49
Gravy: rich wot gets the g. 18:5
  Sir Humphrey Davy detested g.
   33:18
Great: all things both g. and small
   106:64
  brilliant chief, irregularly g. 76:53
  but far above the g. 156:45
  even g. men have ... poor relations
   119:35
  g. is Diana of the Ephesians 56:21
  g. is Truth, and mighty 31:37
  g. men are almost always bad men
   9:1
  g. men ... not commonly ... g.
   scholars 164:51
  g. ones eat up the little ones 347:27
  madness in g. ones 310:2
  rightly to be g. ... g. argument
   311:24
  rule of men entirely g. 76:54
  some are born g., some achieve greatness 360:91
  such g. men as these 18:6
  to be g. is to be misunderstood
   133:37
Great War: what did you do in the
   G.? 11:25
Greater: feel that we are g. than we
   know 413:14
  there is no g. sorrow 116:3
  thy necessity is g. than mine 373:88
Greatest: g. happiness of the g. number
   33:14
  g. talkers ... least doers 279:8
  sooner fail than not be among the g.
   187:61
Greatness: farewell, to all my g. 322:80
  highest point of all my g. 322:79
  some achieve g. 360:91
  some have g. thrust upon them
   360:91
  thinks ... his g. is a-ripening 322:80
Greece: citizen not of Athens or G.
   375:20
  dream'd that G. ... be free 84–5:78
  G., Italy and England did adorn
   128:66
  the glory that was G. 247:66
  the isles of G., the isles of G.! 84:77

Greedy: not g. of filthy lucre 59:87
Greek: it is G. to me 265:48
  it was G. to me 324:96
  must carve in Latin or in G. 398:18
  paid at the G. Kalends 86:5
  small Latin and less G. 179:56
  when his wife talks G. 178:45
Greeks: G. had a word for it 10:14
  I fear the G. 397:99
  when G. joined G. 195:67
  which came first, the G. or the Romans 123:1
Green: a dyspeptic mint g. 395:80
  a g. and yellow melancholy 360:89
  and all the trees are g. 189:88
  drives my g. age 390:19
  flourishing like a g. bay-tree 42:4
  g. grow the rashes O 80:7
  g. thought in a g. shade 206:99
  in England's g. and pleasant land 67:38
  laurel is g. for a season 383:23
  making the g. one red 334:43
  salad days, when I was g. 298:53
  the memory be g. 305:37
  their heads are g. 194:58
  there is a g. hill far away 11:20
  through the g. fuse drives the flower 390:19
  upon England's mountains g. 67:38
  voices of children are heard on the g. 68:52
  when woods are getting g. 93:88
  whiten the g. plains under 368:22
Greenery-yallery ... young man 146:18
Greenland: from G.'s icy mountains 159:86
Greensleeves: G. was all my joy 16:83
  who but Lady G.? 16:83
Greet: how shd. I g. thee? 86:1
Grenadier: for the British G. 18:6
Grew: where only one g. before 381:2
Grey: by thy long g. beard 104:42
  lend me yr. g. mare 19:12
  that g. iniquity 314:68
Greyhounds: stand like g. in the slips 319:47
Grief: after long g. and pain 388:88
  but for our g., as if it had not been 367:12
  g. and pain for promis'd joy. 80:18
  g. itself be mortal 367:12
  g. returns with the revolving year 367:10
  g., with a glass that ran 382:16
  hopeless g. is passionless 73:12
  past help shd. be past g. 361:14
  silent manliness of g. 150:71

Grief (continued)
  smiling at g. 360:89
  time and thinking tame the g. 250:38
  when thou art old ... g. enough 156:48
Griefs: of all the g. that harass 172:54
  secret ... are their g. and fears 24:94
Grin: g. like a dog, and run about 42:12
  taking a fee with a g. 144:84
Grind: my life is one demd horrid g. 120:54
  [ye] g. the faces of the poor 48:32
Grinds: with exactness g. he all 198:99
Grindstone: one's nose to the g. 273:4
Grinning; antic sits ... g. at his pomp 350:54
Grist: bring g. to the mill 265:49
Groan: bitter g. of a martyr's woe 66-7:35
  future ages g. for this foul act 350:56
Groaned: my mother g., my father wept 67:44
Groaning: strong gongs g. 99:71
Grocer: God made the wicked G. 99:76
Groomed: nicely g., like a mushroom 193:47
Grosvenor Gallery ... young man 146:18
Grotesque: so g. a blunder 33-4:19
Ground: betwixt the stirrup and the g. 87:16
  blood of English shall manure the g. 350:56
  children of Israel ... upon the dry g. 36:78
  commit his body to the g. 65:15
  fathom-line cd. never touch the g. 313:54
  let us sit upon the g. 350:54
  massa's in de cold, cold g. 138:3
  native air, in his own g. 251:28
  upon the g., can fall no lower 269:77
  when every rood of g. maintained 150:63
Grovel: souls that g. 87:13
Grovelled: he g. ... and my-lorded 389:13
Groves: o'er shady g. they hover 400:54
Grow: ask me where they do g. 162:15
  g. up with the country 156:47
Growed: I 'spect I g. 380:85
Growled: cracked and g. and roared and howled 105:46

Growth: I cannot give it vital g. again
346:19
Grubstreet ... near Moorfields 172:45
Grudge: feed fat the ancient g. 338:3
Grumble: nothing whatever to g. at
148:40
Grumbling: the g. grew to a ... rumb-
ling 75:40
Grundy, the end of Solomon G.
238:71
Grunt and sweat under a weary life
309:95
Gruntled: he was far from being g.
408:51
Gryphon: called lessons, the G.
remarked 91:61
Guard: Alice is marrying one of the g.
211:54
g. the guards themselves? 180:69
Guards: up, G., and at 'em 401:60
Guerre: la g. ... industrie nationale
224:47
Guess: I g. an' fear 80–1:19
Guest: constant g. is never welcome
258:24
dull fighter and a keen g. 315:84
Guests: the G. star-scattered on the
Grass 136:83
unbidden g. ... welcomest when ...
gone 321:63
Guide: custom ... the great g. 168:91
g. me, O thou great Redeemer
407:40
my g., philosopher and friend
250:19
Guilders: 'will you give me a thousand
g.?' 75:39
Guilt: other pens dwell on g. and
misery 23:71
what art can wash her g.? 152:2
Guilty: better that ten g. ... escape
66:26
my soul ... g. of dust and sin 161:12
suspicion ... haunts the g. mind
322:72
we make g. of our disasters the sun
327:53
Guinea: worth a g. a box 11:34
Guinness is good for you 11:28
Gulf: a great g. fixed 55:87
Gull's way and the whale's way 208:16
Gum: Arabian trees their med'cinable
g. 346–7:22
Gummidge: Mrs G.'s words 119:37
Gunga Din 190:1
Gunner and his mate lov'd Mall
356:43
Gunpowder treason and plot 15:69

Guns: g. aren't lawful, nooses give
243:23
g. will make us powerful; butter ...
fat 149:58
loaded g. with boys 114:82
strong gongs groaning as the g. boom
far 99:71
Gustibus: de g. non est disputandum
259:53
Gypsies: play with the g. in the wood
236:57
Gyre and gimble in the wabe 91:69

Ha, ha, ha, you and me 16:84
Habit: costly thy h. as thy purse can
buy 306:56
h. is a great deadener 30:76
h. with him was all the test of truth
114:79
honour ... in the meanest h. 355:25
Habitation: local h. and a name
342:53
Habits: h. ... carry them far apart
108:2
needs reforming as other people's h.
394:72
Hackney: see to H. ('A) Marshes 29:66
Haggards ride no more 378:63
Hags: secret, black, and midnight h.
335:60
Hail: h. and farewell 94:6
h., divinest Melancholy! 213:83
h., Holy Light 218:58
h., horrors! h. 216:34
h., wedded Love 219:71
my gracious silence, h.! 303:13
the flail of the lashing h. 368:22
to be h. fellow well met 265:50
Hailed at the twilight's last gleaming
188:79
Hair: beauty draws us with a single h.
251:35
each particular h. to stand on end
307:64
graduates in their golden h. 388:95
her h. was long, her foot was light
183:8
I must sugar my h. 91:64
if a woman have long h. 57:52
Jeanie with the light brown h.
138:2
[letters] serve ... to pin up one's h.
109:11
shall I part my h. behind? 131:4
smooths her h. with automatic hand
131:12
train of thy amber-dropping h.
213:80

Hairs: given me over in my grey h. 408:55

how ill white h. become a ... jester 318:34

to split h. 278:67

Hairy: Esau, my brother, is a h. man 36:59

Hal: why, H., 'tis my vocation, H. 312:47

Half: h. a league onward 385:40

h. a trade and h. an art 170:12

h. as much as ... Mr Toad 153:14

h.-seas over 265:53

knows not how the other h. lives 265:52

the h. that's got my keys 153:9

too civil by h. 372:73

too clever by h. 280:49

yr. servant's cut in h. 153:9

youth shows but h. 75–6:46

Half-a-crown: if I fling h. to a beggar 175:84

Half-a-dozen of the other 206:87, 277:41

Half-way: don't meet trouble h. 272:53

Halifax: from Hell, Hull and H. ... deliver us 266:85

Hall: bride hath paced into the h. 104:45

the Douglas in his h. 296:12

Tom bears logs into the h. 332:20

Hallelujah: h.! I'm alive 242:8

here lies my wife, h.! 13:44

Hallowed: place of justice is an h. place 26:36

Halo? ... one more thing to keep clean 140:32

Halt: how long h. ye between two opinions 40:56

Halves: never do things by h. 266:54

Hamelin town's in Brunswick 75:36

Hamlet: I saw H. Prince of Denmark played 134:54

O H., what a falling off! 307:68

rude forefathers of the h. 155:33

Hamlets brown, and dim-discover'd spires 107:88

Hammock: Drake he's in his h. 230:11

Hampden: some village H. 155:38

Hand: bite the h. that fed them 78:83

captain's h. on his shoulder smote 230:14

cold h. ... warm heart 258:19

come, give me your h. 335:70

discern between ... right h. ... left h. 50:88

Hand (*continued*)

earth, I do salute thee with my h. 349:49

every man's h. against him 35:53

great is the h. that holds dominion 390:20

h. and glove 266:55

h. for h., foot for foot 37:93

h. ... head ... heart of man go together 292:63

h. in h., on ... edge of the sand 195:62

h. open as day for ... charity 317:25

h. that signed the treaty 390:20

have still the upper h. 111:39

having put his h. to the plough 54:74

her h. on his thick skull 127:49

I fear thy skinny h. 105:53

infinity in the palm of your h. 66:27

iron h. in a velvet glove 267:20

leans her cheek upon her h. 353:98

lend thy guiding h. 221:11

let not thy left h. know 52:16

O that I were a glove upon that h. 353:98

one whose h. ... threw a pearl away 346–7:22

our times are in His h. 75:46

reason is our soul's left h. 123:5

smooths ... hair with automatic h. 131:12

the h. of war 348:41

the handle toward my h. 334:40

the larger heart, the kindlier h. 387:71

this blood clean from my h. 334:43

this my h. will rather 334:43

touch of a vanish'd h. 384:37

we are in God's h. 73:14

what immortal h. or eye 68:46

whatsoever thy h. findeth to do 47:7

when I stretched out my h. 379:69

who will stand on either h.? 201:37

will not sweeten this little h. 335:69

Handbag: an ordinary h. in fact 405:11

yes, Lady Bracknell ... a h. 405:11

Handful: just for a h. of silver he left us 74:28

Handle: and I polished up the h. 147:26

the h. toward my hand 334:40

Hands: and then take h. 355:34

by fairy h. their knell is rung 107:90

fall into the h. of the living God 59:98

Hands (*continued*)
he clasps the crag with crooked h. 385:47
if you believe, clap your h. 28:62
into thy h. I commend my spirit 42:96
laid violent h. upon themselves 65:12
large and sinewy h. 199:6
licence my roving h. 123:9
lift not thy h. to It 136:80
many h. make light work 266:57
mischief ... for idle h. 399:36
my h. from picking and stealing 64:98
people who have flabby h. 145:99
right h. of fellowship 58:67
swinken with his h. 96:30
the h. are the h. of Esau 36:60
the horny h. of toil 200:22
their h. are blue 194:58
took water and washed his h. 53:51
with mine own h. I give away my crown 350–1:58
Handsaw: a hawk from a h. 308:83
Handsome: a h., lively young fellow 372:79
h. in three hundred pounds a year 341:32
h. is that h. does 266:59
not h. at twenty ... rich at forty 266:58
Hang: a rope to h. himself 16:85
I think I will not h. myself to-day 98:66
rope enough and he'll h. himself 276:4
she wd. h. on him 305:44
we must indeed all h. together 138:14
we will h. you, never fear 148:36
wretches h. that jury-men may dine 252:37
Hanged: as good be h. for a sheep 266:60
born, bred, and h., ... same parish 13:47
born to be h. 257:57
man knows he is to be h. 177:24
my poor fool is h.! 331:6
not h. for stealing horses 157:56
Hanging: any thing we allow ... short of h. 176:7
good h. prevents a bad marriage 359:78
h. and wiving go (goes) by destiny 266:61, 339:11
Puritane-one h. of his cat 70:74

Hangs: thereby h. a tail 345:4
thereby h. a tale 301:88, 355:23
Hanover: by famous H. city 75:36
Hans Breitmann gife a barty 195:68
Happiest: h. moments of the h. ... minds 371:58
I am h. when I am idle 399:30
Happiness: all the h. mankind can gain 128:64
boring ... somebody else's h. 169:1
divided and minute domestic h. 187:63
greatest h. of the greatest number 33:14
greatest h. of the whole 247:62
h. in marriage ... matter of chance 23:76
h. makes up in height 139:28
h. ... rare in human life 176:13
h. ... wine of the rarest vintage 374:99
in solitude, what h.? 220:87
it is a flaw in h. 181:88
life, liberty, and the pursuit of h. 171:26
lifetime of h.! ... hell on earth 365:78
look into h. ... another man's eyes 303:6
my H. ... not so fine as my Solitude 187:63
no more right to consume h. 364:66
O h.! our being's ... aim 250:15
recall ... h. when in misery 116:3
Happy: a h. bridesmaid makes a h. bride 384:38
be h. and live within our means 399:31
be h. while ... young 19:20
better be h. than wise 255:18
call no man h. until he dies 375:22
h. is England! 185:42, 43
h. issue out of ... afflictions 63:84
h. the man, and h. he alone 128:71
h. the man, whose wish and care 251:28
h. ... to learn the causes 397:5
how h. ... born and taught 416:48
how h. cd. I be with either 142:54
how h. he who crowns in shades 150:64
how to be h. though married 157:63
I cd. be h. with you 407:44
little h. if I cd. say how much 342:64
methinks it were a h. life 321:70
riches of the mind ... make ... h. 276:93

Happy (*continued*)
the duty of being h.   379:79
this h. breed of men   348:41
Harbour: [fog] looking over the h.
293:77
Hard: h. cheese   266:68
how h. ... for women to keep counsel
324:2
nothing's so h. but search will find
162:22
Hardy: Kiss me, H.   230:9
Hare: first catch yr. h.   263:65
h. limp'd trembling through the
frozen grass   181:89
mad as a March h.   271:24
rouse a lion than to start a h.   313:53
run with the h.   276:8
take yr. h. when cased   149:55
Hark: h., h. the lark   304:20
h.! the herald angels sing   402:71
Harlot: wise man that marries a h.
298:39
Harm: do so much h. ... doing good
115:85
drunken folk seldom take h.   261:95
none ... shall h. Macbeth   335:62
when loyalty no h. meant   17:91
Harmony: all discord, h. not understood   250:12
heaven drowsy with the h.   331:15
made quiet by the power of h.
415:33
such h. is in immortal souls   340:22
tie the hidden soul of h.   215:5
touches of sweet h.   340:22
Harness: die with h. on our back
336:77
Harp: David took an h.   39:43
h. not on that string   352:81
h. that once through Tara's halls
226:62
his wild h. slung behind him   226:64
praise the Lord with h.   42:97
Harps: we hanged our h. upon the
willows   44:45
Harrow: lightest word wd. h. up thy
soul   307:64
Harry: cry, God for H.!   319:47
not ... Amurath ... but H., H.
318:31
stain the brow of my young H.
312:44
Harsh: good are so h. to the clever
409:59
pluck yr. berries h. and crude
215:8
Harshness: not enough no h. gives
offence   249:99

Harvest: like a stubble-land at h. home
313:51
seedtime and h. and cold and heat
35:48
Harwich: a steamer from H.   144:92
Haste: daffodils ... h. away so soon
162:18
h. still pays h.   338:94
h. thee Nymph   214:93
marry in h.   271:46
men love in h.   85:84
more h. the less speed   266:70
said in my h., All men are liars
43:32
Hat: faith but ... fashion of his h.
342:57
hath no head, needs no h.   266:74
Hatch, match and despatch   266:72
Hatchet: bury the h.   257:72
I did it with my little h.   399:34
Hate: cherish those hearts that h. thee
323:83
enough religion to make us h.   382:9
generation of them that h. me   37:84
greatest h. ... from the greatest love
265:47
h. him for he is a Christian   338:3
h. the man ... you have hurt   383:28
I h. and love ... and am in torment
94:5
I h. letters   109:11
Juno's unrelenting h.   128:72
love and h. are necessary   68:56
neither beg nor fear ... favours nor ...
h.   333:27
only love sprung from my only h.
353:96
politicians neither love nor h.
126:41
pomp ... of this world, I h. ye   322:81
study of revenge, immortal h.   216:30
Hated: h. wickedness that hinders
loving   74:32
loved well because he h.   74:32
to be h. needs but to be seen   250:14
Hatred: h., and malice, ... uncharitableness   63:77
h. is blind   266:71
h. ... the longest pleasure   85:84
no h. or bitterness   95:7
no rage like love to h. turned   108:6
stalled ox and h. therewith   45:71
Hatter: mad as a h.   271:23
Haul over the coals   266:73
Haunches: fog ... sits ... on silent h.
293:77
Haunt: murmurous h. of flies on summer eves   184:28

Haunt (*continued*)
our life, exempt from public h. 300:75
Haunted: beneath a waning moon was h. 106:72
on summers eves by h. stream 214:3
Have: not good to want and to h. 265:35
to h. and to hold 64:7
what we h. we prize not 343:81
Havens: ports and happy h. 348:36
Haves: the *H.* and the *Have-Nots* 95:10
Havoc: Cry 'H.!' and let slip the dogs of war 324:9
Hawk: I know a h. from a handsaw 308:83
Hawks: all haggard h. will stoop 191:22
Hawthorn: gives not the h. bush a sweeter shade? 322:71
under the h. in the dale 214:98
Hay: dance an antic h. 204:68
make h. while the sun shines 271:27
Haystack: needle in a h. 272:81
He: every h. has ... a she 16:79
Head: a h. grown gray in vain 367:16
better be the h. of a dog 255:20
born about three ... with a white h. 316:99
four angels round my h. 10:13
frost which binds so dear a h. 367:9
hath no h., needs no hat 266:74
heavy weight from off my h. 350:58
here rests his h. upon the lap of earth 155:40
I ... covered up her h. 17:96
I will make you shorter by a h. 132:19
if you can keep yr. h. when all about you 190:2
in the heart or in the h. 339:14
incessantly stand on your h. 90:48
lay your sleeping h., my love 22:60
left it dead and with its h. 92:70
my h. is bending low 138:8
my h. is bloody, but unbowed 160:94
old h. on young shoulders 274:19
on the ... hands little gold h. 211:61
one small h. cd. carry all he knew 150:69
precious jewel in his h. 300:75
rise up before the hoary h. 38:1
shoot ... this old gray h. 403:89
shouting 'Off with his h.!' 91:56
talked ... after his h. was cut off 15:66

Head (*continued*)
thou art a traitor. Off with his h.! 352:75
turns no more his h. 106:60
uneasy lies the h. that wears a crown 317:14
wash ... yr. h. never 282:7
weak h. with strongest bias rules 249:93
what though his h. be empty 382:8
which way the h. lies 286:95
with intention to break his h. 175:84
Headache: awake with a dismal h. 144:91
Heads: bald h. are soon shaven 255:90
h. I win, tails you lose 115:86, 266:75
houseless h. and unfed sides 329:78
mob has many h., but no brains 272:62
stars hide their diminished h. 218:61
their h. are green 194:58
two h. are better than one 281:77
Headstone: become the h. of the corner 44:35
Headstrong: as h. as an allegory 372:72
Head-waiter who's allowed to sit 395:82
Heal: ever h. but by degrees? 345:3
Healed: they have h. also the hurt 49:54
Healing: arise with h. in his wings 51:1
Health: a h. unto his Majesty 16:85
and h. on both! 335:54
good wife and h. ... best wealth 265:37
h.! h.! the blessing of the rich! 179:60
h. is better than wealth 266:76
h. is not valued till sickness 266:77
he that will not drink his h. 16:85
he that will this h. deny 129:78
me? In my state of h.? 180:77
the popular idea of h. 406:27
Healthy: all h. instinct for it 82:46
h. and wealthy and dead 392:42
h. citizens ... greatest asset 101:6
h., wealthy and wise 261:5
imagination of a boy is h. 181:84
nobody is h. in London 23:66
Hear: chink in the floor ... let me h. 383:26
deaf as those who won't h. 260:59
destroyer and preserver, h., oh h.! 369:36

Hear (*continued*)
　do you h. the children weeping?
　　73:11
　few love to h. the sins　347:25
　grossly close it in, we cannot h.
　　340:22
　h. a voice in every wind　154:28
　h. dat mournful sound　138:3
　h. twice before you speak　266:79
　I h. thee and rejoice　415:37
　never merry when I h. sweet music
　　340:23
　the ear begins to h.　71:87
　time ... when you will h. me　122:88
　to h. the lark begin his flight　214:97
Heard: cuckoo is in June, h., not
　　regarded　314:77
　h. a thousand blended notes　411:83
　h. melodies are sweet　183:17
　I h. a maid singing in the valley
　　16:80
　more he h. the less he spoke　285:82
　not a drum was h.　408:52
　voice I h. this passing night was h.
　　184:30
Hearing: I have heard of thee by the h.
　　41:79
Hears: she neither h. nor sees　414:19
Heart: a broken and a contrite h.
　　42:9
　a h. grown cold ... in vain　367:16
　a man after his own h.　39:40
　absence makes h. grow fonder
　　15:72, 29:68
　all that mighty h. is lying still　412:97
　as well as want of H.!　165:62
　awake, my h., to be loved　70:75
　ay, in my h. of h.　310:6
　because my h. is pure　389:3
　blessed are the pure in h.　52:10
　bring with you a h. that watches
　　415:29
　bringing Soviet power into the h. of
　　Western Europe　102:7
　but [give] not yr. h. away　167:81
　but his flaw'd h. ... too weak　330:3
　cold hand ... warm h.　258:19
　comes from the h., goes to the h.
　　107:84
　enter every trembling h.　402:72
　faint h. never won fair lady　263:44
　fair face ... foul h.　262:47
　find Calais lying in my h.　207:10
　fool hath said in his h.　41:84
　give me back my h.　86:95
　Greensleeves was my h. of gold
　　16:83
　hardened Pharaoh's h.　36:76

Heart (*continued*)
　h. and stomach of a king　132:20
　h. of oak are our ships　141:48
　h. shall break into ... flaws　328:69
　h.'s lightness from ... May　181:87
　h. to poke poor Billy　153:11
　h. upon my sleeves for daws
　　344:89
　h. which grief hath cankered　87:12
　heavy purse ... light h.　266:82
　her h. was young and gay　157:58
　his h. is in his mouth　266:81
　his h.'s his mouth　303–4:17
　his tiger's h. wrapped in ... hide
　　156:49
　holiness of the h.'s affection　186:50
　hope deferred maketh ... h. sick
　　45:66
　how my h. grows weary　138:6
　I feel my h. new open'd　322:81
　I said to H., 'How goes it?'　31:97
　I shall light a candle ... in thine h.
　　61:38
　I sleep but my h. waketh　47:25
　if thou didst ever hold me in thy h.
　　312:38
　in the h., not in the knees　171:37
　in the h. or in the head　339:14
　intellect ... fooled by the h.　288:16
　inward fragrance of each other's h.
　　182:3
　it's Oh! in my h.　179:63
　language of the h.　248:87
　light purse ... heavy h.　269:83
　like music on my h.　106:61
　look in thy h. and write　373:84
　love the Lord ... with all thine h.
　　38:6
　many a h. is aching　158:71
　meditation of my h. be acceptable
　　42:89
　merry h. ... cheerful countenance
　　45:70
　merry h. goes all the day　361:19
　my h. aches and a drowsy numbness
　　184:23
　my h. leaps up when I behold　412:98
　my h. untravelled ... turns to thee
　　151:90
　my true love hath my h.　372:83
　nation ... that had the lion h.
　　102:11
　natural language of the h.　297:38
　never a crack in my h.　417:56
　no longer lacerates his h.　382:12
　now cracks a noble h.　312:40
　open not thine h. to every man
　　62:49

Heart (*continued*)
overset the brain, or break the h.
411:88
perilous stuff which weighs upon the
h. 336:72
pity ... in the h. of love 417:57
poor h. that never rejoices 274:50
pourest thy full h. 370:49
quickening life from the earth's h.
367:11
rend yr. h. and not yr. garments
50:78
rose in the deeps of my h. 417:55
serve the Lord ... with all thy h.
38:9
Shakespeare unlocked his h. 412:95
shall command my h. and me
115:84
shot through his h. on Sunday
379:71
so the h. be right 286:95
strike mine eyes but not my h.
179:52
strings, said Mr. Tappertit, in the ...
h. 119:32
take thy beak from out my h.
247:67
tears fall in my h. 396:90
the h. has its reasons 244:28
the larger h., the kindlier hand
387:71
the laughter of her h. 157:58
the Lord looketh on the h. 39:42
the waters of the h. 390:21
them that are of a broken h. 42:1
through the sad h. of Ruth 184:30
to lose your h.'s desire ... to gain it
365:83
warm the cockles of the h. 282:5
way to an Englishman's h. 282:13
wear him in my h.'s core 310:6
wear one's h. on one's sleeve 282:17
what female h. can gold despise?
154:24
what the false h. doth know 333:39
when my h. was young and gay
138:7
where my h. lies 74:33
whose ... complexion and whose h.
362:24
wine that maketh glad the h.
43:24
with a h. for any fate 198:98
with h., and soul, and voice 229:2
with rue my h. is laden 167:84
woman with the h. 389:2
word 'Callous' engraved on her h.
297:31

Heart-ache: to say we end the h.
309:95
Hearts: agonies, the strife of human h.
185:37
apply our h. unto wisdom 43:18
enthroned in the h. of kings 339:15
grows old with their sick h. 180:70
h. are dry as summer dust 409:64
h. at peace, under an English heaven
71:94
kind h. are more than coronets
387:74
men with splendid h. 71:90
our h., though stout and brave
198:96
thousand creeds ... move men's h.
71:85
two h. that beat as one 200:18
wand'ring eyes and heedless h.
154:26
while yr. h. are yearning 137:94
Heat: fear no more the h. o' th' sun
304:29
have neither h. nor light 400:48
h. me these irons hot 327:42
h. not a furnace for your foe 322:74
I know not where is that Promethean
h. 346:19
thinketh on fantastic summer's h.
348:37
Heath: a wind on the h. 69:65
Heathen: why do the h. rage? 41:80
Heaven: a h. in a wild flower 66:27
a H. on Earth 219:65
a new h. and a new earth 61:32
all this and h. too 161:2
brightest h. of invention 318:36
builds a h. in hell's despair 67:43
created the h. and the earth 34:26
differ as H. and earth 385:52
droppeth as the gentle rain from h.
339:15
every purpose under the h. 46:98
fallen from h., O Lucifer 48:38
fantastic tricks before high h.
337:87
first h. ... passed away 61:32
floor of h. is thick inlaid 340:22
friends ... in h. and hell 264:96
gain'd from h. ... a friend 155:41
garden hard by H. 69:68
God is in h. and thou upon earth
46:1
God's in his h. 75:44
h. and earth shall pass away 295:7
h. has no rage like love to hatred
turned 108:6
h. is in these lips 204:63

Heaven (*continued*)

H. itself wd. stoop to her [Virtue] 213:81

H. lies about us in our infancy 410:77

H. tries earth if it be in tune 200:25

Hell I suffer seems a H. 218:62

high H. rejects the lore 409:60

how long ... permit to H. 220:98

I see H.'s glories shine 71:84

in earth ... as it is in h. 52:18

in the nurseries of H. 391:32

joy shall be in h. 54:80

justice be done, though h. fall 263:59

keys of the kingdom of h. 53:35

kingdom of h. is at hand 51:4

leave to H. the measure ... choice 174:71

love is h. and h. is love 295:2

make h. drowsy with the harmony 331:15

marriages are made in h. 274:41

mind ... can make a H. of Hell 216:35

more things in h. and earth 307:69

new Jerusalem ... out of h. 61:33

not mad, sweet h.! 328:60

O h., were men but constant 361:11

open face of h. 186:47

or what's a h. for? 73:15

our conversation is in h. 58:77

over his living head like H. 367:13

parting is all we know of h. 122:82

places that the eye of h. visits 348:36

praise my soul, the King of H. 201:34

progressive virtue, and approving H.! 391:34

puts all H. in a rage 66:28

reign in Hell than serve in H. 216:36

shun the h. that leads men to this hell 363:51

steep and thorny way to h. 306:54

summons thee to h. or to hell 334:41

that from H., or near it 370:49

that h.'s vault shd. crack 330:4

there was silence in h. 61:27

to be young was very H.! 413:9

to seek the ... eye of h. to garnish 327:43

top ... reached to h. 36:61

under an English h. 71:94

watered h. with their tears 68:47

when Britain first, at H.'s command 391:33

Heavens: pure as the naked h. 413:4

spangled h., a shining frame 9:9

the h. declare the glory of God 41:86

the h. themselves, the planets ... observe 358:66

till you are clothed with the h. 392:52

Heaviness foreruns the good event 317:22

Heavy: a light wife doth make a h. husband 340:26

Hebrew: called in the H. tongue Armageddon 61:31

Hector: of H. and Lysander 18:6

Hecuba: what's H. to him or he to H.? 308:90

Hedge: a voice ... from h. to h. 185:42

Heels: if yr. h. are nimble and light 233:36

to cool one's h. 259:27

Heigh! the doxy over the dale 361:17

Heigh-ho: h.! says Rowley 232:30

sing h. unto the green holly 302:91

Height: happiness makes up in h. 139:28

to the h. of this great argument 216:29

Heir: dear son of memory, great h. of fame 216:24

first h. of my invention 364:58

Heiresses: all h. are beautiful 128:65

Helen: dust hath closed H.'s eye 229:99

sweet H., make me immortal 204:63

Helena: all is dross that is not H. 204:63

Hell: a shout that tore H.'s concave 217:40

airs from heaven or blasts from h. 307:60

all H. broke loose 219:74

all we need of h. 122:82

and H. followed with him 61:26

better to reign in H. 216:36

boys, it [war] is all h. 372:81

builds a Heaven in H.'s despair 67:43

down to h.; and say I sent thee 322:73

dunnest smoke of h. 333:33

England ... h. for horses 81:31

gates of h. shall not prevail 53:34

go ... to h. in embroidery' 256:24

heaven that leads men to this h. 363:51

h. and Chancery are always open 266:83

h. is a city ... like London 369:41

Hell (*continued*)

h. itself breathes out contagion 310:13

h. to which hate and fear ... condemn 292:66

into the mouth of H. 385:43

Italy ... h. for women 81:31

jealousy ... injured lover's h. 219:79

lifetime of happiness! ... h. on earth 365:78

make a Heaven of H., a H. of Heaven 216:35

myself am H. 218:62

no redemption from h. 276:82

nor h. a fury like a woman scorned 108:6

prompted ... by heaven and h. 309:93

road to h. is paved ... intentions 266:84

summons thee to heaven or to h. 334:41

the bells of h. go ting-a-ling 16:76

to reign ... though in H. 216:36

though h. shd. bar the way 231:21

ugly h., gape not! come not, Lucifer! 204:66

way down to H. is easy 397:2

way ... that out of H. leads 218:54

when war begins, h. opens 282:3

which way I fly is H. 218:62

women ... as Heaven and H. 385:52

Hellish dark, and smells of cheese! 380:90

Helmsman: so the h. answered 198:1

Help: a very present h. 42:7

H. of the helpless 201:31

h. yourself, heaven will h. you 136:89

hills, from whence cometh my h. 44:37

many of yr. countrymen cannot h. 174:83

not enough to h. the feeble up 357:59

O God, our h. in ages past 399:38

past h. shd. be past grief 361:14

past my h. is past my care 29:72

since there's no h. ... kiss and part 125:34

the rich can h. themselves 264:20

Helpers: when other h. fail 201:31

Helpless: Help of the h., O Abide with me 201:31

h., naked, piping loud 67–8:44

Hemlock: as though of h. I had drunk 184:23

Hen: two Owls and a H. 195:66

yaf nat of that text a pulled h. 96:29

Henry: the chief defect of H. King 31:90

Henry IV Part II: abdicated in favour of H. 297:30

Hens: three French h. 238:73

Heraldry: the boast of h., the pomp of power 155:35

Herbert Spencer: expression ... used by Mr H. 117:8

Herbs: dinner of h. where love is 45:71

Hercules: and some of H. 18:6

let H. ... do what he may 312:34

Herd: lowing h. winds slowly 155:30

Here: h. he lies where he longed to be 379:76

h. is my journey's end, h. is my butt 346:21

h. lie I and ... daughters 12:41

h. lies a man who was killed 12:42

h. lies a poor woman 12:43

h. lies ... Mary Ann Lowder 13:46

h. lies my wife ... hallelujee! 13:44

h. lies my wife: h. let her lie! 127:60

h. lies ... Richard Hind 13:45

h. lies Will Smith 13:47

h. we come gathering nuts in May 16:86

I have been h. before 291:53

the ice was h., the ice was there 105:46

'tis neither h. nor there 346:15

we're h. because we're h. 19:13

Hereafter: she shd. have died h. 336:76

what is love? 'Tis not h. 359:84

what may come h. 382:19

Heresies: begin as h. ... end as superstitions 169:6

Heresy: ancient saying is no h. 339:11

there is no worse h. 9:1

Heretics: Jews, Turks, Infidels, and H. 64:88

Heritage: Americans ... proud of our ancient h. 188:74

Hermit: dwell a weeping h. there! 107–8:90

Hermitage: my gorgeous palace for a h. 350:55

Hermits are contented with their cells 411:89

Hero: be a h. ... must drink brandy 177:31

every h. becomes a bore 133:41

no man is a h. to his valet 111:35

see the conquering h. comes 226:68

Hero (*continued*)
  the grave where our h. we buried
    408:52
  to his ... valet seem'd a h. 83:54
Herod: it out-herods H. 310:4
Heroes: fit country for h. to live in
    197:90
Héros: pas de h. pour son valet 111:35
Hero-worship is strongest where
    376:37
Herring: h. boxes without topses
    225:60
  plague o' these pickle h. 359:79
Hervey: if you call a dog H. 174:73
Hesperus: H. entreats thy light
    178-9:50
  it was the schooner H. 199:9
Hewers of wood and drawers of water
    38:19
Hey: and a h. nonino 303:7
  H. diddle diddle 232:33
Hickory, dickory, dock 232-3:34
Hid: fiend h. in a cloud 67-8:44
  love ... cough cannot be h. 270:8
Hide: let me h. myself in thee 392:51
Hideous: ingratitude ... more h. ... in a
    child 328:57
Hides from himself his state 174:70
High: h. and low mate ill 403:88
  means ... for contempt too h.
    112:47
  when civil fury first grew h. 82:35
  ye'll tak' the h. road 18:2
High churchman: a zealous H. was I
    17:91
Highland: my sweet H. Mary 80:9
  yon solitary H. Lass! 414:20
  your H. Laddie 179:63
Highlands: chieftain to the H. bound
    88:19
  my heart's in the H. 81:20
Hill: apart sat on a h. retired 218:55
  dew of yon high eastward h. 305:36
  h. will not come to Mahomet 25:3
  laughing is heard on the h. 68:52
  there is a green h. far away 11:20
  to sit upon a h. as I do now 321:70
Hills: as old as the h. 273:17
  floats on high o'er vales and h.
    410:67
  halloo yr. name to the reverberate h.
    359:80
  lift up mine eyes unto the h. 44:37
  over the h. and far away 142:53,
    240:82
  the great h. of the South Country
    32:5
  we shall fight in the h. 100–1:94

Him first, h. last, h. midst 219:78
Himself: discommendeth others ...
    commendeth h. 72:98
  man's first duty? ... To be h. 169:11
  none ... liveth ... dieth to h. 57:44
  shd. be the master of h. 208:18
  so lonely 'twas, that God h. 106:62
Hinder end of the spear 40:50
Hindmost: devil take the h. 260:74
Hinky dinky parley-voo 291:57
Hint: upon this h. I spake 344:92
Hip: catch him once upon the h.
    338:3
  smote them h. and thigh 39:28
Hippo: Lord H. 32:3
Hippocrene: the blushful H. 184:24
Hireling: pay given to a state h.
    172:50
Hiss: a dismal universal h. 220:96
  roasted crabs h. in the bowl 332:20
Hissed all my mystery lectures 377:50
*Histoire des grands événements ... h. des
    crimes* 397:13
Histories make men wise 26:34
History: attend to the h. of Rasselas
    173:61
  cd. ever hear by tale or h. 341:36
  ends this strange eventful h. 301:90
  great deal of h. to produce a little
    literature 170:24
  great dust-heap called h. 65:21
  happiest women ... have no h.
    130:86
  happy ... country which has no h.
    266:64
  h. ... essence of innumerable bio-
    graphies 89:38
  h. is ... biography of great men
    89:36
  h. is bunk 137:91
  h. is philosophy teaching 122:87
  h. must be false 398:21
  h. of England ... h. of progress
    202:45
  h. of the great events ... h. of crimes
    397:13
  h. ... register of the crimes, follies
    142:66
  h. repeats itself 266:87
  H. ... will tell lies, as usual 365:70
  no h., only biography 132:31
  Thames is liquid h. 79:94
  there is a h. in all men's lives 317:16
  war makes rattling good h. 158:64
  we learn from h. ... nothing from
    h. 365:85
  woman's ... h. ... h. of the affections
    170:16

History (*continued*)
world h. ... world's judgment 294:86
Hit: a h., a very palpable h. 312:36
    h. the nail on the head 267:88
Hitch yr. wagon to a star 133:43
Hither: come h., come h. 300:83
Hitler has missed the bus 95:17
Hive: a h. for the honey bee 417:52
Hoarded: beauty is nature's coin; must not be h. 213:79
Hobson's choice 267:89
Hodgepodge: our ... tongue a galli-maufry or h. 377:48
Hoist with his own petard 267:90
Holborn: when I was last in H. 352:74
Hold: for ever h. his peace 64:5
    h. fast that which is good 59:85
    to have and to h. 64:7
Hole: a better 'ole 27:47
    Roöötten, Beëëastly, Silly H.! 401:63
Holes where eyes did once inhabit 352:72
Holidays: if ... year were playing h. 313:50
Holiness: go! put off H.! 67:37
    h. of the Heart's affection 186:50
Hollow: we are the h. men 130:94
Holly: heigh-ho unto the green h. 302:91
    the h. and the ivy 16:87
    the h. bears the crown 16-17:87
Holy: an h. and a good thought 63:65
    H. Deadlock 161:10
    h., divine, good, amiable 220:94
    h., fair and wise is she 361:8
    h., h., h., all the Saints adore thee 160:88
    hunters been nat h. men 96:29
    sabbath day – to keep it h. 37:86
    savage place! As h. and enchanted 106:72
    the h. city, new Jerusalem 61:33
    was the h. Lamb of God 67:38
    ye shall be h. ... for I the Lord ... am h. 37:97
Holy Roman Empire was neither holy, nor Roman, nor an Empire 398:14
Holy writ: odd old ends ... of h. 351:70
Homage: hypocrisy ... h. paid by vice 288:17
Home: as much like h. as we can 140:35
    at h. I was in a better place 300:81
    blest by suns of h. 71:93

Home (*continued*)
charity begins at h. 258:96
comin' for to carry me h. 18:8
don't want to go h. in the dark 161:5
dunce that has been kept at h. 113:65
east or west, h. is best 261:7
fools at h. condemn 'em 356:48
God, who is our h. 410:77
his first, best country ... h. 151:91
h. art gone, and ta'en thy wages 304-5:29
h. is heaven 228:90
h. is the sailor, h. from sea 379:76
h. life of our own dear Queen 14:62
h. of the bean and the cod 69:67
h. on the rolling deep 293:81
h ... they have to take you in 139:24
hunter h. from the hill 379:76
I am far from h. 230:16
it's h. and it's h. ... fain wad I be 116:97
keep the h. fires burning 137:94
ladybird, ladybird, fly away h. 234:46
leave them alone, and they'll come h. 234:48
man goeth to his long h. 47:12
our eternal h. 399:38
pillage ... with merry march bring h. 318:39
pleasure never is at h. 182:95
returned h. the previous night 76:52
sick for h., she stood in tears 184:30
Sublimity to welcome me h. 187:63
sweet h. of ... fears and hopes and joys 183:15
that is fit h. for thee 415:39
the old Kentucky H. 138:4
there's no place like h. 245:34
they dream of h. 137:94
this little pig stayed at h. 239:78
what's the good of a h.? 156:52
Homely: home-keeping youth hath ... h. wits 360:4
Homer: seven cities warred for H., being dead 163:26
    shame when the worthy H. nods 166:71
    with the single exception of H. 367:8
Homerus: quandoque ... dormitat H. 166:71
Homes: the stately h. of England! 111:39, 160:90

Homestead, Braddock, Birmingham 293:80

Homines: quot h. tot sententiae 389:7

Honest: armour is his h. thought 416:48

deal with none but h. men 276:87

good to be h. and true 17:93

h. God is the noblest work of man 170:14

h. man sent to lie abroad 416:46

h. man's the noblest work of God 250:16

I am not naturally h. 362:25

she was poor but she was h. 18:3

the world's grown h. 308:79

to be h. ... is to be one man pick'd out 308:76

Honesty: corruption wins not more than h. 323:83

for saving of thine h. 226:67

h. is the best policy 267:94

neither h., manhood, nor ... fellow-ship 312:48

no legacy is so rich as h. 298:45

Honey: and is there h. still for tea? 71:91

civil citizens kneading up the h. 318–19:39

eat our pot of h. on the grave 209:33

flowing with milk and h. 36:70

funny how a bear likes h.? 211:62

gather h. all the day 399:35

I always eat peas with h. 15:63

in the parlour eating bread and h. 238:70

it's no go my h. love 203:55

some h., and plenty of money 195:60

sweeter than h. and the h.-comb 41:88

Tiggers don't like h. 210:50

Honey-dew: he on h. hath fed 107:76

Honeyed middle of the night 181:90

Honi soit qui mal y pense 267:95

Honour: as h., love, obedience 336:71

brilliance ... left to the fighter's h. 160:92

can h. set to a leg? 315:88

desires h. ... not worthy of h. 260:70

drown'd my H. in a shallow Cup 136:82

fewer men, the greater share of h. 320:55

giving h. unto the wife 60:10

his h. rooted in dishonour 385:50

h. a physician with the h. due 62:57

Honour (*continued*)

h. all men ... h. the king 60:9

H. comes, a pilgrim grey 107–8:90

h. for his valour 325:11

h. hath no skill in surgery 315:88

h. is a mere scutcheon 315:88

h. is the subject of my story 323:91

h. of honourable men 395:79

h. peereth in the meanest habit 355:25

h. pricks me on 315:88

h. sinks where commerce ... prevails 151:92

h.'s thought reigns solely 319:40

h. the face of the old man 38:1

h. thy father and thy mother 37:87

I believe it is ... peace with h. 95:16

if I give thee h. due 214:96

if it be a sin to covet h. 320:56

if peace cannot be ... with h. 292:65

jealous in h. 301:90

loss of h. was a wrench 153:12

loved I not H. more 200:17

mine h. is my life 347:30

pledge ... our fortunes, and our sacred h. 171:27

pluck bright h. from the ... moon 313:54

pluck up drowned h. 313:54

take h. from me ... life is done 347:30

the louder he talked of his h. 132:27

there is h. among thieves 267:96

'tis for the h. of England 109:8

to h. we call you 141:48

what is h.? A word 315:88

when h.'s at the stake 311:24

Honourable: Brutus is an h. man 325:13

Honoured: more h. in the breach than the observance 307:59

Honours: bears his blushing h. thick upon him 322:80

mindless of its just h. 412:95

Hood: can drink with him that wears a h. 380:81

Hoofs: wound ... with their horses' h. 349:49

Hook: by h. or by crook 267:97

draw out leviathan with an h. 41:78

he for subscribers baits his h. 100:84

Hook-nos'd fellow of Rome 317:24

Hooks: silken lines and silver h. 123:4

Horses (*continued*)
  some trust in chariots and some in h.
    42:90
  swap h. in mid-stream 196:80
  that h. may not be stolen 157:56
Hose: youthful h. ... a world too wide
    301:90
Host: a h. of golden daffodils 410:67
  a soundless-clapping h. 390:28
Hostages: given h. to fortune 24:96
Hostess: fairer the h., the fouler the
    reckoning 262:50
  sits on's horse back at mine h.' door
    326:35
Hot: h. as hell 384:30
  H., Cold, Moist and Dry 218:57
  soon h., soon cold 278:56
Hotel: living in a vile h. 32:4
Hotspur: the H. of the north 314:62
Hound: a traveller, by the faithful h.
    198:94
Hounds: cry of his h. 154:20
  h. of spring are on winter's traces
    382:15
  hunt with the h. 276:8
  with his h. and his horn in the morn-
    ing? 154:20
Hour: but one bare h. to live 204:65
  dusky h. friendliest to sleep 219:80
  Eternity in an h. 66:27
  fools! for I also had my h. 99:69
  fourscore ... not an h. more nor less
    330:97
  from h. to h. we ripe ... rot 301:88
  he rose in less than half an h. 32:4
  how many makes the h. ... complete
    321:70
  I have known the lightning's h.
    117:15
  improve each shining h. 399:35
  it chanceth in an h. 258:95
  memorial ... to one dead deathless h.
    290:49
  one far fierce h. and sweet 99:69
  that struts and frets his h. 336:76
  the h. is come, but not the man
    296:17
  the h. is ill which severs 368:27
  the wish'd, the trysted h. 80:15
  this was their finest h. 101:95
  wet sea-boy in an h. so rude
    317:14
Hours: a heavy weight of h. has chained
    369:37
  golden h. on angel wings 80:9
  lazy, leaden-stepping h. 223:34
  lose and neglect the creeping h.
    301:89

Hours (*continued*)
  love alters not with his brief h.
    363:48
  six h. in sleep, in ... study six 104:40
  sweetest h. that e'er I spend 80:7
  three h. a day will produce 393:56
  to chase the glowing H. 83:60
  two h.' traffic of our stage 353:89
  worst effect is banishing for h.
    112:53
House: a h. where help wasn't hired
    12:43
  a h. wherein to tarry 255:97
  a man's h. is his castle 104:39
  as a moat defensive to a h. 348-9:41
  call upon my soul within the h.
    359:80
  daughters of my father's h. 360:90
  eaten me out of h. and home
    316:6
  glory of this latter h. 51:94
  h. fell upon the lords, and ... people
    39:30
  h. is a machine for living in 110:31
  h. that Jack built 239:79
  I will build a h. with deep thatch
    32:6
  if a h. be divided ... h. cannot stand
    53:55
  in a little crooked h. 239:74
  in my Father's h. are many mansions
    56:9
  in that H. M.P.'s divide 144:88
  like a h. on fire 267:6
  my h. in the high wood 32:7
  my h. ... the h. of prayer 54:62
  out of the h. of bondage 37:81
  prop that doth sustain my h. 340:20
  set thine h. in order 48:41
  shalt not covet thy neighbour's h.
    37:92
  the h. where I was born 165:60
  wounded in the h. of my friends
    51:97
  you take my h. when you do take the
    prop 340:20
  yr. h. is on fire and yr. children all
    gone 234:46
House of Lords are never in touch
    406:28
House of Peers throughout the war
    144:90
Household: breathing h. laws 412:2
  stables ... real centre of h. 365:72
Houses: a plague o' both your h.
    354:11
  h. are built to live in 26:28
  h. thick and sewers annoy 220:93

Houses (*continued*)
  if it wasn't for the h. in between 29:66
  lawyers' h. ... on the heads of fools 269:60
Housewife: here's to the h. that's thrifty 372:78
Hovel: *prefer* ... a h. to ... marble halls 87:13
Hover through the fog and filthy air 332:23
How: a pretty h. town 116:94
How-de-do: here's a h.! 145:5
Howl, h., h., h., ... men of stones! 330:4
Howled: cracked and growled and roared and h. 105:46
Howling: churlish priest ... when thou liest h. 312:32
  Tom went h. down the street 240:83
Hubbard: old Mother H. 236:59
Hubbub increases more they call out 'Hush!' 182:99
Hue: add another h. unto the rainbow 327:43
  native h. of resolution 309:95
Huffy: not h. or stuffy, nor tiny 161:7
Hull: from Hell, H. and Halifax ... deliver us 266:85
Hum: busy h. of men 214:1
  h. of either army stilly sounds 320:50
  sad-ey'd justice, with his surly h. 318–19:39
Human: a fearful sign of h. frailty 84:74
  Adam was but h. 394:68
  all h. things are subject to decay 128:68
  all that is h. must retrograde 142:67
  climax of all h. ills 84:76
  dignity and worth of the h. person 394:76
  every h. benefit and enjoyment 78:74
  full tide of h. existence ... Charing-Cross 176:9
  [God] ... does a h. form display 66:31
  h. on my faithless arm 22:60
  h. kind cannot bear ... much reality 130:91
  h. race to which ... readers belong 99:78
  I may be devout, but I am h. 224:50
  I wish I loved the H. Race 286:97

Human (*continued*)
  in h. nature ... more of the fool 25:2
  purest of h. pleasures 26:29
  requires the highest type of h. nature 376:33
  the field of h. conflict 101:96
  to err is h. 249:4, 267:7
  where ... least regard for h. freedom 376:37
  women—one half the h. race 27:44
Human being: remember that you are a h. 366:93
Humane: every h. and gentle virtue 78:89
Humanized: distress hath h. my soul 409:62
Humanity: h. i love you because 116:95
  h. with all its fears 197:92
  still, sad music of h. 415:35
Humanum est errare 267:7
Humble: neither too h. nor too great 203:59
  we are so very h. 119:41
  you are *not* his most h. servant 177:34
Humbly: walk h. with thy God 51:91
Humility: h. towards the Public 186:58
  modest stillness and h. 319:45
Humour: deficient in a sense of h. 107:83
  unyok'd h. of yr. idleness 312:49
  was ever woman in this h. woo'd ... won? 351:69
Hump: a woman ... without a positive h. 389:12
  camel's h. is an ugly lump 190:15
  uglier yet is the h. we get 190–91:15
Humpty Dumpty: 93:84–6, 233:37
Hundred: about two h. pounds a year 82:38
  only one religion ... a h. versions 366:92
  uttered it a h. times 164:49
Hunger ... is highly indelicate 148:39
Hungry: if thine enemy be h. 45:81
  makes h. where most she satisfies 299:55
Hunter: h. home from the hill 379:76
  Lo! the H. of the East 134:65
  man is the h. 388:1
  mighty h. before the Lord 35:51
Hunter Dunn: Miss J. H. 34:25
Hunters: seith ... h. been nat holy men 96:29

Hunting: h. he loved but love he laugh'd to scorn 364:59
we daren't go a-h. 11:22
wet and dirty from h. 381:92
Huntress: queen and h. chaste and fair 178:50
Hurlyburly: when the h.'s done 332:22
Hurrah! H.! we bring the Jubilee 416:45
Hurricanes: you cataracts and h., spout 328:71
Hurry: an old man in a h. 100:86
sick h., its divided aims 21:42
Hurt: cd. you h. me, sweet lips? 382:18
give delight and h. not 356:47
hate the man whom you have h. 383:28
h. with the same weapons 339:13
Hurtig: you are h. be 190:14
Husband: actors are...h., and wife and lover 209:32
being a h. ... whole-time job 33:11
good wife makes a good h. 265:38
light wife makes a heavy h. 340:26
Husbands: flirt with their own h. 405:7
h. at chirche-dore she hadde fyve 97:39
why so many h. fail 33:11
Hush: a breathless h. in the Close tonight 230:13
they call out 'H.!' 182:99
Hush-a-bye baby 233:38
Husks that the swine did eat 55:81
Hut: love in a h. 183:11
Hymns: chanting faint h. to ... moon 341:35
Hyperion to a satyr 305:43
Hyphenated Americanism: no room ... for h. 289:38
Hypocrisy: Conservative Government ... organized h. 122:90
h. ... homage ... by vice to virtue 288:17
h. ... homage that vice pays 267:8
Hypocrite: no man is a h. in his pleasures 178:36
plea of the scoundrel, h. 67:36
Hysterica passio, down ... sorrow 328:64

I: blew hither: here am I 167:83
I am I, and you are you 74:27
I am the State 199:12
I came, I saw, I conquered 87:8
I galloped, Dirck galloped 74:26
I have a go ... don't I? 242:5

I (continued)
I, said the Fly 241:88
I, said the Sparrow 241:88
'I', says the Quarterly 86:94
the spot where I made one 136:83
whoso turns as I 74:25
Iacta alea est 87:7
Iago: the pity of it, I.! 346:12
Ice: as chaste as i., as pure as snow 310:98
i. in June 85:91
in skating over thin i. 133:35
like ... i. on a hot stove 139:29
pleasure-dome with caves of i. 107:75
some say the world will end in ... i. 139:25
the i. was here, the i. was there 105:46
thrilling region of thick-ribbed i. 337:90
to smooth the i. 327:43
Icicles: when i. hang by the wall 332:20
Ida: on I.'s shady brow 68:54
Idea: abstract I. I have of Beauty 187:63
between the i. and the reality 130:95
Ideal: the i. man ... non-attached 168:99
Ideas: nice man ... of nasty i. 382:11
ruling i. ... i. of its ruling class 207:8
Idem velle ... nolle, ... firma amicitia 293:73
Ides of March: beware the i. 323:90
Idiosyncrasy: I have no ... i. in ... humour 72:2
Idiot: it is a tale told by an i. 336:76
law is an ass—a i. 120:58
the i. who praises 145:1
Idle: as i. as a painted ship 105:49
be not solitary, be not i. 82:33
for i. hands to do 399:36
happiest when I am i. 399:30
i. that might be better employed 267:9
tears, i. tears 388:99
tongue of i. ... is never i. 280:47
Idleness: i. ... the refuge of weak minds 98:61
unyok'd humour of yr. i. 312:49
Idol: a one-eyed yellow i. 159:76
Idolatries: to its i. a patient knee 83:61
Idolatry: god of our i., the press 113:66

Idols: the i. I have loved so long
136:82
   there are four classes of I. 27:41
If: i. it wasn't for the 'ouses 29:66
   yr. I. is the only peace-maker 303:10
Ifs: if I. and Ans were pots and pans
267:10
   talk'st thou to me of i.? 352:75
Ignorance: art has no enemy except i.
254:76
   from i. our comfort flows 253:52
   hold there is no sin but i. 204:69
   i. is like ... exotic fruit 405:9
   i. is preferable to error 171:32
   i., Madam, pure i. 174:81
   where i. is bliss 154:29
Ignorant: conscious that you are i.
123:97
   most i. of what he's most assur'd
337:87
Ignore: aren't happy with nothing to i.
228:93
Ilium: the topless towers of I. 204:63
Ill: a fool is love ... he thinks no i.
363:39
   better suffer i. than do i. 256:29
   costs more to do i. 259:28
   i. doers are i. thinkers 267:12
   i. fares the land, to ... ills a prey
150:62
   i. gotten, i. spent 267:13
   i.-housed, i.-clad, i.-nourished
289:30
   i. met by moonlight 341:43
   love worketh no i. 57:43
   marries late, marries i. 271:43
   means to do i. deeds make deeds i.
done 327:45
   of every i. a woman is the worst
153:17
   religion an i. man is of 276:83
   the final goal of i. 386:51
   things bad begun make strong ... by
i. 335:52
Ill-bred: nothing so ... i. as audible
laughter 98:59
Illiberal: nothing so i. ... as audible
laughter 98:59
Illiterate him ... from your memory
371:66
Ills: bear those i. we have 309:95
   climax of all human i. 84:76
   i. have no weight 201:33
   to hastening i. a prey 150:62
   what i. the scholar's life assail
173:68
Ill-tempered and queer 194:59
Illumine: what in me is dark i. 216:29

Image: any graven i. 37:83
   are wronging your i. 417:55
   best i. of myself, and dearer half
219:77
   i. of war, without its guilt 375:23
   in the i. of God created 34:28
Imagination: as i. bodies forth the
forms 342:53
   are of i. all compact 342:52
   by bare i. of a feast 348:37
   certain of ... the truth of I. 186:50
   civet ... to sweeten my i. 329:91
   i. of a boy is healthy 181:84
   [indebted to] ... i. for his facts
372:80
   what the I. seizes as Beauty 186:50
Imagined: exhausted worlds and ... i.
new 173:58
Imitate the action of the tiger 319:45
Imitation ... sincerest form of flattery
108:98
Imlac: business of a poet, said I.
173:63
Immanuel: shall call his name I.
48:34
Immaterial: the Brighton line. The line
is i. 405:12
Immortal: a thing i. as itself 307:61
   grow i. as they quote 417:59
   Helen, make me i. with a kiss
204:63
   his biting is i. 299:68
   I have left no i. work 187:68
   i. longings in me 299:70
   lost the i. part of myself 345:1
   my scrip of joy, i. diet 286:94
   such harmony is in i. souls 340:22
   what i. hand or eye 68:46
Immortality: just ourselves and I.
122:84
   nurslings of i. 369:43
Imparadised in one another's arms
219:68
Impatient: surprised by joy, i. as the
Wind 411:91
Impediment: cause or just i. 64:3
Impediments: marriage of true minds
admit i. 363:47
   wife and children ... are i. 24:96
Important: little things ... the most i.
124:18
Imports be more than your exports
178:35
Importunate: rashly i., gone to her
death 165:56
Importune: too proud to i. 156:46
Impossibility: begotten by Despair
upon I. 206:97

Impossible: I wish it were i. 178:40
in two words, i. 152:5
pure and complete sorrow ... i.
392:50
that not i. she 115:84
when you have eliminated the i.
125:25
Impostors: treat those two i. just the
same 190:4
Impotently: rolls i. on as Thou or I
136:80
Impregnable: as if this flesh ... were
brass i. 350:54
Impressions: first i. are most lasting
263:67
Improbable: however i., must be the
truth 125:25
Impropriety: i. is the soul of wit
208:21
use any language ... without i.
144:91
Improve: i. each shining hour 399:35
i. his shining tail 89:45
Impulse: i. of the moment, or ... study
23:78
one i. from a vernal wood 414:28
In: home ... you are never i. it 156:52
they have to take you i. 139:24
Incarnadine: the multitudinous seas i.
334:43
Incense: soft i. hangs upon the boughs
184:27
Inch: ay, every i. a king 329:89
give ... i. ... take an ell 264:7
no painful i. to gain 103:33
Inches: die by famine die by i. 161:1
Incident: curious i. of the dog in the
night 125:23
Inclines to think there is a God 103:27
Include me out 152:6
Income: a good i. is of no avail 374:1
annual i. ... annual expenditure ...
misery 119:40
innate desire ... to live beyond ... i.
82:45
Inconstant: swear not by ... th' i. moon
354:2
Incontestable: what is official is i.
140:33
Inconvenient: i. to be poor 112:51
poverty ... is confoundedly i. 374:6
Incorruptible: the seagreen I. 89:35
Increase: from fairest creatures we
desire i. 362:29
God gave the i. 57:46
good and i. of the world 385:48
Ind: wealth of Ormus and of I.
217:45

Indebted to his memory for his jests
372:80
Indecency: a public i. 95:11
Independence: treacle to the wings of i.
187:66
Independent: poor and i. ... nearly an
impossibility 104:35
India's coral strand 159:86
Indian: like the base I., threw a pearl
away 346–7:22
only good I. is a dead I. 371:61
Indictment against an whole people
78:73
Indifferent: delayed till I am i. 174:78
Indignatio: ubi saeva i.... lacerare nequit
382:12
Indignation: burning i. no longer
lacerates 382:12
Indiscretion: a lover without i. is no
lover 158:65
Individual: no i. cd. resent 381:97
not the i. but the species 173:63
Individualism: American system of
rugged i. 166:66
Individuals: worth of the i. composing
it 210:43
Indivisible: peace is i. 197:84
Industry: avarice, the spur of i. 168:90
i. will improve them [talents] 287:6
i. will supply their deficiency 287:6
Inebriate: cups that cheer but not i.
114:73
Inebriated with the exuberance of ...
verbosity 123:94
Ineffectual: beautiful and i. angel
[Shelley] 21:51
remote and i. don 32:1
Inelegance: a continual state of i,
24:81
Inert: the earth, tideless and i. 27:48
Inevitability: the i. of gradualness
400:42
Inevitable: arguing with the i. 200:27
Inexactitude: without some risk of
terminological i. 100:88
Infamy: thou, whose i. is not thy fame
367:15
Infancy: Heaven lies about us in our i.
410:77
Infant: i., mewling and puking 301:90
the i. child is not aware 167:78
to a little i. ... as painful 24:87
Infection: against i. and the hand of
war 348:41
Inferiority: conscious of an i. 177:22
Infidels: peace ... go sleep with Turks
and i. 350:56
Turks, I., and Hereticks 64:88

Infinite: everything ... as it is, i. 69:64
how i. in faculties! 308:81
i. wrath and i. despair 218:62
Infinity in the palm of your hand 66:27
Infirmities: bear his friend's i. 326:26
bear the i. of the weak 57:45
wine for ... thine often i. 59:90
Infirmity: last i. of noble mind 215:13
Inflammation of his weekly bills 84:76
Influence: bright eyes rain i. 214:2
How to Win Friends and I. People 89:40
Influenza: call it i. if ye like 32:9
my aunt died of i. 366:97
no i. in my young days 32:9
Inform: occasions do i. against me 311:22
Information: I only ask for i. 119:42
i. vegetable, animal 147:31
know where we can find i. 176:14
Infortune: worst kinde of i. 97:51
Ingenious: neither i., sober, nor kind 13:45
Ingratitude: I hate i. more ... than lying 360:1
i., thou marble-hearted fiend 328:57
unkind as man's i. 302:91
Ingratitudes: great-siz'd monster of i. 358:71
Inhabitants: look not like th' i. o' th' earth 332:26
Inherit: all which it i. shall dissolve 356:50
i. the vasty Hall of Death 21:38
Inheritance: king's favour is no i. 268:37
Inhumanity: man's i. to man 80:14
Iniquity: that reverend vice, that grey i. 314:68
the i. of the fathers 37:84
Injury: i. ... sooner forgotten than an insult 98:56
revenge never repairs an i. 276:90
Ink: all the sea were i. 15:65
black as i. 256:39
he hath not drunk i. 331:13
whose sin ... dipt me in i.? 248:80
Inlets: far back through creeks and i. 103:33
Inn: do you remember an i., Miranda? 32:8
no room ... in the i. 54:67
warmest welcome at an i. 371:60
Innisfree: and go to I. 417:52
Innocence: our peace, our fearful i. 412:2

Innocent: better ... guilty ... escape than one i. suffer 66:26
i. of the blood of this just person 53:51
Macbeth doth murder sleep—the i. sleep 334:42
rich shall not be i. 46:88
source of i. merriment 146:7
Innocently employed than in getting money 176:8
Innovator: time is the greatest i. 26:17
Inns: shun the awful shops and go to i. 99:76
Inopem me copia fecit 243:13
Inquest: came together like the coroner's i. 108:7
Insensibility: no, Sir, stark i. 174:72
Insensible, then? Yea, to the dead 315:88
Inside: birds ... i. ... desperate to get out 225:56
returned from the ride ... lady i. 13:52
Insipid to a vulgar taste 374:99
Insisture, course, proportion, season 358:66
Insolence: flown with i. and wine 217:38
the i. of office 309:95
Insomnia: amor vincit i. 140:36
Inspiration: all scripture ... by i. of God 59:94
genius is one per cent i. and 129:79
Inspired: that I i. the nation 102:11
with eyes up-rais'd, as one i. 108:92
Instances: wise saws and modern i. 301:90
Instinct: all healthy i. for it 82:46
overpaying i. is a generous one 364:67
Institutions: neither for nor against i. 403:79
sought to destroy i. 403:79
Instruments: Genius and the mortal i. 324:98
make i. to plague us 330:1
Insult: add i. to injury 267:18
injury ... sooner forgotten than an i. 98:56
Insurrection: suffers ... the nature of an i. 324:98
Integer vitae scelerisque purus 166:75
Intellect: his i. is not replenished 331:13
i. is ... fooled by the heart 288:16
put on i. 67:37

Italian (*continued*)
Turk, or Proosian, or perhaps I.!
147:30
Italy: a man who has not been in I.
177:22
I. a paradise for horses 81:31
thou Paradise of exiles, I.! 368:29
Itch: I would thou didst i. 358:69
inveterate ... i. for writing 180:70
i. of literature ... scratching of a pen
200:19
Itching: condemn'd to have an i. palm
325:23
Iteration: prone to any i. of nuptials
109:19
thou hast damnable i. 312:46
Itself: he was ... the old block i. 78:76
Iuvenes: gaudeamus ... i. dum sumus
19:20
Ivied: sat at her i. door 87:11
Ivy: i. never sere 215:8
the holly and the i. 16:87

Jabberwock: hast thou slain the J.?
92:71
Jack: all work ... makes J. a dull boy
284:56
banish plump J. 314:69
every J. has his Jill 268:22
every J. ... study the knack 149:50
house that J. built 239:79
J. and Jill went up the hill 234:44
J. fell down and broke his crown
234:44
J. of all trades and master of none
268:23
J. Sprat cd, eat no fat 234:45
little J. Horner 235:50
poor J., farewell! 315:92
Jack Robinson: before one can say J.
255:5
Jackdaw sat on the Cardinal's chair
28:52
Jackson standing like a stone wall
30:79
Jacky shall have a new master 237:68
Jacob: J. saw ... corn in Egypt 36:64
sold his birthright unto J. 36:58
the voice is J.'s voice 36:60
Jade: let the galled j. wince 310:10
Jades: hollow pampered j. of Asia
316:9
ye pamper'd j. of Asia! 205:78
Jail: nothing now left but a j. 119:39
taken from the county j. 145:98
want, the patron, and the j. 173:68
Jam to-morrow and j. yesterday 93:83
James, J., Morrison Morrison 211:56

Janvier: Generals J. and Février
230:17
Japan: gentlemen of J. 145:94
Jar: folk ... in front that I j. 134:53
Jardin: il faut cultiver notre j. 397:9
Javan or Gadire 222:18
Jaws: into the j. of Death 385:43
Jealous: am a j. God 37:84
j. for the cause 346:11
j. for they are j. 346:11
one not easily j. 346–7:22
Jealousy: beware, my lord, of j.
345:7
j. is cruel as the grave 47:27
nor j. ... the injured lover's hell
219:79
Jeanie: I dream of J. 138:2
Jehu: J., the son of Nimshi 40:62
like the driving of J. 40:62
Jelly: out, vile j.! 329:83
Jenny kissed me when we met 168:96
Jerusalem: black but comely ... ye
daughters of J. 47:16
if I forget thee, O J. 44:48
the holy city, new J. 61:33
till we have built J. 67:38
Jeshurun waxed fat 38:15
Jessica, look how the floor of heaven
340:22
Jest: a fellow of infinite j. 311:31
a good j. for ever 313:58
his whole wit in a j. 29:70
J. and youthful Jollity 214:93
j.'s prosperity lies in the ear 331:18
life is a j. and all things show it
142:60
most bitter is a scornful j. 172:54
true word is spoken in j. 281:59
Jesting: what is truth? said j. Pilate
24:85
Jests: indebted to his memory for ... j.
372:80
j. at scars that never felt a wound
353:97
Jesu: J. by a nobler deed 95:18
J., thou art all compassion 402:72
Jesus: blood of J. whispers peace
65:19
Gentle J., meek and mild 402:70
J. wept 55:7
stand up for J.! 128:73
the Cross of J. ... on before 28:57
Jesus Christ: J. her little child 10:19
J. ... the same yesterday ... for ever
60:3
the Church's one foundation is J.
380:83
Jeunesse: si j. savait 133:50

Jew: hath not a J. eyes? ... hands
339:13
Jewel: a rich j. in an Ethiop's ear
353:94
  j. ... in a swine's snout 45:64
  j. in a ten-times barred-up chest
  347:30
  the immediate j. of their souls
  345:6
  wears ... precious j. in his head
  300:75
Jewels: dumb j. ... in their silent kind
361:7
  give my j. for a set of beads 350:55
  unvalued j. ... bottom of the sea
  352:72
Jewish: spit upon my J. gaberdine
338:6
Jews, Turks, Infidels 64:88
Jigging veins of rhyming mother-wits
204:72
Jill: Jack and J. 234:44
  make sure of his J. 149:50
Jim: they called him Sunny J. 157:60
Jingo: but by j. if we do 168:93
Joan: greasy J. doth keel the pot
332:20
  J. as my Lady is as good 162:21
Job: as poor as J. 274:49
  being a husband ... whole-time j.
  33:11
  best of a bad j. 255:11
  give us the tools and we will finish the
  j. 101:98
  heard of the patience of J. 60:7
Jobiska: to fish for his Aunt J.'s
195:63
Jocund: be gay in such a j. company
410:70
Joe: 'Poor old J.' 138:8
Jog on, j. on, the footpath way 361:19
John: Don J. of Austria is going to the
  war 99:71
  King J. was not a good man 211:52
  Matthew, Mark, Luke, and J.
  10:13
  some said, J., print it 76:56
John Anderson my jo 80:11
John Bradford: there ... goes J. 70:73
John Brown: J.'s body ... a mould'ring
157:57
  J. is filling his last cavity 13:49
  J. is stowed. He watched the ads.
  228:91
John of Gaunt: old J., time-honoured
  Lancaster 347:28
John Peel: d'ye ken J.? 154:20
Johnny: little J. Green 232:28

Johnny head-in-air: do not despair for
  J. 284:72
Little J. 164:41
Johnson: Dr J. condemns 79:93
  glad, replied J., ... that he thanks
  God 174:79
  great Cham of literature, Samuel J.
  375:18
  J. said ... triumph of hope 176:1
  J. scolded him [Langton] 174:75
  no arguing with J. 152:3
Join: will you j. the dance? 91:63
Joined: shall be j. unto his wife 58:72
  what ... God hath j. together 54:60
Joint: every j. and motive of her body
358:73
  time is out of j. O cursed spite
  307:71
Joking: my way of j. ... to tell the truth
365:75
Jolly: hir j. whistle wel y-wet 97:46
  j. good ale 380:82
  j. tars are our men 141:48
  there was a j. miller once 65:16
Jonah: J., doest thou well to be angry
50:87
  J. was in the belly of the fish 50:86
  lot fell upon J. 50:85
Jonathan: Saul and J. 40:48
Jones: indeed! said Mr J. 153:9
Joneses: keep up with the J. 268:30
Jonson: O rare Ben J. 179:62
Jordan: I looked over J. 18:8
Journey: here is my j.'s end ... my butt
346:21
  is yr. j. really necessary? 11:29
  one of the pleasantest things ... a j.
  159:81
  tired and weary still j. on 193:43
  will the day's j. take ... long day?
  290:46
Journeys end in lovers meeting 359:83
Jours: tous les j. ... vais de mieux en
  mieux 111:37
Jove: daughter of J., relentless Power
155:43
  J. for's power to thunder 303–4:17
  lovelier than the love of J. 204:73
  while J.'s planet rises yonder 74:25
Jowett: my name is J. 30:80
Joy: a j. for ever 181:85
  and snatch a fearful j. 154:28
  dreams of j. and fear 368:32
  dwell in doubtful j. 334:50
  fields where j. for ever dwells 216:34
  glad tidings of great j. 384:35
  God send you j. 265:24
  grief and pain for promis'd j. 80:18

Kin: more than k., and less than kind
305:38

one's own k. and kith   228:89

one touch of nature ... whole world
k.   358:72

Kind: be to her virtues very k.   253:50

cruel only to be k.   311:20

dumb jewels ... in their silent k.
361:7

just the art of being k.   404:93

k. as she is fair   361:9

k. hearts are more than coronets
387:74

more than kin and less than k.
305:38

neither ingenious, sober, nor k.
13:45

what k. of people do they think we
are?   101:99

Kindly: is sure of being k. spoken of
23:67

Kindness: A Woman Killed with K.
163:27

beauty lives with k.   361:9

kill a wife with k.   355:24

k. in another's trouble   152:7

save in the way of k.   392:48

tak' a cup o' k.   79:1

too full o' th' milk of human k.
333:32

unremembered acts of k., love
415:31

Kinds: soft maids and village k.   107:87

King: a little pin bores ... farewell, k.!
350:54

a new k. over Egypt   36:67

all the k.'s horses ... men   93:84,
233:37

as I have served the k.   408:55

ay, every inch a k.   329:89

catch the conscience of the K.
309:94

dainty dish, to set before the K.?
238:70

deny it (repose) to a k.   317:14

discharge my duties as K.   129:81

divinity doth hedge a k.   311:27

glory to the new-born K.   402:71

God save the K.! Will no man say
amen?   350:57

have a k., and officers of sorts   318:39

he that plays the k. ... be welcome
308:82

here lies our sovereign lord the k.
288:21

I'm the k. of the castle   233:41

is the k. dead, the empire unpossess'd?   352:82

King (continued)

Judge that no k. can corrupt   322:78

k. is a thing men have made   297:25

k. is but a man as I am   320:52

K., observing with judicious eyes
393:54

k. of shreds and patches   311:18

K. shall do it ... shall be contented
350:55

k.'s name is a tower of strength
353:84

lad that's born to be k.   69:69

let us sing, Long live the K.   113:61

mortal temples of a k.   350:54

no bishop, no K.   170:21

Old K. Cole   236:58

old, mad, blind ... dying k.   370:53

one-eyed man is k.   256:48

our Gracious K. ... noble K.   88:29

passing brave to be a k.   205:75

so excellent a k.   305:43

sword of an angel k.   66:35

the K. asked the Queen and   211:59

the k. can do no wrong   66:25

the k. himself has followed her
150:73

the K. is strongest   61:36

the k. loved Esther   40:64

the k. never dies   66:24

the k.'s a bawcock ... heart of gold
320:51

the k. sits in Dunfermline   12:37

the K. to Oxford sent   72:8

think the K. knows about me?
211:55

wash the balm off from an anointed
k.   349:50

we will go by the k.'s high way   38:3

whatsoever K. shall reign   17:92

who Pretender is, or who is K.   83:53

with half the zeal I serv'd my k.
323:84

King Charles: in good K.'s golden days
17:91

King James ... call for his old shoes
296:21

King of the Jews: he that is born K.
51:2

Kingdom: for thine is the k.   52:18

keys of the k. of heaven   53:35

k. of heaven is at hand   51:4

my k. for a horse!   353:87

my large k. for a little grave   350:55

my mind to me a k. is   129:77

my new-found land, my k.   123–4:9

of such is the k. of God   54:61

stand upon my k. once again   349:49

state of man, like to a little k.   324:98

Kingdom (*continued*)
teach ... order to a peopled k. 318:39
thy k. come 52:18
thy k. is divided 49:70
Kingdoms: goodly states and k. seen 185:40
Kings: all K. is mostly rapscallions 393:62
captains and the k. depart 190:9
conquering k. their titles take 95:18
divorc'd so many English k. 318:28
dread and fear of k. 339:15
I know the k. of England 147:31
k. for such a tomb wd. ... die 216:25
k. it makes gods, and meaner creatures k. 352:83
k. that fear ... subjects' treachery 322:71
left lonely ... the k. of the sea 20:34
low ambition, and the pride of k. 250:7
mad world! mad k.! 326:36
mirror of all Christian k. 319:40
my throne, bid k. come bow 326:39
of cabbages—and k. 93:80
poor men's hovels ... K.' palaces 166:73
punctuality is the politeness of k. 199:14
sad stories of the death of k. 350:54
scorn to change my state with k. 362:36
showers on her k. barbaric pearl 217:45
such is the breath of K. 348:34
teeming womb of royal k. 348–9:41
the chase, the sport of k. 375:23
this royal throne of k. 348:41
King's English: an old abusing of ... the K. 340:29
Kinquering Congs their titles take 377:49
Kipling: when the Rudyards cease from k. 378:63
Kiss: ae fond k., and then we sever! 79:95
come let us k. and part 125:34
coward does it with a k. 404:94
gin a body k. a body 79:3
I dare not ask a k. ... a smile 162:19
I k. his dirty shoe 320:51
I saw you take his k. 244:31
if you can k. the mistress 268:39
k. and be friends 268:38
k. me, Hardy 230:9
k. me, Kate 355:22
k. me, sweet and twenty 359:84

Kiss (*continued*)
k. me with the kisses of his mouth 47:15
leave a k. but in the cup 178:49
make me immortal with a k. 204:63
pale grew thy cheek ... colder thy k. 86:99
to die upon a k. 347:23
Kissed: but I k. her little sister 225:61
hasn't been k. for forty years 291:57
I k. thee ere I kill'd thee 347:23
k. the girls and made them cry 232:31
k. the maiden all forlorn 239:79
Kisses: beneath the k. of Night 370:46
bread and cheese and k. 254:85
but my k. bring again 337–8:92
give me a thousand k. 94:4
I fear thy k., gentle maiden 370:55
I understand thy k., and thou mine 314:75
k. the joy as it flies 66:34
of many thousand k. the poor last 299:65
play'd at cards for k. 201:29
Kissing: k. don't last: cookery do! 209:36
k. yr. hand may make you feel ... good 199:11
when the k. had to stop 76:48
Kit-bag: troubles in your old k. 22:56
Kitchen: friends in the kennel, but not in the k. 366:90
taste of the k. is better 279:11
way of all flesh ... towards the k. 400:53
Kitten: rather be a k. and cry mew 314:73
Knave: a petty sneaking k. I knew 67:42
K. of Hearts, he stole those tarts 91:66, 237:65
Knee: not loved the world ... nor bow'd ... patient k. 83:61
silver buckles at his k. 231:24
Kneels at the foot of the bed 211:61
Knees: religion's ... not in the k. 171:37
spectacles lay on her aproned k. 87:11
Knell: by fairy hands their k. is rung 107:90
curfew tolls the k. of parting day 155:30
hear it not, Duncan, for it is a k. 334:41
Knew: fell to earth, I k. not where 197:91

Knew (*continued*)

I k. almost as much at eighteen 175:18

I k. him well, and every truant k. 150:68

men fell out they k. not why 82:35

new king ... which k. not Joseph 36:67

one small head cd. carry all he k. 150:69

Knife: cut it without a k. 235:52

cut off their tails ... carving k. 240:80

honey ... keeps them on the k. 15:63

smyler with the k. 97:44

Knight: a verray parfit gentle k. 96:26

gentle k. was pricking on the plain 377:41

k. of the sorrowful countenance 95:8

Knit: k. hands, and beat the ground 212:75

stuff of life to k. me 167:83

Knits up the ravell'd sleave of care 334:42

Knitting: in twisted braids of lilies k. 213:80

Knocked: k. 'em in the Old Kent Road 99:79

k. me down with a feather 268:41

Knocker: tie up the k., say ... I'm dead 248:77

Knocking: k. at Preferment's door 21:41

k. on the moonlit door 118:23

there's k. at the gate 335:70

Knocks you down with the butt end 152:3

Know: all Europe should k. we have blockheads 109:8

all ye need to k. 183:20

and when this we rightly k. 66:30

believe her, though I k. she lies 364:54

but I k. what I like 30:83

do you k. me, my lord? 308:75

does your mother k. you are out? 28:55

every wise man's son doth k. 359:83

he replied, Yes, I k. 13–14:54

I don't know anything ... really 30:83

I k. a bank ... wild thyme blows 341:46

I k. a reasonable woman 251:31

I k. the kings of England 147:31

I k. thee not, old man 318:34

I k. two things about the horse 15:64

Know (*continued*)

I k. you all, and will ... uphold 312:49

I thought so once; but now I k. it 142:60

k. a subject ... k. where ... information 176:14

k. all that there is to be knowed 153:14

k. cause, or just impediment 64:3

k. then thyself 250:13

k. where the shoe pinches 277:31

little do we k. what lays afore us! 120:51

mad, bad, and dangerous to k. 191:24

no knowledge but I k. it 30:80

not to k. me ... yourselves unknown 219:72

not utter what thou dost not k. 313:61

O, that a man might k. the end 326:29

ol' man river ... must k. sumpin' 157:59

pleasant to k. Mr Lear 194:59

she didn't k. what to do 239:76

than the devil you don't k. 256:30

they k. not what they do 55:91

this alone I k. full well 72:96

to k. that which before us lies 220:86

to k. this only, that he nothing knew 221:7

we are greater than we k. 413:14

what I don't k. isn't knowledge 30:80

what shd. they k. of England? 190:97

what the false heart doth k. 333:39

whom truly to k. is everlasting life 64:91

Knoweth: talketh what he k. 24:93

Knowing: as gods, k. good and evil 35:36

k. what shd. not be known 136:84

the misfortune of k. anything 23:73

thinking ... far from k. 280:29

Knowledge: a supercilious k. in accounts 371:70

all k. to be my province 27:39

all our k. is ourselves to know 250:20

conscious ... ignorant is a great step to k. 123:97

continual drinking of K. 186:59

darkeneth counsel by words without k. 41:76

Knowledge (*continued*)
    ever-green tree of diabolical k.
        371:68
    fear of the Lord ... beginning of k.
        44:54
    having any k. of ... social order
        365:84
    his k. of life ... so hazy 242:9
    increaseth k. increaseth sorrow
        46:97
    k. comes, but wisdom lingers 387:82
    k. enormous makes a God 182:2
    k. is of two kinds 176:14
    k. is power 268:46
    k. of God more than burnt offerings
        50:75
    night unto night showeth k. 41:87
    science is organized k. 376:32
    smattering of everything ... k. of
        nothing 121:78
    still climbing after k. infinite 205:76
    Thou ... art still, out-topping k.
        21:44
    to know no more is woman's hap-
        piest k. 219:70
    Zeal without k. is fire without light
        284:71
Known: best that has been k. and said
        21:53
    best that is k. and thought 21:50
    I am k. and do not want [patronage]
        174:78
    k. by the company he keeps 271:33
Knows: a woman conceals what she k.
        not 283:46
    I never k. the children 206:87
    if you k. of a better 'ole 27:47
    k. nought that k. not this 358:65
    no man truly k. another 72:4
    nobody k. how to write letters
        109:11
    the more a man k. 365:74
    travels far, k. much 281:55
    wise father that k. his own child
        339:8
Kubla: in Xanadu did K. Khan
        106:71
    K. heard from far ancestral voices
        107:74
Kyd: Lyly outshine, or sporting K.
        179:55

Labor omnia vicit ... egestas 397:4
Laborare est orare 268:50
Labour: crowns a youth of l. 150:64
    ease and alternate l. 391:34
    l., and do all thy work 37:86
    l. and the wounds are vain 103:32

Labour (*continued*)
    l. night and day to be a pilgrim
        77:65
    l. of an age in piled stones 216:23
    months without ... any kind of l.
        399:30
    persistent l. overcame all things
        397:4
    six days shalt thou l. 37:86
    sore l.'s bath 334:42
    true success is to l. 380:80
    votes L., ought to be locked up
        225:58
    yr. work of faith ... l. of love
        59:83
Labourer: l. is worthy of his hire 54:75
    now the l.'s task is o'er 132:23
Labours: children sweeten l. 24:95
Lack: sigh the l. of many a thing
        362:37
Lacked: being l. and lost ... rack the
        value 343:81
Lacrimae: hinc illae l. 389:4
Lad: and many a lightfoot l. 167:84
    cd. that l. be I? 379:73
    l. that's born to be king 69:69
    song of a l. that is gone 379:73
    when I was a l. I served a term
        147:26
Ladder: a l. set up on the earth 36:61
    down the l. when thou marriest
        264:14
    l. of all high designs 358:67
    wiv a l. and some glasses 29:66
Ladies: a lion among l. ... dreadful
        341:47
    eleven l. dancing 238:73
    good night, sweet l. 311:25
    rhyme themselves into l.' favours
        321:61
    sigh no more, l. 343:68
    store of l., whose bright eyes 214:2
Lads: golden l. and girls ... come to
        dust 304–5:29
    though yr. l. are far away 137:94
    two l. that thought ... to be boy
        eternal 361:12
Lady: a l. of a certain age 85:81
    a l. sweet and kind 18:9
    and in my l.'s chamber 232:32
    courting his l. in the spring 70:76
    faint heart never won fair l. 262:44
    fine l. upon a white horse 237:66
    for secrecy, no l. closer 313:61
    I met a l. in the meads 183:8
    I want to talk like a l. 366:94
    make a l. of my own 415:30
    my l. sweet, arise 304:20

Lap: his head upon the l. of earth 155:40

in thy green l. was Nature's Darling 156:44

Lards the lean earth as he walks 313:59

Large as life, and twice as natural 94:93

Largest: shout with the l. [mob] 121:63

Lark: no l. more blithe than he 65:16

rise with the l. 264:16

the l.'s on the wing 75:44

to hear the l. begin his flight 214:97

Larks: hear the l. so high about us 167:82

two Owls ... four L. and a Wren 195:66

Lars Porsena of Clusium 201:35

Lashed the vice, but spared the name 381:97

Lass: I loved a l., a fair one 408:48

yon solitary Highland L. 414:20

Lasses: come, l. and lads 16:79

he dearly lov'd the l. 80:8

hours ... spent among the l. 80:7

Last: die ... the l. thing I shall do! 243:21

filling his l. cavity 13:49

heard the l. of her ... I wonder! 366:5

it will not l. the night 210:45

kissing don't l.: cookery do! 209:36

l. but not least 268:52

L. of the Mohicans 110:30

l. out a night in Russia 337:83

l. taste of sweets, is sweetest l. 348:39

might be the l., my Mary! 114:76

of many thousand kisses the poor l. 299:65

rash ... blaze of riot cannot l. 348:40

the l. of life, for wh. the first was made 75:46

there is no l. nor first 75:45

well, I cannot l. ever 316:1

Late: better l. than never 256:25

good to marry l. or never 271:47

make haste, and come too l. 348:38

marries l., marries ill 271:43

never too l. to mend 273:88

too l. to save the stamp 153:10

Lately: read any good books l.? 227:76

Latin: away with him! He speaks L. 321:69

must carve in L. or in Greek 398:18

small L. and less Greek 179:56

Latter: meeter to carry off the l. 245:38

Laugh: and l. at gilded butterflies 330:99

if I l. at any mortal thing 85:79

l. and the world l. with you 404:91

l. as I pass in thunder 368:22

l. to scorn the pow'r of man 335:62

l. where we must, be candid 250:8

loud l. that spoke the vacant mind 150:65

love I l. to scorn 71:86

make 'em l. ... cry ... wait 287:2

men that l. and weep 382:19

the l. broke into ... pieces 28:59

who but must l.? 248:84

Laughed: little dog l. to see such sport 232:33

no man who has ... wholly l. 89:39

when the first baby l. 28:59

Laughing is heard on the hill 68:52

Laughs: flabby hands and irritating l. 145:99

he l. best who l. last 269:55

Laughter: drinks his wine 'mid l. free 19:10

I heard the l. of her heart 157:58

invent anything that tends to l. 316:98

it wd. be ... l. for a month 313:58

L. holding both his sides 214:94

l., learnt of friends 71:94

nothing so ... ill-bred as audible l. 98:59

present mirth hath present l. 359:84

ran ... after the ... music with ... l. 75:43

sincerest l. with some pain is fraught 370:50

so is the l. of the fool 46:4

tired of tears and l. 382:19

Laundry: general idea ... in any ... l. 194:53

Laurel: burned is Apollo's l.-bough 204:67

l. is green for a season 383:23

l. outlives not May 383:23

Laurels: the l. all are cut 167:79

yet once more, O ye l. 215:8

Lavinia: she is L. ... must be loved 357:63

Law: against reason, ... of no force in l. 104:38

agree, for the l. is costly 254:63

and the l. doth give it 340:19

and this is l. that I'll maintain 17:92

dusty purlieus of the l. 386:64

every l. is a contract 297:26

glorious uncertainty of the l. 281:85

God is thy l., thou mine 219:70

Law (*continued*)
good of the people ... chief l. 102:15
hard cases make bad l. 266:67
higher l. than the Constitution 297:37
I ... embody the L. 143–4:81
in l.'s grave study 104:40
in vice their l.'s their will 347:26
l. is a bottomless pit 269:56
l. is an ass—a idiot 120:58
l. makers shd. not be l. breakers 269:58
love ... fulfilling of the l. 57:43
love has never known a l. 403:88
may be ... good l. for all that 296:16
much l., but little justice 272:74
nature's l. that man was made to mourn 80:13
necessity hath no l. 272:77
one God, one l., one element 387:73
one l. for the rich 269:57
other sources of international l. 394:76
ought l. to weed it out 24:89
possession is nine points of the l. 275:51
pounds of l., ... not an ounce of love 280:32
rich men rule the l. 151:93
self-preservation is the first l. 277:28
take the l. into one's own hands 279:1
the l. hath not been dead 337:85
the L. is the true embodiment 143:81
the l. of the Yukon 297:35
the L. of Triviality 244:26
the l.'s delay 309:95
the more l., the more offenders 269:59
these ... a l. unto themselves 56:30
this is the l. and the prophets 52:25
this is the L. of the Jungle 190:6
wedded Love, mysterious l. 219:71
windy side of the l. 360:98
wrest once the l. to yr. authority 339:16
Lawn as white as driven snow 362:22
Laws: know not whether l. be right 404:97
l. grind the poor and rich men rule the law 151:93
l. of England are at my command-ment 318:33
l. of the Persians ... Medes 40:63
l. were made to be broken 230:19
let ... l. and learning die 292:68
Nature's L. lay hid in Night 248:88

Laws (*continued*)
religion breathing household l. 412:2
repeal of bad or obnoxious l. 153:16
sweeter manners, purer l. 386:69
Lawyers: few l. die well 262:57
let's kill all the l. 321:67
Lay on, Macduff 336:80
Lazy: liftin' the l. ones on 154:19
mentally l. ... as well be dead 401–2:69
Lead: do scald like molten l. 330:96
l., Kindly Light ... l. thou me on 230:16
strange ... the life he makes us l. 73:14
Leaden-eyed despairs 184:25
Leadeth me beside the still waters 42:92
Leaf: fall'n into the sear, the yellow l. 336:71
lowest boughs ... are in tiny l. 74:21
November's l. is red 295:8
take a l. out of one's book 279:94
turn over a new l. 281:68
where the dead l. fell ... did it rest 182:97
League: half a l. onward 385:40
keep a l. till death 351:60
Lean: his wife cd. eat no l. 234:45
l. and slipper'd pantaloon 301:90
Leap: a great l. in the dark 163:35
methinks it were an easy l. 313:44
Leaps: morn doth break ... l. in the sky 70:75
my heart l. up when I behold 412:98
Leapt: into the dangerous world I l. 67:44
Leap-year: twenty-nine in each l. 239:77
Lear: how pleasant to know Mr L. 194:59
Learn: gladly wolde he l. 97:34
l. by other men's mistakes 283:41
l. to labour and to wait 198:98
live and l. 270:93
they will l. at no other 78:82
we l. nothing from history 365:85
Learned: he was naturally l. 127:59
loads of l. lumber in his head 249:5
that ... grew within this l. man 204:67
that l. body wanted loyalty 393:54
Learning: a little l. is a dangerous thing 249:94
better than a bushel of l. 266:56
l. is but an adjunct to ourself 331:14
l. makes ... better ... worse 269:64

Levellers: yr. l. wish to level down 175:89
Levers to lift me up ... being down? 313:57
Leviathan: canst thou draw out l.? 41:78
Lexicographer.—a harmless drudge 172:46
Lexicography: not yet so lost in l. 172:41
Liar ... when he speaks the truth 269:73
Liars: all men are l. 43:32
great talkers are great l. 265:44
l. ought to [should] have good memories 269:74, 372:82
Libel: greater the truth, the greater the l. 265:46
Liberal: is either a little L. 144:87
Liberté: l., égalité, fraternité 19:15
O L.! que de crimes ... en ton nom! 288:26
Libertine: puff'd and reckless l. 306:54
the air, a charter'd l. 318:38
Liberty: give me l. or ... death 161:6
God hath given l. to man 116:98
L., and Union, now and for ever 400:44
l. cannot long exist 78:86
l., equality, fraternity 19:15
l. is precious ... must be rationed 195:69
l. means responsibility ... men dread it 366:87
l. ... must be limited 78:85
L. of the Press ... the *Palladium* 180:65
l.'s in every blow 81:23
l. to know, to utter 224:44
marries for wealth, sells his l. 271:42
mountain-nymph, sweet L. 214:95
O l., l., what crimes ... in yr. name! 288:26
sweet life of l. 374:5
thy chosen music, L. 412:1
Liberty Hall: this is L. 151:85
Library: a circulating l. in a town 371:68
my l. was dukedom ... enough 355:31
vanity of ... hopes ... public l. 173:60
Libre: l'homme est né l. ... est dans les fers 291:55
Licence: Government l. to print money 391:35
the rest love not freedom, but l. 224:46

Licht: mehr L.! 150:60
Lick: ill cook that cannot l. his own fingers 258:26, 354:16
to l. into shape 269:75
Licked: they l. the platter clean 234:45
Lie: a cat and a l. 394:70
a l. begets a l. 269:76
after all, what is a l.? 85:82
and they all dead did l. 105:55
Father, I cannot tell a l. 399:44
honest man sent to l. abroad 416:46
I knowed it was a l. 393:61
not a stone tell where I l. 251:29
nothing can need a l. 161:11
oft when on my couch I l. 410:71
painters and poets have leave to l. 274:27
seventh, the L. Direct 303:9
the L. with Circumstance 303:9
where my heart lies, let my brain l. 74:33
while you here do snoring l. 356:39
who loves to l. with me 300:83
Lied: Heart replied ... but it l. 31:97
Lies: ask no questions ... be told no l. 254:78
beats all the l. you can invent 66:29
believe her, though I know she l. 364:54
one of the social l. 169:8
one thing is certain ... Rest is L. 135:71
three kinds of l. 393:63
where my heart l. 74:33
Life: a daily beauty in his l. 346:16
a handful of good l. 266:56
a keen observer of l. 22:61
a lad of l., an imp of fame 320:51
a l. like the scriptures 187:64
a l. on the ocean wave 293:81
a space of l. between 181:84
a useless l. is an early death 150:59
after l.'s fitful fever he sleeps well 334:51
all his l. ... speaking the truth 405:16
all the blessings of this l. 64:85
all the voyage of their l. is bound 326:27
all this flesh keeps in a little l. 315:92
and l. is thorny 106:67
any practical part of l. 9:6
anything for a quiet l. 121:77, 254:72
art is long, but l. is short 163:30
as large as l. 268:51
bankrupt of l., yet prodigal of ease 126:40
before us lies in daily l. 220:86

Life (*continued*)

best of l. is but intoxication 84:71
best portion of a good man's l. 415:31
brief l. is here our portion 229:1
cannot tell what you ... think of this l. 323:91
care of human l. ... not their destruction 171:30
commuter—one who spends his l. 402:77
compare human l. to ... Mansion 187:60
custom ... great guide of ... l. 168:91
dear ... as light and l. 80:9
death after l. doth greatly please 377:42
digestion is the great secret of l. 375:12
doth the wingèd l. destroy 66:34
each change of many-colour'd l. 173:58
essential thing in l. is not conquering 111:36
expect more from l. than l. will afford 176:99
fie upon this quiet l.! 314:62
giveth his l. for the sheep 55:6
he that cuts off twenty years of l. 324:4
his name out of the book of l. 61:22
I bear a charmed l. 336:78
I do not set my l. at a pin's fee 307:61
I fall upon the thorns of l. 369:37
I will give thee a crown of l. 60:20
in London all that l. can afford 177:25
in the midst of l. we are in death 65:14
is l. a boon? 148:44
isn't l. a terrible thing? 390:25
its private l. is a disgrace 15:70
I've done it all my l. 15:63
large as l. and twice as natural 94:93
last of l., for which the first 75:46
lay hold on l. 225:53
letter killeth ... spirit giveth l. 58:61
l. for l., eye for eye 37:93
l., force and beauty must ... impart 249:92
l. ... is a continual allegory 187:64
l. is a jest 142:60
l. is as tedious as a twice-told tale 327:41
l. is but a day; a ... dew-drop 185:35
l. is but an empty dream 198:95

Life (*continued*)

l. is just one damned thing after another 168:88
l. is mostly froth and bubble 152:7
l. is ... process of getting tired 82:43
L. is real! L. is earnest 198:95
l. is sweet 269:79
l. is the art of drawing ... conclusions 82:44
l. is very sweet, brother 69:65
l. isn't all beer and skittles 168:89
l., liberty ... pursuit of happiness 171:26
l., like a dome of many-coloured glass 367:19
l. protracted is protracted woe 174:70
l. ... solitary, poor, nasty, brutish 163:34
l., time's fool 315:91
l.'s too short for chess 86:3
live a barren sister all yr. l. 341:35
love is of man's l. a thing apart 84:70
make l., death ... for-ever one ... song 189:86
makes calamity of so long l. 309:95
man's l. is cheap as beast's 328:67
married to a single l. 115:83
measured out my l. with coffee spoons 131:2
mine honour is my l. 347:30
modern l. ... tedious, ... and modern literature 405:5
most of the change ... in l. 139:22
no, no, no l. 331:6
nor love thy l., nor hate 220:98
not so much l. as on a summer's day 182:97
nothing in his l. became him 333:30
O for a L. of Sensations! 186:51
on human l., musing in solitude 409:63
on the Tree of L. ... sat 219:64
one good deed in all my l. 358:64
our l., exempt from public haunt 300:75
our l. is frittered away by detail 391:37
our little l. is rounded ... sleep 356–7:50
my l. is one demd horrid grind 120:54
my way of l. ... the yellow leaf 336:71
pass them for a nobler l. 185:37
people say that L. is the thing 374:3
preach ... doctrine of strenuous l. 289:35

Life (*continued*)

promise them l. and then kill them 395:79

quickening l. from the Earth's heart 367:11

saw l. steadily and ... whole 20:35

sells us l. at a discount 140:33

she is coming, my l., my fate 388:87

short l. and a merry one 277:34

shd. ... have everlasting l. 55:99

so careless of the single l. 386:62

soldier's l. is terrible hard 211:54

spare all I have and take my l. 134:57

spend my l. in driving briskly 177:23

strange disease of modern l. 21:42

stuff of l. to knit me 167:83

sucking his l. out of the dead leaves 193:47

take away my good name ... my l. 279:95

take honour ... and my l. is done 347:30

that a man lay down his l. 56:10

that no l. lives for ever 383:20

that state of l., unto which 64:99

the death of each day's l. 334:42

the l. he makes us lead! 73:14

the l. so short, the craft so long to lerne 97:50

the nobler modes of l. 386:69

the passion and the l. 106:69

the rest of his dull l. 29:70

there are two tragedies in l. 365:83

there is no wealth but l. 292:64

therefore choose l. 38:13

this gives l. to thee 362:34

this long disease, my L. 248:81

those with irrational fear of l. 110:22

thoughts, the slaves of l. 315:91

to the vagrant gypsy l. 208:16

travel on l.'s common way 413:4

travelled l.'s dull round 371:60

treasured up ... to a l. beyond l. 223:38

upright l., unstained by guilt 166:75

useful l., progressive virtue 391:34

variety's ... spice of l. 114:71

warmed both hands before the fire of l. 192:34

way of l. uncertain 181:84

we see into the l. of things 415:33

weariest and most loathed worldly l. 337:91

what is this l. if, full of care 117:11

what kind of l. did you give me? 401:68

while ... l. there is hope 269:80

Life (*continued*)

whom ... to know is everlasting l. 64:91

yr. l. extremely flat 148:40

yr. money or yr. l.! 272:68

yr. money or yr. l.; women require 83:51

Life-in-death: the Night-mare L. was she 105:52

Lifeless: he is l. that is faultless 269:81

Lifetime: lamps ... lit again in our l. 156:51

Lift: l. not thy hands to It 136:80

l. them high ... before you drop them 395:79

oh, l. me as a wave, a leaf 369:37

Light: a certain slant of l. 122:83

apparelled in celestial l. 410:72

casting a dim religious l. 213:88

clear, unchang'd, and universal l. 249:92

come forth into the l. of things 414:27

common as l. is love 369:44

dear ... as l. and life 80:9

God appears, and God is l. 66:31

God said, Let there be l. 34:27

God saw the l. was good 220:84

God's first creature ... l. 27:40

gone into the world of l. 396:85

hail, Holy L., offspring of Heaven 218:58

Heaven's l. forever shines 367:19

Hesperus entreats thy l. 178-9:50

how my l. is spent 223:29

I can again thy former l. restore 346:19

in a Noose of L. 134:65

it gives a lovely l. 210:45

lead, Kindly L. 230:16

Let Newton be! and all was L. 248:88

l. breaks where no sun shines 390:21

l. that never was, on sea or land 409:61

l. the Day ... he named 220:84

more l.! 150:60

out of Hell leads up to l. 218:54

passion for sweetness and l. 21:52

Promethean heat that can thy l. relume 346:19

pursuit of sweetness and l. 21:47

put out the l., and then put out the l. 346:19

shower of l. is poesy 185:38

teach l. to counterfeit a gloom 213:86

the dying of the l. 390:18

Light (*continued*)
 the l. of common day 411:78
 the l. of the world 55:4
 The L. that Failed 191:17
 The people ... have seen a great l. 48:35
 things l. and swoln ... weighty 26:35
 too l. winning, make the prize l. 356:36
 true l. which lighteth every man 55:93
 two noblest ... sweetness and l. 381:95
 what l. through yonder window? 353:97
 when my l. is low 386:60
 who art a l. to guide, a rod 413:7
 wiser than the children of l. 55:84
 with a l. behind her 148:42
Light Brigade: forward, the L. 385:41
Lighten: l. our darkness 63:74
 now, the Lord l. thee! 316:7
Lighter than vanity 77:60
Lighthouse: took the sitivation at the l. 121:77
Lighting a little Hour or two 135:68
Lightly come, l. go 269:84
Lightning: I have known the l.'s hour 117:15
 man who was killed by l. 12:42
 the l. of the nations 369:34
 thunder, l., or in rain 332:22
Lights: l. that do mislead the morn 337–8:92
 turn up the l. ... home in the dark 161:5
Like: a God, or something very l. Him 103:27
 I know what I l. 30:83
 I l. two months of every year 83:55
 I shall not look upon his l. again 306:49
 l. and dislike the same things 293:73
 l. doth quit l., and Measure still for Measure 338:94
 l. to be Beside the Seaside 149:57
 people who l. this sort of thing 197:83
Liked it not, and died 416:47
Liking: I have a l. old for thee 87:15
Lilac: down to Kew in l.-time 230–31:20
 just now the l. is in bloom 71:89
Lilacs out of the dead land 131:10
Lilies: consider the l. of the field 52:21
 in twisted braids of l. knitting 213:80
 l. that fester smell far worse 363:42

Lilies (*continued*)
 peacocks and l. 291:61
 the l. and languors of virtue 382:18
 where roses and white l. grow 88:24
Lily: I am the ... l. of the valleys 47:17
 to paint the l. 327:43
Limb: care I for the l., the thews ... bulk? 317:20
Limbo: into a L. large and broad 218:60
Limbs: your l. they are alive 416:41
Limericks; whose l. never wd. scan 13:54
Lime-tree Bower my prison 107:77
Limited in order to be possessed 78:85
Limits: beyond the l. of a vulgar fate 156:45
Line: l. stretch out to th' crack of doom? 335:64
 must draw the l. somewhere 260:88
 the Brighton l. ... the l. is immaterial 405:12
 to cancel half a l. 136:79
 to l. one's pockets 270:88
 we carved not a l. 408:53
Linen: choose neither ... l. by candle-light 258:3
 old l. wash whitest 400:52
Lines: with silken l. and silver hooks 123:4
Lingering: something l., with boiling oil 146:10
Lingers: borrowing only l. and l. it out 316:3
Linguistics: An Essay in Sociological L. 290:42
Lining: there's a silver l. 137:94
Linnet: a l. courting his lady 70:76
 come, hear the woodland l. 414:26
Lion: a l. among ladies 341:47
 dar'st ... beard the l. ... The Douglas 296:12
 in like a l. ... out like a lamb 271:38
 l. is not so fierce as ... painted 270:89
 nation ... had the l. heart 102:11
 not a more fearful wildfowl than ... l. 341:47
 rouse a l. than to start a hare 313:53
 the devil, as a roaring l. 60:12
 the l. and the unicorn 234:47
 the l. looked at Alice wearily 94:94
Lions: cast him into the den of l. 50:72
 Saul and Jonathan ... stronger than l. 40:48
Lip: keep a stiff upper l. 94:99, 278:76

Lips: beauty's ensign is crimson in thy
l. 354:17
cd. you hurt me, sweet l.? 382:18
dear red curve of her l. 207:11
her l. suck forth my soul 204:63
her l. were red, her looks were free
105:52
take, O, take, those l. away 337:92
their l. were four red roses 352:79
through my l. to unawakened earth
369:38
truth sits upon the l. of dying men
21:45
what l. my l. have kissed 210:46
when I ope my l. let no dog bark
338:98
where my Julia's l. do smile 162:15
Liquefaction of her clothes 162:23
Liquid: Thames is l. history 79:94
Liquidation: preside over the l. of the
British Empire 101:3
Liquor: l. is quicker 229:95
they sell worse kinds of l. 399:28
Lisp of leaves and ripple of rain 382:15
List: I've got a little l. 145:99
I wd. not enter on my l. of friends
114:75
l., l., O, l.! 307:64
Listen: darkling I l. 184:29
l. with credulity to ... fancy 173:61
the world shd. l. then 370:51
Listened: I l., motionless and still
414:22
Listeners hear no good of themselves
270:90
Lit again in our lifetime 156:51
Literature: he has raised the price of l.
174:80
itch of l. comes over a man 200:19
l. flourishes best when it is half a
trade 170:12
that great Cham of l. 375:18
the rest is just l. 396:89
to produce a little l. 170:24
Litter: all her l. but one 316:98
Littérature: tout le reste est l. 396:89
Little: a l. of what you fancy 197:86
a l. still she strove 84:67
comrades, leave me here a l. 387:78
every l. helps 262:26
give according to that l. 62:39
goin' through so much to learn so l.
121:70
great ones eat up the l. ones 347:27
having too l. to do 190–1:15
I thought so l. they rewarded me
147:27
if I'm content with a l. 65:18

Little (*continued*)
it was a very l. one 206:86
knows l., soon repeats it 268:48
knows l. who will tell his wife all
140:39
l. breezes dusk and shiver 387:76
l. drops ... l. grains ... l. minutes
89:41
l. things please l. minds 270:92
l. things ... the most important
124:18
l. we see in nature that is ours 412:93
love me l., love me long 270:18
man wants but l. drink below 164:47
man wants but l., nor that l. long
418:64
many a l. makes a mickle 271:37
no great ones if ... no l. ones 265:43
nor wants that l. long 150:72
obedience is ... seen in l. things
273:15
so l. done, so much to do 287:7
such a l. tail behind 31:89
the l. less, and what worlds away
73:19
the l. more, and how much 73:19
think too l. ... talk too much 126:42
through so much to learn so l.
121:70
wealth is contentment with a l.
282:16
Live: a bachelor, I l. by myself 17:95
anything but – l. for it [religion]
108:96
bear to l. or dare to die 250:15
better to l. rich 177:27
but a short time to l. 65:13
but one bare hour to l. 204:65
come l. with me and be my love
123:4, 205:82
crabbed age and youth cannot l.
together 364:56
desire ... to l. beyond its income
82:45
eat to l. ... not l. to eat 261:12
I had as lief not be as l. 323:91
I marvel how the fishes l. 347:27
I with thee will choose to l. 213:90
in our embers is something that doth
l. 411:80
let me l. unseen, unknown 251:29
l. a fool the rest of his dull life 29:70
l. and learn 270:93
l. and let l. 270:94
l., and move, and have our being
56:20
l. as the Romans do 11:23
l., for the truth is living 383:24

Live (*continued*)

loves to l. i' th' sun   301:85
may l. to fight another day   14:61
Mirth, with thee I mean to l.   215:7
not l. by bread only   38:7
not suffer a witch to l.   37:94
other men l. to eat   375:21
rogues ... want to l. for ever?   139:18
she ... tried to l. without him   416:47
so we'll l., and pray, and sing   330:99
so wise, so young, ... never l. long   352:73
take the means whereby I l.   340:20
threatened men l. long   280:34
to l. is like love   82:46
to l. with her and l. with thee   214:96
to l. with thee and be thy love   286:96
we that l. to please   173:59
what thou liv'st l. well   220:98
will it not l. with the living?   315:88
you might as well l.   243–4:23
Lived: for I have l. to-day   128:71
I have l. long enough   383:22
l. in the odium ... sodium   33:18
l. on, and so did I   105:55
who has never loved has never l.   142:55
Liver: open and notorious evil l.   64:93
Livery: in her sober l. all things clad   219:69
Lives: a history in all men's l.   317:16
all that l. must die   305:40
as a man l., so shall he die   271:34
cat has only nine l.   394:70
constancy l. in realms above   106:67
he l. ... 'tis Death is dead   367:17
he preaches well that l. well   275:59
he who l. more l. than one   404:96
l. in eternity's sunrise   66:34
l. of great men all remind us   198:7
love l. in cottages ... courts   270:15
men lead l. of quiet desperation   391:36
not how a man dies, but how he l.   175:98
one really l. nowhere   79:92
so long l. this, and this gives life   362:34
the music of men's l.   351:63
there l. more faith in ... doubt   386:65
Living: from too much love of l.   383:20
Homer ... who, l., had no roof   163:26
Lady Disdain, are you yet l.?   342:58
live, for the truth is l.   383:24

Living (*continued*)

l. ... eight years with a strange man   169:7
l., shall forfeit fair renown   295:6
plain l. and high thinking   412:2
the l. need charity   20:29
the mother of all l.   35:40
the noble L.   413:10
'tis the l. up to [faith]   389:9
we have gone on l., l. and partly l.   131:16
Livingstone, Dr L., I presume   378:57
Lizzie Borden took an axe   15:67
Load: how to l. and bless with fruit   180:78
Loaf: half a l. is better   265:51
of a cut l. to steal a shive   357–8:63
Loafe: I l. and invite my soul   403:83
Loan oft loses both itself and friend   306:57
Lobster: the voice of the l.   91:64
Lochinvar: never was Knight like ... L.   296:11
young L. is come out of the west   295:10
Lock: l., stock and barrel   270:96
prison with a life-long l.   145:3
Locks: her l. were yellow as gold   105:52
knotted and combined l. to part   307:64
pluck up ... honour by the l.   313:54
shaking her invincible l.   224:43
yr. l. were like the raven   80:11
Locust: years that the l. hath eaten   50:79
Lodge: where thou lodgest, I will l.   39:33
Loftiness: in l. of thought surpass'd   128:66
Lofty and sour to them that lov'd him not   323:87
Log: on a l., expiring frog   121:64
Logic: as it isn't, it ain't. That s l.   92:75
grape that can with L. absolute   135:77
l. and rhetoric [make] able to contend   26:34
un-to l. hadde longe y-go   96:31
Logs: bring me pine l. hither   229:4
Tom bears l. into the hall   332:20
Loitering: alone and palely l.   182:7
Lombard Street to a China orange   270:97
London: a L. particular ... A fog   119:33
as L. is to Paddington   88:28

London (*continued*)
  citizen ... of famous L. town   112:54
  hell is ... much like L.   369:41
  it isn't far from L.   230–1:20
  L., ... flower of Cities all   129:75
  L., that great cesspool   125:27
  L., ... the Clearing-house of the
    World   95:13
  Mr Weller's knowledge of L.   121:66
  no man ... willing to leave L.   177:25
  nobody is healthy in L.   23:66
  our scene is L.   178:47
  to L. to look at the queen   237:64
  when a man is tired of L.   177:25
London Bridge is broken down   235:53
Loneliness of my country and my God
    366:4
Lonely: close to the sun in l. lands
    385:47
  left l. for ever the kings   20:34
  so l. 'twas, that God himself   106:62
  wandered l. as a cloud   410:67
Lonesome: one that on a l. road
    106:60
Long: a l., l. trail a-winding   189:84
  a l. way to Tipperary   407:39
  by thy l. grey beard   104:42
  has been l. in city pent   186:47
  he l. lived the pride   28:54
  how l. or short permit to Heaven
    220:98
  I have lived l. enough   383:22
  it cannot hold you l.   150:75
  it shall be witty and it shan't be l.
    98:64
  l. after it was heard no more   414:22
  l., dark, boggy, dirty ... way   151:84
  l. is the way and hard   218:54
  l. live the king, and Gilpin l. live he
    113:61
  look at them l. and l.   403:84
  love me little, so you love me l.
    162:20
  man goeth to his l. home   47:12
  nor wants that little l.   150:72
  not that the story need be l.   391:40
  Shenandoah, I l. to hear you   18:1
  star-spangled banner! O l. may it
    wave   188:82
  the night is l. that never finds the day
    335:67
  victory however l. ... the road
    100:93
  waiting for the l.-promised invasion
    101:97
Longed: lies where he l. to be   379:76
Longest: hatred is by far the l. pleasure
    85:84

Longest (*continued*)
  Russia, when nights are l. there
    337:83
Longings: I have immortal l. in me
    299:70
Longitude: a l. with no platitude
    140:34
Look; but westward, l., the land is
    bright   104:34
  Cassius has a lean and hungry l.
    324:94
  do it with a bitter l.   404:94
  has a frightened l. in its eye   373:91
  houses are built ... not to l. on   26:28
  I'll be a candle-holder and l. on
    353:91
  just to l. about us and to die   250:7
  let him l. to his bond   339:12
  l. at [animals] long and long   403:84
  l. before you leap   270:2
  l. thy last on all things lovely   118:22
  mountains l. on Marathon   84:78
  only a l. and a voice   198:4
  shall not l. upon his like again
    306:49
  to l. upon verdure ... perfect refresh-
    ment   23:70
  we l. before and after   370:50
Looked: having l. to government for
    bread   78:83
  no sooner l. but they lov'd   302:5
  she l. at me as she did love   183:9
Lookers-on see most of the game
    270:4
Looking-glass: not thank you for a l.
    256:47
Looks: her l. were free   105:52
  how like a ... publican he l.   338:3
  l. the whole world in the face
    199:7
  love l. not with the eyes   341:38
  toward school with heavy l.   354:4
  woman as old as she l.   107:86
Looms: quest and passage through
    these l.   396:86
Loon: private buffoon is a light-hearted
    l.   149:49
  sung ... by a love-lorn l.   148:45
Lord: a ... l., neat, and trimly dress'd
    313:51
  bread which the L. ... hath given
    37:80
  deputy elected by the L.   349:50
  foundation is Jesus Christ her L.
    380:83
  from ghoulies ... good L. deliver us!
    14:60
  I thought ... a L. among wits   174:76

Lord (*continued*)
L. Finchley tried to mend ... light 31:94
L. Hippo suffered fearful loss 32:3
L. Lucky, by a curious fluke 32:4
l. of thy presence and no land 326:33
now, the L. lighten thee! 316:7
O L., thou lover of souls 62:45
one day is with the L. 60:14
praise the L. for he is kind 221:10
sing to the L. with cheerful voice 188:77
speak, L.; for thy servant heareth 39:36
the Angel of the L. came down 384:35
the day thou gavest, L. 132:24
the L. bless thee and keep thee 38:2
the L. ... chasteneth thee 38:8
the L. do so to me 39:34
the L. gave and the L. hath taken 41:65
the L. hardened Pharaoh's heart 36:76
the L. is my shepherd 42:91
the L. ... is one L. 38:5
the L. lift up his countenance 38:2
the L. make his face shine 38:2
the L. our God is good 188:78
the L. set a mark upon Cain 35:42
the L., whom ye seek 51:99
where the dear L. was crucified 11:20
whom the L. loveth he chasteneth 60:1
Lords: twelve l. a-leaping 238:73
Lose: grasp all, l. all 265:41
heads I win, tails you l. 115:86, 266:75
l. and neglect the creeping hours 301:89
l. by over-running 322:74
l. myself in other men's minds 192:29
who wd. l. ... this intellectual being 217:49
Losers: l. are ... in the wrong 270:5
l. seekers, finders keepers 270:6
Loss: buy and sell, and live by the l. 257:79
enow to do our country's l. 320:55
Lord Hippo suffered fearful l. 32:3
l. of honour was a wrench 153:12
Losses: all l. are restor'd 363:38
Lost: and she l. her maiden name 18:3
better to have fought and l. 103:31
better to have loved and l. 83:50, 386:59

Lost (*continued*)
books by which the printers have l. 140:40
field be l.? All is not l. 216:30
how art thou l.! 220:94
I have l. all the names 177:33
I have l. my reputation 345:1
I look upon every day to be l. 178:37
learning without thought is labour l. 108:4
l. causes, forsaken beliefs 21:49
never to have l. at all 83:50
praising ... l. makes the remembrance dear 298:47
sorry when any language is l. 178:39
thou art l. and gone for ever 225:59
wherever we're l. in 140:35
woman that deliberates is l. 9:5
Lot: policeman's l. is not a happy one 148:33
remember L.'s wife 55:88
the l. fell upon Jonah 50:85
Lots: so they cast l. 50:85
Lottery: marriage is a l. 271:40
Loud: I said it very l. and clear 93:91
Louder: the l. he talked of his honour 132:27
Loungers: all the l. of the Empire 125:27
Love: a little l. and good company 134:56
absence sharpens l. 254:53
ah, dearest l., sweet home of all 183:15
Alas! the l. of women 84:72
all is fair in l. and war 254:65
all l. is sweet 369:44
all mankind l. a lover 132:32
all she loves is l. 84:73
am like to l. three more 380:86
an oyster may be crossed in l. 371:64
and when l. speaks 331:15
as honour, l., obedience 336:71
be wise and l. exceeds man's might 358:70
brief ... as woman's l. 310:8
but l. is blind, and lovers cannot see 339:10
choose l. by another's eyes 341:37
comfort in the strength of l. 411:88
corner in the thing I l. 345:8
course of true l. never ... smooth 341:36
cupboard l. 259:42
dinner of herbs where l. is 45:71
dislike ... the l. of a woman ... treacle 187:66
drew them ... with bands of l. 50:77

Love (*continued*)

earth's the right place for l.   139:21
familiar acts are beautiful through l.
369:45
faults are thick where l. is thin
262:56
fear the Lord ... and to l. him
38:9
few l. to hear the sins they l. to act
347:25
folly ... l. did make thee run into
300:82
for ever wilt thou l.   183:18
for I am sick of l.   47:19
for ... them that l. God   56:34
for thy sweet l. rememb'red   362:36
friendly l. perfecteth   25:99
friendship is constant ... save in ... l.
342:62
from too much l. of living   383:20
gave, once, her flowers to l.   71:93
general award of l.   182:4
God is l.   60:16
greater l. hath no man   56:10
greatest hate ... from the greatest l.
265:47
hail, wedded L.   219:71
half in l. with easeful Death   184:29
his banner over me was l.   47:18
hot l. is soon cold   267:1
how have you left the ancient l.
68:55
I cd. not l. thee, Dear, so much
200:17
I do not l. thee, Dr Fell   72:96
I hate and l. ... and am in torment
94:5
I l. a lassie   193:41
I l. everything that's old   151:83
I l. not man the less   84:65
I l. sixpence   233:40
I l. thee true   183:10
I never shall l. the snow   70:77
I think my l. as rare   364:53
if music be the food of l.   358:75
is it ... a crime to l. too well   248:73
leave to come unto my l.   377:39
lest that thy l. prove variable   354:2
let brotherly l. continue   60:2
let l. be without dissimulation   57:37
lightly turns to thoughts of l.   387:79
little brown jug ... I l. thee   16:84
live with me and be my l.   123:4,
205:82
live with thee and be thy l.   286:96
look'd at me as she did l.   183:9
l. all, trust a few   298:41
l. alters not   363:48

Love (*continued*)

l. and a cough cannot be hid   270:8
l. and business teach eloquence
270:9
l. and fame to nothingness   186:49
l. and hate are necessary   68:56
l. and marriage rarely can combine
84:74
l. and meekness ... become a churchman   323:88
l. bade me welcome: yet my soul
drew back   161:12
l. begets l.   270:10
l. built on beauty   123:6
l. but her and l. for ever   79:96
l. ceases to be a pleasure   30:85
l. conquers all   397:3
l. ... differs from gold and clay
368:26
l. Divine, all loves excelling   402:72
L. forgive us—cinders, ashes   183:11
l., free as air, at sight of ... ties
248:75
l. goes toward l. ... but l. from l.
354:4
l. grows bitter with treason   383:23
l. has never known a law   403:88
l. he laughed to scorn   364:59
l. her till I die   18:9
l. I laugh to scorn   71:86
l. in a golden bowl   66:32
l. in a hut with water   183:11
l. in a palace   183:11
l. is blind   270:13
l. is enough   227:72
l. ... is exactly like war   379:71
l. is heaven and heaven is l.   295:2
l. is like the measles   171:34
l. is my religion—I cd. die   187:67
l. is not l. which alters   363:47
l. is ... sour in the ending   270:14
l. is strong as death   47:27
l. is sweet for a day   383:23
l. is the fulfilling of the law   57:43
l. itself shall slumber on   370:54
l. looks not with the eyes   341:38
l. me little, l. me long   270:18
l. me little, so you l. me long   162:20
l. me, l. my dog   270:19
l. of flattery   378:59
l. of money ... root of all evil   59:92
l. rules the court, the camp   295:2
l.'s but the frailty of the mind   109:14
l. seeketh not itself to please   67:43
l. sought is good   360:94
l.'s the noblest frailty of the mind
128:63
l. that moves the sun   117:4

Love (continued)

l. that never told can be 67:40
l. the brotherhood 60:9
l. the Lord ... with all thine heart
38:6
l. thy neighbour as thyself 37:99
l. thyself last 323:83
l. too much that die for l. 271:21
l., we are in God's hand 73:14
l. will find a way 271:22
l. worketh no ill 57:43
l. ye therefore the stranger 38:10
l. you because ... hard up you pawn
116:95
l. your enemies 52:14
lovers' quarrels ... renewal of l.
389:5
loyal cantons of contemned l. 359:80
man's l. ... a thing apart 84:70
many waters cannot quench l. 47:28
marry first and l. will follow 271:45
master-passion ... l. of news 114:81
me and my true l. 18:2
medicines to make me l. him 313:56
men have died ... but not for l.
302:3
men l. in haste ... detest at leisure
85:84
my dear l. sits him down 19:10
my l. and I wd. lie 167:82
my l. climbed up to me 189:85
my l. is like a red red rose 81:21
my l. is like the melodie 81:21
my L. is of a birth as rare 206:97
my l. lies underground 193:48
my only l. sprung from my only hate
353:96
my true l. hath my heart 372:83
my true l. sent to me 238:72, 73
my vegetable l. shd. grow 206:93
my whole course of l. 344:91
nameless ... acts of kindness and of
l. 415:31
never seek to tell thy l. 67:40
no l. sincerer than the l. of food
365:79
no rage like l. to hatred turned 108:6
none to praise ... few to l. 413:15
nor l. thy life, nor hate 220:98
not enough [religion] to make us l.
382:9
not in our power to l. or hate 205:80
nuptial l. maketh mankind 25:99
O l.; has she done this to thee?
201:30
of soup and l., the first 278:59
off with the old l. 17:93
office and affairs of l. 342:62

Love (continued)

old l., cold l. 257:81
one does not l. a place less 23:74
one must not trifle with l. 227:79
open rebuke is better than secret l.
46:86
passing the l. of women 40:49
perfect l. casteth out fear 60:17
pity ... in the heart of l. 417:57
politicians neither l. nor hate 126:41
pounds of law, not an ounce of l.
280:32
pray you, l., remember 311:28
prosperity's the very bond of l.
362:24
prove ... the sports of l. 179:61
regain l. once possessed 222:24
rise up, my l. 47:20
said that the l. of money is the root
82:41
saying 'Farewell, blighted l.' 18:4
seals of l., but seal'd in vain
337–8:92
seen ... that l. hath an end 383:22
she never told her l. 360:89
sighed for the l. of a ladye 148–9:46
so faithful in l. 296:11
so true a fool is l. 363:39
some are fou o' l. divine 80:10
something ... doesn't l. a wall
139:27
support of the woman I l. 129:81
that true self-l. and social are the
same 250:20
that ye l. one another 56:8
the arms of my true l. 388:88
the fool of l., unpractis'd 128:70
the l. that can be reckon'd 298:50
the l. which doth us bind 206:98
the pangs of despis'd l. 309:95
the right true end of l. 123:8
the service of my l. 377:53
there is no fear in l. 60:17
there is tears for his l. 325:11
things that l. might 329:75
this bud of l. may prove a ... flower
354:3
this spring of l. resembleth 361:6
though I can't make her l. me 372:75
through l., through hope, and faith's
413:14
thy l. is better than wine 47:15
thy l. to me was wonderful 40:49
tired of l. ... tired of rhyme 32:98
to do justly and to l. mercy 51:91
to hold my wealth of l. 149:48
to let the warm L. in 185:33
to live is like l. 82:46

Love (*continued*)
to l. and to cherish   64:7
to l. oneself ... lifelong romance   404:3
to see her was to l. her   79:96
true l.'s the gift which God has given   295:4
try thinking of l. or something   140:36
unbounded l. thou art   402:72
wanton l. corrupteth   25:99
weak man who marries for l.   177:19
what is l.? 'Tis not hereafter   359:84
what L. shall never reap   290:50
when I l. thee not, chaos is come   345:5
where both deliberate, the l. is slight   205:81
with l. in summer's wonderland   230-1:20
women ... have ... but two passions, vanity and l.   98:62
work of faith ... labour of l.   59:83
wroth with one we l.   106:67
you must sit down, says L.   161:13
your true l.'s coming   359:83
Loved: Alas! that all we l. of him shd. be   367:12
awake, my heart, to be l.   70:75
better l. ye canna be   228:81
better to have l. and lost   83:50
Dante who l. well   74:32
first he l. her, then he left her   18:3
God so l. the world   55:99
had we never l. so kindly   79:97
he dearly l. the lasses   80:8
he l. gold in special   97:38
I have not l. the world   83:61
I l. a lass, a fair one   408:48
I l. him not, and yet   192:35
I never writ, nor no man ever l.   363:48
I wish I l. the Human Race   286:97
Lavinia, therefore must be l.   357:63
l. her that she did pity them   344:92
l. I not Honour more   200:17
l. three whole days together   380:86
l. well because he hated   74:32
men l. darkness   55:1
Nature I l., and ... art   192:34
no sooner l. but they sigh'd   302:5
one that l. not wisely, but too well   346:22
she l. me for the dangers ... pass'd   344:92
sour to them that l. him not   323:87
the king l. Esther   40:64

Loved (*continued*)
the time and the place and the l. one   74:31
'tis better to have l. and lost   386:59
to be l. needs only to be seen   127:61
to have l. ... thought ... done   20:31
we l., sir—used to meet   73:20
where burning Sappho l. and sung   84:77
who ever l. that l. not at first sight?   205:81
who has never l. has never lived   142:55
Lovelier than the love of Jove   204:73
Loveliest: the l. things of beauty   207:11
Loveliness: enough their simple l.   185:44
glory and l. have pass'd   186:46
her l. I never knew until   104:41
l. which once he made more lovely   367:18
your L. and the hour of my death   187:65
Lovely: a billboard l. as a tree   229:97
a l. and a fearful thing   84:72
and l. is the rose   410:73
as you are l., so be various   154:22
go, l. rose   398:17
he'd make a l. corpse   120:50
I love the l. bully   320:51
look thy last on all things l.   118:22
l. and pleasant in their lives   40:48
more l. and more temperate   362:32
so l. fair and smell'st so sweet   346:14
whatsoever things are l.   58:79
Lover: a l. and his lass   303:7
a l. without indiscretion   158:65
all mankind love a l.   132:32
jealousy ... the injured l.'s hell   219:79
mother and l. of men, the sea   383:25
my fause l. stole my rose   81:28
O Lord, thou l. of souls   62:45
the l., sighing like furnace   301:90
the lunatic, the l., and the poet   342:52
thoughts will slide into a l.'s head   414:24
what is a l., that it can give?   109:13
woman loves her l.   84:73
Lovers: a pair of star-cross'd l.   353:88
all l. young, all l. must   305:30
journeys end in l. meeting   359:83
l. cannot see the pretty follies   339:10
l. fled away into the storm   181:91

Lovers (*continued*)
l., to bed; 'tis almost fairy time 342:55
old l. are soundest 400:52
one makes l. ... as one pleases 109:13
sweet l. love the spring 303:7
Loves: a man l. the meat in his youth 343:69
all she l. is love 84:73
faithful l. ... moralize my song 377:40
fat white woman whom nobody l. 111:34
forebode not any severing of our l. 411:81
I have reigned with yr. l. 132:21
in her first passion woman l. 84:73
kills the thing he l. 404:94
Love Divine, all l. excelling 402:72
one that l. his fellow-men 168:95
show a woman when he l. 74:34
two l. ... of comfort and despair 364:55
who l. to lie with me 300:83
whoever l., ... do not propose 123:8
Love-sick all against our will 146:13
Lovesome: garden is a l. thing 72:97
Loveth: God l. a cheerful giver 58:63
l. him chasteneth him betimes 45:67
the dear God who l. us 106:64
whom the Lord l. he chasteneth 60:1
whom the Lord l. he correcteth 44:55
Loving: Friday's child is l. and giving 235:56
heart be still as l. 86:97
more pleasure in l. than ... loved 274:46
most l. mere folly 302:91
the night was made for l. 86:98
wickedness that hinders l. 74:32
Low: happy l., lie down! 317:14
he that is l. 77:66
her voice ... l.—an excellent thing 331:5
I'll tak' the l. road 18:2
last great Englishman is l. 388:92
sweet and l. 388:96
to cast one's eyes so l. 329:88
too l. for envy 112:47
what is l. raise and support 216:29
when my light is l. 386:60
Lowells talk to the Cabots 69:67
Lowest: matrimony at its l. 379:77
Lowly: better to be l. born 322:75
God made them, high or l. 10:18
me, made l. wise 413:8

Lowly (*continued*)
stood a l. cattle shed 10:19
to order myself l. ... to all my betters 64:97
Loyal: that l. body wanted learning 393:54
Loyalties: home of ... impossible l. [Oxford] 21:49
Loyalty: that learned body wanted l. 393:54
when l. no harm meant 17:91
Lucifer: as proud as L. 275:66
come not, L.! 204:66
falls like L., never to hope again 322-3:81
how art thou fallen ... O L.! 48:38
Luck: better l. next time 256:26
I had the l. to be called upon 102:11
Lucky: better to be born l. 255:16
Lord L., by a curious fluke 32:4
Lucy: if L. shd. be dead! 414:24
Luke: L. began to slacken in his duty 411:87
Matthew, Mark, L. and John 10:13
Lukewarm: because thou art l. 61:23
Lullaby: songs and snatches, and dreamy l. 145:95
Lumber: learned l. in his head 249:5
stowed away in a Montreal l. room 82:47
Luminous: beating ... his l. wings in vain 21:51
Dong with a l. Nose 194:56
Lump: don't like it, you can l. it 269:86
Lunatic, the lover, and the poet 342:52
Luncheon: breakfast, supper, dinner, l. 75:41
Lungs: a custom ... dangerous to the l. 170:19
Lurch: leave in the l. 269:67
Lure it back to cancel half a line 136:79
Lust: for l. of knowing 136:84
l. in action; and till action, l. 363:50
l. of fame was but a dream 71:86
Lustre: where is thy l. now? 329:83
Lustres: unrisen l. slake the o'ertaken moon 70:75
Lute: musical as is Apollo's l. 213:77
Orpheus with his l. 322:77
Luxuries: give us the l. of life 227:73
two l. to brood over 187:65
Lying: let me have no l. 362:26
l., vainness ... drunkenness 360:1
subject we old men are to ... l. 317:21
there is whispering, there is l. 283:29

Lying (*continued*)
to conclude, they are l. knaves
344:87
world is given to l.!   315:94
Lyly: didst our L. outshine   179:55
Lyme: an old party of L.   224:52
Lysander: of Hector and L.   18:6

Mab: I see Queen M. hath been with
you   353:92
Macaroni: and called it m.   241:90
Macaulay: as cocksure ... as Tom M.
is   208:27
Macavity: no one like M.   131:6
Machine: house is a m. for living in
110:31
maison est une m.-à-habiter   110:31
Mackerel: sprat to catch a m.   278:69
Mad: but m. north-north-west   308:83
how sad and bad and m.   73:20
I wd. not be m.!   328:60
m. as a hatter   271:23
m. as a March hare   271:24
m., bad and dangerous to know
191:24
m. world! m. kings! m. composition!
326:36
made me m. to see him shine   313:52
O, fool, I shall go m.!   328:69
O, let me not be m.   328:60
Oh, he is m., is he?   142:61
that he's m., 'tis true   308:74
to destroy, he first makes m.   275:74
we want a few m. people now   366:1
went m. and bit the man   151:76
Madding crowd's ignoble strife   155:39
Made: did he who m. the Lamb make
thee?   68:47
dost thou know who m. thee?   68:50
fearfully and wonderfully m.   44:50
m. and loveth all   106:64
m. him a coat of many colours   36:62
nobody never m. me.   380:85
Mademoiselle from Armenteers   291:57
Madness: devil's m.—War   297:36
great wits ... to m. near allied
126:39
m. in great ones ... not unwatch'd
310:2
m., yet there is method in't   308:78
melancholy and moon-struck m.
220:97
much mirth and no m.   373:93
such harmonious m. from my lips
370:51
that way m. lies   329:77
this is ... midsummer m.   360:95
work like m. in the brain   106:67

Magdalen: fourteen months at M.
College   142:64
Magistrates: some like m. correct at
home   318:39
Magnanimity: in all his m. of thought
418:63
in Victory: M.   102:10
you might curb yr. m.   187:69
Magnificence comes after   192:30
Magnificent: it is m., but it is not war
69:66
Magnifique: c'est m. ... pas la guerre
69:66
Magog: Gog, the land of M.   49:66
Mahomet: hill will not come to M.   25:3
Maid: a fair m. dwellin'   12:36
be good, sweet m.   189:86
chariest m. is prodigal enough
306:53
I heard a m. singing   16:80
m. whom there were none to praise
413:15
Music, heavenly m., was young
108:91
O Music, sphere-descended M.
108:93
slain by a fair cruel m.   359:88
the m. was in the garden   238:70
way of a man with a m.   46:91
where are you going to, my pretty
m.?   241:86
woo a fair young m.   17:95
Maiden: for many a rose-lipt m.
167:84
kissed the m. all forlorn   239:79
m. of bashful fifteen   372:78
m. ... must be slaughtered too   145:5
prithee, pretty m., will you marry
me?   146:17
use a poor m. so   16:80
when a merry m. marries   143:74
Maidens: m. like moths, are ever
caught   83:56
twenty lovesick m. we   146:13
Maids: eight m. a-milking   238:73
m. are May when ... m.   302:4
pretty m. all in a row   235:55
seven m. with seven mops   92:79
three little m. from school   145:2
Maimed and set at naught   82:47
Main: every man ... part of the m.
124:13
Maintaining: died m. his right of way
13:50
Majestic: his face ... m. though in ruin
218:52
Majestical: we do it wrong, being so m.
305:35

Majesty: a strange beginning—'borrowed m.'! 326:32
  attribute to awe and m. 339:15
  busied in his m., surveys 318–19:39
  sight so touching in its m. 412:96
  the next in M. 128:66
  then our M. adorning 143:75
  this earth of m., this seat of Mars
  348:41
  you got no-no-no m. 401:68
Major-General: model of a modern M.
  147:31
Majority: m. never has right on its side
  169:8
  one on God's side is a m. 246:51
  who makes up the m.? 169:8
Make: m. him an help meet 35:32
  makes no mistakes does not m. anything 246:50
  one of them said to his m. 12:39
Makes: the night that either m. me or
  fordoes 346:17
Male: into the ark ... m. and ... female
  35:45
  m. and female created he them 34:28
  more deadly than the m. 190:98
Males: deeds are m. and words are
  females 260:66
Malice: m. never was his aim 381:97
  nor set down aught in m. 346:22
  with m. toward none 196:81
Malignant: a m. and a turban'd Turk
  346–7:22
Malt: m. does more than Milton can
  167:85
  rat that ate the m. 239:79
Mammon: and M. wins his way
  83:56
  m. of unrighteousness 55:85
Man: a better m. than I am 190:1
  a Christian faithful m. 351:71
  a good old m. sir 343:78
  a hairy m. ... a smooth m. 36:59
  a living dead m. 303:12
  a m. after his own heart 39:40
  a m. can die but once 317:19
  a m. can raise a thirst 190:8
  a m. leave his father and mother
  58:72
  a m. more sinn'd against 329:76
  a m. must serve his time 85:90
  a m. of sorrows 48:47
  a m. of such a feeble temper 323:92
  a m.'s a m. for a' that 80:6
  a m.'s [business] to keep unmarried
  365:81
  a m.'s first duty? ... To be himself
  169:11

Man (*continued*)
  a m.'s friendships ... are invalidated
  83:49
  a m.'s reach should exceed his grasp
  73:15
  a m.'s worth something 73:18
  a m. severe he was 150:68
  a m. so various 126:43
  a m. that is young in years 26:26
  a m. that left his family 393:60
  a m. under authority 52:28
  a m. who cd. make so vile a pun
  119:29
  a m. who has not been in Italy
  177:22
  a m. who said 'God' 191:20
  a m. who shaves and takes a train
  402:77
  a m. who's untrue to his wife 22:61
  a m. will ne'er quite understand
  245:32
  a moral, sensible and well-bred m.
  112:52
  a nice m. ... a m. of nasty ideas
  382:11
  a ready m. 26:33
  a sadder and a wiser m. 106:65
  a single-m. ... a good fortune 23:75
  a strong m. after sleep 224:43
  a stupid m. is doing something
  364:65
  a very unclubbable m. 175:93
  'A was a m. 306:49
  a weak m. who marries for love
  177:19
  Adam, the goodliest m. 219:67
  all my faults as m. to m. 365:73
  all that was pleasant in m. 151:80
  an aged aged m. 94:95
  an elder m. not at all 25:98
  an exact m. 26:33
  an honest God ... noblest work of
  m. 170:14
  an old m. and no honester 343:76
  an old m. in a dry month 130:92
  and the last m. in 230:13
  Angry Young M. 245:33
  any m.'s death diminishes me 124:14
  apparel oft proclaims the m. 306:56
  as for m., his days are as grass 43:23
  ash on an old m.'s sleeve 130:97
  at thirty m. suspects 418:63
  away, slight m.! 326:25
  beauty crieth ... no m. regardeth
  82:47
  became a m., I put away childish
  things 57:53
  Benedick the married m. 342:60

Man (*continued*)

better angel is a m. right fair 364:55
better spar'd a better m. 315:92
big assemblance of a m.! 317:20
both m. and bird and beast 106:63
brothers and their murder'd m. 182:5
Brutus is an honourable m. 325:13
busiest m. who has time to spare 244:25
business of the wealthy m. 31:94
by courtesy a m. 24:82
by m. shall his blood be shed 35:49
came to the making of m. 382:16
care not whether a m. is good 67:37
caverns measureless to m. 106:71, 73
child is father of the m. 412:99
cloud ... like a m.'s hand 40:57
condition of m. ... condition of war 163:33
conference [maketh] a ready m. 26:33
crumbs ... from the rich m.'s table 55:86
daring young m. on the flying trapeze 196:71
Darwinian M. ... well-behaved 148:38
deep young m. 146:15
each m. kills ... thing he loves 404:94
every m. did that which was right 39:32
every m. for himself 262:27
every m. has his faults 262:28
every m. is as Heaven made him 95:9
every m. is best known to himself 262:29
every m. is wanted, no m. ... much 133:34
every m. meets his Waterloo 246:52
every m. must play a part 338:96
every m. over forty 366:91
every m.'s hand against him 35:53
every m. that cometh into ... world 55:93
every m. to his taste 262:30
every m. under his vine 50:89
every m. was ... god or devil 126:44
every woman shd. marry ... no m. 123:96
everyone has sat except a m. 115:93
expects every m. ... do his duty 229:7
face of the old m. 38:1
foolish fond old m. 330:97

Man (*continued*)

foolishly-compounded clay, m. 316:98
foot-in-the-grave young m. 146:18
get a new m. 356:44
glory to M. in the highest! 383:21
God created m. in his own image 34:28
God doth not need ... m.'s work 223:30
God made the woman for the m. 385:48
God took the m. and put him 35:31
good for a m. that he bear the yoke 49:62
good name in m. and woman 345:6
greater love hath no m. 56:10
greatest m. you had ... yet seen 178:46
he thinks, good easy m. 322:80
heaven had made her such a m. 344:92
her m. ... he done her wrong 16:81
honest m. sent to lie abroad 416:46
honest m.'s the noblest work of God 250:16
how use doth breed a habit in a m. 361:10
I hate ingratitude ... in a m. 360:1
I love not m. the less 84:65
ideal m. ... non-attached m. 168:99
if a m. will begin with certainties 26:37
if any m. shall add 61:35
if I ever become a rich m. 32:6
if such a m. there be 248:84
if the m. who turnips cries 172:56
I'm truly sorry m.'s dominion 80:17
in the Parliament of m. 387:81
in the spring a young m.'s fancy 387:79
in wit a m.: simplicity a child 248:89
is m. an ape or an angel? 122:91
it is the number of a m. 61:30
It's That M. Again 180:76
laugh to scorn the pow'r of m. 335:62
let no m. despise thy youth 59:89
let no m. put asunder 65:10
let not m. put asunder 54:60
like master, like m. 270:87
looking for a m.'s footprint 30:82
m. and wife together 65:11
m. ... bears in his bodily frame 117:6
m. being too proud to fight 407:45
m. ... born free ... is in chains 291:55

Man (*continued*)

m. delights not me ... nor woman 308:81
m. for the field ... the sword 389:2
m. goeth to his long home 47:12
m. has his will, – but woman 164:48
m. in the moon 271:29
m. in the street 271:30
m. is a noble animal 72:7
m. is ... a political animal 20:26
m. is ... a religious animal 78:79
m. is a tool-making animal 139:17
m. is born unto trouble 41:67
m. is Nature's sole mistake 148:37
m. is not a fly 250:10
m. is the hunter 388:1
m. is the master of things 383:21
m. is the shuttle 396:86
m. ... killed by lightning 12:42
m. looketh on ... outward appearance 39:42
m. made the town 114:69
m. ... must get drunk 84:71
m. of upright life unstained 166:75
m. or mouse 271:35
m. proposes ... God disposes 188:71, 271:36
m., proud m. 337:87
m.'s a ribald ... a rake 148:37
m.'s inhumanity to m. 80:14
m. shall not live by bread 51:7
m. that is born of a woman 41:69, 65:13
m. that lays his hand upon a woman 392:48
m. to afflict his soul 49:52
m. wants but little 418:64
m. wants but little here below 150:72
m. was made for joy and woe 66:30
m. who knows the price 406:21
m. who sees absolutely nothing 404:98
m. who sees both sides 404:98
m. who ... sets foot upon a worm 114:75
m. with the head ... to command 389:2
manners maketh m. 407:38
met a m. who wasn't there 208:24
met a m. with seven wives 231:22
money makes the m. 272:67
Nature might ... say ... 'This was a m.!' 326:31
new m. ... raised up in him 64:94
no great m. lives in vain 89:36
no m. can serve two masters 52:19
no m. dieth to himself 57:44

Man (*continued*)

no m. does [become like his mother] 406:30
no m. ever talked poetry 121:72
no m., having put ... hand to plough 54:74
no m. is an island 124:13
no m. is good enough to govern 196:73
no m. putteth new wine 54:73
no m. truly knows another 72:4
nor no m. ever loved 363:48
not a dinner to ask a m. to 175:92
no-wher so bisy a m. 97:35
O good old m., how well in thee 300:79
o'er all this scene of m. 250:7
of M.'s first disobedience 216:27
old m. in a hurry 100:86
on m., on nature ... life 409:63
one m. ... appointed to buy the meat 297:25
one m. ... plays many parts 301:90
one m.'s meat is another m.'s poison 272:52
only m. is vile 160:87
open not ... heart to every m. 62:49
poor, infirm ... despis'd old m. 329:73
poor m. that hangs on princes' favours 322:81
proper study of Mankind is M. 250:13
reading maketh a full m. 26:33
rejoice, O young m., in ... youth 47:10
reminds a m. he is mortal 117:14
rich m., poor m., beggar m. 240:81
ruins of the noblest m. 324:8
sabbath was made for m. 53:54
safeliest when with one m. m.'d 123–4:9
same tree ... a wise m. sees 69:60
say to ... world, This was a m.! 326:31
shall mortal m. be more just than God 41:66
sleep of a labouring m. 46:2
so can I, or so can any m. 314:72
so unto the m. is woman 198:3
some new race, called M. 218:53
son of m., set thy face against Gog 49:66
stagger like a drunken m. 43:27
state of m., like to a ... kingdom 324:98
style is the m. himself 76:51
that a m. lay down his life 56:10

Man (*continued*)
    that m. was made to mourn 80:13
    the blood of a British m. 329:82
    the childhood shows the m. 221:6
    the fury of a patient man 127:48
    the hour is come, but not the m.
        296:17
    the m. all tattered and torn 239:79
    the m. hath penance done 105:59
    the m. of action is called on 317:12
    the m. perceives it die away 411:78
    the m. that hath no music 340:24
    the m., with soul so dead 295:5
    the most senseless and fit m. 343:74
    the proud m.'s contumely 309:95
    the tongue can no m. tame 60:5
    the whole duty of m. 47:14
    the young m.'s dog with them 62:40
    there came to the making of m.
        382:16
    There once was a m. who said
        'Damn' 158:63
    there was an old m. from Darjeeling
        14:56
    there was an Old M. who said
        'Hush!' 195:65
    there was an Old M. with a beard
        195:66
    there was a young m. of Boulogne
        13:53
    there was a young m. of Japan 13:54
    there was a young m. of Montrose
        33:12
    thinking m. is bound to rebel 169:8
    this is the state of m. 322:80
    till one greater M. restore us 216:27
    'tis strange what a m. may do 389:10
    to be a well-favoured m. 343:73
    to every m. a damsel or two 39:24
    true love's the gift ... to m. alone
        295:4
    valiant m. and free 387:71
    vexing the dull ear of a drowsy m.
        327:41
    wager ... m. ... is absolutely fixed on
        134:59
    was there a m. dismayed 385:41
    water-drops stain my m.'s cheeks
        328:68
    way of a m. with a maid 46:91
    were m. but constant! 361:11
    what a piece of work is a m.! 308:81
    what bloody m. is that? 332:24
    what is m., that thou art mindful
        41:82
    what m. has made of m. 411:84
    what shall it profit a m.? 54:58
    whatsoever a m. soweth 58:70

Man (*continued*)
    when a m. bites a dog 116:1
    when a m. shd. marry 25:98
    when no m. can work 55:5
    when the brains were out the m.
        would die 335:55
    whenever he met a great m. 389:13
    where m. is not, nature is barren
        69:63
    whether ... wise m. or a fool
        67:37
    who kills a m. 223:37
    who sheddeth m.'s blood 35:49
    who's master, who's m. 381:4
    who thicks m.'s blood with cold
        105:52
    whoso wd. be a m. 133:36
    wine ... maketh glad ... heart of m.
        43:24
    wisest m. the warl' saw 80:8
    with cords of a m. 50:77
    woman is the lesser m. 387:83
    wd. this m. ... ask why? 22:58
    you asked this m. to die 22:58
    you'll be a M., my son 190:5
Man Friday: I takes my M. with me
    118:17
Mandalay: on the road to M. 190:7
Mandrake: get with child a m. root
    124:11
Manger: in a m. for His bed 10:19
    in the rude m. lies 215:20
    the babe ... lying in a m. 54:69
Manhood: m. full and fair 70:78
    neither ... m., nor good fellowship
        312:48
Manhoods: and hold their m. cheap
    320:59
Manifold stories ... told not to thy
    credit 87:15
Man-in-the-street ... a keen observer of
    life 22:61
Mankind: amongst the noblest of m.
    87:14
    example is the school of m. 78:82
    gave up what was meant for m.
        151:78
    how beauteous m. is! 357:57
    I am involved in m. 124:14
    love all m., except an American
        177:26
    m. and posterity ... in their debt
        170:13
    not retreat but exclusion from m.
        173:66
    nuptial love maketh m. 25:99
    proper study of M. is Man 250:13
    seems to be all m.'s epitome 126:43

Mankind (*continued*)
survey m. from China to Peru
173:67
to you and all m. 384:35
wd. deserve better of m. 381:2
wisest, brightest, meanest of m.
250:17
Manliness: the silent m. of grief 150:71
Manna: said one to another. It is m.
37:80
though his tongue dropped m.
217:48
Manner: cease to think about the m.
159:85
native here, and to the m. born
307:59
Manners: by nothing ... as by his m.
377:45
graced with polished m. 114:75
m. maketh man 407:38
m. of a dancing-master 174:77
men's evil m. live in brass 323:86
old m., old books, old wine 151:83
sweeter m., purer laws 386:69
Manservant: nor his m., nor his maidservant 37:92
Mansion: life ... M. of many Apartments 187:60
Mansions: build thee more stately m.
164:50
in my Father's house are many m.
56:9
Mantle: cast his m. upon him 40:59
cream and m. like a standing pond
338:97
morn, in russet m. clad 305:36
twitched his m. blue 215:18
Manure: blood of English shall m. the
ground 350:56
Many: have the measels? ... how m.?
399:27
m. are called, but few are chosen
53:42
m. things to fear 25:13
owed by so m. to so few 101:96
the m. change and pass 367:19
the m. men, so beautiful 105:55
ye are m.—they are few 368:31
Many-splendour'd: miss the m. thing
391:31
Maps: generals are already poring over
m. 22:59
Mar: oft we m. what's well 328:59
Marathon: from M. to Waterloo
147:31
M. looks on the sea 84:78
Marble: I dreamt ... I dwelt in m. halls
76:55

Marble (*continued*)
poets that lasting m. seek 398:18
whole as the m., founded as the rock
335:53
your dreary m. halls 87:13
March: beware the Ides of M. 323:90
droghte of M. hath perced 96:25
M. comes in like a lion 271:38
Marched breast forward 73:16
Marches: dreadful m. to delightful
measures 351:65
funeral m. to the grave 198:96
Marching: as we were m. through
Georgia 416:44, 45
his soul is m. on! 157:57
m. as to war 28:57
Mare: lend me yr. grey m. 19:12
patience ... tired m. ... will plod
319:42
to find a m.'s nest 271:39
Maréchal: le bâton de m. de France
228:86
Margin: through a meadow of m.
372:74
Marian: Mall, Meg, and M., and
Margery 356:43
M.'s nose looks red and raw 332:20
Mariner: I fear thee, ancient M.
105:53
it is an ancient M. 104:42
Mariners: ye m. of England 88:21
Marines: tell that to the M. 279:15
Mark: God save the m.! 313:52
love ... an ever-fixed m. 363:47
Matthew, M., Luke, and John 10:13
no drowning m. upon him 355:27
read, m., learn 64:86
Market: chief good and m. of his time
311:22
if fools went not to m. 263:82
school or college, kirk or m. 379:78
send a fool to the m. 263:80
women ... goose make a m. 280:36
Market-place: at noon-day, upon the
m. 324:97
Idols of the M. 27:41
Marks: Signior Benedick; nobody m.
you 342:58
Marlowe: M.'s mighty line 179:55
neat M. 125:33
Marmion: last words of M. 296:15
Marquis: abducted by a French m.
153:12
Marred: young man married ... man
that's m. 298:44
Marriage: care ... more for a m. than
a ministry 27:44
coldly furnish ... m. tables 306:48

Marriage (*continued*)
comedies are ended by a m. 84:75
exclaim ... against second m. 134:59
eyes wide open before m. 268:31
friendships are ... invalidated by m.
83:49
hanging prevents a bad m. 359:78
happiness in m. ... matter of chance
23:76
love and m. rarely can combine
84:74
m. has many pains but celibacy has
no pleasures 173:66
m. is a lottery 271:40
m. is like a cage 225:56
m. is popular because 366:89
m. is the best state for a man 177:18
m. of true minds 363:47
O curse of m. 345:8
takes two to make a m. a success
293:75
won't be a stylish m. 116:99
Married: a woman's business to get m.
365:81
as wellbred as if ... not m. 109:17
Benedick the m. man 342:60
cuckoo ... mocks m. men 332:19
how ... be m. without a wife? 235:52
how to be happy though m. 157:63
if ever we had been m. 141:52
live till I were m. 343:70
man who m. ... did more service
152:96
m. three wives at a time 224:52
unpleasing to a m. ear 332:19
wen you're a m. man, Samivel
121:70
what delight we m. people have
245:42
wd. be m. but I'd have no wife
115:83
wd. be m. to a single life 115:83
young man m. is ... marr'd 298:44
Marries: m. late, m. ill 271:43
person who either m. or dies 23:67
Marry: advise none to m. 254:61
be sure before you m. of a house
255:97
better to m. than to burn 57:50
every woman should m. – and no
man 123:96
he'll come back and m. me 231:24
honest men m. soon 267:93
I can't m. you, my pretty maid
241:87
if men knew ... they'd never m.
161:4
may m. whom she likes 389:12

Marry (*continued*)
now that you are going to m. 176:99
to persons about to m.—Don't
284:73
when a man shd. m. 25:98
while ye may, go m. 162:25
young man shd. not m. yet 284:62
Mars: this seat of M. 348:41
Marshal: the m.'s truncheon nor the
judge's robe 337:84
Martin Elginbrode: here lie I, M.
202:50
Martini: get ... into a dry M. 409:57
Martyr: bitter groan of a m.'s woe
66–7:35
Martyrdom ... in which ... can become
famous 365:69
Martyrs: noble army of M. 63:69
Marvel: I m. how the fishes live 347:27
match me such m. 77:70
they m. more and more 31:89
Marvellous: Chatterton, the m. boy
413:12
Mary: M. had a little lamb 157:55
M., M., quite contrary 235:55
M. was that Mother mild 10:19
might be the last, my M.! 114:76
my sweet Highland M. 80:9
O M., at thy window be 80:15
Mary Ann: M. has gone to rest 13:48
nuts for M. 13:48
Mary Ann Lowder: here lies the body
of M. 13:46
Mary Jane: *What* is the matter with
M.? 211:58
Mary-buds: winking M. begin 304:20
Masons: singing m. building roofs of
gold 318–19:39
Masquerade: the truth in m. 85:82
Mass: Paris is well worth a m. 160:97
Massacre: not as sudden as a m.
393:64
Masses: the m. against the classes
149:53
Mast: bends the gallant m. 116:96
Master: has a new m., get a new man
356:44
has a wife, has a m. 283:31
I am the M. of this College 30:80
in constancy follow the M. 77:64
like m., like man 270:87
man is the m. of things 383:21
M. Mistress of my passion 362:35
money is ... a bad m. 272:65
money ... will be thy m. 272:63
my m.'s lost his fiddlestick 231:26
one for the m. 231:23
that ... I wd. fain call m. 327:55

Master (*continued*)
the m., the swabber, the boatswain 356:43
vice is a m. 250:14
who's m., who's man 381:4
Masterpiece: a friend ... m. of Nature 132:29
Masters: men are m. of their fates 323–4:93
no man can serve two m. 52:19
the people are the m. 78:75
Match: ten to make ... m. to win 230:13
Matched: thy passions, m. with mine 387:83
Mate: high and low m. ill 403:88
Mathematics: m. [make] subtile 26:34
m. possesses ... truth ... beauty 292:67
Matilda: you'll come a-waltzing, M. 244:30
Mating: come ... Only in the m. season 210:48
Matrimony: in m. ... a little aversion 371:67
take m. at its lowest 379:77
Matron: sober-suited m., all in black 354:13
Matter: a Star Chamber m. of it 340:27
all mirth and no m. 343:66
mere m. for a May morning 360:97
more m. with less art 307:73
what is M.? Never Mind 284:77
wretched m. and lame metre 216:26
Matters: where man may read strange m. 333:34
Matthew, Mark, Luke, and John 10:13
Mature in dullness 128:69
Maud: come into the garden, M. 388:86
I had written to Aunt M. 153:10
Maurice: never love the snow ... since M. died 70:77
Mawkishness: thence proceeds m. 181:84
Maxim: an old m. in the schools 381:96
it is my m. ... to enjoy it [world] 375:16
that grounded m. so rife 222:21
the m. of the British people 100:89
Maximum: marriage ... combines m. of temptation 366:89
May: fresh as is the month of M. 96:27
gathering nuts in M. 16:86
laurel outlives not M. 383:23
M. when they are maids 302:4

May (*continued*)
merriment of M. 181:87
more matter for a M. morning 360:97
ne'er a clout till M. be out 257:87
to be Queen of the M. 388:90
when M. follows ... whitethroat builds 74:22
winds do shake the darling buds of M. 362:32
Mayor: astonished M. and Corporation 75:39
Maypole: away to the m. hie 16:79
Maze: a mighty m.! but not without a plan 250:7
Mazes: in wandering m. lost 218:55
Me: blest compared with m. 80:19
but the One was M. 169:4
m. as one who loves his fellow-men 168:95
not m. for the world 375:16
terms too deep for m. 146:15
what shall, alas! become of m.? 201:30
ye have done it unto m. 53:48
Mead: about the new-mown m. 185:42
Meadow: a time when m., grove and stream 410:72
going through m. and village 208:17
meander through a m. of margin 372:74
the sheep's in the m. 234:49
Meadows: O, ye Fountains, M., Hills 411:81
Meads: I met a lady in the m. 183:8
Mean: I m. the Faith's Defender 83:53
in m. men we entitle patience 347:32
it all depends what you m. by 171:39
means just what I choose it to m. 93:86
tears ... I know not what they m. 388:99
try and tell you what I m. 93:88
Meanest: the m. flower that blows 411:82
Meaning: to some faint m. make pretence 128:69
word ... teems with hidden m. 148:41
Means: by honest m. ... by any m. make money 166:72
die beyond my m. 406:34
end justifies the m. 261:19
it m. ... what I choose it to mean 93:86
let us ... live within our m. 399:31
my m. ... too low for envy 112:47

Meant: more is m. than meets the ear 213:87
what those damned dots m. 100:87
Measles: have the m.: ... how many? 399:27
love is like the m. 171:34
Measure: conquests ... shrunk to this little m. 324:6
like doth quit like, and m. still for m. 338:94
m. not the work until 73:9
m. thrice before you cut 272:51
there is a m. in all things 271:50
Measureless: caverns m. to man 106:71, 73
Measures: dreadful marches to delightful m. 351:65
Meat: appointed to buy the m. 297:25
givest them ... m. in due season 44:52
have made worms' m. of me 354:11
I cannot eat but little m. 380:81
it snewed in his hous of m. 97:36
loves the m. in his youth 343:69
mock the m. it feeds on 345:7
one man's m. ... man's poison 272:52
out of the eater came forth m. 39:27
sit down, ... and taste My m. 161:13
some hae m., and canna eat 81:24
Mechanic: poor m. porters crowding in 318–19:39
Meddling with any practical part of life 9:6
Medes and Persians: law of the M., which altereth not 50:71
thy kingdom ... given to the M. 49:70
Medicinable: their m. gum 346–7:22
Medicine: faithful friend is the m. of life 62:47
no other m. but only hope 337:89
Medicines: given me m. to make me love him 313:56
Meditate: strictly m. the thankless Muse? 215:11
Meek: blessed are the m. 51:9
I am m. and gentle 324:8
m. shall inherit the earth 42:2
m. until they be married 271:25
taught us to be calm and m. 164:45
Meekness: love and m. ... become a churchman 323:88
Meet: extremes m. 262:41
God be with you till we m. again 286:98
if I shd. m. thee 86:1

Meet (continued)
if we do m. again ... shall smile 326:28
m. in her aspect and her eyes 86:96
never the twain shall m. 189:92
we loved, sir – used to m. 73:20
will never m. again ... on ... banks 18:2
Meeter to carry off the latter 245:38
Meeting: journeys end in lovers m. 359:83
this m. is drunk 121:73
Meetings: alarums changed to merry m. 351:65
Melancholy: bird ... most musical, most m.! 213:85
green and yellow m. 360:89
hail, divinest M.! 213:83
hence, loathed M. 213:91
m. marked him for her own 155:40
m. ... shd. be diverted 177:20
moping m. 220:97
my cue is villainous m. 327:54
naught so sweet as m. 81:29
not m. once a day 263:79
nothing ... so m. as a battle ... won 401:57
pale M. sat retired 108:92
suck m. out of a song 301:84
these pleasures, M., give 213:90
'tis m. and a fearful sign 84:74
what charm can soothe her m.? 152:2
Melodies: heard m. are sweet 183:17
Melody: from ancient m. have ceas'd 68:54
my love is like the m. 81:21
Melrose: view fair M. aright 295:1
Melted into air, into thin air 356:50
Melts: a moment white, then m. for ever 81:25
Member: ev'ry m. of the force 288:22
Members one of another 57:36
Meminisse: forsan et haec ... m. iuvabit 396:98
Memorable: finding ... he was not m. 297:30
Memorial: m. from the Soul's eternity 290:49
some ... that have no m. 62:61
Memories: creditors ... better m. than debtors 259:34
liars ought to have good m. 372:82
liars shd. have good m. 269:74
Memory: dear son of m., ... heir of fame 216:24
everyone complains of his m. 288:15
m. is the diary we ... carry 405:13

Memory (continued)
m. of the just is blessed   45:62
m. ... the beginning of dowdiness 406:32
mixing m. and desire   131:10
no man ... force can abolish m. 289:33
no woman shd. have a m.   406:32
peaceful hours ... how sweet their m. 113:62
pluck from the m. a rooted sorrow 336:72
shorter in wind, as in m. long   70:72
the m. be green   305:37
the M. of great Men   186:58
vibrates in the m.   370:54
Men: a sort of m. whose visages 338:97
a tide in the affairs of m.   326:27
all sorts and conditions of m.   63:81
all things to all m.   57:51
among new m., strange faces   385:53
appointed unto m. once to die   59:97
are you good m. and true?   343:72
ay, in the catalogue ye go for m. 334:48
best m. are dead   285:85
bodies of unburied m.   400:54
boon and a blessing to m.   11:32
busiest m. ... most leisure   257:73
busy hum of m.   214:1
but m. are m. ... sometimes forget 345:99
common wonder of all m.   72:3
daggers in m.'s smiles   334:47
dead m. don't bite   259:56
dead m. naked shall be one   390:17
dead m. rise up never   383:20
dead m. tell no tales   259:57
deal with none but honest m.   276:87
despised and rejected of m.   48:47
destiny with m. for pieces plays 135:78
down among the dead m.   129:78
dumb m. get no lands   261:1
England ... purgatory of m.   136:86
equal rights of m. and women 394:76
Eve upon the first of M.   165:63
even great m. have ... poor relations 119:35
evil that m. do lives after them 325:12
fair women and brave m.   83:59
fifteen m. on ... dead man's chest 379:74
finds too late that m. betray   152:2
for fear of little m.   11:22

Men (continued)
for m. must work   189:87
give place to better m.   115:90
glory of young m. is their strength 45:78
going to dine with some m.   33:16
good will toward m.   54:70
great m. are almost always bad m. 9:1
great m. are not always wise   41:75
great m. ... not commonly ... great scholars   164:51
have m. about me that are fat   324:94
heaven ... leads m. to this hell 363:51
histories make m. wise   26:34
I said ... All m. are liars   43:32
I speak ... French to m.   96:24
I will make you fishers of m.   51:8
idols which beset m.'s minds   27:41
in mean m. we entitle patience 347:32
in most m.'s power to be agreeable 382:10
it is the m. who make a city   272:54
jolly tars are our m.   141:48
let us now praise famous m.   62:59
lives not three good m. unhang'd 314:64
m. alone ... capable of every wickedness   110:27
m. and women merely players 301:90
m. are April when they woo   302:4
m. are but gilded loam   347:30
m. are capable ... of ... benevolence 292:66
m. are children of a larger growth 127:56
m. at some time are masters of their fates   323–4:93
m. below and saints above   295:2
m. ... differ as heaven and earth 385:52
m. fear death as children ... dark 24:86
m. fell out ... knew not why   82:35
m. have died from time to time 302:3
m. in great places are thrice servants 25:1
m. love in haste ... detest at leisure 85:84
m. may bleed and m. may burn 148:43
m. may come and m. may go   384:39
m. may rise on stepping-stones 386:57

Men (*continued*)

m. must endure their going hence 330:98

m. of few words ... best m.   320:48

m. of good quality 399:33

m. prize the thing ungain'd 358:65

m. seldom make passes 243:22

m. that laugh and weep 382:19

m. that sow to reap 382:19

m. that were boys when I was 32:7

m. were deceivers ever 343:68

m. who borrow and m. who lend 191:25

m. will still say ... their finest hour 101:95

m. will wrangle ... write ... fight 108:96

m. with splendid hearts 71:90

m.'s natures are alike 108:2

mocks married m. 332:19

mother and lover of m. 383:25

my object ... to form Christian m. 22:55

new m., strange faces, other minds 385:53

nor yet favour to m. of skill 47:8

nor yet riches to m. of understanding 47:8

not as other m. are 55:89

not in the roll of common m. 314:71

old m. shall dream dreams 50:80

praise makes ... bad m. worse 275:58

praise makes good m. better 275:58

quit yourselves like m. 39:38

reputed one of the wise m. 25:98

rich m. furnished with ability 62:60

rich m. have no faults 276:91

rule of m. entirely great 76:54

schemes o' mice an' m. 80:18

sleek-headed m., and such as sleep 324:94

so are they all, all honourable m. 325:13

so long as m. can breathe 362:34

so many m., so many opinions 389:7

sons of the prophet ... brave m. 18:7

such m. are dangerous 324:94

talk of censorious old m. 94:3

that all m. are created equal 171:26

that all m. everywhere cd. be free 196:78

the breath of worldly ... m. 349:50

the clever m. at Oxford 153:14

the many m., so beautiful 105:55

the most mighty m. ... in his army 49:67

Men (*continued*)

The War between M. and Women 392:45

they make their steel with m. 293:80

thousand creeds ... move m.'s hearts 71:85

to m.'s business, and bosoms 24:84

to put confidence in m. 43:34

truth ... on the lips of dying m. 21:45

two m. look out through the same bars 193:38

we are the hollow m. ... the stuffed m. 130:94

we cannot be free m. if ... slavery 196:75

we petty m. walk under his huge legs 323:93

wealth accumulates and m. decay 150:62

what m. call gallantry 84:66

whatsoever ye wd. that m. shd. do 52:25

wisest m. have erred 222:15

wives are ... old m.'s nurses 24:97

wives are young m.'s mistresses 24:97

women are more like each other than m. 98:62

wonder m. dare trust th'selves with m. 357:60

you are m. of stones 330:4

young m. shall see visions 50:80

Mend: tried to m. the electric light 31:94

Mended: least said, soonest m. 269:66

Mene, mene, tekel, upharsin 49:68

Mens: m. cuiusque is est quisque 102:18

ut sit m. sana in corpore sano 180:71

Mentioned: and m. me to him 91:67

Merchant: m. to secure his treasure 253:51

that same m.'s flesh 340:19

Merchants: like m., venture trade abroad 318:39

Mercies: all thy faithful m. crown 402:72

His m. ay endure 221:10

Merciful as constant 154:22

Mercuries: as English M. 319:40

Mercury: words of M. are harsh 332:21

Mercy: desired m., and not sacrifice 50:75

doing justice ... leaving m. to heaven 134:63

half so good a grace as m. 337:84

have m. upon us ... sinners 63:76

Mercy (*continued*)
his m. is for ever sure 188:78
m. I asked, m. I found 87:16
m. is above this sceptred sway 339:15
m. is nobility's true badge 357:62
'O m.!' to myself I cried 414:24
peace on earth and m. mild 402:71
quality of m. is not strain'd 339:15
render the deeds of m. 339:15
to love m., and to walk humbly 51:91
we do pray for m. 339:15
when m. seasons justice 339:15
Meridian: from that full m. of my glory 322:79
Merit: fondly we think we honour m. 249:3
I like the Garter ... no damned m. 208:25
men of m. are sought after 317:12
m. wins the soul 252:39
Satan exalted sat, by m. raised 217:45
spurns that patient m. ... takes 309:95
Merits: seek his m. to disclose 155:42
Mermaid: a m. on a dolphin's back 341:44
choicer than the M. Tavern 183:14
seen, done at the M. 29:70
Mermaids: I have heard the m. singing 131:4
Merrier: the more the m. 272:70
Merrily: m. hent the stile-a 361:19
m., m., shall I live now 357:56
tripping and skipping ran m. 75:43
Merriment: borrow ... from the m. of May 181:87
source of innocent m. 146:7
Merry: against ill chances men are ... m. 317:22
God rest you m., gentlemen 16:82
It is good to be m. and wise 17:93
m. heart ... cheerful countenance 45:70
m. heart goes all the day 361:19
m. of soul he sailed 379:73
m. village chime 148:34
m. with the fruitful grape 135:75
m. yarn from ... fellow-rover 208:16
never m. when I hear sweet music 340:23
playing of the m. organ 16–17:87
short life and a m. one 277:34
so I piped into m. cheer 68:49
tonight we'll m. be 16:78
Tu-whit, Tu-who – a m. note 332:20

Merrygoround: it's no go the m. 203:54
Merryman: a m. moping mum 148:46
Message: the electric m. came 24:83
Messing: simply m. about in boats 153:13
Met: no sooner m. but they look'd 302:5
Metal: here's m. more attractive 310:7
touch of sweating m. 117:14
Meteor: shone like a m. streaming 217:39
Method: madness, yet there is m. in't 308:78
m. of making a fortune 156:46
Methods: you know my m., Watson 124:20
Methuselah: all the days of M. 35:43
Mew: rather be a kitten and cry m. 314:73
the cat will m. 312:34
Mewling: infant, m. and puking 301:90
Mexique Bay: Echo beyond the M. 206:90
Micawber, Mr 119:39, 40
Mice: best-laid schemes o' m. and men 80:18
cat is away ... m. will play 283:28
three blind m., see how they run! 240:80
Michelangelo: women come and go talking of M. 131:99
Microbe is so very small 32:2
Microscopic: has not man a m. eye? 250:10
Middle: in the m. of the woods ... Yonghy-Bonghy-Bò 194:55
wives are ... companions for m. age 24:97
Midlands: when I am living in the M. 32:5
Midnight: burn the m. oil 257:71
cease upon the m. with no pain 184:29
consum'd the m. oil 142:56
it came upon the m. clear 296:19
not to be abed after m. 359:82
of Cerberus and blackest M. born 213:91
One hour's sleep before m. 267:5
secret, black, and m. hags 335:60
see her on the bridge at m. 18:4
the iron tongue of m. 342:55
time may cease, and m. never come 204:65
we have heard the chimes at m. 317:18

Midsummer: this is very m. madness
360:95

Midwife: she is the fairies' m.   353:92
the m. laid her hand on ... Skull
127:49

Mid-winter: bleak m., long ago 290:43

Mieux: le m. est l'ennemi du bien
397:11

tout est pour le m.   397:7

Might: first in beauty shd. be first in m.
182:1

m. is right   272:57

saddest [words] ... It m. have been
403:90

'tis m. half-slumbering   185:38

Might-have-been: my name is M.
291:51

you won't be sorry for a m.   286:99

Mightier: God ... make thee m. yet
33:13

in word m. than they in arms
219:82

Mightiest: 'tis m. in the m.   339:15

Mighty: a m. man is he   199:6

death ... some have called thee m.
124:10

fear not, said he, for m. dread
384:35

God who made thee m.   33:13

how are the m. fallen!   40:46

I am weak, but thou art m.   407:40

look on my works, ye M., and despair 369:40

mean and m. rotting together 304:27

m. hunter before the Lord   35:51

this m. sum of things   409:65

Truth ... m. above all things   61:37

Mike O'Day: this is the grave of M.
13:50

Milan: retire me to my M.   357:58

Mile: he walked a crooked m.   239:74

miss is as good as a m.   272:61

yr. sad [heart] tires in a m.-a   361:19

Miles: can ye draw but twenty m. a day
205:78

how many m. to Babylon?   233:36

people come m. to see it   146:9

Miles gloriosus   247:63

Military: war ... too serious ... to be
left to m. men   384:34

Milk: crying over spilt m.   259:41

drunk the m. of Paradise   107:76

flowing with m. and honey   36:70

m. comes frozen home in pail   332:20

no finer investment than ... m. in
babies 101:6

too full o' th' m. of human kindness
333:32

Milking: going a-m., sir, she said
241:86

Milkmaid singeth blithe   214:98

Milky way: twinkle on the m.   410:68

Mill: bring grist to the m.   265:49

God's m. grinds slow but sure
265:27

in Gaza at the m. with slaves   221:12

more water glideth by the m.
357–8:63

Millar: I respect M., Sir   174:80

last sheet [*Johnson's Dictionary*] to
M.   174:79

Miller: more water ... than wots ... m.
of 357–8:63

there was a jolly m. once   65:16

Milliner: perfumed like a m.   313:51

Million: a m. m. spermatozoa   169:4

among so many m. of faces   72:3

the play ... pleas'd not the m.   308:85

Millionaire: I am a M. That is my
religion 365:76

Millions: there are m. of us   401:69

Mills: the m. of God grind slowly
198:99

Millstone ... hanged about his neck
53:38

Milton: faith and morals ... M. held
413:5

malt does more than M. can   167:85

M.! thou shdst. be living   413:3

some mute inglorious M.   155:38

Mimsy were the borogoves   91:69

Mince: they dined on m. and ... quince
195:62

Mind: a m. not to be changed   216:35

a m. quite vacant is a m. distressed
113:67

a miserable state of m.   25:13

a prodigious quantity of m.   393:65

among all the diseases of the m.
378:59

better than P. of M.   284:75

blind ... judgment, and misguide the
m.   249:93

born for the Universe, narrowed his
m.   151:78

cheer of m. ... I was wont to have
353:85

clap yr. padlock on her m.   253:50

distressed, in m., body, or estate
63:83

dread had seized their troubled m.
384:35

education forms the common m.
251:22

fair terms and a villain's m.   339:7

farewell the tranquil m.   345:10

Mirror: best m. is an old friend 272:59
  m. of all Christian kings 319:40
Mirth: all m. and no matter 343:66
  bards of passion and of M. 181:83
  far from all resort of m. 213:86
  M., admit me of thy crew 214:96
  M., with thee I mean to live 215:7
  much m. and no madness 373:93
  no country's m. is better than our
    own 178:47
  old earth must borrow its m. 404:91
  present m. hath present laughter
    359:84
  very tragical m. 342:54
Miscarriage: success and m. are empty
    172:43
Mischief: no m. but a woman ... priest
    is at the bottom 273:94
  Satan finds some m. still 399:36
  to draw new m. on 344:93
  to mourn a m. ... past 344:93
Miserable: a m. state of mind 25:13
  me m.! 218:62
  m. have no other medicine 337:89
Miseries: bound in shallows and in m.
    326:27
  hopes, and joys, and panting m.
    183:15
Misery: dwell on guilt and m. 23:71
  fallen ... into m. and endeth
    wrecchedly 97:47
  gave to m. all he had, a tear 155:41
  man ... is full of m. 65:13
  m. acquaints ... with strange bed-
    fellows 356:41
  my m., the wormwood ... gall 49:60
  recall ... happiness when in m. 116:3
Misfortune: the m. of knowing any-
    thing 23:73
  to lose one parent ... a m. 405:10
Misfortunes: children ... make m. more
    bitter 24:95
  m. never come singly 272:60
  m. of our best friends ... not dis-
    pleasing 288:19
  strength to bear the m. of others
    288:14
Misgivings: I view with profound m.
    the retreat 102:7
Mislead: lights that do m. the morn
    337–8:92
Miss: and mine [heart] he cannot m.
    372:83
  m. is as good as a mile 272:61
Missed: how I m. my Clementine!
    225:61
  society offenders ... who never wd.
    be m. 145:99

Mist: the rank m. they draw 215:16
Mistake: any m. about it in any quarter
    101:3
  man is Nature's sole m. 148:37
Mistakes: learn by other men's m.
    283:41
  the man who makes no m. 246:50
Mistress: art is a jealous m. 132:26
  if you can kiss the m. 268:39
  Master M. of my passion 362:35
  m. of herself, though China fall
    251:25
  m. of the Earl of Craven 407:43
  O m. mine 359:83
  select ... a m. or a friend 368:25
Mistresses: wives are young men's
    m. 24:27
Mists: season of m. and ... fruitfulness
    180:78
Misunderstood: to be great is to be m.
    133:37
Misused the King's press 315:82
Mix: I m. them with my brains, sir
    242:97
Moan: is not paid with m. 390:29
Moaning: no m. at the bar 385:44
Moat: as a m. defensive to a house
    348–9:41
Mob: best ... to do what the m. do
    121:63
  m. has ... no brains 272:62
Mobled queen 308:86
Mobs: suppose there are two m.?
    121:63
Mock: green-ey'd monster wh. doth m.
    345:7
  m. on, m. on, Voltaire 67:39
Mock Turtle: said the M. angrily
    91:59
  the M. replied 91:60
Mocked: be not deceived; God is not
    m. 58:70
Mockery: death itself ... a m. 370:47
Model of a modern Major-General
    147:31
Moderately: love m.; long love doth so
    354:10
Moderation: astonished at my own m.
    103:24
  m. is a fatal thing 406:31
Modes: ring in the nobler m. of life
    386:69
Modesty: O m.! 'twas strictly kept
    244:31
  o'erstep not the m. of nature 310:5
  wore enough for m. 76:50
Mohicans: The Last of the M. 110:30
Mole: wilt thou go ask the m. 66:32

Molehill: mountain out of a m. 272:73

Molly Malone 17:89

Mome raths outgrabe 91:69

Moment: all my possessions for a m. of time 132:22

  happy in the m. that was present 176:13

  m. foreseen may be unexpected 132:18

  pleasing attentions ... impulse of the m. 23:78

  snow falls ... a m. white then melts 81:25

  some m. when the moon was blood 98:67

  sonnet is a m.'s monument 290:49

  spur of the m. 278:71

  to every ... nation comes the m. 200:24

Monan's rill: the moon on M. 294:94

Monarch: becomes the ... m. better than his crown 339:15

  I am m. of all I survey 114:77

Monday: hanging ... cat on M. 70:74

  M.'s child is fair of face 235:56

Monde: se mêler à corriger le m. 224:49

Mondes: meilleur des m. possibles 397:7

Money: abundance of m. ruins youth 254:55

  borrer the m. to do it with 399:31

  business ... may bring m. 23:68

  by any means make m. 166:72

  dally not with m. or women 259:50

  did dream of m.-bags to-night 339:9

  fool ... m. are soon parted 263:76

  Government licence to print m. 391:35

  he lends out m. gratis 338:3

  he that wants m., means 302:93

  I have spent all the m. 177:33

  if m. be not thy servant 272:63

  innocently employed ... getting m. 176:8

  lend yr. m. and lose yr. friend 269:70

  love of m. ... root of all evil 59:92

  marrieth for love without m. 271:44

  merit will not serve ... as m. 175:87

  m. begets m. 272:64

  m. gives me pleasure 32:98

  m. is like muck 25:8

  m. makes marriage 272:66

  m. talks 272:69

  no man ... wrote, except for m. 177:21

  no m., no swiss 273:95

Money (*continued*)

  pays yr. m. ... takes yr. choice 284:74

  purse ... full of other men's m. 261:17

  put m. in thy purse 345:96

  putting m. on a horse 32:3

  remember when ... m. not scarce 133:47

  said that love of m. is the root 82:41

  some honey, and plenty of m. 195:60

  that's the way the m. goes 203:60

  the want of m. is so [root of evil] 82:41

  throw good m. after bad 280:37

  thy m. perish with thee 56:16

  your m. or your life 83:51

Mongrels: greyhounds, m., spaniels, curs 334:48

Monk: the devil a m. wd. be 227:74

Monkey: only a m. shaved 148:38

Monotony: bless articulate m. 378:62

  to chase m. 144:85

Monster: great-siz'd m. of ingratitudes 358:71

  green-ey'd m. wh. doth mock 345:7

Montezuma: knows who imprisoned M. 202:42

Month: April is the cruellest m. 131:10

  ark rested in the seventh m. 35:46

  laughter for a m. ... jest for ever 313:58

  this is the m. ... the happy morn 215:19

Months: cd. live for m. without ... labour 399:30

  go right on ... for numerous more m. 399:30

Montreal: in a M. lumber room 82:47

  O God! O M.! 82:47

Montrose: young man of M. 33:12

Monument: a sonnet is a moment's m. 290:49

  an early but enduring m. 367:13

  he replied, 'Like the M.' 174:74

  if you seek my m. 416:49

  Patience on a m. 360:89

  their only m. the asphalt road 131:8

  thou art a m. 179:54

Monumentum: si m. requiris, circumspice 416:49

Mood: albeit unused to the melting m. 346–7:22

  in vacant or in pensive m. 410:71

  sweet m. when pleasant thoughts bring sad 411:83

  that blessed m. 415:32

Moon: a-roving by the light of the m. 86:98

beneath a waning m. was haunted 106:72

beneath the visiting m.   299:66

course of one revolving m.   126:43

cry for the m.   259:39

danced by the light of the m.   195:62

danced the m. on Monan's Rill 294:94

honour from the pale-fac'd m. 313:54

hymns to the cold fruitless m. 341:35

I see the m. ... m. sees me   234:43

late eclipses in the sun and m. 327:52

lustres slake the o'ertaken m.   70:75

make guilty ... the m.   327:53

man in the m.   271:29

man in the m. ... down too soon 235:54

m. in the valley of Ajalon   38:20

m. when she deserts the night   221:14

moving M. went up the sky   105:56

nor the m. [smite thee] by night 44:38

one with ... the west m.   390:17

Queen-M. is on her throne   184:26

rather be a dog and bay the m. 325:24

slowly, silently, now the m.   118:27

sung to the m. by a ... loon   148:45

swear not by the m., th' inconstant m.   354:2

the cow jumped over the m.   232:33

the m. be still as bright   86:97

the m. doth shine as bright as day 231:25

the m. lies fair   20:30

to bark at the m.   255:92

unmasked her beauty to the m. 306:53

with how sad steps, O M.   373:85

Moonlight: ghost along the m. shade 248:72

go visit it by the pale m.   295:1

how sweet the m. sleeps   340:22

I'll come to thee by m.   231:21

ill met by m., proud Titania   341:43

look for me by m.   231:21

passions ... as m. unto sunlight 387:83

Moonlit: knocking on the m. door 118:23

Moons: some nine m. wasted   344:90

Moonshine: look in the almanack; find out m.   342:48

Mops: seven maids with seven m. 92:79

Moral: a m., if only you can find it 91:57

a m., sensible, and well-bred man 112:52

golf ... a form of m. effort   194:52

grandest m. attribute of a Scotsman 28:64

let us be m. ... contemplate existence 120:48

O m. Gower   98:53

point a m. or adorn a tale   174:69

Morality: give ... a lecture on m. ... a shilling   175:87

gossip made tedious by m.   406:20

m. of an action depends   175:84

periodical fits of m.   202:46

up agen middle class m.   366:96

Moralize: faithful loves shall m. 377:40

Morals: foundation of m. and legislation   33:14

no man's religion ... survives his m. 273:93

teach the m. of a whore   174:77

More: and penance m. will do   105:59

easy to take *m.* than nothing   90:55

enough for modesty—no m.   76:50

m. than somewhat   29:58

Oliver Twist has asked for m.   120:55

you get no m. of me   125:34

Morituri te salutant   380:88

Morn: awake, the m. will never rise 117:10

healthy breath of m.   182:96

lights that do mislead the m. 337–8:92

now M., her rosy steps   219:75

sang from m. till night   65:16

the m., in russet mantle clad   305:36

this the happy m.   215:19

Morning: beauty of the m.; silent, bare   412:96

day's at the morn. M.'s at seven 75:44

early one m. ... sun was rising 16:80

glad, confident m.   74:29

great m. of the world   367:11

hour in the m. is worth two   267:2

in his m. face   150:68

in the m. we will remember them 65:20

it's nice to get up in the m.   193:44

Lucifer, son of the m.   48:38

M. in the Bowl of Night   134:65

on a cold and frosty m.   16:86

Morning (*continued*)
peace ... dropping from the veils of the m. 417:53
sees some m., unaware 74:21
Morrow: good night till it be m. 354:6
never shall sun that m. see 333:34
trusting the m. as little as you can 166:74
Mors: pallida M. aequo ... pede 166:73
Morsel: sweetest m. of the night 316:11
Mortal: he raised a m. to the skies 127:54
her last disorder m. 150:74
reminds a man he is m. 117:14
shall m. man be more just than God? 41:66
Mortality: m., behold and fear 29:71
there's nothing serious in m. 334:46
Mortals: not in m. to command success 9:4
what fools these m. be! 342:50
Mortuis: de m. nil nisi bonum 259:54
Moses: meekness of M. ... strength of Samson 272:55
M. said, ... This is the bread 37:80
persuaded to leave M. out 34:21
Moss: a rolling stone gathers no m. 276:1
Most may err as greatly as the few 127:47
Moth: desire of the m. for the star 371:56
Mother: call me early, m. dear 388:89
dead! and ... never called me m. 409:56
disclaim her for a m. 142:64
does your m. know ... you are out? 28:55
England ... m. of parliaments 71:81
foolish son ... heaviness of his m. 45:61
gave her m. forty whacks 15:67
home to his m.'s house 221:9
I arose a m. in Israel 39:21
I feel no pain, dear m. 17:88
let ... his m. drudge ... at seventy 365:80
like m., like daughter 272:71
Mary was that M. mild 10:19
m. of the free, how shall we extol? 33:13
m., who'd give her booby for another 142:57
m. who talks about her own children 122:92
my m. bore me in ... wild 68:51
my m. said that I never shd. 236:57

Mother (*continued*)
never had any m.? 380:84
the m. of all living 35:40
the m. of months in meadow 382:15
took great care of his m. 211:56
variety ... m. of enjoyment 123:99
where a M. laid her Baby 10:19
whether his m. wd. let him or no 232:30
with the m. first begin 259:51
Mother-in-law remembers not 272:72
Mothers: all women become like their m. 406:30
people's m. always bore me 406:30
Moths ... ever caught by glare 83:56
Motion: between the m. and the act 130:95
in his m. like an angel sings 340:22
in our proper m. we ascend 217:47
no m. has she now, no force 414:19
sensible warm m. to become ... clod 337:90
Motive: morality ... depends on the m. 175:84
Motley: a m. fool 301:87
Mould: splashing the wintry m. 417:55
the m. of form 310:1
Mount: yet shall he m. [Milton] 156:45
Mountain: m. out of a molehill 272:73
robes the m. in its azure hue 88:20
tiptoe on the misty m. tops 354:14
up the airy m. 11:22
Mountains: from Greenland's icy m. 159:86
m. skipped like rams 43:29
the m. look on Marathon 84:78
two voices ... one of the m. 412:1
upon the m. of Ararat 35:46
walk upon England's m. green 67:38
Mountebank: a mere anatomy, a m. 303:12
Mourn: don't m. for me never 12:43
in summer skies to m. 181:88
makes countless thousands m. 80:14
secure, and now can never m. 367:16
that man was made to m. 80:13
to m. a mischief ... past 344:93
Mourning: with my m. very handsome 246:44
Mouse: caught a crooked m. 239:74
frightened a little m. under her chair 237:64
killing of a m. on Sunday 70:74
man or m. 271:35
the m. ran up the clock 232:34
the other caught a m. 195:64
Mouse-trap: make a better m. 133:48

Mouth: a close m. catcheth no flies
258:11
  burnt his m. with ... cold plum
  porridge 235:54
  gift horse in the m. 264:5
  heart is in his m. 266:81
  her m. unclosed in ... kiss 193:48
  if you m. it as many ... players do
  310:3
  into the m. of Hell 385:43
  lo, in her m. ... an olive leaf 35:47
  out of thine own m. ... I judge thee
  55:90
  purple-stained m. 184:24
  set a watch ... before my m. 44:51
  spue thee out of my m. 61:23
  tree whose hungry m. is pressed
  188–9:81
  wd. not melt in his m. 257:77
Mouths: blind m. that scarce ... know
  how 215:15
  have m. but ... speak not 43:30
  made m. in a glass 329:74
Moutons: revenons à nos m. 19:16
Move: but it does m. 141:44
  do m. a woman's mind 361:7
  I will m. the earth 20:24
  languid strings do scarcely m. 68:55
  m. him into the sun 243:17
Moved: not m. with concord of sweet
  sounds 340:24
Moves: and having writ, m. on 136:79
  m., and mates, and slays 135:78
  m. in determinate grooves 158:68
Moving: always m. as the restless
  spheres 205:76
  m. Moon went up the sky 105:56
Mower whets his scythe 214:98
Much: missing so m. and so m. 111:34
  m. may be made of a Scotchman
  176:4
  m. of a muchness 395:84
  m. ... said on both sides 9:8
  so m., to learn so little 121:70
Muck: money is like m. 25:8
Mud: two men look out ... one sees
  the m. 193:38
Muddy, ill-seeming, thick, bereft
  355:26
Mudie's: I keep my books at ... M.
  82:42
Muffet: little Miss M. sat on a tuffet
  235:51
Muffin: one caught a m. 195:64
Multiply: be fruitful, and m. 34:29
Multitudes: against revolted m. 219:82
  I contain m. 403:87
  m. in the valley of decision 50:81

Multitudes (*continued*)
  pestilence-stricken m. 369:35
Multitudinous: the m. seas incarnadine
  334:43
Munch on, crunch on 75:41
Murder: foul and most unnatural m.
  307:65
  I met M. on the way 368:30
  m. most foul ... unnatural 307:66
  m. ... one of the Fine Arts 119:30
  m. shrieks out 400:49
  m. will out 97:48, 272:75
  then m.'s out of tune 346:20
Murdered: death of kings ... all m.
  350:54
  two brothers and their m. man 182:5
Murderer: Aram ... thief ... liar ... m.
  87:14
Murmur: creeping m. and the poring
  dark 320:50
  live m. of a summer's day 21:40
Muse: Fool, said my M. to me 373:84
  O for a M. of fire 318:36
  strictly meditate the thankless M.
  215:11
  the M. but served to ease 248:81
Mushroom: nicely groomed, like a m.
  193:27
Mushrooms: broiled fowl and m.—
  capital! 120:60
Music: a reasonable good ear in m.
  342:51
  and let the sounds of m. creep
  340:22
  deep sea ... m. in its roar 84:65
  fled is that m. 184:32
  have m. wherever she goes 237:66
  how sour sweet m. is! 351:63
  if m. be the food of love 358:75
  like m. on my heart 106:61
  linnet, how sweet his m.! 414:26
  man that hath no m. 340:24
  m. and women I ... give way to
  245:43
  m. has charms to soothe 108:5
  m. that gentlier on the spirit lies
  388:85
  m., when soft voices die 370:54
  never merry when I hear sweet m.
  340:23
  O M., sphere-descended Maid
  108:93
  ran ... after the wonderful m. 75:43
  still, sad m. of humanity 415:35
  the m. in my heart I bore 414:22
  the setting sun, and m. at the close
  348:49
  the soul of m. shed 226:62

Music (*continued*)
  thou hast thy m. too 181:81
  thy chosen m., Liberty! 412:1
  to church ... not for the doctrine, but the m. 249:98
  to hear the sea-maid's m. 341:44
  uproar's your only m. 186:53
  when M., heavenly maid, was young 108:91
  women and m. shd. never be dated 151:88
Musical: most m., most melancholy! 213:85
  we are a m. nation 390:26
Musing there an hour alone 84-5:78
Musty: proverb is something m. 310:11
Mutilators: borrowers of books ... m. of collections 192:26
Muttering: the m. grew to a grumbling 75:40
Mutton: Alice—M.; M.—Alice 94:98
Muzzle: shall not m. the ox 38:12
Myriad-minded: our m. Shakespeare 107:80
Myrtles: ye m. brown, with ivy never sere 215:8
Myself: awe of such a thing as I m. 323:91
  best image of m. 219:77
  deliver me from m. 72:6
  I celebrate m., and sing m. 403:82
  I like to go by m. 159:81
  made m. a speculative statesman 9:6
  said I to m.—said I 144:83
  thought of thinking for m. 147:27
  very well then I contradict m. 403:87
  when I give I give m. 403:85
Mysteries: capable of being in uncertainties, m. 186:52
Mysterious: God moves in a m. way 113:63
Mystery: brave its [sea's] dangers comprehend its m. 198:1
  hissed all my m. lectures 377:50
  riddle ... in a m. inside an enigma 100:91
  [sea's] works ... are wrapped in m. 110:26
  take upon's the m. of things 330:99
  the wicked grocer ... m. and a sign 99:76

Nag: forc'd gait of a shuffling n. 314:74
Nail: and Dick the shepherd blows his n. 332:20

Nail (*continued*)
  dead as a door-n. 259:55
  hit the n. on the head 267:88
Nailed: blessed feet which ... years ago were n. 312:43
Nails: nineteen hundred and forty n. 373:90
Naked: both n. ... and were not ashamed 35:35
  dead men n. they shall be one 390:17
  helpless, n., piping loud 67-8:44
  left me n. to mine enemies 323:84
  n. came I out of ... womb 41:65
Nakedness: and not in utter n. 410:77
Name: a deed without a n. 335:61
  a good n. ... rather than great riches 45:79
  a rose by any other n. 353:1
  and she lost her maiden n. 18:3
  conveys it in a borrowed n. 253:51
  dominion ... by a scribbled n. 390:20
  gathered together in thy N. 63:73
  give a dog a bad n. 264:6
  good n. in man and woman 345:6
  good n. is better than precious ointment 46:3
  halloo yr. n. to the reverberate hills 359:80
  hallowed be thy n. 52:18
  he that filches from me my good n. 345:6
  her n. was Barbara Allen 12:36
  I remember yr. n. perfectly 377:52
  I will not blot out his n. 61:22
  I wd. ... my n. were not so terrible 316:2
  it beareth the n. of Vanity Fair 77:60
  lash'd the vice but spared the n. 381:97
  let me not n. it to you, you chaste stars 346:18
  local habitation and a n. 342:53
  must he lose the n. of king? 350:55
  my n. is Legion 54:57
  my n. is Might-Have-Been 291:51
  my 'oss, my wife, and my n. 381:91
  n., at which the world grew pale 174:69
  n. to all succeeding ages curst 126:38
  nature ... a n. for an effect 114:74
  not take the n. of ... God in vain 37:85
  noteless blot on a remembered n. 367:15
  of every friendless n. the friend 172:53

Name (*continued*)
rouse him at the n. of Crispian 320:57
such weak witness of thy n. 216:24
take ... my good n. ... my life 279:95
tell your n. the livelong day 122:81
the gentleman's n. ... Worldly Wiseman 77:59
the grand old n. of gentleman 387:72
the n. of it called Babel 35:52
the n. of the slough was Despond 77:58
the very n. of [stepmother] sufficeth 278:72
the whistling of a n. 250:17
their n. liveth for evermore 62:62
to see one's n. in print 85:89
tranquility! thou better n. 107:78
what's in a n.? 353:1
what the dickens his n. is 340:31
whose n. was writ in water 187:70
write against your n. 287:9
yet leaving here a n. 376:26
Names: call'd him soft n. 184:29
I have lost all the n. 177:33
no n., no pack drill 273:96
sick men play ... with their n. 349:43
such great n. as these 18:6
unpopular n. and impossible loyalties 21:49
Naming: today we have n. of parts 287:3
Naples: see N. and die 277:22
Napoleon: N.'s armies used to march 297:33
N.'s presence ... forty thousand men 401:58
the N. of crime [Moriarty] 125:22
Narr: blebt ein N. sein Lebelang 200:28
Nasty: a nice man ... of n. ideas 382:11
something n. in the woodshed 142:68
Nation: as the clergy ... so ... rest of the n. 23:69
bind up the n.'s wounds 196:81
dedicate this n. to the policy 289:29
every n. has the govt. it deserves 203:58
hinted that we are a n. of amateurs 290:41
inspired the n. It was the n. 102:11
n. of shopkeepers 228:85, 374:98
n. ... perpetually to be conquered 78:72
n. shall not lift up sword agst. n. 48:31

Nation (*continued*)
no n. was ever ruined by trade 138:11
noble and puissant n. rousing herself 224:43
once to every man and n. 200:24
one third of a n. ill-housed 289:30
righteousness exalteth a n. 45:68
that this n. ... shall have a new birth 196:79
we are a musical n. 390:26
Nations: day of small n. ... passed away 95:14
eclipsed the gaiety of n. 178:43
equal rights ... of n., large and small 394:76
happiest n. have no history 130:86
in thy seed shall all the n. ... blessed 36:57
languages are the pedigree of n. 178:39
lasting peace ... with all n. 196–7:81
lightning of the n. 369:34
many n. and three continents 125:24
n. are as a drop of a bucket 48:43
n. which have put mankind ... in their debt 170:13
Privileged ... People ... Two N. 123:98
Native: content to breathe his n. air 251:28
fast by their n. shore 113:64
my n. Land—Good Night 83:58
n. hue of resolution 309:95
though I am n. here 307:59
Natives: the bulk of your n. ... vermin 381:1
Nativity: in n., chance, or death 341:34
Natural: as n. to die as to be born 24:87
I do it more n. 359:85
in him alone, 'twas n. to please 126:37
n., simple, affecting 151:82
Natural Philosophy [makes men] deep 26:34
Natural Selection: called this principle ... N. 117:7
Naturalists: so, n. observe, a flea 382:5
Naturally: if Poetry come not as n. as the Leaves 186:56
not n. honest 362:25
Nature: a friend ... masterpiece of N. 132:29
accuse not N.! 220:88
all n. is but art 250:12

Nature (*continued*)

allow not n. more than n. needs 328:67

are God and N. then at strife? 386:62

as old and new ... as N.'s self 73:17

broken N.'s social union 80:17

creatures that by a rule in n. teach 318:39

cunning'st pattern of excelling n. 346:19

disguise fair n. with ... rage 319:45

first follow N. 249:92

Force of N. cd. no farther go 128:66

fortress built by N. for herself 348:41

great n.'s second course 334:42

his n. is too noble 303:17

human n. is so well disposed 23:67

I have learned to look on n. 415:35

I love not Man the less, but N. more 84:65

in human n. ... more of the fool 25:2

in thy green lap was N.'s darling 156:44

let N. be your teacher 414:27

little we see in N. 412:93

loathed ... life that age ... can lay on n. 337:91

man is N.'s sole mistake 148:37

mute N. mourns her worshipper 295:3

N. always does contrive 144:87

N. and N.'s Laws lay hid 248:88

N. I loved 192:34

n. in you stands on the very verge 328:65

n. is but a name for an effect 114:74

n. is often hidden, sometimes overcome 26:25

n. is the art of God 72:1

n. lends such evil dreams 386:62

N. might stand up and say 326:31

n. ... must be obeyed 27:42

n. never did betray the heart 415:36

n. of a tragic volume 316:96

n., red in tooth and claw 386:63

n.'s law ... man was made to mourn 80:13

n.'s soft nurse 317:13

N. that framed us 205:76

o'erstep not the modesty of n. 310:5

on N., and on human life, musing 409:63

one touch of n. ... whole world kin 358:72

passing through n. to eternity 305:40

Nature (*continued*)

scenery is fine ... human n. is finer 186:57

spectacles of books to read n. 127:59

that N. yet remembers ... fugitive 411:80

the more man's n. runs to 24:89

the n. of an insurrection 324:98

the purpose and n. of miracles 366:3

the rest [hours] on N. fix 104:40

then N. said, 'A lovelier flower' 415:30

to write and read comes by n. 343:73

true wit is n. to advantage dress'd 249:97

unerring N., still divinely bright 249:92

where man is not, n. is barren 69:63

whose body N. is, and God the soul 250:11

woman ... one of N.'s agreeable blunders 112:48

words, like N., half reveal 386:58

yet do I fear thy n. 333:32

youth ... still is N.'s priest 411:78

Natures: men's n. are alike 108:2

Naught: it is n., it is n., saith the buyer 45:77

Naughty: a n. night to swim in 329:80

good deed in a n. world 340:25

n. girl to disobey 236:57

Navy: Ruler of the Queen's N. 147:26, 27

Nazareth: can ... any good thing come out of N.? 55:96

Neaera: tangles of N.'s hair 215:12

Near: call ... while he is n. 48:50

he seems so n. and yet so far 386:66

Nearer, my God, to thee 9:3

Neat: still to be n. ... be drest 179:51

Necessary: is yr. journey really n.? 11:5

Necessities: give us the luxuries ... will dispense with ... n. 227:73

Necessity: by n. ... we all quote 133:40

make a virtue of n. 282:96

n. hath no law 272:77

n. ... is the argument of tyrants 246:56

n. is the mother of invention 272:78

no virtue like n. 348:36

sworn brother ... to grim N. 351:60

teach thy n. to reason thus 348:36

thy n. is greater than mine 373:88

Neck: a n. God made for other use 167:80

Neck (*continued*)
England will have her n. wrung 101:1
my n. is very short   226:67
n. or nothing   272:79
some chicken! Some n.!   101:1
Need: all we n. of hell   122:82
friend in n. is a friend indeed   263:92
in thy most n. ... by thy side   14:58
n. to pray for fair weather   25:7
O, reason not the n.   328:67
Needle: man for the sword and for the n. she   389:2
plying her n. and thread   166:64
through the eye of a n.   53:41
Needlessly sets foot upon a worm   114:75
Needs: all this sad world n.   404:93
more than nature n.   328:67
to each according to his n.   207:6
Negative Capability   186:52
Negatives: two n. make an affirmative   281:79
Neglect: n. the creeping hours   301:89
such sweet n. more taketh me   179:52
Negligent: celerity ... admir'd than by the n.   299:59
Neiges: où sont les n. d'antan?   396:95
Neighbour: false witness against thy n.   37:91
lov'd his wicked n. as himself   126:46
love thy n. as thyself   37:99
policy of a good n.   289:29
thy n.'s wife ... manservant ... ox ... ass   37:92
worketh no ill to his n.   57:43
Neighbours: good fences make good n.   139:26
in peace ... as good n.   394:76
live without friends ... not without ... n.   270:95
Nelly: let not poor N. starve   96:22
Neptune: do choose the ebbing N.   357:54
envious siege of wat'ry N.   349:42
he wd. not flatter N.   303:17
will all great N.'s ocean wash this blood?   334:43
Nerissa, my little body is aweary   338:1
Nerves: when ... the n. prick   386:60
Nervous: Bradshaw—n. and terse but limited   125:28
Nest: to find a mare's n.   271:39
Nests: birds in their little n. agree   399:37
birds in their ... n. agree with Chinamen   32:99
built their n. in my beard   195:66

Nettle: out of this n., danger   313:60
Never: and ... n. called me mother   409:56
better late than n.   256:25
books n. die   289:33
dead men rise up n.   383:20
don't mourn for me n.   12:43
I n. shall love the snow again   70:77
limericks n. wd. scan   13:54
love that n. told can be   67:40
me and my true love will n. meet   18:2
my apple trees will n.   139:26
n. a spray of yew   21:37
n. begin than n. make an end   256:27
n. broke the Sabbath, but for gain   126:45
n. glad confident morning again   74:29
n., I ween, was a prouder   28:53
n. lov'd ... met ... parted   79:97
n., n., n., n., n.   331:6
n., n. thinks of me   19:10
n. seek to tell thy love   67:40
n. send to know for whom the bell   124:14
n. the time and the place   74:31
n. the twain shall meet   189:92
n. to have lost at all   83:50
n. to have loved at all   386:59
n. turned his back ... n. doubted   73:16
seldom or n. the two hit it off   409:59
This England n. did nor n. shall   327:47
what, n.? No, n.!   147:22
who n. made a foe   385:51
Nevermore: quoth the Raven, N.   247:67
New: a n. broom sweeps clean   273:91
a n. commandment I give   56:8
a n. heaven and a n. earth   61:32
a n. master—get a n. man   356:44
among n. men, strange faces   385:53
as old and n. ... as Nature's self   73:17
before you are on with the n.   17:93
called the N. World into existence   88:26
[compassions] are n. every morning   49:61
conservatism? ... is ... against the n.   196:77
how strange it seems, and n.!   74:30
n. king ... knew not Joseph   36:67
n. man ... raised up in him   64:94
n. nobility ... act of power   25:6

New (continued)
- n. philosophy calls all in doubt 123:3
- n. wine into old bottles 54:73
- no n. thing under the sun 46:96
- old lamps for n. 20:22
- old order ... yielding place to n. 385:54
- piping songs for ever n. 183:19
- ring in the n. 386:68
- sing unto him a n. song 42:98
- will not apply n. remedies 26:17

New Way to Pay Old Debts 208:19

Newcastle: coals to N. 257:85

Newcomer: O, blithe N.!...415:37

New-fangled: May's n. shows 331:11
- their garments, though n. ill 363:41

News: all the n. that's fit to print 242:95
- first bringer of unwelcome n. 316:97
- for there is good n. yet to hear 99:74
- good n. from a far country 45:82
- he that tells his wife n. 279:17
- ill n. comes too soon 267:14
- man bites a dog, that is n. 116:1
- master-passion ... love of n. 114:81
- nature of bad n. infects 298:51
- never good to bring bad n. 299:56
- no n. is good n. 273:97
- nowadays truth ... greatest n. 273:14
- talk of court n. 330:99

Newspapers: n. always excite curiosity 192:31
- successful n. are ceaselessly querulous 208:28

Newton: another N., a new Donne 169:4
- God said, Let N. be! 248:88

Nice: a n. man ... of nasty ideas 382:11
- n. to get up in the mornin' 193:44
- sugar and spice and all that's n. 240:85
- too n. for a statesman 151:79

Nicely: n.-calculated less or more 409:60
- sick men play so n. with their names 349:43

Nickname: a n. is the heaviest stone 159:84

Nigh: the Lord is n. 42:1

Night: a braw, bricht, moonlicht n. 193:42
- a casement ope at n. 185:33
- a naughty n. to swim in 329:80
- afraid for the terror by n. 43:20
- all n. long ... on sentry-go 144:85

Night (continued)
- and darkness N. he named 220:84
- a-roving so late into the n. 86:97
- as a watch in the n. 43:16
- beneath the kisses of n. 370:46
- calmest and most stillest n. 317:14
- come, civil n. 354:13
- come, thick n. 333:33
- desire ... of the n. for the morrow 371:56
- dog in the n.-time 125:23
- done by n. appears by day 260:85
- doom'd ... to walk the n. 307:63
- Friday n. is Amami n. 11:27
- from morn to n., my friend 290:46
- gentle into that good n. 390:18
- gwine to run all n. ... all day 137:1
- honey'd middle of the n. 181:90
- I ask of thee, beloved N. 369:33
- I read much of the n. 131:11
- in the Bowl of N. 134:65
- in the forests of the n. 68:46
- it [candle] will not last the n. 210:45
- labour n. and day to be a pilgrim 77:65
- let's have one other gaudy n. 299:61
- like the n. of cloudless climes 86:96
- moonless n. in the small town 390:23
- my delight on a shining n. 18:98
- ne'er saw true beauty till this n. 353:95
- n. cometh, when no man can work 55:5
- n. is drawing nigh 28:56
- n. is long that never finds the day 335:67
- n. makes no difference 162:21
- n. neddying among the snuggeries 390:24
- n.'s candles are burnt out 354:14
- n. unto n. sheweth knowledge 41:87
- odd ... it was the middle of the n. 92:76
- out of the n. that covers me 160:93
- pass'd a miserable n. 351:71
- perils and dangers of this n. 63:75
- poor souls who dwell in N. 66:31
- reign of Chaos and old N. 217:40
- remain together ... it will be good n. 368:27
- returned home the previous n. 76:52
- shades of n. were falling fast 197:93
- she hangs upon the cheek of n. 353:94
- ships that pass in the n. 198:4
- silver-sweet ... lovers' tongues by n. 354:5

Night (*continued*)
  sing ... even in the dead of n. 359:80
  singing, startle the dull n. 214:97
  soft stillness and the n. 340:22
  sound of revelry by n. 83:59
  Spirit of N.! 368:32
  stood that n. against my fire 330:95
  sweetest morsel of the n. 316:11
  tender is the n. 184:26
  the bird of n. did sit 324:97
  the black bat, n. 388:86
  the n. has a thousand eyes 69:70
  the n. is dark ... far from home 230:16
  the n. was made for loving 86:98
  the n. we went to Birmingham 99:73
  the shadow of our n. 367:16
  there's n. and day, brother 69:65
  things that go bump in the n. 14:60
  things that love n. 329:75
  this is the n. that ... makes me or fordoes 346:17
  this will last out a n. in Russia 337:83
  to many a watchful n.! 317:27
  upon a tranced summer-n. 182:98
  voice I hear this passing n. 184:30
  watch that ends the n. 399:39
  watchman, what of the n.? 48:39
  weeping may endure for a n. 42:95
  what hath n. to do with sleep? 212:74
  when n. darkens the streets 217:38
  wide womb of uncreated N. 217:49
  witching time of n. 310:13
  wd. not spend another such a n. 351–2:71
Nightingale: spoils the singing of the n. 181:88
Nightmare: the n. Life-in-Death was she 105:52
Nights: Chequer-Board of N. and Days 135:78
  days of danger, n. of waking 295:97
  Nile: allegory on the banks of the N. 372:72
  my serpent of old N.? 298:52
  pour the waters of the N. 89–90:45
Nimble: words that have been so n. 29:70
Nimrod: even as N. the mighty hunter 35:51
Nine: a cat has n. lives 257:90
  a cat has only n. lives 394:70
  how many beans make n. 268:47
  n. bean rows will I have 417:52
  stitch in time saves n. 278:81

Nineveh: shd. not I spare N.? 50:88
Nip: I'll n. him in the bud 288:13
No: some said ... print it ... others ... N. 76:56
Noah: and N. he often said to his wife 99:77
  but one poor N. 169:4
  unto N. into the ark 35:45
Nobility: leave us still our old n. 292:68
  mercy is n.'s true badge 357:62
  new n. ... ancient n. 25:6
  n. imposes its own obligations 196:70
Noble: do n. things, not dream 189:86
  how n. in reason! 308:81
  man is a n. animal 72:7
  never enjoys h'self except for a n. purpose 161:9
  n. army of Martyrs 63:69
  n. Living and the n. dead 413:10
Nobleman: celebrated, cultivated ... n. 143:70
  live cleanly as a n. shd. 315:95
Nobler: n. in the mind to suffer 309:95
  n. than attending for a check 304:23
Noblesse oblige 196:70
Noblest: n. Roman of them all 326:30
  ruins of the n. man 324:8
  the two n. of things 381:95
Nobly: both parties n. are subdu'd 317:23
  n., n., Cape Saint Vincent 74:24
Nobody: don't think n. never made me 380:85
  I care for n., not I 65:17
  n. asked you, sir, she said 241:87
  n. feels for my poor nerves 23:79
  n. gets old ... godly ... crafty 417:54
  n. is on my side 23:79
  nothing happens, n. comes 30:74
Nod: Old N. the shepherd goes 118:25
Nodding by the fire, take down this book 417:58
Nods: N. and Becks and ... Smiles 214:93
  shame when the worthy Homer n. 166:71
Nohow: looked at for nothing. N.! 92:73
Noise: a loud n. at one end 191:21
  an incessant n. like ... water-mill 381:98
  dreadful n. of waters 352:72
  Fifth Symphony ... most sublime n. 137:97

Noise (*continued*)
 never valued till they make a n.
 114:82
Noises: like n. in a swound 105:46
 this isle is full of n. 356:47
Noll: for shortness called N. 141:49
No-More, Too-Late, Farewell 291:51
Nonconformist: whoso wd. be a man
 must be a n. 133:36
None: n. of us liveth to himself 57:44
 n. that ... trust in him shall be overcome 63:63
 so the poor dog had n. 236:59
 some believe they've n. at all 82:40
 then n. was for a party 201:38
 this little pig had n. 239:78
Nonsense: sounds like n., my dear
 296:16
 through ... realms of N. absolute
 128:68
Noon: dark, amid the blaze of n.
 221:13
 far from the fiery n. 182:96
 from morn to n. he fell 217:44
 sun has not attained his n. 162:18
Noon-day, upon the market-place
 324:97
Noose: in a N. of Light 134:65
 naked to the hangman's n. 167:80
Normal, yes, thank God, we're n.
 242:7
Norman: simple faith than N. blood
 387:74
North-north-west: am but mad n.
 308:83
Nor(o)way: to N., N. ... o'er the faem
 12:38
Norwich: asked his way to N. 235:54
Nose: custom ... hateful to the n.
 170:19
 cut off one's n. to spite one's face
 259:46
 Dong with a luminous N. 194:56
 ever and anon he gave his n. 313:51
 had Cleopatra's n. been shorter
 244:27
 led by the n. with gold 362:27
 Marian's n. looks red and raw
 332:20
 n. was as sharp as a pen 319:44
 one's n. to the grindstone 273:4
 pay through the n. 33:12, 274:32
 ring at the end of his n. 195:61
 snapped off her n. 238:70
 to turn up one's n. 281:70
 wipe a bloody n. 142:58
Noses: athwart men's n. as they lie
 asleep 353:92

Noses (*continued*)
 n., ... but they smell not 43:31
 nothing pay for wearing our own n.
 304:21
Note: as the gen'l'm'n said to the fi'
 pun' n. 121:69
 his merry n. unto ... bird's throat
 300:83
 not a funeral n. 408:52
 when found, make a n. 120:46
Notes: I heard a thousand blended n.
 411:83
 the sound is forced, the n. are few
 68:55
Nothing: book although there's n. in't
 85:89
 certain of n. but ... holiness 186:50
 civility costs n. 258:7
 days ... when ... n. goes wrong
 148:40
 devil, having n. else to do 31:96
 did n. in particular 144:90
 do n. for ever and ever 12:43
 doing n. for a bribe 304:23
 doings without charity are n. worth
 64:87
 easy to take *more* than n. 90:55
 everything by starts and n. long
 126:43
 gives to airy n. ... habitation 342:53
 he n. common did or mean 207:3
 he that knows n., doubts n. 268:49
 I am n. if not critical 345:97
 I do n. upon myself 124:12
 is it n. to ... ye that pass by? 49:59
 know this only, that he n. knew
 221:7
 learnt n., and forgotten n. 384:31
 let n. you dismay 16:82
 looked at for n. Nohow! 92:73
 mind's cluttered up with n. 401:68
 neck or n. 272:79
 n. a year, paid quarterly 381:93
 n – absolutely n. – half so much
 worth doing 153:13
 n. begins and n. ends 390:29
 n. beside remains. Round the decay
 369:40
 n. can bring you peace 133:38
 n. destroyeth authority so much
 25:14
 n. except a battle lost 401:57
 n. for n. 273:6
 n. for n. 'ere 285:80
 n. great ... without enthusiasm
 132:28
 n. happens, nobody comes 30:74
 n. in excess 19:17

Nothing (*continued*)
- n. in his life became him   333:30
- n. is certain but death and taxes 139:16
- n. is certain but uncertainty   273:7
- n. is had for n.   103:25
- n. is ours but time   273:8
- n. of him that doth fade   355:35
- n. of itself will come   409:65
- n. pay for wearing our own noses 304:21
- n. seek, n. find   273:10
- n. so absurd but some philosopher has said it   102:14
- n. so sharply reminds   117:14
- n.'s truer than them [taxes]   120:43
- n. succeeds like excess   406:31
- n. succeeds like success   273:11
- n. to declare except my genius 406:33
- n. to do but work   189:83
- n. to eat but food   189:83
- n. to look backward [forward] to 139:23
- n. to say—say n.   108:97
- n. to wear but clothes   189:83
- n. venture, n. win   273:13
- n. ... violent is permanent   273:12
- n. went unrewarded but Desert 126:44
- n. whatever to grumble at   148:40
- n. will come of n.   327:49
- questioneth n., n. learneth   273:9
- sea ... n. but to make him sick 123:8
- smattering of everything ... knowledge of n.   121:78
- sound and fury signifying n.   336:76
- speak ... as I am; n. extenuate 346:22
- think n. done while aught remains 288:24
- 'tis something, n.   345:6
- we brought n. into this world   59:91
- yeomanry ... with whom ... n. to do 23:64

Nothingness: love and fame to n. 186:49
- will never pass into n.   181:85

Notice ... you have been pleased to take   174:78

Notorious: open and n. evil liver 64:95

Nought: knows n. that knows not this 358:65

Noun: talk of a n. and a verb   321:68

Nourished: how begot, how n.   339:14

Novel: I've read in many a n.   87:13

Novel (*continued*)
- only obligation to which ... we may hold a n.   170:23
- when I want to read a n.   123:2

Novels: catalogue ... more entertaining than ... n.   208:22
- how much wd. n. gain   85:87

November's sky ... November's leaf 295:8

Novice: young, a N. in the Trade 128:70

Now: in England – n.!   74:21

Nowhere: and n. did abide   105:56
- one really lives n.   79:92

Nude: keep one from going n.   189:83

Nuisances who write for autographs 145:99

Number: count the n. of the beast 61:30
- greatest happiness of the greatest n. 33:14
- so teach us to n. our days   43:18

Numbers: achiever brings home full n. 342:56
- divinity in odd n.   341:34
- I lisp'd in n., for the n. came   248:80
- perhaps the plaintive n. flow   414:21
- tell me not, in mournful n.   198:95

Numbness: drowsy n. pains my sense 184:23

Nun: holy time is quiet as a n.   412:92

Nuncheon: crunch on, take your n. 75:41

Nunnery: get thee to a n.   310:97
- n. of thy chaste breast   199:16

Nuns fret not at ... narrow cell   411:89

Nuptials: prone to any iteration of n. 109:19

Nurse: baby ... that sucks the n. asleep 300:71
- nature's soft n.   317:13
- this n., this teeming womb of ... kings   348–9:41

Nurseries: in the n. of Heaven   391:32
- n. of all vice and immorality   134:62

Nurses: wives are ... old men's n. 24:97

Nursing the unconquerable hope 21:43

Nursling: I am ... the n. of the Sky 368:23

Nurslings of immortality   369:43

Nut: hard n. to crack   266:69
- I had a little n. tree   233:39

Nutmeg: silver n. and a golden pear 233:39

Nuts: Brazil, where the n. come from 389:16

Nuts (*continued*)
gathering n. in May 16:86
may be n. for Mary Ann 13:48
Nymph: haste thee, N. 214:93
mountain-n., sweet Liberty 214:95

O: cram within this wooden O 318:37
Oak: bend a knotted o. 108:5
grave where English o. and holly
158:72
hearts of o. are our ships 141:48
Oaks: tall o., branch-charmed 182:98
Oars: the o. were silver 298:54
with falling o. ... kept the time
206:91
Oath: a good mouth-filling o. 314:76
Oaths: full of strange o. 301:90
o. are but words 82:37
Oats: o. ... in England ... given to
horses 172:48
sow one's wild o. 283:32
Obedience: as honour, love, o. 336:71
o. is ... seen in little things 273:15
resistance to tyrants is o. to God
171:31
Obey: safer to o. than to rule 188:73
to love, cherish, and to o. 64:8
woman to o. 389:2
Object: my o. all sublime 146:6
only legitimate o. of government
171:30
'tis for o. strange and high 206:97
Obligation: only o. to which ... we may
hold a novel 170:23
Obligations: nobility imposes its own
o. 196:70
respect for the o. arising from treaties
394:76
Oblivion: put alms for o. 358:71
second childishness and mere o.
301–2:90
the rest ... commend to cold o.
368:25
Oblivious: some sweet o. antidote
336:72
Obsequies: Nature ... celebrates his o.
295:3
Observance: more honour'd in the
breach than the o. 307:59
with this special o. 310:5
Observation: let o. with extensive view
173:67
Observations which ourselves we make
251:21
Observed: the o. of all observers
310:1
Obstruction: to lie in cold o. and to rot
337:90

Occasion: courage mounteth with o.
326:34
Occasions: all o. do inform against me
311:22
there is o. and causes 321:60
Occupation: absence of o. is not rest
113:67
line of o. in the central sector 102:7
Occupations: worse o. in the world
379:67
Occupied: how my parents were o. and
all 292:71
Ocean: a life on the o. wave 293:81
dark unfathom'd caves of o. 155:37
great Neptune's o. wash this blood
334:43
in the o.'s bosom unespied 206:89
make the mighty o. 89:41
on the o. of life we pass 198:4
painted ship upon a painted o.
105:49
pores of the o. and shores 368:23
we sail the o. blue 146:19
Odd: creators of o. volumes 192:26
divinity in o. numbers 341:34
o. because ... middle of the night
92:76
scarcely o. because they'd eaten
every one 93:82
think it exceedingly o. 191:20
Odds: die better than facing fearful o.
201:36
the o. is gone 299:66
Odi et amo. Quare ... nescio 94:5
Odium: the o. of having discovered
sodium 33:18
Odorous: comparisons are o. 343:77
Odour: in the o. of sanctity died 28:54
stealing and giving o. 358–9:75
Odours, when sweet violets sicken
370:54
O'erpeer: for truth to o. 303:15
Off: o. with his head! 91:56
o. with the old love 17:93
only that when ... o. [stage] he was
acting 151:82
Offence: beauty ... after o. returning
222:24
dire o. from am'rous causes springs
251:33
my o. is rank 311:15
Offend: if thine eye o. thee 53:39
o. one of these little ones 53:38
Offended: for him have I o. 325:11
Offender: Clinker ... a most notorious
o. 375:14
Offenders: little list of Society o.
145:99

Offenders (*continued*)
the more laws, the more o. 269:59
Offer: never refuse a good o. 273:86
nothing to o. but blood, toil, tears
100:92
Office: hath but a losing o. 316:97
heresy ... that ... o. sanctifies 9:1
o. and affairs of love 342:62
o. and custom, in all line 358:66
the insolence of o. 309:95
Office boy: as o. to an Attorney's firm
147:26
Officers: a King, and o. of sorts 318:39
Official: what is o. is incontestable
140:33
Officious, innocent, sincere 172:53
Officiously to keep alive 103:29
Offspring: o. of Heaven first-born!
218:58
true source of human o. 219:71
Oft: many a time and o. 338:5
o., when on my couch I lie 410:71
Oil: lingering, with boiling o. 146:10
o'er books consumed the midnight o.
142:56
pour o. upon the waters 273:16
Ointment: good name ... better than
precious o. 46:3
Old: a liking o. for thee 87:15
adherence to the o. and tried 196:77
all things worn out and o. 417:55
an o. abusing of ... patience 340:29
an o. man in a dry month 130:92
an o. man in a hurry 100:86
an o. maxim in the schools 381:96
as o. and new ... as Nature's self
73:17
call for his o. shoes 296:21
grow o. along with me 75:46
grow o. with a good grace 378:60
half as o. as time 77:70
I grow o. ... I grow o. 131:3
I love everything that's o. 151:83
if I ever grow to be o. 32:6
man ... as o. as he's feeling
107:86
never too o. to learn 273:89
new book is published, read an o.
one 288:23
o. age shd. burn 390:18
o. and godly and grave 417:54
o. as he feels ... o. as she looks
271:32
o. as the hills 273:17
o. books, o. wine 151:83
o. friends and o. wine are best
273:18
o. friends are best 296:21

Old (*continued*)
o. friends, o. times, o. manners
151:83
o. head on young shoulders 274:19
o. lamps for new 20:22
o. men forget 320:58
o. poacher ... good game-keeper
274:20
o. soldiers ... only fade away 18:99
o. soldiers, sweethearts ... lovers
400:52
o., unhappy, far-off things 414:21
o. wine ... o. pippins ... o. wood
400:52
one of them is fat and grows o.
314:64
ring out the o. 386:68
so o., and so profane 318:34
summits o. in story 388:97
tell me the o., o. story 157:61
the grand o. name of gentleman
387:72
the mighty minds of o. 376:25
the o. gang 100:85
the o. order changeth 385:54
the thousand wars of o. 386:70
they shall grow not o. 65:20
they think he is growing o. 170:15
when thou art o. ... grief enough
156:48
when you are o. and grey 417:58
woman as o. as she looks 107:86
young in years ... o. in hours 26:26
Old Bailey: say the bells of O. 236:61
Old Kent Road: knock'd 'em in the O.
99:79
Old Testament: prosperity is the blessing of the O. 24:90
Olive-leaf: an o. he brings, pacific sign
221:1
in her mouth was an o. 35:47
Oliver Twist has asked for more
120:55
Olivia: air cry out 'O.!' 359:80
Olympiades: l'important dans ces o.
111:36
Olympic Games: important thing in
the O. is 111:36
Omnia vincit amor ... cedamus 397:3
On: before you are o. with the new
17:93
o. o., you noblest English 319:46
o., Stanley, o.! 296:15
Once: children ... call yet o. 20:33
One: all for o., and o. for all
129:74
animals went in o. by o. 15:73
but the O. was Me 169:4

One (*continued*)

clock struck o., the mouse ran down 232–3:34

dead men ... shall be o.   390:17

he replied, O.'s absurd   224–5:52

how to be o. up   252:44

Liberty and Union ... o. and inseparable   400:44

o. for the master ... o. for the dame 231:23

o. God, o. law, o. element   387:73

o. ... is rather coarse   15:64

o. more river to cross   15:73

o. thing ... worse than being talked about   406:23

O., two, buckle my shoe   236:60

o. to watch and o. to pray   10:13

the O. remains, the many change 367:19

to lose o. parent   405:10

true it is she had o. failing   80:12

two hearts that beat as o.   200:18

One-and-twenty: long expected, o. ... is flown   173:57

when I was o.   167:81

Oneself: to love o. ... lifelong romance 404:3

Only: not by eastern windows o. 104:34

o. thing that I ever did wrong 17:95

Onward: a little o. lend thy ... hand 221:11

O. Christian soldiers   28:57

O., the sailors cry   69:69

Open: o. and notorious evil liver   64:93

o. not thine heart   62:49

o. Sesame!   20:23

Ophir: quinquireme ... from distant O. 207:12

Opinion: error of o. may be tolerated 171:28

never in touch with public o.   406:28

no o. of God at all   25:11

of his own o. still   82:39

think the last o. right   249:2

Opinions: halt ye between two o. 40:56

proper o. for the time of year   22:62

so many men, so many o.   389:7

stiff in o., ... in the wrong   126:43

Opium: religion ... is the o. of the people   207:7

Opportunity makes the thief   274:23

Opposed: bear't that th' o. may beware 306:56

Opposing: sea of troubles and by o., end them   309:95

Opposition: conjunction of the mind and o. of the stars   206:98

Oppression: lack gall to make o. bitter 309:92

Oppressor: who wd. bear ... th' o.'s wrong?   309:95

Oracle: I am Sir O.   338:98

Orange: ruled by an O.   297:32

Oranges and lemons   236:61

Orator: beauty ... doth ... persuade ... without an o.   364:60

Orb: monthly changes in her circled o. 354:2

smallest o. which thou behold'st 340:22

Orchard: chaffinch sings on the o. bough   74:21

Order: good o. is the foundation   78:81

in all line of o.   358:66

o. ... this matter better in France 378:64

stand not upon the o. of your going 335:56

the old o. changeth   385:54

to o. myself ... reverently   64:97

words in the (their) best o.   107:82

Ordered: God ... o. their estate   10:18

Ore: load ... yr. subject with o. 187:69

Organ: O. Morgan ... o. o. all the time 390:27

playing of the merry o.   16–17:87

Organism to live beyond its income 82:45

Organized: no mind is thoroughly well o.   107:83

Organs: hath not a Jew hands, o.? 339:13

Orgies are vile   228:90

Origin: dancing? Oh, dreadful! ... of savage o.   79:91

indelible stamp of his lowly o.   117:6

Original: a thought is often o.   164:49

their great O. proclaim   9:9

Originality: all good things ... are the fruits of o.   209:42

Originator: next to the o. of a good sentence   133:39

Orlando: run, run O.   302:92

Ormus: wealth of O. and of Ind   217:45

Ornament: rhyme being no ... true o. 216:26

Ornavit: nullum quod tetigit non o. 178:38

Orpheus with his lute   322:77

Oscar: you will, O., you will   402:76

Ostrich: America cannot be an o. 408:46

Other: after the first death ... no o.
390:22

bunch of o. men's flowers 225:57
or any o. reason why 10:16
o. times, o. manners 254:83
since then I have used no o.
285:84

Others: a corner ... for o.' uses 345:8
be not false to o. 25:16
best and distinguished above o.
165:55
England ... wont to conquer o.
349:42
fly to o. that we know not of 309:95
misfortunes and pains of o. 78:88
o. abide our question 21:44
pleased ourselves, we ... please o.
274:45
some ... are more equal than o.
242:98
to encourage the o. 397:8

Otherwise: some ... wise, and some ...
o. 278:53, 375:15

Ounce: an o. of discretion 274:24

Ours: little we see in nature that is o.
412:93

Ourselves: fault ... not in our stars,
but in o. 323–4:93
praise o. in other men 249:3

Out: include me o. 152:6
mordre wol o. 97:48
murder will o. 272:75
O., damned spot! o., I say! 335:68
o. of sight, o. of mind 274:25
o., o., brief candle! 336:76
o., o., hyaena! 222:19
who's in, who's o. 330:99

Outgrabe: mome raths o. 91:69

Outlive: desire shd. so ... o. performance? 316:10

Outrun: we may o. by violent swiftness
322:74

Outside: I am just going o. 241:93

Outsoared: he has o. the shadow of our
night 367:16

Outward: hope from o. forms to win
106:69
o. and visible sign 64:1

Oven: in the o. for baby and me
237:62

Over: now the day is o. 28:56
'O. the hills and far away' 240:82
until it doth run o. 16:78

Over much: be not righteous o. 47:6

Over-canopied with luscious woodbine
341:46

Overcast: since first our sky was o.
114:76

Overcoat: only argument ... put on yr.
o. 200:27

Overcome: nature ... sometimes o.
26:25
o. evil with good 57:41
to o. pleasure ... greatest pleasure
274:47
what is else not to be o.? 216:30

Overcomes: who o. by force 217:43

O(v)erjoyed was he to find 113:56

Overpaid: high official ... grossly o.
161:8

Overset the brain, or break the heart
411:88

Overthrow: those ... thou thinkest thou
dost o. 124:10

Overwhelm myself in poesy 185:36

Overwhelmed all her litter but one
316:98

Owed: so much o. by so many to so
few 101:96

Owes: he o. not any man 199:7
o. its pleasure to another's pain
114:72

Owl: moping o. does to the moon
complain 155:32
nightly sings the staring o. 332:20
old o. lived in an oak 285:82
o., for all his feathers, was a-cold
181:89
the O. and the Pussy-Cat 195:60

Owls: I couch when o. do fly 357:56
two O. and a Hen 195:66

Own: came unto his o. and his o.
received him not 55:94
every country but his o. 145:1
our watches ... each believes his o.
249:91
room of one's o. 409:58
we mean to hold our o. 101:3

Owner: the o. whereof was Giant
Despair 77:62
the ox knoweth his o. 48:29

Ox: a stalled o. and hatred 45:71
nor his o., nor his ass 37:92
o. knoweth his owner 48:29
thou shalt not muzzle the o. 38:12

Oxenford: a Clerk ther was of O.
96:31

Oxford: ahead ... either O. or Cambridge 375:19
the clever men at O. 153:14
the king to O. sent a troop 72:8
to ... O. I acknowledge no obligation
142:64
to O. sent a troop of horse 393:54

Oxlips and the nodding violet
341:46

Oyster: an o. may be crossed in love
371:64
the world's mine o. 340:30
Oysters: 'O, O.,' said the Carpenter
93:82
poverty and o. 121:68
Ozymandias, king of kings 369:40

P's and Q's: to mind one's P. 274:26
Pace: creeps in this petty p. 336:76
Paced: bride hath p. into the hall
104:45
Pacem: qui desiderat p. 396:88
Paces about her room ... alone 131:12
Pacific: he stared at the P. 185:41
Pack: can p. the cards 25:15
Paddington: as London is to P. 88:28
Paddle: every man p. his own canoe
206:88
Padlock: clap yr. p. on her mind
253:50
wedlock is a p. 282:19
Pagan suckled in a creed outworn
412:94
Pagans: to chase these p. in those holy
fields 312:43
Page: on a beautiful quarto p. 372:74
Pageant: this insubstantial p. faded
356-7:50
Paid: at cards for kisses – Cupid p.
201:29
p. at the Greek Kalends 86:5
two I am sure I have p. 314:65
well p. that is well satisfied 340:21
Pail: to fetch a p. of water 234:44
Pain: a stranger yet to p. 154:27
although p. isn't real 13:51
cease upon the midnight with no p.
184:29
hour of p. ... long as a day 267:3
I feel no p., dear mother 17:88
I love to give p. 109:12
laughter with some p. is fraught
370:50
long grief and p. 388:88
neither shall there be any more p.
61:34
not because it gave p. to the bear
202:47
not in pleasure, but in rest from p.
128:64
one who never inflicts p. 230:15
owes its pleasure to another's p.
114:72
p. clings cruelly to us 181:86
sweet is pleasure after p. 127:53
we are born in others' p. 390:29
what p. it was to drown! 352:72

Pain (*continued*)
when p. and anguish wring the brow
296:14
who wd. lose, though full of p., this
... being 217:49
with p. purchas'd, doth inherit p.
331:9
Painful: no p. inch to gain 103:33
one ... as p. as the other 24:87
Pains: for my p. a world of sighs
344:92
Paint: cheeks are covered with p.
228:88
good face needs no p. 265:32
looking as fresh as p. 374:96
p. my picture truly like me 115:91
p. the meadows with delight 332:19
to p. the lily 327:43
Painted: face with nature's own hand p.
362:35
idle as a p. ship upon a p. ocean
105:49
not so young as ... p. 30:81
Painters and poets ... lie 274:27
Painting a face ... not washing 140:37
Paintings: I have heard of your p.
310:99
Palace: a p. and a prison on each hand
84:62
love in a p. 183:11
my gorgeous p. for a hermitage
350:55
Palaces: cottages, princes' p. 338:2
Pale: p. cold cowardice 347:22
p. grew thy cheek and cold 86:99
Palestine: to haven in sunny P. 207:12
Pall Mall Gazette is written by gentle-
men 389:11
Palladium of all the ... rights 180:65
Palm: an itching p. 325:23
bear the p. alone 323:92
Palms before my feet 99:69
Palpable: a very p. hit 312:36
Pan: what ... doing, the great god P.?
73:13
Pancake: as flat as a p. 263:72
Pangs: more p. ... than wars or women
have 322-3:81
p. of despis'd love 309:95
Panic: what a p.'s in thy breastie 80:16
Pansies, that's for thoughts 311:28
Pantaloon: lean and slipper'd p.
301:90
Paper: both sides of the p. at once
297:34
he hath not eat p. 331:13
if all the world were p. 15:65
make dust our p. 349:53

Paper-mill: thou hast built a p.   321:68
Paradise: a p. to what we fear of death
  337:91
  called the P. of Fools   218:60
  drunk the milk of P.   107:76
  England ... p. of women, the hell of
    horses   81:31, 261:20
  P. of exiles, Italy   368:29
  such are the gates of P.   66:33
  this other Eden, demi-p.   348:41
  to P. by way of Kensal Green   99:74
  weave a p. for a sect   182:93
  Wilderness is P. enow   135:67
Paragon: the p. of animals!   308:81
Parchment: inky blots and rotten p.
  bonds   349:42
Pard: bearded like the p.   301:90
Pardon: bret-ful of p. ... from Rome
  97:43
  never ask p. before ... accused
    273:84
Parent: to lose one p., Mr Worthing
  405:10
Parents: joys of p. are secret   24:94
  of p. good, of fist most valiant
    320:51
  p. we can have but once   175:94
  what p. were created for   228:93
Paris: good Americans ... go to P.
  406:55
  P. is well worth a mass   160:97
  P. vaut bien une messe   160:97
  the last time I saw P.   157:58
Parish: all the world as my p.   402:73
  born ... hanged ... in the same p.
    13:47
Parliament: in the P. of man   387:81
Parliaments: England ... mother of p.
  71:81
Parlour: 'tis the prettiest little p.
  168:86
  will you walk into my p.?   168:86
Parmaceti for an inward bruise   313:52
Parochial: worse than provincial – he
  was p.   170:25
Parody: the devil's walking p.   99:68
*Parole ... donnée à l'homme pour
  déguiser*   384:32
Paroles ... pour déguiser leures pensées
  397:10
Parson: a p. much bemused in beer
  248:78
  coughing drowns the p.'s saw   332:20
Part: every man must play a p.   338:96
  I have forgot my p.   304:18
  if ought but death p. thee and me
    39:34
  kiss and p.   125:34

Part (*continued*)
  p. of education ... p. of experience
    25:12
  till death us do p.   64:7
Parted: when we two p.   86:99
Partial: more p. for the observer's sake
  251:21
Particle: very fiery p. ... snuff'd out
  85:83
Particular: a London p. – fog, miss
  119:33
  called away by p. business   372:77
Particulars: [do good] in Minute P.
  67:36
Parties: both p. nobly are subdu'd
  317:23
  hear all p.   266:78
Parting: do not let this p. grieve thee
  19:11
  p. is all we know of heaven   122:82
  p. is such sweet sorrow   354:6
  stood at the p. of the way   49:64
  this p. was well made   326:28
Partitions: thin p. do their bounds
  divide   126:39
Partridge in a pear tree   238–9:73
Parts: one man ... plays many p.
  301:90
Party: ancient forms of p. strife   386:69
  best number for a dinner p. is two
    157:54
  neither p. loser   317:23
  then none was for a p.   201:38
  there was an old p. of Lyme   224:52
  to p. gave up what was ... for man-
    kind   151:78
  true patriotism is of no p.   375:17
Pass: his ghost. O, let him p.   331:7
  I p. through the pores of the ocean
    368:23
  she may ... p. for forty-three   148:42
  they shall not p.   246:48
Passed: he p. by on the other side
  54:77
  so he p. over   77:67
  [time] wd. have p. in any case   30:75
Passeront: ils ne p. pas   246:48
Passes: everything p. ... perishes ...
  palls   281:53
  p. at girls who wear glasses   243:22
Passing: did but see her p. by   18:9
  P. of the Third Floor Back   171:36
  p. the love of women   40:49
Passing-bells for those who die as
  cattle   243:16
Passion: a master-p. is the love of news
  114:81
  calm of mind, all p. spent   223:27

Passion (*continued*)
  in her first p. woman 84:73
  man that is not p.'s slave 310:6
  master mistress of my p. 362:35
  Queen was in a furious p. 91:56
  ruling p. conquers reason still
    251:27
  strange fits of p. 414:23
  the p. and the life 106:69
Passion-flower: the p. at the gate
  388:87
Passionless: hopeless grief is p. 73:12
Passions: all thy p., match'd with mine
  387:83
  hath not a Jew ... p.? 339:13
  in truth but two p., vanity and love
    98:62
Past: a mischief that is p. and gone
  344:93
  leave thy low-vaulted p. 164:50
  p. and to come seems best 316:4
  p. cure, p. care 274:28
  p. help ... p. grief 361:14
  p. my help ... p. my care 29:72
  remembrance of things p. 362:37
  study the p. ... divine the future
    108:3
'Pastern' as the 'knee of a horse'
  174:81
Pastoral-comical, historical-p. 308:84
Pastors: as some ungracious p. do
  306:54
Pasture: sell the p. now to buy the
  horse 319:40
Pastures: fresh woods, and p. new
  215:18
  lie down in green p. 42:92
  on England's pleasant p. seen 67:38
Pat-a-cake, baker's man 237:62
Path: a beaten p. to his door 133:48
  p. of duty ... way to glory 388:94
Pathetic: That's what it is, P. 212:64
Pathless: pleasure in the p. woods
  84:65
Paths: so many p. that wind 404:93
Patience: abusing of God's p. 340:29
  how poor ... that have not p.l
    345:3
  in mean men we entitle p. 347:32
  p. is a flower 274:29
  p., money ... bring all ... to pass
    274:30
  p. under ... sufferings 63:84
  sat like P. on a monument 360:89
  though p. be a tired mare 319:42
  though with p. He stands waiting
    198:99
  ye have heard of the p. of Job 60:7

Patient: a p. etherized upon a table
  130:98
  fury of a p. man 127:48
Patines: inlaid with p. of bright gold
  340:22
Patria: dulce et decorum est pro p. mori
  167:77
  pro p. ... liberis ... aris 293:74
Patrie: allons, enfants de la p. 291:54
Patriot: for a p., too cool 151:79
  such is the p.'s boast 151:91
Patriotic: if p. sentiment is wanted
  145:96
Patriotism: I realize ... p. is not enough
  95:7
  p. ... last refuge of a scoundrel
    176:12
  true p. is of no party 375:17
Patriots: true p. we 29:65
Patron: a P., ... looks with unconcern
  174:78
  p. ... a wretch ... with insolence
    172:49
Pattern: thou cunning'st p. of ...
  nature 346:19
Paul: one named Peter, the other
  named P. 240:84
  rob Peter to pay P. 276:98
Pause: what dreams ... must give us p.
  309:95
Pawn: p. the Bechstein Grand 111:40
  you p. your intelligence 116:95
Pay: God make me able to p. 245:41
  p. ... in his own coin 274:31
  p. through the nose 274:32
  what one can p. others to do 208:23
  when will you p. me? 236:61
  you ought to p., you know 92:73
Pays: he who p. the piper 274:33
  p. yr. money ... takes yr. choice
    284:74
Peace: a hard and bitter p. 188:74
  a p. above all earthly dignities
    323:82
  a p. I hope with honour 122:93
  all her paths are p. 44:56
  better a lean p. 255:12
  blood of Jesus whispers p. 65:19
  calm world and a long p. 315:83
  cherish a just and lasting p. 196–7:81
  create desolation, call it p. 383:27
  for ever hold his p. 64:5
  for p. comes dropping slow 417:53
  give p. in our time, O Lord 63:70
  I am for p. ... they ... for war 44:36
  I shall have some p. there 417:53
  if p. cannot be ... with honour
    292:65

Peace (*continued*)
  in P., Goodwill 102:10
  in what p. a Christian can die 10:12
  inglorious arts of p. 207:2
  live together in p. ... as good neigh-
    bours 394:76
  never was ... a bad p. 138:15
  no p. ... unto the wicked 48:45
  nothing can bring you p. but your-
    self 133:38
  on earth p., good will 54:70
  our p., our fearful innocence 412:2
  p., commerce, and honest friendship
    171:29
  p. for our time ... p. with honour
    95:16
  p. hath her victories 223:32
  p. is indivisible 197:84
  p. is of the nature of a conquest
    317:23
  p. is poor reading 158:64
  p. makes plenty 274:34
  p. of God ... passeth all understand-
    ing 58:78
  p. on earth and mercy mild 402:71
  p., p., when there is no p. 49:54
  p., perfect p. 65:19
  p. shall go sleep with Turks 350:56
  the Lord ... give thee p. 38:2
  the Prince of P. 48:36
  the soft phrase of p. 344:90
  the thousand years of p. 386:70
  their bodies are buried in p. 62:62
  weak piping time of p. 351:67
  when ... p. he was for p. 22:62
  who desires p., prepare for war
    396:88
Peaceably: living p. in their habitations
    62:60
Peaceful: p. hours I once enjoyed
    113:62
  welcome p. evening in 114:73
Peace-maker: yr. If is the only p.
    303:10
Peach: do I dare to eat a p.? 131:4
  p. was once a bitter almond 394:69
Peacock: as proud as a p. 275:67
Peacocks and lilies for instance 291:61
Pear: and a gold p. 233:39
Pearl: barbaric p. and gold 217:45
  heaps of p., inestimable stones
    352:72
  hillside's dew-p.'d 75:44
  likc the base Indian, threw a p. away
    346–7:22
  one p. of great price 52:31
  sowed the earth with orient p.
    219:75

Pearls: he who wd. search for p. must
    dive 127:55
  neither cast ... p. before swine 52:24
  p. that were his eyes 355:35
  teeth like p. 75:43
Peas: I always eat p. with honey
    15:63
Peccavi [I have Sind] 228:82
Pécher en silence 224:51
Pedigree: languages ... p. of nations
    178:39
Peep about to find ... graves 323:93
Peeping: came p. in at morn 165:60
Peepshow: a ticket for the p. 203:54
Peer: a rhyming p. 248:78
  when daffodils begin to p. 361:17
Peg: take one down a p. 279:97
Pelican: wonderful bird is the p.
    209:38
Pelting: bide the p. of this pitiless storm
    329:78
Pen: before my p. has glean'd 186:48
  biting my truant p. 373:84
  more cruel ... p. is than ... sword
    81:30
  p. is mightier than the sword 76:54
  poet's p. turns them to shapes
    342:53
Pennance: hath p. done and p. more
    will do 105:59
Pence: take care of the p. 279:96
Penny: back again, like a bad p.
    254:86
  I spent a p. ... I lent a p. 233:40
  in for a p., in for a pound 267:17
  not given a p. for a song 417:51
  p. and p. laid up 274:35
  p. for yr. thoughts 274:36
  p. wise, pound foolish 274:37
  shall have but a p. a day 237:68
  show me first yr. p. 237:69
  turn an honest p. 281:66
  two a p., hot cross buns 233:35
Pens: let other p. dwell on guilt 23:71
*Pensée: se servent de la p. ... pour
    autoriser ... injustices* 397:10
Pensées: paroles ... pour déguiser ... p.
    397:10
Pension: p. never enriched a young
    man 274:38
  p. ... pay given to a state hireling
    172:50
Pensive: in vacant or in p. mood
    410:71
Pent: long in city p. 186:47
  long in populous city p 220:93
Penury: age, ache, p., and imprison-
    ment 337:91

People: a glorious p. vibrated again 369:34
  all p. that on earth do dwell 188:77
  among a p. generally corrupt 78:86
  Continental p. have sex life 209:40
  decent godless p. 131:8
  for God's sake look after our p. 294:90
  good of the p. ... chief law 102:15
  good p. all, of every sort 150:75
  government of the p., by the p. 196:79
  if the good p. in their wisdom 196:72
  indictment against an whole p. 78:83
  it is what the p. think so 78:84
  let my p. go 36:73
  no p. do so much harm as 115:85
  no vision, the p. perish 46:89
  nor is the p.'s judgment ... true 127:47
  observe the condition of the p. 180:66
  p. agree with me ... I must be wrong 404:1
  p. are ,.. charming or tedious 405:18
  p. have good food ... table manners 209:39
  p. who like this sort of thing 197:83
  p.'s mothers ... bore me 406:30
  raising up a p. of customers 374:98
  such trivial p. shd. muse 194:49
  the Irish are a fair p. 176:6
  the p. all exulting 403:81
  the p. are the masters 78:75
  the p. that walked in darkness 48:35
  thou art a stiffnecked p. 37:95
  thy p. shall be my p. 39:33
  Top P. 11:33
  voice of the p. 10:15
  what kind of a p. do they think 101:99
  wholesome ... nice English p. 365:72
  win friends and influence p. 89:40
  wd. all have some p. under them 175:89
  you can fool some of the p. 197:82
  you live with rich p. 374:2
Peopled: the world must be p. 343:70
Pepper: enjoy the p. when he pleases 90:52
  peck of pickled p. 237:63
Peppered: I have p. two of them 314:65
Perceives: the Man p. it die away 411:78
Perceiving *how not to do it* 120:47

Perception: if the doors of p. were cleansed 69:64
  p. that something ought to be done 401:66
Percy: I am not yet of P.'s mind 314:62
  old song of P. and Douglas 373:87
Perdition catch my soul 345:5
Perfect: he was a p. cavaliero 83:54
  I had else been p. 335:53
  p. little body 70:78
  practice makes p. 275:56
Perfection: the pursuit of p. ... is 21:47
Performance: provokes desire ... takes away p. 334:45
Perfume: throw a p. on the violet 327:43
Perfumed: he was p. like a milliner 313:51
Perfumes: all the p. of Arabia will not sweeten 335:69
Perhaps: in search of a great p. 285:91
Perilous: bright stars, through the p. fight 188:75
  cleanse ... bosom of that p. stuff 336:72
  thought without learning is p. 108:4
Perils and dangers of this night 63:75
Perish: name ... will not p. in the dust 376:26
  no vision, the people p. 46:89
  shall not p. from the earth 196:79
  they money p. with thee 56:16
  to p. ... swallowed up and lost 217:49
  when your time has come to p. 145:5
  whosoever believeth ... shd. not p. 55:99
Periwig: new p., make a great show 264:44
Perjured, murd'rous, bloody 363:50
Perk'd up in a glist'ring grief 322:75
Perplexed: being wrought, p. in the extreme 346–7:22
  p. in a world of doubts 186:53
Persecuted: I am p. with letters 109:11
Persepolis: in triumph through P.? 205:75
Persians and 'the Medes: among the laws of the P. 40:63
Persons: comprehended two aspicious p. 343:79
  God is no respecter of p. 56:19
  no respect of place, p., nor time 359:86
  should certain p. die before they sing 106:70
  you tossed and gored several p. 175:97

Perspiration: genius ... ninety-nine per cent p. 129:79

Persuade: beauty ... doth of itself p. 364:60

Persuadest: almost thou p. me 56:28

Persuading others we convince ourselves 180:67

Persuasive: case [against wealth] never proved widely p. 141:43

Pert as a school-girl 145:2

Perturbation: O polish'd p.! golden care! 317:27

Peru: mankind from China to P. 173:67

Pestilence: he ... breeds p. 69:59
  p. that walketh in darkness 43:21

Petard: hoist with his own p. 267:90

Peter: dicky birds ... one named P. 240:84
  rob P. to pay Paul 276:98
  Shock-headed P. 164:42
  thou art P., and upon this rock 53:34

Peter Piper picked a peck 237:63

Petty: a p. sneaking knave 67:42

Peut-être: chercher un grand p. 285:91

Phagocytes: stimulate the p. 365:71

Phantasma: like a p. or a hideous dream 324:98

Phantom: she was a P. of delight 414:16

Pharaoh: the Lord hardened P.'s heart 36:76

Philistian: resist P. gold 222:20

Philistines: Barbarians, P., Populace 21:48

Philosopher: all be that he was a p. 96:33
  guide, p. and friend 250:19
  nothing so absurd but some p. has said 102:14
  there was never yet p. 344:86
  tried ... in my time to be a p. 129:82

Philosophers: English are ... the least ... pure p. 27:45

Philosophic: gild the p. pill! 149:47

Philosophy: a little p. inclineth ... to atheism 25:10
  are dreamt of in your p. 307:69
  history is p. teaching by examples 122:87
  how charming is divine P.! 213:77
  mere touch of cold p. 183:12
  new p. calls all in doubt 123:3
  p. is nothing but discretion 296:23
  p. will clip an angel's wings 183:13

Phoebus: and P. 'gins arise 304:20
  Delos rose, and P. sprung 84:77

Phrase: proverb'd with a grandsire p. 353:91
  the soft p. of peace 344:90

Physic: for p. and farces 141:47
  take p., pomp 329:79

Physician: honour a p. 62:57
  is there no p. there? 49:55
  p., heal thyself 54:72
  they that are whole ... no need of the p. 53:53

Physicians: few p. live well 262:57
  p. of the utmost fame 31:91

Pianist: do not shoot the p. 405:17

Piccadilly: good-bye, P. 407:39

Picked a peck of pickled pepper 237:63

Picket: the p.'s off duty forever 30:84

Picking and stealing 64:98

Pickwick: Mr P. 121:63; 65; 121:74
  P., ... Owl ... Waverley pen 11:32

Pictures: book without p. and conversation 89:42
  cutting all the p. out 31:88

Pie: blackbirds baked in a p. 238:70
  eating a Christmas p. 235:50
  finger in the p. 263:62
  some of a pudding ... none of a p. 256:28

Pieces: broke into a thousand p. 28:59

Pie-crust: promises and p. ... to be broken 382:6

Pieman: Simple Simon met a p. 237:69

Pierian spring: taste not the P. 249:94

Pies: eat one of Bellamy's veal p. 247:59

Piety: nor all thy p. nor wit 136:79
  renowned for larnin' and p. 154:18

Pig: a p. in a poke 257:78
  stole a p. and away he run 240:83
  the p. was eat 240:83
  the little p. went to market 239:78

Pigeon: crooning like a bilious p. 366:93

Pigeon-livered: am p., and lack gall 309:92

Piggy-wig: a P. stood 195:61

Pigmy: darling of a p. size 411:79
  fretted the p. body 126:39

Pigs: and whether p. have wings 93:80
  p. might fly: 274:39

Pike-staff: as plain as a p. 274:41

Pilate: P. saith ... What is truth? 56:12
  what is truth? said jesting P. 24:85

Pilgrim: Honour comes, a p. grey 107–8:90
  p. through this barren land 407:40
  the P. of Eternity 367:13
  to be a p. 77:64,65

Placid: animals ... so p. and self-
  contained 403:84
Plague: a p. o' both your houses!
  354:11
  a p. of all cowards! 314:63
  a p. of sighing and grief! 314:67
  make instruments to p. us 330:1
  p. o' these pickle-herring! 359:79
  the red p. rid you 355:33
Plagues: of all p. ... thy wrath can
  send 88:27
  of all the p. ... woman ... worst
  153:17
  p. that are written 61:35
  p. with which mankind are curst
  118:19
Plain: all doctrines p. and clear 82:38
  did you ... see Shelley p.? 74:30
  in meadow or p. 382:15
  p. as a pike-staff 274:41
  p. living and high thinking 412:2
  pricking on the p. 377:41
  virtue is ... best p. set 26:27
Plainly: honest tale ... p. told 352:80
Plaintive: the p. numbers flow 414:21
Plan: mighty maze! but not without a
  p. 250:70
Planet: measure every wandering p.'s
  course 205:76
  when a new p. swims into his ken
  185:41
  while Jove's p. rises 74:25
Planets: the p., and this centre, observe
  degree 358:66
Planned: Who saith 'A whole I p.'
  75–6:46
Plant: A Sensitive P. in a garden grew
  370:46
Planted: feet firmly p. in the air 289:31
  I have p., Apollos watered 57:46
Platitude: a longitude with no p.
  140:34
Plato: attachment *à la* P. 146:16
  P. is dear to me 20:28
Platter: they licked the p. clean 234:45
Play: all work and no p. 284:56
  an hour to p. ... last man in 230:13
  at Christmas p. and make good
  cheer 393:58
  better than a p. 96:23
  boys and girls come out to p. 231:25
  can pack ... cards ... cannot p. well
  25:15
  good p. needs no epilogue 303:11
  I doubt some foul p. 306:52
  learnt to p. when he was young
  240:82
  never ... go to a p. together 109:17

Play (*continued*)
  p. first (second) fiddle 274:42
  p. up! and p. the game 230:14
  p. with the gypsies in the wood
  236:57
  the p. ... pleas'd not the million
  308:85
  the p.'s the thing wherein 309:94
  they p. from ten till four 285:78
  two can p. at that game 281:75
  when the boys came out to p. 232:31
  where every man must p. a part
  338:96
  Zephyrus did softly p. 377:46
Played: marks ... how you p. the game
  287:9
Player: a walking shadow, a poor p.
  336:76
Players: men and women merely p.
  301:90
  mouth it, as ... p. do 310:3
Playing of the merry organ 16–17:87
Playmates: I have had p. ... old familiar
  faces 192:32
Plays: he p. best (well) that wins
  274:43
  old p. begin to disgust 134:54
Plea: general good ... p. of the scoundrel 67:36
Pleasance: youth is full of p. 364:56
Pleasant: a few think him p. enough
  194:59
  a p. fire our souls to regale 68:45
  abridgement of all ... p. in man
  151:80
  green and p. land 67:38
  how p. to know Mr Lear 194:59
  on England's p. pastures seen?
  67:38
  p. in their lives 40:48
  p. thoughts bring sad 411:83
  p. ... to see ... name in print 85:89
  some day be p. to remember 396:98
  songs of p. glee 68:48
  standing on this p. lea 412:94
Pleasantest: one of the p. things ... a
  journey 159:81
Pleasantness: her ways are ways of p.
  44:56
  the p. of an employment 23:80
Please: books cannot always p. 114:30
  in him alone 'twas natural to p.
  126:37
  live to p., must p. to live 173:59
  say what they p. ... do what I p.
  139:19
  seeketh not itself to p. 67:43
Pleased: as p. as Punch 274:44

Pleased (*continued*)
p. with what he gets 301:85
when ... p. ourselves, we ... please 274:45
Pleases: every prospect p. 160:87
one makes lovers ... as one p. 109:13
Pleasing: art of p. ... being pleased 159:83
Pleasure: a p. in the pathless woods 84:65
business before p. 257:75
but the privilege and p. 143:76
dissipation without p. 142:65
drinking is the soldier's p. 127:53
every p. is of itself a good 177:29
friend of P., Wisdom's aid 108:93
gave p. to the spectators 202:47
good, p., ease, content! 250:15
great source of p. is variety 178:42
happiness ... not in p. but in rest from pain 128:64
hatred ... the longest p. 85:84
love ceases to be a p. 30:85
money gives me p. 32:98
more p. in loving than ... loved 274:46
no p. without pain 273:98
no profit ... where is no p. 355:20
owes its p. to another's pain 114:72
p. ... is lost by coveting more 274:48
p. is oft a visitant 181:86
p. never is at home 185:95
p. of the fleeting year 363:43
p.'s a sin ... sin's a p. 84:69
public stock of harmless p. 178:43
refrain from the unholy p. 31:88
short p., long lament 277:35
some to business, some to p. take 251:23
sweet is p. after pain 127:53
though on p. she was bent 113:56
to overcome p. is the greatest p. 274:47
'twas for your p. you came 113:60
variety ... soul of p. 30:86
when Youth and P. meet 83:60
written without effort ... read without p. 178:41
Pleasure-dome: a stately p. 106:71
sunny p. with caves of ice 107:75
Pleasures: all the p. prove 205:82
cannot understand the p. 23:65
can sympathise ... not with their p. 169:1
in unreproved p. free 214:96
'mid p. and palaces 245:34
no man is a hypocrite in his p. 178:36

Pleasures (*continued*)
p. are like poppies spread 81:25
the purest of human p. 26:29
these p., Melancholy, give 213:90
these pretty p. might me move 286:96
we will some new p. prove 123:4
Pledge: I will p. with mine 178:49
p. to each other our lives, our fortunes 171:27
Plenty: however p. silver dollars may become 103:23
in delay there lies no p. 359:84
p. makes me 243:13
wasna fou, but just had p. 79:4
Pleure: il p. dans mon cœur 396:90
Plodders: small have continual p. ... won 331:10
Plot: the sonnet's scanty p. of ground 411:90
this blessed p., this earth 348–9:41
Plough: having put his hand to the p. 54:74
Ploughman: heavy steps of the p. 417:55
the p., near at hand 214:98
Plowman homeward plods 155:30
Pluck: p. from the memory a rooted sorrow 336:72
sin will p. on sin 352:77
we p. this flower, safety 313:60
Plucked: when I have p. thy rose 346:19
Plum: and pulled out a p. 235:50
supping cold p. porridge 235:54
Poacher: a p. is a keeper 189:90
old p. makes a good game-keeper 274:20
Pocket: a p. full of posies 237:67
a p. full of rye 238:70
Pocket borough: by a p. into Parliament 147:27
Pocket-handkerchief: holding his p. 93:81
Pockets: p. in none of his clothes 33:12
to line one's p. 270:88
Poem: I would rather have written that p. 408:54
ought himself to be a true p. 223:36
p. lovely as a tree 188:81
p. must ride on ... melting 139:29
p. ... worked ... not worried 139:29
Poems: dictionaries, and temporary p. 172:45
Gert's p. are bunk 14:57
p. are made by fools like me 189:82
Poesy: drainless shower of light is p. 185:38

Preacher: vanity of vanities, saith the
P. 46:93
Preaches: he p. well that lives well
275:59
Preaching: a woman's p. is like 175:90
Precept: example is better than p.
262:37
Precepts: these few p. in thy memory
306:55
Precise: too p. in every part 162:17
Precisely: thinking too p. on th' event
311:23
Prefer: folks p. ... a hovel to ... marble
halls 87:13
Preferment: and so I got p. 17:91
tired of knocking at P.'s door
21:41
Prejudice: we all decry p., yet 376:35
Prejudices: it p. a man so [reading ...
before reviewing] 375:11
Premises: sufficient conclusions from
insufficient p. 82:44
Prepare to meet Thy God 50:83
Preposterous? A thorough-paced absurdity 146:14
Presbyter: new P. is but old Priest
223:31
Presence: from whose unseen p. the
leaves dead 369:35
lord of thy p. and no land 326:33
p. strengthens [love] 254:53
scanter of yr. maiden p. 307:58
Present: a very p. help in trouble 42:7
both perhaps p. in time future
130:90
no time like the p. 280:41
p. mirth hath p. laughter 359:84
p. only toucheth thee 80:19
things p., worst 316:4
un-birthday p. 93:85
Presents ... endear Absents 192:28
Preservation: creation, p., and all the
blessings 64:85
President: rather be right than be P.
103:22
Press: god of our idolatry, the p.
113:66
misused the King's p. damnably
315:82
written of the power of the p. 395:77
Pressed: if it were p., would run 32:3
power p. too far and relaxed too
much 25:14
Pretender: who P. is, or who is King
83:53
Pretty: where the girls are so p. 17:89
Prevail: gates of hell shall not p. 53:34
passion for making them p. 21:52

Prevention is better than cure 245:37,
275:60
Prey: have they not divided the p.?
39:24
smaller fleas that on him p. 382:5
to hastening ills a p. 150:62
Price: all those men have their p.
398:20
p. of everything ... value of nothing
406:21
p. of wisdom is above rubies 41:73
virtuous woman ... p. ... above
rubies 46:92
Prick: how if honour p. me off? 315:88
if you p. us, do we not bleed? 339:13
no spur to p. the sides of my intent
333:37
pat it and p. it 237:62
when ... the nerves p. 386:60
Pricking: a gentle knight was p. on the
plain 377:41
Pricks: kick against the p. 56:18
Pride: he that is low, no p. 77:66
look backward to with p. 139:23
perished in his p. 413:12
p. goeth before destruction 45:72
p. of kingly sway from out my heart
350:58
p., pomp, and circumstance, of ...
war 345–6:10
p. that licks the dust 248:86
p., the ... vice of fools 249:93
p. will have a fall 275:61
the poet's inward p. 117:15
the p. of that country side 28:54
Priest: am I both p. and clerk? 350:57
free me of this turbulent p. 160:99
I tell thee, churlish p. 312:32
p. all shaven and shorn 239:79
p. is at the bottom of it [mischief]
273:94
youth ... still is Nature's p. 411:78
Priest-craft: ere p. did begin 126:36
Priests: of p. ... a charmin' variety
154:18
Prime: having lost but once yr. p.
162:25
Primrose: p. path of dalliance treads
306:54
p. way to th' everlasting bonfire
334:44
rathe p. that forsaken dies 215:17
Prince: the P. of Peace 48:36
Princes: hangs on p.' favours 322:81
put not yr. trust in p. 44:53
that sweet aspect of p. 322–3:81
Principalities: against p., against
powers ... rulers 58:74

Principle: a p. in life with me, sir 367:7
don't believe in p. ... *do* in interest
200:21
fundamental p. of ... constitution
66:25
what is p. against ... flattery? 372:79
Principles: first, religious and moral p.
22:54
these two p.—right and wrong
196:76
they speak of p.—look out 22:59
Print: some said, John, p. it 76:56
to see one's name in p. 85:89
Printer: almost hear the p. saying damn
395:80
Printers: books by which the p. have
lost 140:40
Printing: barbarous where there is no
p. 176:3
cogent reasons for not p. ... subscribers 177:33
thou hast caused p. to be used
321:68
Priority: observe degree, p., and place
358:66
Prison: come, let's away to p. 330:99
dock in a pestilential p. 145:3
Lime-tree Bower my p. 107:77
palace ... p. on each hand 84:62
stone walls do not a p. make 199:15
this p. where I live 351:62
Prisoner: the jury, passing on the p.'s
life 337:81
Prison-house: secrets of my p. 307:64
shades of the p. begin to close
410–11:77
Prithee, pretty maiden 146:17
Private: to the public good p. respects
... yield 222:21
Privilege: accursed power which stands
on p. 31:95
but the p. and pleasure ... little
errands 143:76
Privileged: the p. and the people ...
two nations 123:98
Prize: men p. the thing ungain'd
358:65
not all that tempts ... is lawful p.
154:26
rain influence, and judge the p.
214:2
the p. we sought is won 403:81
too light winning make the p. light
356:36
what we have we p. not 343:81
Problem: quite a three-pipe p. 124:19
Problems: the p. of victory are more
agreeable 101:5

Proceedings: subsequent p. interested
him no more 158:73
Process: one long p. of getting tired
82:43
Procrastination is the thief of time
418:62
Procreate: we might p. like trees
72:5
Proctors: with prudes for p. 388:95
Prodigal: chariest maid is p. enough
306:53
Shimei, though not p. of pelf 126:46
Profane: O p. one! 70:74
so old, and so p. 318:34
Profaned: province ... desolated and p.
149:52
Profess: all who p. ... themselves
Christians 63:82
Professions: let in some of all p.
334:44
Profit: my p. on't is, I know how to
curse 355:33
no p. ... where ... no pleasure
355:20
the winds will blow the p. 203:55
what p. hath a man of ... labour
46:94
what shall it p. a man? 54:58
Profits: small p. and quick returns
277:47
Progeny: a p. of learning 371:69
Prognostics do not ... prove prophecies
398:24
Progress: all p. ... desire ... to live
beyond ... income 82:45
history of England ... history of p.
202:43
to promote social p. 394:76
Promethean: I know not where is that
P. heat 346:19
Promise of strength and manhood
70:78
Promises: he p. himself too much
175:94
p. and pie-crust ... to be broken
382:6
p. too much ... means nothing
275:62
Promising: pretty Thomasina ... once
... so p. 140:30
Promontory: I sat upon a p. 341:44
Promotion: none will sweat but for p.
300:79
Prone to any iteration of nuptials
109:19
Pronounce: spell better than they p.
394:66
Proof of the pudding 275:63

Prop: you take my house ... take the p.
340:20

Propagate: endeavour to ... p. the best
21:50

Proper words in p. places 381:3

Properties: general p. and large appearances 173:63

Property has its duties ... rights 126:35

Prophecies: prognostics do not always
prove p. 398:24

Prophecy: the trumpet of a p. 369:38

Prophesy: if you crown him, let me p.
350:56

Prophesying: ancestral voices p. war
107:74

Prophet: a p. is not without honour
52:32
   methinks I am a p. new inspir'd
348:40
   sons of the p. were brave 18:7

Prophetess: more than a p. ... uncommon pretty 129:84

Prophetic: O my p. soul 307:67
   to something like p. strain 213:89

Prophets: beware of false p. 52:27
   is Saul ... among the p. 39:39
   wisest p. ... sure of the event first
398:24

Proportion: time is broke and no p.
kept! 351:63

Propose: whoever loves ... do not p.
123:8

Propriety: pleasantness ... does not ...
evince p. 23:80

Proprium humani ingenii ... odisse
383:28

Prose: homely definitions of p. and
poetry 107:82
   in p. and verse was own'd ... absolute
128:68
   je dis de la p. 224:48
   p. run mad 248:82
   talking p. for over forty years 224:48
   unattempted yet in p. or rhyme
216:28

Prospect: noblest p. ... Scotchman ever
sees 175:85
   p. is ... better than possession
275:64
   though every p. pleases 160:87

Prospects: died when his p. ... brightening 12:42
   on p. drear 80:19

Prosper: treason doth never p. 158:70

Prosperity: a jest's p. lies in the ear
331:18
   a man to have been in p. 97–8:51
   him that stood in great p. 97:47

Prosperity (*continued*)
   p. doth best discover vice 24:92
   p. has damned more ... than ...
devils 275:65
   p. is the blessing of the Old Testament 24:90
   p.'s the very bond of love 362:24
   you will see a state of p. 202:52

Prospers: Hope ... turns Ashes—or it
p. 135:68

Protest: the lady doth p. too much
310:9

Proteus rising from the sea 412:94

Protracted: life p. is p. woe 174:70

Proud: Americans ... p. of ... ancient
heritage 188:74
   as p. as Lucifer 275:66
   as p. as a peacock 275:67
   being too p. to fight 407:45
   death, be not p. 124:10
   how apt the poor are to be p. 360:93
   I might grow p. the while 162:19
   p. me no prouds 354:15
   too p. for a wit 151:79
   too p. to importune 156:46

Prouder: never, I ween, was a p. seen
28:53

Prove: might p. anything by figures
89:32
   prov'd true before, p. false again
82:38

Proved: likely ... to have p. most royal
312:41
   p. true before, prove false again
82:38
   which was to be p. 133:51

Proverb: a p. is much matter 140:38
   the p. is something musty 310:11

Providence: assert Eternal P. 216:29
   P. their guide 221:3
   reasoned high of P., Foreknowledge
218:55

Province: all knowledge to be my p.
27:39
   p. they [Turks] have desolated
149:52

Provincial: worse than p.—he was
parochial 170:25

Prudes: with p. for proctors 388:95

Pruning-hooks: swords into plowshares, ... spears into p. 48:31

Prussia: war ... national industry of P.
224:47

Prussian: French, or Turk, or P.
147:30

Psalmist: the sweet p. of Israel 40:52

Psaltery: sing unto him with the p.
42:97

Public: British p. in one of its ... fits
202:46
  deliberation sat, and p. care 218:52
  dislike the favour of the p. 187:66
  how p., like a frog 122:81
  mean, stupid, dastardly, ... p.
  159:82
  never in touch with p. opinion
  406:28
  reasons for ... not speaking in p.
  176:10
  the sound of p. scorn 220:96
  wash dirty linen in p. 282:6
  washing ... clean linen in p. 405:7
Public house: vidders ... if they've kept
  a p. 121:67
Public meeting: speaks ... as if I was a
  p. 396:92
Public opinion: researchers into p.
  22:62
Public schools are the nurseries of vice
  134:62
Publican: how like a fawning p. 338:3
Publish: I'll p., right or wrong 85:88
  p. and be damned 401:62
  p. it not in the streets 40:47
Publisher: now Barabbas was a p.
  88:22
Publishers: with irrational fear of life
  become p. 110:22
Pudding: a p. hath two [ends] 262:33
  better some of a p. 256:28
  proof of the p. is in the eating 275:63
Puff direct ... preliminary ... collateral
  371:62
Puffing is of various sorts 371:62
Puissant et solitaire 396:93
Puking: infant, mewling and p. 301:90
Pullet-sperm: no p. in my brewage
  341:33
Pulse: feeling a woman's p. 379:67
  two people with one p. 203:57
  when the p. begins to throb 71:87
Pumpkins: where the early p. blow
  194:55
Punch: as pleased as P. 274:44
Punctuality is the politeness of kings
  199:14
Punctures: pin ... p. my skin 13:51
Punishment: as I deserve, pay on my p.
  222:17
  the p. fit the crime 146:6
Puppets: God, whose p. ... are we
  75:45
Purchased: thought ... gift of God may
  be p. 56:16
Pure: as p. as snow 310:98
  because my heart is p. 389:3

Pure (*continued*)
  blessed are the p. in heart 52:10
  more p. than his Maker 41:66
  p. as an angel 384:30
  p. as the naked heavens 413:4
  p. unbounded love thou art 402:72
  things are p. ... lovely ... of good
  report 58:79
  unto the p. all things are p. 59:96
Purest: garden ... p. of human
  pleasures 26:29
Purgatory: England ... p. of men
  136:86
  no other p. but a woman 29:73
Purge: I'll p., and leave sack 315:95
  p. me with hyssop 42:8
Puritan: saw a P.-one hanging of his
  cat 70:74
  the P. hated bear-baiting 202:47
Purlieus: dusty p. of the law 386:64
Purple: I never saw a P. Cow 77:68
  I wrote the 'P. Cow' 77:69
  p. the sails, and so perfumed 298:54
Purpose: cite Scripture for his p.
  338:4
Purse: ask thy p. what thou shdst. buy
  254:79
  heavy p. ... light heart 266:82
  light p. ... heavy heart 269:83
  little and often fills the p. 270:91
  p. ... full of other men's money
  261:17
  put money in thy p. 345:96
  remedy against ... consumption of
  the p. 316:3
  silk p. out of a sow's ear 277:39
  who steals my p. steals trash 345:6
Purses: our p. shall be proud 355:25
  wine and wenches empty ... p.
  283:35
Purse-strings are ... common ties
  275:70
Pursuing: faint, yet p. 39:25
Pursuit of perfection ... is the p. of
  sweetness 21:47
Pussy: Owl and the P.-cat 195:60
  P cat, where have you been? 237:64
  P.'s in the well 232:28
Put: p. off holiness and p. on intellect
  67:37
  up with which I will not p. 102:9
Putting milk into babies 101:6
Pye: than shine with P. 85:92
Pyramides: du haut de ces p. 228:83
Pyramids: from the summit of these p.
  228:83
Pyramus: Death of P. and Thisby
  341:39

Quires and places where they sing
63:72
Quiring to the young-ey'd cherubins
340:22
Quit: like doth q. like 338:94
q. yourselves like men 39:38
Quiver: willows whiten, aspens q.
387:76
Quod erat demonstrandum 133:51
Quotation: every q. contributes some-
thing 172:42
Questions: a book that furnishes no q.
245:36
Quote: by necessity ... delight, we all q.
133:40
grow immortal as they q. 417:59
I'll kill you if you q. it 77:69
I q. the fights historical 147:31
Quoter: next to originator ... is the first
q. 133:39

Rabbit: the r. has a charming face
15:70
Race: earth ... will no longer tolerate
the r. 27:48
he rides a r. 113:57
pernicious r. ... of odious vermin
381:1
slow and steady wins the r. 197:89
some new r., called Man 218:53
the human r., to which so many ...
belong 99:78
the r. dwelling all round the globe
102:11
the r. is not to the swift 47:8
whole r. of politicians 381:2
Races: human species ... two distinct
r. 191:25
Rachel weeping for her children
51:3'
Rack: leave not a r. behind 356–7:50
ship has weather'd every r. 403:81
the r. of this tough world 331:7
then we r. the value 343:81
Radical ... with both feet ... in the air
289:31
Rage: disguise ... nature with hard-
favour'd r. 319:45
puts all Heaven in a r. 66:28
r., r., against the dying 390:18
Ragged: though my ryme be r., tattered 373:92
Raggedness: loop'd and window'd r.
329:78
Rags: heaven in r., than to hell in
embroidery 256:24
no scandal like r. 134:55
sat in unwomanly r. 166:64

Rail: I'll r. against ... first-born 301:86
whiles I am a beggar, I will r. 326:38
Rain: being read to ... waiting for r.
130:92
droppeth as the gentle r. from heaven
339:15
hath the r. a father? 41:77
I dissolve it in r. 368:22
in thunder, lightning, or in r. 332:22
nor r., wind, thunder ... my daughters 328:72
r. before seven, fine before eleven
275:75
r., r., go to Spain 275:76
right as r. 276:95
ripple of r. 382:15
rudely r. beaten ... moth-eaten
373:92
sendeth r. on ... just ... unjust 52:15
still falls the r. 373:90
stirring ... roots with spring r.
131:10
the r. came heavily ... in floods
413:11
the r. is full of ghosts 210:46
the r. is over and gone 47:21
the r. it raineth every day 360:3
the r. it raineth on the just 70:71
the wind and the r. 360:3
Rainbow: a r. in the sky 412:98
add another hue unto the r. 327:43
the r. comes and goes 410:73
Rains: it never r. but it pours 275:77
Rainy: lay it up for a r. day 275:78
the weather when it is not r. 83:55
Raisons que la raison ne connaît point
244:28
Rake: every woman is at heart a r.
251:23
excuse for thus playing the r. 226:65
lean as a r. 269:63
lene was his hors as is a r. 96:32
man's a ribald ... a r. 148:37
Rampallion, you r.! 316:5
Rampart: his corse to the r. we hurried
408:52
Ramparts: o'er the r. we watched
188:79
Ran: Georgie Porgie r. away 232:31
grief with a glass that r. 382:16
the sacred river r. 106:71, 73
Ranged with humble livers in content
322:75
Rank is good, and gold is fair 403:88
Rankers: gentlemen r. 190:99
Ranks: all service r. the same with God
75:45
even the r. of Tuscany 202:41

Rap and knock and enter in our soul
73:17

Rapidity: travelling ... dull in ... proportion to its r. 291:59

Rapidly: yes, but not so r. 30:75

Rapscallions: all kings is mostly r.
393:62

Rapture: a r. on the lonely shore 84:65
first fine careless r. 74:23

Raptures: the r. and roses of vice
382:18

Rare: I think my love as r. 364:53
she was indeed a r. one 408:48

Rarely, rarely, comest thou 370:52

Rascal: a dull and muddy-mettl'd r.
308:91
get down you dirty r. 233:41

Rashes: green grow the r. 80:7

Rasselas, prince of Abyssinia 173:61

Rat: a dog, a horse, a r. have life
331:6
a r.? Dead, for a ducat 311:17
cat that killed the r. 239:79
Mr Speaker, I smell a r. 288:13
to smell a r. 277:48

Rate: brings down the r. of usance
338:3

Rated: in the Rialto you have r. me
338:5

Rather: he had r. have a turnip 172:56
I live ... r. as a Spectator 9:6

Rationed: liberty ... so precious ... it
must be r. 195:69

Rats: out ... the r. came tumbling
75:40
r. desert a sinking ship 275:79
r.! they fought the dogs 75:37
rid your town of r. 75:39

Rattle: spoiled his nice new r. 92:74

Rave: old age shd. burn and r. 390:18

Raven: quoth the R., Nevermore
247:67
yr. locks were like the r. 80:11

Ravens: there were three r. 12:39

Ray: gem of purest r. serene 155:37

Raze out the ... troubles of the brain
336:72

Reach: man's r. shd. exceed his grasp
73:15

Read: classic ... everybody wants to
have r. 394:73
classic ... nobody wants to r. 394:73
I r. much of the night 131:11
I've r. in many a novel 87:13
r. ... as inclination leads him 175:86
r., mark, learn 64:86
sins were scarlet ... books were r.
31:93

Read (*continued*)
sooner r. a time-table ... than
nothing 208:22
what do you r., my lord? 308:77
without an intention to r. it
176:5

Reader: last r. reads no more 164:43

Readers: the human race, to which ...
r. belong 99:78

Reading: I prefer r. 374:3
peace is poor r. 158:64
r. is to the mind 378:61
r. maketh a full man 26:33
when ... not walking, I am r. 192:29
writer's time is spent in r. 176:11

Ready: conference [maketh] a r. man
26:33
we always are r. 141:48

Real: although pain isn't r. 13:51

Realistic: when statesmen ... say ... r.
22:59

Reality: between the idea and the r.
130:95
cannot bear very much r. 130:91

Realm: this earth, this r., this England
348–9:41

Realms: constancy lives in r. above
106:67
who dwell in r. of day 66:31

Reap: men that sow to r. 382:19
shall r. the whirlwind 50:76

Reaped: wheat which never shd. be r.
392:53

Reason: all r. is against it 82:46
Cornish men will know the r. why
158–9:74
divorced old barren R. 135:76
do ... r. themselves out again
321:61
have I not r. to lament 411:84
in erring r.'s spite 250:12
no other but a woman's r. 361:5
O, r. not the need 328:67
or any other r. why 10:16
r. and energy, love and hate 68:56
r. is left free to combat it 171:28
r. is our soul's left hand 123:5
r. why I cannot tell 72:96
reasons which r. does not know
244:28
right deed for the wrong reason 132:17
ruling passion conquers r. still
251:27
teach thy necessity to r. thus 348:36
theirs not to r. why 385:42
worse appear the better r. 217:48

Reasonable: a r. good ear in music
342:51

Reasoned high of Providence 218:55

Reasons: the heart has its r. 244:28

Rebel: thinking man is bound to r.
    169:8

Rebellion lay in his way 315:86

Rebels: dear earth ... though r. wound
    thee 349:49

Rebuke: boldly r. vice 64:92

    open r. is better than secret love
    46:86

Recapture: think he never could r.
    74:23

Reckless what I do to spite the world
    334:49

Recommendation: self-praise is no r.
    277:27

Recompense: heaven did a r. ... send
    155:41

Record: puts a r. on the gramophone
    131:12

Recover: die of it do seldom ... r.
    299:68

*Recte: si possis r., si non, quocumque
    modo rem* 166:72

Reculer: il faut r. pour mieux sauter
    267:11

Red: coral is far more r. than her lips'
    r. 364:52

    grace to get ... r. in the face 34:20

    her lips were r., her looks were free
    105:52

    keep the R. Flag flying 109–10:21

    like a r. r. rose 81:21

    making the green one r. 334:43

    nature, r. in tooth and claw 386:63

    r. as a rose 275:80

    r. as a rose is she 104:45

    r. rag to a bull 275:81

    sun ... curtained with cloudy r.
    216:22

    sunset ... one glorious blood-r.
    74:24

    the one in r. cravat 122:85

    the r. plague rid you 355:33

    the R. Queen 94:96, 98

Red brick: not even r., but white tile
    242:10

Red-breast: the r. whistles 181:82

Rede: recks not his own r. 306:54

Redeemer: I know that my r. liveth
    41:72

Redemption: condemn'd into everlast-
    ing r. 344:84

    no r. from hell 276:82

Redress: things past r. ... past care
    349:47

Reed: a bruised r. shall he not break
    48:44

Reed (*continued*)
    r. shaken with the wind 52:29

Reeds: down in the r. by the river
    73:13

Reeking into Cadiz Bay 74:24

Reeling and Writhing 91:60

References: always verify yr. r. 291:56

Reflect: when I r. that God is just
    171:33

Reformation: reforming of R. itself
    224:42

Reforming: nothing so needs r. as ...
    habits 394:72

Refrain: did ... from expensive sins r.
    126:45

Refreshment: the most perfect r. 23:70

Refuge: eternal God is thy r. 38:17

    God is our r. and strength 42:7

    idleness ... r. of weak minds 98:61

Refugees: the guttural sorrow of the r.
    203:56

Regard: where ... least r. for human
    freedom 376:37

Regiment: four elements warring ... for
    r. 205:76

    led his r. from behind 143:69

    Monstrous R. of Women 191:19

Region: in thrilling r. of thick-ribbed
    ice 337:90

Regions: double lived in r. new 181:83

    r. Caesar never knew 112:50

Regret: youth is a blunder ... old age a
    r. 123:95

Regrets: past R. and future Fears
    135:69

Reign: r. in this horrible place 114:78

    whatsoever King shall r. 17:92

Reigned: I have r. with your loves
    132:21

Reinforcement: what r. we may gain
    from hope 216:33

Rejoice: as he was fortunate, I r.
    325:11

    daughters of the Philistines r. 40:47

    from age to age thou didst r. 412:1

    good Christian men, r. 229:2

    I hear thee and r. 415:37

    r. with them that do r. 57:38

Rejoices: a poor heart that never r.
    274:50

Rejoicing: went on his way r. 56:17

Relative: set out ... in a r. way 76:52

Relaxed: power ... r. too much 25:14

Relaxes: damn braces, bless r. 69:61

Relent: shall make him once r. 77:64

Relief: for this r. much thanks 305:33

Religion: bringeth ... minds about to
    r. 25:10

Religion (*continued*)
  enough r. to make us hate 382:9
  good life is the only r. 265:34
  love is my r.—I cd. die for that 187:67
  men will wrangle for r. 108:96
  Millionaire. That is my r. 365:76
  my pollertics, like my r. 398:26
  no man's r. ... survives his morals 273:93
  not a r. for gentlemen 96:21
  one r. is as true as another 82:32
  one's r. is whatever he is ... interested in 28:63
  only one r., though ... a hundred versions 366:92
  pure r. breathing household laws 412:2
  r. but a childish toy 204:69
  r. is allowed to invade 208:26
  r., justice, counsel, and treasure 25:7
  r. of an ill man 276:83
  r. is the best armour ... worst cloak 276:84
  r.'s in the heart, not ... knees 171:37
  r. ... the opium of the people 207:7
  superstition ... r. of feeble minds 78:80
Religious: casting a dim r. light 213:88
  good, but not r. good 158:66
  man is ... a r. animal 78:79
Rely upon a comfortable time-lag 401:66
Remain: as things have been, things r. 103:32
Remained: came to scoff, r. to pray 150:67
Remains: what r. is bestial 345:1
Remarkable: nothing left r. beneath the moon 299:66
Remedies: desperate diseases ... desperate r. 260:71
  he that will not apply new r. 26:17
  our r. oft in ourselves 298:42
Remedy: a r. for all ... but death 276:85
  force is not a r. 71:83
  knew the reason ... sought the r. 302:5
  one unfailing r.—the Tankard 87:12
  r. is worse than the disease 25:9
Remember: and if thou wilt, r. 290:48
  bitter to endure ... sweet to r. 256:38
  do you r. an inn, Miranda? 32:8
  forget and smile ... r. and be sad 290:45
  he'll r., with advantages 320:58

Remember (*continued*)
  I r., I r. 165:60, 61
  I r. your name perfectly 377:52
  I wish our ... poets wd. r. 107:82
  if I do not r. thee 44:49
  in the morning we will r. them 65:20
  it r., whan it passed is 97–8:51
  please to r. the fifth of November 15:69
  r. ... best of friends must part 19:11
  r. Lot's wife, 55:88
  r. me when I am gone away 290:44
  r. now thy Creator 47:11
  r. when ... money not scarce? 133:47
  some day ... pleasant to r. 396:98
Remembered: r. tolling a departed friend 316:97
  when we r. Zion 44:44
  wd. have made myself r. 187:68
Remembering: a soul r. my good friends 349:44
  r. mine affliction ... misery 49:60
Remembers: nature yet r. what was so fugitive 411:80
Remembrance: appear almost a r. 186:55
  praising ... lost makes the r. dear 298:47
  rosemary, that's for r. 311:28
  summon up r. of things past 362:37
  writ in r. more than things long past 348:39
Reminds a man he is mortal 117:14
Remorse: farewell fear, farewell r. 218:63
Remote: r. and ineffectual don 32:1
  r., unfriended, melancholy, slow 151:89
Remover: bends with the r. to remove 363:47
Remuneration: Latin word for three farthings 331:12
Rend yr. heart and not yr. garments 50:78
Render therefore unto Caesar 53:43
Rendezvous: I have a r. with Death 296:20
Renounce the devil ... his works 64:95
Renown: a citizen of credit and r. 112:54
  living, shall forfeit fair r. 295:6
Renowned for larnin' and piety 154:18
Rent: what a r. the envious Casca made 325:18
Repair unto the Bell at Edmonton 113:55
Repay: I will r., saith the Lord 57:40

Repeal of bad or obnoxious laws 153:16

Repent: I do r. it from my very soul 358:64

Repentance: r. comes too late 276:86
Winter Garment of R. fling 135:66

Repented: she strove, and much r. 84:67

Repetitions: use not vain r. 52:17

Replenish: be fruitful ... r. the earth 34:29

Reply: third, the R. Churlish 303:9

Report me and my cause aright 312:37

Reporters: gallery in which the r. sit 202:44

Repose: earned a night's r. 199:8
O partial sleep, give thy r.? 317:14
r. is taboo'd by anxiety 144:91

Reposes: in quiet she r. 21:37

Reprehend: if I r. any thing in this world 372:71

Representation: no taxation without r. 273:3

Reproach: receives r. of being 363:49
sting of a r. ... truth of it 278:79

Reproof: fourth, the R. Valiant 303:9

Reprove: check the erring, and r. 413:7

Republican form of Government is the highest 376:33

Reputation: at every word a r. dies 251:36
if you esteem your own r. 399:33
purest treasure ... spotless r. 347:30
r., r., r., ... lost my r.! 345:1
seeking the bubble r. 301:90
sold my R. for a Song 136:82

Reputations: murdered r. of the week 108:7

Requests: thou wilt grant their r. 63:73

Require: what doth the Lord r.? 51:91

Requires: all the human frame r. 31:92

Researchers: our r. into public opinion 22:62

Resemble: when I r. her to thee 398:17

Resent: no individual cd. r. ... thousands ... meant 381:97

Resist: can r. everything except temptation 405:19
r. the devil and he will flee 60:6

Resisting: not over-fond of r. temptation 30:77

Resolute: be bloody, bold and r. 335:62

Resolution: in War: R. 102:10
native hue of r. 309:95
what r. from despair 216:33

Resolved to live a fool 29:70

Resolves: and re-resolves; then dies the same 418:63

Resort: far from all r. of mirth 213:86

Resource: infinite— r.— and— sagacity 191:16

Respect: is there no r. of place ... time? 359:86
the r. that makes calamity 309:95

Respectable: r. means rich 245:35
when was genius found r.? 73:10

Respecter of persons 56:19

Respects: he that r. not is not respected 276:88

Responsibility: liberty means r. ... men dread it 366:87
no sense of r. (baby) 191:21

Rest: absence of occupation is not r. 113:67
angels, sing thee to thy r. 312:40
far better r. that I go to 121:79
God ... ordain'd no r. 396:86
run far faster than the r. 32:3
set up my everlasting r. 354:18
she's at r. and so am I 127:60
so may he r. 323:85
some ill a-brewing towards my r. 339:9
the r. is silence 312:39
the r. of his dull life 29:70
wear ourselves and never r. 205:76

Restoration: the Church's R. in 1883 34:24

Restraint: firm r. with which they write 87:17

Resumed: democracy r. her reign 31:95

Reticulated or decussated 172:47

Retire me to my Milan 357:58

Retired into ... political Cave of Adullam 71:82

Retirement: short r. urges sweet return 220:92

Retort: first the R. Courteous 303:9

Retreat: let us make an honourable r. 302:94

Return: art gone and never must r. 215:10
departed never to r. 81:27
short retirement urges sweet r. 220:92
unto dust shalt thou r. 35:39

Returns: and the day r. too soon 86:98
small profits and quick r. 277:47

Reveal: words ... half r. ... half conceal 386:58

Reveals: soberness conceals what drunkenness r. 278:52

Revelry: sound of r. by night 83:59

Revels: our r. now are ended 356:50

Revenge: prompted to my r. by heaven 309:93

r., at first though sweet 220:91

r. his foul ... unnatural murder 307:65

r. is a kind of wild justice 24:89

r. is sweet 276:89

r. never repairs 276:90

shall we not r.? 339:13

spur my dull r. 311:22

study of r., immortal hate 216:30

sweet is r.—especially to women 84:68

sweet r. grows harsh 346:20

Revenges: time brings in his r. 360:2

Reverence: none so poor to do him r. 325:15

yet r. ... doth make distinction 304:27

Reviewing: read a book before r. it 375:11

Revolt: a r.? No, Sire, ... a revolution 288:20

inferiors r. in order that 20:27

Révolte: c'est une r.? non ... une révolution 288:20

Revolution: a revolt? No, sire, ... a r. 288:20

Révolution: une révolte? Non ... une r. 288:20

Revolutionist: not a r., is an inferior 365:84

Revolutions: state of mind which creates r. 20:27

Reward: only r. of virtue is virtue 132:30

r. of a thing well done 133:33

the Lord shall r. thee 45:81

virtue is its own r. 282:94

Rheims: Cardinal Lord Archbishop of R. 28:53

Rhetorician: a sophistical r. inebriated [Gladstone] 123:94

Rheumatic of shoulder 70:72

Rhodope: brighter than is ... R. 204:73

Rhyme: build the lofty r. 215:9

r. being no necessary adjunct 216:26

r. themselves into ladies' favours 321:61

soft names in many a mused r. 184:29

still more tired of r. 32:98

though my r. be ragged 373:92

Rialto: in the R. you have rated me 338:5

Rib: r. ... made he a woman 35:33

smote him under the fifth r. 40:50

Riband: just for a r. ... in his coat 74:28

r. in the cap of youth 311:29

Ribstone pippin: right as a R. 31:97

Rich: adversity makes ... not r. 254:59

being r., my virtue ... shall be 326:38

better to live r. than to die r. 177:27

born lucky than r. 255:16

good workmen are seldom r. 265:40

God help the r. 264:21

grew so r. that I was sent 147:27

he is r. that is satisfied 276:92

health! the blessing of the r.! 179:60

if I ever become a r. man 32:6

maketh haste to be r. 46:88

never be handsome, strong, r. 266:58

no sin but to be r. 326:38

one law for the r. 369:57

over the r. Dead 71:88

passing r. with forty pounds a year 150:66

Poor Little R. Girl 112:45

poverty is an anomaly to r. people 27:46

respectable means r. 245:35

r. can help themselves 264:20

r. man to enter ... kingdom of God 53:41

r. men have no faults 276:91

r. men rule the law 151:93

r. not gaudy 306:56

r. what gets the gravy 18:5

seems it r. to die 184:29

the r. man in his castle 10:18

victim of a r. man's game 18:3

when I grow r., say the bells 236:61

widows are always r. 283:30

wretchedness of being r. 374:2

Richard: body of R. Hind 13:45

we came in with R. Conqueror 355:19

Richer: for r. or for poorer 64:7

r. than doing nothing for a bribe 304:23

Riches: infinite r. in a little room 204:70

of great r. ... no real use 26:24

r. are for spending 26:21

r. I hold in light esteem 71:86

r. of the mind ... make ... rich 276:93

to r., dignity and power 32:4

Richly: a lady r. left 338:9
Rickshaw: it's no go the r. 203:54
Rid: idea of getting r. of it [work]
171:35
  if I can r. your town 75:39
Riddle: a r. wrapped in a mystery
100:91
Ride: a poem must r. 139:29
  Haggards r. no more 378:63
  r. a cock-horse 237:66
  r. in triumph through Persepolis
205:75
  went for a r. on a tiger 13:52
  when he next doth r. abroad 113:61
Rideau: tirez le r., la farce est jouée
285:90
Rider: secret ... between a r. and his
horse 381:94
Rides: and r. upon the storm 113:63
Ridicule: easier to r. than commend
276:94
Ridiculous: is not this r.? 146:14
  one step above the r. 243:19
  sublime to the r. 228:84
  the sublime and the r. ... nearly
related 243:19
Riding: r. to and from his wife 402:77
  Yankee Doodle ... r. on a pony
241:90
Ridley: be of good comfort, Master R.
193:40
Rien appris ... oublié 384:31
Rifle all the breathing spring 107:87
Rift: load every r. of yr. subject 187:69
Riga: young lady of Riga 13:52
Right: a r. judgement in all things
64:89
  all goes r. and nothing ... wrong
148:40
  all's r. with the world 75:44
  an earl by r., by courtesy a man
24:82
  defend to the death your r. 398:16
  do the r. deed for the wrong reason
132:17
  earth's the r. place for love 139:21
  great r. ... a little wrong 339:16
  I'll publish r. or wrong 85:88
  it must be r. I've done it from my
youth 114:79
  know not whether laws be r. 404:97
  majority never has r. on its side
169:8
  my r. there is none to dispute 114:77
  never dreamed, though r. were
worsted 73:16
  no r. to strike against the public
safety 110:28

Right (*continued*)
  our country, r. or wrong 118:16
  rather be r. than be President 103:22
  r. as a Ribstone Pippin 31:97
  r. as rain 276:95
  r. divine of kings to govern wrong
247:70
  r. in his own eyes 39:32
  shall not the Judge ... do r.? 35:54
  think at yr. age, it is r.? 90:48
  think the last opinion r. 249:2
  too fond of the r. 151:79
  two wrongs don't make a r. 281:83
  with firmness in the r. 196:81
Righteous: be not r. over much 47:6
  die the death of the r. 38:4
  if I find ... fifty r. 36:55
  judge r. judgment 55:2
  souls of the r. are in the hand of God
62:43
Righteousness: r. exalteth a nation
45:68
  the Sun of r. arise 51:1
Rights: endowed ... with certain un-
alienable r. 171:26
  property has its duties ... its r.
126:35
  reaffirm faith in fundamental ... r.
394:76
Rigol: from this golden r. hath
divorc'd 318:28
Rigour of the game 192:27
Ring: r. at the end of his nose 195:61
  spring ... the only pretty r. time
303:7
  with this r. I thee wed 65:9
Ring-a-ring o' roses 237:67
Rings: my true love sent ... five gold r.
238:73
  r. on her fingers 237:66
Riot: rash fierce blaze of r. cannot last
348:40
  r. and dishonour stain the brow
312:44
Ripe: from hour to hour, we r. and r.
301:88
  scholar ... r. and good one 323:87
Ripeness is all 330:98
Rise: r. up before the hoary head
38:1
  r. up, my love, my fair one 47:20
  some r. by sin ... by virtue fall
337:82
Rises: hoo-ray and up she r. 19:14
  while Jove's planet r. yonder 74:25
Rising: in his r. seemed a pillar 218:52
River: Alph, the sacred r., ran 106:71
  away, you rolling r. 18:1

Rome (*continued*)
I lov'd R. more   325:10
pardoun come from R.   97:43
R. shall fall; and when R. falls   84:64
R. was not built in a day   276:2
the grandeur that was R.   247:66
the hook-nos'd fellow of R.   317:24
when in R., live as the Romans do
11:23
Romeo: wherefore art thou R.?
353:99
Ronald: Lord R. said nothing ... rode
... off   194:51
Rood: when every r. ... maintained its
man   150:63
Roofs: masons building r. of gold
318–19:39
Room: all before my little r.   71:89
although the r. grows chilly   153:11
always r. at the top   400:46
convent's narrow r.   411:89
infinite riches in a little r.   204:70
no r. ... for hyphenated Americanism   289:38
no r. for them in the inn   54:67
not r. to swing a cat   276:3
r. of one's own   409:58
r. with a view—and you   112:41
Roosevelt: here is the answer ... to
President R.   101:98
Roost (Roast): to rule the r.   276:6
Root of all evil, The want of money
82:41
Rooted: pluck from the memory of r.
sorrow   336:72
Roots: stirring dull r. with spring rain
131:10
straight trees have crooked r.   279:84
Rope: a r. to hang himself   16:85
give a thief r. enough   276:4
Ropes: know the r.   268:43
Rose: a sadder ... man he r.   106:65
and lovely is the r.   410:73
as red as a r.   275:80
At Christmas I no more desire a r.
331:11
beauty's r. might never die   362:29
go, lovely r.   398:17
he's mighty lak' a r.   378:58
I am the r. of Sharon   47:17
in a twilight dim with r.   118:25
my fause lover stole my r.   81:28
my love ... like a red red r.   81:21
no r. without a thorn   273:99
not to me returns ... summer's r.
218:59
red as a r. is she   104:45
r. by any other name   353:11

Rose (*continued*)
r. leaves, when the r. is dead   370:54
r. of the fair state   310:1
r. or rue or laurel   382:17
the last r. of summer   226:63
the r. of youth upon him   299:60
when I have pluck'd thy r.   346:19
your image that blossoms a r.   417:55
Rosebuds: gather ye r. while ye may
162:24
r., before they be withered   62:41
Rosemary: for you there's r. and rue
361:20
r., that's for remembrance   311:28
Rose-moles all in stipple upon trout
166:68
Rose-red city half as old as time   77:70
Roses: as soon seek r. in December
85:91
ash the burnt r. leave   130:97
it was r., r., all the way   74:35
raptures and r. of vice   382:18
strew on her r., r.   21:37
their lips were four red r.   352:79
twin r. by the zephyr blown apart
182:3
where r. and white lilies grow   88:24
Rosy cheeks and flaxen curls   75:43
Rot: from hour to hour, we r. and r.
301:88
lie in cold obstruction and to r.
337:90
r. inwardly, and foul contagion
spread   215:16
Rotted: do you think my mind ... r.
early?   228:92
Rotten: something is r. in the state of
Denmark   307:62
soon ripe, soon r.   278:57
Rotting: mean and mighty r. together
304:27
Rough: take the r. with the smooth
276:5
Rough-hew them how we will   312:35
Round: in a light fantastic r.   212:75
Rounded: our little life is r. with a sleep
356–7:50
Rousseau: mock on, Voltaire, R.
67:39
Roving: we'll go no more a r.   86:97,98
Rowland: Child R., to the dark tower
329:82
Rowley, powley, gammon and spinach
232:30
Royal: likely ... to have prov'd most r.
312:41
no r. road to geometry   133:52
Rub: Ay, there's the r.   309:95

Rubies: her price is far above r.   46:92
  wisdom is better than r.   45:58
Rude: r. am I in my speech   344:90
  'very r. of him,' she said   92:77
Rue: nought shall make us r.   327:48
  shall I strew ... rose or r.   382:17
  there's rosemary and r.   361:20
  with r. my heart is laden   167:84
Rues: eye sees not, heart r. not   262:42
Ruffian, that father r.   314:68
Ruhnken: more learn'd professor R.
  252:41
Ruins: I'm one of the r.   197:87
Rule: exception proves the r.   262:38
  golden r. is ... no golden rules
  365:86
  only infallible r. we know   380:89
  r., Britannia, r. the waves   391:33
  r. them with a rod of iron   60:21
  r. youth well for age will r. itself
  276:7
Ruler of the Queen's Navee   147:26,
  27
Rulers: against the r. of the darkness
  58:74
Ruling: the r. ideas ... ideas of its r.
  class   207:8
  the r. passion ... conquers reason
  251:27
Rum: what a R. Go everything is
  401:65
  Yo-ho-ho and a bottle of r.   379:74
Rumble thy bellyful. Spit, fire   328:72
Rumour: listen to popular r.   149:49
Run: gwine to r. all night   137:1
  he may r. that readeth   51:93
  outrun ... that which we r. at   322:74
  r., r., Orlando   302:92
  r. with the hare   276:8
  see how they r.!   240:80
  they ... r. about through the city
  42:12
  until it doth r. over   16:78
  you r. about, my little Maid   416:41
  you've had a pleasant r.   93:82
Runcible cat   195:63
Runcible spoon: ate with a r.   195:62
Running: takes all the r. you can do.
  92:72
  the r. of the deer   16–17:87
Runs: fights and r. away   14:61
Run-stealers flicker to and fro   390:28
Rupert: frank ... rash,—the R. of
  Debate   76:53
Rushy: down the r. glen   11:22
Russia: I cannot forecast ... the action
  of R.   100:91
  R. has two generals   230:17

Russia (continued)
  this will last out a night in R.   337:83
Russian: he might have been a R.
  (Roosian)   147:30
Rust: better to wear out than to r. out
  115:92
  Sunday clears away the r.   9:7
Rustling in unpaid-for silk   304:23
Rusty: my ryme ... r. and mothe eaten
  373:92
Ruth: sad heart of R., when, sick for
  home   184:30
Rye: before the Roman came to R.
  99:72
  comin' through the r.   79:3
  fields of barley and of r.   387:75

Sabbath: child ... born on the s. day
  235–6:56
  never broke the S. but for gain
  126:45
  remember the s. day to keep it holy
  37:86
  s. ... made for man ... not man for s.
  53:54
  seventh day is the s.   37:86
Sabrina fair, listen   213:80
Sack: I'll purge, and leave s.   315:95
  s. the lot!   134:64
  this intolerable deal of s.!   314:70
Sacred: if anything is s. ... body is s.
  403:80
  the s. river ran   106:71, 73
Sacrifice: I desire mercy, and not s.
  50:75
Sacrifices: the s. of God are   42:9
Sad: how s. and bad and mad   73:20
  s. words of tongue or pen   403:90
  when pleasant thoughts bring s.
  411:83
  you shd. remember and be s.   290:45
Sadder: a s. and wiser man   106:65
Sadists: repressed s. ... to become
  policemen   110:22
sadness: s. and gladness succeed each
  other   276:9
  shady s. of a vale   182:96
  sickness is better than s.   277:36
Safe: better s. than sorry   255:19
  I pray you ... see me s. up   226:66
  I wish him s. at home   179:63
  s. ... on Abraham's breast   13:48
  to be s. ... never to be secure   282:14
  world made s. for democracy   408:47
Safely: thro' the world we s. go   66:30
Safer: s. to obey than to rule   188:73
  'tis s. to be that which we destroy
  334:50

Safest: just when we are s. ... a sunset-
touch 73:17
Safety: in ... multitude of counsellors
... is s. 45:63
our s. is in our speed 133:35
strike against the public s. 110:28
we pluck this flower, s. 313:60
Sagacious, bold and turbulent of wit
126:38
Sagacity: infinite—resource—and—s.
191:16
Sage: thou Goddess s. and holy 213:83
Sages: teach you more ... than all the s.
414:28
Said: best ... known and s. in the world
21:53
I hope it may be s. 'His sins' 31:93
Sail: and cried, A s.! A s.! 105:51
full s. ... fan spread ... streamers
109:10
s. near the wind 276:10
s. on, O Ship of State! 197:92
very sea-mark of my utmost s.
346:21
white and rustling s. 116:96
Sailed: they s. away ... year and a day
195:61
Sailing: three ships come s. by 15:74,
233–4:42
what thing ... comes this way s.
222:18
Sailor: drunken s. early in the morning
19:14
home is the s. 379:76
Sails: purple the s., and so perfumed
298:54
when we our s. advance 125:31
wind out of one's s. 279:2
Saint: and never a s. took pity on
105:54
art ... able to corrupt a s. 312:46
my late espoused s. 223:35
open the shrine, that I may see my s.
179:59
s.-seducing gold 353:90
seem a s. when ... play the devil
351:70
young s., old devil 284:65
St. Agnes Eve—Ah, bitter chill 181:89
St. Clement's: say the bells of S.
236:61
St. Crispin: fought ... upon S.'s day
320–21:59
Saint Empire Romain ... ni saint, ni
romain, ni empire 398:14
St. George: for Harry, England, and
S.! 319:47
S., that swing'd the dragon 326:35

St. Ives: as I was going to S. 231:22
St. John: awake, my S. 250:7
St. Martin's: say the bells of S. 236:61
St. Paul's: 'Say I am designing S.'
33:16
Saint Vincent: nobly, nobly, Capt. S.
74:24
Saints: a pair of carved s. 350:55
all the S. adore thee 160:88
Sal: down South for to see my S.
18:97
Salad: my s. days 298:53
Salisbury: Lord S. ... brought back
peace 122:93
Sally: there's none like pretty S. 89:31
Salt: became a pillar of s. 36:56
coaster with a s.-caked smoke-stack
207:13
ye are the s. of the earth 52:11
Salus populi suprema est lex 102:15
Salute: s. the happy morn 83:52
s. thee with my hand 349:49
Salvation: my bottle of s. 286:94
none of us shd. see s. 339:15
visit us with thy s. 402:72
work out yr. own s. 58:75
wot prawce s.? 365:77
Samarkand: the Golden Road to S.
136:84
Same: it's the s. the whole world over
18:5
Jesus Christ the s. ... for ever 60:3
more they are the s. 180:72
no better ... much the s. 24:83
Sammy: vy worn't there a alleybi!
121:76
Samson: better than the strength of S.
272:55
Sanctity: in the odour of s. died 28:54
Sand: a world in a grain of s. 66:27
little grain of s. 89:41
on the edge of the s. 195:62
roll down their golden s. 159:86
such quantities of s. 92:78
throw the s. against the wind 67:39
Sandals were for Clementine 225:60
Sandalwood, cedarwood, ... white
wine 207:12
Sandboy: jolly as a 268:25
Sands: come unto these yellow s.
355:34
golden s., and crystal brooks 123:4
lone and level s. stretch far away
369:40
on the s. with printless foot 357:54
wd. steer too nigh the s. 126:39
Sane: see where the s. ... have landed
us! 366:1

Schemes: best laid s. o' mice and men 80:18

Scholar: he was a s. and a ripe   323:87
   what ills the s.'s life assail   173:68

Scholars: great men ... not commonly ... great s.   164:51
   s. dispute ... case is still before the courts   166:70

School: every day in the life of a s. 194:50
   example ... the s. of mankind   78:82
   extreme busyness ... at s. or college 379:78
   like snail unwillingly to s.   301:90
   s. of Stratford atte Bowe   96:28
   tell tales out of s.   279:4
   toward s. with heavy looks   354:4
   village master taught his little s. 150:68

Schoolboy: every s. knows who imprisoned Montezuma   202:42
   whining s., with his satchel   301:90

Schoolboys: as s. from their books 354:4

Schooldays: in my joyful s.   192:32

Schoolgirl: pert as a s.   145:2
   that s. complexion   11:30

Schoolman's subtle art   248:87

Schoolmaster: average s. ... essentially an ass   209:29

Schools: 'tis an old maxim in the s. 381:96

Schooner: the s. Hesperus   199:9

Science: fair S. frowned not on his ... birth   155:40
   S. is organized knowledge   376:32

Scoff: fools, who came to s.   150:67

Scotting: antic sits s. his state   350:54

Scorer: when the one Great S. comes 287:9

Scorn: fixed figure for the time of s. 346:13
   I can s. and let her go   408:50
   I s. to change my state   362:36
   in s. of eyes, reflecting gems   352:72
   love he laugh'd to s.   364:59
   love I laugh to s.   71:86
   s. not the sonnet   412:95
   the sound of public s.   220:96

Scorned: nor hell a fury like a woman s.   108:6

Scorns: how Stanley s., the glance 76:53

Scorpions: they had tails like unto s. 61:29

Scotchman: a S., if he be caught young 176:4

Scot-free: to go s.   277:17

Scotland: I do indeed come from S. 174:83
   I'll be in S. afore ye   18:2
   oats ... in S., supports the people 172:48
   stands S. where it did?   335:66

Scots: Kills me ... S. at a breakfast 314:62
   S. wha hae wi' Wallace bled   81:22
   S. whom Bruce has ... led   81:22

Scotsman: grandest moral attribute of a S.   28:64

Scott: not even Sir Walter S.   367:8

Scotus or Aquinas   223:40

Scoundrel: every man over forty is a s. 366:91
   general good ... plea of the s.   67:36
   patriotism ... last refuge of a s. 176:12

Scourge: daughter of Jove ... whose iron s.   155-6:43

Scratch: come up to the s.   277:18
   s. my back and I'll s. yours   277:19

Scratching: cure ... but the s. of a pen 200:19
   wd. ... I had the s. of thee   358:69

Scream: a s., a splash   18:4

Screw: a s. loose somewhere   277:20
   s. may twist ... rack may turn   148:43
   s. yr. courage to the sticking place 333:38

Scribble: always s., s., s.! ... Mr Gibbon   149:56

Scrip and scrippage   302:94

Scripture: all s. is ... by inspiration of God   59:94
   devil can cite S. for his purpose 338:4

Scriptures: life like the s.—figurative 187:64

Scruple: some craven s.   311:23
   wd. not s. to pick a pocket   119:29

Scullion: away, you s.!   316:5

Sculpture: beauty cold ... like that of s. 292:67

Scum: [our army] ... s. of the earth 401:59

Scutcheon: honour is a mere s.   315:88

Scylla: between S. and Charybdis 256:33

Scythe: mower whets his s.   214:98

Scythian: snow on S. hills   204:73

Sea: all the s. were ink   15:65
   alone on a wide, wide s.   105:54, 106:62
   and there was no more s.   61:32
   between France and England ... the s.   171:38

Sea (*continued*)
  devil and the deep s. 260:72
  down to a sunless s. 106:71
  down to the s. in ships 43:26
  England ... with the triumphant s. 349:42
  first ... into that silent s. 105:48
  from s. to shining s. 29:67
  into the midst of the s. 36:78
  learn the secret of the s.? 198:1
  mother and lover ... the s. 383:25
  my Bonnie is over the s. 17:94
  never, never sick at s.! 147:22
  not all the water in the rough, rude s. 349:50
  on such a full s. are we now afloat 326:27
  one foot in s. 343:68
  one that goes to s. for nothing 123:8
  out of the s. came he 104:44
  over the s. to Skye 69:69, 379:73
  plants His footsteps in the s. 113:63
  precious stone set in the silver s. 348:41
  sailed the wintry s. 199:9
  scatter'd in the bottom of the s. 352:72
  the kings of the s. 20:34
  the rude s. grew civil 341:44
  the s. is calm to-night 20:30
  the s. never changes 110:26
  the s.! the s.! 416:50
  the wrinkled s. beneath him crawls 385:47
  there is Society ... by the deep s. 84:65
  till the s. ... floweth in yr. veins 392:52
  to s. for nothing but to make him sick 123:8
  to s. in a ... pea-green boat 195:60
  two Voices ... one is of the s. 412:1
  went down into the s. 104:44
  went to s. in a sieve 194:57
  when I put out to s. 385:44
  where no s. runs 390:21
  whose sound was like the s. 413:4
  why the s. is boiling hot 93:80
  wind of the Western S. 388:96
  winds somewhere safe to s. 383:20
  within a walk of the s. 32:7
  worse things happen at s. 284:58
Sea-boy: wet s. in an hour so rude 317:14
Seagreen Incorruptible 89:35
Seal: all right ... you heard a s. bark 392:43
  opened the seventh s. 61:27

Sealing-wax: ships and s. 93:80
Seals of love, but seal'd in vain 337–8:92
Sea-maid: to hear the s.'s music 341:44
Sea-mark: very s. of my utmost sail 346:21
Sea-monster: ingratitude ... more hideous ... than the s. 328:57
Search will find it out 162:22
Seas: foam of perilous s. 184:30
  guard our native s. 88:21
  I must down to the s. again 207–8:14–16
  port after stormy s. 377:42
  the multitudinous s. incarnadine 334:43
  we shall fight on the s. and oceans 100:94
Seaside: I do like to be beside the s. 149:57
Season: a dry brain in a dry s. 130:93
  givest ... meat in due s. 44:52
  in the s. of the year 18:98
  to every thing ... a s. 46:98
Seasons: as the swift s. roll 164:50
  defend you from s. such as these 329:78
  four s. fill the measure 185:45
  four s. in the mind of man 185:45
  thus with the year s. return 218:59
  when mercy s. justice 339:15
Seat: regain the blissful s. 216:27
  this s. of Mars 348:41
Seats: you want the best s.; we have them 11:35
Seconds: sixty s. worth of distance run 190:5
Secrecy: for s., no lady closer 313:61
Secret: bread eaten in s. is pleasant 45:60
  digestion ... great s. of life 375:12
  it [love] ceases to be a s. 30:85
  joys of parents are s. 24:94
  learn the s. of the sea? 198:1
  s., black, and midnight hags! 335:60
  there is no s. so close 381:94
Secrets: s. with girls ... never valued 114:82
  tell the s. of my prison-house 307:64
Sect: attached to that great s. 368:25
  paradise for a s. 182:93
Sects: two-and-seventy jarring s. confute 135:77
Secure: safe ... never to be s. 282:14
  s., and never now can mourn 367:16
Sedge is wither'd from the lake 182:7
See: and no man s. me more 322:79
  blind as those who won't s. 256:45

Shadrach, Meshach, and Abed-nego
  49:67
Shadwell: S. ... my perfect image bears
  128:69
  S. never deviates into sense   128:69
Shady: on Ida's s. brow   68:54
Shafto: Bobby S.'s gone to sea   231:24
Shaken: looks on tempests and is never
  s.   363:47
  so s. as we are, so wan   312:42
  when taken to be well s.   108:95
Shake-scene: is the only s.   156:49
Shakespeare: fashionable topics ...
  pictures ... S.   152:1
  immortal S. rose   173:58
  might have chanced to be S.   169:4
  our myriad-minded S.   107:80
  S. led a life of allegory   187:64
  S. unlocked his heart   412:95
  sweetest S., Fancy's child   214:4
  the tongue that S. spake   413:5
  what needs my S. for his ... bones
  216:23
  when I read S.   194:49
Shall: mark you his absolute 's.'
  303:16
Shallow: Master S., I owe you   318:35
  s. in himself   221:8
Shallows: bound in s. and in miseries
  326:27
Shalott: the Lady of S.   387:77
Shame: ain't it all a bleedin' s.?   18:5
  England ... now bound in with s.
  349:42
  in a waste of s.   363:50
  poverty is not a s.   275:55
  whose glory is their s.   58:76
Shank: too wide for his shrunk s.
  301:90
Shape: com'st in such a questionable s.
  307:60
  S. of Things to Come   401:67
  the other S.—if s. it might be   218:56
  to lick into s.   269:75
  virtue in her s. how lovely   219:73
Share: no one so true did s. it
  359-60:88
  s. and s. alike   277:30
Sharon: I am the rose of S.   47:17
Sharper: a s. played with a dupe
  115:86
  s. than a serpent's tooth   328:58
Sharps: fifty different s. and flats
  75:38
Shatter yr. leaves before the mellowing
  year   215:8
Shaven: bald heads are soon s.   255:90
  if I be s. ... strength will go   39:29

Shaves: a man who s. and takes a train
  402:77
She: has got him a s.   16:79
  that not impossible s.   115:84
  the fair ... and unexpressive s.
  302:92
Sheba: another S. Queen   408:48
Shed: a lowly cattle s.   10:19
  by man shall his blood be s.   35:49
  tears, prepare to s. them now   325:17
  with ... [Edmund Burke] beneath a
  s.   178:46
Sheep: an old half-witted s.   378:62
  baa, baa, black s.   231:23
  black s. in every flock   256:42
  divideth ... s. from ... goats   53:47
  hanged for a s. as a lamb   266:60
  hungry s. look up, and are not fed
  215:16
  Little Bo-peep has lost her s.   234:48
  looking on their silly s.   322:71
  mountain s. are sweeter   245:38
  noble ensample to his s. he yaf
  97:40
  return to our s.   19:16
  strayed from thy ways like lost s.
  63:66
  the s.'s in the meadow   234:49
Sheep-hook: know how to hold a s.
  215:15
Sheet: a wet s. and a flowing sea
  116:96
Sheets: better wear out shoes than s.
  256:32
Shelley: did you once see S. plain?
  74:30
Shelter: I will build a house ... to s. me
  32:6
  our s. from the stormy blast   399:38
Shenandoah: O, S. I long to hear you
  18:1
Shepherd: as a s. divideth his sheep
  53:47
  Dick the s. blows his nail   332:20
  every s. tells his tale   214:98
  go, for they call you, S.   21:39
  good s. giveth his life   55:6
  homely, slighted, s.'s trade   215:11
  Old Nod the s. goes   118:25
  truth in every s.'s tongue   286:96
Shepherds: a sweeter shade to s.   322:71
  s. abiding in the field   54:68
  while s. watched their flocks   384:35
Sheridan was listened to   288:25
Shibboleth: say now S.   39:26
Shift: let me s. for myself   226:66
Shilling: better give a s.   256:23
  cut off with a s.   259:47

Shillings: rather than forty s. ... Book of Songs 340:28

Shimei, though not prodigal of pelf 126:46

Shine: err with Pope ... s. with Pye 85:92

few are qualified to s. 382:10

I see Heaven's glories s. 71:84

moon doth s. as bright as day 231:25

s. so brisk, and smell so sweet 313:52

sun that warms you ... s. on me 348:33

Shines: light ... where no sun s. 390:21

Shining: from sea to s. sea 29:67

s. with all his might 92:76

Ship: a s. in a black storm 401:55

a s. is worse than a gaol 177:16

a stately s. of Tarsus 222:18

all I ask is a tall s. 207:14

as idle as a painted s. 105:49

our saucy s.'s a beauty 146:19

rats desert a sinking s. 275:79

sail on, O S. of State 197:92

the s. has weathered every rack 403:81

Ships: face that launch'd a thousand s. 204:63

I saw three s. come sailing by 233–4:42

our bloody s. today 29:69

seen old s. sail like swans 136:85

s. that pass in the night 198:4

s., towers, domes, theatres 412:96

spied three s. come sailing by 15:74

we've got the s., we've got the men 168:93

Shires and towns from Airly Beacon 189:85

Shirt: no s. or collar ... comes back twice 194:53

Shive: cut loaf to steal a s. 357–8:63

Shiver: little breezes dusk and s. 387:76

Shivering: grass ... s.-sweet to the touch 111:34

Shoal: a s. of fools for tenders 109:10

bank and s. of time 333:36

Shock: short sharp s. 145:3

Shock-headed Peter 164:42

Shocks: natural s. that flesh is heir to 309:95

Shoe: I kiss his dirty s. 320:51

know where the s. pinches 277:31

my dame has lost her s. 231:26

old woman ... lived in a s. 239:76

one, two, buckle my s. 236:60

Shoemakers: brave s. ... of the gentle craft 118:21

Shoe-string: a careless s. in whose tie 162:17

Shoes: better wear out s. than sheets 256:32

her s. were number nine 225:60

old s. ... easiest for his feet 296:21

s. – and ships – and sealing-wax 93:80

Shone like a meteor streaming 217:39

Shoot: do not s. the pianist 405:17

s., if you must, this old gray head 403:89

Shopkeepers: England is a nation of's. 228:85

fit only for a nation of s. 374:98

nation that is governed by s. 374:98

Shops: that men might shun the awful s. 99:76

Shore: adieu, my native s. 83:57

fast by their native s. 113:64

now upon the farther s. 132:23

rapture on the lonely s. 84:65

rocky s. beats back the envious siege 349:42

s. of the wide world 186:49

the lights around the s. 291:53

waves make towards the pebbled s. 363:40

Shoreditch: say the bells of S. 236:61

Short: if you find it wond'rous s. 150:75

s. and sweet 277:32

sweet discourse makes s. days 279:90

take a long while to make it s. 391:40

Shorter: had Cleopatra's nose been s. 244:27

make you s. by a head 132:19

Shortly: I expect a judgment. S. 119:34

Shortness: to spend that s. basely 315:89

Shot: I s. the albatross 105:47

not a soldier discharged his farewell s. 408:52

Shoulder: give the cold s. 258:20

put yr. s. to the wheel 275:72

Shoulder-blade: I have a left s. ... a miracle 146:9

Shoulders: old head on young s. 274:19

Shout: s. that tore Hell's concave 217:40

's. with the largest' [mob] 121:63

there was a s. about my ears 99:69

Shouting: after the ... music with s. and laughter 75:43
all is over bar the s. 254:67
Shovel them [bodies] under and let me work 293:78
Show: s. and gaze o' th' time 336:79
that within which passes s. 305:41
to offer it the s. of violence 305:35
Shower: drainless s. of light is poesy 185:38
this was our finest s.! 242:7
Showers: Aprille with his s. sote 96:25
fresh s. for thirsting flowers 368:21
small s. last long 348:40
Shows: May's new-fangled s. 331:11
Shreds: king of s. and patches 311:18
thing of s. and patches 145:95
Shrieking: with s. and squeaking 75:38
Shrink: all the boards did s. 105:50
Shroud: my s. ... stuck all with yew 359–60:88
Shrug: borne it with a patient s. 338:6
Shuffled off this mortal coil 309:95
Shun: s. the heaven that leads ... to ... hell 363:51
that men might s. the awful shops 99:76
Shut, shut the door, good John 248:77
Shutters: now ... close the s. fast 114:73
Shy: once bitten, twice s. 274:21
you look a little s. 94:98
Sick: can s. men play so nicely? 349:43
for I am s. of love 47:19
hope deferred maketh the heart s. 45:66
I am s. at heart 305:33
never, never s. at sea! 147:22
s. hurry ... divided aims 21:42
the devil was s. 227:74
the enterprise is s.! 358:67
tie up the knocker, say I'm s. 248:77
to sea for nothing but to make him s. 123:8
when ... the heart is s. 386:60
when we are s. in fortune 327:53
Sicklied o'er with the pale cast 309:95
Sickness: he hath the falling s. 324:95
in s. and in health 64:7
s. is better than sadness 277:36
Side: courtesy on one s. only 259:32
hear the other s. 254:81
look on the bright s. 270:3
nobody is on my s. 23:79
trumpets sounded ... on the other s. 77:67
which s. one's bread is buttered 268:42

Sides: buttered on both s. 257:65
laughter holding both his s. 214:94
your ... unfed s. 329:78
Siècles: quarante s. vous contemplent 228:83
Siege: rocky shore beats back the envious s. 349:42
Sieve: carry water in a s. 282:10
in a s. they went to sea 194:57
Sigh: a s. is the sword 66:35
a s. like Tom o' Bedlam 327:54
s. no more, ladies, s. no more 343:68
s. the lack of many a thing 362:37
something ... prompts th' eternal s. 250:15
Sighed: no sooner s. but they ask'd 302:5
she s., she cried 17:96
s. for ... love of a ladye 148–9:46
Sighing: a plague of s. and grief! 314:67
fell a-s. and a-sobbing 241:89
Sighs: for my pains a world of s. 344:92
s. are the natural language 297:38
Sight: a s. to dream of 106:66
and 'tis a shameful s. 399:37
every common s. to me did seem 410:72
Oh the pleasant s. to see 189:85
she gleamed upon my s. 414:16
s. for sore eyes 277:37
s. ... good for sore eyes 382:7
s. of means to do ill deeds 327:45
s. of vernal bloom 218:59
s. so touching in its majesty 412:96
to s. or thought be formed 220:94
who ever lov'd that lov'd not at first s.? 205:81
Sights: such s. as youthful poets dream 214:3
what s. of ugly death! 352:72
Sign: an olive-leaf ... pacific s. 221:1
an outward and visible s. 64:1
God made the wicked Grocer for a ... s. 99:76
Signal: only a s. shown 198:4
Silence: but oh! the s. sank 106:61
darkness again and a s. 198:4
dusky hour friendliest to ... s. 219:80
foster-child of s. 183:16
greet thee? With s. and tears 86:1
let yr. women keep s. in ... churches 57:56
mourn'd in s. and was Di-do-Dum 252:40
my gracious s., hail! 303:13

Silence (*continued*)
no wisdom like s. 283:38
seul le s. est grand 396:94
s. gives consent 277:38
s. is golden 278:65
s., like a poultice, comes 164:44
s. ... perfectest herald of joy 342:64
the rest is s. 312:39
there was s. in heaven 61:27
to sit in solemn s. in ... dock 145:3
Silent: burst into that s. sea 105:48
s. as the moon, when she deserts
221:14
s., flooding in, the main 103:33
s. over Africa 74:25
s. stars go by 72:95
s., upon a peak in Darien 185:41
s. was the flock 181:89
Silently: s., and with how wan a face!
373:85
s., invisibly he took her 67:41
wind does move s., invisibly 67:40
Silk: rustling in unpaid-for s. 304:23
Silken: s. dalliance in the wardrobe lies
319:40
s. lines and silver hooks 123:4
Silks: whenas in s. my Julia goes
162:23
Silver: can wisdom be put in a s. rod?
66:32
every cloud has a s. lining 258:12
how s.-sweet sound lovers' tongues
354:5
just for a handful of s. 74:28
polished up the s. plate 226:70
precious stone set in the s. sea
348:41
seated in thy s. chair 178–9:50
s. and gold have I none 56:15
s. bells and cockle shells 235:55
s. buckles at his knee 231:24
s. nutmeg and a golden pear 233:39
the oars were s. 298:54
the s. Rhodope 204:73
when gold and s. becks me 327:40
Silvia: who is S.? What is she? 361:8
Simon: Simple S. met a pieman 237:69
Simplicity: in low s. he lends out ...
gratis 338:3
in ... s. a child 248:89
pity my s. 402:70
Simplify, simplify 391:37
Sin: a private s. is not so prejudicial
95:11
a s. to covet honour 320:56
as ugly as s. 281:84
before polygamy was made a s.
126:36

Sin (*continued*)
he that is without s. among you 55:3
hold there is no s. but ignorance
204:69
no s. but to be rich 326:38
no s. except stupidity 404:2
no s. to s. in secret 224:51
pleasure's a s. ... s.'s a pleasure
84:69
some rise by s. 337:82
some will pluck on s. 352:77
this dark world of s. 65:19
wages of s. is death 56:32
whose s. ... dipt me in ink? 248:80
Sincere: a wit shd. be no more s. 109:9
Sincerely: comes as s. from the author's
soul 169:3
Sincerity: a little s. is a dangerous thing
404:99
Sind: *Peccavi* (I have S.) 228:82
Sinews: stiffen the s., summon up the
blood 319:45
Sing: and I will s. of the sun 252:48
arms and the man I s. 128:72
himself to s., and build the lofty
rhyme 215:9
I celebrate ... and s. myself 403:82
I do not think that they will s. to me
131:5
I'll s. ... in thy praise 79:98
I s. the Sofa 113:68
Lhude s. Goddamm 252:47
love, and pray, and s. 330:99
more safe I s. 219:83
now let us s., Long live the King
113:61
ord'ring yr. affairs, to s. them too
362:21
Quires and Places where they s.
63:72
s. both high and low 359:83
s., choirs of Angels, s. in exultation
241:92
s., Heavenly Muse 216:27
s. me a song ... lad that is gone
379:73
s. me a song, O! 148:45
s. no sad songs for me 290:47
s. 'polly-wolly-doodle' 18:97
s. them loud ... dead of night 359:80
s. to the Lord with cheerful voice
188:77
swans s. before they die 106:70
used to s. it—fifty thousand strong
416:44
we'd s. and pray ... livelong day
68:45
we'll s. another song 416:44

Sing (*continued*)
when you s., I'd have you buy 362:21
Singe: so hot ... it doth s. yourself 322:74
Singed: I have s. ... king's beard 125:29
Singing: everyone suddenly burst out s. 293:83
I'll be quit of the s. 12:43
maid s. in the valley below 16:80
s. in the Wilderness 135:67
sweet s. in the choir 16–17:87
Single: continued s. ... only talked of population 152:96
Sings: chaffinch s. on the orchard bough 74:21
in his motion like an angel s. 340:22
in me [summer] s. no more 210:47
lark at heaven's gate s. 304:20
s. for his supper 235:52
tell me what she s. 414:21
thrush, he s. each song twice over 74:23
Singularity: surprise by ... excess ... not by S. 186:55
Sinks: it s., and I am ready 192:34
Sinner: joy ... over one s. that repenteth 54:80
Sinners: God and s. reconciled 402:71
mercy upon us miserable s. 63:76
Sinning: more sinn'd against than s. 329:76
Sins: did ... from expensive s. refrain 126:45
few love to hear the s. they love to act 347:25
his s. were scarlet, but his books 31:93
oldest s. the newest kind of ways 318:30
other s. only speak; murder shrieks out 400:49
result of her s. was quadruplets 14:55
the multitude of s. 60:11
though yr. s. be as scarlet 48:30
Sirens: blest pair of S. 212:71
Sisera: stars ... fought against S. 39:22
Sister: a barren s. all your life 341:35
but I kissed her little s. 225:61
Sisters: his s., and his cousins, and his aunts 147:25
sphere-born harmonious s. 212:71
two s. embrace like one brother 287:11
Sit: can s. and look at it [work] for hours 171:35

Sit (*continued*)
here I and sorrows s. 326:39
I will s. down now, but 122:88
If I s. on a pin 13:51
not fit that you shd. s. here 115:90
shall s. and drink with me 32:7
s. every man under his vine 50:89
s. on a cushion and sew 231–2:27
s. upon the murdered reputations 108:7
so I did s. and eat 161:13
test my bath before I s. 229:96
there we s. in peaceful calm 169:5
to s. in ... shade ... look upon verdure 23:70
to s. upon a hill, as I do now 321:70
Sitivation at the lighthouse 121:77
Sitting: thee s. careless on ... granary floor 181:80
Situation excellent. I shall attack 136:87
Six: it's just s. of one 206:87
s. days shalt thou labour 37:86
s. hours in sleep, in ... study s. 104:40
s. of one and half a dozen ... other 277:41
Sixes and sevens: to be at s. 277:42
Sixpence: bang—went s.!!! 285:79
buy a thing that costs even s. 176:5
he found a crooked s. 239:74
I love s., jolly little s. 233:40
nothink for nothink ... little for s. 285:80
sing a song of s. 238:70
Skating over thin ice 133:35
Skies: cloudless climes and starry s. 86:96
for s. of couple-colour 166:68
his watch-tower in the s. 214:97
in summer skies to mourn 181:88
some watcher of the s. 185:41
Skill: simple truth his utmost s. 416:48
Skills: create by means of new s. 292:66
Skin: and it punctures my s. 13:51
by the s. of one's teeth 277:43
can the Ethiopian change his s.? 49:56
her s. was white as leprosy 105:52
I stuff my s. so full within 380:82
saw the skull beneath the s. 131:13
why, my s. hangs about me 314:78
Skins: all ... fancy dress ... except our ... s. 366:6
Skipped: the mountains s. like rams 43:29

Slight: away, s. man! 326:25
  if she s. me when I woo   408:50
Slimy: a thousand thousand s. things
  105:55
Slings and arrows of outrageous fortune 309:95
Slinks out of the race   223:39
Slip 'twixt the cup and the lip   280:20
Slippery: as s. as an eel   277:45
Slips: like greyhounds in the s.   319:47
Sloth: too much time in studies ... s.
  26:31
Slough: name of the s. was Despond
  77:58
Slow: s. and steady   197:89
  s. but sure   277:46
  come he s. or come he fast   295:9
  divine grace was never s.   260:78
  I am s. of study   341:41
  sun climbs s., how slowly   104:34
  too swift ... as tardy as too s.   354:10
  wisely and s.   354:7
Slowly: and s. answered Arthur   385:54
  mills of God grind s.   198:99
  ring out a s. dying cause   386:69
  sun climbs slow, how s.   104:34
Sluggard: go to the ant, thou s.   44:57
  voice of the s.   400:41
Slumber: I must s. again   400:41
  love itself shall s. on   370:54
  ports of s. open wide   317:27
Slumbering: poesy ... 'tis might half-s.
  185:38
Slumbers: golden s. kiss your eyes
  118:20
  soul is dead that s.   198:95
Slung atween the round shot   230:11
Slut: I am not a s.   302:2
Small: all things both great and s.
  106:64
  microbe is so very s.   32:2
  souls of women are so s.   82:40
  when they said, 'Is it s.?'   195:65
  wind ... to fire ... extinguishes the s.
  82:34
  yet they grind exceeding s.   198:99
Smarts so little as a fool   248:79
Smattering of everything   121:78
Smell: here's the s. of the blood still
  335:69
  I know ... the sweet keen s.   291:53
  shine so brisk, and s. so sweet
  313:52
  s. far worse than weeds   363:42
  taste ... better than the s.   279:11
  to s. a rat   277:48
Smells: it s. to heaven   311:15
Smile: and s., s., s.   22:56

Smile (continued)
  did he s. his work to see?   68:47
  fortune ... s. once more   328:63
  grandeur hear with a disdainful s.
  155:34
  I dare not beg a s.   162:19
  if we do meet ... shall s.   326:28
  my wanton, s. upon my knee   156:48
  s. at us, pay us, pass us   99:75
  s. on the face of the tiger   13:52
  that s. we wd. aspire to   322–3:81
  you shd. forget and s.   290:45
Smiled: s. a kind of sickly smile
  158:73
  until she s. on me   104:41
Smiles: daggers in men's s.   334:47
  life is ... sobs, sniffles, and s.   161:3
  Nods and Becks and wreathed S.
  214:93
  s. awake you when you rise   118:20
Smilest: Thou s. and art still   21:44
Smiling: com'st s. from the ... snare
  uncaught?   299:63
  like Patience ... s. at grief   360:89
  Soldan of Byzantium is s.   99:70
Smilingly: flaw'd heart ... burst s.
  330:3
Smite: if the rude caitiff s. the other
  164:45
  whosoever shall s. thee   52:13
Smith: the s., a mighty man is he
  199:6
Smithy: the village s. stands   199:6
Smoke: good cigar is a s.   190:94
  in yr. pipe and s. it   275:71
  no fire without some s.   273:92
  s, and blood is the mix of steel
  293:80
Smokeless: bright and glittering in the
  s. air   412:96
Smooth: I am a s. man   36:59
  take the rough with the s.   276:5
Smote: and s. him—thus   346–7:22
  s. them hip and thigh   39:28
  the Lord s. all the firstborn   36:77
Smyler with the Knyf under the Cloke
  97:44
Snaffle ... curb ... but where's the
  bloody horse?   87:17
Snail: a whiting to a s.   91:62
  like s. unwillingly to school   301:90
  the s.'s on the thorn   75:44
Snake: a s. in the grass   277:49
  earth doth like a s. renew   368:28
Snapper-up of unconsidered trifles
  361:18
Snare: smiling from the world's great s.
  299:63

Snatch: hear a voice ... s. a fearful joy 154:28

Sneer: without sneering, teach the rest to s. 248:83

Sneezed: not to be s. at 278:50

Sneezes: beat him when he s. 90:51

Sniffles: sobs, s. and smiles ... s. predominating 161:3

Snicker-snack: blade went s. 92:70

Snob: impossible ... not to be ... a S. 389:8

Snodgrass: Mr. S. 121:63

Snoring: while you here do s. lie 356:39

Snow: birds sit brooding in the s. 332:20
 bore 'mid s. and ice 197:93
 half-buried in the s. 198:94
 I sh. be whiter than s. 42:8
 like S. upon ... Desert's ... Face 135:68
 like the s. falls in ... river 81:25
 naked in December s. 348:37
 never ... love the s. again 70:77
 [sins] shall be ... white as s. 48:30
 s. had fallen, s. on s. 290:43
 s. in May's new-fangled shows 331:11
 when the s. lay round about 229:3
 where the s. lay dinted 229:5
 white as driven s. 362:22
 whitest s. on Scythian hills 204:73

Snowing: the more it goes on s. 210:49

Snows: where are the s. of yesteryear? 396:95

Snug: Skugg ... s. as a bug in a rug 138:13

So: if it was s. it might be 92:75
 s. far, s. good 278:51

Soap: s. and education ... more deadly 393:64
 used your s. two years ago 285:84

Sober: as s. as a judge 134:60
 be s., be vigilant 60:12
 neither ingenious, s., nor kind 13:45
 tomorrow we'll be s. 16:78

Sobers: drinking largely s. us again 249:94

Sobs: with s. and tears he sorted out 93:81

Social: new stock for every s. occasion 169:2
 one of the s. lies 169:8

Socialists; we are all S. now 157:62

Society: classes into which our s. is divided 21:48
 no s. can surely be flourishing 374:97

Society (continued)
 one great s. alone on earth 413:10
 s. is no comfort 304:26
 s. is now one polished horde 85:86
 s. where none intrudes 84:65
 solitude ... best s. 220:92
 The Affluent S. 140:42
 unfriendly to s.'s chief joys 112:53

Sodden: Midlands ... s. and unkind 32:5

Sodium: odium of having discovered s. 33:18

Sodom: in S. fifty righteous 36:55

Sofa: I sing the s. 113:68
 wheel the s. round 114:73

Soft: her voice was ever s., gentle 331:5
 s. falls the dew 30:84

Soften rocks, or bend ... oak 108:5

Softly: fair and s. goes far 262:45
 s. she was going up 105:56
 sweet Thames! run s. 377:47
 Zephyrus did s. play 377:46

Softness: for s. she 219:66

Soil: fame is no plant ... on mortal s. 215:14
 subject is the fattest s. to weeds 317:26

Soiled: name ... s. with all ignoble use 387:72

Solace: with s. and gladness 373:93

Sold: he s. his birthright unto Jacob 36:58
 s. my Reputation for a Song 136:82

Soldat: tout s. ... porte dans sa giberne 228:86

Soldier: Ben Battle was a s. bold 165:57
 can always tell an old s. 364:62
 drinking is the s.'s pleasure 127:53
 every French s. ... in his cartridge-pouch 228:86
 in the s. is flat blasphemy 337:88
 s., full of strange oaths 301:90
 s., rest! thy warfare o'er 295:97
 s.'s pole is fall'n! 299:66
 statesman, s., merchant 9:6
 the boastful s. 247:63
 very poor s. ... a chocolate cream s. 364:63

Soldiers: like s., armed in their stings 318:39
 old s. never die 18:99
 old s. ... surest 400:52
 onward, Christian s. 28:57

Soliciting: this supernatural s. 333:28

Solitary: be not s., be not idle 82:33
 life of a s. man 173:65

Solitary (*continued*)
the s. child   411:85
took their s. way   221:3
Solitude: a state more gloomy than s.
173:66
as my S. is sublime   187:63
in s. what happiness?   220:87
O S.! where are the charms?   114:78
race ... has ... disturbed its s.   27:48
s. sometimes is best society   220:92
which is the bliss of s.   410:71
whosoever is delighted in s.   26:20
Solitudinem faciunt, pacem appellant
383:27
Solomon: S. Grundy, born on a
Monday   238:71
the wisdom of S.   40:54
Some: S. chicken! S. neck!   101:1
s. ... fou o' love ... s. ... o' brandy
80:10
s. glory in their birth   363:41
s. hae meat ... s. wad eat   81:24
s. talk of Alexander   18:6
Somebody: how dreary to be s.   122:81
s. bet on de bay   137:1
when every one is s.   143:78
Somer: in a s. season   193:39
Something: a man's worth s.   73:18
add s. more to this wonderful year
141:48
always doing s. for posterity   10:11
in our embers is s. that doth live
411:80
s. left to treat my friends   203:59
s. rich and strange   355:35
s. sensational to read in the train
405:14
s. ... that doesn't love a wall   139:27
s. was dead in each of us   404:95
that s. ... which prompts th' eternal
sigh   250:15
time for a little s.   212:66
'tis s., nothing   345:6
what's s. rarish   13:47
Sometime: come up and see me s.
402:74
Somewhat: more than s.   291:58
Somewhere: time was away and s. else
203:57
Son: a foolish s. ... heaviness   45:61
a virgin shall ... bear a s.   48:34
a wise s. ... a glad father   45:61
as a man chasteneth his s.   38:8
he gave his only begotten S.   55:99
Jehu ... s. of Nimshi ... driveth
40:62
marry yr s. when you will   271:49
my s., if thou come to serve   62:46

Son (*continued*)
O Absalom, my s., my s.!   40:51
O Lucifer, s. of the morning   48:38
she will ... renounce me for a s.
142:64
spareth his rod hateth his s.   45:67
unto us a s. is given   48:36
Song: a s. to sing, O!   148:45
broke into a quavering s.   401:63
fierce wars ... shall moralize my s.
377:40
give ear unto my s.   150:75
glorious the s. when God's the theme
374:94
he sings each s. twice over   74:23
let satire be my s.   85:88
not given a penny for a s.   417:51
old s. of Percy and Douglas   373:87
one grand, sweet s.   189:86
pipe a s. about a lamb   68:49
run softly till I end my S.   377:47
sang a most topical s.   13:53
sea grew civil at her s.   341:44
self-same s. that found a path   184:30
sold my Reputation for a S.   136:82
s. for yr. delight   93:87
suck melancholy out of a s.   301:84
that glorious s. of old   296:19
the Lord's s. in a strange land
44:47
this subject for heroic s.   220:90
unlike my subject ... frame my s.
98:64
we'll sing another s.   416:44
Songs: Book of S. and Sonnets here
340:28
for ever piping s. for ever new
183:19
our sweetest s. ... saddest thought
370:50
piping s. of pleasant glee   68:48
sing no sad s. for me   290:47
the s. of Apollo   332:21
their lean and flashy s.   215:16
there shall the Sussex s. be sung
32:6
where are the s. of Spring?   181:81
Sonne: when soft was the s.   193:39
Sonnet: a s. is a moment's monument
290:49
scorn not the s.   412:95
s.'s scanty plot of ground   411:90
Sonnets: onlie begetter of ... insuing s.
362:28
Sons: bears all its s. away   400:40
free as the s. of the waves   141:48
s. of Belial, flown with insolence
217:38

Sons (*continued*)
s. of Belial had a Glorious Time
126:46
the s. of the prophet were brave 18:7
things are the s. of heaven 172:41
Soon: belovèd Night ... come s., s.
369:33
day returns too s. 86:98
it [the future] comes s. enough
129:83
s. as she was gone ... a traveller came
67:41
s. got, s. spent 278:55
s. hot, s. cold 278:56
s. ripe, s. rotten 278:57
you have waked me too s. 400:41
Sooner it's over, the s. to sleep 189:87
Soot: black as s. 256:40
Sooth: poesy ... friend to s. the cares
185:39
Sophisters: age ... of s., economists,
calculators 78:78
Sore: sight ... good for s. eyes 382:7
sleep ... s. labour's bath 334:42
trust in critics who themselves are s.
85:91
Sorrow: and not be in s. too 68:53
and wear a golden s. 322:75
any s. like unto my s. 49:59
brief s., short-lived care 229:1
down, thou climbing s. 328:64
ere the s. comes with years 73:11
from the sphere of our s. 371:56
has brought [war] untold s. to mankind 394:76
I feel it when I s. most 386:59
increaseth knowledge increaseth s.
46:97
more in s. than in anger 306:50
no more death, neither s. 61:34
O S., why dost borrow? 181:87
parting is such sweet s. 354:6
pluck from the memory a rooted s.
336:72
pure and complete s. 392:50
s. comes unsent for 278:58
s. goes, and pleasure tarries 143:74
s. will come fast enough 265:24
the guttural s. of the refugees 203:56
then to come, in spite of s. 214:97
there is no greater s. 116:3
to think is to be full of s. 184:25
truly that hour foretold s. 86:99
write s. on the bosom of the earth
349:53
Sorrows: a man of s. ... acquainted
with grief 48:47
here I and s. sit 326:39

Sorrows (*continued*)
losses are restor'd and s. end 363:38
s. come ... not single spies 311:26
there are few s. ... in which 374:1
when age, disease, or s. strike him
103:27
Sorry: better ... safe than s. 255:19
dreadful s., Clementine 225:59
truly s. man's dominion 80:17
Sort: a s. of men whose visages 338:97
travel, in the younger s. 25:12
Sorts: all s. and conditions of men
63:81
Sought: that I s. to destroy institutions
403:79
the prize we s. is won 403:81
those men that s. him 323:87
Soul: a day for a man to afflict his s.
49:52
a thing which enters ... s. 186:54
all thy heart ... all thy s. 38:9
and his s. sincere 155:41
as if that s. were fled 226:62
asleep in body ... become a living s.
415:33
body Nature is, and God the s.
250:11
body presseth down the s. 62:44
breathes there the man, with s. so
dead 295:5
build ... stately mansions, O my s.
164:50
call upon my s. within the house
359:80
cold waters to a thirsty s. 45:82
confession is good for the s. 258:23
distress hath humanized my s.
409:62
dull wd. he be of s. 412:96
for my s., what can it do to that?
307:61
for my unconquerable s. 160:93
foredoom'd his father's s. to cross
248:78
gain the ... world, and lose his own
s. 54:58
give not thy s. unto a woman 62:50
hae mercy o' my s., Lord God
202:50
half conceal the S. within 386:58
harrow up thy s., freeze thy young
blood 307:64
Helen, ... give me my s. again
204:63
her lips suck forth my s. 204:63
hidden s. of harmony 215:5
his s. is marching on! 157:57
I am black ... my s. is white 68:51

Soul (*continued*)
I am the captain of my s. 160:95
I ... invite my s. 403:83
iron entered [into] his s. 43:25,
    267:19
it is the cause, my s. 346:18
joy's s. lies in the doing 358:65
King Cole was a merry old s.
    236:58
largest and most comprehensive s.
    127:58
lose his own s. 54:58
memorial from the S.'s eternity
    290:49
merit wins the s. 252:39
most offending s. alive 320:56
my prophetic s.! My uncle! 307:67
my s. in agony 105:54
my s. into the boughs does glide
    206:1
my s., like to a ship 401:55
my s., there is a country 396:87
no coward s. is mine 71:84
our s.'s left hand 123:5
perdition catch my s. 345:5
pouring forth thy s. abroad 184:29
praise my s., the King of Heaven
    201:34
pray for my s. 386:55
prepare thy s. for temptation 62:46
rap and knock and enter in our s.
    73:17
sleepless S. that perished 413:12
s. and ... gift of articulate speech
    366:93
s. hath been alone 106:62
s. is dead that slumbers 198:95
s. is in a ferment 181:84
s. is not more than the body 403:86
s. of the Age! 179:53
s. rememb'ring my good friends
    349:44
s. was sad ... glance was glum
    148:46
the s. of Adonais, like a star 368:20
the s. that rises with us 410:77
the s. to feel the flesh 71:87
thou art a s. in bliss 330:96
thy rapt s. sitting in thine eyes
    213:84
thy s. was like a Star 413:4
to bear my s. away 10:13
was not spoken of the s. 198:95
what a dusty answer gets the s.
    209:34
what of s. was left 76:48
with all thy s. ... all thy might 38:6
yet my s. drew back 161:12

Souls: fire our s. to regale 68:45
have ye s. in heaven too? 181:83
immediate jewel of their s. 345:6
Lord, thou lover of s. 62:45
our s., whose faculties can compre-
    hend 205:76
poor s. who dwell in Night 66:31
prosperity has damned more s.
    275:65
s. of Poets dead and gone 183:14
s. of the righteous ... in the hand of
    God 62:43
s. of women are so small 82:40
such harmony is in immortal s.
    340:22
two s. with but a single thought
    200:18
unless they've s. that grovel 87:13
we that have free s. 310:10
ye have left yr. s. on earth 181:83
Sound: full of s. and fury 336:76
hear dat mournful s. 138:3
no s. save the rush of the river 30:84
sighing s., the lights around the shore
    291:53
s. must seem an echo to the sense
    249:99
s. of a voice that is still 384:37
s. of public scorn 220:96
s. of revelry by night 83:59
s. upon the bugle-horn 387:78
the s. is forc'd, the notes are few
    68:55
the s. of his horn 154:20
to heal the blows of s. 164:44
Sounds: s. will take care of themselves
    91:58
with s. that echo still 385:45
Soup: he screamed out, 'Take the s.
    away!' 164:39
of s. and love, the first 278:59
s. of the evening, beautiful s. 91:65
Sour: how s. sweet music is 351:63
lost his taste, sweet is s. 270:7
love is ... s. in the ending 270:14
things sweet ... prove in digestion s.
    348:35
will not taste the s. 260:69
Source: true s. of human offspring
    219:71
South: beaker full of the warm S.
    184:24
he went by the s. 235:54
I ... go s. in the winter 131:11
Oh, I went down S. 18:97
yes, but not in the S. 252:46
South country: great hills of the S.
    32:5

Southern: bore me in the s. wild   68:51
  walls on the s. side   75:36
Sovereign: servants of the s. or state
  25:1
Sovereignest thing on earth   313:52
Soviet power into the heart of W.
  Europe   102:7
Sow (noun): I do ... walk before thee
  like a s.   316:98
  s. that was washed ... wallowing
  60:13
Sow (verb): men that s. to reap   382:19
  s. one's wild oats   283:32
  they that s. in tears   44:40
Soweth: whatsoever ... s. ... shall he
  also reap   58:70
Sown the wind ... reap the whirlwind
  50:76
Spade: call a s. a s. - 257:82
Spain: build castles in S.   257:88
  King of S.'s daughter came to visit
  233:39
  rain, rain, go to S.   275:76
Span: when Adam delved and Eve s.
  27:50
Spaniards: S. seem wiser than they are
  26:19
  win this game ... thrash the S.
  125:30
Spanish: I speak S. to God   96:24
Spare: I will s. all the place   36:55
  s. all I have ... take my life   134:57
  woodman, s. the beechen tree   88:18
Sparkling: pair of s. eyes   143:77
Sparks: born unto trouble as the s. fly
  41:67
Sparrow: I, said the S.   241:88
Speak: did he stop and s. to you?
  74:30
  I only s. right on   325:21
  I s. severely to my boy   90:52
  I s. Spanish to God   96:24
  never s. well of one another   176:6
  now s., or ... hold his peace   64:5
  one to s., ... another to hear   391:39
  other sins only s.; murder shrieks
  400:49
  s. each other in passing   198:4
  s., Lord; for thy servant heareth
  39:36
  s. not of my debts unless   278:61
  s. of me as I am   346:22
  s. roughly to your little boy   90:51
  s. the speech ... as I pronounc'd
  310:3
  s. well of yr. friend   278:62
  s. when you are spoken to   94:96,
  278:63

Speak (continued)
  think to-day and s. tomorrow
  280:26
  when I think, I must s.   302:96
  when you s., ... I'd have you do it
  ever   362:21
Speaking: he ... [Adam] thought him
  still s.   220:85
Speaks: s. ill of his wife   278:64
  when he s., the air ... is still   318:38
Spear: bring me my s.   67:38
Spears: stars threw down their s.   68:47
Species: especially the male of the s.
  193:46
  female of the s. is more deadly
  190:98
  not the individual, but the s.   173:63
  our self-tormented s.   292:66
Spectacles: her s. ... on her aproned
  knees   87:11
  needed not the s. of books   127:59
  s. on nose and pouch on side   301:90
Spectator: I live ... as a S.   9:6
Spectre: grows pale and s.-thin   184:25
Speculator: I was raised by a s.   380:84
Speech: be ... never tax'd for s.   298:41
  found our s. copious without order
  172:40
  freedom of s. and expression   289:32
  let thy s. be short   62:56
  rude am I in my s.   344:90
  soul and ... gift of articulate s.
  366:93
  souninge in moral vertu was his s.
  97:34
  s. ... given to ... disguise thoughts
  384:32
  s. is silver   278:65
Speed: s., bonny boat, like a bird
  69:69
  our safety is in our s.   133:35
  whose s. ... faster than light   76:52
Spell: foreigners always s. better
  394:66
Spend: to s. too much time in studies
  26:30
  what we yet may s.   135:70
Spending: getting and s., we lay waste
  our powers   412:93
  riches are for s.   26:21
Spends: commuter—one who s. his
  life   402:77
Spenser: sage and serious poet S.
  223:40
Spent: all passion s.   223:27
  how my light is s.   223:29
  soon got, soon s.   278:55
Speranza: lasciate ogni s.   116:2

Spermatozoa: a million million s., all
... alive 169:4
Sphere: from the s. of our sorrow
371:56
their motion in one s. 315:90
world's storm-troubled s. 71:84
Spheres: as the restless s. 205:76
stand still, you ever-moving s.
204:65
stars shot madly from their s. 341:44
Spice: variety's the very s. of life
114:71
Spick and span 278:66
Spider: said a s. to a fly 168:86
there came a big s. 235:51
Spies: as if we were God's s. 330:99
sorrows ... come not single s. 311:26
Spires: City with her dreaming s. 21:46
dim-discover'd s. 107:88
Spirit: a bold s. in a loyal breast
347:30
a pardlike S. beautiful and swift
367:14
a S. still, and bright 414:18
a S., yet a Woman too 414:17
expense of s. in a waste 363:50
follow your s., and upon this charge
319:47
give me the s. 317:20
hail to thee, blithe s. 370:49
have not that alacrity of s. 353:85
history of the human s. 21:53
how oft, in s. ... sylvan Wye 415:34
I am thy father's s. 307:63
life-blood of a master s. 223:38
music ... gentlier on the s. lies
388:85
my s. is too deeply laden 370:55
pipe to the s. ditties of no tone
183:17
present in s. 57:47
rarely comest thou, S. of Delight
370:52
same s. that its author writ 249:95
s. ... is willing ... flesh is weak
53:50
s. of health or goblin damn'd 307:60
s. that will start the world along
416:44
s. to bathe in fiery floods 337:90
spur that the clear s. doth raise
215:13
the worser s. ... a woman 364:55
Wild S. ... moving everywhere
369:36
Spirits: actors ... were all s. 356:50
choice and master s. of this age
324:7

Spirits (*continued*)
comfort and despair, which like two
s. 364:55
her wanton s. look out 358:73
I can call s. from the ... deep
314:72
pluck up thy s., man 226:67
Spit: 'Please don't s. on the floor'
14:56
s. fire; spout rain 328:72
s. in my face, call me horse 314:65
s. upon my Jewish gaberdine 338:6
Spite: cursed s., that ... I was born
307:71
cut off ... nose to s. ... face 259:46
reckless what I do to s. the world
334:49
S. of cormorant devouring Time
331:8
s. of pride, in erring reason's s.
250:12
victory in s. of all terror 100:93
Splash: a scream, a s. 18:4
Spleen or Vapors 127:57
Splendid: and by the vision s. 411:78
in ... our s. isolation 152:8
man is ... s. in ashes 72:7
s. tear from the passion-flower
388:87
Splendour: the s. falls on castle walls
388:97
Split: part ... to make all s. 341:40
Spoil: come and s. the fun 92:77
company ... hath been the s. of me
315:79
Spoiled: had s. his nice new rattle
92:74
Spoilers of ... symmetry of shelves
192:26
Spoils: it s. the singing of the nightingale 181:88
Spoke: English as she is s. 393:57
less he s., the more he heard 285:82
put a s. in one's wheel 278:68
Spoken: sure of being kindly s. of
23:67
Spoon: dish ran away with the s.
232:33
have a long s. that sups with the
devil 270:99
silver s. in his mouth 257:58
Spoons: measured out my life with
coffee s. 131:2
the faster we counted our s. 132:27
Sport: detested s., that owes its pleasure
114:72
dog laughed to see such s. 232:33
S. that wrinkled Care derides 214:94

Sport (*continued*)
s. with Amaryllis in the shade 215:12
the chase, the s. of kings 375:23
they kill us for their s. 329:85
to s. wd. be as tedious as to work 313:50
Sported: and by him s. on the green 376:28
Sports: let us prove ... the s. of love 179:61
Spot: Out, damned s.! out, I say! 335:68
Spout: cataracts and hurricanoes s. 328:71
spit fire; s. rain 328:72
Sprang: I s. to the stirrup 74:26
Sprat: a s. to catch a mackerel (whale) 278:69
Spray: never a s. of yew 21:37
Spread: money ... like muck ... be s. 25:8
Sprightly: tossing their heads in s. dance 410:69
Spring: a linnet courting ... in the s. 70:76
absent in the s. 363:44
all the breathing s. 107:87
apparell'd like the s. 347:24
can S. be far behind? 369:38
how this s. of love resembleth 361:6
in s., when woods are getting green 93:88
in the Fire of S. 135:66
in the s. a young man's fancy 387:79
it is s., moonless night 390:23
lived light in the s. 20:31
no s. ... beauty hath such grace 123:7
sweet lovers love the s. 303:7
the year's at the s. 75:44
when the hounds of s. 382:15
where are the songs of S.? 181:81
Springs: four wanton s. end in a word 348:34
steeds to water at those s. 304:20
Sprites: [tale] ... of s. and goblins 361:13
Spur: do not s. a free horse 278:70
fame is the s. 215:13
no s. to prick the sides of my intent 333:37
on the s. of the moment 278:71
Spurns that patient merit ... takes 309:95
Spurs: let the boy win his s. 129:80
Squandering wealth was his peculiar art 126:44

Squeaking: with shrieking and s. 75:38
Squeals: if he s., let him go 232:29
Squeers, Mr Wackford 120:52
Stable: nothing s. in the world 186:53
Stables: the s. are ... centre of the household 365:72
Stabs: with bemock'd-at s. kill ... waters 356.49
Staff: I'll break my s. 357:55
my s. of faith to walk upon 286:94
Stag at eve had drunk his fill 294:94
Stage: after a well-grac'd actor leaves the s. 351:61
all the world's a s. 301:90
frets his hour upon the s. 336:76
if ... played upon a s. now 360:96
mellow glory of the Attic s. 20:35
on the s. he was natural 151:82
s. where every man must play a part 338:96
the wonder of our S. 179:53
to this great s. of fools 330:94
two hours' traffic of our s. 353:89
your daughter on the s. 112:44
Stages: wher'er his s. may have been 371:60
Stagger: they reel ... s. like a drunken man 43:27
Stain: true blue will never s. 281:58
without fault or s. on thee 70:78
Stairs: somebody stopped the moving s. 203:57
Stake: when honour's at the s. 311:24
Stamford: bullocks at S. fair? 317:17
Stamp: s. of his lowly origin 117:6
too late to save the s. 153:10
Stand: s. still, you ever-moving spheres 204:65
s. up for Jesus! 128:73
Sun, s. thou still 38:20
who will s. on either hand? 201:37
Standard: raise the scarlet s. high 109:21
Standing: Jackson s. like a stone wall 30:79
Stanley: here S. meets,—how S. scorns 76:53
on, S., on! 296:15
Stanza: pens a s. when he shd. engross 248:78
Star: and a s. or two beside 105:56
desire of the moth for the s. 371:56
dropped from the zenith, like a falling s. 217:44
eve's one s. 182:96
go and catch a falling s. 124:11
hitch yr. wagon to a s. 133:43

Star (*continued*)

Soul ... rises with us, our life's S. 410:77

s. to steer her by 207:14

there was a s. danc'd 343:67

thy soul was like a S. 413:4

twinkle, twinkle, little s. 384:36

we have seen his s. 51:2

Star Chamber matter of it 340:27

Star-crossed: a pair of s. lovers 353:88

Stare: and all the world wd. s. 113:59

time to stand and s. 117:11

Starry: cloudless climes and s. skies 89:96

Stars: a country far beyond the s. 396:87

and one [sees] the s. 193:38

branch-charmed by the earnest s. 182:98

certain s. shot madly 341:44

clad in the beauty of a thousand s. 204:64

continuous as the s. 410:68

eyes, like s., start from their spheres 307:64

make guilty ... the sun ... the s. 327:53

opposition of the s. 206:98

s. above us govern our conditions 329:87

s. hide their diminished heads 218:61

s., hide your fires 333:31

s. in their courses fought 39:22

s. threw down their spears 68:47

s. through the window-pane are my children 187:63

stone that puts the S. to Flight 134:65

the silent s. go by 72:95

till you are ... crowned with the s. 392:52

true as the s. above 16:81

two s. keep not their motion 315:90

we are ... the s.' tennis balls 400:51

yoke of inauspicious s. 354:18

you chaste s., it is the cause 346:18

Star-spangled banner 188:80

Start: get the s. of the majestic world 323:92

Startle: singing, s. the dull night 214:97

s. it or amaze it with itself 186:54

Starve: let not poor Nelly s. 96:22

State: a continual s. of inelegance 24:81

all were for the s. 201:38

beat a Venetian and traduc'd the s. 346-7:22

State (*continued*)

grant me ... a middle s. 203:59

hides from himself his s. 174:70

his s. is kingly 223:30

I am the S. 199:12

I have done the s. some service 346:22

object in the construction of the s. 247:62

other two ... like us, the s. totters 356:45

the worth of a S. ... individuals 210:43

this is the s. of man 322:80

Stately: a s. pleasure-dome decree 106:71

the s. homes of England 111:39, 160:90

Statements was interesting but tough 393:60

States: many goodly s. and kingdoms 185:40

s. unborn and accents yet unknown 324:5

Statesman: a witty s. said 89:32

chymist, fiddler, s. and buffoon 126:43

speculative s., soldier, merchant 9:6

too nice for a s. 151:79

Statesmen: when s. ... say ... be realistic 22:59

Statistics: lies, damned lies, and s. 393:63

Statues: Epp's s. are junk 14:57

Status quo: restored the s. 378:55

Stay: and here I s. 202:51

without thee here to s. 221:2

wd. not s. for an answer 24:85

Stay-at-home: sweet s. 117:12

Steadily: saw life s. and ... whole 20:35

Steady, boys, steady 141:48

Steaks: smells of s. in passageways 131:7

Steal: cut loaf to s. a shive 357-8:63

shadows ... s. across the sky 28:56

s. from the world, and not a stone 251:29

thou shalt not s. 37:90

Stealing: not hanged for s. horses 157:56

picking and s. 64:98

s. and giving odour 358-9:75

wronging ... s., fighting 361:16

Steals: s. something from the thief 344:94

who s. my purse s. trash 345:6

Steed: his s. was the best 295:10

Steeds: Phoebus 'gins arise, his s. to water 304:20
Steel: clad in complete s. 212:76
   foeman bares his s., tarantara 148:32
   smoke and blood ... mix of s. 293:80
   to thy soul with hoops of s. 306:55
Steeples: spout till you have drench'd our s. 328:71
Steer: happily to s. from grave to gay 250:18
   our ... policy to s. clear 399:32
   s. too nigh the sands 126:39
Stein: wonderful family called S. 14:57
Step: a great s. to knowledge 123:97
   became ... bad in one s. 180:68
Stephen: Feast of S. 229:3
Stepmother: take heed of a s. 278:72
Stepney: say the bells of S. 236:61
Stepping-stones: on s. of their dead selves 386:57
Steps: heavy s. of the ploughman 417:55
   in his master's s. he trod 229:5
   invites my s. and points to yonder glade 248:72
   to these dark s. 221:11
   with how sad s., O Moon 373:85
   with wandering s. and slow 221:3
Stew in one's own juice 278:73
Stick: a riband to s. in his coat 74:28
   fling dirt ... some will s. 263:73
   I am a kind of burr; I shall s. 338:93
Sticking-place: courage to the s. 333:38
Sticks and stones may break my bones 278:74
Stiff: keep a s. upper lip 94:99
   s. in opinions, ... in the wrong 126:43
Stiffnecked: a s. people 37:95
Stile: merrily hent the s.-a 361:19
   sixpence against a crooked s. 239:74
Still: how s. we see thee lie 72:95
   mighty heart is lying s. 412:97
   sound of a voice that is s. 384:37
   Thou smilest and art s. 21:44
Stillness: air a solemn s. holds 155:31
   modest s. and humility 319:45
   soft s. and the night 340:22
Stimulate the phagocytes 365:71
Sting: death, where is thy s.? 57:60
   O Death! where is thy S.? 247:71
   s. is in the tail 278:78
   s. of a reproach ... truth of it 278:79
   where is death's s.? 201:33
Stings: armed in their s. 318:39

Stir: no s. of air was there 182:97
Stirring dull roots with spring rain 131:10
Stirrup: betwixt the s. and the ground 87:16
   I sprang to the s. 74:26
Stitch: a s. in time saves nine 278:81
   s. I s. I s. I 166:64
Stockings: commended the yellow s. 360:92
Stole: fause lover s. my rose 81:28
   I s. the Prince 143:71
   s. a pig and away he run 240:83
Stolen sweets are best 102:13
Stomach: an army marches on its s. 228:87
   have the ... s. ... of a King of England 132:20
   my s. is not good 380:81
Stone: heaviest s. ... the devil can throw 159:84
   kill two birds with one s. 268:34
   leave no s. unturned 269:68
   let him first cast a s. at her 55:3
   not a s. tell where I lie 251:29
   precious s. set in the silver sea 348:41
   rolling s. gathers no moss 276:1
   s. that lieth not in yr. way 278:82
   s. which the builders refused 44:35
   virtue is like a rich s. 26:27
   water like a s. 290:43
   we raised not a s. 408:53
Stones: in glass houses ... never throw s. 264:12
   inestimable s., unvalued jewels 352:72
   labour of an age in piled s. 216:23
   o, ye are men of s. 330:4
   sermons in s. 300:75
   you blocks, you s.! 323:89
Stools: between two s. one falls 256:34
Stop: Shelley ... did he s. and speak? 74:30
   s.; look; listen 395:78
   s. me and buy one 11:31
   time ... must have a s. 315:91
   when the kissing had to s. 76:48
Stopped: he [Death] kindly s. for me 122:44
   it s. short—never to go again 416:43
Stoppeth: he s. one of three 104:42
Store: oft amid thy s. 181:80
   s. of ladies, whose bright eyes 214:2
Storied windows richly dight 213:88
Stories: s. ... not to thy credit 87:15
   tell sad s. of the death of kings 350:54

Storm: after a s. ... a calm 254:62
and rides upon the s. 113:63
any port in a s. 254:71
S. and Stress 191:18
S. in a Teacup 34:23, 278:83
lovers fled ... into the s. 181:91
the pelting of this pitiless s. 329:78
Storms: he sought the s. 126:39
sudden s. are short 348:40
vows made in s. are forgotten 282:97
Story: honour is the subject of my s. 323:91
in pain, to tell my s. 312:38
not that the s. need be long 391:40
our rough island-s. 388:94
place where a s. ended 130:97
shuts up the s. of our days 286:93
summits old in s. 388:97
teach him how to tell my s. 344:92
tell me the old, old s. 157:61
the s. of Sussex told 32:6
Stove: like ... ice on a hot s. 139:29
Straight trees ... crooked roots 279:84
Strain: attain to something like prophetic s. 213:89
that s. again 358:75
Strained: quality of mercy is not s. 339:15
Straining upon the start 319:47
Strains: such s. as wd. have won the ear 215:6
Straits: moon lies fair upon the S. 20:30
Strand: India's coral s. 159:86
let's all go down the S. 94:1
Strange: how s. it seems, and new! 74:30
how s. now, looks the life 73:14
misery acquaints ... with s. bedfellows 356:41
something rich and s. 355:35
s. as if ... married a great while 109:17
'tis s. but true 85:87
truth is always s. 85:87
'twas s., 'twas passing s. 344:92
very s. and wellbred 109:17
Stranger: a s. in a strange land 36:68
a s. yet to pain 154:27
love ye ... the s. 38:10
s. than fiction 85:87
the wiles of the s. 228:89
Strangers: gracious and courteous to s. 25:5
s. in the land of Egypt 38:10
we may be better s. 302:97
Strangling: other use than s. in a string 167:80

Stratford: the scole of S. atte Bowe 96:28
Straw: drowning man ... catch at a s. 260:90
find quarrel in a s. 311:24
headpiece filled with s. 130:94
last s. breaks the camel's back 269:54
scrannel pipes of wretched s. 215:16
Strawberries: feed upon s., sugar and cream 231-2:27
in Holborn I saw good s. 352:74
Straws: errors, like s. 127:55
Stray: if with me you'd fondly s. 142:53
nor ever ... from the Church to s. 68:45
Streaks: number the s. of the tulip 173:63
Stream: hoar leaves in the glassy s. 311:30
still glides the S. 413:13
time, like an ever-rolling s. 400:40
Streamers: sails filled and s. waving 222:18
Streams: fresh showers ... from ... the s. 368:21
thy banner ... s. ... *against* the wind 84:63
Street: have yer bought the s.? 99:79
man in the s. 271:30
Streets: through s. broad and narrow 17:89
we shall fight ... in the s. 100-101:94
Strength: as thy days, so shall thy s. be 38:16
better than the s. of Samson 272:55
Christ is thy s. 225:53
comfort in the s. of love 411:88
fall'n ... that tower of s. 388:93
glory of young men is their s. 45:78
if I be shaven ... s. will go 39:29
Ignorance is S. 242:2
king's name is a tower of s. 353:84
my s. is as the s. of ten 389:3
my s. is made perfect in weakness 58:66
promise of s. and manhood 70:78
s. to bear the misfortunes of others 288:14
their s. labour and sorrow 43:17
they go from s. to s. 43:14
to have a giant's s. 337:86
unity is s. 282:88
we shall fight with growing ... s. 100-101:94
Stretch: upon the rack ... s. him out longer 331:7

Stretched: there was things ... he s. 393:59
 when I s. out my hand 379:69
Strew: shall I s. ... rose or rue or laurel? 382:17
 s. on her roses, roses 21:37
Strife: agonies, the s. of human hearts 185:37
 ancient forms of party s. 386:69
 are God and Nature ... at s. 386:62
 books ... dull and endless s. 414:26
 ignoble s. 155:39
 in the s. of Truth with Falsehood 200:24
 poverty breeds s. 275:53
Strike: no right to s. against the public safety 110:28
 s. while the iron is hot 279:85
 take heed ... thou s. not awry 226:67
String: chewing little bits of s. 31:90
 harp not on that s. 352:81
 provided ..: s. to tie them together 225:57
 strangling in a s. 167:80
 untune that s. 358:68
Strings: the languid s. do scarcely move 68:55
 there are s. in the human heart 119:32
Stripes: whose broad s. and bright stars 188:79
Strive: four champions fierce, s. here 218:57
 s. to set the crooked straight? 227:71
Striving to better, mar what's well 328:59
Strode: out to Severn s. 99:72
Stroke: tune of flutes kept s. 298–9:54
Strong: be s. and of a good courage 38:18
 but wants that little s. 164:47
 out of the s. ... sweetness 39:27
 s.-backed and neat-bound 192:30
 we know ... that the wall is s. 404:97
 we then that are s. 57:45
 what will it help ... once you were s.? 70:72
Strove: a little still she s. 84:67
 I s. with none 192:34
Struggle: manhood a s. 123:95
 say not the s. naught availeth 103:32
Struggling for life in the water 174:78
Strumpet: transform'd into a s.'s fool 298:49
Struts: that s. and frets his hour 336:76
Stubble: chin ... show'd like a s. land 313:51

Stubble (*continued*)
 he lies in the s. 12:42
Studies: s. serve for delight, for ornament 26:30
 too much time in s. 26:31
Study: every Jack ... must s. the knack 149:50
 his s. was but litel on the bible 97:37
 I am slow of s. 341:41
 much s. ... weariness of the flesh 47:13
 proper s. of Mankind is Man 250:13
 s. what you most affect 355:20
Stuff: ambition ... made of sterner s. 325:14
 listen all day to such s. 90:49
 'S. and nonsense!' said Alice 91:68
 s. of life to knit me 167:83
 such s. as dreams are made on 356–7:50
 written such volumes of s.! 194:59
Stumble: they s. that run fast 354:7
Stupidity: confirm'd in full s. 128:69
 no sin except s. 404:2
Sturm und Drang 191:18
Stygian: in S. cave forlorn 213–14:91
 s. smoke of the pit 170:19
Style: le s. est l'homme 76:51
Style: s. is the man himself 76:51
 true definition of a s. 381:3
Subdue: it [force] may s. for a moment 78:72
Subject: every s.'s duty ... soul 320:53
 load every rift of yr. s. 187:69
 poetry ... startle ... with its s. 186:54
 s. to the same diseases 339:13
 s. we old men are to ... lying 317:21
 this s. for heroic song 220:90
Subjects: my s. for a pair of carved saints 350:55
 poorest s. are at this hour asleep! 317:13
Sublime: du s. au ridicule ... un pas 228:84
Sublime: from the s. to the ridiculous 228:84
 my object all s. 146:6
 one step above the s. 243:19
 s. and the ridiculous are ... related 243:19
 we can make our lives s. 198:97
Sublimity: a S. to welcome me home 187:63
Submit: King do now? Must he s.? 350:55
Subscribers: he for s. baits his hook 100:84
 not printing any list of s. 177:33

Substance of things hoped for 59:99
Subtlety is better than force 279:86
Succeed: if at first you don't s. 163:28
  those who ne'er s. 121:80
Succeeds: nothing s. like excess 406:31
  nothing s. like success 273:11
Success: s. and miscarriage are empty
  sounds 172:43
  s. is counted sweetest 121:80
  this ecstasy, is s. in life 244:29
  to command s. 9:4
  to make a marriage a s. 293:75
  true s. is to labour 380:80
  yours [religion] is S. 28:63
Sucked: I s. the blood 105:51
Sucker: a s. born every minute 28:58
Sucks: my baby ... s. the nurse asleep
  300:71
  where the bee s., there suck I 357:56
Sudden storms are short 348:40
Suddenly: shall s. come to his temple
  51:99
Sudetenland is the last ... claim 163:31
Sue: less used to s. than to command
  294:96
  we were not born to s. 347:31
Suez: somewhere East of Suez 190:8
Suffer: but doth s. a sea-change 355:35
  not s. a witch to live 37:94
  s. for the truth's sake 64:92
  s. me to come to thee 402:70
  s. the little children to come 54:61
  than one innocent s. 66:26
  ye s. fools gladly ... yourselves are
  wise 58:64
Sufferance is the badge of all our tribe
  338:6
Suffered: Lord Hippo s. fearful loss
  32:3
  love a place the less for having s.
  23:74
Suffering: been s., nothing but s. 23:74
Sufficiency: an elegant s., content
  391:34
Sufficient: s. conclusions from insufficient premises 82:44
  s. unto the day is the evil 52:22
Sugar: I must s. my hair 91:64
  s. and spice and all that's nice 240:85
Suggests: the word Intellectual s.
  22:61
Suit: silk s. ... cost me much money
  245:41
Sultry: more common where the
  climate's s. 84:66
Summer: a wind in s. 185:34
  after s., merrily, merrily 357:56
  all on a s.'s day 237:65

Summer (continued)
  bud of love by s.'s ripening breath
  354:3
  compare thee to a s.'s day 362:32
  dry as s. dust. 409:64
  eternal s. gilds them 84:77
  haunt of flies on s. eves 184:28
  I only know that s. sang in me
  210:47
  in their s. beauty kiss'd 352:79
  last rose of s. 226:63
  live murmur of a s.'s day 21:40
  on s. eves by haunted stream 214:3
  one swallow does not make a s.
  279:89
  s. and winter ... shall not cease
  35:48
  s. by this sun of York 351:64
  s. has o'er-brimm'd ... clammy cells
  181:79
  s. has set in with ... severity 107:81
  s. is icumen in 15:71
  s.'s lease ... too short a date 362:32
  s.'s velvet buds 318:39
  thinking on fantastic s.'s heat 348:37
  thy eternal s. shall not fade 362:33
  to ... men that sought him sweet as s.
  323:87
  warmed ... by the same ... s. 339:13
  with love in s.'s wonderland
  230–1:20
Summits: snowy s. old in story 388:97
Sun (see also Sonne): all, except their
  s., is set 84:77
  and I will sing of the s. 252:48
  at the going down of the s. 65:20
  before the rising s. 399:39
  between me and the s. 122:86
  birds are faint with the hot s. 185:42
  cannot make our s. stand still 206:96
  close to the s. in lonely lands 385:47
  dominions, on which the s. never
  sets 230:18
  early-rising s. has not attained
  162:18
  eyes are nothing like the s. 364:52
  far from the s. and summer-gale
  156:44
  follow the fair s. 88:23
  furnish'd ... by Aldershot s. 34:25
  glory of the s. will be dimmed 27:48
  go out in the midday s. 112:42
  hath Britain all the s.? 304:25
  I am too much in the s. 305:39
  I gin to be aweary of the s. 336:77
  just as the s. was rising 16:80
  late eclipses in the s. and moon
  327:52

Sun (*continued*)
  light ... dies with the dying s.
    69:70
  light ... where no s. shines 390:21
  love that moves the s. 117:4
  loves to live i' th' s. 301:85
  make guilty ... the s. 327:53
  make hay while the s. shines 271:27
  Mother, give me the s. 169:10
  never shall s. that morrow see
    333:34
  no new thing under the s. 46:96
  now the s. is laid to sleep 178:50
  self-same s. that shines 362:23
  she grew in s. and shower 415:30
  so when the s. in bed 216:22
  s. breaks through the darkest clouds
    355:25
  s. came up upon the left 104:44
  s. climbs slow, how slowly 104:34
  s. go down upon your wrath 58:71
  s. shines upon all alike 279:87
  S., stand thou still 38:20
  s. that warms you ... shine on me
    348:33
  s. was shining on the sea 92:76
  thank heavens, the s. has gone in
    374:4
  the chambers of the s. 68:54
  the maturing s. 180:78
  the rising of the s. 16–17:87
  the s. is lost, and th' earth 123:3
  the s. of righteousness arise 51:1
  the s. shall not smite thee 44:38
  this s. of York 351:64
  to have enjoy'd the s. 20:31
  white founts ... in the Courts of the
    s. 99:70
  with the setting s. dropped from the
    zenith 217:44
Sunday: golf may be played on S.
    194:52
  here of a S. morning 167:82
  killing ... mouse on S. 70:74
  shot through his heart on S. 379:71
  S. clears away the rust 9:7
Sunk: all s. beneath the wave 113:64
Sunless: down to a s. sea 106:71
Sunny Jim: they called him S. 157:60
Sunny pleasure-dome 107:75
Sunrise: in eternity's s. 66:34
Suns: blest by s. of home 71:93
Sunset: s. and evening star 385:44
  s. ran, one glorious blood-red 74:24
Sunshine: no s. but has some shadow
    273:2
  the s. is a glorious birth 410:74
Sup: who sipped no s. 148–9:46

Supercilious: a s. knowledge in ac-
    counts 371:70
Superfluity of good things 11:21
Superfluous: in the poorest thing s.
    328:67
Superior: revolt ... that they may be s.
    20:27
Superiority: one shall acquire an
    evident s. 175:96
Superstition is the religion of feeble
    minds 78:80
Superstitions: new truths ... end as s.
    169:6
Supper: hope is ... a bad s. 26:38
  sings for his s. 235:52
  to s. with a flood of tears 119:39
Support: help the feeble ... s. him after
    357:59
Sure: his mercy is for ever s. 188:78
  s. way to see it lost ... last ditch
    79:90
Surfeit: feast ... where no crude s.
    reigns 213:77
Surfeit-swelled: so s., so old 318:34
Surfeiting: give me excess ... that s.
    358:75
Surfeits: the s. of our own behaviour
    327:53
Surgery: honour hath no skill in s.
    315:88
Surmise: with a wild s. 185:41
Surprise: poetry shd. s. by a fine excess
    186:55
Surprised by joy ... I turned 411:91
Surrender: unconditional and im-
    mediate s. 153:15
  we shall never s. 100–101:94
Survey: monarch of all I s. 114:77
  time that takes s. 315:91
Survival: s. of the fittest 117:8, 376:34
  without victory there is no s. 100:93
Survive: but one ... Noah dare hope to
    s. 169:4
Suspects: man s. himself a fool 418:63
Suspension: willing s. of disbelief
    107:79
Suspicion: Caesar's wife ... above s.
    87:10
  s. ... haunts the guilty mind 322:72
Suspicions amongst thoughts ... bats
    amongst birds 26:23
Sussex: and the story of S. told 32:6
  there shall the S. songs be sung 32:6
Swagman: jolly s. camped by a billa-
    bong 244:30
Swain: no better than a homely s.
    321:70
Swains: all our s. commend her 361:8

Swallow: hope ... flies with s.'s wings 352:83
one s. does not make a summer 279:89
Swallows: gathering s. twitter 181:82
whitethroat builds and all the s. 74:22
Swan: Sweet S. of Avon 179:58
Swanee Ribber: 'way down upon de S. 138:5
Swans: all his geese are s. 264:4
seven s. a-swimming 238:73
s. sing before they die 106:70
Swap horses in mid-stream 196:80
Swat: Akond of S. 194:54
Sway: mercy is above this sceptred s. 339:15
regions ... thy posterity shall s. 112:50
truth ... prevailed with double s. 150:67
Swear: s. me, Kate, like a lady 314:76
when very angry s. 394:71
Sweat: blood, toil, tears and s. 100:92
in the s. of thy face 35:38
none will s. but for promotion 300:79
s. for duty not for meed 300:79
Sweating: quietly s. palm to palm 169:5
Sweats: Falstaff s. to death 313:59
Sweep on, you fat and greasy citizens 300:76
Sweet: a lady s. and kind 18:9
and s. girl-graduates 388:95
back to the great s. mother 383:25
both s. things ... all s. things 69:65
but then, how it was s.! 73:20
by any other name wd. smell as s. 353:1
deserves not the s. 260:69
each op'ning s. of earliest bloom 107:87
how sour s. music is! 351:63
how s. and fair she seems to be 398:17
how s. the moonlight sleeps 340:22
how s. their memory still 113:62
law beyond its own s. will 403:88
little s. ... kill much bitterness 182:4
love is s. for a day 383:23
love is s., given or returned 369:44
naught so s. as Melancholy 81:29
revenge is s. 276:89
sessions of s. silent thought 362:37
sleep of labouring man is s. 46:2
stolen waters are s. 45:60
s. as love 384:30

Sweet (continued)
s. breathing Zephyrus did ... play 377:46
s. is pleasure after pain 127:53
s. is revenge – especially to women 84:68
s. Little Buttercup I 146-7:20
s. singing in the choir · 16-17:87
s. Stay-at-Home, s. Well-content 117:12
s. Thames! run softly 377:47
s. to look into ... face of heaven 186:47
s. to taste ... indigestion sour 348:35
swing low, s. chariot 18:8
the s. o' the year 361:17
to have a s. tooth 279:91
when you speak, s. 362:21
you'll look s. upon the seat 116:99
Sweet and twenty: kiss me, s. 359:84
Sweet-briar: through the s. or the vine 214:97
Sweeten: children s. labours 24:95
civet ... to s. my imagination 329:91
perfumes of Arabia will not s. 335:69
Sweeter: anything to me is s. 164:42
s. manners, purer laws 386:69
s. than the berry 141:51
Sweetest: last taste of sweets is s. last 348:39
s. li'l feller 378:58
s. thing that ever grew 411:86
Sweethearts: old soldiers, s., are surest 400:52
Sweeting: trip no further, pretty s. 359:83
Sweetly flows that liquefaction 162:23
Sweetness: out of the strong came forth s. 39:27
passion for s. and light 21:52
pursuit of s. and light 21:47
two noblest things ... s. and light 381:95
waste its s. on the desert air 155:37
Sweets: as the last taste of s., is sweetest last 348:39
perpetual feast of nectared s. 213:77
stolen s. are best 102:13
s. and a ride in the train 211:58
s. to the sweet; farewell! 312:33
Swept: if seven maids ... s. it 92:79
Swift: Cousin S., you will never be a poet 128:67
too s. ... as tardy as too slow 354:10
Swifter than eagles ... stronger than lions 40:48

Swim: a naughty night to s. in 329:80
  but said I cd. not s. 91:67
Swine: nor yet feed the s. 231–2:27
  pearls before s. 52:24
  s., women and bees cannot be turned
  279:92
Swing low, sweet chariot 18:8
Swoon: at twelve noon the natives s.
  112:42
Swoons: wearied band s. to a waltz
  169:5
Swop for my dear old Dutch 99:80
Sword: a Sigh is the s. of an angel king
  66:35
  believed he had a s. upstairs 417:51
  his father's s. ... girded on 226:64
  I with s. will open 340:30
  is the s. unsway'd? 352:82
  man for the s. 389:2
  more cruel the pen ... than ... s.
  81:30
  nor shall my s. sleep 67:38
  nor the deputed s. 337:84
  pen is mightier than the s. 76:54
Swords: beat ... s. into plowshares
  48:31
  with paper hats and wooden s.
  395:81
Swore: Frankie and Johnny ... s. to be
  true 16:81
Swound: like noises in a s. 105:46
Syllable: last s. of recorded time
  336:76
Symmetry: frame thy fearful s. 68:46
  spoilers of the s. of shelves 192:26
Sympathize: the Walrus said: 'I
  deeply s.' 93:81
  s. with ... pains ... not ... pleasures
  169:1
Sympathy: without feeling or exciting
  s. 173:66
System: energies of our s. will decay
  27:48
Systems: our little s. have their day
  386:56

Ta-ra-ra-boom-de-ay 294:84
Table: crumbs ... from the rich man's
  t. 55:86
Tables: to turn the t. 281:69
Tabor: as to the t.'s sound 410:75
Tail: better ... than the t. of a lion
  255:20
  he's treading on my t. 91:62
  improve his shining t. 89:45
  sting is in the t. 278:78
  such a little t. behind 31:89
  thereby hangs a t. 345:4

Tails: and bring their t. behind them
  234:48
  cut off their t. with a carving knife
  240:80
  frogs and snails and puppy-dogs' t.
  240:85
  stings in their t. 61:29
  t. like unto scorpions 61:29
Take: t. a farthing away 279:93
  t. any man's horses 318:33
  t. away my good name 279:95
Taken: when t. to be well shaken
  108:95
Takes: a man who shaves and t. a train
  402:77
  blesseth ... him that t. 339:15
Talcum: a bit of t. is always walcum
  229:94
Tale: a round unvarnish'd t. 344:91
  an honest t. speeds best 352:80
  cd. ever hear by t. or history 341:36
  every shepherd tells his t. 214:98
  every t. condemns me 353:86
  every tongue brings in a ... t. 353:86
  had we lived, I shd. have had a t.
  294:91
  I cd. a t. unfold 307:64
  it is a t. told by an idiot 336:76
  point a moral, or adorn a t. 174:69
  sad t.'s best for winter 361:13
  t. which holdeth children from play
  327:41
  tedious as a twice-told t. 327:41
  thereby hangs a t. 301:88, 355:23
  with a t. forsooth he cometh 373:86
  yr. t., sir, wd. cure deafness 355:50
Talent: one t. which is death to hide
  223:29
  t. does what it can 209:37
  t. of flattering with delicacy 23:78
Talents: if you have great t. 287:6
Tales: and tell old t., and laugh
  330:99
  dead men tell no t. 259:57
  natural fear ... increased with t.
  24:86
  tell t. out of school 279:4
Talk: Cabots t. only to God 69:67
  I dont want to t. grammar 366:94
  I want to t. like a lady 366:94
  make little fishes t. ... t. like whales
  152:4
  some t. of Alexander 18:6
  t. of censorious old men 94:3
  t. of court news ... t. with them
  330:99
  t. of many things 93:80
  t. of the devil 279:6

Talk (*continued*)
t. so like a waiting-gentlewoman 313:52
t. the hind leg off a donkey 279:5
t. what he knoweth not 24:93
think too little ... t. too much 126:42
to t. about the rest of us 163:36
Talked: being t. about ... not being t. about 406:23
he [Coleridge] t. on for ever 159:78
not to be t. of ... by men 392:41
t. like Poor Poll 141:49
Talkers: great t. are great liars 265:44
greatest t. ... least doers 279:8
Talketh what he knoweth 24:93
Talking: ears burn, someone is t. 261:3
he will be t. ... 'wit is out' 343:78
t. about being a gentleman 380:89
you go on t. and t. 401:68
you will still be t. 342:58
Talks: I wish I liked the way it t. 286:97
t. to himself, speaks to a fool 279:9
Tall: divinely t., and most divinely fair 385:46
Tally: no books but the score and the t. 321:68
Tamburlaine, the scourge of God, must die 205:79
Tameless: too like thee: t., and swift 369:37
Tamer of the human breast 155:43
Tampers with natural ignorance 405:9
Tangles: with the t. of Neaera's hair 215:12
Taper-light: with t. to seek 327:43
Tappertit: 'strings', said Mr T. 119:32
Tara: hangs as mute on T.'s walls 226:62
Tarquin: great house of T. 201:35
Tarred with the same brush 279:10
Tarry: you may for ever t. 162:25
Tarsus: like a stately ship of T. 222:18
Tartarly: Quarterly, so savage and T. 86:94
Tarts: Queen of Hearts, she made some t. 91:66, 237:65
Task: long day's t. is done 299:64
thy worldly t. has done 304–5:29
what he reads as a t. 175:86
Taste: every man to his t. 262:30
last t. of sweets, is sweetest last 348:39
let me t. yr. ware 237:69
lost his t., sweet is sour 270:7
O t. and see ... the Lord is good 42:99
they do t. kind of funny 15:63

Tasted: some books are to be t. 26:32
you have t. two whole worms 377:50
Tastes: no accounting for t. 254:57
no disputing about t. 259:53
Taught: Cristes lore ... he t. 97:42
first he wroghte ... afterwards he t. 97:40
Tortoise because he t. us 91:59
Tavern: enjoy themselves ... at a capital t. 177:17
there is a t. in the town 19:10
Taxation: no t. without representation 273:3
t. without representation is tyranny 243:11
Taxes: nothing is certain but death and t. 139:16
Tea: if this is t. ... I wish for coffee 285:87
is there honey still for t.? 71:91
'take some more t.,' the March Hare said 90:55
Teach: may t. you more of man 414:28
prayer doth t. us all to render 339:15
t. the torches to burn bright 353:94
they t. the morals of a whore 174:77
Teacher: let Nature be your t. 414:27
Teaches: he who cannot, t. 366:88
Tea-cup: a storm in a t. 278:83
A Storm in a T. 34:23
Team of little atomies 353:92
Tear: a t. is an intellectual thing 66:35
all he had, a t. 155:41
and shed a bitter t. 92:79
fallen a splendid t. 388:87
he hath a t. for pity 317:25
part to t. a cat in 341:40
t. him for his bad verses 325:22
Tears: and I look through my t. 390:28
crocodile t. 259:35
drops t. as fast as ... trees ... gum 346–7:22
hence these t. 389:4
if you have t., prepare to shed 325:17
ills ... no weight, and t. no bitterness 201:33
in silence and t. 86:99
in t. amid the alien corn 184:30
nor all thy t. wash out 136:79
nothing to offer but blood, toil, t. 100:92
our t. thaw not the frost 367:9
t. fall in my heart 396:90
t., idle t. 388:99
there is t. for his love 325:11
thoughts ... too deep for t. 411:82
time with a gift of t. 382:16

Things (*continued*)
little t. please little minds 270:92
little t. ... the most important 124:18
look thy last on all t. lovely 118:22
Man is the master of t. 383:21
men may rise ... to higher t. 386:57
mighty sum of t. forever speaking 409:65
more t. are wrought by prayer 386:55
more t. in heaven and earth 307:69
night and day ... both sweet t. 69:65
old, unhappy, far-off t. 414:21
remembrance of t. past 362:37
right judgement in all t. 64:89
river ... drowns t. weighty 26:35
see the t. thou dost not 330:93
set yr. affection on t. above 59:82
Shape of T. to Come 401:67
sweetest t. turn sourest 363:42
sympathizeth with all t. 72:2
take upon's the mystery of t. 330:99
the day of small t. 51:96
the more t. change 180:72
the two noblest of t. 381:95
there was t. ... he stretched 393:59
t. are not what they seem 198:95
t. are the sons of heaven 172:41
t. hoped for ... t. not seen 59:99
t. past redress ... past care 349:47
t. sweet to taste prove ... sour 348:35
t. that go bump in the night 14:60
t. that wd. astonish you 144:86
t. ... true, t. ... honest ... just ... think on these t. 58:79
t. ... we ought not to have done 63:67
t. won are done 358:65
those brave translunary t. 125:33
thou ... art all t. under Heaven 221:2
to talk of many t. 93:80
two t. about the horse 15:64
two t. stand like stone 152:7
unseen t. above 157:61
unto the pure all t. are pure 59:96
what t. ... done at the Mermaid 29:70
you worse than senseless t.! 323:89
you'll understand a good many t. 121:70
Think: books t. for me 192:29
first t., and then speak 263:68
I cannot sit and t. 192:29
I stand alone, and t. 186:49
I t. him so, because I t. him so 361:5

Think (*continued*)
I t., therefore I am 119:31
if ... I t. on thee, dear friend 363:38
not so t. as you drunk 378:56
t. of yr. forefathers ... posterity! 9:2
t. today and speak tomorrow 280:26
t. too little ... talk too much 126:42
t. well of all men 280:27
t. with the wise 280:28
to t. is to be full of sorrow 184:25
we cannot t. alike 127:62
when I t., I must speak 302:96
world is a comedy to those who t. 398:23
Thinking: dogged as does it. It ain't t. 393:55
good or bad, ... t. makes it so 308:80
never thought of t. for myself 147:27
plain living and high t. 412:2
put on one's t. cap 275:68
talk without t. ... shoot without aiming 279:7
t. is very far from knowing 280:29
t. jest what a Rum Go 401:65
t. on fantastic summer's heat 348:37
t. on the frosty Caucasus 348:37
t. too precisely on th' event 311:23
Thinks: he t. too much. Such men are dangerous 324:94
t. what ne'er was, nor is 249:96
you do anything, he t. no ill 363:39
Third: to make a t. she joined the former two 128:66
unto the t. and fourth generation 37:84
Thirst: a man can raise a t. 190:8
Thirsty: if he be t., give him water 45:81
when you are t., to cure it 245:37
Thirteen: the clocks were striking t. 242:99
Thirty: at t. man suspects 418:63
person under ... t. ... not a revolutionist 365:84
t. days hath September 239:77
Thomasin once ... so promising 140:30
Thorn: a t. in the flesh 58:65
day as sharp to them as t. 351:59
figs grew upon t. 98:67
he left the t. wi' me 81:28
no rose without a t. 273:99
snail's on the t. 75:44
Thorns: I fall upon the t. of life! 369:37
Thorny: life is t.; and youth is vain 106:67
Thou: and T. beside me singing 135:67

Three (*continued*)
he stoppeth one of t. 104:42
I have answered t. questions 90:49
I spied t. ships 15:74
in married life t. is company 405:8
indicates that two and one are t. 378:62
is without t. good friends 302:93
lives not t. good men unhanged 314:64
loved t. whole days together 380:86
there are t. sexes 375:9
though he was only t. 211:56
t. acres and a cow 107:85
t. cheers and one cheer more 147:24
t. distinct terms, Barbarians 21:48
t., four, knock at the door 236:60
t. hours a day will produce 393:56
t. is company and two is none 405:8
t. jolly farmers 118:26
t. little maids from school 145:2
t. may keep counsel if two be away 280:35
t. poets in t. distant Ages 128:66
t. ravens sat on a tree 12:39
t. ships come sailing by 233–4:42
t. things I never lends 381:91
t. things ... too wonderful for me 46:91
t. years she grew in sun 415:30
we galloped all t. 74:26
when shall we t. meet again? 332:22
Threefold: at t. cord is not ... broken 46:99
Threescore: the days of our years are t. years and ten 43:17
Threshold: starry t. of Jove's court 212:72
Thrice: men in great places are t. servants 25:1
t. welcome darling of the Spring 415:38
weave a circle round him t. 107:76
Thrift, thrift, Horatio! 306:48
Thrifty: the housewife that's t. 372:78
Thrilling: in t. region of thick-ribbed ice 337:90
Thrive: only the strong shall t. 297:35
Throat: took by the t. the circumcised dog 346–7:22
unto the sweet bird's t. 300:83
Throne: here is my t., bid kings come 326:39
high on a t. of royal state 217:45
Queen-Moon is on her t. 184:26
Throw good money after bad 280:37
Thrush: that's the wise t. 74:23

Thumb: he put in his t. 235:50
'twixt his finger and his t. 313:51
Thunder: glorious the t.'s roar 374:94
laugh as I pass in t. 368:22
t. in such lovely language 194:49
t., lightning, or in rain? 332:22
Thunderbolt: like a t. he falls 385·47
Thunderstorm: dying duck in a t. 261:2
streams like the t. 84:63
Thursday: T.'s child has far to go 235:56
took ill on T. 238:71
Thus: why ... t? ... reason of this thusness? 399:29
Thwackum was for doing justice 134:63
Thyme: the wild t. blows 341:46
Thyself: love thy neighbour as t. 37:99
when T. with shining Foot 136:83
Tiber: Oh, T., father T. 201:40
Tickle: if you t. us, do we not laugh? 339:13
I'll t. your catastrophe 316:5
Tickling commodity 326:37
Tide: a t. in the affairs of men 326:27
a t. in the affairs of women 85:80
call of the running t. 207:15
ev'n at the turning o' th' t. 319:43
lived in the t. of times 324:8
the t. is full, the moon lies fair 20:30
Tidings: glad t. of great joy 384:35
Tie: educational relations ... strongest t. 287:8
Ties: purse-strings ... common t. of friendship 275:70
Tiger: imitate the action of the t. 319:45
smile on the face of the t. 13:52
t., t., burning bright 68:46
·t.'s heart ... in a player's hide 156:49
went for a ride on a t. 13:52
Tigers: there were no t. That was the point 131:14
Tiggers don't like honey 210:50
Time: a man must serve his t. 85:90
a t. for all things 280:40
a t. for such a word 336:76
a t. to every purpose 46:98
a t. when meadow, grove, and stream 410:72
almost fairy t. 342:55
ancient nobility ... act of t. 25:6
and in good t. you gave it 328:66
Art is long, and T. is fleeting 198:96
bank and shoal of t. 333:36
be not coy, but use yr. t. 162:25

Time (continued)
bid t. return 349:51
busiest man who has t. to spare 244:25
but a short t. to live 65:13
conspiracy his t. doth take 356:39
cormorant devouring T. 331:8
creeping hours of t. 301:89
dark backward and abysm of t. 355:29
did those feet in ancient t. 67:38
dust on antique t. 303:15
fixed figure for the t. of scorn 346:13
fleet the t. carelessly 300:72
fly envious T. 223:34
fool all the people all the t. 197:82
footprints in the sands of t. 198:97
friends are thieves of t. 264:95
full of dismal terror was the t. 351–2:71
greatest part of a writer's t. 176:11
half as old as t. 77:70
happiness takes no account of t. 266:62
he hath shook hands with t. 137:92
how long a t. lies in one ... word 348:34
I had liv'd a blessed t. 334:46
in t. all haggard hawks 191:22
in t. small wedges cleave 191:22
in t. the flint is pierced 191:22
in t. the savage bull 191:22
inaudible and noiseless foot of T. 298:48
just going outside ... may be some t. 241:93
life, t.'s fool 315:91
look into the seeds of t. 333:27
many a t. and oft 338:5
never the t. and the place 74:31
new wail my dear t.'s waste 362:37
no t. like the present 280:41
no t. to stand and stare 117:11
not of an age but for all t.! 179:57
nothing is ours but t. 273:8
old in hours if he have lost no t. 26:26
old t. is still a-flying 162:24
panting t. toiled after him 173:58
patience, money and t. 274:30
remember that t. is money 138:10
repeat how T. is slipping 135:74
seen better faces in my t. 328:62
sent before my t. into this ... world 351:66
such is T. that takes in trust 286:93
that passed the t. It wd. have passed 30:75

Time (continued)
that t. may cease, and midnight 204:65
the Bird of T. has but a little way 135:66
the holy t. is quiet as a nun 412:92
the last syllable of recorded t. 336:76
the show and gaze o' th' t. 336:79
'the t. has come,' the Walrus said 93:80
the t. is out of joint 307:71
the t. of our Ford 168:97
the t. will come ... you will hear me 122:88
thief of t. 418:62
this bloody tyrant T. 362:31
T. ambles ... trots ... gallops 302:98
t. and chance happeneth to ... all 47:8
t. and the hour 333:29
t. and thinking tame ... grief 280:38
t. and tide wait for no man 280:39
t. enough to think of the future 366:95
t. flies 280:18
t. future contained in t. past 130:90
t. hath ... a wallet 358:71
t. is broke and no proportion kept 351:63
t. is flying 397:6
t. is on our side 149:51
t. is the greatest innovator 26:17
t., like an ever-rolling stream 400:40
t. ... man is always trying to kill 376:31
t. ... must have a stop 315:91
t. of life is short 315:89
t. of the singing of birds 47:22
t. present and t. past are both 130:90
t. spent on any item of the agenda 244:26
T., ... subtle thief of youth 223:28
t. that takes survey of all the world 315:91
t., the devourer of things 243:14
T. travels in divers paces 302:98
t. was away and somewhere else 203:57
t. will not be ours for ever 179:61
t. will run back 215:21
t., with a gift of tears 382:16
T., you old gypsy man 163:37
T.'s winged chariot 206:94
to choose t. is to save t. 26:18
too much t. in studies is sloth 26:31
want to know the t., ask a P'liceman 288:22
whips and scorns of t. 309:95

Time (*continued*)
whirligig of t. 360:2
with thee conversing I forget all t.
219:70
Time-honoured: old John of Gaunt,
t. Lancaster 347:28
Time-table: sooner read a t. or a catalogue 208:22
Times (see also *The Times*): art not for
fashion of these t. 300:79
cowards die many t. 324:1
in pious t., ere priest-craft 126:36
lived in the tide of t. 324:8
natures of the t. dec.eas'd 317:16
other t., other manners 254:83
our t. are in His hand 75:46
purest treasure mortal t. afford
347:30
remember when the t. were not hard
133:47
the spacious t. of great Elizabeth
385:45
what t.! what customs! 102:19
Timor mortis conturbat me 129:76
Timotheus: let old T. yield the Prize
127:54
Tinker, tailor, soldier, sailor 240:81
Tinkers: there'd be no trade for t.
267:10
Tinklings: drowsy t. lull the distant
folds 155:31
Tiny: are in t. leaf 74:21
Tiny Tim: 'God bless us ...' said T.
119:36
Tipperary: it's a long way to T. 407:39
Tippled: have ye t. drink more fine?
183:14
Tiptoe: jocund day stands t. 354:14
stand a t. when this day is named
320:57
Tired: dinner waits, and we are t.
113:58
I'm t. of love ... t. of rhyme 32:98
life ... process of getting t. 82:43
the t. waves, vainly breaking 103:33
t. eyelids upon t. eyes 388:85
t. of knocking at preferment's door
21:41
woman who was always t. 12:43
Tires: he t. betimes that spurs too fast
348:40
sad [heart] t. in a mile-a 361:19
Titania: ill met by moonlight, proud T.
341:43
Title-leaf: this man's brow, like to a t.
316:96
Titles: conquering kings their t. take
95:18

Titles (*continued*)
thy other t. ... given away 328:56
Titwillow, titwillow! 146:12
Toad: I had rather be a t. 345:8
intelligent Mr T. 153:14
t., ugly and venomous 300:75
Toast: let the t. pass, drink to the lass
372:78
Today: be wise t. 418:61
can call t. his own 128:71
hour t. is worth two tomorrow
267:4
if T. be sweet 135:74
never jam t. 93:83
one t. is worth two to-morrows
280:42
such a day tomorrow as t. 361:12
Toddle safely home and die—in bed
293:82
Toe: catch a nigger by his t. 232:29
on the light fantastic t. 214:94
Toes: bells on her t. 237:66
nobody knows ... how cold my t.
210:49
Together: let us never visit t. 109:17
let us remain t. still 368:27
put Humpty t. again 233:37
t. in a little crooked house 239:74
t. now for forty years 99:80
Toil: each anxious t., each eager strife
173:67
let not ambition mock ... useful t.
155:34
offer ... blood, t., tears and sweat
100:92
sleep after t. 377:42
they t. not, neither ... spin 52:21
t., envy, want, the patron 173:68
Told: t. me you had been to her
91:67
went and t. the sexton 165:59
Tolerable and not to be endured
343:75
Tolerance: practise t. ... live ... in peace
394:76
Tolerate: no longer t. the race 27:48
Toll: t. for the brace 113:64
t. me back from thee to ... self
184:31
Tolled: sexton t. the bell 165:59
Tolls: for whom the bell t. 124:14
it t. for thee 124:14
Tom: 'Come, come,' said T.'s father
226:65
poor T.'s a-cold 329:81
T. bears logs into the hall 332:20
T., he was a piper's son 240:82
T., T., the piper's son 240:83

Tom (*continued*)
T. went howling down the street 240:83
Tom o' Bedlam: a sigh like T. 327:54
Tom Pearse, lend me yr. grey mare 19:12
Tomb: for such a t. wd. wish to die 216:25
monument without a t. 179:54
Tommy: it's T. this, an' T. that 190:11
little T. Stout 232:28
little T. Tucker 235:52
Tom-tit: a little t. sang 'Willow' 146:12
Tomorrow: can say, T. do thy worst 128:71
egg today ... hen t. 255:13
hour today is worth two t. 267:4
never put off till t. 273:85
same flower ... t. will be dying 162:24
such a day t. as today 361:12
think today and speak t. 280:26
t. and t. creeps in this petty pace 336:76
t. blossoms ... bears his blushing honours 322:80
t. is a new day 280:44
t. is our wedding day 113:55
t. never comes 280:43
t. we'll be sober 16:78
T.!—Why, T. I may be 135:69
unborn T. and dead Yesterday 135:74
Tomorrows: one today is worth two t. 280:42
Tone: take the t. of the company 98:57
that t. and gesture bland 294:96
Tongs: the t. and the bones 342:51
touch him with a pair of t. 280:51
Tongue: an understanding, but no t. 306:51
breast forges ... t. must vent 303–4:17
customs, politics and t. 245:32
every t. brings in a ... tale 353:86
eye, t., sword 310:1
fellows of infinite t. 321:61
give thy thoughts no t. 306:55
iron t. of midnight 342:55
keep one's t. between one's teeth 268:29
keep wel thy t. ... keep thy freend 97:49
no venom to that of the t. 282:91
one t. is enough for a woman 280:45
our English t. a gallimaufry 377:48

Tongue (*continued*)
sad words of t. or pen 403:90
sharp t. ... edged tool ... grows keener 170:17
though his t. dropped manna 217:48
t. can no man tame 60:5
t. cleave to ... roof of my mouth 44:49
t. is not steel ... it cuts 280:46
t. of idle people 280:47
t. sounds ... as a sullen bell 316:97
t. that Shakespeare spake 413:5
use of my oracular t. 372:71
virtue dwells not in the t. 282:93
Tongues: conscience ... thousand several t. 353:86
done to death by slanderous t. 344:88
finds t. in trees 300:75
lack t. to praise 363:46
silver-sweet ... lovers' t. by night 354:5
these poor t. ... shall be silent 196:76
Tonight: along the Potomac t. 30:84
t. we'll merry be 16:78
Too: this t., t. solid flesh 305:42
t. nice ... t. proud ... cool ... fond 151:79
Tool: man is a t.-making animal 139:17
sharp tongue ... edged t. ... grows keener 170:17
Tools: bad workman quarrels with his t. 255:88
give us the t. ... finish the job 101:98
t. to woik ... for those who will 200:22
Tooth: a t. for a t. 52:12
Nature, red in t. and claw 386:63
sharper than a serpent's t. 328:58
t. to t., hand for hand 37:93
to have a sweet t. 279:91
thy t. is not so keen 302:91
Toothache: endure the t. patiently 344:86
Top: always room at the t. 400:46
I shall die at the t. 382:13
sleep like a t. 117:9
t. of it reached to heaven 36:61
T. People take *The Times* 11:33
Topical: sang a most t. song 13:53
Topics: high life ... other fashionable t. 152:1
Tops: mountain t. that freeze 322:77
t. were close against the sky 165:61
Topses: herring boxes without t. 225:60

Topsy: persisted T., 'never had no father' 380:84

Torch: a bright t. and a casement 185:33

t. ... passed to a new generation 188:74

Torches: doth teach the t. to burn bright 353:94

Tories own no argument but force 72:8

Torment: love in a palace ... grievous t. 183:11

there shall no t. touch them 62:43

Torments: our t. ... may ... become our elements 217:51

Torn: man all tattered and t. 239:79

Tortoise: why did you call him T.? 91:59

Torture: touch him not and t. not again 367:16

Tory ... with more propriety ... the Conservative 115:87

Tossed: you t. and gored several persons 175:97

Tossing their heads in sprightly dance 410:69

Totter: charming to t. into vogue 398:22

Totters: the state t. 356:45

Touch: men t. them and change 382:18

O for the t. of a vanish'd hand 384:37

one t. of nature 358:72

that I might t. that cheek 353:98

t. him with a pair of tongs 280:51

t. not, taste not, handle not 59:81

t. wood 280:52

unkind as the t. of sweating metal 117:14

Touching: a sight so t. in its majesty 412:96

Toujours gai archy 205:84

Tous pour un, un pour tous 129:74

Tout passe, t. casse, t. lasse 281:53

Toves: the slithy t. 91:69

Tower: fall'n ... that t. of strength 388:93

King's name is a t. of strength 353:84

to the dark t. came 329:82

yonder ivy-mantled t. 155:32

Towers: burnt the topless t. of Ilium? 204:63

cloud-capp'd t., ... gorgeous palaces 356:50

Town: a tavern in the t. 19:10

in Scarlet t., where I was born 12:36

Town (*continued*)

King sits in Dunfermline t. 12:37

lived in a pretty how t. 116:94

O little t. of Bethlehem 72:95

spring, moonless night ... small t. 390:23

t. ... is lighter than vanity 77:60

Town-crier: as lief the t. spoke 310:3

Toy: foolish thing was but a t. 360:3

I count religion ... childish t. 204:69

Toys: all is but t. 334:46

Trace: learned to t. the day's disasters 150:68

Traces: hounds of spring are on winter's t. 382:15

Trade: and now there isn't any t. 161:8

every t. save censure 85:90

half a t. and half an art 170:12

homely, slighted, shepherd's t. 215:11

no nation was ever ruined by t. 138:11

others ... venture t. abroad 318:39

where the old t.'s plying 230:12

Tradesmen: bow, ye t., bow, ye masses 143:80

lying ... becomes none but t. 362:26

Tradition: t. approves all forms of competition 103:30

youth of America ... oldest t. 406:26

Traduced: beat a Venetian and t. the state 346–7:22

Trafalgar Square fountains like Government Clerks 285:78

Traffic: the two hours' t. of our stage 353:89

Tragedies: all t. are finished by a death 84:75

there are two t. in life 365:83

Tragedy: go litel myn t. 98:52

t. is ... a certeyn storie 97:47

world ... a t. to those who feel 398:23

Tragical-historical, t.-comical-historical- 308:84

Trail: long, long t. a-winding 189:84

Train: a man who shaves and takes a t. 402:77

something ... to read in the t. 405:14

Train-band: a t. captain eke was he 112:54

Training is everything 394:69

Traitor: thou art a t. Off with his head! 352:75

Traitors: cowards flinch, and t. jeer 109–10:21

translators, t. 281:54

Tresses: fair t. man's ... race insnare
251:35
wither'd cheek and t. grey 295:99
Trial by jury ... instead of being a
security 119:28
Tribe: badge of all our t. 338:6
Idols of the T. 27:41
pearl ... richer than all his t.
346–7:22
Tribes: two mighty t., the *Bores* and
Bored 85:86
Tribute: to his feet thy t. bring 201:34
Trick: a t. worth two of that 313:55
t. of our English nation 316:1
when in doubt, win the t. 168:87
when the long t.'s over 208:16
Tricks: fantastic t. before high heaven
337:87
frustrate their knavish t. 88:30
hard to teach an old dog t. 279:12
Trident: flatter Neptune for his t.
303:17
Tried to live without him ... died
416:47
Trifle: as 'twere a careless t. 333:30
one must not t. with love 227:79
Trifles: man of sense ... t. ... humours
... flatters 98:60
snapper-up of unconsidered t.
361:18
Trip no further, pretty sweeting 359:83
Tripping hither, t. thither 143:79
Trippingly on the tongue 310:3
Triton: old T. blow his wreathèd horn
412:94
T. of the minnows 303:16
Triumph: I t. still if thou abide 201:33
meet with T. and Disaster 190:4
never dreamed ... wrong wd. t.
73:16
t. of hope over experience 176:1
Triumphs: thy ... glories, t., spoils,
shrunk 324:6
Trivial: contests rise from t. things
251:33
such t. people ... such lovely language 194:49
t. and vulgar ... coition 72:5
Troop: sent a t. of horse 72:8
Troops: farewell the plumed t. 345:10
Trotting: shall we be t. home again?
93:82
Trouble: a very present help in t. 42:7
double, double toil and t. 335:58
has t. enough of its own 404:91
he that seeks t. 277:26
kindness in another's t. 152:7
man is born unto t. 41:67

Trouble (*continued*)
man ... of few days ... full of t. 41:69
never t. t. until t. troubles 273:90
where there's a will, there's t. 283:34
Troubles: arms against a sea of t.
309:95
don't meet t. half-way 272:53
pack up yr. t. 22:56
the written t. of the brain 336:72
Trousers: bottoms of my t. rolled
131:3
I shall wear white flannel t. 131:4
shd. never put on his best t. 169:9
Trout: rose-moles ... upon t. 166:68
Trowel: lay it on with a t. 269:61
that was laid on with a t. 300:73
Truant: a t. disposition 306:47
and every t. knew 150:68
True: a truism ... none the less t.
293:76
as t. ... as taxes is 120:43
be so t. to thyself 25:16
dare to be t. 161:11
faith unfaithful ... falsely t. 385:50
good to be honest and t. 17:93
he's mad, 'tis t.: 'tis t. 'tis pity
308:74
if all be t. that I do think 10:16
me and my t. love 18:2
nor ... people's judgment always t.
127:47
one religion is as t. as another 82:32
ring in the t. 386:68
sad reflection but a t. one 175:88
so young, my lord, and t. 327:50
to thine own self be t. 306:57
t. as the stars above 16:81
which was prov'd t. ... prove false
82:38
Truism: a t. is ... none the less true
293:76
Truly: whom t. to know is everlasting
life 64:91
Trumpet: moved more than with a t.
373:87
the t. of a prophecy! O, Wind
369:38
to blow one's own t. 256:50
Trumpets: all the t. sounded for him
77:67
sound the t., beat the drums 127:52,
226:68
Trumps: to turn up t. 281:71
Truncheon: marshal's t. ... judge's
robe 337:84
Trunk: so large a t. before 31:89
Trust: better to t. in the Lord 43:34
extreme, rude, cruel, not to t. 363:50

Turns: t. no more his head 106:60
 whoso t. as I, this evening 74:25
Turpissimus: nemo repente fuit t.
 180:68
Turret: Sultan's T. in a Noose of Light
 134:65
Turtle: the t. lives 'twixt plated decks
 229:98
 voice of the t. is heard 47:22
Turtle-doves: two t. and a partridge
 238–9:73
Tuscany: even the ranks of T. 202:41
Tutor: irreverent to my t. 174:72
Tweedledee: 'Contrariwise,' continued
 T. 92:75
 Tweedledum and T. 92:74
Twelve: 'a parted ... between t. and
 one 319:43
 at t. noon the natives swoon 112:42
 he in t. found truth in all but one
 350:57
 I, in t. thousand, none 350:57
 in the sworn t. have a thief or two
 337:81
Twenty: expenditure t. pounds ought
 and six 119:40
Twice: a victory is t. itself 342:56
 he sings each song t. over 74:23
 hear t. before you speak once 266:79
 it is t. blest 339:15
Twig: as the t. is bent, the tree's
 inclined 251:22
Twilight: a t. dim with rose 118:25
 at the t.'s last gleaming 188:79
 bats ... they ever fly by t. 26:23
 t. grey ... in her sober livery 219:69
Twin roses by the zephyr blown apart
 182:3
Twinkle: t. on the milky way 410:68
 t., t., little bat 90:53
 t., t., little star 384:36
Twinkling: in the t. of a bed-staff
 298:40
Twins: quadruplets, not t. 14:55
Twist: neither t. wolf's-bane 183:21
Twitched: rose, and t. his mantle blue
 215:18
Two: a trick worth t. of that 313:55
 bicycle made for t. 116:99
 human species ... t. distinct races
 191:25
 I like t. months of every year 83:55
 if t. are in the churchyard laid
 416:41
 in t. words: im-possible 152:5
 only know t. sorts of boys 120:57
 only t. families in the world 95:10
 takes t. to speak the truth 391:39

Two (*continued*)
 the t. noblest of things 381:95
 there went in t. and t. unto Noah
 35:45
 t. can play at that game 281:75
 t. cheers for Democracy 137:98
 t. glasses ... t. chairs ... t. people
 203:57
 t. luxuries to brood over 187:65
 t. men look out 193:38
 t. mites, which make a farthing
 54:63
 t. things stand like stone 152:7
 t. to bear my soul away 10:13
 t. to make a marriage a success
 293:75
 when t. or three are gathered together
 63:73
Type: so careful of the t. she seems
 386:62
Tyrannies: of all the T. on humane
 kind 127:62
Tyrannous to use it like a giant 337:86
Tyranny: ecclesiastic t.'s the worst
 118:19
 taxation without representation is t.
 243:11
Tyrant: little t. of his fields withstood
 155:38
 professed t. to their sex 342:59
 this bloody t., Time 362:31
Tyrants: necessity ... argument of t.
 246:56
 resistance to t. is obedience 171:31
Tyre: village which men still call T.
 136:85

U and Non-U ... Sociological Lin-
 guistics 290:42
Uglier yet is the hump 190:15
Uglification and Derision 91:60
Ugly: beauty ... that makes me u.
 346:16
 The U. Duckling 11:24
Umbrella: unjust steals the just's u.
 70:71
Unadorned: beauty u. 31:87
Unarm, Eros ... day's task is done
 299:64
Unattempted yet in prose or rhyme
 216:28
Unbaptized: any that die u. 65:12
Unbelief: help thou mine u. 54:59
Unbidden guests ... welcomest when ...
 gone 321:63
Un-birthday: an u. present 93:85
Unborn: the children yet u. shall feel
 351:59

Unburied: bodies of u. men 400:54

Uncertain: u., coy, and hard to please 296:14

u. glory of an April day 361:6

Uncharitableness: envy, hatred, ... and all u. 63:77

Uncle: my prophetic soul! My u.! 307:67

u. me no u. 349:45

Uncle Toby: our armies swore ... cried my U. 379:70

Uncle Tom Cobbleigh and all 19:12

Unclubbable: a very u. man 175:93

Uncomely: all things u. and broken 417:55

Uncomfortable: thinks he is moral ... is only u. 365:82

we u. feel 148:32

Uncommon: the thing that's most u. 251:31

Unconfined: let joy be u. 83:60

Unconscionable time dying 96:20

Uncover, dogs, and lap 357:61

Under-belly: the soft u. of the Axis 101:4

Underlings: fault ... in ourselves that we are u. 323–4:93

Underneath are the everlasting arms 38:17

Underpaying: better than the u. instinct 364:67

Underrate ... the duty of being happy 379:79

Understand: a man will ne'er quite u. 245:32

I u. thy kisses, and thou mine 314:75

no one can u. Ein 14:57

one half ... world cannot u. 23:65

Understanding: brute beasts that have no u. 64:4

Donne's verses ... pass all u. 170:20

give it an u., but no tongue 306:51

light a candle of u. 61:38

peace of God, which passeth all u. 58:78

Undeserver may sleep 317:12

Undeserving: Im one of the u. poor 366:96

Undo: pray you u. this button 331:6

Undone: u. those things which we ought to have done 63:67

what's done cannot be u. 335:70

wish th' estate of th' world were now u. 336:77

Uneasy: this swift business I must u. make 356:36

u. lies the head that wears a crown 317:14

Uneatable: in full pursuit of the u. 406:27

Unexpected: moment foreseen may be u. 132:18

the u. ... always happens 282:87

Unfaithful: faith u. ... falsely true 385:50

Unfit: worse man ... u. for the married state 177:18

Unfold: O clouds, u.! 67:38

Unfortunate: one more U., weary of breath 165:56

Unfriendly to society's chief joys 112:53

Unhanged: not three good men u. 314:64

Unhappy: had been very u. in marriage 176:1

instinct for being u. highly developed 292:69

no one till his death ... called u. 73:9

u. family is u. in its own way 392:49

Unheard: heard melodies are sweet, but those u. 183:17

Unholy: refrain from the u. pleasure 31:88

shrieks, and sights u.! 213–14:91

Unicorn: lion and the u. were fighting 234:47

Unintelligible: weary weight of ... this u. world 415:32

Union: broken Nature's social u. 80:17

Liberty and U., now ... for ever ... inseparable 400:44

O U., strong and great! 197:92

Unite: workers of the world, u. 207:9

United Nations: we the peoples of the U. 394:76

Unity: brethren ... swell together in u. 44:43

u. is strength 282:88

Universally acknowledged ... a single man 23:75

Universe: born for the U. [Burke] 151:78

wide vessel of the u. 320:50

Universities: state of both his u. 393:54

University: don't think one 'comes down' from Jimmy's u. 242:10

true U. ... is a collection of books 89:37

we are the U. 378:54

Unjust steals the just's umbrella 70:71

Unkind: Midlands ... sodden and u. 32:5

Unkind (*continued*)
  not so u. as man's ingratitude
  302:91
  tell me not, sweet, I am u. 199:16
  when givers prove u. 310:96
Unkindest: the most u. cut of all
  325:19
Unkindness: I tax not ... elements with
  u. 328:72
Unknown: forms of things u. 342:53
  I travelled among u. men 409:66
  not to know me argues yourselves u.
  219:72
  Paradise of Fools; to few u.
  218:60
Unlamented let me die 251:29
Unlearned, he knew no schoolman's
  ... art 248:87
Unlucky: so u. that he runs into accidents 206:85
  when you shall these u. deeds relate
  346:22
Unnatural: foul, strange, and u.
  307:66
  let me be cruel, not u. 311:14
  poetry's u. 121:72
Unobserved, home to his mother's
  house 221:9
Unperfect, unfinished, inartistic [of
  Thoreau] 170:25
Unpremeditated: my u. verse 220:89
Unprofitable: months ... most idle and
  u. 142:64
  stale, flat, and u. 305:42
Unrespited, unpitied, unreprieved
  217:50
Unrewarded: nothing went u. but
  desert 126:44
  wit shall not go u. 357:51
Unseen: born to blush u. 155:37
  leave the world u. 184:24
Unsought: Beadsman ... u. for slept
  182:92
  [love] given u. 360:94
Unspeakable: the u. in ... pursuit of
  ... uneatable 406:27
Unstable as water 36:66
Unsubstantial: an u. faery place
  415:39
Untaught: better u. than ill-taught
  256:31
Untimely: was from his mother's womb
  u. ripp'd 336:78
Untrue to his wife 22:61
Untruths: they have spoken u. ... are
  slanders 344:87
Untune that string 358:68
Unturned: leave no stone u. 269:68

Unvarnished: a round u. tale deliver
  344:91
Unwept, unhonour'd, and unsung
  295:6
Unworthy: an opinion ... u. of him
  25:11
  spurns that ... merit of th' u. takes
  309:95
Up: they cannot bear levelling u.
  175:89
  U., Guards, and at 'em 401:60
  u. so floating many bells down
  116:94
  U., u.! my friend ... quit your books
  414:25
  u. with which I will not put 102:9
Up-hill: road wind u. all the way?
  290:46
Uphold: will u. the unyok'd humour
  312:49
Upper classes have ... u. hand 111:39
Uproar's your only music 186:53
Upstairs and downstairs 232:32
Urn: bubbling and loud-hissing u.
  114:73
Us: how different from u. 15:68
Usance: rate of u. here ... in Venice
  338:3
Use: beauty too rich for u. 353:94
  great riches ... no real u. 26:24
  how u. doth breed a habit! 361:10
  soil'd with all ignoble u. 387:72
  u. a poor maiden so 16:80
  u. every man after his desert 308:88
  what's the u. of worrying? 22:56
Used: not what there u. to be 34:24
Useless: all art is quite u. 406:22
  most beautiful things ... most u.
  291:61
  talent ... lodged with me u. 223:29
  u. each without the other 198:3
Uses: all the u. of this world! 305:42
  keep a corner ... for others' u.
  345:8
  sweet are the u. of adversity 300:75
Usurpation: I dare, without u. 72:99
Utter: not u. what thou dost not know
  313:61

Vacant: in v. or in pensive mood
  410:71
  loud laugh ... spoke the v. mind
  150:65
Vacations: Dotheboys Hall ... no
  extras, no v. 120:52
Vae victis 197:85
Vaguery: medal inscribed 'For V. in
  the Field' 242:9

Vain: hour when you too learn that all is v. 290:50

labour and the wounds are v. 103:32

mock on, 'tis all in v. 67:39

name of the Lord thy God in v. 37:85

no great man lives in v. 89:36

they labour in v. that build 44:41

use not v. repetitions 52:17

v. are the thousand creeds 71:85

v. for you to rise up early 44:42

Why, all delights are v. 331:9

youth is v. 106:67

Vaincre sans péril ... triomphe sans gloire 110:32

Vainly: tired waves, v. breaking 103:33

Valet: no man is a hero to his v. 111:35

to his very v. ... a hero 83:54

Valiant: as he was v., I honour him 325:11

he who would v. be 77:64

the v. man and free 387:71

v. ... taste of death but once 324:1

Valley: all in the v. of Death 385:40

in the v. of decision 50:81

maid singing in the v. 16:18

v. of the shadow of death 42:93

Valleys: piping down the v. wild 68:48

Valour: better part of v. is discretion 315:93

discretion ... better part of v. 260:76

for contemplation he and v. 219:66

Value: price of everything ... v. of nothing 406:21

then we rack the v. 343:81

Valued: never v. till they make a noise 114:82

Van Dycks have to go 111:40

Vanish: ah, wd. the scandal v. 349:42

Vanished: dream that v. with the morn 71:86

the touch of a v. hand 384:37

Vanity: it beareth the name of V. Fair 77:60

that v. in years 314:68

two passions, v. and love 98:62

v. of vanities, saith the Preacher 46:93

Vanquished: woe to the v. 197:85

Variable: Woman ... v. as the shade 296:14

Variation: each slight v., if useful 117:7

Variety: great source of pleasure is v. 178:42

nor custom stale her infinite v. 299:55

Variety (*continued*)

v. is pleasing 282:89

v. is the mother of enjoyment 123:99

v. is the soul of pleasure 30:86

v.'s the very spice of life 114:71

Various: as you are woman ... so be v. 154:22

so v., that he seem'd ... Epitome 126:43

Varium et mutabile ... femina 397:1

Vase: 'twas on a lofty v.'s side 154:23

Vassals and serfs at my side 76:55

Vasty fields of France 318:37

Vault: that heaven's v. should crack 330:4

Vaults: been in these here v. 12:41

Vegetable: my v. love shd. grow 206:93

v., animal, and mineral 147:31

Vegetate: one does but v. 79:92

Veil: this that was the v. of thee 382:17

V. past which I cd. not see 135:73

Veils: peace ... dropping from the v. of the morning 417:53

Vein: not in the giving v. today 352:78

Veins: jigging v. of rhyming mother-wits 204:72

Venetian: Turk beat a V. 346-7:22

Vengeance: noblest v. is to forgive 282:90

rarer action ... virtue than in v. 357:53

v. is mine ... saith the Lord 57:40

Veni, vidi, vici 87:8

Venice: here with us in V. 338:3

in V., on the Bridge of Sighs 84:62

Venom: no v. to that of the tongue 282:91

Vent: ce qu'est au feu le v. 82:34

Vent: what his breast forges, that his tongue must v. 303-4:17

Venture: nothing v., nothing win 273:13

Ventures: take the current ... or lose our v. 326:27

'Verboojuice': 'Sesquippledan v.' 401:64

Verbum sapienti sat est 282:92

Verdict: Sentence first—v. afterwards 91:68

Verdure: content to see no other v. 185:43

different shades in the v. 173:63

Verge: on the very v. of her confine 328:65

Verified: they have v. unjust things 344:87

Verify: always v. yr. references 291:56

Villain (*continued*)
fair terms and a v.'s mind 339:7
hungry, lean-fac'd v. 303:12
O v. ... condemned into ... redemption 344:84
Villainous: foreheads v. low 357:52
Villains: God shd. go before such v. 344:82
Villainy: thus I clothe my naked v. 351:70
Vinci: they spell it V. 394:66
Vindicate the ways of God to Man 250:8
Vine: Daughter of the V. 135:76
every man under his v. 50:89
Vines: bless with fruit the v. 180:78
our v. have tender grapes 47:23
Vineyard: thou shalt not glean thy v. 37:98
Violence: to offer it the show of v. 305:35
Violent: laid v. hands upon themselves 65:12
nothing ... v. is permanent 273:12
so over v. or over civil 126:44
Violet: the nodding v. grows 341:46
the v. smells to him as ... to me 320:52
throw a perfume on the v. 327:43
Violets: breathes upon a bank of v. 358-9:75
daisies pied and v. blue 332:19
from her ... flesh may v. spring 312:32
odours, when sweet v. sicken 370:54
Vipers: generation of v. 51:6
Virgin: a v. shall conceive, and bear 48:34
Virtue: a fugitive and cloistered v. 223:39
admire v. ... follow not her lore 221:4
assume a v. if you have it not 311:19
enterprises ... of v. or mischief 24:96
every v. ... founded on compromise 78:74
forbearance ceases to be a v. 78:77
if V. feeble were 213:81
lilies and languors of v. 382:18
love V., she alone is free 213:81
much v. in If 303:10
O infinite v., com'st thou smiling? 299:63
only reward of v. is v. 132:30
power ... extirpates ... gentle v. 78:89
rarer ... in v. than in vengeance 357:53

Virtue (*continued*)
saw v. in her shape how lovely 219:73
some rise by sin, and some by v. fall 337:82
there is no v. like necessity 348:36
useful life, progressive v. 391:34
v. dwells not in the tongue 282:93
v. is ... best plain set 26:27
v. is its own reward 282:94
v. never grows old 282:95
v. of necessity 282:96
v. only makes our bliss below 250:20
v. that possession wd. not show 343:81
wars that makes ambition v. 345:10
Virtues: be to her v. very kind 253:50
lady ... of wondrous v. 338:99
their v. we write in water 323:86
world to hide v. in? 359:77
Virtuous: be in general v., and ... happy 138:12
think, because thou art v. 359:87
Visages: whose v. do cream and mantle 338:97
Vision: a v. or a waking dream? 184:32
baseless fabric of this v. 356:50
by the v. splendid ... attended 411:78
not disobedient unto ... heavenly v. 56:27
saw the V. of the world 387:80
where ... no v., the people perish 46:89
write the v., ... make it plain 51:93
Visionary: whither is fled the v. gleam? 410:76
Visions: young men shall see v. 50:80
Visit: let us never v. together 109:17
v. us with thy salvation 402:72
Visiting the iniquity of the fathers 37:84
Vital: I cannot give it v. growth again 346:19
Vitality: extreme busyness ... deficient v. 379:78
Vive: Napoleon's armies ... shouting 'V. l'intérieur' 297:33
Vocabulary: the v. of Bradshaw is nervous 125:28
Vocation: no sin ... to labour in his v. 312:47
'tis my v., Hal 312:47
Vogue: charming to totter into v. 398:22
Voice: a certain what-is-it in his v. 408:51

War (*continued*)
  image of w. without its guilt   375:23
  in w. ... no winners, ... all are losers
    ·95:15
  in W.: Resolution. In Defeat:
    Defiance   102:10
  infection and the hand of w.   348:41
  let slip the dogs of w.   324:9
  looks on w. as all glory   372:81
  love ... is exactly like w.   379:71
  magnificent, but ... not w.   69:66
  marching as to w.   28:57
  my sentence is for open w.   217:46
  neither shall they learn w.   48:31
  never was a good w.   138:15
  pride, pomp, and circumstance of ...
    w.   345–6:10
  so dauntless in w.   296:11
  some ... depos'd, some slain in w.
    350:54
  stupid crime ... devil's madness—W.
    297:36
  succeeding generations from ...
    scourge of w.   394:76
  the arts of w. and peace   84:77
  w. and the pity of w.   243:18
  The W. between Men and Women
    392:45
  to w. and arms I fly   199:16
  w. ... endless w. still breed?   223:33
  w. is done and youth stone dead
    293:82
  w. is ... national industry of Prussia
    224:47
  W. is Peace, Freedom is Slavery
    242:2
  w. makes rattling good history
    158:64
  w. ... too serious ... to be left to
    military   384:34
  w. upon this bloody tyrant, Time
    362:31
  when I speak, they are for w.
    44:36
  when the blast of w. blows   319:45
  when there was w., he went   22:62
  when w. begins, hell opens   282:3
  wither'd is the garland of the w.
    299:66
  Women ... and Power and W.
    189:93
Warble his native wood-notes wild
  214:4
Ward: thou knowest my old w.   314:65
Ware: I shd. dine at W.   113:59
Warm: let the w. Love in   185:33
  this sensible w. motion to become
    337:90

Warmed: w. and cooled ... winter and
  summer   339:13
  w. both hands ... fire of life   192:34
Warn: to w., to comfort, and command
  414:18
Warned: be w. by me that breakfast
  31:92
Warring within our breasts   205:76
Wars: end to the beginnings of all w.
  289:34
  fierce w. and faithful loves   377:40
  let w. give way to peace   102:17
  more ... fears than w. or women
    322–3:81
  still w. and lechery!   358:74
  the thousand w. of old   386:70
  w. and rumours of w.   53:45
  w. bring scars   282:4
  w. that makes ambition virtue
    345:10
Wars of the Roses: leave Moses out of
  the W.   34:21
Warts: roughnesses, pimples, and w.
  115:91
Wash: bid them w. their faces   303:14
  I w. away my balm   350–51:58
  tears ... w. out a word of it   136:79
  w. dirty linen in public   282:6
  w. me ... whiter than snow   42:8
  w. the balm ... from ... anointed
    king   349:50
  w. ... yr. feet seldom ... head never
    282:7
  will all great Neptune's ocean w. this
    blood   334:43
Washed the dishes with his wife   226:70
Washes: river Weser ... w. its wall
  75:36
Washing: no cooking, or w., or sewing
  12:43
  painting a face ... not w. it   140:37
  w. ... clean linen in public   405:7
Waste: barrel of meal shall not w.
  40:55
  in a w. of shame   363:50
  wail my dear time's w.   362:37
  w. not, want not   282:8
Wasted: some nine moons w.   344:90
Wasteful and ridiculous excess   327:43
Wastes: tell her that w. her time and
  me   398:17
Watch: has a w. and chain, of course
  288:22
  keeping w. over ... flock by night
    54:68
  one to w., and one to pray   10:13
  our w. ... have indeed comprehended
    343:79

Way (*continued*)
  travel on life's common w. 413:4
  w. of an eagle ... serpent 46:91
  w. was long, the wind was cold
    295:99
  where there's a will ... a w. 283:33
  which w. shall I fly? 218:62
Ways: among the untrodden w. 413:15
  gave once ... her w. to roam 71:93
  he had his little w. 211:52
  her w. are w. of pleasantness 44:56
  let all her w. be unconfined 253:50
  Mr Facing-both-w. 77:61
  neither are yr. w. my w. 48:51
  oldest sins the newest ... w. 318:30
  when ... w. be foul 332:20
We: put it down a w., my lord 121:75
Weak: bear the infirmities of the w.
    57:45
  concessions of the w. 77:71
  idleness ... refuge of w. minds 98:61
  surely the w. shall perish 297:35
  to be w. is miserable 216:31
  w. and therefore pacifistic 22:59
Weakest goes to the wall 282:15
Weakness: show no more w. than is
    natural 392:41
  silence ... all else is w. 396:94
  w. is thy excuse 222:20
Wealth: as their w. increaseth, so in-
    close 204:70
  bear w. 255:98
  consume w. without producing it
    364:66
  he that marries for w. 271:42
  health is better than w. 266:76
  let w. and commerce ... die 292:68
  love rememb'red such w. brings
    362:36
  neither wit nor w. 16:85
  squandering w. ... his ... art 126:44
  there is no w. but life 292:64
  w. accumulates and men decay
    150:62
  w. is contentment with a little
    282:16
  w. is not without its advantages
    141:43
  w. maketh many friends 45:74
  where w. and freedom reign 151:92
Weapons: hurt with the same w.
    339:13
  in this war ... books are w. 289:33
  women's w., water-drops 328:68
Wear: better to w. out than ... rust out
    115:92
  better w. out shoes than sheets
    256:32

Wear (*continued*)
  if the cap fits, w. it 257:83
  our souls ... will us to w. ourselves
    205:76
  to w. the breeches 282:18
  w. him in my heart's core 310:6
Wearied: wherein have I w. thee?
    50:90
Weariest: even the w. river ... safe to
    sea 383:20
Weariness: much study ... a w. of the
    flesh 47:13
Wearing: everything is the worse for w.
    262:34
Weary: age shall not w. them 65:20
  how my heart grows w. 138:6
  how w., stale ... uses of this world
    305:42
  long w. day have end 377:39
  sae w., fu' o' care 81:26
  Unfortunate, w. of breath 165:56
Weasel: as a w. sucks eggs 301:84
  pop goes the w.! 203:60
Weather: I like the w. 83:55
  if it prove fair w. 380:86
  need to pray for fair w. 25:7
  no enemy but winter and rough w.
    300:83
  the w. the cuckoo likes 158:67
  two Englishmen ... talk is of the w.
    172:51
  what dreadful hot w.! 24:81
  who's there, besides foul w.? 328:70
  you won't hold up the w. 203:55
Weave: tangled web we w. 296:13
  w. a circle round him thrice 107:76
Weaving: I work at the w. trade 17:95
Web: w. of our life ... mingled yarn
    298:46
  what a tangled w. we weave 296:13
Webster was ... possessed by death
    131:13
Wed: with this ring I thee w. 65:9
Wedding: has bought her w. clothes
    9:10
Wedding-day: brightly dawns our w.
    145:4
  said John, 'It is my w.' 113:59
  tomorrow is our w. 113:55
  wager ... w. ... is ... fixed on 134:59
Wedding-gown: I chose my wife, as
    she ... her w. 152:97
Wedding-guest: O W.! this soul hath
    been 106:62
Wedge: thin end of the w. 280:23
Wedges: in time small w. cleave 191:22
  w. of gold, great anchors 352:72
Wedlock is a padlock 282:19

Wednesday: he that died o' W. 315:88
married on W. 238:71
W.'s child is full of woe 235:56
Wee, sleekit, cow'rin' ... beastie 80:16
Wee-wee-wee: little pig cried w. 239:78
Weed: O thou w. who art so lovely
346:14
pernicious w. whose scent ... annoys
112:53
Weeds: her winter w. outworn 368:28
lilies ... smell far worse than w.
363:42
subject is the fattest soil to w. 317:26
worthless as wither'd w. 71:85
Week: in his beak enough food for a
w. 209:38
murdered reputations of the w.
108:7
no admittance till the w. after next
94:97
rust of the whole w. 9:7
takes me as much as a w. 393:65
Weeks: love alters not with ... w.
363:48
Weep: I w. for Adonais – he is dead!
367:9
I w. for joy to stand 349:49
'I w. for you,' the Walrus said 93:81
men that laugh and w. 382:19
no, I'll not w. 328:69
or ere I'll w. ... I shall go mad
328:69
such ... tricks ... the angels w.
337:87
that he shd. w. for her? 308:90
'tis that I may not w. 85:79
w., and you w. alone 404:91
w. no more, my lady 138:4
w. not for little Leonie 153:12
w. not, my wanton, smile 156:48
w. with them that w. 57:38
who wd. not w., if Atticus were he?
248:84
Weeping: all de darkies am a w. 138:3
dwell a w. hermit there 107–8:90
I have full cause of w. 328:69
Rachel w. for her children 51:3
the children w., O my brothers 73:11
w. may endure for a night 42:95
Weeps: our country sinks ... it w., it
bleeds 335:65
Weighed: thou art w. in the balances
49:69
Weight: able and willing to pull his w.
289:36
he carries w.! he rides a race 113:57
heavy ... weary w. ... of ... world
415:32

Weight (continued)
heavy w. from off my head 350:58
w of Cathedral tunes 122:83
Wein, Weib und Gesang: wer nicht
liebt W. 200:28
Welcome: advice is seldom w. 98:58
constant guest is never w. 258:24
eat and w., fast, and heartily w.
261:10
he that plays the king shall be w.
308:82
so let us w. peaceful evening 114:73
thrice w., darling of the Spring
415:38
warmest w. at an inn 371:60
w. is the best cheer 282:20
w. to yr. gory bed 81:22
Welcomes: and w. little fishes in
89–90:45
Well: all is not w. 306:52
all is w. that ends w. 254:68
Chaucer, w. of English undefiled
377:44
deep w. of unconscious cerebration
170:22
did nothing ... did it very w. 144:90
he preaches w. that lives w. 275:59
lov'd not wisely, but too w. 346:22
not feeling very w. myself! 285:85
prayeth w. who loveth w. 106:63
Pussy's in the w. 232:28
worth doing is worth doing w.
283:24
Well-a-way: made every youth cry W.!
12:36
Wellbred: as w. as if ... not married
109:17
moral, sensible, and w. man 112:52
very strange and w. 109:17
w. Captain of the Pinafore 147:24
Well-content: sweet W. 117:12
Weller: Mr W.'s knowledge of London
121:66
Well-favoured: to be a w. man is the
gift of fortune 343:73
Weltgeschichte: die W. ... Weltgericht
294:86
Wen: fate of the great w. [London]
104:36
Wenceslas: good King W. 229:3
Wench: beside the w. is dead 204:71
Wenches: getting w. with child 361:16
Went: and she w., and came, and
gleaned 39:35
when there was war, he w. 22:62
Wept: my mother groan'd, my father
w. 67:44
they w. like anything to see 92:78

West: East is East, and W. is W.
189:92

go W., young man 156:47, 376:24

Lochinvar is come out of the w.
295:10

West port: open the W., and let me
gang free 294:92

Westen: im W. nichts Neues 287:4

Western: All Quiet on the W. Front
287:4

wind of the W. Sea 388:96

Westminster Abbey or victory 229:6

Westward: but w., look, the land is
bright 104:34

Wet: out of ... w. clothes and into a
dry Martini 409:57

to w. one's whistle 283:22

w. and dirty from hunting 381:92

Wetting: saved his friend from a w.
212:70

Whale: gull's way ... w.'s way 208:16

sprat to catch a w. 278:69

very like a w. 310:12

Whales: they wd. talk like w. 152:4

What-is-it: a certain w. in his voice
408:51

Wheat: orient and immortal w. 392:53

Wheel: a w. ... in the midst of a w.
49:63

fortune ... turn thy w. 328:63

put a spoke in one's w. 278:68

put yr. shoulder to the w. 275:72

upon a w. of fire 330:96

w. is come full circle 330:2

Wheelbarrow: as she wheeled her w.
17:89

Wheels: all the w. of Being slow
386:60

w. within w. 283:26

Where: leads – God knows w. 85:80

w. are the snows of yesteryear?
396:95

w. ish dat barty now? 195:68

Wherefore: for every why he had a w.
82:36

never mind the why and w. 147:28

w. stopp'st thou me? 104:42

Whiff: a w. of grapeshot 89:34

Whig: first W. was the Devil 177:28

Whigs: caught the W. bathing 122:89

W. ... no force but argument 72–3:8

Whim: tempted by a private w. 31:96

the strangest w. has seized me 98:66

Whimper: not with a bang but a w.
130:96

'twixt a smile and a w. 369:42

Whipped: she w. them all soundly
239:76

Whipping: who shall 'scape w.?
308:88

Whips and scorns of time 309:95

Whirligig of time brings ... revenges
360:2

Whiskers: runcible cat with crimson w.
195:63

Whisky: freedom and W. ... thegither
79:2

Whisper: hush! hush! w. who dares!
211:61

Whispering: where there is w. ... lying
283:29

w. of fields unsown 243:17

Whispers: blood of Jesus w. peace
65:19

secret w. of each other's watch
320:50

Whist: loved a good game of w. 192:27

Whistle: as clean as a w. 258:8

hir joly w. wel y-wet 97:46

to wet one's w. 283:22

Whistles o'er the furrowed land 214:98

White: a moment w., then melts 81:25

as w. as leprosy 105:52

fleece was w. as snow 157:55

I shall wear w. flannel trousers 131:4

in winter, when the fields are w.
93:87

my soul is w. 68:51

one w., and two khaki 14:55

[sins] shall be ... w. as snow 48:30

some gave them w. bread 234:47

the w. foam flew 105:48

the W. Man's Burden 190:12

two blacks do not make a w. 281:74

w. radiance of Eternity 367:19

yr. hair has become very w. 90:48

Whiten: w. the green plains under
368:22

willows w., aspens quiver 387:76

Whiter: I shall be w. than snow 42:8

Whites: don't fire ... see the w. of their
eyes 253:49

Whitethroat builds, and all the swallows 74:22

Whither: one knows not w. nor why
208:17

soul ... driven ... I know not w.
401:55

w. goest thou? 56:11

w. is fled the visionary gleam?
410:76

Whiting: said a w. to a snail 91:62

Who: w. killed Cock Robin? 241:88

w. kill'd John Keats? 86:94

w., or why, or which 194:54

w. was then the gentleman? 27:50

Whole: all ... parts of one stupendous
w. 250:11
saw life steadily, and saw it w. 20:35
they that are w. 53:53
Who saith 'A w. I planned' 75–6:46
Whooping: wonderful ... out of all w.
302:95
Whore: like a w., unpack my heart
309:93
'Tis Pity She's a W. 137:93
Wicked: God made the w. Grocer
99:76
lov'd his w. neighbour as himself
126:46
no peace ... unto the w. 48:45
pomps ... of this w. world 64:96
Wickedness: men alone ... capable of
every w. 110:27
spiritual w. in high places 58:74
w. of a woman 62:55
Wicklow: chink in the floor of the old
W. house 383:26
Widdicombe Fair: for to go to W.
19:13
Wide: alone on a w. w. sea 105:54,
106:62
Wider still and wider shall thy bounds
be set 33:13
Widow: a certain poor w. ... threw in
two mites 54:63
care for ... his w. and his orphan
196–7:81
here's to the w. of fifty 372:78
Widows: be very careful o' w. (vidders)
121:67
when w. exclaim ... against second
marriage 134:59
w. are always rich 283:30
Wife: a light w., a heavy husband
340:26
all the world and his w. 284:57
and Noah he often said to his w.
99:77
by degrees dwindle into a w. 109:18
Caesar's w. ... above suspicion
87:10
choose a w. ... by yr. ear 258:2
choose my w. ... not for ... glossy
surface 152:97
good w. and health ... best wealth
265:37
good w. makes a good husband
265:38
has a w., has a master 283:31
he that hath w. and children 24:96
he that speaks ill of his w. 278:64
he that tells his w. news 279:17
here lies my w. – hallelujah! 13:44

Wife (continued)
his w. cd. eat no lean 234:45
his w. looked back 36:56
honour unto ... w. as ... weaker
vessel 60:10
horse made ... w. to make 258:1
how ... be married without a w.?
235:52
if w. shd. dine at Edmonton 113:59
Intellectual suggests ... untrue to his
w. 22:61
kill a w. with kindness 355:24
married, but I'd have no w. 115:83
must be in want of a w. 23:75
naked, the man and his w. 35:35
need makes the old w. trot 272:80
never lend 'oss, ... w., ... name
381:91
not covet thy neighbour's w. 37:92
remember Lot's w. 55:88
riding to and from his w. 402:77
roaring of the wind is my w. 187:63
tell his w. all he knows 140:39
this is my w. – look well at her
378:54
took fourpence home to my w.
233:40
when his w. talks Greek 178:45
whose w. shall I take? 226:65
Wights: descriptions of the fairest w.
363:45
Wild: and her eyes were w. 183:8
bore me in the southern w. 68:51
kind of w. justice 24:89
piping down the valleys w. 68:48
Wilderness: one crying in the w. 51:5
scapegoat into the w. 37:96
the w. of this world 76:57
W. is Paradise enow 135:67
Wiles: of w., more unexpert, I boast
not 217:46
Quips and Cranks and wanton W.
214:93
Will: a man's ... w. ... invalidated by
marriage 83:49
complies against his w. 82:39
law beyond its own sweet w. 403:88
man has his w. ... woman has her
way 164:48
puzzles the w. 309:95
serveth not another's w. 416:48
the w.! the w.! ... Caesar's w.!
325:16
the w. to do, the soul to dare 294:95
their law's their w. 347:26
thy w. be done 52:18
unconquerable w., and study of
revenge 216:30

Will (*continued*)

where there's a w. there's a way 283:33

where there's a w., there's trouble 283:34

w. in us is over-rul'd by fate 205:80

William: you are old. Father W. 90:48

Williamanmary ... ruled by an Orange 297:32

Willow: a w. cabin at yr. gate 359:80

a w. grows aslant the brook 311:30

w., titwillow 146:12

w. w. waly 146:17

Willows: our harps upon the w. 44:45

w. whiten, aspens quiver 387:76

Wills: choose executors and talk of w. 349:53

the w. above be done 355:28

women must have their w. 283:52

Wilson: the 14th Mr W. 165:53

Win: heads I w., tails you lose 115:86, 266:75

hope from outward forms to w. 106:69

nothing ... foul to those that w. 315:85

Wind: a roaring in the w. all night 413:11

absence is to love what w. is to fire 82:34

all aloud the w. doth blow 332:20

and the w. shall say 131:8

bayed the whispering w. 150:65

blow, blow, thou winter w. 302:91

blow w., come wrack 336:77

fair stood the w. for France 125:31

frosty w. made moan 290:43

gentle w. does move 67:40

God tempers the w. ... shorn lamb 265:26

hey, ho, the w. and the rain 360:3

hope constancy in w. 85:91

how the w. doth ramm! 252:47

ill w. that blows nobody good 267:15

impatient as the W. 411:91

know which way the w. blows 268:45

like W. I go 135:72

likewise a w. on the heath 69:65

man in the w. 390:17

more gentle than a w. in summer 185:34

O Wild West W. 369:35

only argument ... with an east w. 200:27

readers ... sway in the w. 130:89

Wind (*continued*)

reed shaken with the w. 52:29

roaring of the w. is my wife 187:63

sail near the w. 276:10

shorter in w., as in memory long 70:72

streams ... *against* the w. 84:63

swoln with w. and the rank mist 215:16

tempers the w. ... to the shorn lamb 379:68

the w. of change is blowing 203:53

they have sown the w. 50:76

when the w. is southerly 308:83

where the w. comes from ... goes 211:53

w. bloweth where it listeth 55:98

w. blows it back again 67:39

w. blows, the cradle will rock 233:38

w. of the Western Sea 388:96

w. out of one's sails 279:2

w. that follows fast 116:96

w.'s like a whetted knife 208:16

words but w. 82:37

Window: at my w. bid good morrow 214:97

love comes in at the w. 270:12

the little w. where the sun 165:60

what light through yonder w.? 353:97

Windowed: loop'd and w. raggedness 329:78

Window-panes: fog ... rubs its back upon the w. 131:1

Windows: cleaned the w., ... swept the floor 147:26

not by eastern w. only 104:34

storied w. richly dight 213:88

Winds: blow, w., and crack yr. cheeks 328:71

courted by all the w. 222:18

four-square to all the w. 388:93

rough w. do shake the darling buds 362:32

so perfumed that the w. were love-sick 298:54

the w. will blow the profit 203:55

w. somewhere safe to sea 383:20

wound the loud w. 356:49

young w. fed it with ... dew 370:46

Windy: keep o' th' w. side of the law 360:98

Wine: a little w. for thy stomach's sake 59:90

as water unto w. 387:83

bring me flesh ... wine 229:4

cedarwood, and sweet white w. 207:12

Wisdom (*continued*)
  w. and goodness to the vile   329:86
  w. hath builded her house   45:59
Wise: a word is enough to the w.
    282:92
  all things w. and wonderful   10:17
  be not w. in yr. own conceits   57:39
  be w. today ... madness to defer
    418:61
  be w. with speed   417:60
  better ... happy than w.   255:18
  exceeding w., fair-spoken   323:87
  fool ... holdeth his peace is counted
    w.   45:73
  give unto me made lowly w.   413:8
  good to be merry and w.   17:93
  great men are not always w.   41:75
  he that is not ... w. at fifty   266:58
  histories make men w.   26:34
  holy, fair and w. is she   361:8
  I care whether ... w. man or a fool
    67:37
  I heard a w. man say   167:81
  more of the fool than of the w.   25:2
  nor ever did a w. one   288:21
  reputed one of the w. men   25:98
  same w. ... a w. man sees   69:60
  so w., so young ... never live long
    352:73
  some are w., ... some are otherwise
    278:53
  some folk are w. ... some are other-
    wise   375:15
  that's the w. thrush   74:23
  the least foolish is w.   269:65
  the only wretched are the w.   253:52
  'tis folly to be w.   154:29
  to a w. man ports ... havens   348:36
  to be w. and love   358:70
  w. after the event   261:9
  w. father ... knows his own child
    339:8
  w. man that marries a harlot   298:39
  w. ones [marry] not at all   267:93
Wisely: one that lov'd not w., but too
    well   346–7:22
  thou dost not inquire w.   46:5
Wiser: be w. ... but do not tell   98:54
  French are w. than they seem   26:19
  sadder and a w. man   106:65
  Spaniards seem w. than they are
    26:19
  world would be w. than ever   409:59
Wisest: fool ... ask more than ... w. ...
    can answer   108:99
  in the mouths of w. men   222:21
Wish: I w. I had said that. You will
    402:76

Wish (*continued*)
  I w. our clever young poets   107:82
  my oft-expressed personal w.   196:78
  who wd. w. to die?   69:65
  w. is father to the thought   283:42
  w. was father ... to that thought
    318:29
Wished she had not heard it, yet she
    wished   344:92
Wishes: everything ... exact to my w.
    12:43
Wit: a w. shd. no more be sincere
    109:9
  age is in, the w. is out   343:78
  bold and turbulent of w.   126:38
  brevity is the soul of w.   307:72
  he is only a w. among Lords   174:76
  his whole w. in a jest   29:70
  I wish him neither w. nor wealth
    16:85
  impropriety ... soul of w.   208:21
  in w. a man: simplicity a child
    248:89
  neither w., nor words, nor worth
    325:21
  no man's w. can well direct   123:3
  nor all thy piety nor w.   136:79
  prize of w. or arms   214:2
  too proud for a w.   51:79
  true w. is nature to advantage   249:97
  want of w. is worse   282:2
  wine is in ... w. is out   30:78
  w., if not first, in ... first line   151:81
  w. shall not go unrewarded   357:51
  w. that can creep   248:86
  w. with dunces ... dunce with wits
    247:69
  your men of w. will condescend
    381:96
Witch: not suffer a w. to live   37:94
Witchcraft: only ... w. I have used
    344:92
Witching: very w. time of night   310:13
With: not w. me is against me   52:30
Withal: Time ambles w., ... trots w.
    302:98
Withered: rosebuds, before they be w.
    62:41
  so w., ... wild in their attire   332:26
Withers: our w. are unwrung   310:10
Within: life whose fountains are w.
    106:69
Witness: shalt not bear false w.   37:91
  such weak w. of thy name   216:24
Wits: great w. ... to madness near
    allied   126:39
  home-keeping youth ... homely w.
    360:4

Witty: a w. statesman ... prove anything 89:32
it shall be w. and it shan't be long
98:64
not only w. in myself 316:98
Wive: hard to w. and thrive ... in a
year 283:43
Wives: a man with seven w. 231:22
married three w. at one time
224–5:52
profane and old w.' fables 59:88
sky changes when they are w. 302:4
some poison'd by their w. 350:54
w. are young men's mistresses 24:97
w. must be had ... good or bad
283:44
Wiving: hanging and w. goes by
destiny 339:11
Wobbly: my spelling is w. 212:67
Woe: a thurghfare ful of w. 97:45
all our w., with loss of Eden 216:27
bitter groan of a martyr's w. 66–7:35
can I see another's w.? 68:53
cry w., destruction, ruin 349:52
life protracted is protracted w.
174:70
man was made for joy and w. 66:30
the w.'s to come 351:59
trappings and the suits of w. 305:41
Wednesday's child is full of w.
235:56
w. to the vanquished 197:85
w. to them ... at ease in Zion 50:84
w. unto them that call ... good evil
48:33
Woes: with old w. new wail 362:37
Wold: fields ... that clothe the w.
387:75
Wolf: keep the w. from the door
283:45
to cry 'W.' 259:40
w. ... shall dwell with the lamb
48:37
Wolf's-bane, tight-rooted 183:21
Wolves: inwardly ... ravening w. 52:27
Woman: a fair w. ... without discretion
45:64
a perfect W., nobly planned 414:18
a Spirit, yet a W. too 414:17
a virtuous w. is a crown 45:65
a w. is a foreign land 245:32
a w. is only a w. 190:94
A W. Killed with Kindness 163:27
a w. mov'd ... a fountain troubled
355:26
a w. sat, in unwomanly rags 166:64
a w. seldom asks advice 9:10
a w.'s face ... hast thou 362:35

Woman (continued)
a w.'s preaching is like 175:90
a w.'s whole history 170:16
a w., therefore to be won 321:64
a w. who tells her ... age 406:29
a w. with fair opportunities 389:12
a w. yet think him an angel 389:10
a worthy w. al hir lyve 97:39
a young w. called Starkie 14:55
a uncommon pretty young w.
129:84
as you are w., so be lovely 154:22
believe a w. or an epitaph 85:91
but what is w.? 112:48
but w. has her way 164:48
constant ... but yet a w. 313:61
die because a w.'s fair 408:49
do you not know I am a w.?
302:96
dumb jewels ... move a w.'s mind
361:7
every w. false like thee 222:19
every w. is at heart a rake 251:23
every w. is ... to be gained by ...
flattery 98:63
every w. shd. marry – and no man
123:96
fat white w. whom nobody loves
111:34
frailty, thy name is w. 306:45
give not thy soul unto a w. 62:50
God made the w. for the man 385:48
great glory in a w. 392:41
had a w. ever less? 80:12
her voice ... soft – an excellent thing
in w. 331:5
I could be a good w. if 389:15
I know a reasonable w. 251:31
if a w. have long hair 57:52
in a post-chaise with a pretty w.
177:23
in argument with men a w. 222:22
in her first passion w. 84:73
lays his hand upon a w. 392:48
love and good company improves a
w. 134:56
man that is born of a w. 41:69,
65:13
never yet fair w. but 329:74
no other but a w.'s reason 361:5
no other purgatory but a w. 29:73
no w. shd. ... be quite accurate
405:15
no w. shd. have a memory 406:32
none of w. born shall harm Macbeth
335:62
nor hell a fury like a w. scorned
108:6

Woman (*continued*)

O W.! in our hours of ease 296:14
of every ill, a w. is the worst 153:17
old w. lived under a hill 239:75
old w. who lived in a shoe 239:76
one tongue is enough for a w. 280:45
poor w. who was always tired 12:43
seven [hours' sleep] for a w. 277:40
she is a w., ... may be woo'd ... won 357–8:63
teaches such beauty as a w.'s eye 331:14
the rib ... made he a w. 35:33
the worser spirit a w. colour'd ill 364:55
there's a broken-hearted w. 159:76
this w. to thy wedded wife 64:6
thought does not become a young w. 371:65
'tis w.'s whole existence 84:70
to show a w. when he loves 74:34
wavers ... in a word, she is a w. 285:92
when lovely w. stoops to folly 131:12, 152:2
who can find a virtuous w.? 46:92
wickedness of a w. 62:55
wit no more ... sincere than a w. constant 109:9
without the ... w. I love 129:81
w. as old as she looks 107:86
w. ... at the bottom of [mischief] 273:94
w. conceals what she knows not 283:46
w. ... fickle and changing 397:1
w. for the hearth 389:2
w. ... if she have the misfortune 23:73
w. in this humour woo'd ... won? 351:69
w. is his game 388:1
w. is the lesser man 387:83
w.'s at best a contradiction 251:26
w.'s happiest knowledge 219:70
w. that deliberates is lost 9:5
w. to obey 389:2
w. wailing for her demon-lover 106:72
w. will be the last thing civilized 209:35
w. with the heart 389:2
w.'s work is never done 283:47
worse occupations ... than feeling a w.'s pulse 379:67
yield to one of w. born 336:78
Womb: from his mother's w. untimely ripp'd 336:78

Womb (*continued*)

this teeming w. of royal kings 348–9:41
through the foul w. of night 320:50
Women: a bevy of fair w. 221:99
alas! the love of w. 84:72
an experience of w. which extends 125:24
Bah! I have sung w. 252:48
by bad w. been deceived 222:15
dally not with money or w. 259:50
discreet w. ... neither eyes nor ears 260:75
England ... a paradise for w. 81:31
England is the paradise of w. 136:86, 261:20
fair w. and brave men 83:59
for w. to keep counsel 324:2
from w.'s eyes this doctrine I derive 331:16
goes with w., and champagne 31:95
happiest w. ... have no history 130:86
how w. pass the time when ... alone 161:4
I speak ... Italian to w. 96:24
Italy ... hell for w. 81:31
let your w. keep silence in ... churches 57:56
loved Esther above all the w. 40:64
Monstrous Regiment of W. 191:19
most w. are not so young as ... painted 30:81
music and w. I ... give way to 245:43
other w. cloy the appetites 299:55
passing the love of w. 40:49
souls of w. are so small 82:40
sweet is revenge – especially to w. 84:68
the more w. look in ... glass 283:51
the third wrote, W. are strongest 61:36
three w. ... goose make a market 280:36
tide in the affairs of w. 85:80
where there are w. and geese 283:48
W. and Horses and Power 189:93
w. and music shd. never be dated 151:88
w. are always in extremes 283:49
w. are angels, wooing 358:65
w. are glad to have been asked 243:12
w. are necessary evils 283:50
w. become like their mothers 406:30
w. ... care ... more for a marriage 27:44
w. in London who flirt 405:7

Women (*continued*)

w. ... more like each other than men 98:62

w. must have the last word 283:53

w. must have their wills 283:52

w. must weep 189:87

w. never look so well as when 381:92

w. require both 83:51

w. sit or move to and fro 403:78

w.'s letters ... pith is in the postscript 159:77

w.'s weapons, water-drops 328:68

w. ... talking of Michelangelo 131:99

w., worst and best 385:52

Won: a woman, therefore to be w. 321:64

marks – not that you w. or lost 287:9

melancholy as a battle w. 401:57

prize we sought is w. 403:81

things w. are done 358:65

woman, therefore may be w. 357:63

w. on the playing fields of Eton 401:61

Wonder: all the w. that wd. be 387:80

and still the w. grew 150:69

how I w. what you are! 384:36

how I w. what you're at 90:53

the common w. of all men 72:3

we ... have eyes to w. 363:46

Wonderful: all things wise and w. 10:17

how w. is Death! 368:24

O w., w. ... out of all whooping 302:95

W., Counsellor, The Mighty God 48:36

Wonderment: I'm always moved to w. 229:96

Wonders: His w. to perform 113:63

w. will never cease 283:54

Won't: will you, w. you, will you, w. you? 91:63

Woo: was to w. a fair young maid 17:95

Wood: my house in the high w. 32:7

old w. burn brightest 400:52

one impulse from a vernal w. 414:28

see the w. for the trees 277:23

springeth the w. new 15:71

through w. and dale the sacred river 106:73

Woodbine: over-canopied with luscious w. 341:46

Woodman, spare the beechen tree 88:18

Wood-notes: his native w. wild 214:4

Woods: a pleasure in the pathless w. 84:65

and the w. have no voice 227:72

in spring, when w. are getting green 93:88

senators of mighty w. 182:98

the w. shall to me answer 376:38

though he build his house in the w. 133:48

tomorrow to fresh w. 215:18

we'll to the w. no more 167:79

w. or steepy mountain yields 205:82

Woodshed: something nasty in the w. 142:68

Wooed: beautiful, and therefore to be w. 321:64

woman in this humour w. 351:69

woman, therefore may be w. 357:63

Wooing: a frog he wd. a-w. go 232:30

women are angels, w. 358:65

Wool: have you any w.? 231:23

pull the w. over a person's eyes 284:55

Word: a character dead at every w. 372:76

a tale unfold whose lightest w. 307:64

at every w. a reputation dies 251:36

by water and the W. 380:83

every w. stabs 342:63

every w. that proceedeth 38:7

fairer than that w. 338:99

four ... winters ... springs end in a w. 348:34

Greeks had a w. for it 10:14

his w. was still 'Fie, foh, and fum' 329:82

in the captain's but a choleric w. 337:88

in w. mightier 219:82

Latin w. for three farthings 331:12

let the w. go forth 188:74

many a true w. ... in jest 281:59

Mum's the w. 108:94

nor all thy tears wash out a w. of it 136:79

some with a flattering w. 404:94

suit ... the w. to the action 310:5

that I kept my w., he said 118:24

the W., and the W. was with God 55:92

the W. was made flesh 55:95

there wd. have been a time for such a w. 336:76

what is honour? A w. 315:88

'when I use a w.,' Humpty Dumpty said 93:86

whose w. no man relies on 288:21

Word (*continued*)

women must have the last w.   283:53

w. for w. without book   359:76

w. is as good as his bond   267:92

w. ... teems with hidden meaning
  148:41

yawning at every other w.   94:94

yesterday the w. of Caesar   325:15

Words: actions speak louder than w.
  254:58

all sad w. of tongue or pen   403:90

as many w. into the last line
  13–14:54

best w. in the best order   107:82

comprehending much in few w.
  62:56

dumb jewels ... more than quick w.
  do move   361:7

eat one's w.   261:11

few w. are best   262:58

her last w. on earth   12:43

in two w.: im-possible   152:5

let the w. of my mouth ... be acceptable   42:89

let thy w. be few   46:1

like a whore, unpack my heart with
  w.   309:93

long w. Bother me   212:63

men of few w. ... best men   320:48

much matter decorated into few w.
  140:38

my w. fly up, my thoughts remain
  311:16

neither wit, nor w., nor worth
  325:21

noun ... verb ... abominable w.
  321:68

oaths are but w. ..., w. but wind
  82:37

on the pedestal these w. appear
  369:40

proper w. in proper places   381:3

report thy w. by adding fuel   222:25

scatter ... my w. among mankind
  369:38

the w. of Mercury are harsh   332:21

use ... w. only to conceal ... thoughts
  397:10

what do you read ...? W., w., w.
  308:77

when you let proud w. go   293:79

w. are the daughters of earth   172:41

w., like Nature, half reveal   386:58

w. may be false   297:38

w. ... so nimble ... full of ... flame
  29:70

w. that frightened the birds   13:53

w. will never hurt me   278:74

Words (*continued*)

w. without thoughts never to heaven
  go   311:16

Wore enough for modesty   76:50

Work: a w. that aspires to ... art
  110:25

all in the day's w.   254:64

all things w. together for good   56:34

all w. and no play   284:56

because he can't w. any faster
  237:68

day is short ... w. is long   259:52

doing more w. than I shd. do
  171:35

I have left no immortal w.   187:68

I have protracted my w.   172:43

I like w.; it fascinates me   171:35

I w. at the weaving trade   17:95

if any wd. not w., neither shd. he eat
  59:86

men must w. and women must weep
  189:87

my w. is left behind   32:5

night ... when no man can w.   55:5

no more hard w. for poor old Ned
  138:9

nothing to do but w.   189:83

old Kaspar's w. was done   376:27

smile his w. to see   68:47

so w. the honey bees   318:39

sport wd. be as tedious as to w.
  313:50

strive on to finish the w.   196:81

the way to spread a w.   176:5

there is always w. and tools to w.
  200:22

to w. is to pray   268:50

whose w. is not born with him
  200:22

woman's w. is never done   283:47

w. ... curse of the drinking classes
  406:35

w. expands so as to fill the time
  244:25

w. like madness in the brain   106:67

w. yr. hands from day to day   203:55

Workers of the world, unite   207:9

Workhouse: Christmas Day in the W.
  373:89

Working: another for w.-days   343:65

fiery Soul, which w. out its way
  126:39

Workman: a bad w. quarrels ... tools
  255:88

Workmen: good w. are seldom rich
  265:40

Works: devil and all his w.   64:95

faith without w. is dead   60:4

Works (*continued*)

its [sea's] w. ... are wrapped in mystery 110:26

Saturday's child w. hard for his living 235–6:56

World: a balm upon the w. 182:94

a citizen ... of the w. 375:20

a man if he shall gain the whole w. 54:58

a w. in a grain of sand 66:27

a w. of happy days 351–2:71

a w. too wide for his shrunk shank 301:90

a w. where nothing is had for nothing 103:25

aching void the w. can never fill 113:62

all de w. am sad 138:6

all sorts to make a w. 254:70

all's right with the w. 75:44

all the uses of this w.! 305:42

all the w. and his wife 284:57

all the w. as my parish 402:73

all the w. is queer 243:15

all the w.'s a stage 301:90

all this sad w. needs 404:93

all this the w. well knows 363:51

and all the w. would stare 113:59

another W., the happy seat 218:53

any author in the w. 331:14

any portion of the foreign w. 399:32

any way to perpetuate the w. 72:5

as good be out of the w. 102:12

as they did in the golden w. 300:72

banish ... Jack and banish all the w. 314:69

before my time into this breathing w. 351:66

body is aweary of this great w. 338:1

brave new w. ... such people in't 357:57

Britain is a w. by itself 304:21

called from the w. 13:46

cankers of a calm w. 315:83

Clearing-house of the w. 95:13

commodity, the bias of the w. 326:37

compare this prison ... unto the w. 351:62

consider the w. as made for me 375:16

constant service of the antique w. 300:79

contain and nourish all the w. 331:16

deceits of the w., the flesh, and the devil 63:78

enthusiasm moves the w. 27:49

World (*continued*)

ever shall be: w. without end 63:68

fast, and the w. goes by 404:92

flash in this w. of trouble 12:42

funniest joke in the w. 365:75

gave me ... a w. of sighs 344:92

get the start of the majestic w. 323:92

gone into the w. of light 396:85

greatest thing in the w. 225:54

had we but w. enough, and time 206:92

he doth bestride the narrow w. 323:93

he is a citizen of the w. 25:5

hold the w. but as the w. 338:96

hope before you blacken their w. 395:79

how the w. its veterans rewards 251:24

how this w. is given to lying! 315:94

I called the New W. into existence 88:26

if all the w. were paper 15:65

in this harsh w. draw thy breath in pain 312:38

into the dangerous w. I leapt 67:44

justice ... though the w. perish 134:58

knaves and fools divide the w. 268:40

laugh, and the w. laughs with you 404:91

leaves the w. to darkness and to me 155:30

light of the bright w. dies 69:70

love is enough though the w. 227:72

love makes the w. go round 270:17

mad w.! mad kings! 326:36

more ... wrought by prayer than this w. dreams 386:55

nature is too noble for the w. 303:17

never enjoy the w. aright 392:52

no enjoying the w. without [health] 179:60

not loved the w., nor the w. me 83:61

nothing stable in the w. 186:53

official ... undercuts the problematical w. 140:33

on ... shore of the wide w. 186:49

one half ... w. cannot understand 23:65

reckless what I do to spite the w. 334:49

ring'd with the azure w. he stands 385:47

same the whole w. over 18:5

Saviour of the w. 83:52

Worst (*continued*)
so long as we can say 'This is the w.'
329:84
so much good in the w. of us   163:36
things at the w. will mend   280:25
things present, w.   316:4
whose puppets, best and w.   75:45
women, w. and best   385:52
Worth: doings without charity are
nothing w.   64:87
none was w. my strife   192:34
slow rises w., by poverty depressed
172:55
w. a guinea a box   11:34
w. ... best known by the want
284:60
w. doing ... w. doing well   98:55,
283:24
w. of a State ... w. of ... individuals
210:43
w. reading ... w. buying   291:60
w. seeing ... not w. going to see
177:32
Worthington: daughter on the stage,
Mrs W.   112:44
Worthless as wither'd weeds   71:85
Worthy: labourer is w. of his hire
54:75
Worts: went to W.   252:41
Wound: did help to w. itself   327:47
jests at scars that never felt a w.
353:97
take away the grief of a w.   315:88
what w. did ever heal?   345:3
w. the loud winds   356:49
Wounds: bind up the nation's w.
196:81
faithful ... the w. of a friend   46:87
gash is added to her w.   335:65
labour and the w. are vain   103:32
talk ... of guns ... and w.   313:52
these w. in thine hands   51:97
Wrangle: men will. w. for religion
108:96
Wrapped up in a five-pound note
195:60
Wrath: day of w., that dreadful day
295:7
infinite w. and infinite despair
218:62
sun go down upon your w.   58:71
the w. to come   51:6
Wreck: decay of that colossal w.
369:40
Wrecks: like w. of a dissolving dream
368:28
Wren: four Larks and a W.   195:66
robin redbreast and the w.   400:54

Wren (*continued*)
Sir Christopher W. said   33:16
the w. goes to't   329:90
Wrestle: we w. not against flesh   58:74
Wretch: excellent w.!   345:5
needy, hollow-ey'd ... w.   303:12
patron. – commonly a w.   172:49
w., concentred all in self   295:6
Wretched: scrannel pipes of w. straw
215:16
the only w. are the wise   253:52
the w. child expires   31:92
w. matter and lame metre   216:26
Wretchedness: the w. of being rich
374:2
Wretches: poor naked w., wheresoe'er
you are   329:78
to feel what w. feel   329:79
Wrinkled: the w. sea beneath him
385:47
w. with age ... Old Nod   118:25
Writ: if this be error ... I never w.
363:48
over that same door was ... w.
377:43
Write: as much as a man ought to w.
393:56
contrive to w. so even   23:77
firm restraint with which they w.
87:17
hope to w. well hereafter   223:36
I never read books – I *w*. them
285:83
look in thy heart and w.   373:84
to w. and read comes by nature
343:73
when I want ... novel I w. one   123:2
why did I w.?   248:80
w. God first   344:82
w. me down an ass   344:85
Writers of small histories, dictionaries
172:45
Writes: the moving finger w.   136:79
Writing: in w. or in judging ill   249:90
true ease in w. comes from art
249:99
w. [maketh] an exact man   26:33
Written: what I have w. I have w.
56:13
w. such volumes of stuff   194:59
Wrong: and if you w. us, shall we not
revenge?   339:13
but he done her w.   16:81
fifty million Frenchmen can't be w.
156:53
for telling a man he was w.   104:37
house of Tarquin ... suffer w. no
more   201:35

Wrong (*continued*)

I always feel I must be w. 404:1

King can do no w. 66:25, 268:35

losers are always in the w. 270:5

never dreamed ... w. wd. triumph 73:16

only thing that I ever did w. 17:95

or whether laws be w. 404:97

our country, right or w. 118:16

physical effect is good ... action ... w. 175:84

right divine of kings to govern w. 247:70

something ... w., however slightly 252:44

something w. with ... ships 29:69

stiff in opinions, always in the w. 126:43

to do a great right do a little w. 339:16

we do it w., being so majestical 305:97

w. never comes right 284:61

Wrong number: if I called the w., why ... answer? 392:44

Wrote: no man ... ever w. except for money 177:21

who w. like an angel 141:49

Wroth: to be w. with one we love 106:67

Wrought: being w., perplexed in the extreme 346-7:22

first he w., ... afterwards he taughte 97:40

more things are w. by prayer 386:55

Wye: turned to thee, O sylvan W. 415:34

Xanadu: in X. did Kubla Khan 106:71

Yankee Doodle came to town 241:90

Yarn: all I ask is a merry y. 208:16

web of our life ... a mingled y. 298:46

Year: about two hundred pounds a y. 82:38

add ... to this wonderful y. 141:48

any book ... not a y. old 133:42

before the mellowing y. 215:8

each day is like a y. 404:97

grief returns with the revolving y. 367:10

how many days will finish ... y. 321:70

I like two months of ... y. 83:55

if ... y. were playing holidays 313:50

in the season of the y. 18:98

measure of the y. 185:45

Year (*continued*)

pleasure of the fleeting y. 363:43

proper opinions for ... time of y. 22:62

say no ill of the y. 277:15

stolen ... my three-and-twentieth y. 223:28

sweet o' the y. 361:17

the y. is going, let him go 386:68

the y.'s at the spring 75:44

twentieth y. is well-nigh past 114:76

wive and thrive both in a y. 283:43

Yearning: man of y. ... aspiration 291:52

Yearnings for equal division 132:25

Years: a thousand y. as one day 60:14

age ... not weary ... nor the y. condemn 65:20

alas, Postumus, the fleeting y. 167:76

all the hopes of future y. 197:92

before the beginning of y. 382:16

come to the y. of discretion 64:2

cuts off twenty y. of life 324:4

eight y. with a strange man 169:7

evil days come not ... y. draw nigh 47:11

forty y. on 70:72

fourteen hundred y. ago were nail'd 312:43

hasn't been kissed for forty y. 291:57

if the British Empire ... last for a thousand y. 101:95

Myself with Yesterday's Sev'n Thousand Y. 135:69

O for ten y. 185:36

our hope for y. to come 399:38

parted ... to sever for y. 86:99

sorrow comes with y. 73:11

tell me where all past y. are 124:11

the thousand y. of peace 386:70

three y. she grew in sun and shower 415:30

time-lag of fifty y. 401:66

together now for forty y. 99:80

y. a mortal man may live 321:70

y. that the locust hath eaten 50:79

young in y. ... old in hours 26:26

Yellow: come unto these y. sands 355:44

commended thy y. stockings 360:92

green and y. melancholy 360:89

her locks were y. as gold 105:52

the sear, the y. leaf 336:71

y., and black ... and hectic red 369:35

Yellow (*continued*)

y. god forever gazes down 159:76

Yeomanry ... people with whom 23:64

Yeovil: our H.Q. at Station Road, Y. 252:45

Yes, and back again 233:36

Yesterday: children dear, was it y.? 20:33

dead Y., why fret? 135:74

not born y. 257:60

O, call back y., bid time return 349:51

Yesterdays: all our y. have lighted fools 336:76

Yet: young man shd. not marry y. 284:62

Yew: my shroud ... stuck all with y. 359–60:88

never a spray of y. 21:37

Yield: courage never to submit or y. 216:30

to get rid of temptation ... y. 406:24

Yo-ho-ho and a bottle of rum 379:74

Yoke: our country sinks beneath the y. 335:65

savage bull sustains the y. 191:22

shake the y. of inauspicious stars 354:18

that he bear the y. in his youth 49:62

who best bear his mild y. 223:30

Yonghy-Bonghy-Bò: lived the Y. 194:55

Yorick: a Cock and a Bull, said Y. 379:72

alas, poor Y.! 311:31

York: glorious summer by this sun of Y. 351:64

You: Daddy, what did y. do? 11:25

for y. but not for me 16:76

I am I, and y. are y. 74:27

room with a view – and y. 112:41

sight of y. is good for sore eyes 382:7

y. too, Brutus? 87:9

Young: America ... country of y. men 133:46

compliment him about looking y. 170:15

crime of being a y. man 246:54

happy while we are y. 19:20

I have been y., and now am old 42:3

if ... world and love were y. 286:96

my heart was y. and gay 138:7

no y. man believes he shall ... die 159:80

not so y. as they are painted 30:81

old are more beautiful than the y. 403:78

Young (*continued*)

our clever y. poets 107:82

so y. and so untender? So y. ... and true 327:50

the embarrassing y. 141:50

to be seventy years y. 164:52

to be y. was very Heaven! 413:9

when all the world is y. 189:88

y., and so fair! 165:56

y. blood must have its course 189:89

y. ones ... pistols: ... old ones grub 364:62

Yours: as I y. for ever 154:22

what's mine is y., ... y. is mine 338:95

what's y. is mine 283:25

y. [religion] is Success 28:63

y. is the Earth 190:5

Yourself: *do it y.* 27:51

Youth: a y. of frolics, an old age of cards 251:24

a y. to fortune and to fame unknown 155:40

age ... perform the promises of y. 173:61

crabbed age and y. 364:56

good ... that he bear the yoke in ... y. 49:62

home-keeping y. have ... homely wits 360:4

I wd. ... that y. would sleep 361:16

if only y. knew 133:50

let age approve of y. 76:47

let no man despise thy y. 59:89

loves the meat in his y. 343:69

made every y. cry *Well-a-way!* 12:36

mewing her mighty y. 224:43

must be right ... done it from my y. 114:79

noble y. did dress themselves 316:8

our y., our joys, our all 286:93

rejoice ... in thy y. 47:10

remember ... thy Creator in ... y. 47:11

riband in the cap of y. 311:29

rule y. well 276:7

spirit of y. in every thing 363:44

the hour of thoughtless y. 415:35

the rose of y. upon him 299:60

the y. ... still is Nature's priest 411:78

Time, the subtle thief of y. 223:28

war is done and y. stone dead 293:82

when Y. and Pleasure meet 83:60

y. and age will never agree 284:66

y. grows pale and spectre-thin 184:25

Youth (*continued*)
  y., I do adore thee   364:57
  y. is a blunder   123:95
  y. is full of pleasance   364:56
  y. like summer morn   364:56
  y. of America ... oldest tradition
      406:26
  y. of England are on fire   319:40
  y. of labour ... age of ease   150:64
  y. shows but half   75–6:46
  y. who bore 'mid snow and ice
      197:93
  y. will be served   284:67
  y. will have its course (fling)   284:68
  y.'s a stuff will not endure   359:84
Yukon: this is the law of the Y.   297:35

Zeal: holy, mistaken z. in politics
      180:67
  not too much z.   384:33

Zeal (*continued*)
  serv'd my God with half the z.
      323:84
  z. is ... found mostly in fools   284:69
  z., when ... a virtue   284:70
  z. without knowledge   284:71
Zeal-of-the-Land Busy   178:48
Zed: whoreson z.! ... unnecessary
      letter!   328:61
Zenith: dropped from the z., like a ...
      star   217:44
Zenocrate: fair Z.!—divine Z.!   205:77
  Z., lovelier than the love of Jove
      204:73
Zephyr: roses by the z. blown apart
      182:3
Zion: at ease in Z.   50:84
  one of the songs of Z.   44:46
  wept, when we remembered Z.   44:44
Zuleika on a desert island   30:82

Notes

Notes

Notes

Notes

Notes

Notes

Notes

Everyman's Roget's Thesaurus £1.25
Edited by D. C. Browning

Roget's Thesaurus is one of the English-speaking world's most valuable and celebrated works of reference. It is a treasury of synonyms, antonyms, parallel and related words, designed to help you find the right words or phrase to express your ideas with force and clarity.

This edition preserves the original plan of classification and categories (including the vast and ingenious index) and has been completely revised to bring all words and phrases into accordance with current usage. Over ten thousand more of these have been added, including many technical terms, everyday neologisms, Americanisms and slang.

'Among reference books Roget's Thesaurus stands by itself . . . a treasury upon which writers can draw'
TIMES LITERARY SUPPLEMENT

Chambers Essential English Dictionary 60p
Edited by A. M. MacDonald

A dictionary of the words essential to daily life, with clear, precise and informative definitions ; giving interesting derivations, illustrative examples of usage, and idiomatic expressions.

This is outstanding among small dictionaries for legibility and ease of reference. And although the background of our language makes up the body of the book, it fully reflects modern developments in words, meanings and outlook.

A Dictionary of Economics and Commerce £1.50
Edited by S. E. Stiegeler BSc and
Glyn Thomas BSc (Econ)

An authoritative A–Z of the terms used internationally in the overlapping fields of theoretical economics and practical commerce.

A team of expert contributors provides a formal definition of each word or term, followed by an explanation of its underlying concepts and accompanied by appropriate illustrations. Special attention is paid to such new and rapidly expanding subjects as cost-benefit analysis and welfare economics. And the vocabularies of banking, accounting, insurance, stock exchanges, commodity dealing, shipping, transport and commercial law are all included.

The Universal Encyclopedia
of Mathematics £1.50
With a foreword by James A. Newman

A lucidly written and sensibly arranged mathematical reference book by the compilers of *How Things Work: The Universal Encyclopedia of Machines*.

With over 200 pages of formulae and tables, it will be of the utmost value to parents, teachers, students, engineers, technicians and research workers, as well as to the intelligent layman for whom mathematics retains its fascination.

'The definitions are clear and the treatment just right'
TIMES LITERARY SUPPLEMENT

'Parents blackmailed into helping with the homework, as well as more professional calculators, should find the work invaluable'
DAILY TELEGRAPH

The Story of Language 75p
C. L. Barber

'One of the best books of its kind to appear for years'
TIMES EDUCATIONAL SUPPLEMENT

Beginning with primitive man's first crude attempts at communication by sound, Dr Barber traces the development over thousands of years of organized language and its various families.

From the language groups emerging through the centuries he concentrates on the Indo-European as being of particular interest and describes the growth of the English language as we know it today. From each epoch – Old English, Middle English, the times of Chaucer, of Shakespeare, and later – he introduces pleasing examples of prose and verse to illustrate his arguments.

This new edition of an important book is made still more valuable by revisions and additions including the use of phonetic symbols from the international phonetic alphabet.

The Facts of English 50p
Ronald Ridout and Clifford Witting

An invaluable new edition of an established work of reference that gives the linguistic and literary facts of the English language from adverbs to zeugma.

Thoroughly revised and expanded by Ronald Ridout and Anthony Hern, this edition has been brought up to date with current cultural and commercial usage.

Over 1,000 entries, fully cross-referenced, explained and illustrated with suitable examples, and ranging from the elementary to the specialized, make this an ideal guide for student and expert alike.

The Best English 60p
G. H. Vallins

Dealing with the techniques of composition in poetry, drama and prose, the author shows that words properly used communicate not only with our minds but also with our hearts and our emotions.

The many examples of the uses of language taken from sources as varied as Shakespeare and P. G. Wodehouse, Pepys and George Bernard Shaw, Chaucer and Dylan Thomas, all add enormously to the reader's knowledge and appreciation of the treasures of literature.

'Valuable not only for the sensible criticisms that he makes, not only for the delightful quotations that he introduces, but also for his common sense' OBSERVER

You can buy these and other Pan books from booksellers and newsagents; or direct from the following address:
Pan Books, Cavaye Place, London SW10 9PG
Send purchase price plus 15p for the first book and 5p for each additional book, to allow for postage and packing
Prices quoted are applicable in UK

While every effort is made to keep prices low, it is sometimes necessary to increase prices at short notice. Pan Books reserve the right to show on covers new retail prices which may differ from those advertised in the text or elsewhere